THE BYZANTINE-SLAV LITURGY
OF
ST. JOHN CHRYSOSTOM

CASIMIR KUCHAREK

Priest of the Eparchy of Saskatoon

THE BYZANTINE-SLAV LITURGY

OF

ST. JOHN CHRYSOSTOM

Its Origin and Evolution

ALLELUIA PRESS

By the same author : *The Rite of Holy Matrimony,* According to the Byzan-
tine-Slav Rite
The Divine Liturgy (in collaboration with Rev. A.
Muzyka)
To Settle Your Conscience (in preparation)
Articles in *Our Family* (Canada's Catholic Family
Monthly), in *Svitlo,* in *Ameryka, Shlakh, Svoboda,
Holos Khrysta Chelovikoljubtsa.*

Nihil obstat :   Maximos Salloum, Censor librorum
January 1, 1971

Imprimatur :   + Joseph Raya, Archbishop of Akka, Haifa,
Nazareth and all Galilee
January 6, 1971

Library of Congress Catalog Card Number : 74-147735

ISBN 0-911726-06-3

Published by : Alleluia Press, Box 103, ALLENDALE, N. J. 07401
Combermere, Ontario, Canada.

Printed in Belgium

FOREWORD

In order to appreciate a system of religious ideas and the corresponding human ideals, a study in depth of the background is imperative. The science of Comparative Religion has demonstrated that it is also necessary to discover in such a system the constantly recurring patterns of ritual expression, to analyze them and trace their evolution and development. Only then can the belief and ideals of its followers be rightly appreciated.

All major Christian Bodies have their " ritual patterns." That of the Eucharist is dominant. The Eucharistic Liturgy of St. John Chrysostom is the " ritual pattern " of the Byzantines and the Eastern Slavs. To perceive and appreciate it is to unlock one of the most important doors for understanding the civilization and mentality of the Byzantines and of all the peoples who inherited some of the riches of that civilization. The subject of this book—the Eucharistic Liturgy of St. John Chrysostom—has a significance much wider and deeper than its liturgical, ecclesiastical or devotional interest.

One of the most frustrating difficulties to the student of the Byzantine Eucharistic Liturgy was the lack of an authoritative, comprehensive work on its origin, evolution and theology. The wealth of material available is remarkable, but much of it is scattered and uncoordinated in various articles, publications and books. None of the many good books dealing with the Byzantine Eucharistic Liturgy is comprehensive enough in scope and treatment to meet the requirements of the student or layman interested in the Liturgy as a whole. To compound the difficulty, much of the material is written in Russian, Ukrainian, Greek or Latin— languages unknown to the majority of Western European and American readers.

The object of this work is : to clarify and coordinate the great mass of material on the Byzantine Liturgy of St. John Chrysostom, to interpret and unify, to analyze and synthesize the information available from non-English sources. The results of comparative Liturgy—a relatively recent science—are incalculable. This is the method we have used.

The work is divided into two parts. The first is introductory : it consists in a survey of the Eastern Eucharistic Liturgies as they were celebrated during the first four centuries of the Christian era, and a study of their affinities, and linguistic and national ramifications. Many such historical surveys have been published and this part claims no great originality. It is chiefly intended for the novice, the beginner in the study of Eastern Liturgies.

Part II deals with the Byzantine-Slav recension of the Divine Liturgy of St. John Chrysostom in detail. The text followed is that of the Liturgikon *published in Rome in 1942, since it is acceptable to Catholics and to most Orthodox. Each ceremony, prayer and act is treated separately in its full historical, liturgical and theological aspect. First, the liturgical text is given in its English translation, then a description of the ritual. The exposition of each item seeks to give the reader, not only surface knowledge, but an insight into its essence, course of development and varied shades of meaning. In many cases, the different versions are connected by a common tie, but a more precise insight into origins and motive forces can be gained only by carefully determining the place of origin and the stage of development of each item in particular. Here, the application of the comparative method has proved invaluable. It was never easy, however, to arrange the results of hundreds of detailed investigations, discoveries, hints and controversies in such a way that the exposition would be readable. At times, the task seemed impossibly difficult, yet it was necessary to provide a thorough understanding of the evolution of any given point. For all this diligence, the end product is often a mere paragraph or two, with selected references in the footnotes to offer the critical student a basis for further work.*

Grateful acknowledgment is made to the various University Libraries and their librarians without whose gracious cooperation and patience this work could not have been done. A special debt of gratitude is owed to those librarians who spared no time nor effort in providing microfilms of manuscripts and books otherwise impossible to consult.

It would be practically impossible to name all those who helped me in the ten-year task of assembling and coordinating this material. I wish to embrace them all in the expression of my gratitude. Particular thanks are due, however, to Mr. John Markewich, Mr. Joseph Chicilo, and to Dr. Stephanie Potoski, M.D., without whose help, encouragement, and inspiration this work would have been impossible, and to Baron José de Vinck who tackled the monumental task of preparing the manuscript for publication and who gave such lavish care to the design and execution of the book.

C. K.

TABLE OF CONTENTS

Section II

Liturgy of the Catechumens : Introduction

Section III

Liturgy of the Catechumens : The Service of Readings

Section IV

Liturgy of the Faithful : The Pre-Anaphoral Ritual

Section V

Liturgy of the Faithful : The Anaphora or Eucharistic Prayer

Section VI

Liturgy of the Faithful : The Communion Cycle

KEY TO ABBREVIATIONS

ANF	Ante-Nicene Fathers (Grand Rapids, Mich., U.S.A. : Wm. B. Eerdmans)
BO	Bibliotheca orientalis
BVP	Bibliotheca veterum patrum (Gallandi)
BZ	Byzantinische Zeitschrift
CE	Catholic Encyclopedia
CSCO	Corpus scriptorum christianorum orientalium
CSEL	Corpus scriptorum ecclesiasticorum latinorum
CSHB	Corpus scriptorum historiae byzantinorum
DACL	Dictionnaire d'archéologie chrétienne et de liturgie
DTC	Dictionnaire de théologie catholique
EGM	Ecclesiae graecae monumenta
GCS	Die Griechischen Christlichen Schriftsteller
JbLw	Jahrbuch für Liturgiewissenschaft
JThSt	Journal of Theological Studies
LEW	Liturgies, Eastern and Western (Brightman)
LOC	Liturgiarum orientalium collectio (Renaudot)
LQF	Liturgiegeschichtliche quellen und Forschungen
MBVP	Magna bibliotheca veterum patrum
MGH	Monumenta Germaniae historica
NPB	Nova patrum bibliotheca
NPNF	Nicene and Post-Nicene Fathers (Grand Rapids, Mich., U.S.A. : Wm. B. Eerdmans)
PG	Patrologia graeca (Migne)
PL	Patrologia latina (Migne)
PO	Patrologia orientalis
OC	Orientalia christiana (Rome, 1924-1934)
RAC	Reallexikon für Antike und Christentum
SPCK	Society for Promoting Christian Knowledge

SVNC   Scriptorum veterum nova collectio e Vaticanis codicibus
        edita
TU   Texte und Untersuchungen
ZkTh   Zeitschrift für katholische Theologie

In title abbreviations of lesser known works, especially those written in Russian, only the first word or first several words of the title are cited after the author's name.   For complete title, see Bibliography.

PART ONE

ANCIENT LITURGIES
AND ORIGIN OF RITES

CHAPTER I

THE APOSTOLIC LITURGY

The New Testament accounts, our first and only sources of information about the way in which the Eucharist was celebrated during the lifetime of the Apostles, are scanty and meager to the point of frustration. There are merely a number of allusions, with no fixed order; and none gives a full description of the first Liturgies celebrated by the Apostles and their disciples. The sacred writers took it for granted, as we would have, that their readers had intimate knowledge of such familiar things as the daily celebration of the Eucharist. They felt no need to provide detailed descriptions. Only by studying these allusions separately and collectively, by interpreting them in the light of contemporary practices and by comparing them with subsequent Liturgies have scholars been able to deduce some of the nonessential elements that made up the whole Eucharistic rite in the apostolic era.

Obviously, whatever else was connected with the celebration of the Eucharist, one thing was certain : to obey the Lord's command : *Do this in " anamnesis "* of me. [1] Do what? To do what Christ had just done : take bread, give thanks, bless and break it, say the words of institution, and give it to others; likewise with the chalice of wine. These, then, are the essentials of the Last Supper commemoration performed by the Apostles in obedience to Christ's command. The Apostles had dedicated their lives to spreading his gospel, they were willing to be killed for it; hence they would also obey him in this.

The question remains, however : How did they and their disciples carry out this command? Certainly they carried out the essentials, but what of the nonessentials connected with the celebration of the Eucharist? Because the Gospel accounts omit nearly all the details of the eucharistic supper, we can safely infer that the paschal ritual was not considered essential to it. Furthermore, the paschal meal

---

[1] There is no precise English equivalent of *anamnesis*. See note, p. 58, for discussion of this.

was eaten only once a year, while the Christians celebrated the Eucharist frequently.   To carry out the paschal ceremonial frequently would have contradicted the prescriptions of the Old Law, to which the Apostles still clung.

If the Apostles and the infant Church did not keep to the ritual of the paschal meal in celebrating the Eucharist, did they hold to any meal at all?   Opinions vary, but the overwhelming majority agree that the celebration of the primitive Eucharist was ordinarily connected with a meal. [2]   Of the early Christian writers (from the fourth century on), the Greeks generally held that this meal came before the Eucharist; the Latins, after the Eucharist. [3]   The great John Chrysostom unequivocally states that the meal came after. [4]

Three times the Acts of the Apostles mentions the " breaking of bread " in the Christian community.   This was a fairly common Jewish expression, designating either *having a meal* or the *preliminary ceremony of bread-breaking* at a meal with the usual blessing of the bread and the giving of thanks.   Either way the implication is clear : the meal element cannot be ignored; it was adapted by the first Christians to express a new concept entirely different from the old Jewish one.

According to Acts 2:42, the converts of the first Whitsunday " were persevering in the doctrine of the Apostles and *in the communication of the breaking of bread and in prayer*" and " ...continuing daily with one accord in the temple and breaking bread from house to house, they took their meat with gladness and simplicity of heart " (Acts 2:46).   The meaning here is not the ordinary meal but an essentially religious act, for it is joined with the other elements of Christian doctrine, worship, and way of life.   At the Last Supper the term " breaking of bread " had taken on a completely new

[2] Notable exceptions to this opinion are those of H. Connolly, Coppens, P. Batiffol and L. Thomas.

[3] Cf. *Catholic Commentary on Holy Scriptures* (New York : Nelson, 1953), nn. 652 f., p. 809.

[4] In speaking of this custom in his *Homilia in dictum Apostoli, oportet haereses esse,* 3 (PG 51, 257 AB), St. John Chrysostom says that the people ate this common meal " after having heard the doctrine, after the prayers, *after participating in the mysteries....* "   In another homily *(In I Cor. homilia* 27, 1 [PG 61, 223-224]), he says that it came " after the synaxis was ended, *after the communion of the mysteries....* "   Cf. also his *In sanctum martyrem Iulianum,* 4 (PG 50, 673 D).

meaning, something entirely different from the old concept of having a meal or the preliminary ceremony of bread-breaking at a meal. Christ's command, *Do this in " anamnesis " of me*, would have been redundant and unnecessary were " the breaking of bread " still to mean the same as it always had, for the Apostles, being Jews, would have gone on doing these normal Jewish actions in any case. The use of this expression in the Acts, therefore, has an additional meaning, the new meaning acquired at the Last Supper : now it designates the celebration of the Eucharist. As if to dispel any lingering doubt, St. Paul tells the Corinthians, " And the bread which we break, is it not the partaking of the body of the Lord ? " (I Cor. 10:16).

Another passage from Acts (20:7-11) tells of Paul celebrating Mass in the evening at Troas : " On the first day of the week when we were assembled to break bread, Paul discoursed with them, being about to depart on the morrow. And he continued his speech until midnight. And there were a great number of lamps in the upper chamber where we were assembled. " In modern language it means : " At Sunday Mass, St. Paul preached the sermon, for he was going away the next day. " Clearly here the Christian assembly and Eucharist were held on Sunday, though by Jewish reckoning the evening would be that of Saturday. The building was not a church or synagogue but a private house, for there were many lamps in the *upper room*. Whether by design or coincidence, the circumstances surrounding the Last Supper were literally imitated : it was evening, in an upper room, etc.

There is here a point of human interest : St. Paul preached a long sermon. A young man, Eutychus, who was sitting on the windowsill, feel asleep and tumbled out of the window. It was not a short fall either, three stories down. Paul restored him to life, and then we read of their " going up and breaking bread and tasting. " Here the breaking of bread is interpreted as the Eucharistic service and the tasting as the partaking of Holy Communion. Though nothing more can be gleaned from this passage, more detail concerning the primitive Eucharist is supplied in Paul's First Letter to the Corinthians (I Cor. 11:20-24). It offers the first definite evidence of a meal being connected with the celebration of the

Eucharist. This meal was called the Lord's Supper by Paul. Later it became known as the agape. From Paul's description of the practice at Corinth, we learn of the gross abuses concerning it.

After introducing the topic, Paul immediately condemns two faults : the first was that each little group or clique began supper without spreading out all the provisions in common and without waiting for the whole congregation; the second, by far more reprehensible, that they did not share their food with the poor and the latecomers, who were not attached to any group; instead, they consumed their own supplies with such glaring selfishness that some became drunk while others went hungry! St. Paul minces no words in condemning such unchristian conduct, disgusting enough in itself without its being connected with the celebration of the Eucharist. Seriously, solemnly he recalls to the Corinthians the foundation and the meaning of the Eucharist, reminding them of the close connection that the Eucharist has with Calvary. Without attempting to prove to them that in the Eucharist the bread and wine become Christ's body and blood, but treating it as an accepted fact, he categorically states that anyone who receives it unworthily is guilty of the body and blood of the Lord, i.e., the death of Christ.

Paul does not command discontinuation of the meal itself, but only of the abuses connected with it, as his final words reveal : " Wherefore, my brothers, when you come together to eat, wait for one another. If any man be hungry, let him eat at home... " (I Cor. 11:33-34). Paul introduces the phrase about the chalice with " after he had supped, " that is, after Christ had eaten supper. This is significant. Certainly Paul would not have mentioned this detail had he wanted the meal to be disconnected from the celebration of the Eucharist. It seems, rather, that he wished the meal to be enclosed within the two consecrations, as it had been at the Last Supper. The whole unit, then, could very correctly be spoken of as the *Supper of the Lord*, which is indeed the expression Paul uses in the twentieth verse.

The first Christians probably found it natural to combine the celebration of the Eucharist with a meal. Originally Christ had celebrated it within the framework of a meal. Then, since the Apostles and most of the very first converts were Jewish, they were used to religious meals. Evening meals in every pious Jewish household, especially the *kiddûsh*, those held on the eve of the Sabbath, had a semireligious character. Then there were the more formal suppers, called the *chabûrah* (from *chabûrôth*, the plural form of the singular *chaber*, meaning " friend ") : small private groups of friends and members of a family took part in these formal, corporate suppers on Sabbath or holyday eves. Each one brought his contribution. Whenever the Apostles gathered after Christ's resurrection, it seems that they joined in a common meal. In Jewish eyes, Christ and the Apostles would have been just such a *chabûrôth* group among hundreds of others in Palestine—except perhaps that their bond of union was much closer than most.

Happily, the customs associated with these *chabûrah* suppers are quite well known to scholars from rabbinic sources. [5] The chief meal, supper, in any pious Jewish household was governed by the same regulations and customs as was the *chabûrah*, but in the latter, the regulations were observed with much more exactness and formality.

Since it was elective, the preliminary serving of what we would call relishes or hors-d'œuvre was not considered part of the meal proper; hence each guest said the prescribed blessing over them for himself. But once the guests had washed their hands and the " grace before meals ", had been said, no latecomer was allowed to join. Only those participating in the " grace before meals " were *one company* : they alone could partake of the supper. After this, too, all the prescribed blessings were said for all the participants by the host or leader alone (except for the blessing of the wine during the main course).

Both at the formal *chabûrah* and at every Jewish supper, the " grace before meals " was a beautiful ritual : the father of the house or the leader of the *chabûrah* took bread and broke it while pronouncing the customary blessing of bread, " Blessed art thou, O Lord, our God,

---

[5] Chiefly from the *Berakoth* (Blessings of the Mishnah, c. A.D. 200, but compiled on the basis of first- and second-century authorities). The chabûrôth among the Pharisees concerned themselves for the most part with scrupulous ritual cleanness, but on the other end of the spectrum were the liberal chabûrôth groups, which had assumed an almost exclusive social character.

the King of the world who bringest forth bread from the earth ";
then he ate a piece of it himself and gave a fragment to each person
at table.   Thus, the entire group was drawn together into a unit,
into *one company*, by the blessing and sharing of the one bread.
During the main course which followed, all ate whatever they
wished, but whenever a different kind of food was brought in for
the first time, the host or leader would bless it in the name of all
present.   If wine was served during this main course, however, each
person individually blessed his own cup with the customary blessing
for wine every time it was refilled : " Blessed art thou, O Lord, our
God, the King of the world who createst the fruit of the vine. "
When all had finished eating, water and a towel were brought in;
then all washed their hands.   Sometimes perfume was also offered.

Finally, in the name of all who had eaten the meal, the father
of the house or the leader recited a rather long prayer called the
Blessing or *Benediction*; this was comparable to our grace after meals.
At all *chabûrah* meals and even at all the less formal *kiddûsh* suppers,
this Benediction was recited over a special cup of wine, called the
Cup of the Blessing.   It began with an invitation to drink of this cup,
by the father or leader :

> Let us give thanks... [and when at least a hundred people
> took part, he added]... unto our Lord God.

The guests answered :

> Blessed be the name of the Lord from this time forth for
> evermore.

The leader :

> With the assent of those present we will bless him of whose
> bounty we have partaken.

The guests :

> Blessed be he of whose bounty we have partaken and through
> whose goodness we live.

The father or leader went on to recite the Benediction, parts of
which certainly predate the destruction of Jerusalem :

> Blessed art thou, O Lord, our God, eternal King, who
> feedest the whole world with thy goodness, with grace, with
> loving-kindness and with tender mercy.   Thou givest food

to all flesh, for thy loving-kindness endureth for ever. Through thy great goodness food hath never failed us : O may it not fail us for ever, for thy great name's sake, since thou nourishest and sustainest all living things and dost good unto all, and providest food for all thy creatures whom thou hast created.

Blessed art thou, O Lord, who givest food unto all.

We thank thee, O Lord, our God, because thou didst give as an heritage unto our fathers a desirable, good and ample land, and because thou didst bring us forth, O Lord, our God, from the land of Egypt, and didst deliver us from the house of bondage; as well as for thy Covenant which thou hast sealed in our flesh; for thy law which thou hast taught us; thy statutes which thou hast made known unto us; the life, grace and loving-kindness which thou hast bestowed upon us, and for the food wherewith thou dost constantly feed and sustain us, every day, in every season and at every hour. For all this, O Lord, our God, we thank thee and bless thee. Blessed be thy name by the mouth of all living, continually and for ever; even as it is written " And thou shalt eat and be satisfied, and thou shalt bless the Lord thy God for the good land which he has given thee. "

Blessed art thou, O Lord, for the food and for the land.

Have mercy, O Lord, our God, upon Israel thy people, upon Jerusalem thy city, upon Zion the abiding place of thy glory, upon the kingdom of the house of David thine anointed, and upon the great and holy house that was called by thy name. O our God, our Father, feed us, nourish us, sustain, support and relieve us, and speedily, O Lord, our God, grant us relief from all our troubles. We beseech thee, O Lord, our God, let us not be in need either of the gifts of men or of their loans, but only of thine helping hand, which is full, open, holy and ample, so that we may not be ashamed nor confounded for ever and ever. [6]

Though the foregoing text probably has been expanded and revised since the first century A.D., Jewish scholars generally agree that its first two paragraphs are substantially the same as those used

---

[6] These three paragraphs still appear today in the *Jewish Authorized Daily Prayer Book* (compiled by Rabbi S. Singer [London, 1932], pp. 279 f.) as the focal point of current usage. The additions before and after in the current text are of comparatively recent origin.

in Palestine during Christ's time.   Only the last paragraph has been extensively revised or added entirely after the destruction of Jerusalem in A.D. 70.

After this Benediction, the host or leader sipped a little wine, then passed it around to each of those present.   This final common cup, the Cup of the Blessing, again gave a sense of oneness to the whole group.   Finally, after singing a psalm, the group broke up. Such was the religious character of all formal Jewish suppers, especially the Sabbath meal on Friday evenings, the *chabûrah*.

Such religion-sponsored meals with proper adaptations for Christian use were continued among the first Christians.   Though the controversial chapters IX and X of the *Didache*, or *Teaching of the Twelve Apostles* (c. A.D. 80-100), may prove nothing else, they do prove that the Christians did have such semireligious meals modeled along *chabûrah* lines.   The similarity between the Jewish and Christian usages is startling :

IX. 1. Regarding the thanksgiving (εὐχαριστίας); give thanks (εὐχαριστήσατε) thus :

2. First, concerning the cup : " We give thanks (εὐχαριστοῦμεν) to thee, our Father, for the Holy Vine of David thy servant, which thou hast made known to us through Jesus thy servant. "

To thee be the glory forever.

3. Concerning the broken bread (κλάσμα) : " We give thanks to thee (εὐχαριστοῦμεν), our Father, for the life and knowkedge, which thou hast made known to us through Jesus thy servant. "

To thee be the glory forever.

4. " As this broken bread was scattered upon the tops of the hills and, when gathered, became one, so gather thy Church from the ends of the earth into thy Kingdom.
" For thine is the glory and the power through Jesus Christ forever. "

5. Let no one eat or drink of your thanksgiving

(εὐχαριστία) but those baptized in the name of the Lord. For regarding this, too, the Lord said : " Do not give what is holy to dogs. "

X.　1.　And after you are satiated, give thanks thus :

2.　" We give thanks to thee, O holy Father, for thy holy name which thou hast made to dwell in our hearts and for the knowledge and faith and immortality which thou hast made known to us through Jesus, thy servant. "

To thee be the glory forever.

3.　" Thou, almighty Lord, hast created all things for thy name's sake and hast given food and drink to men for enjoyment, that they might give thanks (εὐχαριστήσωσιν) to thee; but on us thou hast graciously bestowed spiritual food and drink and eternal life through thy Son. "

4.　" Above all, we give thanks (εὐχαριστοῦμεν) to thee because thou art mighty. "

Thine is the glory forever.

5.　" Remember, O Lord, to deliver thy Church from all evil and make it perfect in thy love; and from the four winds gather it, sanctified, in thy Kingdom which thou hast prepared for it. "

For thine is the power and the glory forever.

6.　" Let grace come and let this world pass away. " " Hosanna to the God of David! " " If anyone is holy, let him come nigh; if anyone is not, let him repent. *Maranatha* (Our Lord, come)!　Amen. "

7.　But permit the prophets to give thanks as much as they wish. [7]

---

[7] Our translation made from edit. F. X. Funk, pp. 25-31. We deliberately translated εὐχαριστία, εὐχαριστεῖν as " thanksgiving, " " to give thanks, " etc., though Eucharist (to eucharistize) could have been left intact. The fact that the original text contains the words εὐχαριστεία and εὐχαριστεῖν does not thereby

Whether or not this passage describes the Eucharist, no one knows for sure but it does describe a religion-sponsored meal of the Christians, of that we can be certain, something very similar to the Jewish *chabûrah*. Both the Jews and the Christians had a *cup* (of wine) and bread which was broken. The Christian blessings for both bread and wine were modeled on the Jewish, for both are brief " blessings of God " and not of the wine and bread themselves as we would have expected them to be. True, nothing is taken verbally from the Jewish wine and bread blessings (if we except the use of the word *vine* in the wine-blessing), but proper Christian usage would have demanded such substitutions and adaptations.

The *Thanksgiving* after the meal is similar but again without direct borrowing of text from the Jewish Thanksgiving prayer; however, the sequence of the three ideas remained identical. The Christian gave thanks for the earthly; so did the Jew. The Christian gave thanks for " spiritual food and drink, " which would mean the Eucharist, the center or focal point of the New Dispensation or Covenant; the Jew gave thanks for the Old Covenant whose central point was the Law and circumcision. Finally, the Christian prayed for the Church while the Jew prayed for Jewry, for the " land. "

That the cup preceded the bread (as it did in the Eastern agapes of a century or two later) may be a thoroughly Christian innovation. These Christian table-prayers, beautiful in themselves, must have been composed by men with considerable knowledge and appreciation of Jewish customs and tradition. With such a background, the first Christian converts would have regarded the celebration of the Eucharist within the framework of a supper as a matter of course, especially since Christ set the precedent. When Christ celebrated

mean that the Eucharist is indicated here. It took a long time for the terminology to evolve, and even in the second century, this problem was not solved completely, as is evident from chap. xxvi, 13, of the *Apostolic Tradition*, which states that if there is no cleric present at a Lord's Supper to " eulogize " the bread, the laity should each " eucharistize " the food for themselves. Early Christians used the terms εὐλογεῖν and εὐχαριστεῖν indifferently when translating the Hebrew verb *berakh* (" to bless, " " to give thanks "). When St. Paul speaks of blessing meat which had been bought in a public market, he uses εὐχαριστεῖν, but to express the consecration of the Eucharist he uses εὐλογεῖν. In translating this passage from the *Didache*, therefore, we could have used the terms indifferently, too, but the modern " thanksgiving " and " giving thanks " indicate the truer meaning.

the first Eucharist in the form of the paschal supper, he performed the first consecration at the bread-breaking ceremony and the second at the third cup of wine, the Cup of the Blessing, after the principal course. For the first Christians, the meal quite naturally formed a link between the Last Supper and their own celebration of the Eucharist. Not that the sacramental Eucharist was inevitably celebrated on the occasion of all such religion-sponsored meals : probably sometimes it was and at other times it was not; but whenever the apostolic Eucharist was celebrated, it was within the framework of such a meal.

The nonsacramental Christian prayers of blessing over the bread and wine and the thanksgiving afterward, as described by the *Didache*, were said even if the meal was had without the Eucharist. When the Eucharist was celebrated in conjunction with the meal, these same prayers probably remained and served as the introduction to the properly Eucharistic formulae and narrative. At least later evidence indicates that the thanksgiving after the common meal was the origin of the anaphora texts. [8] Even the prefatory dialogue indicates this, for all the Christian anaphoras were and are introduced by the invitation *Let us give thanks to the Lord* or *Let us give thanks to our Lord God.* [9] This invitation is an almost literal translation of that prescribed by the Mishnah at the *chabûrah* meals attended by at least a hundred people : *Let us give thanks unto our Lord God.* [10] Later, when the Eucharist was celebrated without the meal, a whole new content, though still one of gratitude, had to be given to these ancient Christian meal prayers into which the Eucharistic formulae and narrative were woven. The Christian anaphora, despite everything, is still in its nature a prayer for a meal.

In its historical context, no better sign of oneness and unity would have been linked with the Eucharist than the customary formal Jewish supper with its traditional deep-rooted sign of union

---

[8] Cf. below, pp. 551-556; also A. Baumstark, *Comparative Liturgy* (Westminster : Newman Press, 1958), pp. 46 ff.

[9] E.g., *Apostolic Tradition, Testamentum Domini, Apostolic Constitutions* (VIII), Chrysostom's testimony of Liturgy at Antioch, Cyril of Jerusalem's of the Liturgy there, the Liturgy of St. James, the Liturgy of Basil, etc.

[10] Tractate *Berakoth*, viii, 3.

effected by the ceremonies of bread-breaking and the drinking of the common cup, the Cup of the Blessing. Instead of being merely a sign of oneness and unity, the ceremonies of the formal supper were transformed by the Eucharist into real union and oneness. The fact that the father of the house or leader alone was to pronounce the blessings in the name of all present also fitted in well with the Christian usage : the priest or bishop presided and transubstantiated the bread and wine into the body and blood of Christ.

If we return, now, to St. Paul and his First Letter to the Corinthians, the eleventh chapter becomes much more meaningful and clear. The Jewish regulation was very strict : latecomers not present for the ceremony of bread-breaking could not participate in the rest of the ceremonies, nor in the meal itself. This alone would have warranted Paul's insistence that they " wait for one another. " After all, they could easily consume their own provisions with moderation and still unselfishly share some supplies with the others, but he insists that they " wait for one another. " Aside from the utter selfishness, immoderation, and excess indulged in by each little clique when it consumed its own supplies, the Corinthians had lost all perspective in the celebration of the Eucharist. Instead of being the center and focal point, the Eucharist became merely the occasion of these " get togethers, " an excuse for indulgence and immoderation. The Eucharist was relegated into the background, yet Paul apparently did not want to suppress the meal connected with the Eucharist : if he had, he would have said so in no uncertain terms. He was, after all, capable of unequivocal language. Rather, Paul merely wanted to set all in order, in proper perspective.

There is yet another side to the episode at Corinth. The conduct of the Corinthians, though reprehensible, is less shocking if understood in the proper context. Being Gentiles, the Corinthians had had no previous background or training encouraging them to regard meals as semireligious functions, as had the Jews. True, the Hellenistic *hetairiai* (ἑταιρίαι), or clubs, were associated in a broad sense with a religious meaning, yet they were usually a mere pretext for unethical merry-making. When Paul introduced the Eucharist combined with a meal, the untested, recently converted Gentiles could not shrug off the familiar practice of the *hetairiai* (ἑταιρίαι) even in the " Lord's

Supper. " Secular, unchristian conduct was the result. On the other hand, had the Eucharist been introduced in Corinth already isolated from the meal, purely as a religious function, it is difficult if not impossible to understand how the Corinthians, however fickle they may have been, could have so quickly forgotten its solemn and sacred meaning.

Only by supposing that the Eucharist in the primitive Church was actually combined with a meal does Acts 2:42 mean exactly what it says : " and breaking bread from house to house, they took their meat with gladness and simplicity of heart. "

CHAPTER II

THE APOSTOLIC CATECHETICAL SYNAXIS

Because of its Jewish heritage, the primitive Judeo-Christian community gathered in the Temple. Outside Jerusalem, Christians went to the synagogue for the reading of the Law and the Prophets, to sing the psalms, and to hear the doctrine or explanations of the Scriptures. [1] In fact, the expressions *synagogue* and *to go to the synagogue* were used by the Apostolic Fathers and the Apologists of the very early Christian era to indicate not only the meeting place of the Jews who lived among the Christians but also the assemblies of the Christians, even after their final breach with Judaism. [2]

After A.D. 70, the Christians met less and less in the synagogues. They began to hold their own somewhat modified services (borrowed and adapted from the worship of the synagogue) in their own places of meeting. Later, this instruction-and-prayer service became more formalized and was called the catechetical synaxis. [3] Today it is the first part of the Divine Liturgy, the Mass of the Catechumens.

---

[1] E.g. In the Temple (Acts 3:1; 2:46), at Damascus (Acts 9.20), at Antioch (Acts 13:14), at Iconium (Acts 14:1), at Thessalonica (Acts 17:1-2), at Berea (Acts 17:10), at Athens (Acts 17:17), and at Corinth (Acts 18:4).

[2] Cf. Clement of Alexandria (*Paedagogus* III, 11, 80, 3, edit. O. Stahlin, GCS, I, p. 280); Origen (*Homilia IV in Ieremiam*, edit. E. Klostermann, GCS, III, p. 25, also *Homilia XVIII in Ieremiam, ibid.*, p. 157); Dionysius of Alexandria (*Epist. ad Xystum Romanum*, Eusebius, *Hist. eccl.* VII, 9, 2, edit. E. Schwartz GCS, II, ii, p. 640), etc.

[3] *Synaxis*, a term originating from the word *synagogue*, literally means a gathering or an assembly. It was adopted originally to designate the first part of the Mass, now known as the Mass of the Catechumens, in the third century by Origen (*Homil. in Samuelem* I, 28, 3-25, edit. E. Klosterman, GCS, III, p. 283). Other writers followed suit, e.g., Cyril of Jerusalem (*Catechesis* XIV 24 [PG 33, 856 C]; *Catechesis* I 5-6 [PG 33, 376-377], etc.), Gregory Nazianzen, (*Sermo XIV, Delectione pauperum* 14 [PG 35, 876 AB]), the *Apostolic Constitutions* (II, 39, 6, edit. F. X. Funk, II, p. 129), John Chrysostom, (*Homil. V ad populum Antiochenum* [PG 49, 79]; *Homil. V super inscriptionem altaris* [PG 51, 65-67]; *Homil. IV super Annam* [PG 54, 660]), Eusebius (*Vita Constantini* III, c. 67, edit., I. Heikel, GCS, I, p. 75; *ibid.* IV, c. 45, p. 116, and c. 71, p. 117), etc.

In outline, this service, as we know from New Testament sources among others, consisted of lections or readings from the Scripture (I Tim. 4:13; I Thess. 5:27; Col. 3:16), the singing of psalms (I Cor. 14:26) or hymns (Eph. 5:19; Col. 3:16), a sermon (I Cor. 14:26; Acts 20:7), and prayers (Acts 2:42; I Tim. 2:1-2).

The services of the synagogue, whether held on the mornings and evenings of Sabbaths, on Mondays and Thursdays of each week, or on feast days, were all quite similar in composition. Yet, there were a few differences. The first Christian assemblies patterned their own prayer service on the *Morning Service* of the Sabbath. Though much of the present synagogue usage dates from a period much later than the apostolic era, several parts date back to the third century B.C. On this basis and the evidence contained in the Mishnah and the Talmud, the reconstruction of the first-century synagogue service is possible with a reasonable amount of accuracy. [4]

The general order of the service was directed by an *archisynagogus* (leader of the synagogue). Usually it consisted of the following items :

1. *Prayer*. Introducing the *Shema* was a twofold blessing, announced by the presiding leader with the words *Barku el* (" Bless the Lord "). During these prayers the congregation stood facing Jerusalem. The Shema, a kind of elementary creed professing the Israelite faith in the " true and eternal God, " was then recited. Besides the blessings contained in it, the Shema was composed of extracts from the Pentateuch (Deut. 6:4-9; 11:13-21; and Num. 15:37-41). The solemn recitation of the Shema is one of the most ancient features in Jewish liturgical life.

2. *Reading from the Law*. This selection from the Law, the *Parascha*, was usually chosen by the leader and was translated into the vernacular Aramaic.

3. *Reading or excerpts from the Prophets*, called the *Haftara* ("conclusion," i.e., to the readings), was also translated into Aramaic, by an interpreter for those who did not know the ancient Hebrew.

---

[4] Cf. W. O. E. Oesterley, *The Psalms in the Jewish Church* (London, 1910), c. 8, 144.

4. *Psalms*. These were sung while the scrolls were being put away. [5]

5. The *sermon*, or *Midrash*, was an explanation of the Scriptures just read or an exhortation based upon them. The Midrash was delivered by whomever the leader of the synagogue appointed.

6. The *Eighteen Blessings, Shemoneh Esreh*, said by the " Angel of the Synagogue, " consisted of benedictions with an added element of petition. Each of these ended with a formula common to all.

7. Finally, there was a *prayer-blessing* intoned by a priest or a layman. This consisted of the " Offering of Praise" and the " Aaronic Blessing" (Num. 6:24-26).

Like their Master before them, the Apostles continued to frequent the synagogues. It was the most effective way of reaching the Jews and evangelizing them. [6] Undaunted by bitter opposition and persecution, they still worked for the conversion of the Jews not only in Palestine but in the synagogues of the dispersion. As soon as they arrived in any town or city, they established contact with the Jewish community and preached in the synagogues. The final breach with Judaism was inevitable but it was not the Christians who took the initiative in breaking away. When, later, synagogues of the dispersion became centers of bitter opposition to the doctrines of Christianity, the Jews themselves undoubtedly took the traditional disciplinary steps against the new believers, heretics in their eyes, in form of the *herem* (excommunication) or the *niddui* (temporary exclusion) from the synagogue.

With their exclusion from the synagogues, the Apostles and their followers were forced to organize their own assemblies for prayer and instruction. Unlike the Eucharist, which was celebrated only for the faithful, the baptized alone, these prayer-and-instruction services included the catechumens and inquirers of all descriptions.

---

[5] The singing of psalms in the synagogues of the first century A.D. is now generally agreed upon by scholars. If psalms were not sung, then this detail of the Christian synaxis was taken from the service of the Temple. Cf. Warren, *Liturgy of Ante-Nicene Church*, pp. 205-207.

[6] Among the many references in the Gospels to Jesus' going to the synagogue, Matt. 4:23 also throws light on his reason for doing so : " . . . Jesus went about the length of Galilee, teaching in their synagogues, preaching the gospel of the Kingdom. . . . " For the Apostles, cf. Acts 9:20; 13:14; 14:1-2, 10; 18:4.

The Synaxis was indeed a " public meeting, " as its name suggests.

The Sabbath Morning Service of the Jewish synagogue provided both the inspiration and the pattern for this specifically Christian Synaxis. This is clearly evident from Book VII of the *Apostolic Constitutions* (chaps. 33-38) : there the Christian Synaxis is in effect the whole Greco-Jewish Morning Service for Sabbaths with only a few, somewhat superficial modifications. [7] The double reading from the Law and the Prophets was already Jewish Morning Service usage in the first century A.D.; thus we find St. Paul speaking in the synagogue " after the reading of the Law and the Prophets " (Acts 13:15). The Christians kept these Old Testament readings in their own assemblies but, since the synaxis was a distinctly Christian service, they added readings from the New Testament. One of these was a selection from the Apostolic Letters, or the Epistle; Paul himself ordered it, at least in regard to his own letters (Col. 4:16; I Thess. 5:27). The other was from the Gospels, deemed most important of all, for it contained the very words of the Master. Thus, the total number of readings in the primitive synaxis was four. Traces of this primitive arrangement may be found in several Eastern Liturgies today. The Copts, for example, have preserved the four pericopes, though they replaced the readings from the Old Testament with other texts. [8] The Syrian Nestorians still have the Old Testament readings. [9] The Byzantine Liturgy and its antecedents (i.e., Antiochene, Pontic) formerly had four pericopes; significantly, it reverted to two, the original number in the synagogue. [10]

The singing of the psalms, attested by St. Paul (I Cor. 14:26) was probably borrowed from the Morning Service of the synagogue (see above, p. 32, n. 5). Though the psalmody known as the

---

[7] Cf. Wilhelm Bousset, *Nachrichten der königl. Gesellschaft der Wissenschaften zu Göttingen*, Philolog-histor. Klasse (1915), pp. 435-489.

[8] The present order in the Coptic Liturgy consists in readings : (1) from St. Paul, (2) from the Catholic Epistles, (3) from the Acts, and (4) from the Gospels. Cf. Brightman, *Liturgies Eastern and Western*, pp. 152-155.

[9] Brightman, LEW, p. 76.

[10] Since about the 7th cent. Cf. Jungmann, *The Mass of the Roman Rite* (Benziger, 1951), I, p. 395.

Smiroth does not follow immediately the scriptural readings in present synagogue usage, there is reason to believe that in the first century it did. The Byzantine descendant of this primitive psalmody is the *prokeimenon* (the Slavonic *prokimen*) while its Latin counterpart is the *gradual*.

Taking the place of the Midrash was the Christian sermon or homily (I Cor. 14:26).

In place of the Jewish Eighteen Blessings, the Christians had their own " common " prayers of intercession similar in general content and litanic form to their Jewish counterpart. Just as the Jewish formulary of the Eighteen Blessings was divided by *Amen* responses, so were some of the very ancient litanies of the Eastern Liturgies. [11] Though no conclusive evidence exists that this was universal practice in the primitive Christian assemblies, it may have been. Later, the *Amens* were replaced by the *Kyrie eleisons*. [12]

Something akin to the spirit of the Eighteen Blessings is found in Clement's famous prayer contained in his *Epistle to the Corinthians* (chaps. 59 and 61). All acknowledge that it is a liturgical prayer of some kind, but opinions are far from united regarding its place in the primitive Christian liturgy. Some hold that it is an example of an early Christian thanksgiving. [13] It may be, but too many inconsistencies of text and history seem to preclude such a conclusion. Rather, its place seems to have been in the synaxis as a Christian counterpart to the synagogue's Eighteen Blessings.

First, Clement is not quoting it exactly : rather, he is adapting to his purpose only the basic ideas of this prayer, recited more or less extempore by the celebrant or deacon. Its form may have been litanic, but Clement could not include such a form in his letter without excessive artificiality. As it is, the prayer is admirably and naturally woven into the context of his *Epistle*. Certainly, its general tenor seems to be that of the Eighteen Blessings, the *Shemoneh*

[11] E.g., the great litany of the *Testamentum Domini* (i, 35, edit. I. E. Rahmani, pp. 84-89); also the ancient litanic text in the Nestorian Liturgy (Brightman, LEW, pp. 263-266).

[12] Cf. A. Baumstark, *Comparative Liturgy* (Westminster : Newman Press, 1958), pp. 45-46.

[13] E.g., Duchesne, *Origines*, pp. 49-51; Fortescue, *The Mass, a Study of the Roman Liturgy*, p. 13.

Esreh, where " blessings " and intercessions were combined, that is, an element of petition was added to the praise of God. When the text is divided into distinct petitions, the similarity between them and those of the later Syro-Antiochene litanic forms is immediately apparent :

> . . . that the Creator of the universe may preserve undiminished the established number of his elect in all the world through his beloved Son Jesus Christ, through whom he has called us out of darkness into light, out of ignorance into the full knowledge of the splendor of his name, that we may hope in thy name which gave existence to all creation.
>
> Open the eyes of our heart that we may know thee who alone art highest among the highest and holy among the holy; who humblest the pride of the haughty, destroyest the designs of the heathens; who raisest up the lowly and humblest the lofty, makest rich and makest poor, slayest and bringest to life; who alone art the Benefactor of spirits and the God of all flesh.
>
> Thou beholdest the work of men, the Helper in danger, the Saviour in despair, the Creator and Watcher of every spirit. Thou multipliest the nations upon the earth, and from among all thou hast chosen those that love thee through Jesus Christ, thy beloved Son, through whom thou hast instructed, sanctified, and honored us. We beg thee, O Master, to be our Helper and Protector.
>
> Deliver those of us who are in distress.
>
> Raise up the fallen.
>
> Show thy face to those in need.
>
> Heal the infirm.
>
> Bring back the erring of thy people.
>
> Feed the hungry.
>
> Ransom our prisoners.
>
> Set the infirm upon their feet.
>
> Comfort the fainthearted.
>
> Let all the nations know that thou art the only God, that Jesus Christ is thy Son, that we are thy people and the sheep of thy pasture. For thou hast made known the everlasting constitution of the world through the forces at work in it. Thou, O Lord, hast created the world, thou who art faithful in all generations, right in thy judgments, wonderful in strength and transcendent greatness, wise in creating, and

judicious in establishing what has come into being, beneficent
throughout the visible world and kind toward those that
trust in Thee.

O merciful and compassionate one, forgive us our iniquities
and misdemeanors and transgressions and shortcomings.

Do not consider every sin of thy servants and servant maids;
but cleanse us as only thy truth can cleanse.

And direct our steps to walk in holiness of heart and to do
the things which are good and pleasing in thy sight and in
the sight of our rulers.   Yes, Master, let thy face beam upon
us that we may do good in peace and be sheltered under thy
mighty hand and be delivered from every sin by thy uplifted
arm.

And deliver us from such as hate us without cause.

Grant concord and peace to us as well as to all the inhabitants
of the earth, just as thou didst grant it to our fathers when
they piously called upon thee in faith and truth.

Grant us to be obedient to thy almighty and glorious name,
as well as to our princes and rulers on earth.

Thou, O Master, through thy transcendent and indescribable
sovereignty, hast given them the power of royalty, so that we,
acknowledging the honor and glory conferred upon them by
thee, may bow to them, without in the least opposing thy will.

Grant to them, O Lord, health, peace, concord, and firmness,
so that they may without hindrance exercise the supreme
leadership thou hast conferred upon them.   For it is thou, O
Master, O heavenly King of all ages, that conferest upon the
sons of men glory and honor and authority over the things
which are upon the earth.

Do thou, O Lord, direct their counsels in accord with what
is good and pleasing in thy sight, so that they may piously
exercise in peace and gentleness the authority thou hast
granted them, and thus experience thy graciousness.

To thee, who alone art able to bestow these and even greater
blessings upon us, we render thanks and praise through the
High Priest and Ruler of our souls, Jesus Christ, through
whom be to thee the glory and majesty now and for all
generations and forever and evermore.

Amen. [14]

[14] Trans. by J. A. Kleist, *The Epistles of St. Clement of Rome and St. Ignatius
of Antioch*,   ACW (Westminster : Newman Press, 1946), I, pp. 9-46; cf. also edit.
Funk, *Patres apostolici*, I, pp. 176-180.

Other Liturgical Details

Other liturgical practices existed among the first Christians. Most of them are still apparent today. During services, men were bareheaded, women, veiled or covered (I Cor. 11:6-7). Women were not permitted to speak in the assemblies (I Cor. 14:34-35). There was the *pax*, or kiss of peace (Rom. 16:16; I Cor. 16-20; I Thess. 5:26; I Pet. 5:14), and a public profession of faith (I Tim. 6:12). The people indicated their assent to prayer with the old Hebrew *Amen*. They prayed with uplifted hands (I Tim. 2:8) as does the priest today. An almsgiving or collection for the poor was usually made at the assemblies (I Cor. 16:12; Rom. 15:26). Sunday, as the day of the Resurrection, was probably sanctified in addition to the Sabbath; if this did not happen in all the communities during the lifetime of the Apostles, it did soon afterward.

CHAPTER III

THE SECOND-CENTURY LITURGY

The process of separating the Eucharist from the meal was begun probably within a generation after the lifetime of the Apostles, though the common meal, or agape, was to continue for several more centuries and even longer in the East. [1] The change may have been desired on account of abuses, as happened in Corinth during Paul's time. Perhaps necessity had forced the issue. With an ever-increasing number of converts, the Christian communities became too large and unwieldy for these table-gatherings. The only logical course was to discontinue the meal and to celebrate the Eucharist as an independent liturgical function. With the tables removed from the place of worship, a greater number of faithful could be accommodated in a room.

As long as the Eucharist was connected with a common supper, it was celebrated in the evening. This was not necessarily a literal imitation of the Last Supper; both Jewish and Hellenistic custom had formal evening meals (*chabûrah* and δεῖπνον respectively). But after its separation from the common meal, the Eucharist could be celebrated freely at any other time of day. Another reason, however, made the change desirable. Sunday was being sanctified in addition to the Saturday Sabbath as the Lord's Day in memory of Christ's resurrection. [2] According to the Scriptures, Christ was the Sun of

---

[1] Cf. Clement of Alexandria, *Paedagogus* II, c. 1, 4, 3-4, edit., Stahlin, GCS I, p. 156; also n. 5, *ibid.*, p. 157; n. 6, *ibid.*, p. 157; Origen, *Contra Celsum* 1, I, n. 1, edit. P. Koetschau, GCS I, p. 56. On funerals, cf. Chrysostom, *In sanctum martyrem Iulianum* 4 (PG 50, 673 D); Gregory of Nyssa, *De vita S. Gregorii Thaumaturgi* (PG 46, 953 BC); Gregory Nazianzen, *Carmina* II, 2, 26-29 (PG 38, 97-99).

[2] Those unacquainted with Eastern liturgical history, rather lightly accept the change of the Sabbath to Sunday as an accomplished fact by the time St. Paul wrote to the Corinthians (16:2), or shortly thereafter. Early Christian tradition, on the contrary, points to the Sunday as an extra holy day attached to the Saturday Sabbath and not as a substitute for it. The status of Saturday as a holy day also applied to the laws of fasting; Saturdays as well as Sundays were exempt from fast in Eastern Christian tradition. Even in modern times, the Saturdays in Lent and in other penitential periods are not days of fasting in the Byzantine Church. It is probable that the real substitution of Sunday for the Sabbath dates no earlier than St. Leo's time.

Justice, the Sun of Truth. This idea took deep root in the minds of the early Christians. Since Jesus rose from the dead at dawn on the first Easter Sunday, his rising from the grave coincided with the appearance of the natural sun. Sunrise, therefore, became the symbol of the rising Sun of Justice. The next step was natural. Could not the Eucharist be celebrated at dawn on Sunday morning? Christ, the Sun of Justice and Truth, would then come upon the altar in the Eucharist at the very time the natural sun was rising. Despite subsequent embellishment, the idea originated with the Christians of this era; they, no less than the Christians of the fourth century, were strongly influenced by symbolism.

Whatever the reasons underlying the change, by the beginning of the second century, in a certain number of places, the Christians began to meet before daybreak for their services. About the year A.D. 111-112, Caius Plinius Caecilius Secundus, better known as Pliny the Younger, supplies us not only with many interesting details regarding the government of Bithynia (a Roman province in Asia Minor) but also with a brief sketch of Christian practices in his day.

As governor of Bithynia, Pliny refers the question of investigating the Christians and their punishment to Emperor Trajan. He had received an anonymous statement with a list of persons accused of being Christians. On examination, some denied that they had ever been Christians, others admitted that they had once been, but had forsaken Christianity some years before. All eventually worshiped the image of the deified emperor and the gods. Some even became informers, and told him of their meetings : " They aver that the whole of their fault or error is this : that they were in the habit of meeting on a certain fixed day *(stato die)* before daybreak to sing a hymn in alternate verses *(secum invicem)* to Christ as to a god, and that they bound themselves by a solemn oath not to do any wicked deeds, nor to commit any theft, robbery, or adultery, nor to falsify their word nor to refuse to give up a deposit when they should be called upon to deliver it up. When they had done this it was their custom to depart, and then to meet again to eat food... but ordinary and harmless food. " [3]

[3] For the whole letter, cf. Kirch, *Enchiridion fontium historiae ecclesiasticae antiquae* (Freiburg im. B. : Herder, 1910), pp. 18-19.

Opinion is divided as to whether the second meeting, when the Christians ate their food, was the agape or the celebration of the Eucharist (or both). [4]   The first meeting or service, however, was the Synaxis and took place in the early morning before dawn *(ante lucem)*.   The *carmen Christo quasi deo dicere secum invicem* (" to sing a hymn in alternate verses to Christ as to a god ") can be interpreted in various ways.   Generally, *carmen* meant a hymn or any set form of words even without a metrical rhythm or rhyme.   Latin authors frequently used this word to describe incantations or invocations and, when speaking of religious functions, to denote formulae recited by priests or officials and repeated by others. *Secum invicem* (" in alternate verses ") may imply antiphonal singing, but it can also be interpreted as a litanic form of prayer, one in which the deacon or celebrant " bids " a petition and the congregation responds to each invocation.   To describe adequately and concisely the litanic type of prayer is difficult, especially for someone unfamiliar with this usage, as Pliny was.

The First Detailed Description of Christian Liturgy

The first somewhat detailed description of the Christian Liturgy is contained in Justin's famous " Open Letter to the Government, " his *First Apology*.   It is addressed to Antoninus Pius (A.D. 138-156), to the Senate, and to the Roman people.   St. Justin, martyr and philosopher, wrote the *First Apology* probably at Rome *circa* A.D. 148-155 in order to convince the public at large of the harmlessness of Eucharistic celebrations.   Considering the times and circumstances, his letter is disarmingly frank, but it had no effect on contemporary opinion.

Justin wrote about the Eucharist as it was celebrated in the Rome of his day.   Still, if its celebration were radically different in the East, where he had firsthand experience (he was a Greco-Roman from Sichem, lived at Ephesus for some time and traveled to the various Oriental Churches), he surely would have said so or his very purpose would have been defeated in writing the *Apology*.   He

---

[4] Cf. E. Baumgartner, *Euch. u. Agape*, pp. 247-270.

describes the Eucharistic celebration twice : first, as preceded by baptism (chap. 65), then, as preceded by the Synaxis (chap. 67). Though far from being a complete account of the service, it is a good synopsis of what went on in the mysterious meetings of the Christians :

Chapter 65

Thus, after baptizing him that professes his faith and assents to our doctrine, we lead him into the assembly of those called the brethren to say earnest prayers in common for ourselves, for the newly baptized, and for all others all over the world so that we who have come to the knowledge of the truth may also by the grace of God be found worthy to live a good life by deed and to observe the commandments by which we may gain eternal life.

After finishing the prayers, we greet each other with a kiss.

Then bread and a cup of wine (κρᾶμα, lit. : mixture, but usually used to mean wine) are brought to the one presiding over the brethren. When he takes it, he gives praise and glory to the Father of all in the name of the Son and of the Holy Spirit, and gives thanks at length because he considered us worthy of these gifts.

After he finishes the prayers and thanksgiving, all the people present cry out in agreement : " Amen. " Amen is a Hebrew expression and means So be it. After the one presiding has given thanks (εὐχαριστήσαντος, " has eucharistized ") and all the people have cried out in agreement, the deacons, as they are called by us, distribute the Eucharistic bread and the wine-and-water (ἀπὸ τοῦ εὐχαριστηθέντος ἄρτου καὶ οἴνου καὶ ὕδατος) [5] to every one present so that each may partake, and they (the deacons) carry them to those who are not present.

Chapter 67

And on the day which is called after the sun, all who are in the towns and in the country assemble together in one place

---

[5] Here we definitely know that Justin meant the Eucharist, for in chap. 66, which immediately follows, he states : " And this food itself is known among us as the Eucharist.... For we do not receive these things as common bread or common drink... so we have learned that the food, made Eucharist by a word of prayer, ...by change is the flesh and blood of the incarnate Jesus. " (Cf. edit. Otto, I, pp. 180 f. for original.)

and the commentaries of the Apostles or the writings of the
Prophets are read, for as long as time permits. When the
reader finishes, the one presiding gives a speech in which he
admonishes and exhorts (all) to imitate these beautiful
teachings (in their lives). We all then stand up together and
recite prayers. And when we have finished the prayers
mentioned above, bread and wine-and-water are brought
(ἄρτος προσφέρεται καὶ οἶνος καὶ ὕδωρ) and the one presiding offers up prayers and likewise thanksgivings as much
as he can and the people chime in with " Amen. "   Then to
each one is distributed a portion of the things over which the
thanksgiving had been spoken (ἀπὸ τῶν εὐχαριστηθέντων
ἑκάστῳ γίνεται, lit. : *over which the eucharistizing was made*)
and each one partakes of them, and a share is brought by
the deacons to those who were absent. [6]

Since there is no mention of a common meal being connected
with either description, we may conclude that at least in the West,
the celebration of the Eucharist was no longer connected with any
such meal. Another item of interest is the apparent fusion of the
synaxis with the Eucharist, since nothing in the description indicates
a separation of the two services. The fusion, however, may not have
been accomplished in fact. Aside from later irrefutable testimony,
indirect internal evidence from Justin himself argues for the distinction of the two rites. On occasions of baptisms, the baptismal
ritual took the place of the synaxis. Had the synaxis and the Eucharist already been fused into one, the baptismal rite could not
have rightly been substituted for the synaxis. The first sentence
of chapter 66 corroborates this, for only the baptized who led
virtuous lives could attend the Eucharist and receive it.

Terminology seems to become fixed, for Justin uses no other term
but *Eucharist* for the consecrated bread and wine. From this time
onward, the word *Eucharist* is the technical term exclusively referring
to the consecrated elements. No longer need we fear to translate
Eucharistia as *Eucharist* instead of *Thanksgiving*, since Justin himself
tells us " this food itself is known among us as the Eucharist (ἡ τροφὴ

[6] The earliest manuscripts of the *First Apology* are the *Codex Regius* of 1364,
at the National Library of Paris, and the *Codex Claromontanus* of 1541, at Chel-
tenham, England. Our translation was made from edit. Otto, I, pp. 177-180,
184-188.

αὕτη καλεῖται παρ' ἡμῖν εὐχαριστία)... is both the flesh and blood of the incarnate Jesus " (ἐκείνου τοῦ σαρκοποιηθέντος ᾿Ιησοῦ καὶ σάρκα καὶ αἷμα...εἶναι). [7]

In no uncertain way does Justin emphasize the *Amen* of the congregation after the thanksgiving prayer of the celebrant. Why this prominence or insistence on something which now seems unimportant, almost trivial? The early Christians valued the term and stressed its use. Almost instinctively, they sensed its true meaning of approving, of confirming the celebrant's words. This " stamp of approval" was merely an outward expression of the spirit, the sense of unity and oneness with one another which the early Christians felt so keenly. With the *Amen*, the celebrant's sacrifice became their own; with it, his words of thanksgiving also became theirs. With this one word, they reiterated that unity and oneness urged so forcefully by St. Ignatius of Antioch fifty years previously regarding liturgical functions : " ...when you come together, there should be one prayer, one supplication, one mind, one hope in holy joy." [9] Unfortunately, we have lost much of that spirit of oneness. That is why the *Amen* means so little to so many today, even though Holy Communion is still the most real, the strongest unifying force in the world. If ever the day comes when virtually the whole congregation receives Holy Communion at every Sunday Mass, this spirit of oneness may again prevail in the Catholic community.

Three other writers of the second century provide a few additional items of liturgical information. Of these, Athenagoras of Athens and Theophilus of Antioch offer so very little that the only need for mentioning them is to point out that each one refers to prayers for the emperor, an important element in the intercessory prayers of subsequent Liturgies. [9] Also Athenagoras of Athens, in his comparison of the pagan sacrifices with those of the Christians, mentions that the latter prayed with uplifted hands. [10] St. Irenaeus, on the

---

[7] Justin, *First Apology*, chap. 66. See above, p. 44, n. 5.

[9] Ignatius of Antioch, *Ad magn.*, 7, 1 (PG 3, 711 D [*Series graeca*]).

[9] Cf. Athenagoras, Πρεσβεία περι χριστιανῶν *(Legatio pro christianis)*, 37 (ANF, II, p. 148); Theophilus, *Ad Autolycum*, I, 11 (ANF, II, p. 92).

[10] Athenagoras of Athens, *op. cit.*, 13 (ANF, II, p. 135); however, this can apply to liturgical prayers other than those in the Divine Liturgy.

other hand, fills in more details regarding liturgical functions. Thus, he mentions lections and a homily or sermon, [11] an oblation of bread and wine, [12] a consecration which he calls the *word of invocation, the word of God,* and *the invocation of God,* [13] and that the *Amen* was said by everyone together. [14]

Many things familiar to later Christians were unknown in liturgical functions of the second century. The clergy had no special vestments for the services; they used ordinary clothes, though these particular garments were reserved for exclusive liturgical use. Canonical hours, the cultus of saints, wax tapers, incense were still to be introduced.

[11] Irenaeus, *Ad. haeres.*, IV, 33, 8 (PG 7, 1077-1078).
[12] *Ibid.*, IV, 17, 5 (PG 7, 1023-1024).
[13] *Ibid.*, I, 13, 2 (PG 7, 580 A); IV, 18, 5 (PG 7, 1028 B-1029 A), etc.
[14] *Ibid.*, I, 14, 1 (PG 7, 597).

CHAPTER IV

THE AGAPE

Though the process of separating the Eucharist from the common meal was gradual, it was probably accomplished in most if not all the Churches during the first half of the second century. This does not mean that the common meal was totally abolished, but only that it was held separately from the Eucharist. [1] Even as an independent, semireligious function, the common meal continued to be an important phase of Christian life for several centuries. Fortunately, many details about the ceremonial connected with the agapes have been recorded. Tertullian's writings (A.D. 160?-230?), especially his *Apologeticus*, provide many interesting items. After describing what these Christian reunions were not, he goes on to tell what they were :

> Our repast, by its very name, indicates its purpose. It is called by a name which among the Greeks means "love" (agape)... by this refreshment we comfort the needy.... No one takes his seat at table without first praying to God. They eat as much as appeases their hunger and drink as much as men who are temperate. They satisfy their needs as men who remember that they must still worship God during the night. They take part in conversation but never forget that the Lord can hear all. After the lamps are lit and hands washed, each one, according to his ability to do so, is expected to read the Holy Scriptures or to sing a hymn in the center (of the room). This shows if he drank to excess. The meal likewise ends with a prayer. [2]

[1] Though Clement of Alexandria (fl. A.D. 200) refers several times to the common meal or agape, not once does he hint that the Eucharist was still connected with it (*Paedagogus*, II, 1, edit. Stahlin, GCS, I, p. 156; *ibid.*, 5, 2, edit. cit., p. 157; *ibid.*, 6, 1, edit. cit., p. 157; *ibid.*, 7, 1, edit. cit., pp. 157-158; cf. K. Volker, *Mysterium und Agape, Die gemeinsamen Mahlzeiten in der alten Kirche* [Gotha, 1927], pp. 542-544, for excellent interpretation of these passages). But Alexandria was not alone. The agapes of the other Churches during the third and fourth century were not combined with the Eucharist. This is clear from the various versions of the *Apostolic Tradition*, i.e., the Coptic, Arabic, and Ethiopic (cf. nn. 48-52, Horner, pp. 321-323; nn. 36-38, Horner, pp. 103-104; nn. 37-39, Horner, pp. 25-39), from the *Canons of Hippolytus* (canons 32-34, cf. W. Riedel, *Die Kirchenrechtsquellen*, pp. 221-223), from the *Testamentum Domini* (I, 1, n. xxxiii), etc.

[2] Tertullian, *Apologeticus*, chap. 39 (PL 1, 538-541). Our translation is made from Migne.

In this sketch, Tertullian gives no information regarding the content of the prayers said; hence no comparison can be made between them and the Jewish *chabûrah* suppers. Nor can we, on the basis of what he writes, correlate this common meal with anything specific in the *chabûrah*. The washing of hands and the lighting of lamps (or torches) indeed were *chabûrah* customs, but were they here part of the agape ritual? After all, these in themselves were common practices at evening meals in nearly all the Mediterranean regions. Were the singing of the psalms (or hymns) and the prayer after the meal *chabûrah* vestiges? They could equally well be the natural course of events in any Christian function. After stressing the meaning of brotherly love and affection as the purpose of these common meals, Tertullian strangely forgets to mention one of their most significant symbols, the common cup! The only logical explanation for it is that in his locality this important part of the ceremonial had been eliminated and replaced with the cup of the Eucharist at the time the Eucharist became separated from the meal.

The most complete information on the agape is found in the Egyptian version of the *Apostolic Tradition*. Authorship of the original Greek work is attributed to Hippolytus, the Roman presbyter and controversialist of the third century. He composed it about A.D. 215 but it contains much material from the second century. Though almost unknown in Rome and the West generally—likely owing to the fact that its author had set himself up as an antipope during the reign of Pope Callistus although he was later reconciled to the Church and died a martyr in A.D. 235—the *Apostolic Tradition* has been widely known and copied in the East, especially in Egypt and Syria. Like so many other works, its original Greek version has not survived, except for a few fragments, but its Coptic, Ethiopic, and Arabic versions are extant, as well as a partial Syriac version. How much of these texts are interpolations is difficult to assess. The immense popularity of the original work in the East was due to the belief that it contained (as it claimed) the tradition of the Apostles; also, simply the fact that it originated in Rome, the primal See, may have enhanced its popularity.

At any rate, the *Apostolic Tradition* gives a fairly comprehensive picture of the common meal, which retained all the features of a Christian *chabûrah* even after the Eucharist had been separated from it:

> And he [the bishop], after having broken the bread, must always taste of it and eat with those faithful who are present. And before each takes his own bread, they shall take from the hand of the bishop one fragment of the loaf, for this is the *eulogion* (blessed bread). It is, however, not the Eucharist, as is the Body of the Lord.
>
> And before they drink, let each of those present take a cup, give thanks (εὐχαριστεῖν) and drink. And thus let the baptized have their meal.
>
> But to the catechumens the exorcised bread should be given, and they shall offer a cup each for themselves. A catechumen shall not sit at table at the Lord's supper....
>
> And if the faithful should attend a Lord's supper without a bishop but with a presbyter or a deacon only, they should similarly partake in an orderly way. Let all, however, be careful to receive the blessed bread from the presbyter's or deacon's hand; a catechumen shall receive the exorcised bread in like manner. If [only] laymen are present without a cleric, let them eat with understanding, for a layman cannot make the blessed bread. But after giving thanks (εὐχαριστήσας) for himself, each should eat in the name of the Lord.... [3]

Comparison of the agape as described above with the old Jewish *chabûrah* meal provides some exciting parallels which leave little doubt of the agape's obvious Jewish derivation even after a century and a half of change.

Jewish Chabûrah Meal	*The Christian Agape*
1. Only the host or leader of the *chabûrah* was to begin the meal by saying the " grace before meals. "	1. It was the bishop (or the presbyter or deacon) alone who had the right to say the formal grace or bless the bread which began the agape, " for a layman cannot make the blessed bread. " [4]

---

[3] Our translation from xxv and xxvi of *Ap. Trad.* Brackets supplied for clearer meaning. Cf. Horner, *The Statutes of the Apostles or Canones Ecclesiastici* (London, 1904), 48-52, pp. 321-323, for complete Coptic recension of parallel passages.

[4] So also Ignatius of Antioch : " Without the bishop, it is not lawful... to hold the agape " (*Smyrn.*, viii. 2. edit., F. X. Funk, II, p. 150).

2. This "grace before meals" consisted of the leader taking bread, breaking it, reciting the customary blessing of the bread, and eating a piece of it.

3. After eating a particle of the bread, the leader of the *chabûrah* gave a fragment to each of those present at table.

4. This ritual of bread-blessing and breaking was the formal beginning of the *chabûrah* meal.

5. Each of the guests could bless his own cup of wine during the main course of the *chabûrah* meal.

6. The old rabbinical regulations forbid eating with " uncircumcised men " (Acts 11:13).

7. Jewish custom, however, permitted Gentiles to drink in presence of the *chabûrah*.

8. The *chabûrah* suppers were religion-sponsored or semi-religious functions, as is evident from all the religious ceremonial connected with them.

2. This grace consisted of the bishop (or presbyter or deacon) taking bread, breaking it, blessing it, and tasting of it.

3. After tasting it, the bishop (or presbyter or deacon) gave a fragment of the loaf to each of the faithful who were present.

4. This ceremony of bread-blessing and breaking also began the Christian agape.

5. Each of those present also blessed his own wine-cup during the agape, " And before they drink, let each of those present take a cup and give thanks and drink. "

6. The Christians apparently had a similar rule : " A catechumen shall not sit at table at the Lord's supper.... "

7. The catechumens not having been initiated into the Church, though they had to eat apart from the faithful, were allowed to receive " exorcised bread " (not blessed bread, however).

8. The Christian agapes were also religion-sponsored meals.

The " blessed bread " of the agape, or Lord's Supper, was not the Eucharist " as is the body of the Lord, " nor were the cups of wine over which each of those present gave thanks individually. Again, in the agape described, no parallel " thanksgiving " was said over a Cup of the Blessing, a really important element at Jewish *chabûrah* meals. Evidently, when the Christian parallel to the Cup of the Blessing had become the chalice of the Eucharist in a separate service (where it was conjoined to the institution narrative and the Eucharistic formulae to form the consecration of the wine), no substitute took its place in the meal.

In the East, where the finer distinctions of Jewish practice were generally much better known and appreciated than in the West, the agape even after its separation from the Eucharist did have a common cup. Its Jewish parallel was not the Cup of the Blessing (which was transferred to the Eucharistic service) but the *kiddûsh* cup. The agape found in the Ethiopic version of the *Apostolic Tradition*, into which it had been interpolated from an unknown Eastern source had, for example, such a common cup as well as as several other items of Jewish *chabûrah* derivation :

Concerning the bringing in of lamps at the supper of the congregation. When the evening has come, the bishop being there, the deacon shall bring in a lamp, and standing in the midst of all the Faithful, being about to give thanks, the bishop shall first give the salutation, thus saying : The Lord (be) with you all. And the people also shall say : With thy spirit. And the bishop shall say : Let us give thanks to the Lord. And the people shall say : Right and just, both greatness and exaltation with glory are due to him. And they shall not say : Lift up your hearts, because that shall be said at the time of the Oblation. And he prays thus, saying : We give thee thanks, God, through thy Son Jesus Christ our Lord, because thou hast enlightened us by revealing the incorruptible light, we having therefore finished the length of a day and having come to the beginning of the night, and having been satiated with the light of the day which thou hast created for our satisfaction, and now since we have not been deficient of the light of the evening by thy grace, we sanctify thee and we glorify thee through thine only Son our Lord Jesus Christ, through whom to thee with him (be) glory and might and honour with the Holy Spirit now, etc. And they shall all say : Amen. And having risen up therefore after supper, the children and virgins having prayed, they shall say the psalms : and afterwards the deacon, holding the mingled cup of the Prosfora, shall say the psalm from that in which (is) written Hālē luyā, (and) after that the presbyter

has commanded : " And likewise from those psalms. " And
afterwards the bishop having offered the cup, as is proper
for the cup, he shall say the psalm Hālē luyā; and all of them
as he recites the psalms shall say Hālē luyā, which is to say :
We praise him who is God most high : glorified and praised
is he who founded all the world with one word. And likewise,
the psalm having been completed, he shall give thanks over
the cup, and shall give of the fragments to the Faithful. And
as they are eating their supper the believers shall take a little
bread from the hand of the bishop before they partake of
their own bread, for it is Eulogia and not Eucharist as of
our Lord. [5]

This is a fine example, we believe, of the ceremonial connected
with the agape in the pre-Nicene East, though the actual composition
is of later date. [6] The special Jewish *chabûrah* suppers held on
certain festivals, on Friday and Saturday evenings (beginning and
ending the Sabbath) had several items added to those of the ordinary
chabûrah. The Christian parallel to this special *chabûrah* is the
agape described in the Ethiopic version of the *Apostolic Tradition*.

A. Just before the birth of Christ, *lighting, bringing in and
blessing* the lamp had become an integral part of the *chabûrah* ceremonial for these specially formal occasions; this is evident from the
rabbinic schools of Shammai and Hillel which debated the exact
point in the meal when this should be done, [7] and whether the word
lamp(s) in the blessing should be singular or plural : " Blessed art
Thou, O Lord, our God, King of the world, who createst the lamp(s)
of fire. " The Ethiopic version has a parallel ceremonial of the
lamp-blessing, though the blessing itself has been thoroughly

[5] Translation from the Ethiopic text is taken from G. Horner, *The Statutes of
the Apostles or Canones Ecclesiastici* (London, 1904), Statute, 36, pp. 159-161.
[6] The date of the passage in question cannot have been much later than Hippolytus' original, since it was already widely circulated throughout the East in the
fourth and fifth centuries. It was incorporated into the fourth or fifth century
Greek text of the *Apostolic Tradition* (the remote source of the Ethiopic version)
and also into the text of the *Testamentum Domini*. The compiler of the *Apostolic
Constitutions* (VIII), may also have known it; certainly, the author of the *Canons
of Hippolytus* did. The date of the passage is therefore thought to have been no
later than the third century.
[7] Cf. *Berakoth*, M., viii, 6.

remodeled along Christian lines. [8] Unfortunately the text does not tell us whether this ceremonial was carried out at all Eastern agapes or only at those of Sunday. The lamp-blessing was shifted by the Christians from the end of the proceedings to the beginning—understandably, since the Cup of the Blessing and the accompanying thanksgiving were transferred to the Eucharistic service.

B. In the festal *chabûrah*, besides the Cup of the Blessing, the Jews blessed and partook of an additional common cup called the *kiddûsh* cup. [9] Precisely at what point in the meal the *kiddûsh* cup was blessed and passed around in the first century A.D. is still a matter of dispute, but one thing is certain : the *Cup of the Blessing* never preceded the breaking of bread. From this fact we can deduce that the common cup of the Eastern Christians, described in the Ethiopic text, was the Christian parallel, not of the Cup of the Blessing but of the *kiddûsh* cup of the Jews. In the East, therefore, no less than in the West, the Christian parallel of the Cup of the Blessing had been transferred to the Eucharistic celebration after its separation from the meal—where the words of institution and the consecratory formula were pronounced over it to confect the Eucharist. The other common cup, the *kiddûsh*, remained in the agape.

C. What are we to make of the " alleluia " psalms mentioned by the Ethiopic translator? The confusion is more apparent than real. In Jewish practice, the festal *chabûrah* suppers, that is, those held on the eighteen Jewish feasts such as the Passover, Pentecost, Tabernacles, etc., included the song of the *hallel*. The *hallel* as part of the ceremonial of the Passover supper certainly dates back

---

[8] Vestiges of this ancient practice may be found in the East even today, not to mention the ceremony of the Lucernarium in Milan and Toledo. The Armenian Rite still has a Vesper prayer whose complete structure is that of the Jewish *Berakah* and still contains a formal allusion to the *lumen lucernae* of this ancient ceremonial (cf. *Breviarium Armenium*, p. 214). Great emphasis was placed in the Armenian Church on the ceremony of lighting the lamps, which took place at the tenth hour (cf. F. C. Conybeare, *Rituale Armenorum*, Oxford, 1905, p. 494).

[9] These two cups must be carefully distinguished : in Jewish practice, both were common cups, blessed and passed around by the host, but each differed as to the words of its blessing and its position relative to the parts of the *chabûrah* supper.

before our Lord's time; [10] its extension to the other feasts dates
back at least to the second century A.D. [11]   Since all such changes
are gradual, the latter practice was probably introduced earlier.   The
hallel on such occasions included : *(a)* Psalms 111-118 (Vulgate
112-117), which, when taken as a single unit, were called the *Small
hallel* or the *Egyptian hallel*, originally so-called because of its
recitation during the meal on the night of the Passover; *(b)* Psalms
135 and 136, called the *Great hallel*.   In the Egyptian hallel we
find the alleluias a prominent feature.   The " alleluia " psalms sung
by the Eastern Christians at their agapes were probably none other
than the psalms of the Egyptian hallel.   This also explains the
apparent confusing shift from the singular " psalm " to the plural
" psalms " in the text : taken as a unit the Egyptian hallel was indeed
sometimes called a " psalm "; on the other hand, when taken dis-
jointly, the Egyptian hallel could be termed " psalms, " for that is
what it was, several psalms.

Liturgical Language

Until the latter part of the second century, the liturgical language
in the Eastern as well as the Western Churches was generally Greek.
In this, the infant Church adopted the practice of the Jews in the
diaspora.   Palestinian Jews probably never had a strictly vernacular
service either in the Temple or in the synagogues around the countryside; Hebrew, not the vernacular Aramaic, was their liturgical
language until about the second century A.D.   The Jews of the
diaspora, however, did hold their synagogue services in Greek, the
general vernacular of the Levant already in the first century of the
Christian era.   When the Church spread beyond the confines of
Palestine, it simply took over this practice of using Greek in its
services, except for a few Hebrew words such as *Amen, Alleluia,
Hosanna*, etc.   In the first two centuries, Greek was the vernacular
of most Christians in all the large Eastern cities (e.g., Alexandria,
Antioch, Jerusalem, etc.); it was also the language of the first
Christians in Rome, the majority of whom were Greek-speaking

---

[10] Cf. *Pesachim*, Mishnah, x, 6.
[11] Cf. *Sukkoth, Tos.*, iv, 1.

Levantines living in the foreign quarter. At first, the question of a special liturgical language never arose. Greek was used simply because it was understood by most of the early converts, even at Rome.

Latin as a liturgical language was introduced first in the African Church at the close of the second century. Rome and the Western Church in general probably adopted it some time during the third or fourth century; opinions vary on this. [12] The change occurred because Greek ceased to be used and understood by the Christians of the Western Church. When the language of the people changed, so did the language in the Liturgy. The transition, in any case, was a gradual one. From the third to the fifth centuries, Greek and Latin seem to have been used side by side in the Churches of the West. [13] During this period of transition most people probably knew both languages; the rest, either one or the other.

In most Eastern Churches, on the other hand, the problem was less complicated, for some time at least. As the centuries slipped by, however, one Church after another replaced Greek with its national language. In Greece, of course, no such change was ever necessary.

---

[12] Some of the dates given are : latter half of the second century (G. Dix, *The Shape of the Liturgy* [London : Dacre Press, 1960], p. 617; the second half of the third century (F. Kattenbusch, *Das apostolische Symbol* [Leipzig, 1900], ii, 331, n. 108); from the third to the sixth century (J. A. Jungmann, *The Mass of the Roman Rite*, I, p. 50); the end of the fourth century (G. Rietschel, *Lehrbuch der Liturgik* [Berlin, 1900], i, 337-338; Probst, *Abendländische Messe* [Münster, 1896], pp. 5 f.; I. Watterich, *Konsekrationsmoment* [Heidelberg, 1896), pp. 131 f.).

[13] In the fourth century (c. A.D. 360), for example, the Roman rhetorician Marius Victorinus Africanus writes in Latin but still quotes a liturgical prayer (from the Roman *oratio oblationis* of his day) in Greek. As late as the sixth or seventh century, the Gelasian sacramentary states that the creed at baptism may be said either in Greek or in Latin by the convert. At Rome itself on certain days, e.g. Holy Saturday, the lections were read in Greek along with the Latin until the eighth century; so were some of the psalms (cf. PL, lxxviii, 955, 966, 968).

CHAPTER V

PRE-NICENE UNIFORMITY-DIVERSITY

Despite the great variations of detail, expected of the more-or-less extemporary character of all pre-Nicene prayer, the celebration of the Eucharist in the second century can still be considered uniform. This uniformity consisted not only in the general ideas *(identity of meaning)* contained in those extemporary prayers, but also in the order or arrangement of their component parts. That is why Pope Anicetus (*c.* A.D. 157-158) could have " granted the (celebration of the) Eucharist in church to Polycarp as a mark of honor "[1] when the latter came to Rome. Had the celebration of the Eucharist been radically different at Rome and at Polycarp's hometown of Smyrna, the incident surely would have aroused comment at Rome. The various extemporary details in the prayers themselves were no cause for comment either, since this was the accepted practice among the local clergy at that time.

With the third century, however, although general uniformity was observed, traces of differentiating practices may be found in every Church. These eventually evolved into distinct Rites within the universal Church. Authors generally relegate the separation of the Liturgies (and the ancient Rites) to the fourth century, but the movement began in the third century.

Before the Council of Nicaea, there may have been local differences as regards timing of worship, division of services, and physical attitudes of the worshipers. Yet, a definite uniformity was maintained throughout Christendom both in the order and in the content of the cult. This uniformity most probably represents the genuine tradition received from Christ and the apostles. St. Clement of Rome expresses it well : " It behooves us to do all things in [their proper] order which the Lord has commanded us to perform at stated times. "[2] Justin indicates the same belief : after describing the Eucharistic rite, he says Christ appeared to his

---

[1] From the Letter of Irenaeus to Pope Victor I, in Eusebius, *Hist. eccl.*, V, 24. 17 (PG 13, 201 C [*Series graeca*]).
[2] Clement of Rome, *First Epistle to the Corinthians*, chap. xl (ANF, I, p. 16).

apostles and disciples on Easter and " taught them these things. " [3]

Whether or not this belief was founded on historical fact, it caused the generations that followed the apostles scrupulously to observe the original uniformity of order and arrangement within the service. Habit also was an important factor in preserving the original order and arrangement. People learned when to expect the readings, the psalms, the sermon, when to stand, when to go up for Holy Communion, and so forth. Any sudden reversal of order would have disturbed them. Thus, sufficient similarity was preserved and a classification of distinct ritual entities or rites is unwarranted in the pre-Nicene Church.

Paradoxical as it may seem, many authors do describe this era as one of many separate " local rites. " This is easy to explain because of the general freedom in matters of ritual detail. The general order in the synaxis was similar if not identical in all the Churches, yet, especially in the Eastern Churches, the number of lections varied and also their Old Testament sources. The outline or sequence of the component parts of the celebration of the Eucharist remained uniform in all the Churches at this early date, yet there was no set, standardized form. The general ideas to be included in the major prayers were similar, but the actual wording differed with each celebrant since he was free to extemporize as he went along. [4] The freedom to extemporize is the reason why many prefer to call this the era of " many local rites. " This was probably one of the things which St. Firmilian, Bishop of Caesarea, had in mind when he wrote to St. Cyprian (c. A.D. 250), giving his opinion on Pope Stephen I's insistence on Roman customs for other Churches : " There are differences in regard to many of the divine sacraments; nor are all things observed there [at Rome] as at Jerusalem; indeed, in the other provinces many things are different according to the diversity of men and places, yet there is no division from the peace and unity of the universal Church because of this. " [5]

[3] Justin Martyr, *First Apology*, chap. 67 (ANF, p. 186); also cf. Eusebius, *Vita Constantini*, 3, 43 (PG 20, 1104 [*Series graeca*, 13, 379]).

[4] Thus, the *Didache* states that the " prophets give thanks as much as they wish " (10, 7; for full rite, see all of chaps. 9-10, edit. F. X. Funk, pp. 24-32); thus also Justin Martyr (*First Apology*, 67; see above, p. 42).

[5] Firmilian, *ad Cyprianum*, 75, 6 (Hartel, CSEL, p. 818). Our translation.

It was only from about the middle of the third century that liturgical forms began to be crystallized. In theory, until then, each celebrant could pray as he wished provided he included at least the same general ideas in his prayer—even in the Eucharistic prayer. Somewhat of a parallel may be seen when, given a certain topic, different preachers necessarily give different sermons. The testimony of Hippolytus is clear and to the point : " It is absolutely not necessary for the bishop to use the exact wording... as if he were learning them by heart for his thanksgiving to God. Rather each one should pray according to his capability. If he is ready to pronounce a grand and solemn prayer, that is well; if on the contrary he should say a prayer according to a set form, no one may hinder him! But the prayer must be correct and orthodox. " [6]

True, certain brief forms or expressions from the Scriptures were known and used by the early Christians when they prayed. Such expressions as *Thanks be to God, Blessed art thou, O Lord our God, Forever and ever, Lord, have mercy, Amen, Alleluia* were used extensively. Early Christian language in fact was permeated with them. [7] Public prayer was no exception. Given the same general ideas of what to pray for and a fixed framework as in the Eucharistic celebration, these expressions automatically found their way into liturgical prayer. Such prayers then, despite their extempore character, had a semblance of uniformity.

Understandably, uniformity was greater within a local Church— Rome, Antioch, or Alexandria—than between the various Churches of Christendom. After attending the Eucharistic service for years before his ordination, the young priest would quite naturally tend to do what he had seen being done and use the same expressions as his predecessors (all liturgical prayers were said aloud at the time). When other churches and missions were founded from the mother church, the missionaries would celebrate the Liturgy for their converts in much the same way as in the mother church. Besides,

---

[6] Edit. Dix, *The treatise on the Apostolic Tradition of St. Hippolytus of Rome* (London, 1937), 19. Cf. also J. Lebreton in Fliche et Martin, *Histoire de l'Église*, II (1935), 70, n. 3.

[7] A good example of this, though again not entirely parallel, is the instance of St. Clement of Rome's *Letter to the Corinthians*. It includes many liturgical allusions which evidently pertained to the Roman liturgy, and which Clement obviously expected the people of Corinth to understand and appreciate.

the intense loyalty for the mother church, which we know existed in those early days, would have prompted them carefully to observe what was being done there.

During the first centuries, liturgical functions had almost no ceremonial attached to them. This also aided uniformity. Liturgical action was dictated purely by utility or necessity. Anything that needed to be done was done in the simplest, most practical way. Bread and wine, for example, were brought and set down near the celebrant without ceremony or pomp. Later, when ceremonial developed and increased, uniformity decreased proportionately.

Keeping all this in mind, we may now introduce what is regarded as the most important source of information on the Liturgy in the pre-Nicene Church, the only pre-Nicene text of the Eucharistic Prayer which has not undergone subsequent extensive revision. Contained in the *Apostolic Tradition* of Hippolytus, it represents only the local tradition of Rome but, insofar as the general framework of ideas (identity of meaning) was still uniform throughout Christendom, it may represent to a degree the pre-Nicene traditions of all the Churches. The text includes the consecration of a bishop. When that is finished, the deacons bring up the gifts *(prosphora)*. Then, accompanied by the presbyters, the bishops extend their hands over the gifts and begin the opening dialogue and Eucharistic Prayer :

> The Lord be with you.
> And with thy spirit.
> Lift up your hearts.
> We have [lifted them] unto the Lord.
> Let us give thanks to the Lord.
> It is meet and right.

And he shall proceed thus :

We give thee thanks, O God, through thy beloved Servant Jesus Christ, whom thou didst send in recent times as Saviour, Redeemer and the Angel-messenger of thy counsel. He is thine inseparable Word through whom thou madest all things and in whom thou wast well pleased. Him thou didst send from heaven into the Virgin's womb; he was conceived within her, was made flesh, and was shown to be thy Son in being born of the Holy Spirit and the Virgin. In carrying out thy will and acquiring for thee a holy people he stretched

forth his hands to suffer that he might release from sufferings
those who believed in thee.

When he was delivered up to voluntary suffering that he
might abolish death, rend the bonds of the devil, tread down
hell, enlighten the righteous, establish what was decreed and
show forth the resurrection, taking bread [and] giving thanks
to thee, he said : Take, eat, this is my body which is broken for
you.   Likewise also the cup, saying : This is my blood which
is shed for you.   When you do this, do it in commemoration
of me [or, make ye my *anamnesis*].

Therefore, doing it now in commemoration [or, making the
anamnesis] of his death and resurrection, we offer to thee the
bread and the cup by giving thanks unto thee for making us
worthy to stand before thee and to minister unto thee.
And we pray thee (to send thy Holy Spirit upon the oblation
of thy holy Church) to gather together in unity all thy holy
ones who partake of it that they may be filled with the Holy
Spirit for strengthening [their] faith in truth, that we may
praise and glorify thee through thy Servant Jesus, through
whom honor and glory [be] to thee with the Holy Spirit in
thy holy Church now and forever and ever.

Amen. [8]

This prayer of Hippolytus is not and was not intended to be a
verbatim type of third-century Eucharisitc Prayer; it is only a
suggested text to serve as a model for the clergy to help them extemporize.   Hippolytus himself stresses this right of every celebrant.
The train of thought, the ideas alone should be fixed (identity of
meaning), whereas the words to express them should be composed
by the celebrant himself (verbal diversity); this was the true pre-
Nicene tradition.

[8] Our translation, from the Latin (Hauler, *Didascalia apostolorum fragmenta
Veronensia* [Leipzig, 1900], pp. 106 ff.).   Bracketed words are supplied to make
the meaning of the original clearer.   The clause in parentheses indicates a probable
fourth-century addition.   *Make ye my anamnesis* is undoubtedly a better technical
expression than *Do it in commemoration of me*, to indicate the true meaning of the
original, but it would perhaps be incomprehensible to most readers.   Our translation as *Do it in commemoration of me* follows the Douay Version.   There is no
precise English equivalent of *anamnesis*; " commemoration, " " remembrance, "
" memorial " or " memory " have a connotation of something which is mentally
remembered without the thing itself being present in any other way, whereas in
the Scriptures *anamnesis* (and its verbal form) means " recalling " or " remembrance " or " representing " before God a past event in that it is operative in its
effects here and now (cf. III Kings 17; 18; Heb. 10:3-4, etc.).   This then is the
sense of " in commemoration of " used at this point.

CHAPTER VI

THE LAST CENTURY
OF THE PRE-NICENE EUCHARIST

Originally distinct from one another, the synaxis and the Eucharist not only had different origins but served two different purposes. Until a person was baptized and accepted into the *ecclesia*, he had no hope of ever attending the Eucharist, the Liturgy of the body of Christ, for that was only for the members of that body. Once baptized, the Christian had the grave obligation of attending the Eucharist on every Lord's Day even at the risk of his life, a risk terrifyingly real for over two hundred years (from Nero to Diocletian, A.D. 65 to A.D. 313). He did this as a member of Christ's body, the *ecclesia*, to participate in *the* vital act of that body, the Divine Sacrifice. It was unthinkable to act otherwise.

Attendance at the Sunday synaxis was hardly less strict : the redeemed were expected to participate in it as a corporate witness to the fact of the redemption. Except for casual inquirers, those enrolled in the catechumenate were obliged to attend the synaxis, for they could not hope to be accepted into the body, by baptism, unless they could prove their fidelity, at least to a certain extent. To be faithful meant sincere willingness to observe all the obligations of the Christian, one of which was attendance at the corporate worship. [1] Furthermore, attendance at the synaxis was the normal way of learning the salutory truths of the redemption and other doctrines necessary for acceptance into the Body, the *ecclesia*.

On the basis of pre-Nicene evidence, we can piece together and reconstruct the general form of the synaxis and the Eucharistic rite, and the arrangement of their component parts. Nothing like it can be attempted in the century after Nicaea, for by then the rites of each Church had evolved into separate, distinct entities warranting

---

[1] The period of probation was shortened or extended according to the individual catechumen's good or bad conduct : " If a man be earnest and persevere well... because it is not the time that is judged but the conduct (let him be received) "; Dix, *The Apostolic Tradition*, 28, v. 2.

separate classification. The evidence, necessarily scanty on account of the *disciplina arcani*, does provide sufficient data to form a correct though perhaps far from complete picture of the pre-Nicene Liturgy. In outline, the general order or arrangement of the two services was as follows :

The Synaxis	*The Eucharist*
1. Opening Greeting	1. Greeting and Kiss of Peace
2. Readings and Psalms	2. Offertory
3. Gospel	3. Eucharistic Prayer
4. Sermon or Sermons	4. Fraction
5. Dismissal of Catechumens	5. Communion
6. Intercessory Prayers of the Faithful	6. Ablutions and Dismissal

The Synaxis or Fore-Mass

1. *Opening Greeting.* When the congregation had assembled, the service began with a greeting exchanged between the celebrant and the whole congregation. [2] One of two forms was used : *The Lord be with you* or *Peace be unto you* (or *to all*). Both are of Jewish origin (cf. pp. 408 ff., for history). This preliminary was at once a greeting of welcome to the people and a signal to start the proceedings.

2. *Readings and Psalms.* The lector then began the readings (lections or lessons) from the Old Testament, [3] usually from the Law and the Prophets. [4] The practice in Jewish synagogues had been to arrange the readings from Scripture in descending order of their importance. Since the Law of Moses was the most revered of the Scriptures, it was read first; then, after the psalmody, one or more of the lections from the Prophets. The order used in the Christian synaxis was the exact opposite, ascending in the order of importance. Since the Gospel containing the Lord's own words

---

[2] The modern term " celebrant " is used instead of the pre-Nicene " president " or " the one presiding " to indicate the bishop or presbyter who held the service.

[3] Cf. Clement of Alexandria (c. A. D. 200), *Cohortatio ad gentes* (PG 8, 239 BC); *Stromata*, 7, 7 (PG 9, 469); Origen (c. A.D. 254-255), *In Genes. homil.*, I, 17 (PG 12, 160).

[4] Tertullian, *De Praescript.*, 36 (PL 2, 49); also *Apolog.*, 22 (PL 1, 408).

and deeds was the paramount reading for Christians, it was read last. Next in importance were the apostolic writings or Epistles; they were read immediately before the Gospel. Texts from the Old Testament were read first. When more than one Old Testament reading was made, these too were arranged in this new ascending order of importance. Thus, for a time the Law of Moses seems to have retained some of its Jewish precedence over the rest of the Old Testament; hence, it was read last, i.e., immediately before the Epistle. Later, when the purely chronological order was introduced for Old Testament readings, the Law was read first, then the Prophets etc. In this way the Church reverted to the original Jewish order, though for a different reason.

Between the readings, cantors sang the psalms or other canticles from the Scriptures. [5] The psalms, selected as a " comment " on the Scriptures just read, were sung by soloists and not by alternating choirs, as was usual after the fourth century. [6] The corporate ideal, however, was not lacking, for the people " repeated the last words, " that is, joined as a chorus in a simple refrain. [7] As is the case with today's reading the Epistle could be replaced by a reading from the Acts. [8] In some localities the bishop's pastoral letters might be read at this point. [9]

3. *Gospel.* The Gospel was read by either a deacon or a priest; during its reading all stood in silence. [10]

4. *Sermon or Sermons.* Immediately after the Gospel reading

---

[5] The singing of psalms in general is attested by Clement of Alexandria (*Paedagogus*, 2, 4 [PG 8, 444]); by Origen (*In Iudic. homil.*, 6, 2 [PG 12, 974]; here he mentions psalms and hymns); by Tertullian (*Ad uxor.*, 2, 9 [PL 1, 1304] and *De anima*, 9 [PL 1, 408]) where he states : " *Prout scripturae leguntur aut psalmi canuntur aut allocutiones proferuntur aut petitiones delegantur,* " i.e., lessons, psalms, sermon(s) and prayers).

[6] This type of psalmody by two alternating choirs was introduced into Christian use at Antioch by a society of laymen about A.D. 347-348. From there, it spread rapidly to the other Churches.

[7] Cf. Brightman, LEW, p. 29.

[8] Cf. Tertullian, *De praescript.*, 36 (PL 2, 48-50).

[9] Cyprian, *Ep. xi*, 7 (edit. Hartel, 2, 500); Tertullian, *De pud.*, 1 (PL 2, 981) and *De praescrip.*, 51 (PL 2, 71).

[10] Origen, *In luc. hom.*, 1 (PG 13, 1003); *Homil.*, 7 to end (PG 13, 1819); *Homil.*, 8 (PG 13, 1819 C); Tertullian, *De praescrip.*, 36 (PL 2, 49-50); Cyprian, *Ep.*, 38 (Hartel, 2, 583-584), etc.

there followed the sermon(s). [11]   Often, in addition to the bishop-celebrant, other preachers delivered sermons; in such cases, the bishop was the last to speak.   The early Christians firmly believed that the bishop received a special gift (χάρισμα) at his consecration, not only for liturgical prayers and services but also for his office of preaching.   By his consecration he became a quasi-inspired " prophetic teacher " for his flock, as the faithful of Smyrna aptly described one who was their bishop, Polycarp, in A.D. 156. [12]

Despite the presence of more able preachers, it was the bishop who spoke the authentic mind of the Church in all matters because he alone, it was felt, was endowed by the power of the Holy Spirit to do this.   The sermon was an integral part of the Synaxis.   Without it, the service was regarded as liturgically incomplete.   The bishop always preached in his official capacity, sitting on the throne behind the altar.   This throne was his teacher's chair in more than a figurative way.   He spoke from it as the representative of God, imparting divine wisdom to the world.   That is why, as preacher at the synaxis, he could not be replaced even by the best of his presbyters except in the direst of emergencies.

5.   *Dismissal of Catechumens.*   Catechumens and penitents were dismissed after the sermon. [13]   Doorkeepers (and deaconesses) guarded the doors so that only the faithful remained for the Eucharistic sacrifice.   Probably before each class was asked to leave the assembly, a prayer-blessing was imparted to them. [14]   A dismissal-blessing from fourth-century Egypt, attributed to Sarapion (c. A.D. 340), probably represents the type used in pre-Nicene times.   First the deacon proclaimed : " Bow your heads for a blessing. "   Then the bishop extended his hands over the catechumens and said :

[11] Clement of Alexandria, *Strom.*, 6, 14 (PG 9, 337); Origen, *In Genes. homil.*, 10, 1 (PG 12, 215) and *In Exod. homil.*, 7, 8 (PG 12, 249) and *In Levit. homil.*, 4, 9 (PG 12, 444); also Cyprian, *De mortalitate*, 1 (Hartel, 1, 297), where he says that he is preaching on the lessons just read.

[12] *Mart. Polycarp.*, chap. 16 (ANF, I, p. 42).

[13] Cyprian, *Ep.*, 63, 8 (Hartel, 2, 706-707); Tertullian, *De praescrip.*, 40 (PL 1, 56); also his *Apol.*, 39 (PL 1, 469).

[14] Though pre-Nicene sources contain very few hints of such a prayer, some of Origen's sermons leave the impression that a prayer followed the sermon, e.g., " let us arise and pray. "

We raise our hand, O Lord, and pray that the divine and lifegiving hand be raised for a blessing unto this people, for unto thee, eternal Father, have they bowed their heads through thine only begotten Son. Bless this people unto the blessing of knowledge and piety, unto the blessing of thy mysteries; through thy only-begotten Son, Jesus Christ, by whom glory and might be unto thee in the Holy Ghost now and throughout all ages. Amen. [15]

Later the dismissals evolved into a complex ritual. Before Nicaea, Syria already had an elaborate penitential system; hence, the dismissals there were much more developed than in the other Churches. First the *hearers* were dismissed without a prayer; [16] then, the catechumens, the *energumens* (ἐνεργούμενοι, those possessed by evil spirits) and, finally, the *kneelers* after a prayer. [17]

6. *Intercessory Prayers of the Faithful.* These prayers, which followed the dismissal of the catechumens, were still part of the synaxis. When the Eucharist was held immediately after the synaxis, however, the same prayers can be regarded as belonging to the Eucharistic celebration. In fact, they were recited by the faithful, the " initiated " alone; as such they were the *office* or *function* of the baptized who alone had the right to participate in them and in the Eucharist.

The content of these common prayers of intercession can be surmised. The lengthy prayer that Clement of Rome included in his *Letter to the Corinthians* was probably from this part of the service : [18] in it are petitions for the sick and the weak, for the faint-

---

[15] *Bishop Sarapion's Prayer-Book*, trans. John Wordsworth (London, 1923), p. 92.

[16] Gregory the Wonderworker, *Ep. can.*, 11 (PG 10, 1048 AB).

[17] Council of Ancyra (c. A.D. 314), can. 9 (NPNF, Series II, XIV, pp. 66-67). Gregory the Wonderworker (*Ep. can.*, 11 [PG 10, 1048 AB]) only states that the kneelers were dismissed " along with the catechumens " and does not give the relative order of their dismissal. Canon 9 of the Ancyra Council does not mention a prayer for the catechumens but Gregory the Wonderworker implies it. The dismissal of *energumens* (those possessed by an evil spirit) is not mentioned either but may safely be assumed, since their attendance at the synaxis was indicated. Later fourth century sources corroborate this, e.g., Chrysostom at Antioch, the *Apostolic Constitutions* (VIII), the Council of Laodicea, the *Peregrinatio* of Etheria, etc. Cf. Bingham, *Antiquities*, VI, pp. 443 f.

[18] Chaps. 59 and 61. See above, pp. 35-360.

hearted, for peace, for princes and governors and civil authorities generally. Tertullian, who gives much incidental information about the third-century rite in Africa, also gives some of the petitions contained in the common prayers used in that area : " Lifting up our hands... we pray always for all the emperors, that they may have a long life, loyal people, a quiet territory and whatever else may be desired by men and by Caesar. " [19]   These prayers are usually centered on the temporal aspects of life.

The Eucharist Celebration

1. *Greeting and Kiss of Peace.*   The Eucharistic proceedings always began with a *greeting* and the *kiss of peace*. [20]   The greeting was similar to that beginning the synaxis. The " holy kiss, " or the " kiss of love, " was a token of brotherhood among the Christians since the apostolic era. It was exchanged by the bishop with the clergy standing around the throne behind the altar. The faithfu exchanged it in church, men with men, women with women. [21]

2. *Offertory.*   After the kiss of peace, the deacon(s) spread a linen cloth over the whole altar table. This had a purely utilitarian purpose : the " spreading of the table cloth " on which the offerings were to be placed. In the Latin Rite the linen corporal is still unfolded at this point in the Mass, although its present size is merely a fraction of the original. When the offerings of bread and wine were brought and placed on the altar, the bishop and presbyters laid their hands over the oblations in silent prayer. [22]   Though the pre-Nicene offertory was a ritual act with a meaning all its own and an integral part of the whole Eucharistic celebration, its significance was not always sharply distinguished from what followed. In pre-Nicene tradition the offertory, consecration, and Communion were all very closely connected; they were never considered as separate units, only as constituting a single whole.

---

[19] Tertullian, *De orat.*, 18 (PL 1, 1176-1178); cf. also *Ad uxor.*, 5 (PL 1, 1295).

[20] Both Justin (*First Apology*, chap. 65, see above, p. 41) and Hippolytus (*Apost. Trad.*, 17, 4, cf. Dix. 29 f.) refer to the kiss at this point after the common prayers.

[21] Hippolytus, *Apost. Trad.*, 17, 4 (Dix, 29).

[22] *Ibid.* (Dix, 6).

The Greek terminology of pre-Nicene writers usually does not vary from one writer to another. Προσενέγκειν is used for the Christian who is also a communicant at every Eucharist to indicate his part of the liturgy *to bring* the *prosphora*; ἀναφέρειν is used of the deacon when he *presents it* or *brings it up*; and προσφέρειν, of the bishop or celebrant when he *offers it* (or what Western usage terms the offertory proper). [23]

3. *Eucharistic Prayer* (or *Anaphora*). This prayer always began with the prefatory dialogue and ended with a solemn doxology (see above, pp. 27, 41, 42). The people confirmed it with the *Amen*. After the first-century attempts to translate the Hebrew *Amen* by the Greek ἀληθινός (genuine, true), the *Amen* was left in its original Hebrew form. Its full meaning proved untranslatable. *Amen* is derived from the Hebrew root 'MN, which originally meant steadfast, fixed, or settled, and hence " true. " Because the Jews were convinced that God was a transcendental being, they also recognized him as the absolute standard of truth; accordingly, when the Jews translated the Old Testament into Greek, they translated the Hebrew *Amen* almost always as " Would that it might be so, " or " So be it ", an expression at once a wish and an affirmation.

4. *Fraction.* Bread was broken at the Jewish *chabûrah* so that it could be distributed among the participants; insofar as the fragments were all broken and shared from the one bread, it expressed unity and union. In the Christian Eucharist, a single loaf was also used. For Communion, it was broken into fragments and distributed to all : " For we, being many, are one bread, one body : all that partake of one bread " (I Cor. 10:17). St. Ignatius of Antioch, in demonstrating the unity of the Church, writes to the Philadelphians that " one loaf also is broken to all (the communicants), and one cup is distributed among them all. " [24]

By the end of the third century, in some Churches the symbolism of the fraction was replaced with that of breaking Christ's body in the Passion. By that time, the congregations, especially in the East,

---

[23] Cf. Canons 1, 2, and 3, of the Council of Ancyra (c. A.D., 314), in Mans II, 513 ff., or NPNF, Series II, Vol. XIV, pp. 63-64.

[24] Ignatius of Antioch, *Ep. ad Philadel.*, 3, 2 (PG 4, 681 A [*Series graeca*]).

increased to the extent that no one loaf regardless of its size within practical limits, could accommodate the great number of communicants.   When more than one loaf had to be used, the original symbolism of the fraction obviously had to be replaced.   As an independent function, the Eucharistic celebration concentrated on " recalling " the Lord's death; when necessity forced the change to more than one loaf, the fraction took on the symbolism connected with the death of Christ, the breaking of his body (cf. pp. 671 f.).

Early in the second century there arose the touching custom of the *fermentum*.   A fragment of the consecrated bread from the bishop's Eucharist was carried to other, lesser churches of the city where the presbyters were celebrating the Liturgy, to express the bishop's supremacy or " presidency " over his whole church.   In the East, this custom probably died out in the fourth century.   In Rome itself, however, it survived till the eighth or ninth century.

5.   *Communion*.   When the bread was broken, all received Communion standing; first the clergy around the altar, then all the people before the altar.   Even the laity received under both species of bread and wine.   The bread was given by the bishop " with his own hand, " [25] and the chalice was administered by the presbyters (by deacons only if there were not enough presbyters present). [26] Though Justin gives little or no detail in his description of the rite, Hippolytus provides a wonderfully vivid account of the Communion rite at the Baptismal Eucharist :

> And when the bishop breaks the bread, he shall say in distributing a fragment to each : " The bread of heaven in Christ Jesus. "   And the recipient shall say, " Amen. "
> And the presbyters—if, however, there are not enough of them, the deacons also—shall hold the cups and stand by in good order and with reverence; first, he that holds the water, second he that holds the milk, third he that holds the wine. And they who partake shall taste of each cup three times. He who gives it, says : " In God the Father Almighty " and he who receives it says, " Amen "; [The second says] " And in the Lord Jesus Christ, " and he [the recipient] shall say, " Amen "; [The third says] " And in the Holy Spirit [which

[25] Hippolytus, *Apostolic Tradition*, 23 (Dix, 41).
[26] *Ibid*.

is] in the holy Church," and he [the recipient] shall say, "Amen." [27]

At the Baptismal Eucharist, the first communicants received, in addition to the usual chalice of the Eucharist (i.e., the consecrated wine), a chalice with water only " for a sign of the laver that the inner man... may receive the same cleansing as the body," and a chalice containing milk-and-honey mixed as a sign of their entry into the " promised land " of the Church.

The pre-Nicene Christians were fully aware of the effects of the worthy reception of Holy Communion. The primitive formula of administration, " The bread of heaven in Christ Jesus," obviously stresses " the bread which cometh from heaven... if any man eat of this bread, he shall live forever " (John 6:50-52). Far from minimizing the fact that the Eucharist was the body and blood of Christ, this attitude proves their absolute recognition of it. Immortality was effected by a worthy reception of this heavenly bread precisely because it was, as Justin put it, " the Flesh and Blood of that Jesus who was made flesh. " [28] Ignatius of Antioch calls it " the drug of immortality, the remedy that we should not die, " [29] and Irenaeus says that " Our bodies receiving the Eucharist are no longer corruptible, having the hope of eternal resurrection. " [30] In the fourth century, perhaps in some places even in the third, the Johannine formula of administration was replaced by the more synoptic form " The Body of Christ, " " The Blood of Christ. " The reason for this change is both fascinating and elusive but too complex for discussion here (cf. p. 699).

6. *Ablutions and Dismissal.* After the distribution of Communion, the rite of the Eucharist was in fact completed. What followed was merely the cleansing of the sacred vessels and the dismissal of the *ecclesia.* The cleansing of the vessels expressed both a practical necessity and profound respect for the sacrament. An interesting parallel is found in Judaism, where the tidying of the

[27] *Ibid.,* 23, 5 ff. (Our trans. from Hauler; for full rite, cf. Hauler 111-121 or Dix, 40-42).

[28] Justin Martyr, *First Apology,* chap. 65 (edit. Otto, p. 180).

[29] Ignatius of Antioch, *Ep.* 20, 1 (PG 3, 709 A [*Series graeca*]).

[30] Irenaeus, *Adv. haer.,* 4, 18, 5 (cf. PG 7, 1026 f., for full statement).

room after the *chabûrah* supper was one of prescribed customs. [31]
At what precise moment of the Liturgy did the faithful receive some
of the consecrated bread to carry home with them for their weekday
Communion? Was it at the Communion rite itself or later? And
when did the deacons take the sacrament to the sick and to those
who could not be present? No one really knows, but obviously it
must have been *before* the cleansing of the vessels or ablutions.
Otherwise, the cleansing would have to be repeated. The dismissal
formally closed the service before the people left.

So ended the rite of the Eucharist, a simple, forthright service
that probably took not much longer than ten or fifteen minutes
(excluding the synaxis). For the most part, the pre-Nicene celebration of the Eucharist was uncomplicated by any devotional
elaboration. Yet, it was solemn and dignified. Everything was
done in the simplest, most practical way without ceremony. We
may look in vain through all pre-Nicene sources for anything that
could even remotely be designed to stir the senses or arouse the
emotions. The Liturgy was designed to impress the mind with but
one object, the reality of the Eucharist. There were no liturgical
ornaments, no elaborate music or choral singing, not even a special
style of vestments for the celebration.

An element of solemnity was given to the rite by the chants.
Probably the participants sang the prayers as did the Jews, for most
of the early writers use the expression *carmen dicere* (lit. : to say a
song) to designate this type of recitative chant. The simple almost
plaintive chants of many Eastern Churches are traditional, dating
back to pre-Nicene times. Some of the ancient Byzantine melodies,
for example, derive from the music of Antioch and Jerusalem and
ultimately trace their origin to the music of the Jews. [32] The preface-
chant of the Latin Rite also approximates this early type of recitative
singing. It neither arouses the emotions nor stirs the senses. It is
solemn, but not emotional, thus reflecting the style of the whole
corporate rite of the Eucharist.

On these grounds alone we should reject the theory that the rites

---

[31] Cf. *Berakoth*, vii. 3.

[32] Cf. E. Wellesz, *A History of Byzantine Music and Hymnography* (Oxford :
Clarendon Press, 1961), pp. 35-45.

of the Eucharistic celebration were borrowed from the pagan mysteries. The pagan mysteries always tried to stir, arouse, and frankly play upon religious emotion either by elaborate ceremonial, mystical symbols, pageantry, the alternation of light and darkness, or by downright repulsive and weird means. Even the long periods of preparation and fasting before pagan celebrations were designed to put the initiate into a receptive frame of mind. There was always something of the near-hypnotic, the psychologically thrilling in pagan mysteries. The celebration of the early Eucharistic Liturgy, in its austere simplicity, may be seen as the exact opposite.

CHAPTER VII

THE PERSECUTIONS
AND THE EUCHARIST

We cannot properly understand and appreciate the pre-Nicene Liturgy if we forget the very real and in some ways horrifying threat of torture and death which faced every Christian during the Roman persecutions. Many things will become intelligible and explicable if we remember the two and a half centuries of Rome's totalitarian regime and its iron law of *non licet esse christianos*, "Christians are not allowed to exist!" Certainly we will miss what the Eucharistic rite actually meant to the early Christians and how it was the very heart of the Church's life unless we recognize the intense hatred, slander, calumny, and actual danger which the Christian had to face in his normal daily life.

The obligation of Catholics, for example, to be present at Sunday Mass under pain of serious sin, which appears so formalistic and mechanical now to the average Protestant mind, was something that was burned into the Christian conscience in the centuries between Nero and Diocletian. It is not mere historical memory of the Last Supper that explains the fact that men, women, and children willingly ran the risk of arrest, imprisonment, and death every week of their lives just to be at the Eucharistic service. They did it because they were convinced of the absolute necessity to take their own part in the self-oblation of Christ, a necessity which to them was even more binding than the instinct of self-preservation. This conviction was based on the whole doctrine of redemption and on the last command of Jesus to his own at the Last Supper. It was based on the will of Christ who intends by his sacrificial-atoning death to draw all men unto himself and in a most special way the members of his mystical body, the Church.

Nor was it yet a longing for personal communion with God that brought the individual Christian to the Eucharistic service every Sunday at the risk of life and limb; he could and did unite his heart and soul to the Eucharistic Lord by his daily Communion from the reserved sacrament in his own home. No, what brought him to the Eucharistic sacrifice was the profound conviction that as a member of the body, the Church, he had to take his own part in the fulfillment of the will of God who in an unbloody way offered himself anew every Sunday for the redemption of mankind. Sooner or later any scholar worthy of the name is forced into this conclusion by a serious study of the Pre-Nicene centuries of Christianity.

There were some periods of comparative quiet and uneasy toleration, but from Nero to Valerian (*c.* A.D. 65 to A.D. 260) attendance at Christian worship was a capital crime. Only when the central government in Rome was otherwise occupied with war, rivalry for the imperial throne, etc., or when local authorities chose to " look the other way " did Christians enjoy uneasy peace. At times, the persecutions continued unabated for years. But always, whether from civil authorities or from the mob, the challenge of *Art thou a Christian*? brought swift martyrdom or apostasy to the individual Christian.

Up to A.D. 252, the Church's discipline remained unyielding : if the courage of a Christian failed even momentarily and he burned incense before the idols (or before a picture of the deified emperor), he was excluded from the corporate worship of the Church until death. It made little difference whether or not he did life-long penance for his momentary, single act of apostasy. If a man standing before his pagan Judge pleaded guilty of being a Christian, condemnation and execution were completed on the same day—or he was imprisoned if the arena needed candidates for titillating the senses of a populace who enjoyed the spectacle of living men, women, and children being torn limb from limb by wild beasts or smeared with pitch and turned into living torches. At other times, upon instruction from the administration, the sentences were " mitigated " into servitude for life in one of the imperial mines where, as a rule, the prisoners died within two or three years. There was in those days no comfortable way of leading a Christian life. In fact life and Christianity were incompatible. One or the other had to be sacrificed. To affirm one's belief without proving it every week by cautiously treading one's way through the empty streets in the predawn to the corporate act of worship, the Eucharist, was merely empty talk, pointless and fruitless.   If one were a Christian, one simply took such a risk in spite of the constant threat to freedom and life.

After A.D. 260, the civil law against Christians or, rather, against the Christian assembly, was relaxed somewhat.   Yet, to be a Christian was still *laesa maiestas*, high treason.   In this period of comparative peace and toleration, martyrdom or apostasy still depended upon whether one was accused or not.   A Christian was far from secure : an angry neighbor, an envious competitor or even a bitter child might make the fatal accusation.   We read, for instance, in contemporary records of Marinus, a soldier who was good enough in his profession to be promoted to a centurion : an envious comrade makes the deadly charge against him and within three hours he is dead. [1]   Or the betrayed Tiburtius, who was tortured and then beheaded on the Lavican Road three miles outside Rome; St. Susanna who was accused, probably by her suitor, because she refused to marry.   Anyone could accuse, anything could induce such a charge, and Christians died by the thousands.   Almost always, however, the storm center of the blood baths was the Eucharist because much risk could have been avoided had not attendance been obligatory.

The sheer heroism of many is staggering.   Eyewitness accounts are not lacking.   " We ourselves, " Eusebius tells us, " witnessed a great crowd of people who in one single day endured beheading or the punishment of fire; the orgy went on so long that the deadly blade became blunt and killed by its weight.   The executioners themselves became exhausted and took turns at their work.   We also saw a most marvelous inspiration, a truly divine force, the readiness of those who believed in Christ God.   Immediately when sentence had been pronounced on one group, another came before the tribunal from the opposite side acknowledging themselves Christians and remaining steadfast in face of dangers and torments of all kinds... they received with joy the final sentence of death. They sang hymns and thanked the God of all till their last breath. " [2]

Aside from official persecution, aside from perpetually fearing the charge of *Christian* being leveled at him from any quarter, the

[1] Eusebius, *Eccl. hist.*, VII, 15 (PG 13, 270 [*Series graeca*]).
[2] *Ibid.*, VIII, 9, 1-5 (PG 13, 309-310 [*Series graeca*]).

Christian still had to face a lifetime of suspicion and ostracism from his neighbors, the opposition of his own relatives if not his immediate family, and the intense hatred of the populace at large for the alleged polluted doctrines and disgusting practices of his faith.   Sometimes even apostate Christians were not safe from the frenzied mob, as in Lyons in A.D. 177.

It was not merely a few fanatically cruel and ignorant pagans who believed the gruesome stories and rumors of Christian ritual murder and cannibal feasts based on a misunderstanding of the Eucharist : this was the general opinion, even of decent-minded pagans.   A pagan not sincerely convinced of the actuality of Christian orgies, promiscuous vice and even incest was a rare exception.   It is no wonder that the *disciplina arcani* was applied with all the rigor and force at the command of a struggling Church.   We can readily understand the suspicion caused by any unguarded Christian talk of " receiving the most precious body and blood " or by an indiscreet remark about the " kiss " of brothers and sisters!   Christians were helpless against calumny.   The most effective defense would have been an open and public celebration of the Eucharist, but it would have brought swift death to all participants.   Besides, the whole idea of primitive Christianity about the absolute separateness of the *ecclesia* and the Eucharist would not have allowed this.

To get an idea of what went on in the public mind about the Christians we only have to read Tertullian :

> They think that the Christians are the cause of every disaster to the state and are at the bottom of every misfortune of the people.   If the Tiber floods the city or if the Nile fails to fill the fields, if there are portents in heaven or earthquakes on earth, if a famine comes or a plague, they clamour instantly, " Throw the Christians to the lion. "   So many to one lion? [3]

His irony is even more biting when he counters the popular rumors about the orgies at the Christian Eucharist and demands a show of factual evidence for the charges; he demands, " how many babies any particular person has eaten, how many times anyone has committed incest, who the cooks were... " and immediately adds,

[3] Tertullian, *Apologeticus*, xl (PL I, 542-543 A).   Our translation.

" What a boast for any governor if he actually caught a man who had
eaten a hundred babies! " [4]   And he goes on :

> Suppose for a moment that these things were true.   I ask
> you, then, whether in believing such things you would think
> it worth while to attain eternal life with such a conscience.
> Come now!   Plunge your knife into the baby, guilty though it
> is of nothing, enemy to no one, everybody's son... or maybe
> that's some other Christian's job.... stand here, then, beside
> this human being gasping in death before it has really lived;
> wait for its new little soul to flit away.   Take the fresh
> young blood and soak your bread in it.   Then gulp it down
> with zest!
>
> Meanwhile, as you recline at table, note the place where
> your mother is, where your sister.   Note it carefully, so
> that you make no mistake when the dogs [which were chained
> to the lamps] plunge all in darkness, for you will be guilty of
> a crime if you fail to commit incest.
>
> Initiated and confirmed in mysteries such as these you will
> live forever!   Tell me now, is eternity worth all this; if it
> isn't, then these things shouldn't be believed.   But even if
> you believed them, I deny that you would want to commit
> them.   And even if you wanted to, I tell you, you couldn't.
> Why is it then that others can, if you cannot?   Why cannot
> you, if others can?   I suppose we have a different nature....
> I suppose we have a different sort of teeth, have different
> muscles for incestuous lust!   You believe that men can do
> these things?   Then you should be able to do them too; you
> are a man yourself like the Christian.   If you could not bring
> yourself to do these things, you should not believe that the
> Christians can, for a Christian is a man too just like you.
>
> " But, " you say, " not knowing anything about it, they are
> deceived and imposed upon.   They were unaware that
> anything of the sort was imputed to the Christians.... "
> Yet, I suppose, it is usual for those who want to be initiated
> to go first to the master of these sacred rites to inquire what
> preparations must be made.   In such a case no doubt he
> would say, " Well, you need a baby, a little tiny one who does
> not know yet what it is to die and can smile under your
> knife... and bread with which to catch its juicy blood.
> Besides this, you need candlesticks, lamps, a few dogs and
> bits of meat to draw them on to overturn the lamps.   And

[4] *Ibid.*, ii (PL I, 318-321).

most important of all you must bring your mother and your
sister. " But what if mother and sister do not want to come
or what if you have no mother or sister? What about the
Christians without any close female relatives? I suppose,
then, a man cannot really be a Christian unless he is someone's
brother or son?

Maybe these preparations are made without the foreknowl-
edge of those concerned? At any rate, after once going
through the experience they know the procedure, support it,
and condone it. " They are afraid of being punished, " you
say, " if they reveal it. ". . . Come now, granted that they
are afraid, why do they persevere? The only logical conclusion is that you would no longer want to be that which
you would not have been at all had you known ahead of time
what it was. [5]

Such was the stigma of being a Christian, the price of regularly
attending the Eucharist. Certainly, the government, especially the
central government at Rome, was better informed than the populace,
but like any totalitarian regime it took strong measures to protect
itself from what it considered a potential political enemy. Political
expediency dictated discreet nurturing of such gross misconceptions
of Christianity.

Government officials and policy-makers were perfectly aware that
the single act of offering sacrifice to idols or to the deified emperor,
which apostates were compelled to perform, would not change
their beliefs or conviction. The apostates would still remain
convinced Christians at heart. The government understood this
but it also understood very well the discipline of the Church which
would exclude for life from the *ecclesia* any Christian who let himself
be pressured into even a single act of apostasy. That is why it did
not initiate any organized propaganda to defend pagan beliefs until
the latter part of the third century. Just how well the small circle
of government officials and high policy-makers knew the facts from
their investigations of Christianity can be seen from the writings of
the Neoplatonist Porphyry. [6] They are far from being gratuitous

---

[5] *Ibid.*, viii. Our translation, from PL I, 363-365.

[6] Porphyry wrote fifteen books " against the Christians. " Unfortunately, little
of this tremendous work is extant; this deficiency is somewhat made up by the
numerous quotations cited by various Christian authors.

assertions about the principles of Christianity; in fact, so well-informed was he of some doctrines of Christianity that some writers, without any real proof, saw in him an apostate Christian. No less well-informed was the prefect of Bithynia (and later governor of Egypt), Hierocles, whose *Friendly Discourse on Truth to the Christians* shows considerable knowledge of Christian teachings.

Toward the middle of the third century, the well-organized persecution of Decius raged with especially savage fury and shrewdly made apostasy unprecedentedly easy, causing the lapse of many Christians. The government had reason to congratulate itself on its effectiveness. But in A.D. 252, the Church countered, not without opposition from some of its own members, by changing its iron policy of lifetime exclusion from the *ecclesia* into one of restored membership to the repentant after a suitable period of penance. The penances imposed for various lapses were severe indeed, but now those the Church lost through apostasy were restored at least in part through reconciliation. The writings of St. Cyprian bear ample evidence of the eager droves of apostate Christians coming back into the Church. It was a weakness in courage, not in faith, that had led them to defection. The continued strength of their belief is evidenced by the eagerness and sincerity with which they sought to resume their Christian life. Many of these lapsed Christians later sealed their faith with martyrdom.

This change in Church policy baffled the government. It waged a second wave of persecution under Valerian (A.D. 254-259), to stamp out the Christian revival, but this time with little effect : the pagans were forced to admit defeat, at least temporarily. When the empire found itself engaged in foreign war, the whole problem was laid aside for a while, with relief to both persecutors and persecuted.

In A.D. 260, the edict of Gallienus granted virtual freedom of worship to the Christians and a restoration of their property. The legal position, however, was still far from clear : by law, the Christians could " use their *ecclesiai*, " but since Christianity was not a legal religion, the charge of high treason could still be made against individual Christians.

This somewhat ambiguous toleration, such as it was, afforded the struggling Church a precious opportunity to increase, organize, and prosper. In many cities and towns, special buildings were set up for worship. [7] In some places, for instance, in Asia Minor, because of the large numbers of Christians, it was an open secret who the clergy were and where the Eucharist was celebrated. In other places, where the Christians were still a definite minority, secrecy and discretion were the order of the day. During forty years of comparative quiet, the government chose merely to ignore the whole problem unless forced to deal with specific accusations against individual Christians.

Then it came—the longest and bitterest storm of persecution that the infant Church ever had to face. For ten years, under Diocletian (A.D. 303-313), the blood of Christians flowed unabated. Arrests were much easier to make because who the Christians were, who the clergy were, was semipublic knowledge—and they died by the thousands. Gradually, but irrevocably, the clergy was decimated, mostly by martyrdom but occasionally by apostasy. For a time, it seemed that Christian worship would disappear from entire provinces. The fury of the storm was unleashed against everything Christian : organized ideological warfare, in the form of fierce intellectual propaganda, aimed at discrediting Christian beliefs, while Christian literature was being systematically destroyed.

The persecution began in Nicomedia, where Emperor Diocletian resided during the winter of A.D. 302-303. Contemporary testimony desbribes it thus : " People of both sexes and of all ages were thrown into the fire; not one at a time, but whole groups of them were bound together and burned; slaves were flung into the sea with a great stone tied to their necks... the prisons were full to overflowing while new kinds of torture were an hourly invention. " [8] The conflagration spread rapidly to the outlying territories. Almost

---

[7] Generally, the divine services were still held in private dwellings, though in some places special buildings were being set up specifically for worship. To date, I believe, the only pre-Nicene church found in the East is that at Dura-Europos in Mesopotamia (c. A.D. 230-260). It seems to have been remodeled from a private house. The baptistry had been painted with Old and New Testament scenes, but the assembly hall had not yet been decorated when it was destroyed. Cf. *Excavations at Dura-Europos, Preliminary Report of V. Season of Work*, 1931-1932 (New Haven : Yale, 1934), pp. 238-288.

[8] Lactantius, *De mortibus persecut.*, 15 (PL 7, 216 A-217 B).

simultaneously, Galerius, who had influenced Diocletian to turn persecutor, extended the scourge to his own territories along the Danube. On orders from Diocletian, Maximinian did likewise in Italy and Africa. The milder Constantius alone endeavored to find means of avoiding the carnage in Gaul, Spain and Britain.

Destruction of the Christians' sacred books became an essential goal of this final persecution, so that the obligation arose to defend them even at the cost of one's life. Since the imperial edict ordered the Christians to surrender *(tradere)* the books to the authorities, those who obeyed this command were *traditores* (" those who surrendered "). The names *surrenderers* and *traitors* became synonymous in the Christian mind. The political authorities were implacably efficient in their work. None of the great uncial codices of Scripture still extant dates back before the fourth century. Like the Jews of modern-day Europe who tried to save their sacred books under Hitler, Christians tried to hide their sacred rolls, bringing them on their persons to distant, safer places. In Thessalonica, some women—Agape, Irene, and Chione—made it their special task to preserve the sacred Scriptures. Written accounts of such searches and confiscations have come down to us. [9] As time went on, the twenty, thirty or more million Christians who lived within the confines of the Roman empire at the beginning of the fourth century showed no signs of giving in. The continual slaughter was of such vast proportions that even the pagans began to sicken of it. This perhaps more than anything else dictated the subsequent change of policy into something considered " lenient " : commutation of the death penalty to that of forced labor in the imperial mines and quarries, which provided an almost inexhaustible labor force for this lethal work. Those condemned to the mines *(ad metalla)* were called *confessores metallici* (" mining confessors ") by the Church, for it was no less horrifying and in a way more so, than slow martyrdom.

---

[9] E.g., the protocol of the confiscatory action at Cirta in North Africa (now Constantine, in Algeria). The inventory of items seized included two golden chalices, six silver chalices, six silver dishes, seven silver lamps, seven short bronze candlesticks with their lamps, torches and many other articles useful to the Christians. When the imperial officials demanded the sacred books, however, these had already been transported to safety. The bookcases were found empty (cf. PL 8, 730-732).

The substarvation level of sustenance coupled with the severity of hard labor took their toll in a slower though no less inexorable way than the sword and the arena. The porphyry quarries of the Thebaid area alongside the Red Sea, the marble quarries of Pannonia and Cilicia, the copper mines of Palestine and Cyprus, the lead mines of Sardinia—all consumed their hapless victims within a few years at most. When a Christian was sentenced to one of these mines, he was also mutilated in some way; usually his right eye was cut out with a knife and the wound burned with a hot iron; the tendon of his left foot was also cut to thwart escape. [10] Transfer from one mine to another took further devastating toll. Long lines of human skeletons, the " mining confessors, " would trudge for hundreds of weary miles through the desert under the burning sun; those who fell along the way—and they were many—served to feed the jackals and other beasts of prey.

Silent and uncomplaining, these living martyrs kept up their religious practices as best they could—and even made converts, as happened in the marble quarries of Pannonia! Sometimes the influx of prisoner-workers was so great that many huts and sheds had to be built. When this happened at the mines of Phoeno in Palestine, the Christians took this opportunity to build themselves one more shed to be used as a church. The superintendent discovered it, but surprisingly, he allowed them to use it provided the day's work was done. [11] This happy state of affairs did not last long, however, for we read further that after the governor came to the mines, he ordered the Christians transferred elsewhere. Thirty-nine, too weak for work, were beheaded. [12] Undoubtedly those who were transferred would still meet for the Eucharist wherever they happened to be, just as a St. Denys and his flock had done a little more than fifty years before : " And every spot where we were afflicted became to us a place of assembly for the feast... field, desert, ship, inn, prison. " [13]

---

[10] Eusebius, De mart. Palaest., vii, 3-4 (PG 13, 625-626); Hist. eccl., viii, 12, 10, etc. (PG 13, 313-314, etc.). Both Series graeca.

[11] Cf. Hist. eccl., viii, 13 (PG 13, 315-316 [Series graeca]); De mart. Palaest., vii, 3; xiii, 4-5 (PG 13, 638-639 [Series graeca]),

[12] De mart. Palest., xiii, 10 (PG 13, 640 B [Series graeca]).

[13] Cf. Eusebius, Hist. eccl., VII, xxii, 4 (PG 13, 275 C [Series graeca]).

Roman law respected the condemned person and allowed even criminals to be buried in decent tombs. As Eusebius points out, the tombs of Christians might become places of veneration for the faithful. That is why the bodies of martyrs, even those of officicals of the imperial court who had been executed and buried, were exhumed and flung into the sea. [14]

What happened in Caesarea probably happened in other places : Governor Firmilian ordered that the bodies of the martyrs be left in their place of execution to be devoured by vultures or wild beasts. Because the Christians, relatives, and friends of the deceased were forbidden to take away the bodies, and the wild animals had all they could eat, the vicinity of Caesarea became one huge charnel. Eusebius, who saw it, describes it thus : " All around the city lay scattered bowels and human bones.... very close to the city gates was a sight surpassing all words and tragic description, for human flesh remained undevoured not just in one place but was flung about in all directions. Some said that even within the city gates, they had seen whole human limbs, pieces of flesh and lengths of bowels. " [15]

This was the great baptism of blood, the passion of fire, the Good Friday which the Church had to endure before it could finally rise from the ashes to organize, build up, and flourish. Her glorious resurrection began with the Edict of Toleration published in all territories under the jurisdiction of Galerius, Licinius, and Constantine, and was confirmed two years later by the Edict of Milan.

At long last the Church was free. No longer did a Christian have to fear that he would never come home when he set out to attend the Eucharist. No longer did he have to dread the numbing challenge, " *Art thou a Christian?* " The gnawing feeling of fear that perpetually gripped his stomach was finally gone. He could now worship his God in peace, without listening for the footsteps of soldiers who might come to take all away and bring swift death to him and his dear ones—or, worse still, having to face the frightening alternative of apostasy to which he was never quite sure that he would not succomb. Dizzy, perhaps, with happiness, he realized that the long persecution was over.

[14] Eusebius, *Hist. eccl.*, viii, 6, 7 (PG 13, 306-309 [*Series graeca*]).
[15] *De mart. Palaest.*, ix, 10-11 (PG 13, 631 [*Series graeca*]).

CHAPTER VIII

THE SEPARATION OF THE LITURGIES

The peace of Constantine and the first general Council of Nicaea in A.D. 325 introduce an entirely different era in the history of the Liturgy, an era characterized by major changes in Christian worship and organization. Places of worship and the very religion of the Christians were now legal; Christianity was free to grow, organize, and develop.

In the beginning, as the Apostles went forth to preach the gospel to the whole Roman world, no question ever arose regarding the limits of local juridiction of any given bishop. Jewish communities were invariably confined to the cities and towns, so were the infant Christian groups. The cities of the empire, whose limits were clearly marked by the census, also conveniently served as the basis of a bishop's jurisdiction. St. Paul could speak of the Churches of Corinth, Ephesus, Colossae, etc. The areas of episcopal jurisdiction, coinciding as they did with that of a city—with or without its suburbs or countryside—were naturally unequal in extent. As a rule, the larger the city and the more numerous its Christian community, the greater its prestige, although the historical or civic importance of a city influenced the rating of its See. The founding and growth of the more important cities of the empire depended upon favorable geographical features. The missionary activities of such centers in Christian times were also conditioned by them. Christians from major cities evangelized the surrounding countryside, thus establishing daughter Churches that were bound in loyalty and fealty to the mother Church.

Almost from the beginning of Christianity, the bishops of the larger Sees exercised jurisdiction over other bishops, especially over those whom they themselves had consecrated and set over new Christian communities. This principle of the consecrating bishop having jurisdiction over the one consecrated by him is very important and decisive in the ecclesiastical history of the East. It resulted eventually in the establishment of the extremely important offices of metropolitan and patriarch, and to corresponding territorial divisions.

In the East, for example, Alexandria and Antioch, the oldest Christian communities in the Greek world, became centers of the earliest missions in Egypt, northern Syria, Asia Minor, Mesopotamia, and Persia. In Africa, excluding Egypt, Carthage became the center of Christian organization and development. Soon, however, the authority of some of the missionary centers, came into conflict, particularly in Asia where rivalry existed between several important cities even in pre-Christian times.

For a long time after its destruction by Titus, Jerusalem remained obscure and unimportant. Despite the small group of Christians who had managed to exist there, the Holy City was not destined to become a great center of Christianity until much later. In its place, the inscrutable will of God had chosen the great Babylon of the West, Rome, as *the* Holy See of Christendom. Divine inspiration aside, Rome was also the logical capital of the Church. Rome was, after all, the capital of the whole *orbis Romanus*, the center toward which the world of those days gravitated. If Christianity sought for its goal to embrace the whole world—and it did—then Rome was its only logical choice. Be that as it may, it was to this Babylon of the Roman world that Peter came and there that he established his See. During the first centuries of Christianity, the uncontested capital of the empire also became the uncontested metropolis of the Church.

The primacy of the Bishop of Rome was recognized as a primacy not merely of *honor* but also of *jurisdiction*. During the first three centuries, the Churches of the East, which were later to contest this primacy, recognized this fact without raising any difficulty. This is all the more surprising when we remember that the Apostle John lived in their midst long after the other apostles had gone to their deserved reward; yet, it was to the successor of Peter at Rome that they had recourse in dogmatic or disciplinary matters, and not to John.

Toward the end of the first century, for example, through Pope Clement (Clement of Rome) the " Church which sojourneth in Rome " came forward as a peacemaker to settle a dispute in the

Church of Corinth, at a time when John was still living. Clement's *Epistle to the Corinthians* not only had the authority to settle the dispute at hand but was publicly read from time to time at Corinth. By the fourth century, the usage of appealing to Rome had spread to other Churches of the East.

St. Ignatius, the martyred Bishop of Antioch, draws attention to the supremacy of the Church of Rome when he calls it the head of the union of charity, i.e., of Christendom.

Likewise, in the second century, it was to Rome that the whole of Christendom flocked—apologists, bishops, Christians from Asia Minor, from Syria, from the Pontus, Palestine, and Egypt. Rome was indeed the center of gravity whose attraction lay chiefly in its supreme authority, the primacy of jurisdiction exercised by its Bishop over all the other Churches, as well as in its honorary pre-eminence. Thus, at the end of the second century, when the bishops of Caesarea, Aelia, Ptolemais, Tyre, and others came to Syria to deal with the Easter controversy, Pope Victor had the authority to command them under pain of excommunication to conform with the common usage of the Church regarding the feast. [1] In the next century, Pope Stephen compelled the African and Asiatic bishops to desist from rebaptizing those baptized by heretics. Mere primacy of honor would not have commanded such power.

The Church of Rome was recognized both in the East and in the West as the center of faith because its bishop was acknowledged as the successor of Peter, the head of the Apostles. When St. Cyprian wrote, " He who resists the Church, he who abandons the chair of Peter on which the Church is founded, shall he flatter himself that he is in the Church? " he was reflecting the attitude and conviction of the whole Christian world of the time.

Even in the fourth century, when some of the other Churches matured and rose in eminence, prestige, and renown, none of them claimed the authority and supreme jurisdiction of the See of Peter. When, for example, trouble broke out in their own Sees, some of the Eastern bishops appealed to the popes to defend their rights : " When the controversy [on the divinity of the Holy Ghost] broke

---

[1] Cf. Eusebius, *Hist. eccl.*, v. 24 (PG 13, 197-201 [*Series graeca*]).

out, " writes Sozomen, " the bishop of Rome [Liberius, who died in A.D. 366] wrote to the churches of the East that they should with the bishops of the West confess the three Persons in God, equal in substance and in dignity. All submitted, since the case was decided by the Church of Rome, and thus the controversy was ended. " [2]

During the first centuries of Christianity, always and everywhere the authority of the Bishop of Rome ruled supreme. Although the other Churches prospered and grew, they ruled only over their own respective territories, over their own daughter Churches. A bishop of any large ecclesiastical center had no pretense of authority over bishops other than those consecrated by him and set over one of his daughter Churches even though, as time went on, some of these centers increased the extent of their territorial jurisdiction enormously.

Prior to the third century, there is no real tendency for grouping the various Churches into dioceses according to the divisions of the civil provinces. Very little is known of the councils in those early days, but enough to prove that the ecclesiastical areas and metropolitan Sees were not modeled on the civil divisions of the empire. There were, it is true, some groupings of bishoprics around a metropolitan See or center which approximated the territory of a civil division, but these exceptions were conditioned by the same geographical and historical influences which had determined the civil division; in this sense some assimilation between the two was inevitable.

By the time of Nicaea (A.D. 325), however, there was already in the East a grouping of bishops according to provinces and their subordination to the bishop of the civil metropolis; [3] these ecclesiastical provinces corresponded to those civil divisions in existence at the time, i.e., since the reorganization of the empire by Diocletian. Ecclesiastically, therefore, we have in the fourth century the grouping of Churches of a province under a single head who was, as a rule, the bishop of the civil capital city. He was known as the metropolitan bishop. The Council of Nicaea did not establish these

---

[2] Sozomen, *Hist. eccl.*, VI, 22 (PG 25, 1370 D-1371 A [*Series graeca*]). Our brackets.

[3] Council of Nicaea, Canons 4-7 (NPNF, Series II, vol. XIV, pp. 11-17).

ecclesiastical divisions, for they were already taken for granted at
the time. [4] Simultaneously with this metropolitan system arose the
practice of grouping together the Churches of a number of contiguous
provinces under the leadership of the bishop of the most important
See with a kind of patriarchal authority.   This stage of ecclesiastical
organization had evolved only in the East at this time; the West
developed much slower in this respect, if we except Numidia in Africa.

Thus, at the time of the Nicene Council, we have in the East the
Church of Alexandria ruling over all of Egypt, the Church of Antioch
over what was called the diocese of the Orient, the Church of
Caesarea over the Pontus, the Church of Ephesus over the diocese
of Asia, and the Church of Heraclea over Thrace.   After the persecutions, when this system of church organization was stabilized, it
corresponded more or less to the civil divisions of the empire at the
time. [5]   Later, the organization of the whole Eastern Church into
metropolitanates, and especially into the superior units of church
administration, directly influenced the development and differentiation of the liturgies.

After Constantine moved his capital to the East, Constantinople
gradually rose to pre-eminence over Heraclea (de facto, not by law).
At the Council of Constantinople in A.D. 381, the Bishop of Constantinople was ranked in precedence over all, except the Bishop of
Rome. [6] This decision, however, was not accepted by Rome, nor
was its confirmation seventy years later by the Council of Chalcedon.

At the latter council (A.D. 451), there was a further reshuffling of
organization and authority.   Four patriarchates were established in
the East : [7] 1) Constantinople, whose jurisdiction was extended to

----

[4] Cf. Canons 4, 6, 7 (NPNF, Vol. XIV, pp. 11, 15, 17).

[5] The civil administration of the empire in the East consisted in the following
units of government :

	The Orient (East)....	15 provinces
Prefecture	Egypt	6 provinces
of	Asia	11 provinces
the East	Pontus	11 provinces
	Thrace	6 provinces

[6] Cf. Canon 3 of First Council of Constantinople (NPNF, Vol. XIV, p. 178).

[7] Actually, the terms still used at Chalcedon were not " patriarchates " and
" patriarchs, " but " exarchates " and " exarchs "; it was not until the seventh
century that the former terms were fixed.   We use these terms here only in view
of later developments.

include the political dioceses of Thrace, Asia, and the Pontus (cf. Canon 28 of the council), [8] 2) Alexandria, 3) Antioch and, finally, 4) Jerusalem, which was given jurisdiction over three provinces in Palestine (An unsuccessful attempt to establish a patriarchate of Jerusalem had been made twenty years earlier at the Council of Ephesus by Juvenal, Bishop of Jerusalem).

Rome, the patriarchate of the West, remained and retained its supreme authority and pre-eminence. The borders of its immediate jurisdiction roughly included the north coast of Africa, everything west of a line from the eastern part of Crete to Danzig, although some of this territory, especially Illyricum, was disputed with Constantinople. With this division of the Church (corresponding to that of the empire) into Western and Eastern parts, originated the expressions *Eastern Church*, *Western Church* and eventually, *Eastern Rites*, etc. The difference was more than geographical and ritual : it was also temperamental and cultural. This, of course, is still true today, but to a lesser degree.

Liturgically, from a more or less common pre-Nicene tradition with its two characteristics of *diversity of form* (verbal diversity) and a fundamental *identity of meaning*, the Christian Liturgy developed into separate, distinct Rites within the universal Church. In other words, the old uniform but fluid pre-Nicene Rite crystallized into different types of Liturgies or Rites in different territories. Whereas till this time the formation of Christian ritual had been influenced by the Jewish heritage and the new Christian ideas, now the period of greatest Hellenistic influence begins. [9] This change, or what we may call crystallization, was not instantaneous, but slow and gradual. Traces of different practices can be noted in the various Churches in the third century; after Nicaea, these differences evolved into distinct Liturgies or Rites.

The direct influence of the Council of Nicaea on this great liturgical change was minor if not entirely nil. The Council of Nicaea is merely a point of reference in dating general trends in liturgical history, for want of a better standard. The evolution, changes, and

[8] NPNF, Series II, Vol. XIV, p. 287.

[9] Cf. A. Baumstark, *Vom geschiehtlichen Werden der Liturgie* (Freiburg, 1923), chaps. 3-4.

development of Christian ritual in the Church's life and practice are processes which must be measured in periods of years rather than by single dates, and usually quite independently of any council. If anything, the end of the persecutions could serve as a point of reference perhaps even better than Nicaea, since, with the coming of peace and legality, the Church could better afford to turn its attention to liturgical matters. However, besides being a lesser-known date, it is indefinite in some parts of the empire. The persecuted Church required some time to get back on its feet, as it were. Hence, Nicaea is the favored date for the beginning of a significant era in the Church's liturgical life.

As regards the separation of the Liturgies and Rites, one thing is certain : in the fourth century there are enough marked differences in the Liturgies of various Churches or ecclesiastical centers to necessitate their separate classification—and this, despite unmistakable marks of their common descent, i.e., the same general outline or order of their component parts. No less significant are the complicated and sometimes curious signs of mutual influence among them. So complex is the evidence of mutual influence and interdependence of these Rites that there are almost as many theories of relationship as there are scholars in the field. Certainly, all agree that the old, fluid pre-Nicene Rite crystallized into different forms in the various centers of Christianity, but few agree on their derivation.

Differences of opinion regarding the relative importance of non-essential parts of the Liturgy account for its evolution into distinct forms. Some of these non-essential parts were emphasized and lengthened, others down-graded and shortened, in a way that varied from Church to Church. Practical considerations of local churches also influenced the order of succession of prayers and other details. Until liturgical prayers were written down and read from a book, it was only natural, too, that extempore recitation could not induce uniformity even among the dependent bishoprics of a metropolitan See, much less among the metropolitan Sees themselves. Liturgical separation and differentiation, already firmly established during the third century in the most important Churches of pre-Nicene times, became more evident as time went on.

The liturgical influence of these major Sees permeated the surrounding countryside and their dependent dioceses. Aside from the question of jurisdiction, dependent bishops naturally imitated their leader, the metropolitan or exarch in these matters. Three ancient patriarchal Sees, Rome, Alexandria, and Antioch, emerged as the most influential in diffusing the Liturgies developed within their domains. These Liturgies together with that of Gaul, seem to be the parent types of all later forms. The origin of the Gallican Rite remains a mystery.

These parent types, however, were not absolutely consistent within themselves, for being more or less fluid they were subject to development and change. Daughter Churches, especially those in outlying areas, would adapt the parent type to the circumstances of its own territory, changing some items, expanding others, and in general adding peculiarities of their own. These are the derived Liturgies, the daughter Rites, each descended from one of the four great parent types, related to each other if they belong to the same family, yet really different enough to be classified as distinct Rites. Again, out of some of these daughter Rites came forth yet other Liturgies which also must be classified as separate entities. All of the different forms, parent types, daughter Rites, and other derived Liturgies, influenced each other not only by borrowing and exchanging details, but in some instances by a general interchange of the ritual or its parts—so much so that tracing their derivation still remains elusive and complex.

At any rate, in the East there were two great families of Liturgies, of which Antioch and Alexandria were the parent types. [10] The Liturgies of the other Eastern Churches certainly evolved definite

[10] In the West, the parent Rites were the Gallican and the Roman. Opinions regarding classification differ. Duchesne gives four parent Rites as we do, but he suggests that they may be reduced to two (*Origines du culte chrétien*, p. 54). P. Drews seems to point to Antioch alone (*Untersuchungen über di sogen, clementinische Liturgie* [Tübingen, 1906], p. 126). A. Baumstark gives four in the East alone : those of West Syria, East Syria, Asia Minor, and Egypt (*Die Messe im Morgenland* [Kempten and Munich, 1906], pp. 48-52). E. Bishop sees two main types (cf. Dom R. Connolly, *Liturgical Homilies of Narsai*, p. 154). A. Maltzeff gives seven altogether, three in the East alone (*Die Liturgien der Orthodox-katolischen Kirche* [Berlin, 1894], pp. 234-235). F. Cabrol divides them into two Eastern families and five Western (*Anaphore*, DACL, I, 1899). Essentially the same reality is being subdivided into different categories.

peculiarities of their own, but all in one way or another derive from these two parent types; they are all children, as it were, of two families. There may have existed other Liturgies descended from these parent types, but only those are listed which have survived the accidents of history in anything more than vague and scanty references.

CHAPTER IX

THE POST-NICENE ALEXANDRIAN AND ETHIOPIAN LITURGIES

A. ANCIENT LITURGIES OF ALEXANDRIA AND EGYPT

Although less influential than the Antiochene Liturgy, covered in the next chapter, the Alexandrian did leave its unmistakable mark on the Liturgies of other Churches. Despite cleavage of race and language between the native Copts and the large population of immigrant Greeks, Alexandria exercised its leadership over most of Egypt even in pre-Christian times. With the coming of Christianity, it soon became one of the major ecclesiastical centers.

The Liturgy of Alexandria, like that of other regions, remained fluid until the fourth century. Certain parts were then put into writing. The celebrant could follow the suggested model, or he could use portions of it and still extemporize the rest.

One of the earliest collections of Egyptian liturgical prayers thus written down and copied was the so-called Sacramentary or *Euchologion* of Sarapion. [1] Discovered in 1894 at the Lavra Monastery on Mount Athos, this is undoubtedly one of the most important liturgical finds of modern times. With it the task of reconstructing the course of liturgical development in the Egyptian Church is rendered immeasurably easier. Authorship of this unique collection is ascribed to Sarapion, the Bishop of Thmuis in the Nile delta of lower Egypt, [2] a friend of St. Athanasius and St. Anthony.

The Sacramentary of Sarapion appears to have been written some time between A.D. 353 and 356, but contains older elements, possibly

---

[1] More correctly, the Ἀρχιερατικόν, i.e., a bishop's Sacramentary. For the complete text, see Wobbermin's *Altchristliche liturgische Stücke in Texte u. Untersuchungen, Neue folge*, ii. 3 b (Leipzig, 1898). As rearranged by Funk, see his *Didascalia*, ii, pp. 158-195 (Paderborn, 1905). The MS. in which Sarapion's *Euchologion* is contained is No. 149 of the Lavra Monastery of Mount Athos. Its period is thought to be the eleventh century.

[2] In the delta between the Mindesian and the Tanitic branches of the Nile, near Menzaleh.

dating back to the third century. At least some of its features definitely belong to the third century since they correspond to Eucharistic passages in third-century Egyptian texts.

The collection consists of thirty liturgical compositions intended primarily for the use of a bishop. Except for the headings of the prayers and the final " All these prayers precede that of the Oblation, " there are no rubrics; hence, their proper order is uncertain. Some prayers are related to baptism (7-11); others to ordination (12-14), the blessing of oil (15-17), or funeral services (18). Others again are for the Sunday office or Proanaphoral Prayers (19-30) and the Eucharistic Liturgy (1-6). Since only the latter two series (1-6, 19-30) refer to the Eucharistic Liturgy, our interest is centered upon them. The problem of their proper order still remains unsolved (especially 22, 27, 29, and 30).

These prayers probably are not the official prayers of the Alexandrian Liturgy, nor even perhaps of the Church of Thmuis, but merely a type which could be used if desired. Except for the anaphora (1-4), whose significance and Eucharistic use is obvious, perhaps all of them could have been used for non-liturgical services as well. There is nothing in their make-up or form which would indicate their applicability to the Mass alone. If their arrangement without proper order means anything, it would, rather, indicate their use on any occasion besides the Mass. For example, the prayer for the blessing of oil and water and the benediction of the people after this blessing (5-6) could very well have been used before the administration of baptism.

When used for the Divine Liturgy, these prayers were probably used in the following order (suggested by Brightman) :

Liturgy of the Catechumens

1. " *First Prayer of the Sunday* " (19), an introductory prayer of supplication for a correct understanding and interpretation of the Scriptures.

2. Prayer after the sermon (20).

3. Prayer for the catechumens (21).

4. Benediction of (hands extended over) the catechumens (28), probably used at their dismissal.

The Liturgy of the Faithful

A litany, which is not included in the Sacramentary, was probably said by the deacon and then the bishop would " complete the prayer " with the following :

1.   Prayer " for the people " (27) in which are included the well-being of the faithful, the peace of the state, tranquillity of the Church, prayers for the slaves, the poor, the aged, travelers, the sick, etc. [3]

2.   Benediction of (hands extended over) the faithful (29).

3.   Prayer for the sick (22).

4.   Benediction of (hands extended over) the sick (30).

5.   Prayer for fruitfulness (23).

6.   Prayer for the local Church (24).

7.   Prayer for the bishop and the various members of the Church (25), including priests, deacons, subdeacons, lectors, interpreters (those who translated the Greek into Coptic for the people), ascetics, virgins, etc.

8.   Prayer of genuflection or " Prayer of the bending of the knee " (26), dealing with the names inscribed in the *book of life,* i.e., in the diptych of the living.

The richness and number of the prayers mentioned above seem to be forerunners of the very full intercessions at this part of the Liturgy so characteristic of the Egyptian Rites. [4]

Only the bishop's prayers are included in the Sacramentary; the rest of the Liturgy pertaining to the other clergy, the deacon, and people are omitted.   For these we must turn to other sources, scanty and uncertain though some of them may be, or else make guarded inferences from later sources of the Alexandrian Rite such as the Liturgy of St. Mark.   Thus, for example, there is no mention of the Kiss of Peace in Sarapion, though we know from Clement of Alexandria and Origen that it was part of the local Liturgy.   Nor

---

[3] J. Wordsworth, however, places this prayer before the " Prayer for the Bending of the Knee "; cf. *Bishop Sarapion's Prayer-Book,* Society for Promoting Christian Knowledge (London, 1923), p. 39.

[4] In other fourth-century sources we find " three prayers of the faithful " mentioned in Canon 19 of the Council of Laodicea or the deacon's litany and the bishop's prayer in the *Apostolic Constitutions* in a corresponding position.

is the offertory mentioned (which is not surprising in view of the general absence of rubrics in the Sacramentary), but we know that there must have been one, for there is an allusion to those " who have offered the offerings " in the prayers of the anaphora, entitled the " Offertory prayer of Bishop Sarapion " (1) in the Sacramentary.

9. The text of the anaphora. As translated by J. Wordsworth, the Bishop of Salisbury, it reads :

> It is meet and right to praise, to hymn, to glorify Thee the uncreated Father of the only-begotten Jesus Christ. [5] We praise Thee, O uncreated God, who art unsearchable, ineffable, incomprehensible by any created substance. We praise Thee who art known of Thy Son, the only-begotten, who through Him art spoken of and interpreted and made known to created nature. We praise Thee who knowest the Son and revealest to the saints the glories that are about Him : who art known of Thy begotten Word, and art brought to the sight and interpreted to the understanding of the saints. We praise Thee, O unseen Father, provider of immortality. Thou art the Fount of life, the Fount of light, the Fount of all grace and all truth, O lover of men, O lover of the poor, who reconcilest Thyself to all, and drawest all to Thyself through the advent of Thy beloved Son. We beseech Thee, make us living men. Give us a Spirit of light, that " we may know Thee the True [God] and Him whom Thou didst send, [even] Jesus Christ. Give us Holy Spirit, that we may be able to tell forth and to enunciate Thy unspeakable mysteries. May the Lord Jesus speak in us and Holy Spirit, and hymn Thee through us.
>
> * For Thou art " far above all rule and authority and power and dominion, and every name that is named, not only in this world, but also in that which is to come. " Beside Thee stand thousand thousands and myriad myriads of angels, archangels, thrones, dominions, principalities, powers [lit. : rules, authorities] : by Thee stand the two most honourable six-winged seraphim, with two wings covering the face, and with two the feet, and with two flying and crying " Holy, " with whom receive also our cry of " Holy " as we say : Holy, holy, holy, Lord of Sabaoth, full is the heaven and the earth of Thy glory.

[5] The opening words, " It is meet and right... " imply the usual framework of this portion of the Liturgy; hence, even though the *Sursum corda* is not mentioned in the Sacramentary, we may rightly infer its inclusion in the Liturgy.

Full is the heaven, full also is the earth of Thy excellent glory. [6] Lord of hosts [lit. : powers], *fill also this sacrifice with Thy power and Thy participation :* for to Thee have we offered this living sacrifice, this bloodless oblation. To Thee we have offered this bread the likeness of the Body of the Only-begotten. This bread is the likeness of the Holy Body, *because the Lord Jesus Christ in the night in which He was betrayed* took bread and broke and gave to His disciples saying, " Take ye and eat, this is My Body, which is being broken for you for remission of sins. " [7] Wherefore we also making the likeness of the death have offered the bread, and beseech Thee through this sacrifice, to be reconciled to all of us and to be merciful, O God of Truth; and as this bread had been scattered on the top of mountains and gathered together came to be one, so also gather Thy holy Church out of [8] every nation and every country and every city and village

---

[6] The passage between asterisks, beginning " For Thou art far above all rule... " is substantially the same as the corresponding text of both the Greek and Coptic St. Mark. St. Mark has an intercession interpolated before these words and the (Greek) St. Mark also has elaborations inserted in its text following the words spoken of the cherubim and seraphim, " with flying... " (cf. LEW, p. 131, line 25-p. 132, line 5); these elaborations are a later addition borrowed in part from the Lit. of St. James (LEW, p. 50, lines 26 ff.) and in part independent. Despite slight retouching, the Coptic St. Mark (cf. LEW, p. 175, lines 29-30) is closer to the text in Sarapion than its Greek counterpart. The *Sanctus* itself is evidently taken from Isaiah vi : 3 with which it agrees completely, except that it speaks of heaven and earth being full of glory, whereas Isaiah mentions only the earth. In this, Sarapion and St. Mark are identical; so also the Ethiopian Liturgy except that it adds " holy " before " glory. " None of the Egyptian Liturgies contains the additional *Hosanna* and *Benedictus qui venit*, which seems to be a Gallic innovation of the seventh century, and adopted by later Syrian, Byzantine, and Roman forms.

The Egyptian characteristic of taking up the cue of the *Sanctus* from the word " full " for resuming the Eucharistic Prayer in Sarapion agrees perfectly with that of St. Mark; thus, " full is the heaven, full also is the earth of Thy excellent glory.... " In the Syrian form (e.g. *Apostolic Constitutions*, St. James, and St. Basil, etc.) the cue is taken from the word " holy " and resumes, " holy art thou..., " etc.

[7] The words in italics, in that they a) contain a preliminary form of the Invocation before the recital of the Institution and b) combine the Institution with the *purpose* of offering the gifts, thus resemble the forms in St. Mark; not so, however, the Syrian form contained in the *Apostolic Constitutions*.

Further parallels between Sarapion and St. Mark as well as the later Egyptian Liturgies are found in the recital of the Institution : thus, after " body " is added " which is broken for the remission of sins " (cf. St. Mark in LEW, p. 132, line 30 and the Coptic in LEW, p. 177, line 5); also " He gave to his disciples " (cf. St. Mark, LEW, p. 132, lines 22 ff. and Coptic, LEW, p. 177, lines 1 ff.).

[8] The words between asterisks are similar to those found in the *Didache* (ix. 4).

and house and make one living Catholic Church. We have offered also the cup, the likeness of the Blood, because the Lord Jesus Christ, taking a cup after supper, said to His own disciples, [9] " Take ye, drink, this is the new covenant, which is My Blood, which is being shed for you for remission of sins. " [10] Wherefore we have also offered the cup, presenting a likeness of the blood.

O God of Truth, let Thy Holy Word come upon this bread, that the bread may become Body of the Word, and upon this cup that the cup may become Blood of the Truth; [11] and make all who communicate to receive a medicine of life for the healing of every sickness and for the strengthening of all advancement and virtue, not for condemnation, O God of Truth, and not for censure and reproach. For we have invoked Thee, the uncreated, through the Only-begotten in Holy Spirit.

Let this people receive mercy, let it be counted worthy of advancement, let angels be sent forth as companions to the people for bringing to naught of the evil one and for establishment of the Church.

We intercede also on behalf of all who have been laid to rest, whose memorial we are making.

After the recitation of names : [12] Sanctify these souls : for Thou knowest all, Sanctify all [souls] laid to rest in the Lord. And number them with all Thy holy powers, and give to them a place and a mansion in Thy kingdom.

Receive also the thanksgiving [eucharist] of the people, and bless those who have offered the offerings and the thanksgivings, and grant health and soundness and cheerfulness and all advancement of soul and body to this whole people through the only-begotten Jesus Christ in Holy Spirit; as it was and is and shall be to generations of generations and to all the ages of the ages. Amen. [13]

[9] For similarity in St. Mark and the Coptic Lit., cf. LEW, p. 132, line 22 and p. 177, lines 1 ff.

[10] For parallel of " take " before " drink " in Coptic, cf. LEW, p. 177, line 23.

[11] The invocation of what corresponds to the Epiclesis is for the operation of the *Word* and not the Holy Spirit as in the fourth century Syrian sources or in the Ethiopic Church Order; this is in line with the Alexandrian tradition in Clement of Alexandria, Origen, and Athanasius.

[12] This rubric appears in the manuscript.

[13] John Wordsworth, D.D., *Bishop Sarapion's Prayer-Book* (London, 1923), pp. 60-68.

So ends the Sarapion anaphora.   The rest of the Liturgy follows :

10.   Prayer of the Fraction (2).   This is essentially an Egyptian feature, but here it is given as preparatory to Holy Communion whereas the corresponding prayer in the Coptic Liturgy [14] serves as an introduction to the Lord's Prayer.   It may be that the Lord's Prayer came first in Sarapion's Liturgy if the words contained in the rubric of the Sacramentary, " after the prayer comes the Fraction and in the Fraction a prayer " actually refer to the Lord's Prayer. They could refer to the Eucharistic Prayer.

11.   Prayer of benediction of the people before Holy Communion but after the Communion of the clergy (3).

12.   Prayer of thanksgiving after the Communion of the people (4).

13.   Prayer or blessing of oil and water (5) entitled " Prayer concerning the oils and waters that are offered. "   The oil is for anointing, of course, and the water is to be drunk. [15]

14.   The final benediction of the people or, as the Sacramentary puts it, " Benediction of the people after the blessing of oil and water " (6).   This final blessing would undoubtedly be given at the dismissal.

The order of these final prayers corresponds to that of the later Egyptian and Syrian usages.   There is still no mention of the " Holy Things to holy people " (Τὰ ἅγια τοῖς ἁγίοις).

Sarapion's Liturgy is the earliest source for the recitation of the names of the dead.   The practice was probably adopted in his day. Older liturgical forms had the post-invocation prayers centered on Communion, while the intercessory prayers preceded the anaphora. Sarapion preserves this ancient characteristic up to a point, but by adding the final intercessory aspects of the anaphora, he bears witness to the new liturgical trend in the Eastern Churches of his time.

In 1907, another discovery helped to establish several important

---

[14] Cf. LEW, p. 181, lines 15 f.

[15] A similar prayer is found in the *Canons of Hippolytus* and in the Ethiopic *Church Order*, but its position is at the end of the anaphora; it is also found in the *Testamentum Domini* (cf. LEW, p. 190, lines 24 f.) where it appears immediately after the account of the Liturgy.   The *Apostolic Constitutions* (VIII), 29 also gives a similar prayer but does not indicate its position in the Liturgy.

points in the early Egyptian Liturgy : this was the finding of a manuscript at Deir Balizeh near Asyut in Upper Egypt. The manuscript belongs to the seventh or the eighth century, but the text is much older, probably reaching back to the third century. [16]

Although the Common Prayer of the Church (Prayer of the Faithful, Fol. 1 r-v) and the Prayer for the Fruits of Communion (Fol. 3 r) are too fragmentary to be restored with certainty, the Eucharistic Prayer (Fol. 1 v-2v) with the *Sanctus* (but no *Benedictus*), invocation, institution, and anamnesis are less fragmentary and show a marked resemblance to the corresponding portions of the Liturgy in Sarapion as well as to the Liturgy of St. Mark. [17]

We compare these three ancient parallel texts, Sarapion, Deir Balizeh and St. Mark, below : [18]

Sarapion	*Deir Balizeh*	*St. Mark*
...by thee stand the two most honourable six-winged seraphim, with two wings covering the face, and with two the feet, and with two flying and crying " Holy, " with whom also receive our cry of " Holy " as we say : Holy, holy, holy, Lord of Sabaoth, full is the heaven and the earth of thy glory. Full is the heaven, full also is the earth of thy excellent	Around thee stand the seraphim, the one (has six wings), a(nd the other has si)x (wings). And with twain they covered their face, and with twain their feet, and with twain they did fly. All things always hallow thee, but along with all who hallow thee, receive also our hallowing, as we say to thee, Holy, holy, holy, Lord of hosts. Full is the heaven and the earth	Behind thee stand the two most honourable living creatures, the many-eyed cherubim, and the six-winged seraphim, with two wings covering their faces and with two their feet, and with two flying.... All things always hallow thee, but along with all who hallow thee, receive also our hallowing... as we sing with them and say Holy, holy, holy, Lord of hosts.

[16] The text is in Greek. For a description, see Dom P. de Puniet, *Report of the Nineteenth Eucharistic Congress* (Westminster, Sept. 1908), London, 1909, pp. 367-401, and his article in the *Revue bénédictine*, XXVI (1909), pp. 34-51. As edited by T. Schermann, see *Der liturgische Papyrus von Der-Balyzeh*, in *Texte u. Untersuch.*, XXXVI. 1 b (Leipzig, 1910).

[17] The words in some of these prayers (especially in the Prayer of the Faithful) resemble the clauses in I Clem. lix-lxi. This would tend to confirm the theory of an original universal rite (see pp. 54 ff., above). There is also a short creed (Fol. 3 v) resembling the baptismal creed of the Ethiopic Church Order (Horner, p. 173) and the early Roman forms (Apostles' Creed) rather than that of Nicaea : " I believe in God the almighty Father, and in his only-begotten Son our Lord Jesus Christ, and in Holy Spirit, and resurrection of flesh and a holy Catholic Church. " Note that it has *I believe* rather than the usual Eastern *we believe*.

[18] The text of *Deir Balizeh* is that reconstructed by Dom P. de Puniet. Where reconstruction is conjectural, it is in parentheses.

glory. Lord of hosts, fill also this sacrifice with thy power and thy participation : for to thee have we offered this living sacrifice, this bloodless oblation. To thee we have offered this bread, the likeness of the body of the Only-begotten. This bread is the likeness of the holy body, because the Lord Jesus Christ in the night in which he was betrayed took bread and broke and gave to his disciples saying, " Take ye and eat, this is my body, which is being broken for you for remission of sins." Wherefore we also making the likeness of the death have offered the bread, and beseech thee through this sacrifice, to be reconciled to all of us and to be merciful, O God of Truth; and as this bread had been scattered on the top of the mountains and gathered together came to be one, so also gather thy holy Church out of every nation and every country and every city and village and house and make one living Catholic Church. We have offered also the cup, the likeness of the blood, because the Lord Jesus Christ, taking a cup after supper, said to his own disciples, " Take ye, drink, this is the new covenant, which is my blood, which is being shed for you for remission of sins." Wherefore we have also offered the cup, presenting a likeness of the blood.

of thy glory. Fill also us with the glory that is with thee, and vouchsafe to send thy Holy Spirit upon these creatures and (make) the bread the body of our (Lord and) Saviour Jesus Christ, and the cup the blood of the new covenant. For our Lord Jesus Christ in the night (in which he was being betrayed took bread and gave than)ks, a(nd when he had blessed it, he brake it and gave it) to his di(sciples and apost)les, saying, T(ake, eat all o)f it. This (is my) body, which is being given for you unto remission of sins. Lik(ewise aft)ter supper he took the cup, a(nd) when he had blessed it and had drunk, he gave it to them saying, Take, drink all of it. This is my blood which is being shed for you unto remission of sins. As (often) as ye eat this bread, and drink this cup, ye proclaim my death, ye confess my resurrection. We p(roclaim) thy death, we (confess) thy resurrection, and entreat. . . .

Full is the heaven and the earth of thy holy glory. . . . Fill, O God, also this sacrifice with the blessing which is from thee. . . that he may make the bread the body, and the cup the blood of the new covenant of our very Lord and God and Saviour. . . For our Lord. . . Jesus Christ. . . distributed it to his holy and blessed disciples and apostles saying, Take, eat. This is my body, which is being broken for you and distributed unto remission of sins. Likewise also after he had supped, taking the cup. . . when he had given thanks and blessed it. . . . Drink all of it. This is my blood of the new covenant which is being shed for you and for many. . . unto remission of sins. . . . For as often as ye eat this bread and drink this cup, ye proclaim my death and ye confess my resurrection (and ascension) until I come. Proclaiming the death. . . of thy only-begotten Son, and confessing his. . . resurrection and ascension. . . .

Comparison of the Deir Balizeh fragment with Sarapion and St. Mark shows considerable similarity. It is closer, however, to St. Mark than to Sarapion, especially in its more developed form of the anamnesis. In general, the fragment lacks many of the early characteristics of Sarapion. The invocation, for example, calls for the operation of the Holy Spirit and not for the Logos, the Word, as in Sarapion. It also lacks the prayer from the *Didache*, " bread scattered on the top of the mountains,... etc., " which in Sarapion is interposed between the two parts of the institution; likewise wanting is the description of the bread and the cup as a " likeness of the body " and " a likeness of the blood. " All this would point to a date later than Sarapion. On the other hand, it does preserve the ancient, more subjective character of the prayer, " Fill also *us* with the glory which is from Thee, " which in Sarapion reads " fill *this sacrifice* with thy power..."

The position of the invocation *before* instead of *after* the institution has aroused much comment among scholars; however, no certain conclusions can be drawn from this fact since the document is a fragment and no one knows whether or not it contained any further invocation in the normal place. St. Mark, after all, has a preliminary invocation in this position, [19] in addition to that after the institution.

To summarize, the characteristic Egyptian features stand out in Deir Balizeh fragment just as they do in Sarapion and St. Mark.

The student of the liturgy will also be interested in other early Egyptian liturgical fragments, especially the so-called Borgian Fragments ranging from the eighth to the twelfth centuries. These are actually parts of five different Liturgies and have been published from Coptic manuscripts. [20]

Incidental information concerning the Alexandrine Rite contained in Egyptian texts of the fourth and fifth centuries, although scanty, is valuable as corroborative evidence and for additional points of interest. We have, for example, the reading of the lessons and

---

[19] Cf. Brightman, LEW, p. 132, lines 13 f.

[20] Cf. Abbé Hyvernat, in *Romische Quartalschrift*, I (1887), 330-345, and II (1888), 20-27; also Crum, *Coptic Ostraca* (London, 1902), Nos. 19-27. Also Giorgi, *Fragmentum Evangelii S. Johannis* (Rome, 1789).

psalmody mentioned by Athanasius and Macarius; [21] the reading of
the Gospel, [22] which at least at Alexandria was the exclusive right
of the archdeacon. [23]   Contrary to the custom of other churches
where the bishop rose for the Gospel and took off his pallium, [24] at
Alexandria the bishop did not rise at the reading of the Gospel. [25]
Although not explicitly mentioned, the dismissal of the catechumens
is implied. [26]   Various proclamations and directions are imparted
by the deacon. [27]   There is abundant evidence of prayer for the
emperor. [28]   The salutation, " Peace be with you all, " and its
response is given by Cyril of Alexandria at " the very beginning of
the mysteries. " [29]   The presentation and offering of the oblations
are attested by several writers, [30] though the position of these in the
service is not indicated.   Most likely the hymn of the Seraphim
was said, since Athanasius alludes to this practice in the churches
of both East and West. [31]

There can hardly be any doubt that Cyril of Alexandria was
referring to the anamnesis of the Liturgy when he said : " Proclaiming
the death after the flesh *of the only-begotten Son* of God... and
confessing his return to life from the dead and his assumption into

[21] Athanasius, *Hist. Arian.*, 81 (PG 15, 1240 [*Series graeca*]); *De fuga*, 24 (PG
15, 1183 AB [*Series graeca*]); Macarius, *De charitate*, 29 (PG 34, 932 C).

[22] Athanasius, *Vita Antonii*, 2. 3 (PG 16, 355 B, 356 A [*Series graeca*]).

[23] Sozomen, *Hist. eccl.*, vii, 19 (PG 25, 1432 A).

[24] S. Isid. Pel., *Epp.*, i. 136 (PG 78, 272, or PG 40, 1022 B [*Series graeca*]).

[25] Sozomen, *Hist. eccl.*, vii, 19 (PG 25, 1431 C-1432 A [*Series graeca*]).

[26] We say it is implied because Athanasius (*Ap. c. Arian.*, 28, PG 15, 1013;
1029 [*Series graeca*]) mentions that they were not allowed to be present at the mysteries, while Cyril of Alexandria speaks of their departure before the more solemn
parts of the service (*De ador. in spir. et verit.*, xii [PG 68, 781 or edit. Aubert,
i, 444]).

[27] Cyril of Alexandria, *op. cit.*, xiii (PG 68, 848 BC).   Most of the directions
now existing in the Coptic texts could be construed to have been included in this
passage.

[28] E.g. Athanasius, *Apol. ad Constant.*, 16 (PG 15, 1155 C [*Series graeca*]);
De Synodis (PG 16, 286 A); *ibid.* (PG 16, 326 B, etc. [*Series graeca*]).

[29] Cyril of Alexandria, *In Ioann.*, xii, 1, edit. Aubert, iv. 1093.

[30] Isidore of Pel., *Epp.*, i. 123 (PG 40, 1018 C [*Series graeca*]); Cyril of Alexandria, *In Luc.*, xxii. 19 (PG 72, 908 B); Athanasius, *Apol. contra Arian.*, 28
(PG 15, 1013 C [*Series graeca*]).

[31] Athanasius, *De Trini. et sp. sanct.*, 16 (PG 16, 546 [*Series graeca*]); cf. also
Didym., *De Trini.*, ii. 77 A (PG 31, 545 B or PG 22, 301 D [*Series graeca*]) and
Isidore of Pelusium, *Epp.*, i. 151 (PG 40, 1027 C [*Series graeca*]).

Heaven, we celebrate the unbloody sacrifice in our churches, and thus approach the mystic blessings, and are sanctified, becoming partakers of the holy flesh, and the precious blood of Christ the Saviour of us all. " [32]

The older Alexandrine tradition of effecting the consecration by the operation of the Logos (as Clement and Origen have it) is also attested by Athanasius when he says : " When the great prayers and holy supplications have been sent up, the Word comes down into the bread and the cup, and they become his body. " [33] His successor, however, apparently refers to the invocation of the Holy Spirit when he speaks of the " holy altar where we invoke the descent of the Holy Spirit. " [34] If so, he is the earliest of the Egyptian writers who speaks of the epiclesis or invocation to the Holy Ghost. Otherwise, Theophilus of Alexandria is the first when he speaks in unequivocal terms of " the invocation and advent of the Holy Spirit. " [35]

Except in the works of Synesius (A.D. c. 373-c. 414), the Bishop of Ptolemais in the Libyan Pentapolis, there is no reference to the Lord's Prayer in the Alexandrine Liturgy by fourth-and fifth-century Egyptian writers. [36] Neither is there any explicit testimony of the *Sancta sanctis* in this period, except by Cyril. [37] Cyril also alludes to the Fraction before Holy Communion. [38] Finally, the dismissal after the Eucharistic Liturgy is attested by Athanasius. [39]

After the Council of Chalcedon, which condemned the Monophysite heresy (which claimed one nature in Christ, the divine only), the Church of Egypt was split into two groups : the dissident, heretical Monophysites and the Catholic Melkites. In A.D. 567,

---

[32] Cyril of Alexandria, *Ep. oecum. ad Nestor.*, ii. edit. Aubert, V, 72 C. Parallelism with the *anamnesis* in the Liturgy of St. Mark (cf. LEW, p. 133, lines 22 f.) is indicated by our italics. Both the Coptic and Ethiopian Liturgies also contain references to the ascension, though they lack the phrase " from the dead. "

[33] Athanasius, *Ad nuper baptizatos* (PG 26, 1325).

[34] Cf. Theodoret, *Hist. eccl.*, iv. 19 (PG 42, 1414 D [*Series greaca*]).

[35] Theophilus of Alexandria, *Lib. paschal.*, I (in Jerome, *Ep.* xcviii, 13), PL 22, 801-802.

[36] Cf. Synesius, *De regno* (PG 66, 1053 ff.).

[37] Cyril of Alexandria, *In Ioann.*, xii (edit. Aubert, iv. 1086). Didymus shows that he is familiar with it but does not specifically connect it with the Divine Liturgy, cf. LEW, p. 509, n. 26.

[38] Cf. *catena* quoted in LEW, p. 508, n. 21.

[39] Athanasius, *Hist. Arian.*, 55 (PG 15, 1225 A [*Series graeca*]).

two lines of patriarchs were established. As time went on, the Melkite group, originally supported by Byzantine officialdom (as indicated by its etymology, "party of the king" or "malik"), gradually conformed its Liturgy with that of Constantinople, until finally it was completely displaced by the latter. The Monophysite Church, on the other hand, supported chiefly by the people, continued to swing further and further away from official Byzantine usage. It gradually discarded the Greek language from its Liturgy and substituted the Coptic vernacular.

The classical text of the so-called Liturgy of St. Mark (which is to the Alexandrine rite what St. James is to the Syrian) is found in both the Greek and the Coptic. Its basic text probably dates back to the fifth century and some of its parts perhaps to the fourth. The old Alexandrine Rite is preserved almost intact in the Coptic St. Mark. [40] The Greek St. Mark, on the other hand, whose earliest manuscripts are of the twelfth and thirteenth centuries, has been extensively modified by Byzantine influence; however, its essential parts agree with the style and tenor of the best Coptic texts. Today the Greek St. Mark is no longer used. Comparing both the Coptic and the Greek St. Mark and the Ethiopian Liturgy of the Twelve Apostles, and selecting all that is common to the three, is an invaluable aid in the reconstruction of the ancient Alexandrine Rite. Fundamentally, the three are a single Liturgy whose variations arise merely from later modifications.

The present-day Coptic Liturgies also include the alternative anaphorae of St. Gregory Nazianzen and that of St. Basil (not to be confused with the Byzantine Liturgy of the same name). These, however, are Syrian imports and are of little value for studying the ancient usage of Alexandria. Both are translated from the Greek.

B. THE ANCIENT LITURGY OF THE ETHIOPIAN CHURCH

Beyond the frontiers of the empire and even beyond the southern borders of the Alexandrian Patriarchate itself lived the Ethiopians,

---

[40] More correctly, the ordinary of the Coptic Mass, conjoined with what the Monophysite Copts call the anaphora of St. Cyril (of Alexandria), produces the exact counterpart of the Greek St. Mark; hence, many liturgists prefer to call it the Coptic St. Mark.

a people believed to be of Semitic stock who probably had emigrated to Africa from southern Arabia. The evangelization of the Ethiopians apparently does not date back further than the time of St. Athanasius (A.D. 296?-373) who had consecrated St. Frumentius bishop of that people. At the time of its foundation, the Church of Ethiopia was subject to the great See of Alexandria. [41] About a century and a half later, nine monks, probably Monophysites from Syria, now known as the Nine Saints, revitalized the Ethiopian mission. The conflict between Catholics and Monophysites in Egypt had a direct bearing on the Ethiopian Church : when the Monophysites emerged supreme in the Alexandrian Patriarchate, its Ethiopian dependency also became and for the most part remained Monophysite. Its liturgical language, however, has always been Geez, the classical language of Ethiopia.

The early liturgy of Ethiopia is shrouded in mystery and obscurity. The so-called Egyptian Church Order consisting of what used to be known as the Coptic Church Order and the Ethiopian Church Order, [42] including the Latin Verona fragments [43] of the same, are nothing more than the *Apostolic Tradition* of Hippolytus in different versions. Though the Ethiopic version (formerly known as the Ethiopic Church Order) was naturalized in the Ethiopic Church to the extent that it forms the foundation of the normal anaphora of that Church today, it is not of Ethiopic origin and therefore cannot rightly be considered in the study of the early Ethiopic Liturgy except incidentally.

The *Testamentum Domini*, [44] from which the present-day Ethiopian anaphora of our Lord derives, is not of Ethiopic origin either : it is Syriac. Actually, the *Testamentum Domini* is also a recasting of the

[41] Even to this day, the Ethiopian Metropolitan is consecrated by the Patriarch of Alexandria.

[42] Complete English translation of these is in G. Horner, *Statutes of the Apostles* (London, 1904),

[43] Discovered by E. Hauler at Verona in 1900 and published by him in *Didascaliae apostolorum fragmenta Veronensia latina, accedunt canonum qui dicuntur apostolorum et aegyptiorum reliquiae* (Lipsiae, 1900).

[44] Translation from the Greek, seventh century; first published by Ignatius Ephrem II Rahmani, the Catholic Syrian Patriarch of Antioch, *Testamentum Domini nostri*, with Latin version and notes (Mainz, 1899). English translation by J. Cooper and A. J. Maclean, *Testament of Our Lord* (Edinburgh, 1902).

Apostolic Tradition mentioned above, or else its compiler has based his text almost entirely on a Liturgy identical with that of the *Apostolic Tradition,* although he generously interspersed portions of it with his own interpolations and expansions. The date of this compilation is either the fourth or the fifth century. Only insofar as the *Testamentum Domini* has been assimilated into the Ethiopian Rite can it find a place in the study of the Eucharistic Liturgy of this Church. Since its direct origin is Syrian, it legitimately belongs to the chapter on the early Syrian Liturgy.

Today, as many as seventeen alternative anaphorae may be used in the Ethiopian Church; they are listed on p. 181, n. 2.

CHAPTER X

THE POST-NICENE LITURGY
OF ANTIOCH AND SYRIA

Syria, a land much divided since prehistoric times on account of the diversity of its races, cultures, religions, and languages, was never politically welded into one solid state. Yet, Antioch, its administrative and ecclesiastical capital, became the greatest single center of liturgical influence in the East—perhaps even in the whole universal Church—in the latter part of the third and in the fourth centuries. There is no Rite in all of Christendom which in one way or another has not been influenced by the Liturgy of Syria.

Antioch was the Christian heir to the Seleucid tradition of leadership of all Syria in the path of Hellenism. But the Seleucids (B.C. *c.* 250-150) failed in their attempt to unify their country by the introduction of Hellenism as a general solvent of the diverse local traditions; nor did their Hellenism succeed in acquiring any real influence and prestige beyond their borders. How, then, did Antioch succeed in establishing itself as one of the greatest liturgical centers of influence in the Christian world? The reason seems to be the special ecclesiastical circumstances.

Because of the many councils held at Antioch during this era, its Church was certainly put into a position of influence and prestige in relation to the Churches of Cappadocia, Asia, Pontus, and even Thrace. Their relationship was close in any case by reason of their Antiochene origin. Antioch no less than Cappadocia influenced Constantinople during the latter's ascendancy by providing it with bishops. These factors at least partially explain why the Churches of Cappadocia, Asia, Pontus, and Constantinople have many Antiochene (or Syrian) characteristics in their respective Liturgies. Any Church with dependencies in as many territories would naturally dominate other Churches of Christendom.

Another factor which undoubtedly influenced the spread of the Antiochene Rite during the third and fourth centuries was the situation in Palestine and Jerusalem. Even before becoming a separate patriarchate, Jerusalem (and Palestine) attracted many visitors and pilgrims as the "Holy Land." These pilgrims from other lands were understandably impressed and influenced by the religious practices and ritual of Jerusalem, which belonged to the Antiochene family. On returning home, they incorporated some of these practices into their own Rites. For almost the same reason the monasteries of Syria and Palestine attracted visitors and thus exerted their influence on other Rites, although perhaps to a much lesser degree than did the Holy Land.

The original Rite of the Antiochene Church is undoubtedly the progenitor of the whole Antiochene (Syrian) family of Rites. Unfortunately, it is only imperfectly known, since Antioch itself did not preserve it, but borrowed instead one of its daughter Rites.

In the Antiochene as in the other Churches at the time of the Council of Nicaea, the crystallization of the Divine Liturgy was only beginning; the prayers of the Liturgy were for the most part still recited extempore by the celebrant, although ideal or model forms were beginning to be put into writing. The celebrant could, if he wished, make use of these models; he could adapt them to local circumstances, even incorporate his own ideas, tastes, and preferences into the Liturgy. All these possibilities make it difficult to trace the Rite of a given See. Antioch and Syria were no exception to this rule. We can learn much, however, about the Antiochene Rite of the fourth century from the so-called Clementine Liturgy found in Book VIII of the *Apostolic Constitutions*. [1] The Clementine Liturgy, as could have been expected, is not the official text of Antioch and Syria but only a suggested model or ideal form written

---

[1] The *Apostolic Constitutions*, the most famous of the "Church Orders," consists of eight books. Books I through VI are a Greek reproduction, with considerable modifications by the compiler, of the *Didascalia* of the Apostles, of which only the Latin fragments and Syriac version have survived (for the Syriac, cf. *Didascalia apostolorum syriacae*, edit. P. de Lagarde [Leipzig, 1854]; for the Latin, cf. F. X. Funk, *Didascalia et constitutiones apostolorum*, 2 vols. [Paderborn, 1905]). Book VII is a fusion of the *Didache* (which is much attenuated here) and other liturgical matter of an unknown source. Book VIII contains the Clementine Liturgy described above as well as the 85 Apostolic Canons which conclude the book.

down more for guidance than for application as such. [2] In its structure and legal regulations, Book VIII of the *Apostolic Constitutions*, is actually a recasting of the *Apostolic Tradition* by Hippolytus, but in the Liturgy which it contains, the traces of Hippolytus are faint. It is fairly certain now that the date of the whole composition is late fourth century.

Comparison of this Liturgy with the Antiochene writings of John Chrysostom leaves little doubt that the redactor had indeed drawn heavily on current Antiochene usages and forms. For example, great similarity and even identical phrasing exist in the litanies or *ektenes*, in the intercessions of the anaphora, in the Eucharistic Prayer, etc. The invocation is directly inspired by that of the Ethiopic version of the *Apostolic Tradition* (formerly known as the *Ethiopic Church Order*). All this indicates that the redactor has drawn freely on existing sources but, since he paraphrased and expanded them in line with his own ideas, the Clementine Liturgy can be considered his own composition. This is especially true of the Eucharistic Prayer where the author's personal style, known from his other works, is particularly noticeable. Textually, then, this Liturgy is the redactor's own creation, but its great value lies in corroborating and supplementing the evidence of other Syrian sources, especially Chrysostom's Antiochene writings (A.D. 360-398).

In attempting to reconstitute the old Rite of Antioch regarding the Divine Liturgy, special emphasis must be laid on the most reliable source, i.e., Chrysostom, [3] and only when that is lacking must guarded and qualified efforts be made to complement that source with the so-called Clementine Liturgy. We have attempted to correlate them into corresponding, parallel columns even if it

[2] The facts (1) that preference is given to Antioch (VIII, x. 7, etc.), (2) that Christmas is mentioned (VIII, xxxiii. 6), which feast was kept at an earlier date at Antioch than in most of the other Eastern Churches, and (3) that the Antiochene duration of Lent including Holy Week is given as seven weeks (V, xiii. 3) are valid arguments for the composition's Antiochene origin. Cf. Maclean, *Ancient Church Orders* (Cambridge, 1910), p. 150; Funk, *Die apostolischen Konstitutionen* (Rottenburg, 1891), pp. 96 ff, 164 f., 314, etc.

[3] The project of collecting these scattered data was first undertaken by J. Bingham. Later, other experts, notably Hammond, G. Bickell, and F. Probst, continued the work. Brightman culminated the work of his predecessors in his *Liturgies Eastern adn Western* (Oxford, 1896), Vol. I.

meant breaking up some of them to suit the purpose at hand.   The
Greek texts from which our translation was made are from Brightman : [4]

A.   LITURGY OF THE CATECHUMENS

Chrysostom   *Apostolic Constitutions,*
                                               Book VIII

1.   *Opening Greeting*

Celebrant : " Peace be with you. "
People : " And with thy spirit. "
(*In Matt.* 32:9 [vii. 374 A].)

2.   *Lections*

Lections from :   Lections from :
  a) the Prophets   *a*) the Law
  b) the Epistles, or   *b*) the Prophets
      the Acts (in Eastertime)   *c*) the Epistles
                                        d) and the Acts

(*In Rom.* 24:3 [ix. 697 E],
De baptismo Christi, 2 [ii. 369 C]
Cur in pentecoste, 5 [iii. 89 D].)

Psalmody?

There is no certain evidence of   No   mention   of   psalms   in
any psalms being sung between   Book VIII but Book II of *Apos-*
the lections, but there are some   *tolic Constitutions* mentions them,
indications in *In I Cor.* 36:7   with the people taking up the
(x. 342 C, etc.).   refrains (A.C. ii. 57.6).

---

[4] Brightman, LEW, pp. 3-27 and Appendix C, pp. 470-475. As reconstructed
from these sources, inadequate though they are, a certain definite stage of
development can be seen in the old Rite of Antioch before the close of the fourth
century.   For example, liturgical formulae are becoming more fixed; the Eucharist
itself is regarded with growing awe, reverence, and fear; the splendor of the
churches is increasing, with the altar or " holy table " sometimes made of silver
(Chrysostom, *In Matt.*, 1 al. 52, 3 [7, 518 B]; *In I Cor.*, 41, 4 [10, 392 E]; *De
poenitent.*, 9, 1 [2, 349 D]; *De prodit. Judae,* 1, 6 [2, 384 B]; etc.); costly vessels
of gold, set with jewels, candelabrum (*In Matt.*, 1 al, 51, 3 [7, 518 A]; *In Matt.*,
32, 6 [7, 373 C], etc.).   Chrysostom also mentions the bishop's throne (*Adv. Jud.*,
3, 6 [1, 614 C]).   Special liturgical vestments seem to be coming into their own,
e.g., albs for the ministers (*In Matt.*, 82 al, 83, 6 ([7, 789 D]), stoles for the
deacons, etc. (*De Fil. prod.*, 3 [8, app. 37 A]).   Brightman used the Montfaucon
edition (Paris, 1718-1738, in 13 vols.) of Chrysostom's works.

3. *The Gospel*

Priest or deacon sings the Gospel, during which all stand.
(*In Joan.* x. al. xi. 1 [viii. 62 B]; *In Matt.* 1:6 [vii. 13 B].)

Priest or deacon sings the Gospel, during which all stand.

4. *Homily Instructions*

Salutation by the celebrant :

Peace be to all.

Let the one that is ordained salute the Church, saying :

The grace of our Lord Jesus Christ, the love of God and the Father, and the communion of the Holy Ghost, be with you all.

The people respond :
And with thy spirit.
(*Adv. jud.* iii. 6. [i. 614 C]; *In I Cor.* 36:4 [x. 339 D].)

And they all should answer :
And with thy spirit.

Sermon or sermons

(*In I Cor.* 36:4 [x. 339 D]; *Adv. jud.* iii. 6 [i. 614 C]; *In I Cor.*, etc.).

After these words let him (the celebrant) speak the words of exhortation to the people.

5. *The Dismissals*

The catechumens lie on the ground and the deacon says :

When he finishes his word of doctrine... while all are standing up, the deacon should step up on some elevated rostrum and proclaim :

Let none of the hearers, let none of the unbelievers remain.

And when there is silence, let him say...

Ye catechumens, pray.

Let us earnestly pray for the catechumens

People : Lord, have mercy.

Deacon :

Let us stand properly. Let us pray

Let all the faithful mentally pray for them, saying...

Lord, have mercy.

And let the deacon request prayers for them, saying...

Let us all earnestly pray to God for the catechumens

That the all-merciful and compassionate God hear their prayers,

That he open the ears of their hearts and teach them the word of truth,

That he implant in them his fear and strengthen his faith in their minds,

That he reveal to them the gospel of righteousness,

That he give them a spirit of holiness, a sound mind, a virtuous manner of living, so that they may always know the things that are his, understand the things that are his, meditate on the things that are his, that they may exercise themselves in his law day and night, that they remember his commands and preserve his precepts.

Again let us pray for them more earnestly,

That he deliver them from every wicked and injurious deed, from every malicious sin and from all distress of adversity,

That he make them worthy in proper time of the laver of regeneration, of the remission of sins, of the robe of immortality,

That he bless their comings and their goings, their whole life, their homes and their families,

That he bless the growth of their children and make them wise according to the measure of their age,

That he who is good and the lover of mankind will mercifully hear their prayers and supplications,

And that he accept their petitions so as to help them,

And that he give them those desires of their hearts which are for their good,

That he reveal to them the Gospel of his Christ,

That he may instruct and teach them wisdom,

That he teach them his commands and precepts,

That he implant in them his pure and saving fear.

May he open the ears of their hearts that they may exercise themselves in his law day and night,

That he strengthen them in piety,

That he unite and number them with his holy flock,

That he make them worthy of the laver of regeneration, and of the robe of immortality which is the true life,

That he deliver them from all wickedness and give no quarter to their adversary,

That he cleanse them from all filth of flesh and spirit, dwell in them and move in them through his Christ,

That he bless their comings and their goings,

And that he order their affairs for their good.

That he order all their affairs according to their good.

Again let us earnestly pray for them,

That when they will obtain the forgiveness of their transgressions through their admission [into the Church], [5] they be thought worthy of the holy mysteries and of constant communion with the saints.

Arise

Beseech [for yourselves] an angel of peace,

Ye catechumens, rise up.

Beseech [for yourselves] the peace of God through his Christ.

[Beseech] that all your affairs be peaceful for you,

[Beseech] that this day and the whole of your life be peaceful and sinless,

Beseech that your present day and all the days of your life be peaceful,

[Beseech] a Christian end [to your life],

[Beseech] a Christian end (to your life),

[Beseech] that which is good and salutary.

[Beseech] that God be compassionate and merciful [to you],

[Beseech] the forgiveness of your transgressions.

Commend yourselves to the living God and to His Christ.

Commend yourselves to the only unbegotten God through his Christ.

Bow down your heads.

Bow down and receive the blessing.

As we have said before, at each of these that the deacon mentions, the people should say :

Lord, have mercy.

and the children should say it before all and, when they have bowed down their heads, the newly ordained bishop should bless them with this blessing :

O almighty God, unbegotten and inaccessible, who art the

Priest or bishop : Peace be to all.
People : And to thy spirit.

---

[5] Brackets are added to clarify the meaning.

112   CHAPTER X

Such is the beginning of the blessing.

All exclaim : Amen.

(*De incompr. Dei nat.* iii. 7 [i. 471 A].)
For rubrics and formula cf. *in II Cor.* 2:5 ff. [x. 435-440].
For implication of *Lord, have mercy* being the response to each petition, cf. *In Matt.* lxxi al. lxxii. 4 [vii. 699 E]; also *Dei nat.* iv. 4 [i. 477 C]; *ibid.* iii. 7 [i. 470 E] and *In II Cor.* 18:3 [x. 568 B].)

Deacon : [Let us earnestly pray] for the energumens.
People : Lord, have mercy.

. . . .

. . . .

only true God, God the Father of thy Christ, thine only begotten Son, the sender of the Paraclete and Lord of all, who through Christ didst appoint thy disciples to be the teachers of piety, do thou now also look down upon thy Servants who are being instructed in the Gospel of thy Christ, and give them a new heart and renew within their bowels a right spirit that they may both know and do thy will with a completely sincere purpose and with a willing soul. Vouchsafe them a holy admission and unite them to thy holy Church, and make them partakers of thy divine mysteries, through Christ, our hope, who died for them, through whom may glory and worship be given to thee in the Holy Spirit forever. Amen.

And after this, the deacon should say :
Catechumens, depart in peace.

And after they are gone, he should say :
Energumens afflicted with unclean spirits, pray :
Let us all earnestly pray for them,
That God, the lover of mankind, rebuke the unclean and wicked spirits through Christ,
And that he deliver his implorers from the tyranny of the adversary,
That he who had rebuked a legion of demons and the devil, the author of evil, also

now rebuke these apostates from piety,

And that he deliver his own works from their power,

And that he cleanse these creatures whom he has made with great wisdom.

Again let us pray earnestly for them :

Save them, O God, and raise them up by thy power.

Bow down your heads.

Energumens, bow down your heads and receive the blessing.

Priest or Bishop : Peace be to all.

People : And to thy spirit.

Such is the beginning of the blessing.

. . . .

. . . .

(*In Matt.* lxxi al, lxxii, 4 [vii. 699 E]; *De incompr. Dei nat.* iv. 4 [i. 477 C], *ibid.* iii. 7 [i. 470 E]; *In II Cor.* 18:3 [x. 568 B].)

And the bishop should pray, saying :

Thou, who hast bound the strong one and rifled all that was in his house, who hast given us the power to tread upon serpents and scorpions and upon all the might of the enemy; who hast handed over to us the bound murderer-serpent as a little sparrow to children; whom all things dread and before whose might all things tremble; who hast cast him down as lightning from heaven to earth with a downfall not from a place but from a position of honor to disgrace because of his voluntary evil disposition; whose glance dries the abyss and whose threat melts the mountains and whose truth remains forever; whom the infants praise and sucking babes bless; to whom angels sing hymns and whom they adore; who lookest upon the earth and makest it tremble; who touchest the mountains, and they smoke; who threatenest the sea and driest it

up and who makest all the rivers
as a desert, and the clouds are
the dust of thy feet; who walkest
upon the sea as on firm ground,
O only begotten God, the Son
of the great Father : rebuke
these wicked spirits and deliver
the works of thy hands from the
power of the adverse spirit. For
glory, honor, and worship are
due to thee and, through thee,
to the Father in the Holy Spirit
forever. Amen.

And the deacon should say :
Energumens, depart.

*And after they go out, he should
loudly proclaim :*
Ye that are to be illumined,
  pray.
Let us all, the faithful, earnestly
  pray for them,
That the Lord make them worthy, when they are initiated
  into the death of Christ, to
  rise with him and to become
  partakers of his Kingdom and
  participators of his mysteries.
Unite and number them among
  those that are safe in his holy
  Church.
Again let us earnestly pray for
  them :
Save and raise them up by thy
  grace.

*And when they are being pledged
to God through his Christ, let
them bow down their head and
receive this blessing from the
bishop :*
  Thou who hast once said
through the holy prophets to

those to be initiated, " Wash, ye, become clean " and hast ordained spiritual regeneration through Christ, do thou also now look down upon these who are baptized and bless them, sanctify and prepare them to become worthy of thy spiritual gift and of thy true adoption, of thy spiritual mysteries, of being gathered together with those who are saved through Christ, our Saviour, by whom glory, honor, and worship are due to thee in the Holy Spirit forever. Amen.

And the deacon should say :

Those who are to be illumined, depart.

Deacon :

And after this, he should proclaim :

Penitents, pray.

Let us earnestly pray for the penitents.

People : Lord, have mercy.

. . . .

Let us all earnestly pray for our penitent brothers,

That God who loves compassion will show them the way of repentance,

That he accept their return and their confession,

And that he speedily crush Satan under their feet,

And that he deliver them from the snare of the devil and from the harm of demons,

And that he free them from every unlawful word, from every improper practice and from wicked throughts,

And that he forgive them all their offenses, both voluntary and involuntary,

And that he blot out the handwriting that is against them,
And that he inscribe them in
the Book of Life.
That he cleanse them from all
filth of flesh and spirit,
And that he restore and unite
them to his holy flock.

> For he knoweth our frame.
> For who can glory that he
> has a clean heart? And
> who can boldly say that he
> is pure from sin? For all
> of us are among the blame-
> worthy.

Again let us pray for them more
earnestly, for there is joy in
heaven over one sinner that
repenteth,
That, being converted from
every evil work, they may
proceed to every good act,
That God, the lover of men,
will speedily, benevolently accept their petitions and will
restore them to their former
state,
And that he give them the joy
of salvation and strengthen
them with his noble spirit so
that they may no longer be
wavering in their steps but
may be deemed worthy to
become sharers of his sacred
sacrifices and partakers of his
divine mysteries,
That, being made worthy of his
adoption, they may obtain
eternal life.
Again let us all earnestly say,
Lord have mercy for them.
Save them, O God, and raise
them up by thy mercy.

Rise up and bow your heads to God through his Christ and receive the blessing.

Bishop or Priest :

Peace be to all.

People : And to thy spirit.

Such is the beginning of the blessing.

. . . .

. . . .

(*In Matt.* lxxi al, lxxii. 4 [vii. 699 E], and same as above for energumens.)

The bishop should then pray :

O almighty, eternal God, Lord of the whole world, creator and ruler of all things, who hast shown man as the pride of the world through Christ and didst give him a law both innate and written so that he would live according to it as a rational creature and, when he sinned, thou gavest thy goodness as an inducement for his repentance : Look down upon these who have bent the neck of their soul and body to thee, for thou desirest not the death of a sinner but his repentance so that he turn from his wicked ways and live. Thou who didst accept the repentance of the Ninevites, who willest that all men be saved and come to the knowledge of the truth, who didst accept the son who had consumed his substance in riotous living with the heart of a father because of his repentance : do thou now also accept the repentance of thy suppliants, since there is no man that will not sin, for if thou, O God, wilt mark iniquities, Lord, who shall stand? For with thee there is reconciliation. And do thou restore them to thy holy Church, to their former dignity and honor, through Christ our God and Saviour, by whom glory and adoration are due to thee in the Holy Spirit forever. Amen.

Deacon :

All penitents, depart.

(*In Eph.* 3:4 [xi. 23 A], but cf.
S. Chrys. homiliae in Gal. et Eph.
in *Biblioth. patrum* Oxon. 1852,
p. 133 and note p. 388.)

The doors are closed.

(*In Matt.* 23:3 [vii. 288 C], *De
resur.* 3 [ii. 441 E].)

Then the deacon should say :

Penitents, depart.

LITURGY OF THE FAITHFUL

1.   *Prayers of the Faithful*

*All likewise prostrate themselves
on the ground.*
(*In II Cor.* 18:3 [x. 568 B].)

Deacon :

Let us pray for the whole world.

People and Children :

Lord, have mercy.

(Let us pray) for the Church
  which is spread as far as the
  ends of the world.

And he (the deacon) should add :

Let none of those, who should
  not, draw near.

Let all of us faithful kneel down.

Let us entreat God through his
  Christ.

Let us all earnestly beseech God
  through his Christ.

Let us pray for the peace and
  stability of the world and of
  the holy Churches, that the
  God of the whole world may
  grant us his everlasting peace
  which may not be taken away
  [from us], [6] that he keep us
  in the full perfection of virtue
  even unto godliness.

Let us pray for the holy, catholic
  and apostolic Church which
  extends from one end of the
  earth to the other, that the
  Lord preserve and keep it

[6] Our brackets.

stable and free from the waves of this life as built upon a rock until the end of the world.

Let us pray for this holy parish, that the Lord of the whole world may unfailingly grant us to seek his heavenly trust and unceasingly pay him the debt of our prayer.

(Let us pray) for all the bishops, for the priests, for their help and that they rightly dispense the word of truth.

Let us pray for every bishopric that is under heaven, the bishopric of those who rightly dispense the word of truth.

Let us pray for our bishop James and his parishes, for our bishop Clement and his parishes, for our bishop Euodius and his parishes, for our bishop Annianus and his parishes, that the compassionate God let them continue in his holy Churches in health, honor, and long life, and that he grant them an honorable old age in piety and righteousness.

And let us pray for our priests that the Lord deliver them from every improper and wicked action and that he grant them both a sound and an honorable ministry.

Let us pray for all the deacons and ministers in Christ, that the Lord grant them blameless ministration.

Let us pray for the readers, singers, virgins, widows, and orphans.

Let us pray for the married and those in child-bearing, that the Lord have mercy upon them all.

(Let us pray) for the kings and
rulers.

(Let us pray) for all who are
here and everywhere.

(Let us pray) for the energumens.

(Let us pray) for those in sickness, in the mines, for those
in bitter servitude.

(Let us pray) for the land and
the sea.

(Let us pray) for the weather.

(*De prophet. obscurit.* ii. 5 [vi.
188 A]; *In Matt.* lxxi al. lxxii. 4.
[vii. 699 E]; *In II Cor.* 2:8
[x. 440 E]; also *de incompre. Dei
nat.* iii. 6 [i. 468 E].)

Let us pray for the princes who
lead a pious life.

Let us pray for those who are
continent and prudent.

Let us pray for those who do
good in the holy Church and
for those who give alms to the
poor.

And let us pray for those who
bring offerings and sacrifices
to the Lord our God, that
God, the source of all goodness, repay them with his
heavenly gifts and give them
an hundredfold in this world
and life everlasting in the
world to come, and that he
grant them eternal goods for
those that are temporal, heavenly goods for those that are
earthly.

Let us pray for our newly enlightened brothers : that the
Lord may strengthen and for-
tify them.

Let us pray for our brothers who
are tried with sickness, that
the Lord deliver them from
every sickness and disease and
that he restore them in health
to his holy Church.

Let us pray for those who travel
by sea or by land.

Let us pray for those who are
in the mines, in banishment,
in prisons and in chains for
the name of the Lord.

Let us pray for those who are in
bitter servitude.

Let us pray for our enemies and
for those who hate us.

Let us pray for those who persecute us for the name of the

Lord, that the Lord calm their anger and dispel their wrath against us.

Let us pray for those who are out [of the Church] and for those who have gone astray, that the Lord convert them.

Let us remember the Church's infants, that the Lord may perfect them in his reverence and bring them to maturity.

Let us pray for one another, that the Lord keep us and guard us by his grace till the end and deliver us from the evil one and from all the scandals of those that work iniquity, and save us for his heavenly Kingdom.

Let us pray for every Christian soul.

Save us and raise us up, O God, by thy mercy.

Let us arise

Let us earnestly pray and commend ourselves and one another to the living God, through his Christ.

The bishop should add to this prayer, and say :

O almighty Lord, the Highest who dwellest on high, the Holy who reposest in holy places, King from all eternity, who through Christ hast entrusted us with the preaching of knowledge for an avowal of thy glory and thy name which he has made known to us that we might comprehend, do thou now also through Christ look down upon this thy flock and deliver it from

Similarily, we all arise.

Deacon : Let us beseech for an angel of peace

Let us beseech that all [our] affairs be peaceful.

Priest or Bishop :

Peace be to all.

People : And with thy spirit.

Such is the beginning of the blessing.

(Adv. Jud. iii. 6 [i. 614 C]; *in ascensione* 1 [ii. 448 D].)

. . . .

. . . .

all ignorance and evil habit, and grant that we may reverence thee in earnest and love thee with real affection and have due regard for thy glory. Be kind and merciful to them; be attentive to their prayers; keep them just, blameless, and irreproachable, that they be holy in body and soul, not having spot or wrinkle or any such thing but that they be perfect and that none of them be either defective or empty. Our mighty impartial defender, become the protector of this thy people whom thou hast chosen from among thousands, whom thou hast redeemed with the precious blood of thy Christ; be thou their protector, helper, provider, and guardian, their strong wall of defense, their bulwark and security, for no one can snatch [them] out of thy hand; nor is there any other God like thee while our trust is in thee. Sanctify them in truth, for thy word is truth. Thou who dost nothing for favor, whom no one can deceive, deliver them from every sickness, every disease and every offense, every injury and deceit; deliver them from the fear of the enemy, from the arrow that flieth in the day, from the trouble that walketh about in the darkness; grant them that everlasting life which is in Christ thy only begotten Son, our God and Saviour, through whom glory and adoration are due to thee in the Holy Spirit, now and always and forever and ever. Amen.

2. The Kiss of Peace

And after this the deacon should say :

Let us be attentive.

And the bishop should salute the congregation and say :

The peace of God be with you all.

And the people should answer :

And with thy spirit.

And the deacon should say to all :

Greet one another with the holy kiss.

They embrace one another before the gift is offered,
(De compunct. ad Demetr. i. 3 [l. 127 A B].)

And the clergy should greet the bishop, the laymen should greet the laymen, the women the women.

3. The Offertory

And the children should stand at the reading-desk and another deacon should stand by them that they may not be disorderly. Other deacons should walk about and watch the men and women that no disturbance be made and that no one nod, or whisper, or sleep. Deacons should also stand at the doors of the men and subdeacons at the doors of the women so that no one go out, nor any door be opened even for any of the faithful during the sacrifice.

Then a subdeacon should bring water to the priests for their hands, as a symbol of the purity of souls dedicated to God.

I, James, the brother of John, the son of Zebedee, declare that the deacon should justly say :

Let none of the catechumens, none of the hearers, none of the unbelievers, none of the heretics remain here.

Deacon : Those who cannot pray, depart.

Those who have prayed the preceding prayer, depart. [7]

Let the mothers take their children in hand.

Be reconciled with one another.

Let no one have anything against anyone; let no one remain here in hypocrisy.

Let us stand upright as is fitting.

Let us stand up straight before the Lord with fear and trembling to offer [the oblation].

(*In Eph*. 3:4 [xi. 23 A]; *Adv. Jud*. i. 4 [i. 593 B]; *De incompr. Dei nat*. iv. 5 [i. 478 C]; the position of these proclamations, however, is not clear.)

When this is done, the deacons should bring the gifts to the bishop at the altar.

4.   *The Anaphora*

And the priests should stand on his right and on his left as disciples before their Master. Two deacons, on each side of the altar, should hold a fan, made of small thin membranes or of peacock feathers or of fine cloth, and should silently drive away the small insects flying about so that they may not come near the chalices. [8]

a.   The Thanksgiving

And then the celebrant himself should pray together with the priests; he should vest in a splendid garment, stand at the altar, make the sign of the cross

[7] The non-communicating faithful were not allowed to remain for the rest of the Liturgy.

[8] In ancient times, more than one chalice was used because of the great number of communicants.

Priest : The grace of our Lord Jesus Christ and the love of God and the Father and the communion of the Holy Spirit be with you all.

People :
And with thy spirit.
(*De s. Pentecoste.* i. 4 [ii. 463 B].)

Priest :
Let us lift up our minds and hearts.

People : We lift them up to the Lord.

Priest :
Let us give thanks to the Lord.

People :
It is meet and right [to do so].

Then the priest begins the thanksgiving :
(*De poenitentia* ix. 1 [ii. 349 C] and *In II Cor.* 18:3 [x. 568 B].)

Whenever I say the thanksgiving, I open all the treasure of God's benefits and I call to mind those great gifts.   And while

on his forehead [9] *with his hand and say :*
The grace of almighty God and the love of our Lord Jesus Christ and the communion of the Holy Spirit be with you all.

And all should say together :
And with thy spirit.

The celebrant :
Lift up your mind.

And all the people : We lift it up to the Lord.

And the celebrant :
Let us give thanks to the Lord.

All the people :
It is meet and right [to do so].

Then the celebrant should say :
It is truly meet and right above all to praise thee who art the true God, who art before all things, from whom all paternity in heaven and earth is named, who alone art unbegotten, without beginning, without a ruler and without a master, who art in need of nothing, the giver of every good, who art above all cause and generation, always and immutably the same, from whom all things came into being as from their proper source.   Thou art eternal knowledge, everlasting vision, unbegotten hearing, untaught wisdom, first by na-

---

[9] The common text has here " before all the people. "

repeating over the chalice the ineffable blessings of God and whatever benefits we enjoy, we offer it thus and partake of it while we are thanking him that he hath freed mankind, that when we were far off he hath made us close [to himself], that when we were without hope and without God in this world, he hath made us brothers and co-heirs.   For these and all similar blessings we give him thanks and thus draw close [to him].

(*In I Cor.* 24:1 [x. 212 D E] also comp. *ibid.* 313 A.)

(Also *Ad eos qui scandalizantur* 7 ff. [ii. 482 B ff] is modeled on the Thanksgiving and may be regarded as loosely paraphrasing this section of the Liturgy)

ture, the measure of being and above all number; who didst bring into being all things out of nothing by thine only-begotten Son, the same whom thou didst beget before all ages by thy will, by thy power and thy goodness without an intermediary, the only begotten Son, God the Word, the living wisdom, the first-born of every creature, the angel of thy great Counsel, and thy High Priest, the King and Lord of every intellectual and sentient creature, who art before all things, by whom all things are.   For thou, O eternal God, didst make all things by him, and through him thou dost bestow thy fitting care over the whole world; it is through the very same one by whom thou didst give being that thou didst also bestow well-being.   God and Father of thy only-begotten Son, who didst make through him first of all the Seraphim and the Cherubim, the Aeons and the Powers, the Virtues and the Dominations, the Principalities and the Thrones, the Archangels, and the Angels; after all these thou didst make through him this visible world and all the things that are in it. For thou art he who didst raise the cope of heaven as a dome and didst stretch it out like the covering of a tent and didst establish the earth on nothing by thy mere will; thou art he who didst bring light out of thy treasures and on its suppression didst bring on the darkness to rest the living creatures that move in the world, who didst appoint the sun in the sky to rule over the day, and the moon to rule over the night, and didst prescribe the choir of stars in the heavens to praise thy glorious majesty. Thou art he who didst make water for drinking and cleansing, life-giving air for breathing and for carrying the sound of the voice made by the tongue striking the air, and for the auditory sense which works together therewith in such a way as to perceive speech when it meets and is received by it. Thou art he who madest fire for dispelling the gloom, for supplying our need so that we might be warmed and receive light from it, he who didst separate the great sea from the land and didst render the former navigable and the latter fit for walking... the sea thou didst fill with living creatures small and large and the land thou didst supply with animals both tame and wild and didst cover it with various plants, didst crown it with herbs, didst beautify it with flowers, and didst enrich it with seeds. Thou art he who didst create the great abyss and didst encircle it with a mighty cavity containing the seas of salt waters massed together and didst bind them all around with straits of the finest sand. Sometimes thou dost swell the sea to the height of mountains by the winds, sometimes thou dost smooth it like a plain; sometimes thou dost enrage it with a storm, sometimes thou dost still it with a calm so that it be mild for the voyages of seafaring men. With rivers thou didst gird the world made by thee through Christ, and didst water it with streams and didst fill it with unfailing springs. Thou didst gird the earth around with mountains for its firm and secure support. Thou hast filled up thy world and adorned it with sweet-smelling, healing herbs, with many various living creatures, both strong and weak, tame and wild, for food and work. Thou hast filled it with the hissing of creeping reptiles, with the cries of various birds. Thou hast supplied it with yearly cycles, with numerous months and days, with regular seasons, with the precipitation of rain clouds for fruit-growing and the sustenance of animals. Thou hast also appointed the prescribed limit of the winds that blow when commanded by thee and abundance of plants and herbs. Thou hast not only created the world itself but hast also made for it a citizen, man, whom thou hast designated as the glory of the world, for thou didst say to thy wisdom : Let us make man according to our image and according to our likeness; and let them have dominion over the fish of the sea and the fowls of the air. Thereupon, thou hast made him of an immortal soul and a corruptible body, the former created from nothing,

the latter from the four elements.... for his soul thou hast
given him rational knowledge,
the differentiation of piety and
impiety and an alertness for right
and wrong; for his body thou
hast bestowed upon him the five
senses and the power of loco-
motion.   Then through Christ,
O thou almighty God, thou hast
planted a paradise in Eden
toward the East, adorned with
all kinds of edible plants and
didst bring him into it as into
a rich banquet. In creating him,
thou gavest him a law implanted
within him so that he might have
the seeds of divine knowledge
from himself and within himself.   Nevertheless, when thou
hadst brought him into the paradise of pleasure, thou didst allow
him the privilege of enjoying all
things but in hope of greater
blessings, thou didst forbid him
to taste of one tree so that, provided he kept the commandment,
he would receive its reward, immortality. But when he disregarded that commandment because of the seduction of the
serpent and the advice of his
wife and tasted of the forbidden
fruit, thou didst justly drive him
out of paradise.   Yet in thy
goodness thou didst not despise
him when he was entirely miserable, since he was thy creature;
but thou didst subject the world
to him and didst command him
to earn his food by his own sweat
and labors while thou thyself
didst all the growing, the multi-
plying, and the ripening. When

thou hadst laid him to sleep for
awhile, thou didst call him to a
new birth again with an oath,
didst loose the bond of death,
and didst promise him life after
the resurrection. And not only
this, but when thou hadst increased his posterity to an in-
numerable people, thou didst
glorify those that continued with
thee and didst punish those that
turned away from thee. While
thou didst accept the sacrifice
of Abel as from a truly holy
person, thou didst reject the gifts
of Cain, the murderer of his
brother, as from a wicked wretch.
Moreover, thou didst accept
Seth and Enos and didst take
Enoch, for thou art the creator
of men, the giver of life, the
provider in need, the giver of
laws, the rewarder of those who
keep them and the avenger of
those who transgress them.
Thou didst bring the great flood
upon the world because of the
many wicked people and thou
didst deliver from this flood virtuous Noah together with eight
people in an ark, so that he
would be the end of the foregoing generations and the beginning of the future ones. Thou
didst kindle a fearful fire against
the five cities of Sodom and didst
turn a fruitful land into a salt
lake for the wickedness of them
that dwelt therein, but thou
didst rescue righteous Lot from
the conflagration. Thou art he
who didst deliver Abraham from
the ungodliness of his forefathers
and didst appoint him the heir

of the world and didst reveal to him thy Christ. Thou didst ordain Melchizedek a high priest for thy worship. Thou didst designate thy patient servant, Job, the victor over the serpent, the author of evil. Thou madest Isaac the son of the promise and Jacob, the father of twelve sons, and didst vastly increase his posterity and didst bring him into Egypt with seventy-five people. Thou, O Lord, didst not overlook Joseph but didst grant him command over the Egyptians as a reward of his chastity for thy sake. Thou, O Lord, didst not neglect the Hebrews when they were oppressed by the Egyptians, because of the promises made to their fathers; but thou didst deliver them and didst punish the Egyptians. When men had corrupted the law of nature, sometimes regarding it as the effect of chance and sometimes honoring it more than they should have, and equated it with thee, the God of the universe, thou didst not let them go astray but didst raise up thy holy servant, Moses, and through him didst reveal that creation was thy work and didst drive out the error of polytheism. Thou didst honor Aaron and his posterity with the priesthood and didst punish the Hebrews when they sinned and didst receive them again when they turned back to thee. Thou didst punish the Egyptians with the ten plagues. After dividing the sea, thou didst lead them through it and didst destroy by drowning those Egyptians who were pursuing them. Thou didst sweeten bitter water with wood, didst bring water out of the hardest rock, and didst rain manna from heaven and quails as meat out of the air. Thou didst give them a pillar of fire by night to give them light and a pillar of cloud by day to shade them from the heat. Thou didst designate Joshua as general of the army and, through him, didst overthrow the seven nations of Canaan; thou didst divide the Jordan, didst dry up the rivers of Ethan and didst pull down walls without tools or the hand of man. For all this, glory to thee, almighty Lord! It is thee the uncounted hosts of Angels, Archangels, Thrones, Dominations, Principalities, Virtues, and Powers, thy everlasting armies, adore. The Cherubim and the six-winged Seraphim, who with two wings cover their feet, with two their heads, and with two fly, together with a thousand thousand Archangels and ten thousand times ten thousand Angels without ceasing and without becoming silent cry out :

Consider with whom thou standest during the time of the mysteries, with the Cherubim, with the Seraphim... how canst thou say with them :

Holy, holy, holy (*In Eph.* 14:4 [xi. 108 A], also compare *In illud Vidi Dominum* i. 1 [vi. 95 D] and *In II Cor.* 18:3 [x. 568 B].)

Heaven and earth are filled with his glory. (*In illud vidi Dominum* i. 3 [vi. 98 E].)

And all the people should say together :

Holy, holy, holy Lord of Sabbath

heaven and earth are full of his glory

Be praised forever!

Amen.

And the bishop continues :

For thou art truly holy and all-holy, the highest and most exalted in eternity. Holy also is thine only-begotten Son, our Lord and God, Jesus Christ, who in all things served Thee, his God and Father, both in thy excellent creation and in thy fitting providence... who has not disdained the human race that was lost but, after the natural law, after the admonitions regarding the law, after prophetic rebukes and angels' warning (when men had perverted both the positive and the natural law and had dispelled from their minds the memory of the flood, the burning of Sodom, the plagues of the Egyptians, and the butchery of the Palestinians, and just when they were about to perish entirely), he who was the creator of man was pleased by thy good will to become man, he who was the lawmaker, to be subject to the law, he who was the high priest, to become a sacrifice, he who was the shepherd, to be a sheep! And he did appease thee, his God and Father; he did reconcile thee to the world and freed all men from the wrath to come. He who was born of a virgin, born in the flesh, was God the Word, the beloved Son, the first-born of every creature who according to the prophecies foretold by himself concerning himself was of the seed of David and Abraham, of the tribe of Judah. And he who made all men who are born

into the world was conceived in
the womb of a virgin, he who
was without flesh became incarnate, he who was begotten in
eternity was born in time. He
lived a holy life and taught according to the law. He drove
away every sickness and every
weakness from men. He
wrought signs and wonders
among the people. He who
nourishes all that need food and
fills every living creature with
his goodness, himself partook
of meat, drink, and sleep. He
manifested his name to those
that knew it not. He dispelled
ignorance, restored piety, fulfilled thy will, and completed
the work which thou gavest him
to do. When he had settled all
these things, he was seized with
the hands of the ungodly, the
high priests and priests falsely
so-called and the sinful people,
through the betrayal of him who
was diseased with wickedness.
He suffered much from them.
He endured all sorts of shame
by thy consent. He was turned
over to the governor, Pilate, and
he, the Judge, was judged; he,
the Saviour, was condemned;
he, who was not subject to suffering, was nailed to the cross;
he, who by nature is immortal,
died; he that is the giver of life
was buried so that he might
conquer suffering, that he might
tear away from death those for
whose sake he had come and
that he might loose the bonds
of the devil and free mankind
from his deceit. He arose again

from the dead on the third day. After spending forty days with his disciples, he ascended into heaven and was seated on the right hand of thee, his God and Father.

Remembering what he suffered for us, we give thee thanks, O almighty God, not in the way we should but in as much as we can, and we are fulfilling his command. For on the night in which he was betrayed, he took bread in his holy and undefiled hands and, looking up to thee his God and Father, he broke it and gave it to his disciples, saying : This is the mystery of the New Testament, take of it and eat. This is my body, which is broken for many, for the remission of sins.   In like manner

The sacrifice is this.... what Christ has given to the disciples is also that which the priests do now... for the very words which God spoke are those very same ones which the priest now also says; this then is the sacrifice. (*In II Tim.* 2:4 [xi. 671 E], cf. also *De prodit. Judae* i. 6 [ii. 384 B].)

also the chalice—He mixed wine and water and sanctified it and gave to them, saying : Drink ye all of this; for this is my blood which is shed for many for the remission of sins; do this in commemoration of me. For as often as ye eat this bread and drink this cup, ye shall show forth my death until I come.

The Anamnesis

Recalling, therefore, his passion and death and resurrection from the dead and his return to heaven and his future Second Coming when he will come to judge the living and the dead and to render to every man according to his works, we offer thee, King and God, according to his command, this bread and this chalice by giving thee thanks for having considered us worthy to stand before thee and to officiate to thee as a priest.

The Epiclesis

The priest stands before the altar. Lifting his hands to heaven, he invokes the Holy Spirit to come and touch the gifts which have been offered... that grace descend on the sacrifice, that through it he may enkindle the souls of all and that he make them brighter than a piece of silver purified by fire.

(*In coemet. appelat.* 3 [ii. 401 D]; *De sacerdot.* iii. 4 [i. 383 A]; also cf. *De s. Pentecoste* i. 4 [ii. 463 C].)

And we entreat thee to look with favor upon these gifts that are set here before thee, thou God of riches, and do thou accept them for the honor of thy Christ and deign to send down upon this sacrifice thy Holy Spirit, the witness of the Passion of the Lord Jesus that he might show this bread to be the body of thy Christ and this chalice to be the blood of thy Christ, so that those who partake of it may grow in piety, obtain the forgiveness of their sins, be freed from the devil and his deceit, and that they be filled with the Holy Spirit, be made worthy of thy Christ and obtain eternal life after being reconciled to them, almighty Lord.

The Intercession

The priest makes the sign of the cross over the offerings. (Quod Christus sit Deus 9 [i. 571 A].)

(The Intercessions)

The common atoning sacrifice of the world lies before us; therefore with boldness then do we entreat for the whole world... for the Catholic Church, which is spread from one end of the earth to the other....

We further entreat thee, Lord, for thy holy Church which extends from one end of the earth to the other and which thou hast redeemed with the precious blood of thy Christ, that thou preserve and keep it stable till the end of the world, and for every bishopric that rightly dispenses the word of truth.

We further entreat thee also for my unworthy self who am

[The priest] approaches praying to God that he stop wars everywhere, that he put an end to all troubles. He prays for peace, for good protection, for a swift deliverance from each and every pressing evil both private and public.

(*In I Cor*. 41:5 [x. 393 B]; *Hom. in Eustathium* 3 [ii. 607 C]; *de sacerdot*. vi. 4 [i. 424 A].)

We make a commemoration of the departed during the time of the holy mysteries and, praying for them, we approach the Lamb that lies here and who taketh away the sins of the world.

(*In I Cor*. 41:4 [x. 392 E].)

. . . .

offering to thee, for all the priests, for the deacons, and all the clergy, that thou make all of them wise and fill them with the Holy Spirit.

We further beseech thee, Lord, for the king and all those in authority, the whole army, that they keep their peace toward us so that, living the whole time of our life in tranquillity and in harmony, we may glorify thee through Jesus Christ who is our hope.

Moreover, we offer to thee [this sacrifice] also for all those holy people who have given thee great satisfaction from the beginning of the world, patriarchs, prophets, just men, apostles, martyrs, confessors, bishops, priests, deacons, subdeacons, readers, singers, virgins, widows, the laity, and all whose names thou thyself knowest.

Moreover, we offer to thee [this sacrifice] for this people, that thou designate them for the glory of thy Christ, for the royal priesthood and a holy nation; for those in the state of virginity and purity, for the widows of the Church, for the honorably married and those in childbearing, for thy people's infants, that thou wilt not permit any of us to become castaways.

Moreover, we beseech thee also for this city and its inhabitants, for the sick, for those in bitter servitude, for those in banishment, for those in prison, for those who travel by sea or land, that thou the helper of all men also be their protector.

Moreover, we beseech thee for those that hate us and persecute us for thy name's sake, for those who are out [of the Church] and for those who have gone astray, that thou turn them back toward goodness and calm their anger.

Moreover, we entreat thee also for the Church's catechumens, for those that are distressed by the adversary, and for our brothers in penitence, that thou perfect the catechumens in the faith, that thou free the others from the power of the devil and accept the repentance of the penitent, and that thou forgive both our sins and theirs.

Moreover, we offer to thee [this sacrifice] for good weather and the abundance of fruits, so that, by always enjoying the good things from thee, we may unceasingly praise thee who didst give food to all flesh.

Moreover, we entreat thee also for those who are not here because of a good reason, that thou keep us all in piety and gather us together in the Kingdom of thy Christ, the God of all sensory and intelligent nature, our King, who would keep us firm, innocent, and blameless.

For to thee is due all glory, worship, thanksgiving, honor, and adoration, to the Father, to the Son, and to the Holy Spirit, both now and always, and for ever and ever.

(The intercessions end with)
...for ever and ever.

People : Amen.

(*In I Cor.* 35:3 [x. 325 E].)

And all the people should say :
Amen.

The Blessing

And the bishop should say :
May the peace of God be with all of you.

And all the people should answer :
And with thy spirit.

The Lords Prayer

Priest and People : Our Father who art in heaven....

(*In Gen.* 27:8 [iv. 268].)

The Inclination

The deacon, standing before the altar of sacrifice, proclaims :

Let us all pray together :

. . . .

. . . .

And the deacon again should proclaim :

Again and again let us pray to God through his Christ :

For the gift which was offered to the Lord God, let us pray that the good God through the mediation of his Christ accept it on his heavenly altar as an odor of sweetness.

For this holy church and people, let us pray to the Lord.

For every bishopric, every priestly ministry, every diaconate in Christ, for all the people of the Church, let us pray that the Lord keep and save them all.

For kings and those in authority, let us pray that they keep their peace toward us, so that having a quiet and peaceful life, we may lead it in all piety and honesty.

Let us remember the holy martyrs, that we may be deemed worthy to share their trial.

For all those who have fallen asleep in Christ and for those who commemorate them :

. . . .

. . . .

(*In Eph.* 3:5 [xi. 23 D]; *In I Cor.* 41:4 [x. 392 E]; *In I Cor.* 24:2 [x. 213 C]; this reconstruction is far from certain, though the parallel seems to indicate its position here.)

For those who have died in the faith, let us pray.

Let us pray for good weather and productive crops.

Let us pray for those who are newly enlightened, that they be strengthened in the faith.

Let us all pray for one another.

Raise us up, O God, by thy grace.

Let us stand up and dedicate ourselves to God through his Christ.

And the bishop should say :

O God, who art mighty and whose name is mighty, who art great in design and powerful in works, the God and Father of thy holy child Jesus, our Saviour : look down upon us and upon this thy flock which thou hast chosen through him for the glory of thy name; sanctify our soul and body, grant us that we be made pure from all filth of flesh and spirit, obtain the good things laid up for us, and do not judge any of us unworthy, but be thou our comforter, helper, and protector, through thy Christ with whom glory, honor, praise, acclaim, and thanksgiving be to thee and to the Holy Spirit forever.   Amen.

The priest breaks the bread.
(*Ibid.* Again the position of the fraction here is not certain.)

The Elevation

The curtains are drawn open and the oblation is brought forth.
(*Ibid.* and cf. *In I Cor.* 36:6 [x. 340 E].)

After all have said " Amen " the deacon should say :

Let us be attentive.

And the bishop should say the following to the people :

Priest : Holy things to the holy.
(*In Matt.* 7:6 [vii. 114 A].)

Holy things to the holy.

The people should answer :

There is one holy, one Lord, Jesus Christ, for the glory of God the Father, blessed forever. Amen.

Glory to God in the highest and on earth peace, good will among men.

Hosanna to the Son of David. Blessed is he that cometh in the name of the Lord.   God is the Lord and hath appeared to us. Hosanna in the highest.

The Communion

The bishop should communicate after this, then the priests, deacons, subdeacons, the readers, singers, and the ascetics.   Then, from among the women, the deaconesses, the widows.   Then the children, and finally all the people in order, with reverence and godly fear, without noise.   And the bishop should give the prosphora [*the host*], *saying :*

The body of Christ.

The recipient should answer :

Amen.

The faithful approach and the deacons distribute the gifts.

(*In Matt.* lxxxii al. lxxxiii. 6 [vii. 789 C]; *In Matt.* l al. li. 2 [vii. 516 E].)

The deacon should take the chalice and when he administers it, he should say :

The blood of Christ, the chalice of life.

And he who drinks it should answer :

Amen.

The cantors sing Ps. 144 :

I will extol Thee, my God, my King.

The people sing after each verse :

The eyes of all wait for thee, and thou givest them their food in due season.

(*In Ps.* 144:1 [v. 466 E].)

Psalm 33 should be sung while the rest are receiving.

When all, even the women, have received, the deacons should carry what remains into the sacristy.

The Thanksgiving

The final thanksgiving.

(*De bapt. Christi* 4 [ii. 374 C ff.].)

When the singer is finished, the deacon should say :

After receiving the precious body and the precious blood of Christ, let us give thanks to him who has deemed us worthy to partake of his holy mysteries. Let us beseech him that it be not for our condemnation but for our salvation, for the benefit of our soul and body, for the safeguarding of piety, the remission of sins and for life everlasting.

Let us arise.

By the grace of Christ let us dedicate ourselves to the only unbegotten God and to his Christ.

And the bishop should say :

Lord, God almighty, the Father of thy Christ, thy blessed Son, who hearest those who call upon thee with righteousness, who also understand the supplications of the silent, we thank thee that thou hast deemed us worthy to partake of thy holy mysteries which thou hast given us for the full assurance of the things which we have rightly known, for the safeguarding of piety, for the forgiveness of our sins because the name of thy Christ is invoked by us and we are dedicated to thee. Thou who hast separated us from the company of the ungodly, unite us with those who are consecrated to thee in holiness, strengthen us in truth with the help of the Holy Spirit, reveal to us those things about which we do not know, supply the things in which we are wanting and strengthen us in the things which we already know. Keep the priests blameless in thy service, preserve the kings in peace and the rulers in righteousness, the weather at a good temperature, the fruits in abundance, the world in an all-powerfull care; make the warring nations to be at peace, turn back those who have gone astray, sanctify thy people, guard the virgins, preserve the married in the faith, strengthen the pure, bring the infants to maturity, brace the newly admitted [into the Church], teach the catechumens and make them worthy of admission [into the Church], and gather us all together into thy heavenly Kingdom, through Jesus Christ, our Lord, with whom glory, honor, and worship be to thee in the Holy Spirit, forever. Amen.

The Dismissal

And the deacon should say :

Bow down to God through his Christ and receive the blessing.

And the bishop should add the following prayer and say :

O almighty God, the incomparable and true God, who art everywhere and in all things, who art in nothing as something which is, who art not confined to a place, nor made old by time; who art not terminated by ages, deceived by words, or subjected to generation; who needest no guardian, who art above all corruption, free from all change, and unchangeable by nature; who inhabitest light inaccessible, who art by nature invisible yet art known to all intelligent creatures seeking thee with good will, who art understood by those who seek thee with a good mind, who art the God of Israel, [the God] of the people who truly see and who have believed in Christ: be kind to me and listen to me for thy name's sake, bless those who bow down their head to thee, grant them their sincere petitions—those which are for their good—and do not refuse any of them into thy Kingdom but sanctify, guard, protect, help them, deliver them from the adversary and from every enemy, guard their homes and protect their comings and their goings. For to thee is due honor, praise, glory, worship, and adoration and to thy Son Jesus, thy Christ, our Lord and God and King, and to the Holy Spirit, now and always, forever and ever. Amen.

Deacon :   *And the deacon says :*
Go in peace.   Go in peace.
Adv. jud. iii. 6 [i. 614 C].)

A supplementary source of evidence pertaining to the Antiochene
Liturgy is found in Book II of the *Apostolic Constitutions.* In itself,
the work does not propose to give the text of the Liturgy but merely
a short description of the Rite, or what we may call the rubrics for
its celebration. The directions (which we shall omit) for ordering
or arranging the congregation are long and involved. They probably
date from the third century, but the order of the service itself is
from the fourth.

The Liturgy is described thus : [10]

I.   The Mass of the Catechumens

i

The reader should stand on some elevated place in the middle
[of the church] and should read the books of Moses, Joshua
the son of Nun, Judges, Kings, Chronicles, and those written
after the return from captivity; besides these [he should also
read] the books of Job, Solomon, and the sixteen other
prophets. When two lessons have been read individually,
some other person should sing the hymns of David and the
people should join in at the conclusion of the verses.

After this, the Acts should be read and the Epistles of Paul,
our fellow worker, which he sent to the Churches under the
guidance of the Holy Spirit. Afterwards a deacon or a priest
should read the Gospels, both those which I, Matthew, and
John have entrusted to you and those which Luke and Mark,
Paul's fellow workers, have left to you. While the Gospel
is being read, all the priests, deacons, and people should
stand up in deep silence, for it is written : " Be silent and
hear, O Israel, " and again, " But do thou stand there and
hear. "

ii

Next, the priests should separately, one by one, exhort the
people and last of all the bishop as a commander.

[10] Our translation from the Greek text in Brightman, LEW, pp. 29-30.

iii

(Dismissal of the catechumens and penitents)

II.   The Mass of the Faithful

i

Then, after the catechumens and penitents are gone, after
rising up together and looking toward the East, all should
pray to God who also ascended toward the East into the
heaven of heavens; this also recalls the ancient position of
paradise in the East from where the first man was banished
after yielding to the advice of the serpent and disobeying the
command of God.

ii

After the prayer is over, some of the deacons should carefully
attend to the oblation of the Eucharist, ministering to the
Lord's body with fear; the other deacons should watch the
people and keep them quiet.

iii

The deacon who stands near the celebrant should say to the
people :

> Let no one have anything against another;
> let no one be in hypocrisy.

Then the men should salute the men, and the women the
women, with the Lord's kiss, but no one should do it deceitfully, like Judas, who betrayed the Lord with a kiss.

iv

After this, the deacon should say :

> For the whole Church, for the entire world
> and the countries and produce that are in it.

> For the priests and rulers.

For the high priest and king and for peace in general.
Afterwards in entreating peace for the people, the high priest
should bless them (as Moses commanded the priests to bless
the people in these words : " The Lord bless thee, and keep

thee : the Lord make his face to shine upon thee and have mercy on thee; the Lord lift his countenance upon thee and give thee peace "). The bishop should pray for the people and say :

> Save thy people, O Lord, and bless thine inheritance, which thou hast obtained with the precious blood of thy Christ and hast called a royal priesthood and a holy nation.

The Anaphora

i

The sacrifice should follow after this while all the people stand and silently pray.

ii

And when the sacrifice has been offered, every row should receive by itself the Lord's body and precious blood in order and should come with reverence and holy fear as to the body of their king. The women should come up with their heads covered as becomes their modesty; the door should be watched lest any unbeliever or unbaptized come in.

CHAPTER XI

SYRIAN DERIVATIVES :
THE MAIN PALESTINE AND JERUSALEM

Palestine and Jerusalem belonged to the jurisdiction of Antioch until the middle of the fifth century (i.e., till the Council of Chalcedon, A.D. 451). As a neighboring Church dependent on Antioch, Jerusalem undoubtedly used the rite of the patriarchal Church, but with modifications of its own. Within each patriarchate there was still much variety—just how much variety in the case of Jerusalem can be gleaned from the catechetical writings of Cyril of Jerusalem and from the *Pilgrimage of Etheria*. These Palestinian sources, especially those of Cyril, are of paramount importance if we accept the thesis that during the first half of the fourth century, the Liturgy of Palestine had supplanted it's parent Rite at Antioch, and eventually in all of the West Syrian Church, in the form of the Liturgy of St. James the Brother of the Lord.

By no means can we categorically state that the Liturgy of Palestine as described by St. Cyril was that of St. James. But there are good reasons for justifying the conclusion that the Liturgy of St. James did indeed originate in Palestine some time during the fourth century and, since Cyril was describing the Liturgy as it was celebrated in Jerusalem during his time (also the fourth century), the two may easily be one and the same Liturgy. Evidence is not wanting : undeniable parallels and identical phrasings exist in both Liturgies. If St. James is not an expansion of the Palestinian Liturgy as described by Cyril, then it certainly incorporated many of its features. Both generally follow the main lines of the Liturgy found in the Antiochene *Apostolic Constitutions*. To summarize : the Liturgy of St. James, which completely replaced the ancient and original rite of Antioch, descends from an Antiochene source and is an expansion of the fourth-century rite of Jerusalem.

When exactly did Antioch adopt the Liturgy of St. James? Certainly not before Chrysostom left Antioch in A.D. 397; on the other hand, hardly after A.D. 431 when relations between Antioch and Jerusalem became greatly embittered by Juvenal, Bishop of Jerusalem, in his attempts to establish his See as an independent entity—not only that, but as having jurisdiction over Antioch itself. The date, therefore, must be placed somewhere between A.D. 397 and A.D. 431. The process of adoption was probably gradual, that is, the various parish churches of the Antiochene See probably accepted it at different dates and, even then, perhaps as an additional Liturgy for use on special occasions only. The fact that this Liturgy was incorporated in the Syrian Catholic and Monophysite Churches shows that its use at Antioch must have been solidly entrenched before the Monophysite schism in the latter half of the fifth century.

Why did Antioch adopt the Liturgy of St. James? No one really knows. The main reason seems to be the ever-growing prestige and importance of Jerusalem as the Holy City and the model of liturgical usage—so much so, in fact, that during the latter part of the fourth century and the early part of the fifth, many other Churches of Christendom adopted several of the liturgical practices current there. At any rate, whatever the reason (or reasons) for its acceptance at Antioch, the Liturgy of St. James became what might be termed the patriarchal Rite of Antioch. Antioch modified it and expanded it somewhat, but essentially it remained the same. However, the text of its Eucharistic Prayer never seemed to have achieved the same prescriptive force as the rest of its ritual. As many as seventy-two alternative anaphoras (or Eucharistic Prayers) had subsequently evolved in the various parts of the Syrian patriarchate (ranging in dates from the fourth or fifth centuries to the fifteenth; for the list of them, see Appendix B).

The Liturgy of St. James is found in both the Greek and the Syriac editions. The Greek version is the older of the two. Syria, a mosaic of languages and cultures, needed both texts : the Greek for most of its cities which were more or less hellenized, and the Syriac, in the outlying towns and villages impervious to Hellenism. Unfortunately, the earliest extant manuscript of the Greek St. James is from as late as the tenth century; [1] when it had already been

---

[1] This is a roll, *Vat. gr.*, 2282, edit. I. Cozza-Luzi in A. Mai's NPB, X, ii, pp. 27-110. Brightman's opinion (*The Journal of Theological Studies*, XII, p. 311) that it is of the tenth century seems to be the most probable, though Baumstark/

modified considerably by Byzantine influences. The Syriac
St. James, while differing somewhat from its Greek counterpart up
to the Kiss of Peace, is almost identical from that point onward.
The earliest manuscript of this version dates from the eighth
century. [2]

The fourth-century Rite of Jerusalem, on the other hand, is known
chiefly from the *Catecheses* of Cyril, a presbyter and subsequently
Bishop of Jerusalem. These sermons were delivered during Easter
week, A.D. 348, by Cyril to the newly confirmed who were attending
the Eucharistic celebration for the first time. His account, therefore,
is only of the Eucharistic part of the Liturgy, since this alone was
unfamiliar to the newly baptized. Additional fragments of information regarding liturgical usage are furnished by Etheria, a nun
from Spain or Gaul, who had the opportunity of participating in the
various ceremonies of the Holy City. In writing to her fellow sisters
at home, Etheria unfortunately does not describe the celebration of
the Eucharistic Liturgy, but she does give an interesting account of
the synaxis and the daily offices. From these, some of the liturgical
characteristics pertaining to the Eucharistic Liturgy can be gleaned
but they are too involved to warrant discussion here.

In the interest of brevity, only the texts of the Eucharistic Prayer,
or anaphora, are given in the comparison below. Material not found
in the Syriac is set off in parentheses ( ); passages set off in brackets
[ ] are Syriac interpolations not found in the earliest manuscripts
of the Liturgy.

Schermann (*Oriens christianus*, III, pp. 214-219), E. Bishop (*The Journal of
Theological Studies*, X, p. 598), and R. H. Connolly (*The liturgical homilies of
Narsai*, TS. VIII, i, p. 119) assign it to the seventh or eighth century. Also
belonging to the latter part of the tenth century is a parchment roll, *Graec.*, 177,
at the University Library, Messina. Another manuscript, of about two centuries
later, is parchment, *Vat. gr.* 1970 *olim Basilianus cryptoferratensis ix* at the Vatican
Library. The next oldest is a fifteenth century *Graec.*, 2509 at the National
Library in Paris. All of these are given in Swainson, *The Greek Liturgies Chiefly
from Original Authorities* (Cambridge, 1884), pp. 214-232.

[2] A manuscript of the anaphora in the British Museum (*Add.*, 14523) is from the
eighth or ninth century; another (*Add.*, 14518) found there is from the ninth or
tenth century; also from the tenth century is the Brit. Mus. *Add.*, 14523(3)-14525.
There are many later manuscripts in the British Museum as well as in Berlin,
Oxford's Bodleian Library, and Paris. Cf. Brightman, LEW, p. ix.

Cyril of Jerusalem, *Catechesis*

Liturgy of St. James

Preface :
Priest : Lift up your hearts.

Preface :
Priest : Let us lift up our mind and hearts.

People : We lift them up to the Lord.

People : We lift them up to the Lord.

Priest : Let us give thanks to the Lord.
People : It is meet and right.
(*Cat.* xxiii. 4.5 P. 50.85)

Priest : Let us give thanks to the Lord.
People : It is meet and right.

Priest :

Priest : It is truly meet and right, fitting and our bounden duty to praise thee, to extol thee, to bless thee, to adore thee, to glorify thee, to give thanks to thee, the Creator of every creature visible and invisible (treasury of eternal good things, the source of life and immortality, the God and Lord of all) whom the heavens, the heavens of heaven and all their powers praise, the sun and moon, all the choir of stars, the earth, the sea and all that is in them, the heavenly (assembly of) Jerusalem, the Church of the firstborn *whose members* are written in the heavens (the spirits of the just and prophets, the souls of martyrs and Apostles), the Angels, Archangels, Thrones, Dominations, Principalities, Virtues, and the dreadful Powers, [3] the many-eyed Cherubim and the six-winged Seraphim who with two wings cover their faces and with two their feet and with two they fly, and cry one to another with unceasing voices

After this, we mention heaven, the earth, the sea, the sun and moon, the stars and all rational and irrational, visible and invisible creation; the Angels, Archangels, Powers, Principalities, Virtues, Dominations, Thrones, the many-faced Cherubim, while we say in a loud voice the words of David, " O magnify the Lord with me. " We also mention the Seraphim whom Isaiah in the Holy Spirit

---

[3] The Syriac has " angels, archangels, principalities, powers, thrones, dominations, the virtues above the world, the heavenly armies. "

beheld standing around the
throne of God while with two
wings they cover the face, with
two the feet and with two they
fly, and say :

Holy, holy, holy, Lord of Sabaoth.

We, therefore, say this praise
of God, which we have been
taught by the Seraphim, that we
may become partakers in the
praises of the armies of heaven.
(*Cat.* xxiii. 5)

For truly we are bound to give
thanks for he hath called us,
who are unworthy, to so much
grace, because he reconciled us
who were rejected, because he
hath deemed us worthy of the
spirit of adoption. For when
we give thanks we do a thing
which is fitting and right. For
in doing not merely what was

and unsilenced praising the victorious hymn of thine excellent
glory, with clear voice singing,
shouting, (glorifying), crying out
and saying :

People : Holy, holy, holy, Lord
of Sabaoth. Heaven and earth
are full of thy glory. [4]

Hosanna in the highest.

Blessed is he that [came and]
cometh in the name of the Lord.

Hosanna in the highest.

Priest : [Even as in truth] holy
art thou, O king of the ages,
both Lord and giver of all holiness, holy also is thine only begotten Son our Lord Jesus
Christ [and God and Saviour]
(through whom thou madest all
things) and holy is thine all-
holy [5] Spirit who searcheth all
things, even the deep things of
thee, O God [and Father]. Holy
art thou, ruler of all things, almighty, good, terrible, merciful,
who art especially compassionate
to thy creature, who dist make
man from the earth in thine own
image (and likeness), who didst
bestow on him the enjoyment
of paradise, but when he trans-
gressed thy command and was
banished, thou, O good *God,*
didst not despise nor forsake
him, but as a compassionate
father thou didst chasten him;
thou didst call him through the
Law and didst instruct him

---

[4] The Syriac : " Of whose **majesty's** glory and honor heaven and earth are
full. "

[5] The Syriac simply has " holy " for " all-holy. "

fitting but beyond what was fitting, he was beneficent to us and did make us worthy of such good things. (*Cat.* xxiii, 5)

In the night in which our Lord Jesus Christ was betrayed, when he took bread and after giving thanks, he broke it and gave it to his disciples, saying : Take, eat; this is my body. And when he took the chalice, and after giving thanks, he said : Take ye, drink ye; this is my blood, (*Cat.* xxii, 1), which is shed for many for the remission of sins (*Cat.* xxii, 7).

through the Prophets. Finally, thou didst send thine only begotten Son (our Lord Jesus Christ) into the world that by his coming he might renew thine image *in men*; who, when he came down from heaven and became incarnate of the Holy Spirit and Mary the Virgin-Mother of God, lived among men and accomplished all things for the salvation of our race. And when he who was sinless for the sake of us sinners was about to accept his voluntary (and lifegiving) death (by the cross), in the night in which he was betrayed (or rather gave himself up) for the life and salvation of the world, took bread into his (holy and) undefiled and blameless (and immortal) hands, after (looking up to heaven and) showing it to thee, God and Father, after giving thanks, blessing, [hallowing] and breaking it, gave to his holy disciples and apostles, saying :

(*The deacons join in :* For the remission of sins and life everlasting.)

Take, eat : this is my body which is broken for you [and for many] and given for the remission of sins [and life everlasting].

People : Amen.

Likewise when he had supped, taking the chalice and, after mixing wine and water, (and looking up to heaven and showing it to thee, God and Father),

after giving thanks, blessing it,
hallowing it (and filling it with
the Holy Spirit), he gave to his
holy (and blessed) disciples [and
apostles], saying : Drink ye all
of it; this is my blood of the
New Testament, which is shed
for you and for many and is
delivered for the remission of
sins [and for life eternal].

People : Amen.

Priest : Do this in commemoration of me; for as often as ye
do eat this bread and drink of
this chalice, ye do proclaim the
death of the Son of man and
confess his resurrection until he
come. [6]

(*Deacons :* We believe and confess :)

People : Thy death, O Lord, do
we proclaim and thy resurrection we confess [and thy Second
Coming do we look for, and of
thee we ask mercy and compassion and we implore the forgiveness of sins. Thy mercies
be upon us all].

Priest : And we sinners commemorate his life-giving sufferings, his (saving cross,) death,
(burial,) resurrection from the
dead, ascension into heaven, his
sitting at the right hand of thee,
God and Father, and his second
glorious and fearful coming when
he shall come with glory to judge
the living and the dead, when
he shall recompense everyone

---

[6] The Syriac has the first person : " ye do proclaim my death and confess my
resurrection until I come. "

according to his works. [7] (O Lord our God, forgive us rather according to his compassion). We offer to thee, O Lord, this fearful and unbloody sacrifice beseeching that thou deal not with us according to our sins nor repay us according to our iniquities but according to thy kindness and thy [great and] ineffable love for mankind; (remove and) blot out the handwriting against us, thy suppliants. [8] Grant us thy heavenly and eternal gifts which eye hath not seen nor ear heard, neither hath it entered into the heart of man what things God hath prepared for them that love Him, (and cast not away thy people because of me and our sins, O Lord, the Lover of mankind), for thy people and thy Church entreat thee [and through thee and with thee the Father, saying] :

People : Have mercy on us, O Lord God the Father almighty [have mercy on us].

[*Priest :* We too, O Lord, receiving thy grace, weak and sinful, thy servants, give thanks to thee and praise thee for all things, and because of all things.]

[*People :* We glorify thee, we bless thee, we adore thee, we

---

[7] The Syriac addresses the *anamnesis* to the Second Person of the Trinity : " Commemorating, therefore, O Lord, thy death and thy resurrection on the third day from the tomb and thine ascension into heaven and thy sitting at the right hand of God the Father as well as thy second fearful and glorious coming wherein thou shalt judge the world in righteousness, when thou shalt render to every one according to his works. " Note also the slightly different wording.

[8] The Syriac simply has " ...blot out the sins of us thy servants who entreat thee ".

believe in thee, we pray thee : be propitious, O Lord, God, have mercy on us and hear us.]

[*Deacon :* In silence and fear stand and pray. The peace and tranquillity of God the Father of us all be with us. Thrice we cry and say, Kurillison, Kurillison, Kurillison.]

Then, after sanctifying ourselves with these spiritual hymns, we beseech God, the Lover of mankind, that he send forth the Holy Spirit (*Cat.* xxiii. 7),... who did speak in the Law and the Prophets in the Old and New Testaments, who came down upon the Lord Jesus Christ in the form of a dove, who at Pentecost descended upon the apostles in the form of fiery tongues here in Jerusalem in the upper church of the apostles (*Cat.* iv. 16, xvi. 4)... upon the gifts that are laid out, that he make the bread the body of Christ and the wine the blood of Christ (xxiii. 7, concluded). For whatever comes in contact with the Holy Spirit is sanctified and transformed.

Priest : Have mercy on us, O almighty God [the Father], (have mercy on us, O God our Saviour, have mercy on us, O God, according to thy great mercy), and send forth upon us and upon these gifts that are laid out [before thee] thy (all-) holy Spirit, the Lord and giver of life, who shareth thy throne with thee, O God the Father, and who reigneth with thine only begotten Son, who is of one substance and co-eternal, who did speak through the Law and the Prophets and thy New Testament, who descended in the form of a dove on our Lord Jesus Christ in the river Jordan (and remained in him), who descended on the holy apostles in the form of fiery tongues (in the upper room of the holy and glorious Sion on holy Pentecost day).

[Hear me, O Lord; hear me, O Lord; hear me, O Lord, and have mercy on us : and may thy holy and living Spirit, O Lord, come and descend on me and on this oblation.]

[*People :* Kurillison.]

(Send down, O Lord, on us and on these gifts that are laid

out the all-holy selfsame Spirit that, having come down, with his holy and good and glorious presence, he may bless and make this bread the holy body of Christ). [9]

People : Amen.

(*Priest :* And this chalice, the precious blood of Christ.) [10]

People : Amen.

Priest : That they be to all who partake of them (for the forgiveness of sins and for life everlasting, for) the sanctification of souls and bodies, (for) fruitfulness in good works, for the stability of thy holy (catholic and apostolic) Church which thou hast founded upon the rock of the faith, (that) [11] the gates of hell shall not prevail against it, delivering it from all heresy and scandal of those that work iniquity, (preserving it) till the end of the world by the grace and mercy and love toward mankind of thine only Son through whom and with whom to thee is due glory, honor, and dominion with thy Spirit all-holy, good, adorable, life-giving, and consubstantial with thee now and always and for ever and ever.

People : Amen.

[9] The Syriac puts it this way : " that coming down he may make of this bread the lifegiving body, the redeeming body, the heavenly body, the body which set free our souls and bodies, the body of our Lord God and Saviour Jesus Christ for the remission of sins and eternal life to those who receive. Amen. "

[10] The Syriac has : " And the mixture that is in this chailce, the blood of the New Testament, the redeeming blood, the lifegiving blood, the heavenly blood which sets free our souls and bodies, the blood of our Lord and Saviour Jesus Christ for the remission of sins and etenal life to those who receive it. Amen. "

[11] The Syriac has " and " instead of " that ".

The Intercession

The Intercession follows in both the Greek and Syriac texts : here we shall give only the English translation of the Greek text, since it reproduces the fourth-century Jerusalem Rite more faithfully than does its more embellished Syriac counterpart. Also omitted are the obviously interpolated Byzantine petitions or parts thereof.

Then, after the spiritual sacrifice is perfected, the unbloody worship,

We offer to thee, O Lord, this sacrifice for thy holy places which thou hast glorified by the divine manifestation of thy Christ and the visitation of thine all-holy Spirit, and especially for the holy and glorious Sion the mother of all the Churches, and for thy holy, catholic and apostolic Church throughout all the world. Do thou, O Lord, grant her the rich gifts of thine all-holy Spirit.

we entreat God over this sacrifice of propitiation for the common peace of the Churches,

Remember, O Lord, also those within her, our holy fathers and bishops throughout the world who rightly and truly dispense the word of thy truth.

Remember, O Lord, also me, thy humble and unworthy servant, according to the fullness of thy mercy and compassion, and remember the deacons who stand around thy holy altar and grant them a blameless life, preserve their office of deacon unblemished and make them worthy of good promotions.

for the stability of the world,

Remember, O Lord, the holy city of God and its sovereign authority, remember every city

for the emperors, for the army and the allies,

and land and those of the orthodox faith who live in them, remember their peace and safety.

Remember, O Lord, our most pious and Christ-loving emperors, the pious and Christ-loving empress, all their household and armies, and grant them heavenly help and victory; take hold of armor and shield and raise up to help them, conquer for them all the warlike and barbaric peoples who enjoy war, change their purpose, that we may lead a peaceful and quiet life in all piety and reverence. [12]

for the sick, and possessed,

Remember, O Lord, the diseased and sick, and those possessed by evil spirits, grant them a divine, speedy cure and deliverance.

Remember, O Lord, every Christian soul that is troubled and distressed, and who needs thy mercy and help, O God, and and convert those who are in error.

Remember, O Lord, those of our fathers and brothers who toil and minister unto us for thy holy name's sake.

and in general for all who need help, we all pray and offer this sacrifice.

Remember, O Lord, all good men, have mercy on them all, O Lord, and be reconciled with us all. [13]

Then, we commemorate also those who have fallen asleep be-

Vouchsafe to remember also, O Lord, those who have been

[12] Then follows an interpolated petition from the Antiochene or Byzantine Rite. Then :

[13] Again a Byzantine interpolation follows in the Greek text, consisting of several petitions. Then :

fore us, first the patriarchs, prophets, apostles, and martyrs,

that God receive by their prayers
and entreaties our supplication.

Then, also for our holy fathers
and bishops who have fallen
asleep before us and in general,
for all who have fallen asleep
among us.
(*Cat.* xxxiii. 8, 9)

pleasing to thee from the beginning of time through generations and generations, our holy
fathers, the patriarchs, prophets,
apostles, martyrs. [14]

Hail, [O Woman] full of
grace, the Lord is with thee;
blessed art thou among women
and blessed is the fruit of thy
womb, because thou didst bear
the Saviour of our souls. [15]

...not because we are worthy
to commemorate all their blessedness but that they also who
are present near thy fearful and
dreadful tribunal may in turn
mention our wretchedness and
that we may find grace and mercy
before thee, O Lord, for help
in time of need.

Remember, O Lord, God of
spirits and of all flesh, those of
the orthodox faith whom we
have mentioned and have not
mentioned, from righteous Abel
until this very day. Do thou
thyself refresh them in the land
of the living, in thy Kingdom,
in the enjoyment of paradise, in
the bosom of Abraham, Isaac,
and Jacob, our holy fathers,
whence pain, sorrow and lamen-
tation are fled, where the light
of thy countenance watches and
shines on everything. [16]

[14] Again interpolated from the Byzantine Rite are a few more categories of holy
men after the word " martyrs. "   Then :

[15] The foregoing is also interpolated from some non-Byzantine source. After
this follow the diptychs, beginning with Mary the Mother of God and St. John
the Baptist (from the Byzantine Rite) going on with the naming of all the apostles
and evangelists, and ending with " and all thy holy saints from the foundation
of the world " (taken from the Jerusalem diptychs of a later date).

[16] After this, there is another petition interpolated from the Byzantine Rite.
Then :

...we offer Christ sacrificed for our sins, appeasing God, the Lover of mankind on their behalf and on our own.

(*Cat.* xxiii. 10)

Through thine only-begotten Son, our Lord and God and Saviour Jesus Christ, for he alone of us has appeared upon the earth without sin, through whom as a good God and Lover of mankind both to us and to them.

People : Remit, forgive, pardon, O God, our sins both voluntary and involuntary, those known and unknown to us.

Priest : By the grace, compassion, and love of mankind of thine only-begotten Son, with whom blessed be thou and glorified with thine all-holy, good, and life-giving Spirit, now and always, and forever and ever.

People : Amen.

CHAPTER XII

THE WEST SYRIAN DERIVATIVES : BYZANTIUM AND ARMENIA

Included in the West Syrian derivatives are the Liturgies of Asia Minor generally (Cappadocia, Pontus, Asia), Byzantium (Constantinople), and Armenia. Each of these regions had received the faith directly or indirectly from Antioch and Syria. During the latter part of the third century and throughout the fourth, they had been in close, frequent relation with the See of Antioch. It is not surprising, therefore, that their Liturgies reproduced all the essential features of the Antiochene prototype. The Church of Byzantium is no exception; it received its ancient organization from bishops who came either from Antioch or from Caesarea : Chrysostom, Gregory Nazianzen, Nectarius, and Nestorius, to mention but a few.

These Churches produced distinctive, yet closely similar Greek Liturgies within the Antiochene family. Synthesized in Byzantium, the common text was to become the most influential of all the Eastern Liturgies. Not only did it Byzantinize in one way or another the older Liturgies of Antioch-Jerusalem (e.g., St. James) and of Alexandria (e.g., St. Mark), but in many instances it replaced them completely. The greatest single reason for this, of course, was the tremendous influence, prestige, and occasional constraint exerted over the whole East by Byzantium after it had became the most powerful See of the Oriental Church. We shall deal with the Byzantine Liturgy in full detail later (Chaps. XVIII to end of book).

The only sources regarding the Liturgy of the Asian Church (in the province of Asia) are the scanty details supplied by the Canons of Laodicea. [1] From these Canons, it is barely possible to reconstruct some of the leading features of the Rite, but almost impossible to ascertain its relation with the other fourth century Antiochene types. On the basis of the fragmentary evidence available, it seems that the Asian Liturgy was different from others of the Syrian family.

---

[1] From the Council of Laodicea, c. A.D. 363.

However, judging from the absence of any serious liturgical repercussions following the absorption of the Asian See into that of Byzantium, the difference must have been insignificant. The little information derived from the Canons of Laodicea is outlined below.

Synaxis—Liturgy of the Catechumens

1. The entrance of the bishop and priests into the sanctuary.
2. The lections, consisting probably of a prophecy and Epistle, are read by the lectors; the psalms are chanted by the cantors from the ambo (pulpit). The psalms were probably alternated with the lections, since this principle obtained in the divine office there.
3. The Gospel followed.
4. The homily or sermon of the bishop came next.
5. The dismissals were made thus : a prayer was said for the catechumens and then they were dismissed; a prayer was also said for the penitents, a blessing was bestowed on them, and finally they too were dismissed.

The Mass of the Faithful

6. " Three prayers of the faithful " followed; of these the first was said in silence and the other two aloud. This is usually interpreted to mean that the silent prayer was said by the celebrant and the others by the deacon. [2]
7. After the prayers of the faithful, the Kiss of Peace was exchanged by the bishop and the priests, while the people imparted the kiss to each other.
8. The offertory followed; then the anaphora and Communion. The clergy communicated in the sanctuary; the others outside the sanctuary.
9. The Eulogia was distributed. [3]

[2] Some scholars, however, believe that all the prayers were said by the celebrant, e.g., cf. Palmer, *Origines*, I, 107 (edit. 4., London, 1845).

[3] For the *Mass of the Catechumens* cf. (1) Can. 56 and 20, (2) Can. 59 and 17 where the reference is primarily made to the offices, but the principle of alternating the psalms with the lections probably applies also to the Liturgy, (3) Can. 16, (4) Can. 19, (5) Can. 19.

For the *Mass of the Faithful*, cf. (6) Can. 19, (7) Can 19, (8) Can. 19, (9) Can. 32, which is usually interpreted to mean not the *eulogia* distributed to the faithful after the Liturgy but, rather, the bread that was interchanged between one church and another in sign of communion (thus, cf. Brightman, LEW, p. 521; Hanssens, *Institutiones Lit. de Ritibus Orientalibus* [Rome, 1930], Vol. II, p. 432).

In the Asian See, the custom of celebrating the Divine Liturgy in private homes had somehow survived until the Council, for the Fathers of the Council deemed it necessary explicitly to forbid the practice (Can. 58). Mass was also forbidden in Lent, except on Saturdays and Sundays (Can. 49).

THE ARMENIAN LITURGY

The Armenians have the distinction of being the first nation to have embraced Christianity officially and as a whole. This was due largely to the efforts of St. Gregory the Illuminator, who had been consecrated bishop in A.D. 294 by the Metropolitan of Caesarea in Cappadocia. Since Armenia received it faith from Caesarea, its Liturgy is naturally basically Syrian and has many of the old Cappadocian characteristics. This resemblance is especially great in the prayer after the Sanctus. The text of this Armenian prayer as given by Faustinus Byzantinus (A.D. 392), when compared with its Cappadocian counterpart in the Liturgy of St. Basil, is identical not only in the general meaning, but also in much of its wording :

Armenian Liturgy [4] (Faustinus Byzantinus)	*Liturgy of St. Basil* [5]
O Lord God of Powers, who hast made all things out of nothing and hast created living and incorruptible man from the dust, they (men) have transgressed thy commands and have fallen under the [pain of] death. Both because of their own transgression and forthwith by thy just judgment, thou hast driven them from the paradise of delights back to this earth, from which thou hast made [them], and hast	With these blessed Powers, O Master... Thou has ordered all things for us. When thou formed man by taking dust from the earth and honored him with thine own image, O God, thou didst put him in the paradise of delights, promising him life everlasting and the enjoyment of eternal good things for keeping thy commands. But when he (man) disobeyed thee, the true God, who had created him, and

[4] Text taken from *Historia Armenorum*, V, 28 [Venice, 1832], pp. 223-224. Our translation.

[5] Text from Brightman's reconstruction of an eighth- or ninth century Liturgy of Basil, LEW, pp. 324-326. Our translation.

subjected them to the condemnation of death. But thou hast not forsaken [them], O God, entirely by the providence and grace of thine only-begotten Son, thou hast regenerated thy creatures by a regeneration and thou hast visited thy creatures in many ways. Thou hast sent forth the prophets; thou hast given many varied portents and signs through thy saints who pleased thee with various deeds; thou hast given the Laws to help [them]; thou hast sent forth the angels as guides. And when the time limit was come, thou hast spoken to us by thine only-begotten Son through whom thou hast made the world, who is the image of thy glory and the form of thine essence and who sustains all things by the power of [his] word, who hath thought it no robbery [to have] the essential nature of the Father and an equal glory [to the Father], but as God immortal, he appeared upon the earth, dwelt among men, became incarnate of the holy Virgin, took on the form of a servant and was made in the likeness of our weakness in order to make us like unto his glory....

when he was led astray by the guile of the serpent and was rendered subject to death by his own transgressions, in thy just judgment, O God, thou didst banish him from paradise to this world and didst turn him back to the earth from which he was taken while providing for him the salvation of regeneration which is in thy Christ himself. For thou didst not turn completely away from thine creature whom thou hadst made, O Good One, nor didst thou forget the work of thy hands, but thou didst visit him in various ways through the tender compassion of thy mercy. Thou didst send forth the prophets; thou didst perform mighty works through thy saints who in every generation were well-pleasing to thee; thou didst speak to us by the mouths of thy servants the prophets who foretold unto us the salvation which was to come; thou didst give the Law to help [us]; thou didst appoint angels as guardians. And when the fullness of time was come, thou didst speak to us by thy Son himself, through whom also thou didst make the ages, who, being the reflection of thy glory and the express image of thy Being and the one who sustains all things by the word of his power, thought it no robbery to be equal to thee, God and Father; but as God immortal, he appeared upon the earth and dwelt among men, and in becoming incarnate of the holy

>Virgin, he emptied himself by taking on the form of a servant, by being made similar to the body of our lowliness in order to make us like to the image of his glory....

Until the fifth century in most parts of Armenia, the Divine Liturgy was celebrated in the Greek according to the Cappadocian form; however, in several districts of Armenia the Liturgy was celebrated in Syriac according to the East Syrian Rite. Jerusalem, too, had exerted its influence on the early Armenian Church, not so much in the Divine Liturgy itself but in other liturgical usages. [6]

In A.D. 374, the Armenian Church separated from the Church of Cappadocia and established its own *katholikos* or primate, while retaining its subjection to the Supreme Pontiff of Rome. [7]

Early in the fifth century, the Liturgy was reformed along more thoroughly Byzantine lines and translated into Armenian. [8] It kept many of the old Cappadocian features that were later to be discarded by the Byzantine Rite itself. It retained, for example, the three lessons in the Mass of the Catechumens, i.e., a reading from the Old Testament, an Epistle, and a Gospel. [9]

Its over-all similarity to the Byzantine, however, is great.

---

[6] Cf. F. C. Conybeare, *Rituale Armenorum* (Oxford, 1905), pp. 507-532.

[7] About fifty years after the Council of Chalcedon, the Armenian Church went into schism by repudiating the Council. This repudiation, however, seems to have been made under a misapprehension, since the Armenian Church apparently never embraced the Monophysite heresy.

[8] This work is attributed to St. Isaac the Great, or *Sahak*.

[9] An excellent comparison of the early Armenian Liturgy with its Byzantine counterpart is found in J. Catergian and J. Dašian, *Die Liturgien bei den Armeniern. Fünfzehn und Untersuchungen* (Wien, 1897), pp. 165-168.

CHAPTER XIII

THE EAST SYRIAN DERIVATIVES : PERSIA AND MESOPOTAMIA

The beginnings of Christianity in Persia and Mesopotamia are shrouded in doubt and obscurity. It seems fairly probable, however, that the Church at Edessa was established before the end of the second century. The missionaries who evangelized these regions came from West Syria. During the third century, Edessa and Nisibis where the two great centers of faith of Persia and Mesopotamia.

These centers soon developed their own distinct liturgical and ecclesiastical traditions—related to yet divergent from those of Antioch, their mother Church. Of all Syrian ritual derivatives, the *Liturgy of SS. Addai and Mari* is by far the furthest removed from its Antiochene progenitor. [1] Even in its earliest Christian history, Edessa, where the Liturgy of SS. Addai and Mari was born, was not bound to Antioch by so close a tie as that which connected Caesarea or the Pontus to their mother Church. Edessa remained both a strong center of Semitic cultural traditions and a diffusive source of Hellenism. These factors substantially influenced its standard Liturgy.

That this Liturgy was not more thoroughly hellenized subsequently is explained by the rugged history of the Church in which it was used. The people of these regions spoke Aramaic dialects. Their Jewish communities became quite numerous after the destruction of Jerusalem by Titus. That so many Semitic traits were kept in the Liturgy is probably due to these first Jewish Churches. In A.D. 424, at the Synod of Markabta, the Persian Church, whose own chief Metropolitan resided at Seleucia-Ctesiphon, proclaimed its independence from Antioch. This, together with national politics, caused the Persian Church to shut itself off from nearly all the other

---

[1] Sts. Addai and Mari are the reputed apostles of the East Syrians and Persians; Addai, according to their tradition, was one of the seventy-two disciples appointed by the Lord (Luke 10:1), and Mari was a disciple of Addai.

Churches of the Christian world; thus, there was little if any exchange of ideas with the other Rites.   Anti-imperialist political considerations also played a major role in deciding most of the Persian and East Syrian Christians not to accept the condemnation of Nestorianism by the Council of Ephesus in A.D. 431.

Whatever may be said for the motives prompting the schism, the missionary zeal of this Nestorian Church for the next eight hundred years was unquestionably genuine; it can hardly be equaled by any other national Church in either the magnitude of its scope or the magnificence of its success.   Just before the Mongol invasions under Timur in the fourteenth century, the Nestorian Church had twenty-five metropolitan Sees, or provinces, about a hundred and fifty bishoprics, and perhaps as many or more monasteries, extending from Persia to India and even China. [2]   After the Mongolian conquest, only Malabar was salvaged in its Eastern domain, while the scattered remnants of the Western half could do no more than survive by isolating themselves in the mountains of Kurdistan.

Segments of the Nestorian Church have rejoined the Catholic Church in the course of the last four hundred years.   These are known as Chaldean Catholics, or Catholics of the Chaldean Rite. (Obviously, they cannot be called Nestorian Catholics!)

Little is known of the early liturgical history of this Rite.   Fragmentary evidence of the Edessene use is given by St. Ephrem (A.D. d. 373), who is also a Doctor of the universal Church.   No one so far has attempted an exhaustive study of Edessene liturgical sources prior to its schism (and heresy).   It is certain, however, that among the integral parts of the Eucharistic Rite at Edessa were included the anamnesis, the invocation of the Holy Spirit (although these prayers were directed to God the Father), the fraction, and

---

[2] Besides dioceses in Eastern Syria, Armenia and Persia, the Nestorian Church also had others in Halavan in Media, Merv in Khorasan, Herat, Tashkent, Samarkand, Baluk, Kashgar; Peking and Singan fu Hsi'en fu in China, as well as Cranganore in India.   China (probably in Shensi Province) and India even had metropolitans of their own; this we know from the canon of Theodore of Edessa (c. A.D. 800) which allowed the metropolitans of China, India, and other distant lands to send their reports to the *katholikos* every six years.

[3] At least this much is gathered from the hymn, *De sacerdotio*, of St. Ephrem; cf. *I Fasti della chiesa patriarcale Antiochena*, edit. I. E. Rahmani (Rome, 1920), pp. VII-X.

Communion under both species. [3]   The hymns of St. Ephrem, who opposed Nestorianism, are still being sung in Nestorian services.

Presumably, the Persian Church did have its own ritual peculiarities, but the Rite itself could not have been too dissimilar from its East Syrian counterparts.   This is evident from legislation regarding the celebration of the Divine Liturgy in the Persian Church enacted at its first Synod at Seleucia in A.D. 410 :

> Now and in the future, all of us shall perform the ministry uniformly according to the occidental ministry [i.e., of the province of Mesopotamia which was in the diocese of Antioch] which the bishops Isaac [Bishop of Seleucia] and Maruta [Bishop of Matyropolis, which city, although situated in Armenia, belonged to the ecclesiastical province of Mesopotamia] taught us—everything that we saw them do in the church of Seleucia.   In each city the deacon shall make the " proclamation " just as it is done in it [i.e., in the Church of Seleucia]; the pure and holy oblation shall be offered in all of the churches on one altar... . [4]

The earliest extant document pertaining to the Persian Liturgy proper seems to be a fragment of an anaphora (sixth century) now preserved at the British Museum. [5]   Elements of this anaphora undoubtedly reach back to the fifth century.   As given in Brightman, the following prayers are easily discernible in it : (1) the last part of the prayer before the Sanctus, (2) the Sanctus itself, (3) the prayer after the Sanctus, praising the divine excellence and the work of redemption, (4) the narrative of the institution but without the words of Christ (because of the fragmentary nature of the manuscript it is impossible to determine with any degee of certainty whether or not they were included in this anaphora), (5) part of the prayer of intercession, (6) part of an invocation (epiclesis) after the prayer of intercession (but again it is impossible to determine which

---

[4] Canon 13, cf. edit. I. B. Chabot, Synodicon orientale (Paris, 1902), p. 27 (266-267) (Our translation).
[5] MS. Brit. Mus. Add., 14669 ff. 20 sq.   Bickell was the first to attempt deciphering these two sheets of Syriac writing; the results of his labors were published in his Conspectus rei syrorum literariae (Munster, 1871, pp. 71-73) and then in Liturgies Eastern and Western (Oxford, 1879).   Brightman gives it on pp. 511-518 in LEW.

person of the Blessed Trinity was addressed), and (7) the final
doxology. [6]

The liturgical homilies of Narsai, the celebrated teacher of the
School of Nisibis (A.D. 502?) are an invaluable source of information
regarding the fifth and sixth centuries in the East Syrian Church. [7]

Although this evidence actually dates from the sixth century, most
of the ritual described belongs undoubtedly to the fifth. Just how
much was common to both the Mesopotamian and the Persian
Churches is still a matter of conjecture. In view of the legislation
enacted by the Persian Church in its Synod of A.D. 410, probably
both Churches had substantially the same ritual, at least in the
Eucharistic Prayers. Homily XXI (Mingana) contains a fairly comprehensive picture of these prayers :

> ...A mystery of death he shews first to mortal man; and then
> he reveals the power of life that is hidden in his words.
> As for one dead, he strews a bed with the sacred vessels; and
> he brings up, he sets thereon the bread and wine as a
> corpse.... Two deacons he places like a rank [of soldiers]
> on this side and that, that they may be guarding the dread
> Mystery of the King of kings. Awe and love lie upon the
> faculties of their minds while they look intently upon the
> bread and wine, as upon the King. With bright apparel
> they are clothed exteriorly upon their bodies; and by their
> garments they shew the beauty of their minds. By their
> stoles (oraria) they depict a sign of the heavenly beings that
> were clothed in beauteous garments at the temple of the
> tomb. Two angels the disciples saw in the tomb of our Lord,
> who were attending the place of His body as though it were
> His body [itself].... After the manner of the two watchers
> the two deacons are standing now to hover over the Mysteries.

---

[6] The following are the references for the above in Brightman, LEW (Vol. 1) :
(1) I, 1-24, pp. 511-512; (2) I, 25, p. 512; (3) I, 26-V, 20, pp. 512-515; (4) V,
20-35, p. 515; (5) VI, 14-33, p. 516; (6) VII, 14-VIII, 20; (7) VIII, 21-23. Comparisons may be made with the Nestorian anaphora in E. Renaudot, LOC, II,
pp. 622-628.

[7] The liturgical homilies of Narsai are four out of a total of forty-seven sermons
first collected and published in the Syriac by Alphonse Mingana (Dominican
Press, Mossul, 1905). Their English translation is found in R. H. Connolly
(The Liturgical Homilies of Narsai, TS, VIII [Cambridge, 1909]). The above-
mentioned liturgical homilies are : (1) a commentary on the Eucharistic Sacrifice
(Mingana, xvii), (2) a description of the baptismal ceremonies (Mingana, xxi and
xxiii), and (3) a description of the ordination ritual (Mingana, xxxii).

The priest fills the place of a mouth for all mouths; and as a mediator his voice interprets in secret. He calls upon the Hidden One to send him hidden power, that he may give power in the bread and wine to give life. He turns the gaze of all minds towards that which is hidden, that they may be looking upon secret things by means of visible things.

"Let your minds be aloft," he cries and says to them of earth.

And they answer : "Unto Thee, Lord, who art hidden in the height."

He recites and says what is the cause of gazing aloft, and "Look," he says, "O men, upon the offering of the sacrifice which is for you, which the Divinity accepts with love on behalf of your lives. Look steadfastly upon the bread and wine that are upon the table, which the power of the Spirit changes into the Body and Blood. See the outward things with the outward senses of your members, and depict things hidden by hidden faculties of your minds. Recall your deaths by the sign that is full of death and life, and praise and magnify him that sets power in things feeble.

As with a signet they seal his words with their voices, "Meet and right and becoming and holy is the sacrifice of our life." As [with] a pen he writes the words with the tip of his tongue; and they subscribe with the saying : "Yea, they are true." They bear witness to the words [uttered] on their behalf; and with Amen for a signet they seal the mystery of their life. . . . With the oblation the priest sends up the prayer of the people, and he sanctifies it [the people] by the participation of the living Mystery. With great earnestness he prays for himself and for all men, that his word may be an acceptable sacrifice before the Most High.

He imitates the spiritual beings by his words while he is making supplication; and holily teaches the people to cry "Holy." The utterance of sanctification of the heavenly beings he recites to men, that they may be crying : "Holy, Holy, Holy, Lord."

That saying which the seraphim cried three times—the same he utters in the ears of the people at the hour of the Mysteries. Like Isaiah he also is in anguish when he utters it, remembering how greatly the vileness of men has been advanced. The meaning of that which the prophet saw mystically he [now] discerns in the reality by faith. A coal of fire Isaiah saw coming towards him, which the seraph of fire held in a hand of fire. It touched his mouth—though in truth it did

not touch it—and blotted out the iniquity of his body and
his soul in truth.   It was not a sensible vision that the seer
saw; nor did the spiritual one bring towards him a material
coal.   An intimation he saw in the coal of the Mystery of the
Body and Blood which, like fire, consumes the iniquity of
mortal man.   The power of that mystery which the prophet
saw, the priest interprets; and as with the tongs he holds fire
in his hand with the bread.... *(The author of the homily
goes on at length to interpret and explain this mystery; then
resumes)* :

Body and soul he nourishes with the food of power of the
Mystery; and from [being] mortal makes men immortal.   His
voice does away with the authority of Death from mortals,
and the dominion of the Evil One it looses [and] removes
from mankind.   With food the Evil One slew us in the
beginning and made us slaves; and by food the Creator has
now willed to quicken us.   By the hand that plucked the
fruit in Eden wickedly—by the same He has reached out to
us the fruit of life wisely.   In Adam He cursed us and gave
us for food to gluttonous Death; and by a Son of Adam He
has opened to us the spring of His sweetness.   In our very
nature He performed His will and shewed His love, that that
saying in which He called us His image might be confirmed
for us.   To us He gave to eat the Pledge of life in our mortality; that according to our will we might minister to ourselves by the power of His will.   By the power of His will
the priest distributes life in the Bread, and drives out iniquity
and makes the Spirit to dwell in the midst of the members
[of the body].   The power of the Spirit comes down unto
mortal man, and dwells in the bread and consecrates it by
the might of His power.   O marvel, that, whereas. He is the
Spirit with which everything is filled....   He is the Spirit,
with all in all, in the height and the depth : and He is hidden
and concealed, and the priest points Him out by his words.

...His power lights down upon the visible table, and bestows
power upon the bread and wine to give life.   His power
strengthens the hand of the priest that it may take hold of
His power; and feeble flesh is not burned up by His blaze.

A corporeal being takes hold with his hands of the Spirit in
the Bread; and he lifts up his gaze towards the height, and
then he breaks it.   He breaks the Bread and casts [it] into
the Wine, and he signs and says : " In the name of the Father
and the Son and the Spirit, and equal nature. "

With the name of the Divinity, three hypostases, he completes his words; and as one dead he raises the mystery.... On a sudden the bread and wine acquire new life; and forgiveness of iniquity they give on a sudden to them that receive them. He [the priest] makes the Bread and Wine one by participation, foreasmuch as the blood mingles with the body in all senses [of man]. Wine and water he casts into the cup before he consecrates, foreasmuch as water also is mingled with the blood in things created.

With these [elements] the priest celebrates the perfect mysteries; then he makes [his] voice heard, full of love and mercy. Love and mercy are hidden in the voice of the word of his mouth; that the creatures may call the Creator his Father. In the way of his voice run the voices of them that are become obedient, while they are made ready to call the hidden Divinity " Our Father. "

...By their petitions they shew the love of their minds—how greatly they desire to be partakers of the things that are to come.

With the voice of praise they seal the words of the completion of the Mysteries; and they render holiness to the Father and to the Son and to the Holy Spirit : " Holy is the Father, and holy is His begotten, and the Spirit who is from Him [sc. the Father]; and to them is due holiness and praise from all mouths. "

After the utterance of sanctification and the rendering praise they stretch the gaze of their minds towards the Gift... and, as it were the King, they bear in triumph the Sacrament in the midst of their palms. They hold it sure that the Body of the King dwells in the visible bread; and in it the resurrection of the dead is preached to him that eats of it.

" The Body, " says the priest also when he gives it; and " The Blood " he calls the mingled Wine in the midst of the cup. He gives the Bread, and says, " The Body of the King Messiah " [or " of Christ the King "]; and he gives to drink the Wine and in like manner [he says] : " The Blood of Christ. "

He believes that the Bread and the Wine are the Body and the Blood; and exceedingly sure is it to giver and receiver. Forgiveness of iniquity and the resurrection of the dead he preaches with it.... " [8]

[8] R. H. Connolly, *The Liturgical Homilies of Narsai*, TS, VIII (Cambridge, 1909), pp. 55-61.

Another Homily, XVII (Mingana), doubtful as the work of Narsai himself, describes the principal points contained in the modern Chaldean Eucharistic Liturgy including the order and the silent prayers. This homily was probably written after the sixth century. What is of great interest and importance, however, is the fact that it *does* include the narrative of the institution and the words of Christ.

> ...He commanded us to perform this Mystery with bread and wine....
>
> For when the time of the passion of the Lifegiver of all was arrived, He ate the legal passover with His disciples. He took bread and blessed and brake and gave to His disciples, and said, This is my Body in truth, without doubt. And He took the cup and gave thanks and blessed and gave to His Apostles, and said, This is my true Blood which is for you. And He commanded them to receive [and] drink of it, all of them, that it might be making atonement for their debts for ever. [9]

The Liturgy of the Holy Apostles Addai and Mari, whatever its historical evolution and the traces of hellenistic influence it may contain, is still basically semitic. It preserved its Oriental characteristics because of the gradual and finally complete isolation of this Church from the rest of Christendom. With certain qualification, it reaches back to the early centuries of the Church.

Preface and Eucharistic Prayer of SS. Addai and Mari

Priest : Lift up your minds.

People : Unto thee, O God of Abraham and of Isaac and of Israel, O glorious king.

Priest : The offering is being offered unto God the Lord of all.

People : It is fit and right.

Deacon : Peace be with us.

After a short silent prayer the priest says :

Worthy of praise from every mouth (repeat) and of confession from every tongue and of worship and exaltation from every

---

[9] *Ibid.*, p. 16.

creature is the adorable and glorious name of thy glorious Trinity, O Father and Son and Holy Ghost, who didst create the world by thy grace and its inhabiters by thy mercifulness and didst save mankind by thy compassion and give great grace unto mortals. Thy majesty, O my Lord, thousand thousands of those on high bow down and worship and ten thousand times ten thousand holy angels and hosts of spiritual beings, ministers of fire and spirit, praise thy name with holy cherubim and spiritual seraphim offering worship to thy sovereignty, shouting and praising without ceasing and crying one to another and saying,

> Holy, holy, holy, Lord God of Hosts
> heaven and earth are full of his praises and of the nature of his being and of the excellency of his glorious splendor.
> Hosanna in the highest and Hosanna to the Son of David.
> Blessed is he that came and cometh in the name of the Lord.
> Hosanna in the highest.

And with these heavenly hosts we give thanks to thee, O my Lord (repeat), even we thy servants weak and frail and miserable, for that thou hast given us great grace past recompense in that thou didst put on our manhood that thou mightest quicken it by thy godhead, and hast exalted our low estate and restored our fall and raised our mortality and forgiven our trespasses and justified our sinfulness and enlightened our knowledge and, O our Lord and our God, hast condemned our enemies and granted victory to the weakness of our frail nature in the overflowing mercies of thy grace. And for all thine helps and graces towards us let us raise to thee praise and honour and confession and worship now and ever and world without end.

People : Amen.

The Intercession

Do thou, O my Lord, in thy many and unspeakable mercies (repeat) make a good and acceptable memorial for all the just and righteous fathers who have been well-pleasing in thy sight, in the commemoration of the body and blood of thy Christ which we offer unto thee on thy pure and holy altar as thou hast taught us, and grant us thy tranquillity and thy

peace all the days of the world.   Yea, O our Lord and our
God, grant us thy tranquillity and thy peace all the days of
the world (repeat) that all the inhabitants of the earth may
know thee that thou art the only true God the Father and
that thou hast sent our Lord Jesus Christ thy Son and thy
beloved.   And he our Lord and our God came and in his
lifegiving gospel taught us all the purity and holiness of the
prophets and the apostles and the martyrs and the confessors
and the bishops and the doctors and the presbyters and the
deacons and all the children of the holy catholic church, even
them that thave been signed with the living sign of holy
baptism

The Invocation

And we also, O my Lord (repeat three times), thy weak and
frail and miserable servants who are gathered together in thy
name, both stand before thee at this time and have received
the example which is from thee delivered unto us, rejoicing
and praising and exalting and commemorating and celebrating
this great and fearful and holy and lifegiving and divine
mystery of the passion and the death and the burial and the
resurrection of our Lord and Saviour Jesus Christ.
And may there come, O my Lord, thine Holy Spirit and rest
upon this offering of thy servants, and bless it and hallow
it that it be to us, O my Lord, for the pardon of offenses and
the remission of sins and for the great hope of resurrection
from the dead and for new life in the kingdom of heaven with
all those who have been well-pleasing in thy sight.   And for
all this great and marvellous dispensation towards us we will
give thee thanks and praise thee without ceasing in thy church
redeemed by the precious blood of thy Christ with unclosed
mouths and open faces lifting up praise and honour and
confession and worship to thy living and holy and lifegiving
name now and ever and world without end.
People : Amen. [10]

This ancient Nestorian anaphora suffers from a very serious
dogmatic deficiency, in that it contains no consecratory formula or
even the narrative itself of the institution. [11]   Various indications

[10] Brightman's translation, LEW, pp. 283-288.

[11] Likewise, the sixth century fragments of the Persian anaphora, first published
by Bickell (*Conspectus rei syrorum literariae* (Münster, 1871], pp. 71-73) and revised
by Connolly, *Oriens Christianus*, N.S., xii/xiv [1922-24], pp. 99-128 contain only
a short paraphrase of it.

show that the primitive text of this Liturgy did include these elements;[12] only later were they dropped. Narsai tends to confirm this supposition. (See above, p. 174). The other two anaphoras used in the Nestorian Church (those of *Nestorius* himself and *Theodore the Interpreter*) do have the narrative of the institution and the words of Christ. Various reasons for the disappearance of these elements from the anaphora of SS. Addai and Mari have been suggested : Semitic reverential awe and fear of profaning the sacred words;[13] exaggerated esteem for the epiclesis.[14] The Catholic Chaldeans have inserted the Maronite narrative of the institution and consecratory formula (but without genuflections or elevations) into this anaphora just before the intercessions.[15]

[12] Cf. B. Botte, " L'Anaphore chaldéenne des Apôtres," OCP, XV (1949), 259-276; Lietzmann, *Messe und Herrenmahl* (Bonn, 1923), 33.

[13] Thus, Lietzmann, *op. cit.*, 33.

[14] Thus, A. Raes, S.J., " Le récit de l'institution eucharistique dans l'anaphore chaldéenne et malabare des Apôtres," O.C.P., 10 (1944), 216-226; B. Botte, " L'anaphore chaldéenne des Apôtres," *ibid.*, 15 (1949), 259-276.

[15] Cf. Raes, S.J., *Introductio in liturgiam orientalem* (Rome, 1935), pp. 81, 98 f.

THE EASTERN CHURCH

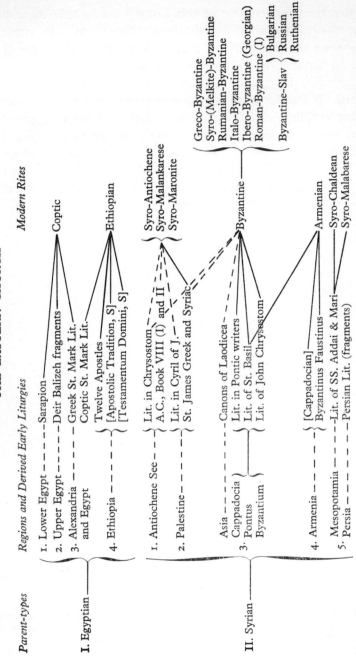

Parent-types   *Regions and Derived Early Liturgies*   *Modern Rites*

I. Egyptian

1. Lower Egypt — Sarapion
2. Upper Egypt — Deir Balizeh fragments
3. Alexandria and Egypt — Greek St. Mark Lit. — Coptic St. Mark Lit. — Coptic
4. Ethiopia — Twelve Apostles — [Apostolic Tradition, S] — [Testamentum Domini, S] — Ethiopian

II. Syrian

1. Antiochene See — Lit. in Chrysostom — A.C., Book VIII (I) and II — Syro-Antiochene / Syro-Malankarese
2. Palestine — Lit. in Cyril of J. — St. James Greek and Syriac — Syro-Maronite

3. Asia — Canons of Laodicea — Byzantine
   Cappadocia — Lit. in Pontic writers
   Pontus — Lit. of St. Basil
   Byzantium — Lit. of John Chrysostom

Byzantine:
Greco-Byzantine
Syro-(Melkite)-Byzantine
Rumanian-Byzantine
Italo-Byzantine
Ibero-Byzantine (Georgian)
Roman-Byzantine (I)
Byzantine-Slav — Bulgarian / Russian / Ruthenian

4. Armenia — [Cappadocian] — Byzantinus Faustinus — Armenian
5. Mesopotamia — Lit. of SS. Addai & Mari — Syro-Chaldean
   Persia — Persian Lit. (fragments) — Syro-Malabarese

Key: Direct antecedents assimilated into modern Rites are indicated by solid lines; indirect antecedents or heavy influences are indicated by broken lines. Brackets indicate imports. S. For Syrian. R. For Roman.

CHAPTER XIV

THE ORIENTAL RITES TODAY

The liturgical forms of worship in the most important Churches became norms for the lesser ones associated with or dependent upon them. This continued to hold true throughout the centuries until modern times. After the patriarchal divisions established by the Councils of Constantinople (A.D. 381) and Chalcedon (A.D. 451), the Alexandrian and Antiochene Sees still retained much of their former authority and prestige but the two newly established Sees of Jerusalem and Byzantium gradually rose in prominence. Byzantium especially vied with the others, so much so that a few centuries later it challenged the supreme authority of Rome itself.

With these four great territorial divisions in the Eastern Church, one might also expect the formation of four major Rites. In fact, there were only three. Some time earlier, before the Council of Chalcedon, Antioch had adopted its Palestinian (Jerusalem) daughter-Rite. Alexandria consolidated its Rite in all of Egypt. Byzantium amalgamated the Rites of Asia Minor (and Antioch) and evolved a more or less " combined Rite " of its own—the Byzantine—which, as the centuries passed, became the most widespread of all the Oriental Rites. The Armenian is now usually placed in a separate category. We may call it a minor Rite, not because it is of lesser value, but because it exerted the least influence outside its own territories. [1] The major ancient Rites not only continued to exist : they actually grew and, through the intervening centuries, developed branches. Today we have the following :

---

[1] The Armenian Rite may now be called *sui generis*. Originally, of course, the Armenians received their ritual observances and practices from Cappadocia. Then, their liturgical usages were modified, not only by Syrian and Constantinopolitan influences, but later also by the Latin, even though Armenian was made the liturgical language. Some authors list the Armenian Rite as a subdivision of the Byzantine. If anything, it is a cross between the Byzantine and the West-Syrian.

I. Egyptian Rite { 1. Coptic Rite
    (Alexandrian)   { 2. Ethiopian Rite

                                                      ⎧ a. Syro-Antiochene
                            1. West Syrian   ⎨ b. Syro-Malankarese
II. Syrian Rite   {   ⎩ c. Syro-Maronite
     (Antiochene)   {   ⎧ a. Syro-Chaldean
                            2. East Syrian   ⎨ b. Syro-Malabarese

III. Armenian Rite

                            ⎧ 1. Greco-Byzantine
                            ⎪ 2. Syro (Melkite)—Byzantine
                            ⎪ 3. Rumanian-Byzantine
IV. Byzantine Rite   ⎨ 4. Italo-Byzantine
                            ⎪ 5. Ibero-Byzantine or Georgian
                            ⎪ 6. (Roman-Byzantine)
                            ⎪   ⎧ a. Bulgarian
                            ⎩ 7. Byzantine-Slav   ⎨ b. Russian
                                                                 ⎩ c. Ruthenian

A comprehensive treatment of the present Oriental Rites may be found in many excellent works. However, a brief synopsis of each will be useful here.

I. *The Egyptian, or Alexandrian, Rite* comprises the *Coptic* and the *Ethiopian.*

a) The Coptic Rite, Catholic and dissident. Its liturgical language is ancient Coptic with many Greek words and phrases; however, Arabic is used frequently. In the celebration of the Eucharist, the Liturgy of St. Cyril of Alexandria is used. It is, in fact, the ancient version of the Greek Liturgy of St. Mark (cf. p. 102) with three alternative anaphoras : namely, an adaptation of the Byzantine of St. Basil, for use on ordinary days and Sundays; that of St. Cyril (or St. Mark) used on St. Cyril's feasts and the consecration of a bishop; that of St. Gregory Nazianzen for all other major feasts.

Holy Communion is now generally received kneeling and under one species, although sometimes it is received standing and under both species, either separately or by intinction. Leavened bread is used.

Liturgical vestments are of the general Byzantine style with some distinctive features. They have added a sort of amice *(kidaris)* and bishops wear the Latin miter and no *sakkos*.

The dissidents separated from the Catholic Church in A.D. 451 when they refused to accept the condemnation of the Monophysite heresy (one nature in Christ, the divine only) by the Council of Chalcedon. In A.D. 567, two lines of patriarchs were definitely established, one for the Monophysites and one for the Catholics.

Today, there are about 2,500,000 dissidents and 80,000 Catholics.

B) *The Ethiopian Rite*, Catholic and dissident. The liturgical language of this Rite is Geez (sometimes called classical Ethiopian), a Semitic language allied to the Arabic. The Ethiopian Rite is substantially that of the Copts. The *common* of their Mass is a form of the Alexandrian Liturgy of St. Mark, " according to the order of our fathers the Egyptians." There are as many as seventeen anaphoras; [2] of these, the Anaphora of the Apostles is the most commonly used.

Holy Communion is distributed always under both species at a solemn Liturgy (the consecrated wine is received from a spoon). At a " Low Mass," it is customary among the Catholics to receive under one species only. Leavened bread is generally used at a solemn Liturgy; unleavened, at a " Low Mass."

The Catholic clergy wear Byzantine vestments, with some variants. Instead of the Byzantine *felonion*, for example, there is a chasuble-like vestment, very full, with an embroidered shoulder-cape. The dissident Ethiopian bishop wears a " crown," the Catholic bishop wears a Roman miter and uses a crozier.

There are at present about 9,000,000 dissidents and 60,000 Catholics.

---

[2] The anaphoras used or known in the Ethiopian Rite are those of : (1) *The Apostles*, (2) *St. John the Evangelist*, (3) *Our Lady Mary*, (4) *Our Lord Jesus Christ*, (5) *St. Dionysius*, known as *St. Dioscorus* among the dissidents, (6) *St. John Chrysostom*, (7) *The CCCXVIII Orthodox* (i.e., the Nicene Fathers), (8) *St. Athanasius*, (9) *St. James the Brother of the Lord*,* (10) *St. Epiphanius*, (11) *St. Gregory Nazianzen*, (12) *Mount Olivet*, known as that of *James of Serugh* among the dissidents, (13) *St. Cyril, I*, (14) *St. Cyril, II*, (15) *St. Gregory the Armenian*, (16 *St. Basil* (trans. of Coptic St. Basil), (17) *St. Mark*.*

It is not certain whether those marked by an asterisk were ever in actual use among the Ethiopians.

II. *The Syrian or Antiochene Rite*, Catholic and dissident. This is divided into *West Syrian* and *East Syrian* Rites. These in turn are subdivided as follows :

1. The *West Syrian* family comprises the *Syro-Antiochene*, the *Syro-Malankarese*, and the *Syro-Maronite* Rites.

A) The *Syro-Antiochene Rite* (also known as the *Syrian Rite*). This Rite uses the language which Jesus spoke, Aramaic (or the Edessene dialect of the Syriac), but with modern Western pronunciation and characters. Some of the prayers and scriptural readings are in Arabic. The most widely used Eucharistic Liturgy is that of St. James as modified through the centuries. Many anaphoras may be used. Authors vary in their listings and groupings, and even the best scholars disagree. There seem to be at least seventy-four, of which sixty-four are sufficiently dissimilar to be distinguished. [3] Seven are used by Syrian Catholics. [4]

The bread used for Holy Communion is leavened and slightly salted. The communicants stand to receive under both species (the consecrated bread is dipped in consecrated wine).

The vestments are of the usual Eastern style, but Catholic bishops use the Roman miter and crozier.

When the Council of Chalcedon (A.D. 451) condemned the Monophysite heresy, those who refused to accept the decision became dissidents; a little later, the Monophysites were called Jacobites, a name given to them on account of their leader Jacob Baradai.

The Catholics of this Rite number about 80,000, the Jacobites, about 130,000. In the United States, there are about 10,000 Syrian Catholics.

b) The Syro-Malankarese Rite (or simply the *Malankarese Rite*), Catholic and dissident. The liturgical usages of this Rite are essentially those of the *Syro-Antiochene Rite* (i.e., without the modifications introduced by the Catholic Syrians). In the Eucharistic Liturgy, the priest's prayers, said in a low voice, are in Syriac. The

---

[3] See Appendix B for listing.

[4] Besides the *Anaphora of St. James the Brother of the Lord*, the others used by the Catholics are those of : (1) *St. John the Evangelist*, (2) *St. Mark the Evangelist*, (3) *The Twelve Apostles*, (4) *St. Eustathius of Antioch*, (5) *St. Cyril of Jerusalem*, and (6) *St. Basil of Caesarea*.

other parts such as the scriptural lessons, hymns, etc., are in the vernacular Malayalem.

There are about 125,000 Malankarese Catholics, almost all of them in the province of Malankara of Malabar on the South-West coast of India. The dissidents of this Rite are called Malabar Jacobites. They number about 700,000, with an additional 250,000 who have kept the Rite after becoming Protestant.

C) *The Syro-Maronite Rite* (or simply the *Maronite Rite*), Catholic only. Their liturgical language is Syriac, with lessons and some of the prayers in Arabic.

The Maronites celebrate the Liturgy of St. James (modified by Roman usages) with eight possible anaphoras. [5] Historically, there were about as many different anaphoras in the Maronite Rite as in the Syro-Antiochene (cf. p. 182), since they were common to both Rites, but most of them are never used, nor are they found in liturgical books.

The altar bread used in Communion is unleavened. Since the synod of 1736, lay people receive under only one species. The priests wear purely Roman vestments, adding only the Eastern epimanikia, or cuffs. Deacons and subdeacons generally wear Syrian-type vestments; so do the bishops usually (but with Roman miter and crozier).

There are about 850,000 Maronites today. This Rite and the Italo-Byzantine hold the distinction of being the only Eastern Rites without dissidents. Lebanon has about 470,000 faithful. The United States, about 125,000.

2. *The East Syrian Rite* is subdivided into the *Syro-Chaldean* and the *Syro-Malabar Rites*.

a) *The Syro-Chaldean Rite* or simply the *Chaldean Rite*, Catholic and dissident. Like the Syro-Antiochene Rite, the Chaldean also uses the Edessene dialect of the Syriac, but with Chaldean pronunciation and characters. The ordinary Liturgy is that " composed

---

[5] Besides the *Anaphora of St. James the Brother of the Lord,* they are those of : (1) *St. Peter,* (2) *The Twelve Apostles,* (3) *St. John the Evangelist,* (4) *St. Xystus,* (5) *St. Mark the Evangelist,* (6) *St. John Maro* (Patriarch of Antioch), and (7) *Holy Roman Church.*

by Addai and Mari, the Holy Apostles. " There are two anaphoras in addition to the common form, or " First Hallowing " : that of *Theodore the Interpreter*, and that of *Nestorius*. The Catholics never refer to them as such, of course, but use, instead, the terms " Second Hallowing " and " Third Hallowing. " The former is celebrated on Sundays and feasts from Advent to Palm Sunday, and the latter, five times a year on special days.

Holy Communion is now usually received under one species, sometimes under both (either separately or with the host dipped into the chalice). The bread is leavened and slightly salted.

Vestments are similar to those of the Syrians but without the cuffs. Bishops wear the Western miter, pectoral cross, and ring (no *omophorion*), and hold the Roman crozier.

The dissidents originally broke with the Church when they refused to accept the condemnation of the Nestorian heresy (two Persons in Christ) by the Council of Ephesus in A.D. 431. Catholics of this Rite number about 190,000, and dissident Nestorians, about 75,000.

B) *The Syro-Malabar Rite* (or simply *Malabarese Rite*), Catholic and dissident. The members of this Rite have always called themselves " Christians of St. Thomas "; they may have been evangelized by that apostle, but there is nothing to either prove or disprove it. Since the earliest times, their liturgy has been Chaldean and its language, Syriac. The Malabarese seem to have been Catholic until 1653. St. Francis Xavier did not question their Catholicity when he was at Cranganore in 1549, nor did the Portuguese, when they arrived in 1498. In fact, from the very beginning the Malabarese regarded the Portugese as their brothers in religion.

The Latinizing by Portuguese of the sixteenth century is one of the greatest tragedies suffered by any of the Oriental Rites. At the Synod of Diamper (Udiamparur) in 1599, many Latin innovations were introduced, resulting in a mutilated Liturgy, Roman vestments, Communion under one species, celibacy of the clergy, and the abolition of the Syrian Pontifical and Ritual. The Holy See never formally confirmed this Synod since some of its acts were completely contrary to existing Pontifical decrees. The Portuguese, however, managed to impose their will.

After several fruitless attempts at redress, almost the whole body of the Malabarese seceded from Rome in 1653. By 1662, however, 84 of the 116 parishes had returned to Catholic unity. Those who did not are now known as the Malabar Jacobites.

Catholic Malabarese number about 1,400,000, dissidents, about 5,000.

Syriac is the liturgical language. The Eucharistic Liturgy of the Catholics is the Chaldean Liturgy but with only one anaphora, that of Addai and Mari, the Holy Apostles, revised by the Synod of Diamper. Except for the Divine Office, there is nothing in the Rite which has not been Latinized. The liturgical vestments are Latin, liturgical books correspond to the Roman texts, Holy Communion is received under one species, the altar bread is unleavened, and there is no concelebration. The sacraments are administered in Syriac, but according to Latin forms. There are hardly any external differences between the Malabarese and the Latin Rites.

III. *The Armenian Rite*, Catholic and dissident. The Mass of this Rite is essentially the Greek Liturgy of St. Basil modified under Syrian, Constantinopolitan, and Latin influences. The language is classical Armenian. While the Armenian Liturgy of today bears no author's name, most manuscripts attribute it to St. Athanasius. [6]

Since about a hundred years, Holy Communion among the Catholic Armenians has been received kneeling and under one species, although it is lawful in that Rite to receive it under both. The altar bread is unleavened.

The liturgical vestments are of mixed style, corresponding mostly to the Byzantine. There are, however, some differences : priests wear a tall, stiff collar and the *saghavard*, which is really the Byzantine episcopal crown. The *saghavard* was adopted by priests when their

---

[6] The anaphora alone can be properly attributed to " St. Athanasius ", while the Common or Ordinary of the Mass might be attributed to St. John Chrysostom because of its close relation with the same in the Greek. Also found in manuscript form are the complete Liturgies of : (1) *St. James called the Brother of the Lord, Lord*, abridged from the Syriac of the same name, (2) *St. John Chrysostom*, an older form of the present Greek Liturgy of St. John Chrysostom, (3) *St. Basil*, an older form of present Greek Liturgy of St. Basil, (4) *The Presanctified Liturgy*, also from the Greek, (5) *The Roman*, from the Latin with some adaptations; also found in manuscript form are the anaphoras of (1) *St. Ignatius*, (2) *St. Gregory Nazianzen*, (3) *St. Gregory the Illuminator*, (4) *St. Cyril of Alexandria*, and (5) *St. Isaac the Great, the Parthian*.

bishops began wearing Latin miters since the Crusades. The bishops also use the Latin crozier.

There are about 150,000 Armenian Catholics, including about 50,000 in Soviet dominated territories. The dissident Monophysite Armenians number about 1,600,000. In the United States, there are about 8,000 Catholic Armenians.

IV. *The Byzantine Rite* is subdivided into many branches, all of which use three Liturgies : St. John Chrysostom, St. Basil the Great, and the Presanctified Gifts (also known as the Liturgy of St. Gregory Dialogos). [7] The branches of the Byzantine Rite are distinct because of their liturgical language and/or national customs.

The name *Greek Rite* is often used because Greek was its original language. It is misleading, however, and should be avoided. *Byzantine Rite*, is better, the name given to the system and forms of worship which were proper to the Church of Constantinople, or Byzantium, and its dependencies.

Byzantine usages and practices are fundamentally the same in all branches and subdivisions, with some minor variants.

1. *The Greco-Byzantine, or Greek Rite* properly so-called, Catholic and Orthodox. Its members are *Greek* by nationality. Catholics number about 3,000 only, most of them living in Greece. Their Orthodox brethren number about 9,500,000. Their ancenstors broke with Rome in 1054.

They follow pure Constantinopolitan usage without any Western modification.

2. The *Syro-Byzantine* Rite, Catholic (Melkite) and Orthodox. When Emperor Marcian (A.D. 450-457) made the decrees of the Council of Chalcedon the law of the empire, those who professed the religion of the emperor were called *Melkites* by the Monophysites (from the work *malka* in Syrian, *malik* in Arabic, meaning " emperor, " " king "). After the seventh century, they came under the influence of Constantinople and adopted the Byzantine rite,

---

[7] On the feast of St. James, the Liturgy of St. James the Brother of the Lord is celebrated in the Melkite church in Jerusalem.

although ethnically they are Syro-Arabs. Their patriarch is still called the " Patriarch of Antioch and of all the East. " [8]

There are about 400,000 Syro-Byzantine Catholics (Melkites), and 600,000 Orthodox. In the United States, there are about 50,000 Melkites, some of whom call themselves Syrian Greek Catholics.

The liturgical language of this Rite is Arabic. In the United States, both Arabic and English are used.

3. The *Rumano-Byzantine*, or *Rumanian* Rite, Catholic and Orthodox. The Rumanians were at first Latin Rite Catholics, but after the conquest of their country by the Bulgars in the ninth century, they were subject to Byzantine bishops who imposed their own Rite on them. After Constantinople broke with Rome, they too became separated.

In 1697, about 200,000 reunited with Rome, retaining their own " discipline, church ritual, Liturgy, fasts, and customs. " Today, there should be about 1,500,000 Catholics of the Rumanian Rite, if the Communist occupation of that country since World War II has not decimated them. Orthodox Rumanians number about 16 million. In the United States, there are about 60,000 Orthodox and 10,000 Catholic Rumanians.

Their liturgical language has been Rumanian since the seventeenth century. In the United States, English is also used.

4. *The Italo-Byzantine, or Italo-Greek, Rite*, Catholic only. More correctly the Italo-Greeks should be called *Italo-Greek-Albanians* or *Italo-Albanians*. In origin, they are the descendants of early Greek colonists of Sicily and southern Italy, especially the provinces of Calabria and Apulia.

After the Norman conquest of these territories, several eparchies (dioceses) were suppressed and large elements of these Byzantine Catholics were Latinized (sometimes by force). The influx of Byzantine Catholics from Albania in the fifteenth and sixteenth centuries saved the dying Rite from extinction.

---

[8] In fact, since the time of Maximos III, every patriarch had the personal privilege of adding the titles of Alexandria and Jerusalem. Even now, it is correct to add, " of Cilicia, Syria, and Iberia; of Arabia, Mesopotamia, and the Pentapolis; of Ethiopia, Egypt, and all the East... "

Today, there remain about 70,000 Italo-Greek-Albanian Catholics, mostly in southern Italy and Sicily. There are no dissidents. Their liturgical language is Greek. This Rite underwent many modifications in southern Italy, but in Sicily it is better preserved. There is actually a small group of Albanians of the Byzantine Rite in Albania itself. They reunited with Rome in 1920.

5. *The Ibero-Byzantine, or Georgian, Rite*, Catholic and Orthodox. It is not known how many Catholics of this Rite are left. Before the Communist Revolution, there were in Georgia about 40,000 Catholics. Of these, 32,000 were of the Latin Rite and about 8,000 of the Armenian Rite. There are, however, several hundred Georgians of the Byzantine Rite outside of Georgia itself. Their liturgical language is Georgian. There were about two and a half million Orthodox Georgians before the revolution of 1917.

6. *Roman-Byzantine Rite*. It consists, not in any group of people, but in the *Euchologion* of Pope Benedict XIV (edit. Rome, 1754). Its purpose was to give Byzantine Catholics liturgical guidance and direction.

7. *The Byzantine-Slav Rite* is subdivided into the *Bulgarian*, the *Russian*, and the *Ruthenian* (Ukrainian) *Rites*, Catholic and Orthodox. All of them, had church Slavonic as their liturgical language for centuries as a common bond. [9]

A) *Bulgarian Rite*. Though the Bulgarians are not Slavs ethnically but Finno-Turkish, they accepted Christianity from Constantinople through their Tsar Boris in the ninth century. Some decades later, they adopted Slavonic as their liturgical language, This came about when some of the followers of St. Methodius in Moravia and Pannonia emigrated to Bulgaria because of German pressure (c. A.D. 885), and helped to evangelize the pagans there.

Political circumstances mostly involved the Bulgarians in separating themselves from the Holy See and casting their lot with Byzantium. Under direct control of Constantinople from 1767 to 1856, the Bulgarian Church was subjected to a ruthless process of Hellenization, and Greek superseded church Slavonic as the

---

[9] At present the Ruthenians are using the vernacular more and more frequently; the Russians, perhaps less.

liturgical language. In 1870, the **Bulgarians** obtained an autonomous national Church and reverted to their own liturgical practices.

In the course of the last two centuries, there were several attempts at reunion with Rome, all frustrated by political forces.

Before the Communist takeover in 1944, there were about 9,000 Catholics of the Bulgarian Rite, while the Orthodox numbered about 6,000,000. Present statistics are unavailable. This Rite is relatively free of hybridization.

B) *The Russian Rite*, Catholic and Orthodox. Because Russia received its faith, its Rite, and its hierarchical dependency either directly or indirectly from Constantinople, its separation from Rome was almost inevitable after 1054. For the Russian Church, however, it came about gradually and by degrees, rather by accident than through any direct severing of ties. There is no date, no outstanding event to mark it as a specific event.

The religious history of Christian Russians is about the same as that of the Ukrainians (" Ruthenians ") until 1443. Both Russians and Ukrainians claim St. Vladimir as their Apostle; it is he who " christened " the people of the Kievan state. Kiev, the capital, is in the heart of what is now known as the Ukraine. When Christianity came to these Eastern Slavs, there existed no such sharp distinction as there is now between Russians and Ukrainians : they were one people, known as the Rus.

From A.D. 991 when it received its first bishop until it was sacked by the Mongols in 1237, Kiev was the political and ecclesiastical center, not only of what is now the Ukraine, but also of Russia. In fact, for two centuries, the metropolitans, while residing in Moscow, still called themselves Metropolitans of Kiev!

At the Council of Florence (1438-1439) both the Ukraine and Russia were represented in the person of Isidore, Metropolitan of Kiev, for his jurisdiction included what is modern Russia and the Ukraine. Because he accepted union with Rome (1439) and wanted to confirm it in his territories, he was forced by the Grand Prince of Muscovy, Basil II, to flee to Rome.

Since that time, Ukrainian and Russian ecclesiastical histories have gone their separate ways, hierarchically at least. A distinct

patriarchate of the Orthodox Church, with its See in Moscow, the
" Third Rome," was acknowledged by the Patriarch of Constantinople, Jeremiah II, in 1589.

During the subsequent centuries, there were very few Russian
Catholics of the Byzantine Rite. Tsarist Russia, even after the Edict
of Religious Toleration of 1905, made it unlawful for a Byzantine
Rite Christian to be a Catholic; every Byzantine *had* to be Orthodox.[10]
Despite every difficulty, for several decades before the revolution
there were some scattered groups of them in Russia. These heroic
little bands of faithful deserve the highest praise for their perseverance in face of unbearable suffering and imprisonment. Leonidas
Fedorov, for example, their Exarch just before the revolution, was
imprisoned first by the Tsars for being a Byzantine Catholic, then
by the Bolsheviks for being a Christian. He died in a slave labor
camp after having spent fourteen of his twenty-two years of priestly
life in prison. There are other examples of heroism, out of all
proportion with the small number of Russian Catholics. No one
knows how many are alive in the Soviet Union today : very few
perhaps, if any at all.

Just before World War II, there were about 25,000 Russian
Catholics of the Byzantine Rite all over the world, several thousand
of them in China and Manchuria before the Communists took over
these countries. In Western Europe, they were about 1,500. The
United States has several Russian Catholic parishes.

Orthodox Russians number from 100,000,000 to 150,000,000, but
it is impossible to give exact figures, since most are in the Soviet
Union. In 1961, the Patriarchate of Moscow gave the figure of
50,000,000. These figures include the Old Russians and the Reformed Russian (Synodal). The Old Russians or *Starovery* are
those who disagreed with the reforms of Patriarch Nikon in 1650.
The Russian Orthodox in the United States number about 805,000
faithful in 430 parishes. Western Europe has about 100,000.

Liturgically, the Russians are very careful to avoid " hybridization," and to preserve their formal religious practices in strict

---

[10] The tsars tolerated Latin Catholics, who numbered about three million
within the borders of imperial Russia before the revolution. Only a small number
of these were Russian by nationality.

accordance with their ritual prescriptions. This holds true of both Catholic and Orthodox. Their liturgical language is Church Slavonic, though in some places the vernacular is used also.

C) *The Ruthenian Rite*, Catholic and Orthodox. The word " Ruthenian " is the official ecclesiastical term used by the Holy See for centuries to designate the Catholics of the Byzantine-Slav-Rite from the Western Ukraine, or Galicia (under Polish domination between the two world wars), Podcarpathia, or Podkarpatska Rus (parts of Czechoslovakia and Hungary between the world wars) and the province of Bucovina (under Rumania, now part of the Ukrainian S.S.R.). This term may also be applied to the people of White Russia (formerly White Ruthenia). The same term applies to these people and their descendants wherever they may have emigrated—the United States, Canada, Brazil, etc.

Today, Catholic Ruthenians are often called Ukrainian Catholics or Catholics of the Ukrainian Rite. They themselves prefer this title, by reason of national rather than religious motives. When in this book we use the terms " Ruthenian " or " Ukrainian, " they are without any political significance. " Ruthenian " is generally used because it is still the official ecclesiastical designation of the Rite. The " Rusins " of Podcarpathia, for example, would resent being called Ukrainians as much as the Irish would dislike being called English. The same is true of the Hungarians of this Rite who, although originally Ruthenians or Rusins from the Carpathian Mountain area, have lost their language and become completely Magyarized. The same applies also to many of those belonging to the Rite in Yugoslavia, etc.

Until the Council of Florence (convened in 1438), the religious history of the Ukrainians was substantially the same as that of the Russians, with their almost unwitting yet tragic withdrawal from communion with the Holy See. From then on, Ukrainians and Russians went their separate ways. After the Union of Florence, part of the Ukraine enjoyed temporary union with Rome. [11] In 1595

[11] Including eight eparchies (dioceses) of the ecclesiastical province of Kiev then under the suzerainty of Poland-Lithuania, — that is, Kiev and the territory west of it. They separated again at the beginning of the sixteenth century.

at Brest-Litovsk, the Metropolitan of Kiev, Michael Ragoza, and the bishops of Vladimir, Lutsk, Polotsk, Pinsk, and Kholm were again united with Rome. Credit for this union must go to the Jesuits and their ecumenical work during the latter part of the sixteenth century. In 1692, the Bishop of Przemyśl (or Peremyshl) brought his eparchy into the Church; in 1700, the Bishop of Lvov (Lviv, or Lwów) did the same. [12]

Several decades after the partition of Poland in the eighteenth century, when most of the Ukrainian and White Russian territories passed into Russian hands, the Ruthenian Church was suppressed and died a slow death by deportation, confiscation, and persecution. In Galicia, however, under Austrian domination, it remained unmolested. In the district of Kholm, ceded to Russia by Austria a little later, the persecution was less severe for a time. Again, it was the Jesuits who tried to preserve what was left of the Church there, and this despite real danger to their lives.

When the Edict of Religious Toleration was signed in 1905, over 300,000 of these " ex-Catholics " and their children returned at once to the Catholic Church. Even after the edict, it was illegal to be a Byzantine Rite Catholic; hence, these people had to become Latins. Anyone acquainted with the history of Eastern Europe will know the intense sacrifice this required, since to many minds it was the same thing as becoming a Pole and therefore a traitor.

Of all the Eparchies to join the Union of Brest, only those of Lvov and Przemyśl survived. They did so because of the more benign Austrian rule. In 1885, a new Eparchy, Stanislavov, was formed from that of Lvov. In 1652, most of the Podcarpathians were united with Rome. Later, in 1771, because of the conflicts of jurisdiction, Pope Clement XIV erected the Ruthenian eparchy of Mukachevo (Munkács) which was subject to the primate of Hungary.

With the capture of most of Galicia during World War I by the Russians, immediate steps were taken to abolish the Ruthenian Church there and to force amalgamation with the Russian Orthodox Church. While the pressure applied cannot compare with the

---

[12] The spelling is that of standard reference works. No political signification or connotation is intended.

Communist brutality of the post-World War II years, yet an incredible number of men, women, children, and invalids were deported to Siberia. [13]

It is to the credit of Ruthenian Catholics in Galicia who survived these trials that, of the eighteen hundred parishes, only about a hundred allowed themselves to be pressured into severing their ties with the Holy See, and this only temporarily. Of the twenty-nine priests who defected, twenty-seven were driven out of their parishes by their own flocks!

After the Russian occupation, more trials and hardships awaited them in the war with Poland in 1918. There was bitter fighting and murderous vengeance on both sides, but the sacking of Ruthenian churches, the desecration of sacred vestments, vessels, and even of the Blessed Sacrament itself by the Catholic Polish soldiers are inexcusable. In 1919, Bolshevik troops occupied the eastern part of Galicia (almost to Lvov itself), bringing about more suffering and trials. In some deaneries, only eight per cent of the priests were still alive in 1920. The rest were lost through execution, deportation, and disease.

From 1920 to World War II, the Ruthenian Church made an almost miraculous recovery, not only inspired, but in many ways directly activated by the saintly and able Metropolitan Andrew Sheptytsky. His deeds, like those of all great saints, would fill a large volume, yet he knew how to reconcile his tremendous activity with inner spirituality and holiness. He offered himself to Christ for the salvation of his flock and died under Soviet occupation on

---

[13] Nor can this persecution of Catholic Ruthenians be minimized. The painful record of it is expressed by Pope Benedict XV : " It is with the deepest grief that we think of the Ruthenians, remembering their fair cities pillaged, quiet villages burnt to the ground, the rich countryside crossed and recrossed by armies fighting to the last. Our thoughts go out not only to the people, but to the ruined churches, the holy images shattered, the sacred vestments defiled, and worse than all, the heart-breaking thought that the Eucharistic species are trodden underfoot by ignorant fanatics. We think of the horrors of famine, the inclement season, mortal sickness, frightful punishments dealt out, the imprisonment of which you, yourself Venerable Brother, bear the scars even now, the slaughter of venerable priests, of aged non-combatants, weak women, and of the flower of youth, all alike guilty of showing attachment to their own rite.... " (Pope Benedict XV, *Il dolore*, *Ad R.P.D. Andream de Szeptycki*, Acta Apostolicae Sedis, Vol. XIII [1921], pp. 218-220).

November 1, 1944. The cause for his beatification has been opened in Rome. [14]

A short time before the outbreak of hostilities in 1939, the Ruthenian Church in Galicia was organized into one ecclesiatical province, consisting of three large eparchies—Lvov, Stanislavov, and Przemyśl—and two territories, that of the Apostolic Administrator of Lemki, and that of the Apostolic Visitator of Volyn.

Eight bishops, an Apostolic Administrator, and about 2,400 priests served approximately 3,500,000 faithful. In spite of grave difficulties, the seminaries were full (with about 400 seminarians), and the schools flourishing.

In the Podcarpathian and Slovakian parts of Czechoslovakia, the Ruthenian Church was also having its success. The Eparchy of Mukachevo had nearly 500,000 faithful, organized into 416 parishes and missions, with 354 priests and 85 seminarians. The Eparchy of Preshov, served by two bishops, numbered about 321,000 faithful, 241 parishes, 311 priests, and 54 seminarians.

In the eparchies and territories mentioned above, there were altogether 3,040 parishes (with 4,440 churches and chapels), 195 religious houses, 9,900 Catholic elementary schools, 380 secondary schools, and 56 institutes of higher learning. The Catholic Press had 38 publications. The Ruthenian Church had made a miraculous recovery indeed in the nineteen years following World War I.

Then came the tragedy of World War II, when an entirely new chapter began in the history of the Ruthenian Church, a chapter that is still far from finished. It is even now being written in the blood and tears of martyrdom within modern Russia.

IN NORTH AMERICA

The Ukrainian immigration to the United States began in 1879; to Canada in 1891. When the trickle of Ukrainian immigrants to the New World swelled into a veritable flood of seemingly endless

---

[14] In 1952, Pope Pius XII had this to say about him : " His name will be forever recorded in the blessings of the Church of God, which will always commemorate his ardent zeal for souls and his virile and generous courage. . . " (Pope Pius XII, *L'Osservatore Romano*, Nov. 16, 1952, n. 269 (28.177), p. 1).

masses, they were for the most part priestless. Father Ivan Valansky established the first Byzantine-Slav rite church in America in 1886. [15] One priest among literally thousands of souls scattered throughout many states! In Canada, matters were even worse. Although a church—Ss. Vladimir and Olga's—was opened in Winnipeg in 1900 under the direction of a Slovak priest (the Reverend Damascene Polivka), it was to be years before the thousands who had settled on the priaries of Manitoba, Saskatchewan and Alberta would have a priest of their own rite. Every day, trainloads of men in sheepskin coats continued to pour out on the vast stretches of the Canadian West, but always priestless. [16]

For years and years, the spiritual tragedy of this priestless people would be re-enacted over and over again. It was not so very long ago, for example, that in many communities they used to gather in each other's homes and sing the chant of the Liturgy by themselves without a priest. Then they would sit and weep bitterly because they had been without a priest for months, for years sometimes since they had come from the old country some twenty, thirty years before. There was no one to confess them, no one to bless them. Sundays became days of spiritual torture for such people. Deeply religious when they immigrated, they would take off their caps and bow as they passed a church, anybody's church; with tears in their eyes, they would pray aloud in public places with their faces turned toward the East, as did the Christians of the early centuries.

Left to themselves, they groped in the darkness, desperately trying to hold the pierced hands of Christ; they stumbled on, lonely and forlorn. With no sacraments to nourish their souls, they weakened and starved spiritually. Then the time came when many fell by the wayside. Even the gentle Master seemed to have forsaken them. There was no one to pick them up, bruised and bleeding. And they lay there... unwanted, uncared for. Thousands wandered far from

[15] At Shenandoah, Pennsylvania.

[16] Between 1896 and 1914, the number of Ukrainian immigrants according to the Department of Immigration in Canada, is 170,000. This figure, however, is misleading since many thousands of Ukrainians still listed themselves as Poles, Austrians Russians, etc., depending upon which country ruled the districts of the Western Ukraine from which they had come. In 1908, for example, there was an estimated 200,000 Ukrainians in Canada.

the only true Church of Christ and lost the priceless heritage of their forefathers.

Even in the towns and cities where there was a Latin rite church in the early years, the Ukrainians felt alone and insecure. Their souls cried out in spiritual anguish over their plight. Just to quote from a letter of one of the early immigrants in Winnipeg to the old country :

> " I write to you this first letter from Canada to tell you that though existence here is good for the flesh, yet the soul is hungry and has not wherewith to nourish itself. Having no home of its own (sic. church), it must stand in the home of the stranger (sic. Latin rite church), and cannot understand the language he speaks. There are people from many countries of the world in Winnipeg, and each faith has its own House of God in which it may assemble for prayer and for the celebration of its sacred days. Only our rite has none... and this is bitter for us, since our children must grow up without religious instruction. Think of our souls here in Canada. Help...!

' Think of our souls here.... Help! ' This pathetic, desperate plea could also have been heard from anyone of the steel cities and coal towns of Pennsylvania and Ohio, from the factory centers of New Jersey and New York. The spiritual plight of the Ukrainians in the United States was only slightly less tragic than in Canada.

It is a credit, however, to the Ukrainians in the New World that the vast majority of them did remain faithful to the Church despite the utter lack of religious instructions and spiritual guidance. They held on despite all obstacles and difficulties. And obstacles there were : if priests were lacking, there was no dearth of other proselytizers.

It is not that the Ukrainian immigrants did not try to obtain priests. They did. They left no stone unturned in their efforts. When all other means failed, they even wrote letters to the goverment in Ottawa that priests be sent to them. In 1901, the faithful around Sifton, Manitoba even drew up a petition to Queen Victoria for a priest! It was written in Ukrainian, the only language they knew. One of the most dramatic but little known efforts was made in 1900 by a humble Black Robe of the Canadian Northwest, Father Lacombe, at the glittering court of Emperor Franz Joseph. Delegated by the Latin Catholic bishops of Western Canada who saw the religious needs of the Ukrainians in their territories, Father Lacombe traveled to Europe to plead their cause. At a conference in Vienna, this ' man of great soul ' as he was called by the Indians, pleaded for the Ukrainians :

> " I met them in our missions and wept more than once in thinking of their fate. If at least we were able to understand them, to give them some consolation! But no, their language is unknown to us. All the same, we have learned to love them, because they are good.... "

Finally, in 1902, three Basilian priests and four Basilian Sisters came to Canada. [17] These priests traveled many hundreds of miles on horseback and ox-cart, from one tiny community to another, where they would celebrate the Divine Liturgy, baptize the babies, hear confessions, marry the young and instruct the faithful. People would flock from miles around on these occasions. The tiny, low-ceilinged houses were always packed to the limit and, likely as not for lack of room, many of the people had to stand outside where they could neither see nor hear the priest. As the Divine Liturgy was being celebrated, they stood for hours, rooted to the spot, tears streaming down their faces, lifting their voices in the responses—and waiting for a chance to catch even a glimpse of the motions of the priest's hand. It was soul-moving to see them, these humble people of God, in such rare moments of sterling joy which saturated their soul-hunger, quenched the thirst of their parched spirit.

In 1910, Metropolitan Andrew Sheptytsky came to Canada for an episcopal visitation. As a result of this visit, the first Ukrainian bishop was appointed for Canada. This was the Most Reverend Nicetas Budka whose episcopal see was the city of Winnipeg, but whose personal jurisdiction included all of Canada. It was the beginning of better things to come, but for many years, only ten priests were available to the Ukrainian-Canadian population of over a quarter million souls. In no small way are the Ukrainian Catholics of Canada indebted to the small band of Redemptorist Fathers who

[17] They were the Reverend Fathers Platonid Filias, Sozont Didik and Anton Strotski; the Sisters were Ambrosia, Isidora, Emilia, and Taida.

had changed from the Latin to the Byzantine rite in order to work among the Ukrainians of Saskatchewan; by truly heroic work, this handful of priests, mostly Belgians, saved vast sections of the province for Christ and the Church.   In Alberta, it was the early efforts of the Basilian Fathers which had preserved the faith among the thousands scattered in the central parts of the province.

At present, there is one Byzantine-Slav Ecclesiastical Province in Canada; this includes the Archeparchy of Winnipeg and three suffragan eparchies (Western Canada, Saskatoon, and Eastern Canada). One hundred seventy-seven secular and seventy-four regular clergy serve the needs of 225,917 faithful in 149 parishes and 448 missions. [18] In all, there are some 54 Ukrainian Catholic schools and institutions.

The Ukrainian Autocephalous Church in Canada is also organized into a Metropolitan See and three suffragan eparchies (Edmonton, Toronto, and Saskatoon), whose faithful number about 100,000.

In the United States where the shortage of clergy in the early days was not quite as acute as in Canada, the growth and development of the Byzantine-Slav Church was truly phenomenal.   The first Byzantine-Slav church in the United States is said to have been that at Shenandoah, Pennsylvania in 1886. [19]   By 1907, the number of Byzantine-Slav Catholics so increased, chiefly through immigration from Galicia, Podcarpathia, Bucovina, etc., that a bishop was appointed for them; he was the Most Reverend Stephen Soter Ortynsky.   In 1924, the Holy See established two exarchates for Byzantine-Slav Catholics : one under the jurisdiction of the Apostolic Exarch, Bishop Constantine Bohachevsky, had its see in Philadelphia,

---

[18] These statistics, taken from the 1961 *Catholic Directory*, vary greatly from those given by the *Oriente Cattolico* (published by the Sacred Congregation for the Oriental Church; Vatican, 1962); the latter gives 200,917 as the total Catholic Ukrainian population for all the Canadian eparchies (pp. 341-343) and 201,512 when it includes the Slovaks and Hungarians of the Byzantine Rite then under jurisdiction of Ukrainian eparchs (p. 446).   This discrepancy is explained by the number of Catholics belonging to other Eastern Rites, about 24,000.   There remains an unexplained discrepancy, however, between the 1961 *Catholic Directory* statistics (225.917 Ukrainian Catholics) and those of the last available Canadian census (1961).   According to the latter, the total Ukrainian Catholic population is given as 189,653 — a difference of 36,264!

[19] D. Attwater, *The Catholic Eastern Churches* (Milwakee : Bruce, 1935), p. 86. Some Ukrainians, however, claim that the first parish was founded in Freeland, Pa., in 1884.

Pa.; the other, under the Apostolic Exarch, Bishop Basil Takach, made it headquarters at Homestead (a suburb of Pittsburgh), Pa. The jurisdiction of these two exarchs was personal, mutually superimposed and extending over all of the U.S.A. The spiritual subjects of the Philadelphia exarch were those Catholics of the Byzantine rite who immigrated to the United States from Galicia, Bucovina and other Ukrainian provinces as well as their descendents. The subjects of the other exarch were all Byzantine Rite Catholics of Rusin (Podcarpathian), Hungarian (Magyar) and Croatian nationalities. Despite setbacks, national difficulties and rivalries (especially between the Rusins and Galicians) both Sees can boast of a record second to none.

What was once the Byzantine Exarchate of Pittsburgh is now a Metropolitan See with two suffragan eparchies (Passaic, N.J. and Parma, Ohio), with about 259 secular priests serving 196 parishes and 7 missions. There is one major seminary with about 110 students.

Their Orthodox counterparts are organized into : (1) The Carpatho-Ruthenian Eparchy of America (under the jurisdiction of the Patriarch of Constantinople) which has 53 priests serving about 100,000 faithful in 55 parishes, and (2) The Carpatho-Ruthenian Administration within the independent Russian-American Metropolitan See, consisting of about 12,500 faithful in 7 parishes.

The original Ukrainian Catholic exarchate of Philadelphia has also become a Metropolitan See with two suffragan eparchies (Stamford, Conn. and Chicago), with about 201 secular priests and 47 religious priests serving 200,000 faithful in 185 parishes and 13 missions. There are four monasteries, a major seminary, and about 75 schools.

The Ukrainian Orthodox in the United States are organized into four jurisdictions, about 135,000 faithful and 160 priests.

Other Ukrainian Catholic Jurisdictions

Jugoslavia. In Jugoslavia the Eparchy of Krijevtsi (Krizevci), according to the *Marytium Croatiae* (Rome, 1946), is organized into 11 deaneries and 50 parishes. The faithful there number more than 56,000 and are served by 53 priests. It also has a monastery with 15 monks and two Basilian convents with 48 nuns. Krijevtsi was reunited with Rome in 1611 when Bishop Simon Vratanja made his formal profession of faith before Cardinal Robert Bellarmine.

Brazil. The country's 86,500 Catholic Ukrainians now have their own bishop, who resides at Curitiba, Parana. The exarchate's 12 parishes and 3 missions (37 churches and 61 chapels) are served by 7 secular and 27 religious priests.

Argentina. In 1961, the Holy See appointed an Apostolic Visitator for the 92,000 Catholic Ukrainians of Argentina. Their 7 parishes (11 churches and 17 chapels) are served by 6 secular and 11 religious priests.

Australia. Since the end of hostilities in 1945, many of the Ukrainians who found themselves in the free world began emigrating to the continent of Australia. By May 10th, 1958, when a separate exarchate was established for them, they numbered about 21,000 in 6 parishes. The priests serving these people number only ten (8 secular and 2 religious).

Great Britain. The post-World War II influx of Ukrainians into the British Isles accounts for most of the 19,250 Catholic Ukrainians there. In 1957, a separate exarchate was created for them. Fourteen priests serve the 7 parishes and 4 missions there.

France. In 1960, the 16,040 Catholic Ukrainians of France received their own bishop, his residence is Paris. Fourteen priests serve the 2 parishes and 10 missions there.

Germany. Due to the influx of workers and refugees during and after World War II, the Catholic Ukrainian population increased rapidly in Germany. In April of 1959, an exarchate was established for them. Seventeen secular and two religious priests serve the 18,000 faithful there.

Western Europe. Catholic Ukrainians scattered in other countries of Western Europe, such as Italy, Spain, Holland, Belgium, etc. In all, they number about 10,000.

PART TWO

THE DIVINE LITURGY
IN DETAIL

THE RITE OF PREPARATION

CHAPTER XV

THE FORMS OF CELEBRATION

In the primitive Church at a time when Christianity was still predominantly urban, the Sunday Eucharist was usually celebrated by the bishop surrounded by his clergy with the whole Christian community participating. [1] This ideal form is very much alive in the Oriental Churches of today. The sense of oneness, complete community, and self-oblation, is the reason for the custom of celebrating only one Eucharistic Liturgy on one altar on any given day. Unless the need of the faithful demands it, two celebrations of the Eucharistic Liturgy at the same altar on the same day are regarded as a sign of disunion.

If a church has side-chapels or *parecclesiae*, only the solemn Liturgy is to be celebrated at the main altar, where it is marked with as much solemnity as possible. If more than one priest is present, they concelebrate, with the assistance of deacons and acolytes whenever possible. *Parecclesiae*, or sidechapels, whether in the shadow of large churches, in cemeteries or in monasteries, exist not to accommodate many priests, nor because there is anything wrong with concelebration, but because certain circumstances demand the

---

[1] Ignatius of Antioch must have had this collective, common Eucharist in mind when he stated : " Take care, then, to partake of one Eucharist; for one is the flesh of our Lord Jesus Christ, and one the cup to unite us with his blood, and one altar, just as there is one bishop assisted by the presbyters and the deacons, my fellow servants " (*Ad Philad.*, 4, edit. Kleist [Westminster : Newman, 1946], p. 86). Cf. also Justin, *First Apology*, chaps. 65, 67; Hippolytus, *Apostolic Tradition* (Dix, 6:40 ff.); *Canons of Hippolytus*, c. 3; *Apostolic Constitutions*, II and VIII; *Didascalia*, II, 57; Ps.-Dionysius, *De eccl. hierarch.*, III, 2 : Narsai, *Homil.*, 17, etc.

celebration of a special Liturgy at a particular place for a particular purpose. Thus, for instance, the chapels flanking the *katholikon*, or main parish church, are used for funerals or family occasions; chapels over the entrances to monasteries serve as special shrines to protect that monastery, while others at the graves of saints serve the pilgrims.

There is, of course, a less elaborate type of Liturgy, celebrated by one priest who is assisted by a deacon. Most Eastern Churches have deacons attached to parishes wherever possible and have retained the Sunday Liturgy with the assistance of one deacon as the most common parish type. Although in Ruthenian churches a deacon is seldom available, the " common from " of the Liturgy still calls for one. In ancient Christian practice, there existed what may be termed the Presbyter's Liturgy, that of one priest assisted by a deacon. In the pre-Nicene Church, a bishop generally had only one parish as his " diocese; " the presbyter/priests, deacons, etc., were his assistants in that parish. By the end of the third century, every bishop had under his care at least several parishes, each with their own presbyter and minor clergy; the practice of the *fermentum* proves this (see p. 66 for history). Care of the main parish belonged to the bishop, while the administration of the others, the " lesser parishes, " was delegated to presbyters and other minor clergy. Since most people whether living in urban areas or in the outlying villages belonged to these " lesser " parishes, we may conclude that the most frequent type of Liturgy in both East and West was the Presbyter's. [2] Cyprian takes it for granted that priests celebrating the Eucharist for prisoners were accompanied by a deacon. [3] John Chrysostom demanded of the Christians who owned entire villages that they not only provide churches, but also a priest and a deacon for each. [4] In the West, the letters of Gregory the Great often mention the need to ordain presbyters *and* deacons

[2] Eusebius, for example, states that during the time of Pope Cornelius (d. A.D. 253) there were forty-six presbyters in Rome. *Hist. eccl.*, VI, 43 (PG 13, 248 B [*Series graeca*]).

[3] Cyprian, *Ep.*, 5, 2 (CSEL, III, 479).

[4] Chrysostom, *In Acta ap. hom.*, 18, 4 f. (PG 60, 147 f. or edit. Montfaucon 9, 149 f.).

for churches which had no bishop. [5] Not until the Middle Ages was this practice discontinued in the Latin Church. [6]

At the present time, Ruthenian and Ukrainian Catholics do have a " Low, " or Recited, Liturgy. It is of recent origin and is entirely unknown in many other Oriental Churches. [7] Many Russian Catholics, for example, have never participated in a " recited, " Liturgy. Even on weekdays, when only a few people are present, the Russians sing their service. The practice of celebrating the Divine Liturgy out of personal devotion, without any of the faithful in attendance, never seems to have gained the general approval and widespread use in the East that it has in the West. Since the earliest days of Christian antiquity, the Eucharist was celebrated only for the sake of the faithful, either for the whole community or for small domestic groups. This spirit, despite exceptions, still pervades Eastern Christians. In many Oriental Rites, the priest will celebrate for the sake of his own personal piety or as his own sacrifice, but only when the utility of the faithful is at stake. " Private " or semi-public Masses are never " solitary, " for an Oriental Rite priest will never celebrate without a group of faithful being present. Nor will he do so to satisfy the obligation of a stipend as is the case in the Latin Rite, especially in religious institutions or monasteries. This is the main reason why many of the Oriental Rites have preserved the old tradition of having only a sung Liturgy. Even when the Holy Sacrifice is celebrated for " private " reasons, it is still

[5] Gregory the Great, *Ep.*, I, 15, 78; II, 43; IV, 41, etc.

[6] There is at present in the Latin Rite a movement in favor of renewing this type of Mass with one deacon, especially in monastic orders and congregations, e.g., Carthusians, Cistercians, not to mention the post-Vatican II developments. The Latin *missa cantata* may perhaps be classified as a modern counterpart of the ancient practice, though it is not exactly parallel; so is the simple Byzantine Liturgy sung by one priest but without the assistance of a deacon.

[7] The " Low, " or Recited, Liturgy seems to have been adopted from the Latin Rite by some Ruthenian priests in the beginning of the seventeenth century; later, it was approved by the Synod of Zamosc in 1720 and again by the Synod of Lvov in 1891. The other Oriental Catholics who have adopted the " Low Mass " are the Italo-Byzantines, by the Constitution *Etsi pastoralis* of Benedict XIV in 1742; the Maronites, in the Synod of Mount Lebanon, 1736; the Copts, in the Synod of Alexandria, 1898; the Malabarese, in Synod of Diamper (Udiamparur), 1599; the Syrians, in the Synod of Sharfeh, 1888; and the Melkites, first in the Synod of S. Salvator in 1790 and later in those of Karkafah in 1806 and Jerusalem in 1849.

with a number of people participating, singing the responses, etc.

There have always been purely domestic celebrations of the Eucharist for private or semiprivate circles. Evidence of this is relatively abundant : the Acts of the Apostles speak of " breaking bread from house to house " (Acts 2:46); various apocryphal histories of the apostles and other later works bear ample testimony to the practice. [8]   Cyprian, for example, speaks of an evening Eucharist for a small group; [9] Basil the Great tells us of priests who were allowed to exercise their priestly functions only in private homes because of misdeameanors; [10] Gregory Nazianzen refers to the Eucharistic Liturgies in his sister's house, etc. [11]   The Synod of Laodicea (c. A.D. 370) issued a proclamation forbidding the celebration of the Divine Liturgy in private homes, but this only proves that it was being done. [12]   Subsequent legislation in the East renewed this prohibition, [13] and then sanctioned it. [14]

This, of course, is not the private Mass strictly so called, that is, a Mass celebrated by the priest alone with the prescribed server. Isolated instances may have existed, but the evidence is scanty and uncertain in ancient documents. [15]   By contrast, at least one Eastern bishop of the sixth century unequivocally states that a solitary Eucharistic Liturgy is invalid. [16]   Its validity was affirmed by the

---

[8] C. Quasten, *Mon.*, 339-345.

[9] Cyprian, *Ep.*, 63, 16 (CSEL, III, 714).

[10] Basil, *Ep.*, 199 (PG 32, 716 f.).

[11] Gregory Nazianzen, *Or.*, 8 al. 11, 18 (PG 35, 809).

[12] Canon 58 (Mansi, 2, 574 C).   For interpretation of this canon see Balsamon, Zonaras and Aristenes, *Commentarios* (PG 137, 1417 B-D and 616 B).   Cf. also Synod of Seleucia-Ctesiphon (A.D. 410), can. 13 (O. Braun, *Das Buch der Synhados* [Stuttgart, 1900], p. 21).

[13] I.e., in the sixth century, Justinian (A.D. 527-565) in *Novella*, 68 (30, X, 537), edit. R. Schoell-G. Kroll, *Corpus Juris Civilis*, III, *Novellae*, pp. 314-315.

[14] In the seventh century, the Council of Trullo, 692 c. 31 (Mansi, 11, 956 DE) at least implicitly gave its sanction with the proviso that permission be had from one's bishop.   In the ninth century, the *Novella* of Leo the Philosopher gave general approval to all (cf. PG 107, 432).

[15] Possible instances in the first ten centuries may be the one recounted by Evagrius (c. A.D. 590) and cited in *Hist. eccl.* I, 13 (PG 86, 2453 f.) and that related by Mari Ben Sulaiman (c. 1135) in the Chaldean Church of the sixth century, *Liber arcis*, BO III, 433, (also recounted by Amru Ben Mathij, *Liber arcis*, BO III, 433, n. 2).

[16] Cf. Moyses Charkensis (c. A.D. 540), *Liber bonorum morum*, cited by Elias of Damascus (p. 900), *Nomocanon*, BO III, 276, n. 2.

Council of Trent [17] but none of the Oriental rites has adopted the practice until modern times. In Latin monasteries, the problem of many priests living under one roof without a " parish " had to be solved centuries ago—otherwise priest-monks could celebrate only very infrequently. The solution was the private or solitary Masses. By the ninth century, such Masses by priest-monks were an accepted practice in the West. [18] But in Oriental Churches, the problem never arose, even in monasteries with many priests, for the simple reason that concelebration was an accepted practice. For many centuries, in the Latin Rite, concelebration was reserved for the ordination Mass. [19]

Another reason why private or solitary Masses increased in the West was the growing desire of the faithful for Votive Masses, that is, Masses for special intentions or wishes (*vota*, " wishes, " " desires "). When these increased to the extent that no one church could offer the number of Masses the faithful desired, their celebration was transferred to parish oratories or to monasteries where the celebrant would often offer the Holy Sacrifice alone.

In both East and West, Masses for the dead were known in Christian antiquity. In the fourth century, for example it was customary to have a memorial Mass celebrated for the deceased on certain fixed days. [20] In some places this was done on the thirtieth day; in others on the seventh or ninth day; and in others on the

[17] Session 22, can. 6 (Denzinger, 944).

[18] Cf. Hariulfus, *Chron. Cent.*, 11, 7 (PL 174, 1250).

[19] Here, we refer to concelebration properly so called where all the concelebrants pronounce the words of consecration with the principal celebrant (and each prays all the silent prayers of the Liturgy pertaining to the priest). Some authors contend that the Latin Rite concelebration in the ordination Mass is not a genuine remnant of this ancient Christian practice (e.g., J. A. Jungmann, *The Mass of the Roman Rite* [Benziger Brothers, 1959], p. 148). There is another form of concelebration in the Eastern Church, one that is only *ceremonial*, nonsacramental; this consists of the concelebrants merely assisting the celebrant without pronouncing the words of consecration with him. It is difficult to ascertain even the approximate date when concelebration strictly so called was discontinued in the Latin Church, for it is uncertain whether many of the Latin authors attesting to concelebration mean real sacramental concelebration or merely ceremonial. Since Vatican II, true concelebration is again permitted and even urged in the Latin Church.

[20] First mention of such a Liturgy comes from Asia Minor, c. A.D. 170, in the apocryphal *Acts of John*, chap. 85 f. (*Acta ap. apocr.*, edit. Lipsius-Bonnet, II, p. 193).

fortieth day after the person's death (This is still done in Russian and Ukrainian Churches). Anniversary Masses for the dead are equally ancient. [21] These practices had a pre-Christian origin. On fixed dates (depending on the locality), it was customary for pious pagans to offer sacrifices for the dead, and sometimes also to have memorial meals at the graveside. The Church replaced the pagan sacrifice with the Christian Sacrifice, the intercessory Mass for the dead. When true concelebration disappeared in the West, votive Masses multiplied and further impetus was given to private or solitary celebration. In the East, on the contrary any number of votive Masses could be accommodated in one church where many priests concelebrated. Such Liturgies were always sung because concelebration ensured the participation of a group.

[21] Cf. *Martyrium Polycarpi*, 18, 3 (ANF, I, p. 43); also Tertullian, *De corona mil.*, chap. 3 (CSEL, 70, 158).

CHAPTER XVI

THE SETTING OF THE EUCHARIST BEHIND THE ICONOSTAS

Because the sanctuary is the dwelling-place of God on earth and is made holy by the Eucharistic presence of Christ himself, the Byzantine Church calls it the *Holy Place* or the *Holy of Holies*. That is why it is separated from the church proper by the iconostas, a solid, richly ornamented screen, covered with icons. The iconostas represents one of the main differences between the Latin and the Byzantine Churches in their approach to God.

There are three openings in the iconostas. At the center, the double doors are called *Royal Doors* or *Holy Doors* because at the Eucharistic Liturgy the King of Glory comes forth through them to feed his flock with his own body and blood. Only the ordained may pass through them, and only at the proper points of the divine services as indicated by the rubrics. On the sides are the smaller, *Deacon's Doors*, used mostly by deacons during the services.

The iconostas bears representations of the inhabitants of heaven, of which the sanctuary is a symbol. More specifically, the iconostas represents the general judgment. As Christ in his glory is surrounded by rows of heavenly beings on the iconostas, so at the Last Judgment Christ, surrounded by the choirs of angels, will come to judge the living and the dead, to separate those who will live eternally in heaven from those who will be excluded from it forever. The meaning of the iconostas, however, is far from merely static or symbolic : its primary role is dynamic, functional; it separates the sanctuary, the *Holy Place*, the *Holy of Holies* from the body of the church. As only the ordained were allowed to enter the Holy of Holies in the Temple at Jerusalem, now none of the faithful are permitted into the sanctuary unless they are appointed to serve there. No woman, whatever her age or social position, may enter the sanctuary at any time.[1]

---

[1] *Ordo Celebrationis* (Rome, 1944), pp. 4-5, n. 7.

Besides emphasizing the awesome sacredness of the sanctuary
as the abode of Christ in the Eucharist, the iconostas ' hides ' this
holy place (and all the sacred Mysteries taking place within it) from
our unworthy eyes. We cannot appreciate the true significance of
the iconostas unless we understand the theology, the devotional
tradition and spirituality which induced it. Its origin goes back
to the churches of Syria where a veil hid the sanctuary at the close
of the fourth century already. When he speaks of to the Divine
Liturgy at Antioch about A.D. 390, St. John Chrysostom refers to
the veil used there as if it were an established custom : " . . . when
you hear, ' Let us all entreat together... ', when you see the veil
drawn aside... then bethink you that heaven is rent asunder from
above and the angels are descending. " [2]

The true explanation for this veil is not the Old Testament
precedent (except perhaps only indirectly) but the idea, the whole
frame of mind regarding the Sacrament being " terrifying " or
" awful " emphasized in Syrian devotion by the *language of fear* in
the sermons of the time; thus, we witness the use of such expressions
by Cyril of Jerusalem, Chrysostom, Theodore of Mopsuestia, and
others. [3] In Syrian tradition, the notion of " the holy " had long
been associated with that of " the dangerous. " Because of the terror
inspired by the Eucharist, combined with its mystery, veils were
introduced to *hide* and *separate* it from the faithful.

After the Arian controversy and the Nicaean dogma, fuller appreciation of the divinity of Christ also had much to do with the hiding
of the Eucharist. Because of the greater awareness of who Christ
was, the familiar approach of Mary Magdalen and the Samaritan

---

[2] Chrysostom, *In Ephes.*, III, 5 (edit. Montfaucon, 11, 23 D); Gregory Nazianzen
speaks of the sanctuary being enclosed with cancelli (*Insomn.*, 14, *de vita sua*, 39
[PG 20, 169 C, *Series graeca*]) and a veil (*Or.*, xliii, 53 [PG 20, 1001 C, *Series
graeca*]); Theodoret, *Hist. eccl.*, 4, 16 (PG 42, 1411 C [*Series graeca*]).

[3] The idea of the Eucharist being " most dread " (φρικωδεστάτος, lit. : what
makes one's hair stand on end) and other such " fearful " expressions seem to have
originated with St. Cyril of Jerusalem. It was further expanded in Chrysostom's
sermons and writings where such terms are relatively numerous. Theodore of
Mopsuestia, who received his training at Antioch, also uses such language in
speaking of the Eucharist; thus, for example, he instructs the faithful to " be
afraid to draw nigh unto the sacrament without a mediator and this is the priest
who with his hand gives you the sacrament " (*Catecheses*, VI, edit. Mingana,
p. 119, c. A.D. 400).

woman disappeared.   Furthermore, at the time of mass-conversions, both the established faithful and the clergy considered that the bulk of these new Christians was not worthy to indulge in that familiarity with holy things to which the small Christian flock had been entitled in the days of the persecutions.

The iconostas has an architectural parent : the *cancelli*, or chancel, found in fourth century churches in Rome, Syria and Palestine.   It propably originated from the same sense of fear and consisted in a trellis wall of marble, some three to five feet high, dividing the sanctuary from the rest of the church and pierced with gates.

When Justinian rebuilt the incomparable cathedral of Hagia Sophia in Constantinople during the first half of the sixth century, he somewhat modified the original *cancelli*. [4]   The Hagia Sophia has a straight, uninterrupted low wall running along a very large sanctuary or *bema*, and three doors follow each other in a row.   On top of this low wall was a row of silver columns which in turn supported a *trabes* or beam, running the entire width of the sanctuary and surmounted with statues of the Twelve Apostles.   The *trabes* also supported the curtain and its rod.   Many churches of the Byzantine world, in Serbia, Rumania, the Ukraine, and Russia, imitated in one way or another the " great church " of Hagia Sophia.

The space between the doors was still left open.   If icons were used, they were placed on the crown of the wall or on top of the beam, but this came much later.   The solid partition characteristic of the Byzantine iconostas took centuries to develop.   The present carefully prescribed arrangement seems to have been introduced early in the fourteenth century in the richly wooded areas around Novgorod where the inhabitants were fine carvers. [5]   The Novgo-

---

[4] Cf. K. Holl, *Archiv. f. Religionswissenschaft*, ix (1906), 365 ff., for architecture of the Hagia Sophia.

[5] Greek iconostases are generally lower than the Russian or Ukrainian where icons are arranged according to a definite plan or order and in rows or tiers.   No set number of these tiers is prescribed; they may range from one to six (depending on the height of the iconostas) but the usual number is four.   The bottom row has the *icon of the Saviour* immediately to the right of the *holy doors* (the epistle side in Latin churches) and next to it, the deacon's south door, then the *icon of the patron saint* of the church.   Immediately to the left of the *holy doors* is the *icon of the Mother of God*, then the deacon's north door, finally the *icon of St. Nicholas of Myra*.   If the patron of the church happens to be St. Nicholas, the

rodian iconographers were masters of their art and endowed with an exceptional sense of color.   Their school of icon painting is the chief glory of Russian art.   The Novgorodians' deep love of icons probably led them to give the iconostas an additional purpose—as a place to hang icons.   Its ornateness did not detract from the original purpose of the waist-high barrier made of columns found in early Greek churches; if anything, it emphasized it.

The desire for greater adornment extended throughout Russia and the Ukraine, so that within a century or two, the iconostas became almost exactly what it is today. [6]   Behind the idea of the iconostas and all its implications is the notion of the awesome Godhead, the Pantocrator, the Heavenly Tsar, the Lawgiver and Judge—combined with that of the repentant humiliation of fallen man striving for ascetic purification.   The consuming fire of the unutterable Yahweh became tolerable only through the veil of the iconostas.

icon of St. John the Baptist is placed there, while that of St. Nicholas is placed where the patron of the church should be.

Usually, smaller churches have only this bottom row of icons and an *image of the Last Supper* over the *holy doors*.   The more elaborate iconostases of the larger churches have more rows or tiers, the second of which has the following arrangement : above the *holy doors*, a large icon of the *Last Supper*; to its left and right, twelve icons depicting the *twelve major feasts* of the Lord and his Mother.   The icon of the Last Supper has this place of honor above the *holy doors* to remind the faithful that those wishing to gain entrance into the Kindgom of heaven must be accounted worthy to partake of the Lord's Supper prepared behind those doors and given to the faithful in front of them.

In the third tier or row stand the icons of the *twelve Apostles* with Christ as King and High Priest in the center.

The icons of the fourth tier are usually of the *major and minor prophets* of the Old Testament.   Surmounting the iconostas and in its center is the *crucifixion scene* : the crucified Christ, his Mother, and St. John the Apostle standing by the cross.

On the *holy doors* themselves, which represent the gates of heaven, is the scene of the Annunciation, the prelude to man's redemption and salvation; also, icons of the *four evangelists* who, like the archangel Gabriel, announced to the world the " good news " of the Saviour.   On the *deacons' doors* are depicted either *angels*, messengers of God, sent to serve all wishing to attain salvation or *holy deacons*, earthly counterparts of angels, who have charge of the sanctuary into which those doors lead.   Many Ukrainian churches, however, have an icon of St. Stephen, the first deacon, on the north door and that of St. Lawrence or an angel on the south door.

[6] Novgorod, Ladoga, and Kiev were the undisputed queens of iconography.

CHAPTER XVII

THE PRELIMINARY PREPARATIONS
OF THE MINISTERS

The preliminary preparation for the Eucharistic Sacrifice takes place the evening before. Like its Old Testament Jewish counterpart, the Byzantine liturgical day extends from sunset to sunset. Its apex is the Divine Liturgy. Revolving around it are the canonical hours of the Divine Office.

Daily worship begins with the Vesper Service in which the Old Testament is seen as prefiguring the New, the coming of the Messiah, Jesus Christ, and his life on earth. Likewise, the Vesper Service precedes and prefigures the Eucharistic Liturgy wherein the life of Christ is repeated symbolically, his atoning, redemptive death being re-enacted in an unbloody manner. All of the canonical hours are, in a sense, an introduction to the Eucharistic Liturgy.

The Divine Office, a systematic form of private prayer among the pre-Nicene ascetics, became the prayer of monastic communities first organized by St. Pachomius in Egypt c. A.D. 335. It was then adopted as part of public worship in the secular churches of the fourth and fifth centuries. Its close connection with the Eucharistic Liturgy at Jerusalem may be seen from a description made by Etheria in A.D. 385. [1]

Before the end of the fourth century, Lauds and Vespers were definitely established in almost all the secular churches of Christendom. Since that time also the All-Night Vigils were almost

[1] When Cyril of Jerusalem delivered his *Catecheses* while still a priest in Jerusalem some time during the spring, A.D. 347-348, he did not mention any of the public offices. It is inconceivable that Cyril would not have mentioned them had they existed then. On the other hand, during her pilgrimage to the Holy City in A.D. 385, Etheria witnessed a complete set of Offices : the Night Office, beginning an hour or two after midnight and lasting till Matin-Lauds at dawn, then Sext and None (public Tierce was reserved for Lent, as is the custom in the Byzantine Rite today), followed by the Eucharistic Liturgy. It seems, then, that the organization of the Divine Office in Jerusalem must be credited to St. Cyril after he became its bishop c. A.D. 350.

universally kept before Sundays and great feasts. [2] The Slav Church, no less than the Byzantine, continued in the Syrian tradition in extending the monastic Office to the laity. The early Kievan rules of worship for the laity contained in the literature of the " Collections " (translated from the Greek) insist on frequent attendance at church. Xenophon, for example, required attendance three times a day : in the morning, at noon, and in the evening. Theodora advises prayers at the third, sixth, and ninth hours, in addition to Matins and Vespers. These, however, may be interpreted as home prayers. Lucas Zhidiata, the second Bishop of Novgorod (the first of Russian origin) insists, " Do not shirk going to church for Matins, Mass and Vespers. " [3] The *Euchologion* became the most common prayerbook for every literate person in old Russia and the Ukraine. This sharply contrasts with the practice of the Latin Church, where the corresponding Breviary remained the exclusive domain of the clergy and monastic congregations.

The secular clergy is no longer strictly required to recite these Offices, yet they are still the best preparation for Eucharistic Sacrifice. These services, especially Vespers and Matins, are still celebrated in public in many Byzantine-Slav parish churches. There is another preparation for Mass which is carefully prescribed for every Byzantine-Slav priest : " The priest who is about to celebrate the Divine Liturgy should, first of all, be reconciled with everyone and not hold anything against anyone; he should, according to his ability, preserve his heart from evil thoughts. From the evening before, he must abstain and keep the fast until the time of celebration and prepare himself with prayers for the Sacrifice. " [4] This is a list

[2] When the " All-Night Vigil " is read and chanted slowly in its entirety, it lasts till dawn. This is still the practice in the great Eastern and Slav monasteries. On visiting seventeenth-century Russia, Paul of Aleppo wrote in his diary : " God help us for the length of their prayers and chants and Masses, for we suffered great pain, so that our very souls were tortured with fatigue and anguish. " Alarmed at the length of the Holy Week services, he exclaims : " God grant us his special aid to get through the whole of this present week ! As for the Muscovites, their feet must surely be of iron. " *The Travels of Macarius* (ed. L. Ridding [London, 1936], pp. 14, 46).

[3] In his only extant sermon. Cf. G. P. Fedotov, *The Russian Religious Mind* (New York, 1946), p. 229.

[4] This prescription of the *Ordo Celebrationis, iuxta Recensionem Ruthenorum* (Rome, 1944), p. 48, n. 99, and in the Ruthenian *Liturgikon/Sluzhebnyk*, (Rome,

of the moral qualifications prescribed for the celebrant by ancient Byzantine moral-ascetic theology. The rubric is taken word for word from the *Constitutions* of Philotheus, Patriarch of Constantinople (1354-1376). [5]

All these prescriptions are clear and intelligible except one : the question of fast *and* abstinence may seem puzzling or at least redundant to the Western mind. The Eucharistic fast, of course, presents no difficulty, since it is the same as that of the Latin Church. The question of abstinence, however, has a different meaning here from that usually associated with preparation for the reception of the Eucharist. This abstinence pertains to the married clergy and marital relations. Though few, if any, would now hold that abstinence from marital relations from the evening prior to celebrating the Divine Liturgy binds the priest *de praecepto*, such abstinence is at least exhortative. Formerly, the Byzantine-Slav canonical prescription prohibiting a priest from celebrating the Divine Liturgy the morning after marital relations was strict. This was not unique to the Slav Church, but rather was common to the Eastern Churches where there were married priests. This may be seen as an Eastern parallel to Latin emphasis on celibacy. Such " partial celibacy, " if we may call it so, is less than the total abstention prescribed by the Western Church. Such Eastern canonical prescriptions, perhaps vestiges of Mosaic Law, do not deny the holiness of marriage. They merely indicate marital relations as a source of *ritual* uncleanness. Marital relations and their concomitant acts are in themselves sinless—the Byzantine Church was very clear on this point—but they became sins when put in contact with sacred things. This called for a complicated system of precautions to regulate sexual

1942), p. 161, is absolutely identical with that for the Russian clergy, cf. Russian recension of the *Sluzhebnyk* (Rome, 1942), p. 169. Virtually the same directives are found in nearly all of the Byzantine-Slav *Sluzhebnyky* of the last two centuries. The *Motu Proprio* of Pope Pius XII (March 25 th, 1957), and later Eucharistic legislation also apply to the Byzantine-Slav Rite; hence, the Eucharistic fast is now the same as that in the Latin Rite, i.e. natural water does not break the fast, food and liquids may be taken by the clergy and faithful up to one hour before the reception of Holy Communion. True medicine, either in liquid or in solid form, may be taken at any time.

[5] Cf. Krasnoseltzev, *Svidinia o nikotorikh liturgicheskikh rukopis'akh Vatikanskoi biblioteki* (Kazan, 1885), p. 265. Also cf. Constantin Triantaphyllides, Εὐλογὴ ἑλληνικῶν ἀνεκδότων, (Venice, 1874).

life, not only for the married priests but also for the laity.   To cite
a few ancient Slav canonical obligations : " A priest who has been
with his wife may read the Gospel outside the sanctuary and eat the
blessed bread " [6] (the inference being that he could not read the
Gospel within the sanctuary itself), but " A secular priest [married]
who was with his wife during the day preceding the celebration
[of the Divine Liturgy] may celebrate after having washed himself
up to the waist, without prostrations and without bathing. " [7]   The
meaning of this uncleannes was entirely religio-physical rather than
moral, just as it was in Judaic times, for washing removes the stain,
the uncleanness.   On the other hand, the canonical obligation of
washing before celebrating the Divine Liturgy, if not fulfilled,
would result in sin; hence, it was morally binding.

The rich ritualistic content of Kievan canonical documents as
well as those of the more exaggerated pre-Mongolian Novgorodian
era are among the most interesting in the pages of Byzantine-Slav
history. [8]   The Russian belief, for example, in the inferiority of
woman developed more out of the idea of ritual uncleanness than
out of any other consideration.   In fact, woman was considered so
ritually unclean that the question was asked in all sincerity by Sabbas,

---

[6] *Kirik*, 27.   One of the best-known question and-answer compositions of
Novgorodian priests; Kirik lived sometime during the twelfth century.

[7] *Kirik*, 28.

[8] Some of them read like Mosaic or Hebraic Law applied to Christianity.   The
old Slav Church, for example, considered a woman unclean for forty days after
childbearing : " The mother after the birth shall not enter the church for forty
days " (*Kirik*, 42).   Both mother and child must be presented in the church on the
fortieth day : to remove this uncleanness, the priest recited a special prayer of
purification over mother and child.   Modern Ruthenian and Russian *Trebnyky*
(Rituals) still contain such prayers.   These prayers, however, are usually recited
over the mother and child immediately after baptism, even if only a few days after
the child's birth.   On the other hand, not a vestige has been left of the old regulation : " When a woman gives birth to a child, it is forbidden for others to eat
with her " (*Precept of the Holy Fathers to the Confessing Sons and Daughters*, 62);
likewise the regulation which stated that unclean is the house or room where the
mother gave birth and where it was forbidden to enter for three days.   Such a
room or house was purified by the same prayer as was said over an unclean vessel
(*Kirik*, 46).   Nor has a trace been left of the canon, formerly so well known that
it was seldom mentioned in Ukrainian-Russian documents, which made the
woman unworthy, because of menstruation, not only of communicating but even
of eating blessed bread (*antidoron*), kissing the Gospel Book, or entering the
church itself (*Kirik-Sabbas*, 23).

the famous Novgorod priest : " If a piece of woman's cloth happens to be sewed into the vestment of a priest, is it legitimate to celebrate in this vestment? " Such matters of ritual uncleanness would not be worth mentioning had they not been an integral part of the Slav national religious mind and tradition.

CHAPTER XVIII

THE PRAYERS BEFORE
THE ICONOSTAS : TEXT

Both the Byzantine and Latin Rites prescribe a proximate preparation for the ministers about to celebrate the Eucharistic
Liturgy. In the Latin Rite, the prescribed prayers are entirely
private, that is, the priest may say them by himself and anywhere
he pleases. [1] In the Byzantine Rite, on the contrary, the prescribed
preparatory prayers are included in every *Liturgikon* (missal); they
must be said in church before the iconostas.

*On entering the church to celebrate the Divine Liturgy, the priest pro-
ceeds to the iconostas which separates the church proper from the sanctuary.
The deacon joins him and stands at his right (the deacon's place is always
at the priest's right, unless the rubrics prescribe otherwise).* [2]

Then, in a moderate voice, the deacon says to the priest :

Bless, sir !

Priest : **Blessed be our God always, now and for ever and
ever.**

Deacon : **Amen.**

*The deacon then continues to recite what is the customary beginning,
called the* Nachalo Obychne, *of any divine service or official prayers of
the Byzantine-Slav Church :*

Glory to You, our God, glory to You.

**O heavenly King, Consoler, Spirit of Truth, everywhere
present and permeating all things, Treasury of blessings and**

---

[1] *The Code of Canon Law* (c. 810) decrees that the priest must not omit to dispose
himself for Mass with fervent prayers : *Sacerdos ne omittat ad Eucharistici Scrificia
oblationem sese piis precibus disponere, eoque expleto gratiam Deo pro tanto beneficio
agere.* Besides this general directive, no specific prayers are imposed. The Latin
Missal offers a set of prayers, the recitation of which is left to the private choice
and devotion of the celebrant.

[2] *Ordo celebrationis* (Rome, 1944), p. 11, n. 25. In the following version of the
Liturgy, the ancient forms, " thou ", " thy," etc. have been replaced by " you, "
" your, " more commonly used in present-day services.

Giver of life, come and dwell within us, cleanse us from every stain and save our souls O gracious One.

Holy God, holy mighty One, holy and immortal One, have mercy on us. *(Thrice.)*

Glory be to the Father and to the Son and to the Holy Spirit, now and always, and for ever and ever. Amen.

Most holy Trinity, have mercy on us. O Lord, wash away our sins. O Master, forgive us our wickedness. O holy One, visit us and heal our infirmities, for your name's sake.

Lord, have mercy. *(Thrice.)*

Glory be to the Father and to the Son and to the Holy Spirit, now and always, and for ever and ever. Amen.

Our Father, who are in heaven, hallowed be your name; your Kingdom come; your will be done on earth as it is in heaven. Give us this day our daily bread, and forgive us our trespasses as we forgive those who trespass against us. And lead us not into temptation, but deliver us from evil.

Priest : For yours is the Kingdom, and the power, and the glory, of the Father and of the Son and of the Holy Spirit, now and always, and for ever and ever.

(Matt. 6:13, Septuagint)

Deacon : Amen.

Then both recite the tropars of penitence :

Have mercy on us, O Lord, have mercy on us. Without any defense as sinners, we offer to you, Master, this supplication : have mercy on us.

Glory be to the Father and to the Son and to the Holy Spirit.

Have mercy on us, O Lord, because we have trusted in you. Be not very angry with us, nor remember our wicked deeds; but as a kind God look down upon us even now and deliver us from our enemies, for you are our God and we are your people, we are all the work of your hand and we call upon your name.

Now and always, and for ever and ever. Amen.

Open the door of mercy for us, O Blessed Mother of God.
We are putting our hope in you; let us not perish but may
we be delivered from all adversity through you, for you are
the salvation of Christian people.

They go before the icon of our Lord, bow and kiss it while saying :

Entreating forgiveness of our offenses, O Christ God, we
bow down before your most pure image, O Gracious One.
In order that you might deliver from enemy bondage those
whom you have made, you graciously consented to ascend
the cross in the flesh. Because of this, we cry aloud to you
with gratitude. Our Saviour, you have filled all things with
joy in coming to save the world.

*Then, they venerate and kiss the icon of the Mother of God while
they recite :*

You are the fount of mercy, O Mother of God, bestow your
compassion on us. Look down upon the people who have
sinned; show your power as always. Because we are placing
our hope in you, we cry aloud to you, Hail, as once did Gabriel
the leader of bodiless beings.

*After the prayer before the icon of our Lady, both priest and deacon
return to the center and stand before the Royal Doors with heads
bowed. While the deacon remains silent, the priest addresses Christ
present in the sanctuary and pleads for strength to offer the Sacrifice
blamelessly :*

Lord, stretch forth your hand from the height of your
holy dwelling place and strengthen me for your appointed
service that I may stand blamelessly before your dread altar
and offer the unbloody sacrifice; for the power is yours for
ever and ever. Amen.

*The priest and deacon bow to the people, both to the right and to
the left, and enter the sanctuary : the priest enters through the southern
deacon's door and the deacon through the northern. In the meanwhile
both recite Psalm 5 :*

I will enter into your house; I will bow in your holy temple
in your fear. Guide me, Lord, with your righteousness;

because of my enemies, make straight my path before you. For there is no truth in their mouth; their heart is vain; their throat is an open sepulcher; with their tongues have they dealt deceitfully. Judge them, O God, let them fall from their devices. According to the multitude of their iniquities cast them out, for they have provoked you exceedingly, O Lord. And let all be joyful who trust in you; they shall rejoice forever, and you shall dwell in them; and those who love your name shall glory in you. For you, O Lord, will bless the just man : as with the shield of benevolence have you crowned us (Ps. 5:8-13).

After they enter the sanctuary, the priest and deacon make three small bows before the altar. Then they approach it. The priest kisses the Gospel Book and the hand cross; the deacon kisses the altar and the hand cross.

The entrance of the priest and deacon with its accompanying words of Psalm 5 is reminiscent of the old entrance ceremony in the Latin Mass at the *Introibo ad altare Dei*. How easy it would be to identify this also with the ancient entrance rite, common to all the Churches of the East and West, whereby, on arrival at the church where Mass was to be celebrated, the bishop was led in solemn procession by all the concelebrants through the church into the sanctuary. The ancient entrance rite, however, corresponds, not with this, but with the Little Entrance (see p. 382).

The preliminary entrance rite was introduced into the Liturgy some time between the tenth and the twelfth centuries, hundreds of years later. In the original Greek Church, entering the sanctuary for the Divine Liturgy was simple and forthright; it remained uncomplicated until the fourteenth century. Before entering the sanctuary to vest, the priest made three bows (cf. above) and recited a prayer or prayers. Many thirteenth-century sources indicate only one such prayer : " O Lord, our God, send me help from your holy dwelling place...." [3] One source, however, gives

[3] Thus, the *Typik of S. Sabba*, MS. Athono-Protat., N. 72 (A. Dmitrievsky, *Opysanie liturgicheskikh rukopisej khraniaschikhsia v bibliotekakh pravoslavnago vostoka*, Vol. III, part 1, *Typika* (St. Petersbourg, 1917), p. 117, and the *Euchologion*

a more developed form : the priest " makes three bows, kisses the holy images and reads the prayer, ' O heavenly King, ' three times, then the prayer ' O God, our, God, invisible to the Cherubim and incomprehensible to the Seraphim ' "; when he finishes this rather long prayer he goes into the sanctuary, makes three bows and kisses the holy Gospel Book. [4]   Another thirteenth-century rubric directs the priest to wash his hands before venerating the sacred images, though this was probably a local usage. [5]

Prayers in the various *Euchologia* from the eleventh to the four-teenth centuries were seemingly to be said out of devotion rather than out of any strict obligation or prescription. [6]

The history of the ceremonial for entering the sanctuary for the Divine Liturgy in the Byzantine-Slav Rite is much different from that in the Greco-Byzantine Rite.   This seems to be one of the few instances where the two Rites have evolved separately, at least for several centuries.   The oldest Slav reference to any ceremonial connected with this entrance is contained in the *Prague Fragments* of a Glagolitic Missal (Fragment 1) of the tenth-eleventh century. The following prayers were to be said in entering the sanctuary : (1) the prayer " I will enter into Your house, " etc. and (2) Psalm 107; in addition, (3) the prayer " Lord Jesus Christ, our Saviour, who

---

of *Patmos*, 719 (*ibid.*).   The wording of the prayer is slightly different in others. For example, the fourteenth century *Euchologion* of Grottaferrata, B.Γ. III (*ibid.*) has, "Lord, our God, send me strength from the height of your holy dwelling place." A similar prayer is found in the *Cod. Sinaiticus*, 959, of the eleventh century, fol. 78 (Dmitrievsky, *op. cit.*, Vol. II, *Euchologia* [Kiev, 1901], p. 53); though not at the entrance of the priest into the sanctuary for the Divine Liturgy, but among other prayers for various occasions, with the rubric : " Prayer when the priest puts on his stole and prepares for liturgical services. "   This prayer begins : " Master, Lord God of our fathers, send me strength from on high.... "   The thirteenth century *Cod. Sinaiticus*, 966 (Dmitrievsky, *op. cit.*, p. 205) has a similar prayer, but puts it at the beginning of the *Euchologion* with the rubric, " Prayer for the priest when he puts on the priestly stole. "   It reads : " Master, Lord God and Father of our Lord Jesus Christ, during the time of wearing the priestly stole, send me, your sinful servant, strength from on high.... "

[4] *Euchologion of Patmos*, 719; cf. A. Dmitrievsky, *Opysanie*, Vol. II, *Euchologia*, p. 170.

[5] *Cod.* from the Monastery of S. Panteleimon; cf. Krasnoseltsev, *Materialy dlja istorii chinoposlidovania liturgii sv. Ioanna Zlatoustago* (Kazan, 1889), pp. 9-10.

[6] This seems to be indicated in MS. N. 362 (607) from the Patriarchal Library of Jerusalem; cf. Dmitrievsky, *op. cit.*, p. 319.

for us didst suffer torments on the cross " was to be recited by the priest when kissing the cross. [7]

Later, in the twelfth and thirteenth centuries, five prayers were prescribed : (1) " Master, Lord, almighty God, who do not wish the death of a sinner, " (2) " Master, Lord, our God, no one wishes to approach, " (3) " I beseech you, Lord, take away from me my wickedness, " (4) " Benefactor of all and Creator of all things, " (5) " Lord, true God, hear us. " [8]   As the ceremonial became more complicated, it also became more widely different in the different churches.   Some books of the fourteenth century would have the priest, on entering the church to celebrate the Divine Liturgy, say : " Rejoice, O divine portal, O impassable doors, mystical sign, O Blessed Mother of God...."   On approaching the holy doors of the sanctuary he was to recite : " We bow before your immaculate image..." and on entering the sanctuary itself : Psalms 14 and 22, the Trisagion, the Lord's Prayer, " Have mercy on us, O Lord...", the " Glory be... Now and always..., Open the door of mercy for us, O Blessed Mother of God, " the *tropar* of the saint of the day and that of the church's patron; only then would he proceed to wash his hands while reciting Psalm 50. [9]   Another fourteenth-century version of this Rite is slightly different : Psalm 50 is added after Psalm 22; the prayers, " Lord, stretch down your hand " and " Master, Lord almighty God, who do not wish the death of a sinner " are added after the Lord's Prayer and " Have mercy on us, O Lord. " [10]

Other liturgical books, however, prescribed a different order and different prayers. [11]   Many books, it is true, followed the ritual observances as given in the Slav version of the *Constitution* of

[7] I. Sreznevskij, *Otryvki iz prevnjago glagolicheskago slurzebnika*, *Zapiski imperatorskoj Akademii nauk*, Vol. IV, fasc. 1 (St. Petersburg, 1863), pp. 20 ff.

[8] Thus, the Barlaam of Khutinsk missal († 1192) in the Synodal Library of Moscow, 343; cf. A. Gorsky - K. Nevostrujev, *Opysanie slavianskikh rukopisej Moskovskoj Synodalnoj biblioteki*, Vol. III, i (Moscow, 1859), pp. 5 ff.

[9] MS. from Library of S. Sophia N. 523, 1-9; cf. A. Petrovsky, *Histoire de la rédaction slave de la liturgie de S. Jean Chrysostome*, XPYCOCTOMIKA (Rome, 1908), p. 879.

[10] *Euchologion* from Library of S. Sophia, N. 522; cf. A. Petrovsky, *ibid.*, pp. 879-880.

[11] Cf. Petrovsky, *ibid.*, p. 880.

Philotheus which had been introduced into the churches of Russia and Bulgaria at the end of the fourteenth century.   In at least one of the fifteenth-century *Euchologia*, we have the Common Beginning (much as it is today except the " Lord, have mercy " was to be said twelve times) before the prayer, " Lord, stretch forth your hand. " [12] This is not to say that uniformity was thereby assured.   Far from it, the various *Euchologia* of the fifteenth and sixteenth centuries differed in kind, number, and order of prayers prescribed.   Some had as many as twenty prayers, while others had only two, three, four, or five, as had been the earlier practice. [13]

Uniformity was ultimately attained in the Ruthenian Church and, if there remained any doubt as to the kind or number of prayers to be said, the Synod of Lvov (Tit. V) settled it in 1891 when it prescribed the order that is still followed today.

---

[12] The *Euchologion* of S. Sophia Library 527, f. 1; cf. A. Petrovsky, *ibid.*, p. 891.
[13] Petrovsky, *op. cit.*, pp. 915-917.

CHAPTER XIX

THE PRAYERS BEFORE
THE ICONOSTAS : INTERPRETATION

The priest and deacon venture to enter the Holy Place, the sanctuary, only after they have purified themselves with prayers of penitence and pleas for mercy. We can appreciate the absolute necessity of such a purification only if we attempt to understand the tremendous awe, reverence, and fear that the Eastern Greeks and Slavs had for the sanctuary. It was the respect and awe of the ancient Jews for Yahweh, before whom the heavens trembled and the earth shook. Even the names given to the sanctuary paralleled the Jewish : the Holy Place, the Holy of Holies. These were not empty phrases. It was indeed the dwelling-place of God on earth. This was not the mysterious, mystical presence of the Godhead in sacred objects, in icons : this was the real presence of the Eucharistic Christ.

To approach the divine presence in any form, one had to be ritually pure. The lengths to which the " bad *Nomocanons*, " the canonical apocrypha, went to preserve ritual purity is fantastic, but even the " good, " the authentic were severe by our standards (cf. above, p. 218, n. 8). Unfortunately, the ancient Slavs were frequently unable to distinguish between the good and the spurious and, hence, all were obeyed at one time or another. Dominating all was the fear of ritual impurity, physical, physiological, or moral. The canonical precision (ἀκρίβεια) of ritual purity demanded for such lesser actions as kissing the Gospels, eating blessed bread *(antidoron)* or even entering the church was not simply counseled or exhortative for greater perfection : it was obligatory with moral guilt attached for any infraction, because of the tremendous risk of approaching the Godhead unworthily. If there was awe in small matters, entrance into the sanctuary, into the very presence of God himself, was terrifying. It was regarded as the dwelling-place, not of the compassionate, loving Christ, but of the Pantocrator, the Tsar of all heaven and earth—in a word, of the God of the Old Testament. The origin of the iconostas and all its psychological meaning were based on this conviction. The One who dictated " Put off the shoes from thy feet; for the place whereon thou standest is holy ground " (Exod. 3:5) was the same God who dwelt in the sanctuary.

In this context, the prayers before the iconostas take on added meaning. Purification by sorrow, penitence, and cries for mercy becomes urgent and all-important. Phrases like " let us not perish, " " Lord, stretch forth your hand from the height of your holy dwelling-place, " and " that I may stand blamelessly before your dread altar " are not verbalism but authentic Byzantine tradition, to be taken quite literally. Even angelic purity is demanded of one offering the Sacrifice :

> When the priest calls upon the Holy Spirit and offers the tremendous sacrifice, tell me in what rank should we place him? What purity shall we require of him, what reverence? Then reflect how those hands should be constituted which perform such services! What should that tongue be which pronounces such words...? At this moment the very angels encompass the priest, and the whole choir of heavenly powers lend their presence and take up the entire space around the altar, to honor Him who lies thereon in sacrifice.... [1]

The first group of prayers including the " Our Father " constitutes the ordinary beginning of any divine service in the Byzantine Rite. It gives the priest a formal, official introduction for his office of acting as mediator between God and man. It is the introductory protocol of an ambassador at court; in this instance, an ambassador with a dual role, as representative of God-Pantocrator before the people and of the people before him. Assigned to obtain favor from a foreign court, an ambassador will not immediately plead his case, but will first introduce himself with gracious amenities. The priest-ambassador here does not immediately begin asking God for favors : he must first carry out the official formalities. These consist of praise and compliment to the Almighty : " Blessed be our God always..., Glory to You, our God..., O heavenly King, Consoler..., " etc. Only after these courtesies is there a request for favor, for being cleansed from sin, and for mercy. Every petition

---

[1] Chrysostom, *De sacerdot.*, 6, 4 (edit. Montfaucon 1, 424 AB).

in this group of prayers is preceded by some form of glorification or praise, be it only a single word of compliment, " O Lord " or " O Master. " All these short prayers are modeled on the incomparable " Our Father, " taught us by the Master-Mediator. The Lord's Prayer first praises God before asking anything from him. Praise or glorification of the divine name was, of course, the standard for beginning all Jewish liturgical prayer even before the birth of Christ. The early Christians formulated their liturgical prayers accordingly.

Tropars of Penitence

The Eastern Christian approached his God with fear, in trembling prostration, but never without hope. His fear was never despairing, since he knew that Christ was understanding and compassionate. On the one hand, the tremendous menace of the Last Judgment forever seared his consciousness; on the other, the image of a meek and loving Saviour, destitute and suffering, poured healing balm of repentance into his soul. Though the fabric of Eastern asceticism has always been interwoven with an acute sense of personal guilt, sin, and repentance, it was also embroidered with hope. This state of mind is admirably illustrated in the penitential *tropars*.

Like all *tropars* and *kondaks* translated from the Greek, they show an extraordinary economy of words (see below, p. 388 ff., for meaning). They are like near-abstractionist paintings, depicting in a few deft strokes what generally requires many. They are beautiful in their simplicity and humility. They plead, they beg, they yearn for acceptance by God in a sense that a wayward child does of its father : " Have mercy... because we have trusted in You.... Be not very angry with us. " The reason why God should be compassionate is unique : because He is our God![2] No better theological reason could in fact be given. A child, when it has offended its father and

---

[2] The same theological reason for mercy is given in the penitential *Canon of St. Andrew of Crete* : " All my transgressions willing and unwilling, manifest and hidden, known and unknown, O Saviour, forgive them all, for you are God... " (Canticle I, stanza 20); or even more clearly : " Being human, I, I alone have sinned, O Lover of mankind, I have sinned more than anybody but since you are the Lord-God of all powers, you have the power to forgive sins " (Canticle IV, *Hirmos*, 3, stanza 2).

wants forgiveness, especially for some offense unpardonable to others, will say : " You will forgive me for you are my father. " Nothing more is needed. Nothing more will suffice. Only a father is capable of such forgiveness to the child begotten by him. God made us. We are all the work of his hand and, hence, no matter what we have done, we call upon his name. He will be kind because he is God!

The Byzantine-Slav Liturgy glories in calling the Mother of Jesus, *Bohorodytsja Divo*, literally the *Virgin Birthgiver of God*. Of all her names, this is the one by which she is most honored. In one way or another all her titles stem from her divine maternity. She is known to the Slav by many names, but in his heart she is always the *Mother of God* and hence all-powerful. That is why he trusts her completely, that is why he loves and honors her. The Liturgy of Byzantium inspired his great devotion to her and continues to nurture it. Indeed, devotion to the *Theotokos* has always been one of the deepest in the Byzantine Church. Thousands of hymns not only in form of *troparia* and *kondakia* but other chants and songs of praise to her were composed and translated into the Slavonic. The Eastern Church calendar has a Marian feast for every day throughout the year, that is, 365 feasts relating to her or to her miracles. One of the predominant concerns of ancient Byzantine liturgists was to introduce her name and glory into all possible liturgical prayers. Of the hundreds of *troparia* composed in her honor, this is among the best known and loved. Most priests and many faithful know it by heart for it is chanted together with the preceding penitential ones as *eisodika*, or entrance songs, in the Eucharistic Liturgy " for every need ", as well as in the daily Office of Compline. Thus these *troparia* were familiar to all long before they became part of the ritual preparation for the clergy before the Eucharistic Liturgy.

Tropars before the Icons of Christ and His Mother

There is a fundamental difference between Byzantines and Westerners in the interpretation of sacred images. The latter merely regard them as representations of one whose presence is elsewhere, in heaven. For the Byzantine Christian, the icon is a veritable theophany, a dynamic manifestation of divine energy at work on earth.   The person represented is in some spiritual way actually present in the icon. [3]   From this presence flow streams of grace upon the sinful world, purifying and sanctifying it.

How explain this mysterious presence in the icon?   To define this presence would be as difficult as explaining the *Shekinah* or the mysterious presence of Christ amid two or three gathered together in his name (Matt. 18:20; cf. p. 582 f.).   Yet such a presence was no less true.   The mystical teaching concerning icons stems from the master idea of all Eastern typology, the idea of the church building as " Heaven on earth. "   Gregory of Nyssa was probably the first to set out the main lines of such teaching. [4]   His doctrine was taken up and developed by others.   The author of the eighth-century *Rerum ecclesiasticarum contemplatio,* for example, expresses it boldly : " The heaven wherein the Triune God lives and moves on earth is the Christian holy place, the church...." [5]   The presence of heaven passed easily from church to icon.

The West never understood the iconoclastic controversy.   It did not see the veneration of icons as a dogmatic matter but simply as a disciplinary matter.   The Byzantine East, on the other hand, saw clearly in the decision of the seventh general council a contribution toward a better understanding of the mystery of the Incarnation or, more precisely, the mystery of God's communication of himself to the world and to man in particular. [6]   That is why iconography was always such a serious science.   It was never merely an art form. To be worthy of the task, the ancient icon painters prayed and fasted for days before taking up their brush—only then could they communicate the Divine through their image-making.   Because icons represent human forms that have been " regenerated into eternity, "

---

[3] This explains the perplexity of conscience raised by the twelfth century Novgorodian priest Kirik : " If one keeps icons or the precious cross in a room *(klet')*, is it lawful to be with one's wife [i.e., have marital relations] ? "   Though the answer of Bishop Niphont is in the affirmative (*Kirik-Sabbas*, 4), Muscovites were of another opinion.

[4] Gregory of Nyssa, *Life of Moses* (PG 24, 181-246 [*Series graeca*]).

[5] Ps.-Germanus, *Rerum eccl. contempl.* (PG 98, 384-385), for full description of the church, a masterpiece of typology.

[6] This communication is actualized first of all in Christ, by the hypostatic union, but it is extended by grace and by all the means through which grace is imparted, the sacraments, the liturgy, and the icons.

holy bodies of persons transformed, transfigured by grace in prayer, iconographers attempted to convey theological meanings through symbolical colors and forms. Saints, for example, are represented facing forward so that their entire face is showing, for a spiritual man cannot be incomplete, with one eye only. "A soul that has been illuminated by divine glory," teaches Macarius the Great, "becomes all light and all face... and has no part with that which is behind but stands altogether facing forward."[7]

The actual though mysterious presence in icons of the holy ones depicted is the underlying reason for their intense veneration by the Slavs. Icons would be placed in the east corner of a room, in a small shrine, the *Kivot* (even the word *kivot* is the same as that of the altar tabernacle), encased in glass and lined with silk or velvet. Such a corner was called "red," synonymous with "beautiful" in the Old Slavonic language. It is still sometimes used to denote something extraordinary, festive, or exceptionally important. [8] Even the most humble peasant tried to decorate this corner in the nicest way he knew, with immaculate linen towels elaborately embroidered at both ends. Before the icon(s), a small altar lamp burned day and night like the sanctuary lamp of Western churches. Belief in the mysterious presence of Christ, his Mother, or the saint in the icon is the reason why in Christian Russia and the Ukraine everyone entering his own home or visiting a friend would bow before the icon(s) and make the sign of the cross before greeting his family or host. The same "presence" forestalled any unseemly conduct, for it is difficult to lie, cheat, or be brutal before an icon, "in front of the saints." How deeply ingrained this feeling was in the lives of ordinary people is shown by the old proverb : Before committing a foul deed, "carry out the saints," i.e., the holy icons.

Special efficacy is hoped for by saying the *tropars* to Christ and his Mother before their icons, in their "presence." The *tropars* said before their icons are the same as those recited in the Canonical

---

[7] Macarius, *Fifty Spiritual Homilies*, I, 2 (PG 19, 1169 C [*Series graeca*]). These *Homilies* were traditionally attributed to St. Macarius of Egypt (fourth century?), but are now thought to be the work of an anonymous author from the first half of the fifth century.

[8] Red Square in Moscow, for example, is not a Communist expression but the old name of the largest and most beautiful square of the tsar's capital.

Office in Sext during the Great Lent. Again, their meaning is primarily penitential. Forgiveness is asked of Christ, the " Gracious One, " because that is why he took on flesh and chose to ascend the cross. " Here the voluntariness of the Passion is stressed, as it is in many Oriental accounts of the institution. [9] The evident note of joy ending the first *tropar* illustrates the Eastern attitude to Christ's cross : sorrow and joy. Sorrow because he suffered and died. Joy because he vanquished death by death, and his resurrection is associated with ours. The theme recurs in the chants of Holy Week, in the Exaltation of the Holy Cross, in Matins of Easter morning, and in the tropar of Easter-time : " Christ is risen from the dead, by his death vanquishing death and giving life to those in the grave. "

In the second tropar, to the Theotokos, the emphasis is not on her role as *our* Mother but as the Mother *of God* and the power of that position : " Bestow your compassion on us "—not *on us your children*—and " look down upon the people "—not *upon your people*—. Her great power stems from her position as the Mother of God. Power, if possessed by a friend, inspires confidence and hope : " Show your power as always. " Unswerving confidence in her power makes her a logical choice as protectress. For the ancient Slav, no less than the Greek before him, Mary's victory-giving power was not merely spiritual but extended to the physical, and even to the purely military. This is clear from the countless instances of protection attributed to the Mother of God by the ancient chroniclers. Her role of Νίκη (Victory), the military patroness of the city, explains why nearly every ancient Slav town and city had at least one church dedicated to her.

Bows of Reconciliation

Just before entering the sanctuary, the priest and deacon bow to the faithful on the right and on the left of the church. These bows plead for pardon and forgiveness from all, a required condition before entering the sanctuary. This is a purely evangelical idea : " If therefore thou offer thy gift at the altar, and there thou remember

[9] Cf. Hamm, *Die liturgischen Ensetzungberichte im Sinne vergleichener Liturgieforschung untersuch* (L.Q.F., 23 [Munster, 1928], 39-42.

that thy brother hath anything against thee, leave there thy offering before the altar and go first to be reconciled to thy brother : and then coming thou shalt offer thy gift " (Matt. 5:23-24). The faithful bow in return to express their pardon. Penitence is hollow if not accompanied by reconciliation.

These two bows to the people became general practice in the sixteenth century. [10] Long before that, members of the old Kievan eparchies were forbidden to enter the church as long as they bore any wrath in their hearts. [11] On entering the church, the faithful would bow first to the inconostas and then to both sides of the congregation as a greeting of love and peace, and as a sign of reconciliation.

Kissing the Gospel Book, Altar and Hand Cross

The priest kisses the Gospel Book because it contains the teaching and counsels of God, very often in the very words of Christ. In a sense, therefore, the Gospel Book takes the place of Christ. That is why it is accorded the place of honor in the front-center of the altar, the " throne, " where nothing else is allowed to stand except the chalice and *diskos* (paten) of the Eucharist. Now discontinued in the Latin Church, this practice was common to both Churches for hundreds of years. [12] The same high regard for the Gospel Book shared by both Churches was shown in another way, in the care and wealth expended on Gospel manuscripts. For centuries, they were decorated with miniatures, some even written in gold or silver script on a purple ground. Later, the bindings were adorned with gems, gold, silver or ivory. [13] Byzantine Churches still continue the practice. However humble a Russian or Ukrainian parish may be,

---

[10] Cf. *Euchologion* (Rome, 1526 and Paris, 1560 [C. A. Swainson, *The Greek Liturgies Chiefly from Original Authorities*, London, 1884, pp. 102, 69]); however, see the thirteenth century *Euchologion* of Patmos, *Cod.*, 719 (Dmitrievsky, *Opysanie liturgicheskikh rukopisej khraniaschikhsia v bibliotekakh pravoslavnago vostoka*, Vol. II, *Euchologia* [Kiev, 1901], p. 170).

[11] G. P. Fedotov, *The Russian Religious Mind* (New York : Harper & Bros., 1960), p. 217.

[12] Cf. H. Leclercq, *Evangéliaire* (DACL, V, 778).

[13] For the Latin Rite, see F. Cabrol, *Books of the Latin Liturgy* (London, 1933), pp. 144-147; also S. Beissel, *Geschichte der Evangelienbücher in der ersten Halfte des Mittelalters* (Freiburg, 1906).

its Gospel Book is covered with rich ornaments, including five miniature icons, of the Four Evangelists and Christ the Teacher.

To emphasize the high esteem for Christ in his Word, the kissing of the Gospel Book is reserved to the priest; the deacon kisses the hand cross. Since the altar does not represent the Lord himself but only his throne, it is kissed by both.

The hand cross which lies on the altar is a crucifix with engraved corpus. It has a handle so that it can be easily held whenever the rubrics prescribe it. The ministers kiss it, as all Christians kiss the cross, because it is the instrument of Christ's death, the source of all grace, and a sign of victory over the powers of evil.

It is the *power* of the cross that impresses the Byzantine Christian. Ever since the conversion of Constantine, the cross had become a sign of political might, appearing on imperial banners with the words *In hoc signo vinces* (By this sign, you shall be victorious). In the newly converted Kievan lands, both notions—of reverence and power—found fertile ground. "Kissing the cross" became the gravest oath and the seal to any pact between feudal principalities of the Kievan-Rus. The breaking of a political oath was regarded as a profanation of the holy cross itself. Punishment was swift and terrible, as may be seen in ancient Chronicles.[14] The lessons from Byzantium were never forgotten. "God and the cross" or the "power of the cross" remained the basis of Tsarist political ethics.

[14] The main subject of the ancient *Chronicles* or *Annals* is the political history of the Kievan principalities. All are unfortunately anonymous. Cf. A. Shakhmatov, *Razyskaniya o drevnieishikh russkikh lietopisnikh svodakh* (St. Petersburg, 1908).

CHAPTER XX

THE VESTING FOR THE SACRIFICE

The priest and deacon now go to the vestment table where they are to vest for the Eucharistic Sacrifice. They may vest either in the sanctuary itself, or in the sacristy. If the vestment table is in the sanctuary, it stands on the south side (the Latin Epistle side).

Liturgical vestments are the official vesture for sacred functions as were those of the Jewish high priests of the Old Testament. There is, however, no link of continuity since during the first three centuries Christians had no special vestments for liturgical functions. Priests celebrating the Eucharist wore ordinary clothing. They were expected to be scrupulously clean and perhaps of finer quality than everyday wear. This is all that is learned from the few references to clerical vesture in the records of the period. The so-called "Canons of Hippolytus," for example, state : "As often as the bishops would partake of the Mysteries, the presbyters and deacons shall gather round him in white clothes, particularly clean, more beautiful than those of the rest of the people. [1]

From the second century on, the Roman *toga virilis* was used less and less, even in the ordinary meetings of the senate. The upper classes adopted a costume, probably of Ionian origin, consisting in three main garments : the *linea*, a linen shift covering the body from neck to feet; the *colobium* or *tunica*, a short-sleeved tunic reaching down to the knees; and the *paenula*, a circular or bell-shaped overgarment with a hole in the center for the head, draping the whole body in folds down to the knees. [2] The *paenula* was worn on formal occasions and outdoors during cold or inclement weather. All were used during liturgical functions, but they had to be clean and in good condition. [3]

[1] Canon 37 (for another translation, see ANF, V, p. 258). Cf. also Clement of Alexandria, *Paed.*, 3, 11 (PG 8, 657).

[2] The *paenula* was also called the *planeta*, *casula*, and even sometimes *lacerna*. There is some doubt about the last, however, since that was also used to designate an open cloak.

[3] In his commentary on Ezek. 44:19, St. Jerome says : "We too ought not to

When St. Cyprian was martyred in A.D. 258, he was wearing this same attire. On reaching the place of execution, " he took off the red *lacerna* that he was wearing, folded it, knelt down upon it, and prostrated himself in prayer to the Lord. And when he had taken off his *tunica* and handed it to the deacons, he stood up in his *linea* and awaited the executioners. " [4] Cyprian was not wearing sacred vestments (aside from other evidence, he would not have knelt down on the *lacerna* were it exclusively reserved for sacred functions) but the ordinary dress of the layman of his day.

In the last part of the fourth century, styles changed to the more military *tunica lanicata* and *chlamys*, or cloak, but the church kept to the *linea, tunica,* and *paenula.* [5]

From the East, from Jerusalem, comes the earliest mention of a special liturgical garment for Christian worship. We know from Theodoret that about A.D. 330 Constantine had given a " sacred robe " of gold texture to his new cathedral church at Jerusalem; this vesture was to be worn by the bishop at solemn baptisms of the paschal vigil. [6] While the robe is a special one used exclusively for liturgical functions, its shape was no different from that of ordinary clothing of the day. A few decades later, a rubric in the *Apostolic Constitutions* insists only that the bishop who will celebrate the Eucharist be " clad in splendid raiment. " [7] The word ἐσθῆτα, is usually interpreted as just that : costly vesture for a lay member of the period's upper classes. It has no connotation of a special liturgical vestment. [8] During the fourth century, therefore, the vestments used for liturgical services were identical in form with secular holiday

enter the Holy of Holies defiled in our everyday garments... when they have become defiled from use of ordinary life, but with a clean conscience, and in clean garments, hold in our hands the sacrament of the Lord. "

[4] *Acta Proconsularia S. Cypriani*, 5 (PL 3, 1564 A).

[5] By a law of A.D. 397 (*Codex Theodosianus*, xiv. 10, I) the senators had to revert to the former civilian style of *paenula, tunica,* and *linea,* which was to be ungirdled; by virtue of the same law, civil servants were to wear the *paenula* over the girdled *linea* as part of their full dress.

[6] Theodoret, Eccl. hist., ii, 23 (PG 42, 1371 AB [*Series graeca*]).

[7] Brightman, LEW, p. 14, 1, 8.

[8] John the Deacon in his *Vita S. Gregorii* (IV, 83) also refers to the sumptuousness of the bishop's vesture, but nothing more can be inferred. Origen, on the other hand, simply states that the priest should be clothed in white linen (*Lev. hom.*, iv, 6 [PG 12, 440 D]).

clothing, but they were exclusively reserved for religious functions. In other words, the clergy could not celebrate the Eucharist in their ordinary clothing, nor could they go out into the streets in the vesture used in church.

About the year A.D. 400, Isidore of Pelusium gives the first indication of a distinctive liturgical vestment, the *omophorion,* worn by bishops as a symbol of their duties as shepherds of their flocks. [9] Some time later, bishops of the Western Church began adopting it under the name of *pallium.* This was still the exception rather than the rule about A.D. 425, since Pope Celestine I rebuked the bishops of Southern France in no uncertain terms for using the pallium and cincture in divine services. After accusing them of violating the Church's custom by introducing these two items, he urges : " We bishops must be distinguished from the people and others by our learning and not by our dress, by our life and not by our robes, by purity of heart and not by elegance.... " [10] To the argument that the cincture corresponded literally to the " girded loins " enjoined by the Gospels, he shrewdly replied that, to be consistent, they must also stand at the altar with a burning lamp in one hand and a staff in the other.

As late as the sixth century, the *orarion* (or stole) and *omophorion* (or pallium) were the only distinctively liturgical vestments. [11] Then the secular fashions changed while the Church retained the traditional garments of the late Roman empire.

According to present-day rubrics, not only do sacred ministers wear special garments for liturgical functions, they must also clothe themselves spiritually with whatever virtue each vestment represents. There must be both internal and external splendor. In putting on each vestment, they must also say the prescribed prayers which, for the Byzantine clergy, usually consist in accommodated verses from

---

[9] Isidore of Pelusium, *Ep.,* 1, 136 (PG 78, 272, or PG 40, 1022 B [*Series graeca*]).

[10] Celestine I, *Ep.,* iv., 1, 2 (PL 50, 430 B-431 A).

[11] Today the *omophorion* is worn by bishops of the Byzantine, Armenian, Coptic and (in a different form) Syrian Rites. It is a band (usually about six inches wide) of silk or velvet, embroidered with crosses and other emblems. When worn, it is twisted loosely around the neck so that the ends hang down in front and behind nearly to the ground. It is worn over the *sakkos* (a short tunic with half-sleeves, similar to a dalmatic).

the Psalms. In this manner, a function as prosaic as dressing is sanctified with appropriate thoughts of God and his service.

When the priest and the deacon come to the vestment table, each takes his stikhar [12] *and bows three times toward the East while privately saying the words :*

O God, be merciful to me a sinner (Luke 18:13).

Then the deacon goes up to the priest and, holding the stikhar, orar, *and* narukavnytsi *in his right hand, he says with head bowed :*

Sir, bless the stikhar with the orar.

Then the priest blesses these vestments with the words :

Blessed be our God always, now and forever and through all eternity.

Deacon : **Amen.**

The deacon then goes to another part of the sanctuary to vest, while the priest remains at the vestment table. After taking the stikhar in his left hand, the priest makes three small bows toward the East and blesses the stikhar with the same words he used in blessing the stikhar of the deacon :

Blessed be our God always, now and forever and through all eternity. Amen.

Then he puts it on, as he says :

My soul shall be exalted in the Lord, for he has clothed me with the robe of salvation and he has arrayed me with the garment of joy; he has put a crown on my head as on a bridegroom and he has adorned me with jewels as a bride (Isaiah 61:10).

Corresponding to the alb in the Latin Rite, the stikhar is a long flowing garment, reaching to the ankles. Unlike the Latin alb, however, the stikhar may be of any color except black. Where the Latin Church insists on linen for the alb, the Byzantine insists on fine quality, though not necessarily linen. Originally, the stikhar

---

[12] Vestments are indicated here by their Byzantine-Slav names, slightly different from the Greek.

and the alb were identical because they were the same garment, the ancient *linea*. For the first nine centuries, there was nothing to distinguish this standard garment either for street wear or for liturgical functions. [13]

The stikhar is a symbol of a pure conscience, a blameless life, and of the spiritual joy that flows from such a conscience. It serves as a constant reminder to the priest that he must always try to keep himself away from sin and all worldly, dangerous inclinations. To wear the stikhar worthily, he must steadfastly strive by watchfulness, humility, and a penitential spirit to increase the grace of God in his soul. Doing this, he will clothe himself with happiness, the supreme joy of the soul, and he will attain salvation. His soul shall rejoice in the Lord, will be exalted in him, for the Lord will have clothed him with sanctifying grace, the robe of salvation. That is why the stikhar is also called " the robe of salvation " and " the garment of joy. "

Putting on the Epitrakhil

The *epitrakhil*, a vestment similar to the Latin stole but much longer, is worn around the neck and is sewn together from the neck down. As its name signifies (from the Greek, ἐπί + τράχηλος on the neck), the epitrakhil is the yoke of the Lord.

" Receive thou the yoke of the Lord, " the ordaining bishop says to the ordinand as he hands him the epitrakhil, " for his yoke is sweet and his burden light. " [14]

The deacon's stole, called the *orar*, looks somewhat different from that of the priest : it is a long, narrow band and hangs over his left shoulder. [15] Though no conclusive evidence exists regarding its exact origin, the orar is mentioned by the Council of Laodicea (A.D. 343-381) as a special mark of distinction for the deacon. [16] It

---

[13] In fact, until the thirteenth century, it was known in Rome as the *linea* or *camisia*, not by its present name, alb.

[14] This holds true only for the Ruthenian Rite.

[15] Originally, the Latin Church had the same stole for its deacons, even using the same name, *orarium*, for it. Cf. N. Gihr, *The Holy Sacrifice of the Mass* (St. Louis, 1955), p. 133.

[16] Canon 22 (NPNF, XIV, p. 140).

was introduced into the West from the East probably through Spain and Gaul. The custom of deacons wearing the orar on their left shoulder, with its ends falling straight in front and back, probably originated in Antioch. [17]   Deacons in all Byzantine Churches still wear it in this manner : hanging over the shoulder, so that it flutters like a wing when they walk or move.   According to Theodore of Mopsuestia, that is what the deacon's orar symbolizes : the flying of angels. [18]   Since the function of the deacon is to assist, to serve, it corresponds with that of the angels in heaven.

The priest's epitrakhil is the same as the deacon's orar but worn around the neck, and sewn together in front.   This indicates the twofold nature of the sacerdotal office, that of priest and that of deacon.   The origin of the epitrakhil is shrouded in obscurity. Theories abound but nothing definite is known.   Probably after the deacon's stole became his insignia in the East, the priestly stole was first used to indicate his office.   It may have had no more significance than an insignia, the symbol of a function.   It may have originated from the fourth-century pallium worn by the emperor and consuls and later granted to numerous other officials.   Probably first adopted by the higher clergy in the East, its use spread to the lower ranks. As originally worn by the clergy of all Rites, it hung in two loose bands over the breast.   In this form it was introduced in the West, where it is still worn in this way.

Besides serving as the mark of his office, the priest's epitrakhil symbolizes the grace of the priesthood being poured from above. When viewed from the front, it represents a twofold stream flowing down from the priest's shoulders.

When putting on this vestment, the priest (first blessing it with the sign of the cross) says the following prayer :

Blessed is God, who pours out grace on his priests like an ointment on the head, an ointment which runs down upon the beard, as it did on the beard of Aaron, down to the hem of his garment (Ps. 132:2).

[17] Cf. Pseudo-Chrysostom, *De fil. prod.*, 3 (VIII, *append.*, 37 A); also Theodore of Mopsuestia, *Catecheses* (edit. Mingana, p. 84).

[18] Theodore of Mopsuestia, *Catecheses* (edit. Mingana, p. 84).

The book of Exodus describes the consecration of Aaron, the brother of Moses, performed through the pouring of the oil of unction upon his head (Exod. 29:7). The anointing and consecration of this priest in the Old Law prefigured the sacrament of Holy Orders in the New. Like all sacraments, Holy Orders pours grace into the soul of the recipient. In the prayers of the epitrakhil, the priest blesses God for the abundance of grace being poured into his soul in no less a measure than the oil of unction poured upon the head of Aaron, which ran down his venerable beard, down to the hem of his garment (Ps. 132:2).

The epitrakhil, in as much as it hangs around the neck of the priest and rests on his shoulders, symbolizes the yoke of the Lord, the burden of service in the sanctuary. But it is a yoke made light and sweet by the outpouring of priestly grace. Though heavy with responsibilities and cares, his burden is not oppressive because the hand of God, grace, eases the load. The oil of unction soothes the shoulders so as to prevent bruising and chafing. Yet, the priest's yoke of office is heavier than the deacon's; hence, the priest wears his epitrakhil on both shoulders and not the way in which the deacon does, on one shoulder.

The Poyas, or Girdle

As he girds himself with the poyas *the priest says :*

Blessed be God who girds me with strength and has made my path blameless, who has made my feet as fleet as those of a deer and has set me on high places (Ps. 17:33-34).

Functionally corresponding to the Latin cincture, the *poyas* resembles a belt more than its Latin counterpart. Made of the same rich, durable material as the epitrakhil and the rest of the vestment set—except the stikhar—the poyas looks like a belt that is tied at the back. Its practical purpose is to gather up the long and broad stikhar so that it will fit more closely. To gird oneself, as the priest does with the poyas, is an act often repeated in Sacred Scripture (e.g., John 13:4; Eph. 6:14). It is an expression of readiness and preparedness for combat, toil, or travel. In ancient times, warriors, laborers, and travelers used to gird themselves in order to gather up their loose, wide garments and hold them securely; thus, their movements were freer and easier in whatever they were to do.

Exactly when the *cingulum* or belt was introduced as part of the sacred vesture is unknown. In the secular life of the year A.D. 387, the *cingulum* was still the badge of the military as opposed to civil office. The officials *(officiales)* ranking as *militia* were subject to military law, and therefore were to wear the girdle, but senators as civilians were not. At the beginning of the fifth century, some bishops were wearing the *cingulum* or girdle in celebrating the Eucharist (understandably enough, since many bishops had been recruited from the magistracy at the time), for this practice is included in the reprimand of Pope Celestine (see above, p. 236). The custom of wearing the belt or *cingulum* was adopted universally, perhaps because of its great practical utility.

The priest is girded by God with strength, of which the poyas is a symbol. He is thus prepared for life's toil and is ready to fight its battles. The imagery of life as a time of labor and warfare is scriptural (e.g., Job 7:1 ff.; Matt. 20; etc.). By being girded, the priest is left free in his movements to work for Christ and to do battle for him. He needs strength for both, and he receives it from God. By arming him with necessary strength, God makes his journey of life, his path, blameless. Strength also gives agility, the nimbleness of a deer. Continuing the same imagery, strength and agility enable him to attain the high ground—strategically important in any battle.

The Narukavnytsi *or Cuffs*

The maniple is not used in the Byzantine Rite nor is there an exact parallel to it in the Byzantine Church. [19] Entirely different in

---

[19] Originally, the Latin maniple was a linen cloth or a kind of large handkerchief for wiping and cleansing the face and hands. Called *mappula*, it was carried by consuls and other magistrates in their hand or laid across the arm. As an ecclesiastical vestment, it came into general use only in the eleventh century, though the *mappula* was used by the clergy of Rome as early as the sixth century, and even earlier in Egypt, by deacons, as a badge of distinction (cf. Isidore of Pelusium, c. A.D. 410, *Ep.*, 1, 136 [PG 78, 272]). The maniple as such was never used in the Byzantine Rite. The Eastern bishops' *epigonation*, however, may be considered somewhat of an equivalent, for it too was carried in the hand until the ninth century.

origin and purpose, the Byzantine *epimanikia* or Slav *narukavnytsi* are simply sleevelets or special cuffs made of the same material as the rest of the vestment set. They are worn over the ends of the sleeves of the stikhar. Their purpose is the very practical one of tucking in the wide sleeves of the stikhar so that these will not encumber the actions of the priest or be in the way when he is handling the sacred vessels. Being identical, the cuffs may be worn interchangeably on either the left or right wrist.

Originally, the epimanikia were exclusively part of the Byzantine emperor's dress. Later patriarchs adopted them. Later, still bishops began wearing them, and finally, ordinary priests, arch-deacons, and protodeacons. Deacons were accorded the privilege of wearing the epimanikia in the seventeenth century. [20]

In vesting for the Divine Liturgy, the priest first puts on the liturgical cuff on his right wrist and says :

Your right hand, O Lord, is glorified in strength, your right hand, O Lord, has shattered the enemy, and with the abundance of your glory you have crushed the adversaries (Exod. 15:6-7).

As he puts the cuff on his left wrist, he says :

Your hands have made and formed me. Give me under-standing and I will learn your commandments (Ps. 118:73).

The epimanikia, or the narukavnytsi, symbolize the strength, the power of God. The accompanying verses, the *Epinicia*, the magni-ficent *Canticle of Moses*, make this clear. The priest trusts the same Power that once vanquished the Egyptian Pharaoh to shatter, to " dash into pieces, " the enemy of his soul. He recognizes his own innate weakness. The more he will trust the strength of God, the more he will distrust his own : " He that thinketh himself to stand, let him take heed lest he fall... " (I Cor. 10:12).

Now it is attached at the height of the right knee (whence its name, from the Greek ἐπί + γόνατος, " on the knee ") by a ribbon to the poyas or zone. Its origin is uncertain.

[20] Cf. A. Neselovsky, *Chyny chyrotej i chyrotonij* (Kamenetz-Podolsk, 1906), p. 161; also P. Bernadakis, " Les ornements liturgiques chez les Grecs, " Echos d'Orient, V (1902), p. 13.

With the second prayer, the priest calls on God, whose hands have made and fashioned him, to give enlightenment in whatever he commands. Enlightenment is necessary for any man of God. The spiritual way is strewn with many pitfalls of self-deception. Unless God gives enlightenment, no one can really be free from self-deceit.

The Phelon

Where the Latin rite has the chasuble, the Byzantine-Slav has the *phelon*, an outer, cloaklike, sleeveless garment covering the other vestments. In its etymological sense *phelonion*, a Cretan word, means a *garment covering all*. It is also known as the *polistaurion* (from the Greek πολύς, meaning " many " and σταυρός, " cross ") because it is decorated with a number of crosses. (The custom of decorating the *phelonion* with many crosses arose late in the eleventh century).

This vestment has its origin in the Greek *phelonys* (φελόνης) or the Roman *paenula*, which had almost entirely replaced the Roman toga in the Greco-Roman world after the second century : this, as we have seen, was a circular, bell-shaped, overgarment worn during cold and inclement weather or when traveling. That is precisely what the phelon (and the ancient form of the Latin chasuble) was : a bell-shaped vestment with an opening in the middle for the head, with all its sides of even length falling in loose folds below the knees almost to the ankles. When the priest wanted to use his hands, he had to gather up the front into folds and hold them on his forearms. This form of phelon is still used in Greece.

While both the phelon of the Byzantine-Slav Rite and the chasuble of the Latin had a common origin in the *phelonys* or *paenula*, both underwent gradual modifications prompted mostly by their obvious difficulty during the celebration of the holy mysteries. After the eleventh century in the West, it was shortened at both sides to allow freer use of the arms—also perhaps because oval outlines suited the Gothic taste and style of the period. Thus, the so-called Gothic chasuble came into being. Gradually, however, more and more was cut away until the Gothic chasuble gave way to the well-known shorter and less graceful, fiddle-shape introduced during the Baroque period which seemed to prefer heavy, stiff brocades to the flowing folds of soft material previously used. The tendency of the Latin Rite is to revert to the Gothic flowing type of vestment. In the Byzantine Church, the phelon has undergone a similar but less radical modification : to be less cumbersome, the front half was shortened to facilitate the movement of the hands.

The phelon is the principal vestment of the priest; its width and length are sufficient to cover all his other vestments. [21] In all liturgical services, in all his pastoral work, the priest represents Christ, who gave himself for the people that they might be saved. Just as the phelon covers all the other vestments, so the spirit of Christ in the priest should clothe every fiber of his being, his every thought, his every word and deed. In putting on the phelon, he is to " put on the Lord Jesus Christ " (Rom. 13:14). He, no less than Paul, should be able to say, " And I live, now not I, but Christ liveth in me " (Gal. 2:20). As the phelon encloses all the other vestments of the priest, so the spirit of Christ encompasses all virtue : mercy, benignity, humility, modesty, patience, bearing with one another, forgiving one another, charity (Col. 3:12-14).

The priest blesses, kisses, and puts on the phelon, saying :

Your priests, O Lord, shall clothe themselves with righteousness, and your faithful shall rejoice with gladness always, now and for ever, and through all eternity (Ps. 131:9).

Historically, there is no other order of putting on the sacred vestments than that used today. The very nature of the vestments and their use preclude divergence on this point. Before the introduction of the *Constitution* of Philotheus into the Slav Church, there were no special prayers that the priest had to say in vesting himself in the sacred garments. [22] Later, however, there was much diversity in regard to both the order and the text of the prayers to be said.

---

[21] The *phelon* is not so specifically a Eucharistic vestment as the chasuble is in the Latin Rite. It is worn not only at the Eucharistic Liturgy but also at other solemn functions, e.g., Vesper Service, Matins, in processions, at the administration of sacraments, etc.

[22] According to the twelfth century Missal of Barlaam of Khutinsk, the priest puts on the sacred vestments in silence (MS. of Synodal Library of Moscow N. 343; Gorsky-Nevostrujev, *Opysanie slavianskikh rukopisej Moskovskoj Synodalnoj biblioteki*, III, 1, 6). Some of the Slav missals of the fourteenth century, however,

After the evolution of special liturgical vestments (fourth century on), vesting was still a purely utilitarian function, without ceremony, without mystical or symbolical meaning. Like many other liturgical actions, purely utilitarian in origin and nature, the simple action of vesting was eventually embellished with ceremony and mystical interpretation. In the Greco-Byzantine Rite, this began some time before the thirteenth century when a prayer was to be said by the priest before vesting. [23] The practice of reciting a separate prayer while putting on each vestment arose during the thirteenth and fourteenth centuries. [24] At first, then, the idea of reciting separate prayers for putting on each vestment was adopted into the Slav Church from its parent, the Greco-Byzantine Rite. The prayer for putting on the phelon has remained almost the same for seven hundred years, although a special prayer has been prescribed for the celebrant of the *proskomidia*, when he lets down the ends of the phelon from his shoulders. [26] The present prayer for the poyas is that of the fifteenth century, said when putting on the epitrakhil; [27]

did prescribe the second of the five preparatory prayers generally included in the twelfth century missals; this was to be said before vesting; cf. A. Petrovsky, *Histoire de la rédaction slave de la liturgie de S. Jean Chrysostome*, XPYCOCTOMIKA, pp. 863, 873, 880.

[23] The vesting itself, however, was still done in silence; thus the thirteenth century *Sinaiticus Roll*, 966 (A. Dmitrievsky, *Opysanie liturgischeskikh rukopisej khraniaschikhsia v bibliotekakh pravoslavnago vostoka*, Vol. II, *Euchologia* (Kiev, 1901), p. 205). Today, the prayer, " Lord, stretch forth your hand, " is said by the priest just before entering the sanctuary. Not all missals contained the same prayer, however, for the thirteenth century *Codex* 719 of the Patmos Library gives a different prayer, a lengthy prayer which begins, " O God, our God who. . . . " Cf. Dmitrievsky, *op. cit.*, pp. 170-171.

[24] E.g., *Patmos Roll*, 719 (Dmitrievsky, *op. cit.*, p. 171), *Codex* of Panteleimon Monastery (N. Krasnoseltsev, *Materialy dlja istorii chinoposlidovania liturgii sv. Ioanna Zlatoustago* [Kazan, 1889], p. 10); *Codex* of Esphigmenon Monastery N. 1306 (Dmitrievsky, *op. cit.*, pp. 262-263). Though all these contain a separate prayer for each vestment, not all the prayers are the same. The early eighth century Armenian Liturgy of Chrysostom contains two separate prayers for vesting : one for putting on the cincture and *orarion* and the other for vesting in the cloak *(phelonion)*; cf. G. Aucher, *La versione armena della liturgia di S. Giovanni Crisostomo fatta sul principio dell'VIII secolo*, XPYCOCTOMIKA, p. 372.

[25] At least we are led to believe this by *Codex* of Patmos 719 (Dmitrievsky, *op. cit.*, pp. 170-171), which has one prayer before the beginning of vesting and separate prayers for each vestment.

[26] *Cod. Panteleimon*, 719; cf. Dmitrievsky, *op. cit.*, p. 171.

[27] MS. of Patriarch of Jerusalem Library; cf. Krasnoseltsev, *op. cit.*, p. 83.

on the other hand, what was once said for putting on the poyas or cincture is now recited for the bishop's epigonation. [28]

The Deacon's Vesting

The deacon vests at the same time as the priest. In putting on the stikhar, he says the same prayer as the priest. The deacon's stikhar has the same symbolic meaning as that of the priest, but is cut differently and is made of a stiffer material.

As the deacon takes the orar, he kisses it and puts it on his left shoulder without saying anything. The orar or stole is generally worn over the left shoulder but is crossed upon the chest and back, during the Eucharistic Liturgy, from the Lord's Prayer until after Holy Communion. [29] The deacon represents the Cherubim and the Seraphim : his orar, their wings. The deacon's ministry, like that of angels, consists in serving at the altar of the Most High. According to ancient Christian tradition, angels participated in the work of redemption and they participate in the Eucharistic Sacrifice whenever it is celebrated. Chrysostom, for example, teaches : that " at that solemn moment, the priest is surrounded with angels, and the choir of the heavenly powers unites with him; they occupy the entire space around the altar, to honor Him who lies there as a sacrifice. " [30]

In putting on the narukavnytsi or cuffs, first on the right hand then on the left, the deacon says the same prayers as the priest; their symbolism and meaning are the same. When he is finished vesting, he goes to the *proskomidia* table [31] to prepare the sacred utensils for the divine service : he unfolds the *illiton* (Greek εἰλητόν), [32] sets the chalice and *diskos* (paten) on it, the chalice on the right and the

---

[28] *Codex* of Patmos 719, of the thirteenth century; cf. Dmitrievsky, *op. cit.*, p. 171. Also *Cod. Falascae*; cf. Goar, *Euchologion, sive Rituale Graecorum* (2nd edit., Venice, 1730), p. 100. The *epigonation*, worn by bishops and all deserving dignitaries, is a diamond-shaped piece of stiff material with a cross or embroidered image; it is suspended, by a corner, just at or above the knee by a ribbon attached to the poyas or to the shoulder.

[29] Unlike the deacon, the subdeacon *always* wears his *orar* crossed. He is thus " bound " to meekness and continence.

[30] Chrysostom, *De Sacerdot.*, 6, 4 (edit. Montfaucon 1, 424 C).

[31] Also known as the *proskomidijnyk*, table of oblation or *prothesis*.

[32] Equivalent to the Latin corporal.

diskos on the left, and readies the lance (liturgical knife), *asterisk* (see below p. 314 for meaning), veils, and linens for the Rite of *proskomidia*.

Prior to the thirteenth century, the deacon, like the priest, vested in silence. The custom of asking the priest for a blessing before vesting dates back to the thirteenth or fourteenth century. [33] The present practice of reciting separate prayers for each vestment was obviously borrowed from the vesting ritual prescribed for the priest; however, it was probably not stabilized until the sixteenth century. [34]

[33] *Cod.* N. 381 of Synodal Library of Moscow, cf. Krasnoseltsev, *op. cit.*, p. 19.

[34] E.g., the fifteenth century *Cod. Vat.* N. 1213 (Krasnoseltsev, *Svidinia o niko-torikh liturgicheskikh rukopisakh Vatikanskoi biblioteki* [Kazan, 1885], p. 128) still does not require the deacon to recite separate prayers for each vestment.

CHAPTER XXI

THE WASHING OF THE HANDS

A*fter vesting, both priest and deacon wash their hands at the* Proskomidia *Table and recite :*

I will wash my hands among the innocent and I will walk around your altar, O Lord, that I may hear the voice of your praise and tell of all your wondrous deeds. Lord, I have loved the beauty of your house and the dwelling place of your glory. Destroy not my soul with the wicked, nor my life with men of blood, in whose hands are iniquities; whose right hand is filled with bribes. But I have walked in my innocence; redeem me, O Lord, and have mercy on me. My foot has been set in righteousness; in the churches I will bless you, O Lord (Ps. 25:6-12).

In almost all the Oriental Rites, the priest washes his hands at least twice when celebrating Mass. The first washing of hands takes place during the rite of preparation, the second, at the offertory. Chaldean Nestorians also wash their hands a third time just before the fraction. In the Byzantine Rite, however, there is only one washing of the hands, during the rite of preparation. In the Syrian Rite, also, there is only one, but at the offertory.

Religious motives rather than utility prompted the Jewish custom of washing before the Thanksgiving at the end of a meal. Our Lord, for example, took advantage of this custom to wash the feet of the apostles at the end of the Last Supper; his action, too, was symbolic rather than practical (John 13:2-12). In a sense, the meal was offered to God through the *berakah*, the blessing. Since the uncleansed could not offer it, the participants washed their hands. In fact, every pious Jew washed his hands before he prayed. Evidence of similar ablutions appear in Christian antiquity. Thus, Christians washed their hands before praying, even before private prayer. [1] Early Christians also washed their hands on entering the

---

[1] Cf. Hippolytus, *Apost. Tradition*, 35, 1, 8, 10 (Dix, 65); *Canones Basilii*, chap. 28 (Riedel, 246); Tertullian, *De oratione*, 13 (CSEL 20, 188 f.).

church. [2] Large basins were placed by the doors of the church or
of the room where the Eucharist was to be celebrated. [3] Hands
could have become soiled in bringing offerings to church. Propriety
demanded that hands be scrupulously clean, for communicants would
receive the Holy Communion on their palms. But there was
another and higher reason for the washing : that of symbolizing
freedom from all stain of sin. [4] The twofold purpose of these
ablutions was probably due to both the Jewish heritage and natural
feeling or instinct. Certainly, the hand that touched the Blessed
Sacrament was to be clean physically and spiritually. Early Christians considered the hand as the principal instrument, the privileged
member in which the strength and activity of the person were
concentrated. Hence the whole person was represented by it. That
is why the outward washing of hands symbolized the internal purification from all that sullied both body and soul. [5] After the custom
of receiving Holy Communion in the hand had been discontinued,
together with that of bringing offerings of bread, wine, or oil to
church, there was no longer any pressing need for the faithful to
wash their hands before Mass.

Whether the celebrant and the other clergy washed their hands
on entering the church is unknown. Good reasons exist for concluding that they did, and other good reasons for presuming that
they did not. In any case, the celebrant and concelebrating priests
washed their hands at the offertory. [6] Its utilitarian purpose and
symbolism, however, were the same as they are today in the rite of

---

[2] Chrysostom, *In Johannem hom.*, 73, 3 (edit. Montfaucon 8, 433 C) : " Then
we wash our hands when we enter into church.... "

[3] Cf. Eusebius, *Eccl. hist.*, 10, 4, 40 (PG 13, 356 BC [*Series graeca*]); Chrysostom,
De verbis Habentes eundem spiritum, 3, 2 (edit. Montfaucon 3, 289 D). Cf. also
Beiseel, *Bilder aus der Geschichte der altchristlichen Kunst und Liturgie in Italien*
(Freiburg, 1899), pp. 254 f.

[4] Cyril of Jerusalem, *Catechesis*, XXIII (*mystag.*, V) 2, (PG 33, 1109) : " The
washing of hands therefore is a symbol of immunity (ἀνυπεύθυνος) from sin. "
Similarly Chrysostom in *In Johannem hom.*, 73, 3 (edit. Montfaucon 8, 433 CD).

[5] The scriptural basis of the handwashing as a sign of innocence was probably
Deut. 21:6, Ps. 72:13, and Matt. 27:24.

[6] Cyril of Jerusalem (*Catecheses XXIII, mystag.*, V, 2 [PG 33, 1109]) places
the washing of hands just before the kiss of peace; so does Ps.-Dionysius the
Areopagite (*De eccles. hierarch.*, 3, 2 [PG 3, 425 D]); the *Apostolic Constitutions*,
VIII, 11, 12 (edit. Funk, 494) gives it after the kiss.

preparation before the Divine Liturgy.   After receiving and handling
the offerings of the people, the deacon, or the celebrant (if no deacon
were present), washed his hands so that they would again be clean.
Yet, from the very beginning, it was the symbolism of spiritual
purity or washing as the " symbol of the purity of souls dedicated
to God, " [7] rather than practical utility that was stressed.   Cyril of
Jerusalem, in fact, emphasizes this mystical sense when he says the
washing of hands " designates the purity and blamelessness of our
actions. "   He seems to exclude its practical utility entirely, " for we
did not come into the *ecclesia* covered with dirt! " [8]   No less does
Chrysostom minimize the outward washing of the hands when he
stresses the cleanliness of the soul that should go with it.   " We wash
our hands when we enter into church, and shall we not wash our
hearts also? " he asks.   " Why?   Is it our hands that speak?   It is
the soul that utters the words; it is to it that God pays attention;
cleanness of the body is of no use, if it [the soul] is defiled... while
we are fearful about trifles, we care not for important matters.   To
pray with unwashed hands is a matter indifferent, but to do it with
an unwashed mind, that is the extreme of all evils. " [9]

Originally, the Byzantine Liturgy and its antecedents also had the
hand-washing at the offertory. [10]   Some time before the eighth or
ninth century, " the Office of Preparation of the Gifts " was transferred from its original position before the offertory to the beginning
of the Liturgy. [11]   The washing of the hands, however, remained
at the offertory until the thirteenth century, when it was transferred

[7] *Apostolic Constitutions*, VIII, 11, 12 (edit. Funk, 494).

[8] Cyril of Jerusalem, *Catecheses*, XXIII (*mystag.*, V), 2 (PG 33, 1109).

[9] Chrysostom, *In Johannem hom.*, 73, e (edit. Montfaucon 8, 433 D).

[10] Theodore of Mopsuestia, *Sermones catech.*, V (Rücker, 25); Ps.-Dionysius
the Areopagite, *De eccles. hierarch.*, III, 2 (PG 3, 425 D); the *Apostolic Constitutions*,
VII (edit. Funk, 494).   The ancient Greek Liturgies of St. James and St. Mark
do not mention the washing of hands at all; since no prayer was prescribed for
the hand-washing in early Christian antiquity, their text understandably would
omit it.

[11] The eighth or ninth century *Codex Barberini*, 336 (Brightman, LEW, pp. 309-
310) is the first Byzantine source to have the prothesis at the beginning of the
Liturgy.   The Armenian version of Chrysostom's Liturgy also had it in the early
eighth century; cf. Aucher, *La versione armena della liturgia di S. Giovanni Crisostomo fatta sul principio dell'VIII secolo*, XPYCOCTOMIKA, pp. 371-373.

to its present position at the beginning of the rite of preparation. [12]

The Slav branch of the Byzantine Rite followed its mother Rite in this. The twelfth and thirteenth century Slav missals still have the washing of the hands associated with the " Bringing in of the Gifts " at the Great Entrance, [13] but those of the next two centuries have it in the present position before the *proskomidia*. [14]

At any rate, the washing of the hands in the rite of preparation still has the same purpose and symbolism as it had in its original place at the offertory. The hands of the priest will touch the very sacrament of the body of Christ, and so they should be clean. But physical purification is not the only purpose. The verses of Psalm 25,

[12] The interpolated *Commentary* of Germanus of Constantinople (PG 98, 424 CD) still has the washing of the hands between the Great Entrance and the Prayer of Offertory. The thirteenth century *Typikon of S. Sabba* from *Codex Athono-Protat.*, 72 (Dmitrievsky, *Opysanie liturgicheskikh rukopisej khraniaschikhsia v bibliotekakh pravoslavnago vostoka*, Vol. III, *Tipika*, part II [St. Petersburg, 1917], p. 117), and the *Constitution* of Philotheus (1376) have it in its present position. In the Esphigmenon Roll of year 1306 (Dmitrievsky, *op. cit.*, Vol. II, *Euchologia* [Kiev, 1901], p. 262) the hands are to be washed " at the beginning of the Liturgy. " The thirteenth century MS. of Panteleimon Monastery (Krasnoseltsev, *Materialy dlja istorii chinoposlidovania liturgii sv. Ioanna Zlatoustago* [Kazan, 1889], pp. 9-10) puts the washing of hands before the veneration of icons, but this is probably a local usage. Although the prothesis is placed before the Divine Liturgy in the *Commentary* of Ps.-Sophronius, no mention is made of hand-washing; whether any mention was made of hand-washing at the offertory cannot be ascertained because of the mutilated condition of the work. Theodore of Andida and Cabasilas (1371) do not refer to the washing of the hands in their commentaries (PG 140, 417-468 and PG 150, 368-492).

[13] E.g., The twelfth century *Sluzhebnyky* of Anthony the Roman and Barlaam of Khutinsk (MSS. Nos. 342 and 343 of Moscow Synodal Library, cf. Gorsky-Nevostrujev, *Opysanie slavianskikh rukopisej Moskovskoj Synodal'noj biblioteky*, Vol. III [Moscow, 1885], 1, 2, 6), and the thirteenth century MSS. Nos. 518 and 524 of Sophia Library (Petrovsky, *Histoire de la rédaction slave de la liturgie de S. Jean Chrysostome*, XPYCOCTOMIKA, p. 875); also the fourteenth century *Molytovnyk-Sluzhebnyk* (edit. P. Kowaliv [New York, 1960], pp. 18-19 of its text, and the fifteenth century *Ustav* in Metropolitan Isidore's *Liturgikon*, MS. *Vat. Slav.*, N. 14, p. 115. Vestiges of this practice are still found in the Pontifical Liturgy when the bishop washes his hands before the Great Entrance. Cf. K. Nikolsky, *Posobie k izucheniu Ustava Bogosluzhenia pravoslavnoi tserkvy* (St. Petersburg, 1907), p. 422, note 2.

[14] E.g., The fourteenth century MS. N. 522 of Sophia Library (Petrovsky, *op. cit.*, p. 879); MS. N. 127 of Moscow Synodal Library, p. 3 (Petrovsky, *op. cit.*, p. 881). While some fifteenth century missals do not mention any hand-washing (e.g., MSS. Nos. 527, 528, and 531 of Sophia Library [Petrovsky, *op. cit.*, p. 897, n. 1], MS. N. 986 of Sinai Library [Dmitrievsky, *op. cit.*, p. 603]), most do either before or after the *proskomidia*, e.g., MSS. Nos. 590 (p. 23) and 544 (p. 66) of Sophia Library (Petrovsky, *op. cit.*, p. 897, n. 1).

which the priest recites during the washing of hands, stress the higher, mystical meaning : spiritual cleanness. He will wash his hands among the innocent; since the hands represent the whole person, the cleansing symbolically encompasses his whole being. In this spotless purity of the innocent, he will serve or " walk around the altar. " In this innocence, he will hear God's praise and recount God's wondrous deeds. The priest loves the beauty of God's house, the dwelling-place of God's glory; he loves it because God lives there. He begs God to save his soul, not to destroy it with the wicked, with men of blood, nor with those whose hands (i.e., whole being) are soiled with all manner of evil. He ends his prayer by reiterating his innocence of which the hand-washing is a symbol, and with the promise to praise the Lord in his assemblies.

The first clear reference to Psalm 25 in connection with the hand-washing in the Byzantine Liturgy comes from the fourteenth century. [15] Does this mean that prior to that century no accompanying prayer was said? The answer cannot be given definitively. Probably most rites had some accompanying formula said out of personal devotion. Cyril of Jerusalem does refer to Psalm 25, *I will wash my hands among the innocent*, in this connection. [16] All the Liturgies have associated some kind of formula with the hand-washing as an expression of purification for service at the altar; [17] to have attained such universality, this need for verbal expression must have been felt at an early period. The Chaldean Nestorian Liturgy, for example, has verse 6 of Psalm 25 at the third hand-washing (before the fraction); [18] the Armenian Liturgy has the same at the hand-washing both in the rite of preparation and at the offertory. [19] The

---

[15] The *Constitution* of Philotheus (1371), cf. Hanssens, *Institutiones liturgicae de ritibus orientalibus, De Missa rituum orientalium*, III (Rome, 1932), p. 10; also MS. N. 127 of Moscow Synodal Library, p. 3, cf. Petrosvky, *op. cit.*, p. 831.

[16] Cyril of Jerusalem, *Catecheses*, XXIII (*mystag.*, V) 2 (PG 33, 1109).

[17] Cf. Hanssens, *op. cit.*, pp. 7-8, for Eastern Liturgies; Jungmann, *The Mass of the Roman Rite*, I, p. 277 (New York : Benziger, 1951), and II, pp. 76-82 (1955), for the Western.

[18] Cf. Brightman, LEW, p. 289; Hanssens, *op. cit.*, III, p. 8.

[19] Brightman, LEW, pp. 415, 432. The early eighth century Armenian version of Chrysostom's Liturgy, however, still has only one washing, at the offertory; its formula was : " I will wash my hands in a holy manner " (Aucher, *op. cit.*, p. 385). The Maronite Liturgy has a similar formula today, accompanying the hand-washing at the offertory : " I will wash my hands in purity " (Hanssens, *op. cit.*, III, p. 8.

Latin Rite's *Lavabo* (Ps. 25:6-12) in its various arrangements traces its roots at least to the ninth century. [20] The Liturgy of the Coptic Jacobites uses verse 6 in combination with Psalm 50:9 just before the prothesis. [21] While the formulae for hand-washing in the Syrian and Ethiopian Liturgies are different, they express the same longing for purification. [22] A common origin alone can explain such universality. Some kind of formula seems to have accompanied the washing of the hands as a devotional option long before any missal prescribed an official prayer.

[20] Cf. Sacramentary of Amiens, which originated in the ninth century (Leroquais, " L'*Ordo missae* du sacramentaire d'Amiens, " *Eph. liturg.*, XLI [1927], 439 f.); also Martène, *De antiquis Ecclesiae ritibus* (2d. ed. [Antwerp, 1736]) 1, 4, VI ff. (I, 528 E; 534 E; 537 E).

[21] Brightman, LEW, p. 145. The Byzantine-Slav Liturgy also used Psalm 50 in connection with the washing of hands during the fourteenth century in some localities (e.g., MS. N. 522 of Sophia Library; cf. Petrovsky, *op. cit.*, p. 879, n. 1).

[22] Cf. Hanssens, *op. cit.*, III, pp. 7-8.

CHAPTER XXII

THE RITUAL PREPARATION
OF THE GIFTS : GENERAL HISTORY

In a church built according to rubrical prescriptions, the *table of preparation* (Greek πρόθεσις, Slav *Proskomedijnyk*) always stands on the northern side of the sanctuary; [1] if not, it still stands on the left side of the sanctuary (as one faces the East, the Latin Gospel side). At this table, the priest performs the *proskomidia*. The word *proskomidia* from the Greek verb προσκομίζειν (" to bring ") means " those things which have been brought " (offerings), or the ritual preparation of the gifts of bread and wine for use in the Eucharistic Sacrifice.

In the very beginnings of the Christian era, when the celebration of the Eucharist was still joined to the common meal, the bread and wine along with the rest of the provisions were brought in by the faithful and placed on the table presumably when it was being set before the meal. There was no special ritual or prayer. After the Eucharist became separated from the common meal, donating the bread and wine and setting them on the altar remained simple acts without ceremony.

To understand the basic evolution and meaning of the prosko-midia, we must go back to the ancient offertory rite. Toward the end of the pre-Nicene era, the terminology of the offertory was already settled. Essentially, it was performed by the bishop (or priest), but deacons and faithful had their part or " liturgy " (service). The " liturgy " of the bishop was to " offer the gifts (προσφέρειν τά δῶρα) of the Holy Church. " [2] The deacon's was to bring up (ἀναφέρειν) " that which was offered (προσφόρα) to thee by thine

---

[1] From the very beginning, Byzantine churches were built with the sanctuary toward the East; the congregation always faces the East when it prays—as did the Christians of the primitive era (see, p. 146). Cf. also Quasten, *Mon.* 35, 184, and Dölger, *Sol salutis, Gebet und Gesang im christlichen altertum* (Münster am W., 1920), 136 ff.

[2] Clement of Rome (I Clem. 44) clearly states that the " bishop's office " is to " offer the gifts " (προσφέρειν τά δῶρα); so does the *Apostolic Tradition*, iii, 4 (cf. Dix, 53 ff.). St. Paul says the same in his Epistle to the Hebrews (5:1).

ordained priest. " [3]   The Council of Ancyra (c. A.D. 314) expresses a long-standing and accepted usage when it says that the bishop is to " offer (προσφέρειν) the oblation (προσφορά)," the deacon to " bring it up " (ἀναφέρειν), and the communicant to " bring it to the church (προσενέγκειν). " [4]   Latin terminological counterparts of the Greek are not as clear, but certainly the " liturgies " of the different classes are easily distinguishable.

The bishop or priest alone is the minister of the offertory, but deacons and faithful are his assistants. The whole rite is a true, corporate offering by the Church in its organic, hierarchic unity. Bishops by their consecration, priests by their ordination, deacons by their orders, and the faithful by the holy character of baptism partake, each in his own special way, in the Church's authentic offering. Only a vivid awareness of the mystical body of Christ in its hierarchic, organic and living totality could explain such clear understanding of each part to be played by the different members of the Ecclesia. Participation in the Liturgy and the reception of Holy Communion were reserved for full members of the Church. [5]

No one knows at what particular point in the pre-Nicene Church the deacons received the offerings of the faithful. This may seem unimportant, yet from it stem some of the greatest differences between Eastern and Western offertory rituals. These differences appear as early as the fifth, or even the fourth century. In the East, the offerings were made before the beginning of the service. The gifts were placed either in a side room or in the church itself on special tables designated for this purpose. [6]   The bread and wine

---

[3] This is the definition of his " liturgy " in the ordination prayer of a deacon in the *Apostolic Tradition*, ix. 11 (see Dix, 17-18 for full prayer).

[4] Canons 1, 2, 3 (Mansi, II, 513 ff., or NPNF, Series II, Vol. XIV, pp. 63-64).

[5] E.g., The Syrian *Didascalia*, IV, 5-8 (Funk, I, 222-228) enjoins bishops and deacons to be on guard from whom they accept the offerings. The gifts of those openly living in sin, i.e., public sinners, thieves, the unchaste, usurers, and even Roman officials who had stained their hands with blood were to be refused. The Council of Ancyra (Can. 5) decreed that suspended laymen, though repentant, may attend the Eucharist but " without the prosphora " (and therefore without communicating); by Canon 2, it decreed that suspended deacons are " to cease from all their holy liturgy, that of presenting the bread or the chalice.... "; NPNF, Series II, Vol. XIV, p. 65 (Can. 5) and p. 63 (Can. 2).

[6] Cf. Fifth century, *Testamentum Domini*, I, 19 (Quasten, *Mon.* 237); *Apostolic Constitutions*, II, 57 (Quasten, 181).

for the Eucharistic Sacrifice were transferred to the altar by the deacons at the offertory (at the beginning of the properly Eucharistic service).   In the West generally (except in the Gallo-Frankish Church), the faithful kept their gifts until the offertory itself, at which time they came forward, either to place them on the designated tables, or to give them directly to the deacons.   Almost immediately, the deacons would take the bread and wine to the altar.

There is no reason why Christians would have deviated from the *chabûrah* custom in the primitive era.   The provisions for the meal, including the bread and probably the wine, would be placed on the table before the meal began. [7]   The difference between Eastern and Western usages seems to have arisen after the Eucharist became separated from the common meal.   Even then, the difference would not have been evident whenever the Eucharist was celebrated without the catechetical synaxis.   The faithful would come into the *ecclesia*, exchange the kiss of peace (as a form of greeting), hand their gifts of bread and wine to the deacons directly or place them on the designated tables, and the offertory would follow immediately.

When the Eucharist was preceded by either the synaxis or baptism, would the faithful hand over their gifts before the synaxis or at the offertory?   Aside from one passage (see below, p. 492), pre-Nicene evidence is silent on the point.   The passing reference to the offertory by Justin, for example, is typically obscure : " bread and a cup of mixed wine and water are brought to the one presiding over the brethren. " [8]   Deacons are not mentioned, but this can be explained on the grounds that this description written for the information of pagans required no details.   But did the faithful bring the gifts before the offertory, as they do in later Western usage, or had they already done it as later Eastern custom dictates?   There is one tenuous clue : before speaking of the offertory, Justin uses the first-person active construction in describing the various events : " We lead him into... so that we who have come to the knowledge of the truth may also... ; " " we greet each other with a kiss, " etc.   Then, abruptly, he switches to the impersonal passive : " Then bread and

---

[7] The wine, if not already on the table, would have been served during the meal.

[8] Justin Martyr, *First Apology*, chap. 65; cf. above, p. 41.

a cup of wine and water mixed are brought to...." This may indicate that the faithful did not bring up the gifts at this point, but had deposited them before the service began, and that someone else (the deacons) brought them up to the celebrant at the offertory. Otherwise, it would have been natural for Justin to have continued the first-person construction : " and we bring up the bread and wine and water mixed. " [9]

The only clear pre-Nicene evidence regarding the reception of the gifts comes from Syria. The *Testamentum Domini* (material from mid-third century) states : " One [of the deacons] should continually stand by the oblations of the Eucharist and the other [deacon] should stand without by the door and observe those who come in. Afterward, when you offer, they should minister together in the church. " [10] The gifts had been handed over to the deacons before the service began, for the deacon was to stand by them. This, however, still leaves many questions unanswered. Was this practice proper to Syria? Or was it universal? Was it a custom of long standing, or a Syrian innovation which later spread to other Eastern Churches? There is no positive evidence pointing in either way, nor do documents of later centuries throw any light on the matter.

In the fifth and sixth centuries, however, doubt no longer exists : Eastern practice differs from Western, and each is widespread. Some have argued that the Western practice originated in or around Rome during the fourth century. This may be, but there is no conclusive evidence. Its use in the fourth and fifth centuries seems to suggest a pre-Nicene origin. [11]

---

[9] The *Apostolic Tradition* of Hippolytus, although the first to describe the offertory in any detail, also leaves this point completely obscure : " To (the bishop) then let the deacons bring up the oblation, and he, with all the presbyters laying his hand on the oblation, shall say..., " etc. Deacons bring up the gifts, but from where? From the tables where the faithful deposited them before the service? Or from the hands of the faithful, who bring them to the chancel at this time? Cf. Dix, 6.

[10] *Testamentum Domini*, I, 19 (Rahmani, 23; Quasten, *Mon.*, 237); cf. also *Didascalia*, IV, 5-8 (Funk, I, 222-228) for discussion outlining the duties of bishops and deacons to watch from whom they accept a gift.

[11] Thus, at Milan during Ambrose's time (*Expos. in Ps. cxviii, Prol.*, 2 [CSEL, LXII, 4]); certainly in fifth-century Africa (Victor of Vita, *Hist. pers. Afric.*, II, 51 [CSEL, VII, 44]). It was traditional in Gaul by A.D. 585 (Council of Macon, Can. 4 [Mansi, IV, 95]). Evidence of this " Western " practice exists in fourth-

In the West, the preparation of the gifts ultimately consisted in the mere placing of the host on the paten and the cruets of wine and water on the credence table, without prayer or ceremony.   In the East, this same preparation developed into the long and complicated *proskomidia (prothesis)* with symbolical anticipation of the immolation of the Lamb of God, the placing on the *diskos* of a number of particles representing the *offerentes* of the Church militant, the Church suffering, and the Church triumphant, and the accompanying magnificent prayers.   The same original difference in the timing of the gifts explains the marked contrast between the present Eastern and Western offertory ritual within the Mass itself.   The Western offertory is simple : the priest pours some wine and a few drops of water into the chalice and makes the offering in silent prayer, while the choir sings a mere verse or two of a psalm and the congregation sits through it all.   The Eastern offertory consists in a complicated ceremonial, the *Great Entrance*.   Preceded by torch and incense bearers, the gifts are carried in procession by the deacon and the priest from the table of preparation, through the iconostas, into the nave of the church, and back into the sanctuary—all of which mystically anticipates the real presence of the Lord in the holy sacrament as the King of all, escorted by unseen angelic hosts. Meanwhile, the Cherubic Hymn is sung by the people who reverently stand at attention or, in some places, prostrate themselves in homage.

Of the many gifts offered by the faithful (oil, grapes, flowers, etc., were also offered, see page 488), only a small portion could be used for the Sacrifice.   Among the chief duties of the deacons was the selection of bread and wine to be consecrated.   Only the finest were chosen.   The rest were set aside with the other gifts for the needs of the clergy and for the poor.   This selection took place immediately before the offertory.   After the fourth century, when congregations had become large and the gifts numerous, this could take time. Therefore, the selection was shifted to the beginning of the Mass,

century Asia Minor (cf. Brightman, LEW, p. 529) and even in Egypt at one time (Brightman, LEW, p. 164), since the Coptic Liturgy still keeps the deacon's thrice-repeated commands for the faithful to bring up their gifts at the former time, at the offertory, although for centuries the preparation of gifts has been made before the Liturgy as the Byzantine Rite has it.

giving rise to the *proskomidia* or *prothesis* of Syro-Byzantine Liturgies. It is not known exactly at what time this shift took place, although it occurred certainly before the end of the eighth century, as shown by documentary evidence, but perhaps not at the same time everywhere. [12] There was nothing to prevent this shift at that time. The catechumenate and the penitential systems had long been abrogated or changed, so that the distinction between the Liturgy of the Catechumens and that of the Faithful had ceased to be important.

At the time of the transference, the *proskomidia* was not the same rich, fully developed ceremonial that it is today. The first Byzantine manuscript to mention it as taking place before the Divine Liturgy contains a single prayer recited by the celebrant while the bread was being placed on the *diskos*. [13] In some localities, at least by the beginning of the ninth century, the sign of the cross was made over the bread with the liturgical lance. [14] But mixing of wine and water was done without any ceremonial. [15] Time brought about much change and development, the history of which concerns the individual prayers and component parts of the *proskomidia*.

[12] E.g., the *Codex Barberini*, *gr.* 336 (Brightman, LEW, pp. 309-310); the *Commentary* of S. Germanus, nn. 20 ff. (edit. N. Borgia, *Il commentario liturgico di s. Germano Patriarca Constantinopolitano e la versione latina di Anastasio Bibliotecario* [Grottaferrata, 1912], pp. 18-20); St. Theodore of Studion, *Explicatio divinae liturgiae praesanctificatorum* (PG 99, 1689 C). Gregory Decapolis in his *Historical Discourse* (A.D. 820) also writes as if the prothesis were a separate action before the beginning of the Divine Liturgy (PG 100, 1201). Since the early eighth century Armenian version of Chrysostom's Liturgy has it before the Divine Liturgy (cf. Aucher, *La versione armena della liturgia di S. Giovanni Crisostomo, fatta sul principio dell'VIII secolo*, XPYCOCTOMIKA, pp. 371-373), it must have been shifted to this position during the seventh century at the latest.

[13] I.e., *Codex Barberini*, *gr.*, 336 (Brightman, LEW, pp. 309-310). A slightly more developed version of the prothesis is found already in the eighth century Armenian Liturgy of Chrysostom. Besides containing the *Prayer of Offering* (almost identical with that of today and found in *Cod. Barberini* in Basil's Liturgy), it has the words, " In memory of our Lord, Jesus Christ " said when the bread is put on the *diskos*. The wine is poured in the form of a cross accompanied with the words : " Through the memory of the salutary economy of our Lord God and Saviour Jesus Christ. " After the *Prayer of Offering*, the Gifts are incensed, While incensing, the priest recites : " The Lord is King and He is robed in majesty. etc. " and a prayer identical with that said by the priest today in blessing the incense (cf. Aucher, *op. cit.*, pp. 372-373).

[14] Cf. Theodore of Studion, *Adv. iconomachas*, I (PG 99, 489).

[15] In fact, Nicephorus I, Patriarch of Constantinople (806-815) forbids his priests to make the sign of the cross over the chalice; cf. I. B. Pitra, *Iuris Eccl. Graecorum historia et monumenta*, Vol. II (Rome, 1868), p. 330.

CHAPTER XXIII

THE PREPARATION
OF THE MAIN BREAD, THE LAMB

T*he priest and deacon begin the* proskomidia *by making three small bows before the table of preparation and both say :*

O God, be merciful to me a sinner (Luke 18:13).

You have redeemed us from the curse of the Law (Gal. 3:13) **by your precious blood. Nailed to the cross and pierced with a lance, you have bestowed immortality upon men. Our Saviour, glory be to you.**

The prelude is a plea to God for mercy in the words of the publican in the Gospel parable. Though brief, this prayer is full of the pathos of a sinful but humble man deeply conscious of his guilt. What justified the publican, i.e., "made him right" (with God), δεδικαιωμένος, [1] was probably not the words themselves, but his humble spirit and deeply felt need. Christ chose his opposite carefully, the vainly complacent Pharisee. The name *Perushim* ("the separated ones") signifies a class apart because of its deep and genuine piety. By our Lord's time, the majority of the Pharisees had become proud, self-righteous hypocrites. Josephus describes them as "a sect of Jews who esteemed themselves more religious than others and thought their interpretation of the Law more accurate." [2] The Pharisee's prayer also typifies his spirit. In contrast, the Publican beats his breast repeatedly and expresses his dire need of divine mercy. Justification can be attained only by a contrite and humble spirit.

There are passages of the Scriptures easier to understand than Paul's "curse of the Law," mentioned in the next prayer. Its meaning must be gleaned from the whole context of Gal. 3:10-14. Those, he says, who rely solely on the deeds prescribed by the Law

---

[1] It relates to "trusted in themselves as just" of verse 9 in same chapter (Luke 18).

[2] Cf. J. Bonsirven, *Judaïsme palestinien au temps de J. C.*, I (Paris, 1934), 5, 2.

are under a curse, and he quotes Deuteronomy 27:26 to prove it. His argument is elliptical. He presupposes that no human can perfectly and at all times observe all the prescriptions of the Law if left to his own resources. God can bestow the necessary aid but the Law itself does not have, nor did it offer, such aid for man. Therefore, left to his own strength and to mere Law, man is doomed to fail and thus to fall under the curse leveled against transgressors. The Law could only reveal the deficiences of human conduct; it could not cure them nor atone for them. Christ's redemption has freed man from this curse not only by taking away all value from legal observances but by actually atoning for all of mankind's transgressions. His redemption, accomplished by his Passion and death (the shedding of his precious blood, by being nailed to the cross, being pierced with a lance) gives immortality, eternal life, to man. The prayer ends by glorifying the Saviour who accomplished all this.

After this prayer, the deacon says :

Bless, sir.

Priest : **Blessed be our God at all times, now and always and for ever and ever.**

Deacon : **Amen.**

Taking the prosphora *(a small loaf) into his left hand and the* kopia *or lance into his right, the priest makes the sign of the cross with it over the bread; this he does three times, and each time he repeats the words :*

In remembrance of our Lord and God and Saviour, Jesus Christ.

Thrusting the lance into the right side of the imprint on top of the loaf, he cuts it and says :

He was led as a sheep to the slaughter (Isaiah 53:7).

Then he cuts the left side and says :

And as a spotless lamb is silent before his shearers, so he did not open his mouth (Isaiah 53:7).

As he cuts the upper side, he says :

In his humiliation his judgment was taken away (Acts 8:33).

Then, cutting the lower side, he says :

Who shall indeed describe his generation? (Isaiah 53:8).

In the meantime the deacon, reverently looking on and holding his orar *in his right hand, says at each incision :*

Let us pray to the Lord.

When the priest finishes cutting the four sides, the deacon says :

Lift up, sir.

The priest thrusts the lance sideways into the bread and cuts off the crust at the bottom ; then, lifting out the cube of bread with the inscription on top, he says :

For his life shall be taken away from the earth (Acts 8:33).

He lays the bread on the diskos *with the inscription downward, while the deacon says :*

Sacrifice, sir.

As the priest cuts the sign of the cross into the bread, he says :

The Lamb of God who takes away the sin of the world is sacrificed for the life and salvation of the world (John 1:29).

While the priest turns the bread over, the deacon says :

Pierce, sir.

The priest pierces the holy bread with the lance in the upper-right corner where the letters IC are imprinted ; as he does this, he says :

One of the soldiers pierced his side with a lance and immediately there came forth blood and water. And he who saw it bore witness, and his testimony is true (John 19:34-35).

Unlike the Latin priest who uses precut, dried hosts of unleavened bread for Mass, the Byzantine priest cuts out the hosts from small loaves of fresh, leavened bread for each Eucharistic Liturgy during the *proskomidia*. These small loaves of bread are called by their ancient name, *prosphory* (sing. *prosphora*). Five are used (one for the large host, and the others for the small hosts) to represent the five loaves with which Christ fed the Five Thousand People. [3]

The word *prosphora* derives from the Greek word for *offering* (see above, p. 65), and that is just what these loaves of bread were in ancient times, the bread which the priest offered in the Eucharistic Sacrifice. [4] The bread which Christ used at the Last Supper must have been unleavened, since the Last Supper, a paschal meal, was celebrated on the " feast of the Azymes, " i.e. " of the unleavened bread. " [5] If our Lord celebrated the paschal supper at all he would have used unleavened bread. [6] The Gospel accounts simply call it ἄρτος, a word which means either leavened or unleavened bread. In any case, the Apostles did not attach any importance to this particular paschal practice of using only unleavened bread, for both kinds of bread were considered lawful matter for the Eucharist from the earliest times. If anything, leavened bread probably was used more frequently for the simple reason that it was more readily available to the early Christians. The faithful merely took bread from their household supply and brought it to the Eucharistic service. [7] From pictorial illustrations and written accounts, we

---

[3] The use of precut " dried hosts " is absolutely forbidden; the bread must be fresh. The Russians almost always use five loaves when they celebrate the Liturgy with more solemn ceremony. The Old Believers use seven, a practice dating back at least to 1100 when the *Typikon* of Empress Irene ordered that seven loaves be used (PG 127, 1056). The Ruthenians have traditionally used five loaves, but can use three or even one. The most recent tendency among the Ruthenians is to use one and the same loaf for several Liturgies; this was officially permitted by a Circular Letter of the Sacred Congregation for the Oriental Church, Sept. 10, 1941, to the Protoarchimandrite of the Basilians and to the Rector of the Ruthenian College in Rome, *Prot.* N. 1219/28. Cf. *Ordo Celebrationis (iuxta recensionem Ruthenorum)*, Rome, 1941, p. 47, n. 98.

[4] Technically, the word προσφορά or προσφέρειν, its verbal form, is now used to denote any of the three presentations or offerings : (1) by the layman to the priest, (2) by the deacons to the priest or bishop at the Great Entrance, and (3) by the priest or bishop to God during the *anaphora*.

[5] While the " feast of the Azymes " was celebrated during the whole week from the evening of the 14th Nisan to the evening of 21st Nisan, the term was applied in particular to the first day of the week's feast, that is, from sunset 14th Nisan to sunset 15th Nisan.

[6] Christ and the Galilean pilgrims probably celebrated the paschal supper on the day before the Jerusalemites (for John 18:28 clearly indicates that Christ's enemies celebrated their paschal supper on the evening of the following day, Friday). Even so, it would have been with unleavened bread, unless Christ would have deviated from paschal custom. This is conceivable but unlikely.

[7] The finest loaves were selected.

know that the Eucharistic loaves did not differ from those used in
the home. [8]

Among the various shapes used by the Romans for domestic use
were small round loaves bearing two crossed incisions *(panis decus-
tus, panis quadratus)*. The early Christians gave preference to this
type of loaf for Eucharistic use because they saw the image of the
cross in the incisions. [9] The original purpose of these incisions—to
facilitate division—also lent itself to Christian use.

Until the seventh century, ecclesiastical writers never concerned
themselves with the distinction between leavened and unleavened
bread in the Sacrifice. From that time on, in the West, unleavened
bread gradually came to be preferred. [10] The custom spread until
the ninth century, when some local churches imposed the exclusive
use of unleavened bread. [11] Even so, it was not until about the
middle of the eleventh century that the use of unleavened bread was
universally established. The Byzantine Church showed equally
strong preference for leavened bread from the sixth century on. Too
much has been made of the different usages. During the first ten
centuries, no dispute ever arose between East and West. [12] The
Councils never raised the question. Writers never disputed it.
Even Photius, so eager to find matters for contention with the
Latins, is silent about it. The first dispute occurred in the middle
of the eleventh century, under circumstances which make it look
like a pretext for schism created by Michael Cerularius. [13] In 1439,
the Council of Florence declared both uses legitimate. [14] Not all
Eastern Rites use leavened bread even now, though most of them do
(see above, chap. XIV, for particulars).

---

[8] Cf. Dölger, *Antike u. Christentum*, I (1929), 1-46; also R. M. Wooley, *The
Bread of the Eucharist* (London, 1913).

[9] *Ibid.*, 39-43. Two Ravenna mosaics, however, picture the bread shaped
into a twisted, braid-like circlet or crown. Gregory the Great refers to this corona-
shaped bread (*Dial.*, IV, 55 [PL 77, 417 B]).

[10] Cf. A. Michel, *Byzant. Zeitschrift*, 36 (1936), 119 f.

[11] Alcuin, *Ep.*, 69 (PL 100, 289); Rabanus Maurus, *De inst. cler.*, I, 31 (PL 107,
318 D). Cf. F. Cabrol, " Azymes, " DACL I, 3254-3260.

[12] During that period, however, the use of leaven had been the subject of a
dispute between the Byzantine and the Armenian Churches.

[13] Cf. A. Michel, *Humbert und Kerullarius*, II (Paderborn, 1930).

[14] Denzinger-Umberg, n. 693.

When unleavened bread began to supplant leavened bread in the West, the faithful gradually discontinued providing it. In the East, out of reverence for the Blessed Sacrament, the making of altar bread was entrusted to the clergy alone. [15] It was made sometimes by sacristans, but almost never by women. [16] Countless documents from almost every one of the Eastern Churches stress the care to be exercised in the making and baking of altar bread, and its freshness.

A vestige of the ancient custom has remained in many churches in Russia on major feasts : before the Divine Liturgy, the faithful give loaves of wheat bread to the priest, who takes a small piece of each and puts it on the *diskos*, for the intentions of the giver.

The word *prosphora* has generally come to mean only the small loaf of wheat bread from which the hosts are cut. On top of this small loaf is an impression made before baking, using a bread-stamp showing a cross with the inscription IC XC NI KA. [17]

These letters are an abbreviation of the Greek works 'IHCOY̆C XPICTÓC, and NIKÁ, meaning, *Jesus* (IC) *Christ* (XC) *conquers* (NIKA). The explanation generally given is that this " seal "

[15] E.g., for the Armenians, cf. the Canons of Sion I (eighth century), Canon 12 (A. Mai, SVNC, X, ii, p. 308); for the Chaldeans, cf. John V Bar Abgarus (patri-arch, 900-905), Canon 3, (BO III, p. 239); *ibid.*, Canon 5, p. 240; for the Copts, cf. Cyril III Ibn Laclac (Coptic patriarch, 1235-1243), *Constitutions* (E. Renaudot, LOC, I, p. 172); for the Ethiopians, cf. Emmanuel d'Almeida, *Historia de Ethiopia*, I, VI (edit. C. Beccari), Vol. VI, p. 162, etc.

[16] In North America, the Ruthenians allow nuns to bake the Eucharistic bread.

[17] The Russian and Ukrainian Orthodox have an identical imprint. That of the Old Believers or Old Ritualists consists in a cross around which are the words, " This is the Lamb of God who taketh away the sins of the world. " This was the imprint of the whole Russian Orthodox Church before the reform of Patriarch Nikon in 1655.

represents the sign that Constantine the Great saw in the heavens :
a flaming cross bearing the inscription *In hoc signo vinces* (" In this
sign thou shalt conquer "). Under the standard of the cross, Constantine vanquished the army of Maxentius beneath the very walls
of Rome and entered the city in triumph. There is, however, no
historical evidence concerning the time of its first use on altar breads.
Pagans often stamped their bread with symbols or inscriptions.
A bread-stamp dating from the fourth-fifth century, evidently
Christian, has a superimposed XP symbol. [18] This could have been
used for the Eucharist, but it could equally have been for purely
domestic use. In the following centuries, Eucharistic bread was
probably imprinted in various ways, generally with some form of
cross. [19] The first references in the Byzantine Liturgy to an imprint
or " seal " date from the eleventh century. [20]

Since the very beginning, the preparation of the bread and wine
was the function of the deacon. The celebrant would prepare them
only if he were alone. [21] The deacon mixed the wine and water in
the chalice, and in the Church of Constantinople, he cut the host out
of the loaf and placed it on the *diskos* (paten) after cutting it crosswise. The covering of the gifts and the prayer of offering were
reserved to the priest. [22] At present, the whole rite of preparation
is performed by the priest, even when he is assisted by a deacon.
The change probably took place in the fifteenth century or just

---

[18] Dölger, *Antike und Christentum,* 1 (1929), 17-20.

[19] *Ibid.,* 21-29.

[20] Cf. Nicolas Grammaticus, Patriarch of Constantinople (1084-1111); cf.
A. S. Pavlov, *Nomokanon pry bolshem trebnyku,* p. 411; also *Ad Paulum Hypopsephium Gallipolitanum,* written by an anonymous Patriarch of Constantinople of
the eleventh century (in Mai, NPB, X, ii, p. 166).

[21] Thus even up to the twelfth century, it was the deacon who was charged
with performing the *proskomidia.* This is attested, for example, by the Missal
of Barlaam of Khutinsk (twelfth century), MS. of the Synodal Library of Moscow,
N. 343; cf. Gorsky-Nevostrujev, *Opysanie slavianskikh rukopisej Moskovskoj
Synodal'noj biblioteky,* III (Moscow, 1859), 1, 6; so also a twelfth century MS. of
the Studion which states, " the deacon... celebrates the *proskomidia,* " MS. of
the Synodal Library of Moscow, N. 380, Gorsky-Nevostrujev, *op. cit.,* p. 248.

[22] This is attested by several authors, e.g., the interpolator of the *Commentary*
of St. Germanus of Constantinople (PG 98, 397 D-400 A); Theodore of Andida
(thirteenth century) in his *Commentaria liturgica,* 10 (PG 140, 429 BC); likewise,
the eleventh century Liturgy of St. John Chrysostom, translated by Leo Thuscus,
Liturgiae sive missae sanctorum patrum (Paris, 1560), p. 52.

before, since Arcudius tells us that Simeon of Thessalonica ruled that " the deacons must not offer the particles, for they do not have the grace of offering to God. " [23]

As already indicated, the priest, after taking the *prosphora* into his hand to cut out the large host, first makes the sign of the cross with the liturgical lance or *kopia* over it. Every time he does so, he repeats the prayer : " In remembrance of our Lord and God and Saviour, Jesus Christ. " An almost identical rubric is shown in an eleventh- or tenth-century description of the *proskomidia*. [24]

With these words, the priest emphasizes the fact that the transubstantiation will occur precisely because of Christ, that the power and words of the consecration will be exercised in virtue of Christ's commission to the apostles at the Last Supper when he said : " Do this for a commemoration of me " (Luke 22:19).

Then the priest cuts the bread on the four sides, first the right, then the left, then the top, and finally the bottom. While doing so, he recites some of the prophecies of Isaiah concerning the passion and death of Christ (Isa. 53:7-8). St. Philip quoted the same passage to the eunuch, as recounted by St. Luke in the Acts of the Apostles (8:32-33). In fact, the words as used in the rite of preparation were probably taken from the Acts as quoted from Isaiah.

The coming of the Messiah and his death were foretold by the prophets hundreds of years before the actual events. These same prophetical words introduce the Eucharistic Liturgy, which is an unbloody commemoration of the passion.

" He was led as a sheep to the slaughter " (Isa. 53:7). This pro-

---

[23] Arcudius, *De concordia Ecclesiae occidentalis et orientalis in septem sacramentorum administratione*, I. III, chap. 17, pp. 180 f.

[24] " Therefore, the priest or the deacon... when he approaches the holy *prothesis* and takes the sacred bread into his hand and with the other the lance... with devotion and faith, signs the bread thrice in the form of the cross with the lance, exclaiming : ' (In) the name of our Lord and God and Saviour, Jesus Christ, who has been sacrificed for the salvation of the world. ' " This rubric is found in the document *Ad Paulum Hypopsephium Gallipolitanum*, written by an unknown Patriarch of Constantinople of the eleventh century (edit. A. Mai [A. Rocchi], NPB, X, ii, pp. 166-169.) The translation is ours.

At least two centuries before this, Theodore of Studion mentions the custom of tracing the sign of the cross over the bread with the liturgical lance. Cf. n. 14, p. 259, above.

phecy was fulfilled when Christ was led unprotesting to his death.

"And as a spotless lamb is silent before his shearers, so he did not open his mouth" (Isa. 53:7). At the house of Caiphas, where the first trial of Christ was held, the chief priests and the whole council brought in many false witnesses to testify against Jesus so that they might put him to death. "But Jesus held his peace," as Matthew is careful to point out (Matt. 26:63). Thus also, Christ "answered nothing" (Luke 23:9) to the many questions of Herod. After the cowardice of Pilate was revealed in that he had the innocent Jesus scourged and mocked by the soldiers, Jesus refused to answer him, as St. John tells us : "But Jesus gave him no answer" (John 19:9). Indeed, the Lamb of God was uncomplaining in all that they did to him during his passion.

"In his humiliation his judgment was taken away" (Acts. 8:33; Isa. 53:8). The meaning perhaps is better understood if this is rendered : "In his humiliation, justice was denied him." There was no greater humiliation in the history of mankind than in Christ, for in him God himself was spat upon, mocked, and suffered what was then considered the most shameful death, crucifixion on a cross, a death reserved for the lowest criminals. This was also the most shameful travesty of justice that man had known, for not only was the God-man Christ completely innocent but, being God, he could do no evil!

"Who shall indeed describe his generation?" (Isa. 53:8). This passage is difficult to explain. If we take "generation" as "begetting" or in the sense of ancestry as a single stage in the succession of natural descent, the Jews certainly did not know the generation of Christ, because he is begotten by the Father in heaven without a mother, and on earth he was conceived in time by a mother but without a human father. In the Gospel we read : "Is not this the carpenter, the son of Mary, the brother of James and Joseph and Jude and Simon? Are not also his sisters here with us? And they were scandalized in regard to him" (Mark 6:3). Hence, most Jews had not even an inkling of his true generation, or refused to believe it. This whole explanation is unacceptable because the Hebrew *dôr* cannot indicate the act of generating, the eternal or temporal generation of Christ, since it usually means " generation " in the sense of a lifetime or a group of contemporaries, as, for instance, in the expression " this modern generation. "

The rest of the sentence from the Acts would seem to give a hint of the true explanation, " for his life shall be taken away from the earth " (Acts. 8:33), or as Isaiah has it, " Because he is cut off out of the land of the living " (Isa. 53:8). The translation would then be : " Who can describe the wickedness of his generation, which has taken his life ? "

After cutting the four sides, the priest then cuts sideways into the loaf and lifts out the square piece or cube of bread bearing the imprint, and says : " For his life shall be taken away from the earth. " In other words, the earthly life of the Messiah was to be shortened by violent death; the Messiah would be killed, his life would be taken, or as Isaiah put it, " he is cut off out of the land of the living. " In the Divine Liturgy, of which the *proskomidia* is a preparation, Christ will also die in an unbloody manner. In the *proskomidia*, then, the priest acts as a prophet of the unbloody death of Christ to be re-enacted in the Eucharistic Sacrifice.

With minor exceptions, this part of the *proskomidia* remained unchanged for over a thousand years, as is evident from a description written between A.D. 867 and 886 : " Thereupon, the priest, after receiving the *prosphora* on the *diskos* from the deacon or subdeacon, takes the lance and cleanses it. Then, after marking it [the *prosphora*] with the sign of the cross, he says : " As a sheep going to the slaughter... is dumb...." Then, after putting the bread on the *diskos*, he adds, while pointing with his finger : ' So he opened not his mouth... his life is taken away from the earth. ' [25]

When the priest has cut out the center cube bearing the inscription IC XC NIKA, he places it on the *diskos* with the inscription down. This will be the large host for the Eucharistic Sacrifice. In Greek, it is called ὁ ἅγιος (ἄρτος), the *holy (bread)*, in Slavonic

---

[25] From the interpolated text of the *Commentary* of St. Germanus, as translated into the Latin by Anastasius Bibliothecarius (edit. N. Borgia, *Il commentario liturgico di S. Germano Patriarca Constantinopolitano e la versione latina di Anastasio Bibliotecario* [Grottaferrata, 1912], p. 20). The translation from the Anastasian version is ours.

ahnets, the *lamb,* an expression borrowed from the Scriptures. St. John in his mystical Apocalypse calls the Son of God a *lamb* about twenty-seven times. In his Gospel, he specifically includes the testimony of the Baptist who revealed Christ as the *Lamb of God.* " Look, " he said, " there is the Lamb of God who takes away the sin of the world " (John 1:29). The full meaning of the expression implied victimhood, for only thus could Jesus take away sin. In the Old Law, a lamb was offered in the Temple for the sins of the people both in the morning and in the evening. If the memory of this practice failed to suggest the victim-image of Christ as the Lamb of God, then surely the prophecy of Isaiah (53:7) would be clear. The paschal lamb prefigured Christ very specially. God commanded the Israelites to kill an unblemished lamb and sprinkle its blood over the doorposts so that the avenging angel would " pass over " the houses thus marked (Exod. 12). The blood of the lamb saved the firstborn of the Israelites from the avenging angel. Mankind was saved from a more terrible fate by the " blood of Christ, that unblemished and spotless Lamb " (I Pet. 1:19). In the Divine Liturgy, the bread and wine will be changed into the body and blood of Christ and offered as the Victim-Sacrifice of the New Law. With every reason, therefore, the Eucharistic Bread can be called the *lamb,* the *ahnets.* Even in the *proskomidia,* before it becomes the Eucharistic Christ, the main host is called the *lamb* because of what is to come. The *proskomidia* rite prepares, prophesies, and prefigures what will take place in the Eucharistic Sacrifice just as the Old Testament was a time of preparation, prophecy, and prefiguration as regards the historical events of the redemption. The role of sacrificial lamb in the Old Law was the same as that of the *ahnets* in the *proskomidia;* prefiguring the Lamb of God who takes away the sin of the world. The prophecies of Isaiah apply in both instances.

The *proskomidia* carries the prophetic imagery further by act and word in the next action of the priest : with the liturgical lance the priest now cuts the sign of the cross into the *ahnets* (by making two deep incisions crosswise, thus cutting the host into four equal parts). While making the incisions, he says : " The Lamb of God who takes away the sin of the world is sacrificed for the life and salvation of

the world. " Here is prophecy in liturgical action relative to the
Eucharistic Sacrifice : the bread, which is still not the Eucharist, is
called the Lamb of God sacrificed for mankind. A definite sense
of immolation and sacrifice is present already in the words of the
deacon when he says, " Sacrifice, sir. " In a vivid, graphic way,
the cutting of the cross into the bread prefigures the unbloody
Sacrifice of the Eucharistic Lamb that will not only be present on
the altar but will truly be immolated. The celebrant, no less than
St. John when he wrote the Apocalypse, beholds in mystical ecstasy
Jesus as the Lamb that was slain, that purchased souls for God out
of all tribes and nations, that washed them clean in his blood. From
this bread, from this *ahnets*, will stream forth blessing, grace, salvation, and redemption.

This sense of oblation and immolation of the Lamb was present
in the eighth century, at which early time the incisions in the bread
were already being made during the *proskomidia* rite. [26]   St. Gregory
the Decapolitan refers to this some time before A.D. 820 when he
tells of the Saracen miracle. [27]   No one knows at what period in
history the words were added to this ritual, but they certainly date
back to the eleventh if not the tenth century. [28]

The host is turned over and the priest pierces it with the lance in
the upper-right corner, where the letters IC are imprinted, while
saying : " One of the soldiers pierced his side with a lance, " etc. [29]

[26] Cf. Germanus of Constantinople, *Commentary*, Nos. 20, 30 (edit. N. Borgia,
op. cit., pp. 19-20, 28).   The sense of immolation is evident also in the eighth or
ninth century *Codex Barberini*, gr. 336 (Brightman, LEW, p. 309) whose prayer
of the *poskomidia* calls the bread " the immaculate lamb sacrificed for the welfare
of the world. "

[27] Gregory the Decapolitan, *Sermone historico* (PG 100, 1201 C-1203 C).

[28] We know this from the following description of the rite contained in the
document, *Ad Paulum Hypopsephium Gallipolitanum* (edit. A. Mai, NPB, X, ii,
pp. 166-169) : " Afterwards, they put down the particle cut out by hand in such
a way that its fleshy part is showing and with the sacred lance they make an incision
[in it] in the form of a cross, saying, ' Sacrificed is the Lamb of God, who takes
away the sin of the world. '   Then they lay the bread on the diskos, but turned
over, the fleshy part beneath, the seal on top. "   The translation is ours.

[29] The words " there came forth from his side blood and water, and he who
saw it bore witness, and his testimony is true " were found in the ninth-century
proskomidia, but they were said by the priest when the deacon poured wine and
water into the chalice (cf. the Anastasian version of interpolated *Commentary* of
St. Germanus, edit. N. Borgia, *op. cit.*, p. 20).   This would indicate that the piercing of the large host was introduced into the rite some time later.   The same
symbolical sense, however, held true.

These words are taken from St. John's account of the Passion and death of Christ (John 19:34-35). St. John reports the facts as he saw them on Calvary, and here he specifically states that he saw the piercing of Christ's side. The usual Roman practice was the *crurifragium* or the breaking of the legs with a hammer or club to bring about immediate death, and shorten the suffering of dying men. In the case of Jesus, the soldiers came under orders to hasten his death at the request of the Jews, who feared that the Passover might begin before the crucified men were dead and removed, which would have constituted a legal impurity for the whole city.

When the soldiers came, they broke the legs of the two robbers, but when they found Jesus already dead, one of the soldiers thrust his lance into his side, to make certain that he was dead. Thus it was that the prophecies of the Scriptures were fulfilled almost as if by accident. It was foretold, as St. John is careful to point out, that " they shall look on him whom they pierced " and " you shall not break a bone of him " (John 19:36). The former is in Zechariah (Zech. 12:10), the latter, in Exodus (12:46) and the book of Numbers (9:12), which concern themselves directly with the paschal lamb and indirectly with Christ himself.

The piercing of the bread with the liturgical lance has its obvious symbolism, as had the actual piercing of Christ's side on Calvary. In the *proskomidia*, the lance thrust is once more prophecy in action as regards the forthcoming Sacrifice.

CHAPTER XXIV

THE POURING OF WINE AND WATER

*A*s *soon as the priest has pierced the host, the deacon takes the cruets of wine and water and says to the priest :*

Sir, bless the holy union.

The priest blesses the cruets. Either he or the deacon pours wine into the chalice and adds a little water.

John the Apostle saw what happened on Golgotha. He was there. When one of the soldiers opened the side of Jesus with his spear, " immediately there came out blood and water " (John 19:34). The piercing and the outpouring were phases of the same event. In the *Proskomidia* the *ahnets bread* is pierced, and immediately wine and water are poured into the chalice. Forming one complete whole, both liturgical actions portray what John described as happening at the crucifixion, except that in the *proskomidia* rite, it is still in the realm of prophecy relative to the Eucharistic Sacrifice.

To the Fathers of the Church, the stream of blood and water was providential, full of mystical meaning, symbolic of all the blessings and graces streaming upon mankind by the power of Christ's Passion and death. The water symbolized baptism, which washes away all stain of sin and the blood, and also the Eucharist, the life-giving fountain of reconciliation and the food of eternal life. [1] Baptism is the beginning and the Eucharist the complement of all the other sacraments; hence, all the sacraments are mystically represented here in baptism and the Eucharist. The sacraments derive the fullness of grace and power from the sacrificial death of Christ expressed in the outpouring of the blood and water from his side.

The Fathers also saw in the pierced side of Jesus the divine origin of the Church when they said that from the opened side of the second Adam, sleeping in death on the cross, was formed and came forth the new Eve (the Church). The reason for this is that the Church,

---

[1] Thus, Chrysostom, *Hom.* 85 *in Io.*, 3 (edit. Montfaucon 8, 507 DE); Canon 32 of Council in Trullo (Mansi II, 956-957).

as symbolized by the outpouring of the blood and water from the side of Christ, is the only lawful possessor and administrator of the sacraments by virtue of which it is ever undergoing purification and sanctification in its members.

There is further symbolism contained in the commingling of the wine and water in the chalice : the mystical relationship of Christ with his Church. Christ is represented by the wine, and the members of the Church, by the water. This symbolism probably originated in the earliest days of the Church, for St. John, writing the Apocalyse some sixty-four years after Christ's ascension, already spoke of the water which he saw as a figure of the nations. [2] Since the drops of water are mixed into the wine and diffused in it, they merge with the wine and take on its qualities, all of which will later be transformed into the blood of Christ. So also the members of the Church are incorporated into Christ. This belief echoes the words of St. Peter (II Pet. 1:4), that we may be made partakers of the divine nature. This same mystery, taught by many of the early Fathers, [3] is beautifully expressed by Cyprian in his letter to Caecilius :

> For since Christ who bore our sins, bore us all, we see that the water represents the people, but the wine signifies the blood of Christ. When the water is mixed with the wine in the cup, the people are united to Christ : the believing nation is joined and united to Him in whom it had believed. This mingling and union of the water and wine in the Lord's chalice are effected in such a way that the elements can no longer be separated from one another; so also nothing can separate the Church, that is, the people formed into the Church and faithfully, firmly persevering in its faith, from Christ. [4]

Still another mystical meaning is expressed by the commingling of the water and wine : the union of the divine and human natures

---

[2] Rev. 17:15. This symbolical interpretation is one of the reasons given by the Council of Trent (Sess. 22, 7) for the admixture of water to the wine (cf. Denzinger, 945).

[3] Irenaeus (A.D. 202), *Adv. haer.*, 5, 2, 3 (PG 7, 1125 B); Clement of Alexandria, *Paedagogus*, 2, 2 (PG 8, 409 f.); Chrysostom, *Hom. 46 in Io.*, 3 (edit. Montfaucon 8, 272 D-273 C); Gregory of Nyssa, *Oratio catechetica*, 37 (PG 45, 96 BC).

[4] Cyprian, *Ep. 62 ad Caecilium*, 13 (PL 4, 383-384).

in one Person, the incarnate Son of God. This interpretation arose in the Orient where its roots are firmly embedded in the christological strife against Monophysitism, the heretical belief that there is but one nature, the divine, in Christ. [5] It is mostly for this reason that the Armenian Church, after accepting Monophysitism, rejected the admixture of water into the wine—and this, as far back as the sixth century, certainly before A.D. 632. [6] This same point has remained an obstacle to union not only with Rome, but also with the Byzantine Church. [7] This selfsame symbolism with all its implications had led the Catholic Armenians to carefully maintain the mixing.

Did the custom come about for the sole purpose of symbolism? Probably not. The practice was carried out from the earliest days of the Church. At the Last Supper, Jesus consecrated wine mixed with water. [8] Palestinian Jews added water to their wine at all their meals, including the paschal supper. This custom, a Greek import rather than Palestinian, was nevertheless universally practiced in Palestine during Christ's time. [9] That this was the usage of the Church from the earliest times is clear from the testimony of the early writers and Fathers. Justin mentions it twice, Irenaeus and Clement of Alexandria repeat it, Pope Julius I in writing to the bishops of Egypt presupposes it. [10] Almost all the Eastern Liturgies tell of Christ mixing water with the wine before the consecration; for example, the Clementine Liturgy of the *Apostolic Constitutions*,

---

[5] Euthymius Zigabenus, *Panoplia dogmat.*, tit. XXIII (PG 130, 1184); Isaac, *Oratio invectiva contra Armen.*, I (PG 132, 1176 BC); Simeon of Thessalonica, *Dialogus*, chap. 93 (PG 155, 276 B).

[6] Cf. Hanssens, *Institutiones liturgicae de ritibus orientalibus, De Missa rituum orientalium*, II (Rome, 1930), pp. 250-271.

[7] The mingling of the water with wine is not *de necessitate sacramenti neque praecepti divini* but only *de necessitate praecepti ecclesiastici, i.e., apostolici*; hence, in itself the mere admixture of water to the wine would not have been such an insurmountable obstacle to union had it not been for theological considerations which have been annexed to this practice in the Orient.

[8] Cf. G. Beer, *Pesachim (Ostern) Text, Übersetzung und Erklärung. Nebst einem textkritischen Anhang* (Giessen, 1912), pp. 71-72, 106.

[9] However, cf. Prov. 9:2, 5; Rev. 18:6; Deut. 32:14; also Beer, *ibid.*, pp. 71-72.

[10] Justin, *First Apology*, chaps. 65-67 (cf. however, F. X. Funk, " Die Abendmahlselemente bei Justin," T.Q., 74 [1892], pp. 643-659). Irenaeus, *Adv. haeres.*, I, 13, 2 (PG 7, 580); IV, 33, 2 (PG 7, 1073 B); V, 2, 3 (PG 7, 1125 B); Clement of Alexandria, *Paedagogus*, II, 2 (PG 8, 409 f.); Pope Julius I (337-352), *Epistula ad episcopos per Ægyptum* (PL 8, 970 B-D).

the Greek anaphora of St. James, the anaphora of St. Basil, etc. [11]
The clergy in celebrating the Eucharistic Mysteries would not
deviate from what they believed was a practice established by Christ
himself. [12]

Most of the Catholic Orientals add somewhat more water to the
wine than do the Latins. Yet, they are conforming with the rule of
the Council of Florence, which states that " a little water " is to be
added to the wine. [13]   The practice of dissident Eastern Churches
is difficult to assess.   The rule followed in most Russian churches,
for example, is that of the *Ustav* : the amount of water to be added

---

[11] The Clementine Liturgy, Book VIII, 12, 37 (edit. F. X. Funk, *Didascalia et
Constitutiones Apostolorum*, I [Paderborn, 1905], p. 508) has : " In like manner
also the chalice; he mixed it of wine and water and sanctified it and gave to them,
saying : Drink ye all of this.... "   The Greek Anaphora of St. James (cf. Brightman, LEW, p. 52) : " In like manner after he had supped, when he took the chalice
and mixed the wine and water.... "   The Byzantine St. Basil (cf. Brightman,
LEW, p. 328) puts it : " Likewise taking the chalice of the fruit of the vine and,
when he had mixed it and had given thanks.... "   Our translations from the
Greek.   For the exceptions see Hanssens, *op. cit.*, I, p. 233.

[12] Despite the proven general practice of the early Church, there is an element
of doubt whether or not water was added to the wine either before Mass or at
any time before the consecration in the Byzantine Church (outside the Italo-
Greek churches) before the twelfth century.   This element of doubt rests mainly
on the discussions between Anselm of Havelberg and Nicetas of Nicomedia in
the year 1136 (cf. *Dialogus*, I, III, chap. 20, *De commixtione vini et aquae in calice,
quod aliter Graeci aliter Latini faciunt* [PL 188, 1241-1245]).   Anselm of Havelberg
certainly believed that the Greeks did not do so, as is evident from his words :
" Pray, tell me, why do you not offer during the Sacrifice of the altar wine and water
poured and mixed together in the chalice ?   Why do you consecrate only the wine
without the water ? "   What is more disconcerting, Nicetas did not deny the
charge; his lack of denial is therefore usually considered tantamount to silent
admission.   Yet, Anselm of Havelberg was mistaken on this point.   Because
of the uniquely Byzantine custom of pouring warm water into the chalice just
before Communion, he seems to have concluded that the Byzantine Church did
not add any water at the *proskomidia*.   Nicetas, on the other hand, in his excessive
zeal to defend the practice of adding warm water, concerned himself only with
providing arguments justifying this same custom.   One very weighty piece of
evidence, among others, which definitely proves that the Byzantine Church did
add water to the wine at some point before the consecration and not merely just
before Communion, is offered by Euthymius Zigabenus (fl. 1100) when he writes
against the Armenian usage : " In the Sacrifice, again, they (the Armenians) do
not offer wine mixed with water but merely the wine without any admixture of
water....   We, on the other hand, mix the wine with water and sacrifice it and
partake of it.... "   (Euthymius Zigabenus, *Panoplia dogmatica*, tit. XXIII,
Contra Armenos [PG 130, 1181 D]).   There can hardly be any doubt from this
passage that the Byzantine Church did commingle the wine with water before
consecrating it.

[13] *Decretum pro Armenis* (Mansi, 31, 1056).

at the *proskomidia* (and just before Holy Communion) must not be so great that the taste of wine would be lost, i.e., changed into the taste of water. [14] This is generally understood as no more than one-third water. Dissident Coptic priests add " a little water "; again, this seems to be interpreted as not more than one-third water. Syrian Jacobites, since ancient times, use equal quantities of water and wine. [15]

The Symbolical Bethlehem

The major events of Christ's life, his passion, and his death were heralded and signified to mankind by types, figures, and prophecies. The Byzantine Liturgy does the same in word, ceremonial, and ritual. It begins in the *proskomidia* with the sacrificial prophecies pronounced over the bread destined to become that true Bread which is Christ crucified and sacrificed. " The words and actions performed over the bread which signify the death of the Lord are only a description and a symbol. The bread, therefore, remains bread and has received no more than the capacity to be offered to God. This is why it typifies the Lord's body in his early years, for... he himself was an offering from his birth onwards. " [16] Christ received the capacity to be offered to God, to suffer, to die, when he was born; indeed he became an offering from his birth onward. In the Liturgy, when the large particle is removed from the *prosphora*, it formally becomes the *ahnets*, destined to be offered to God, to become Christ's body crucified and sacrificed; that is why the action of removing the *ahnets* from the loaf mystically represents Christ's birth. As the flesh of Christ was separated from that of his Virgin Mother at birth, so the *ahnets* is separated and removed from the *prosphora*. It is then placed on the *diskos*, which portrays the placing of the Christ Child in the manger at Bethlehem. Like Simeon of old, who linked the divine Infant

[14] Cf. K. Nikolsky, *Posobie k izucheniu Ustava Bogosluzhenia pravoslavnoi tserkvy* (St. Petersburg, 1907), p. 365.

[15] For an excellent discussion and bibliography concerning this matter, see I. M. Hanssens, *op. cit.*, II, pp. 244-250.

[16] Cabasilas, *Commentary*; trans. Hussey and McNulty, *A Commentary on the Divine Liturgy* (London : SPCK, 1960), 11, p. 41.

with the sacrifice of the cross (Luke 2:22-35), the sacrificial prophecies accompanying the cutting and removing of the *ahnets* from the loaf represent the redemptive and sacrificial role Christ had from the moment of his birth.

CHAPTER XXV

THE FIRST COMMEMORATION

Continuing with the rite of preparation, or proskomidia, *the priest takes another* prosphora *in his hands,*[1] *and commemorates the* Mother of God, *saying :*

In honor and in memory of our Most Blessed Lady, the Mother of God and ever-virgin Mary, through whose prayers, O Lord, accept this sacrifice upon your own altar in heaven.

He cuts out a small particle from the prosphora *and places it on the* diskos *to the right of the holy bread (the priest's left, however, as he stands facing the* diskos); *as he does this, he says :*

At your right hand stood the Queen dressed in golden vesture adorned with many colors (Ps. 44:10).

This is the first of many commemorations made with the particles of bread. Appropriately, it is in honor of the Mother of God. The practice of commemorating the Mother of God, the saints, the living and the dead in the intercessions of the anaphora is indeed ancient; it dates back to the fourth century at least.[2]   Even older is the offertory practice of " naming " the living and the dead " at the altar with the oblation. "[3]   In other words, a small loaf of bread was presented for the sacrifice by each family or individual in their own name; relatives and friends of the deceased also offered a small loaf in the name of the departed who had died in communion with the Church. The " naming, " commemorations, and intercessions were done immediately before the offertory, during the preparation of the gifts of bread and wine. At some point before the eighth or

---

[1] If only one *prosphora* is available, the small particles or hosts are cut from it.

[2] E.g., Sarapion's *Euchologion* (cf. above, p. 95); Cyril of Jerusalem, *Cat. mystag.*, V, 9 (Quasten, *Mon.*, 102), etc.

[3] E.g., Cyprian, *Ep.*, LXV, 2 (edit. Ante-Nicene Fathers, p. 367 [Oxford edit., *Ep.*, I]); Ep. XVI, 2 (CSEL, 3, 519); Council of Elvira, Canon 29 (Hefele-Leclercq, I, 237); Ps.-Dionysius, *De hierarchia eccl.*, 3, ii (PG 3, 425); the ancient Liturgy of SS. Addai and Mari (Brightman, LEW, pp. 275-281); Narsai (Connolly, *The Liturgical Homilies of Narsai* [Cambridge, 1909], pp. 10-11), etc. For detailed history, see below, pp. 518, 527, 625.

ninth century, the preparation of the gifts was shifted from its original position to the beginning of the Divine Liturgy, [4] but the "naming" and commemorations remained in their original place. In the ninth century, however, commemorations for the living and the dead were included also in the *proskomidia* : a whole loaf was offered for each group. This much we know from the implicit testimony of Nicephorus I, Patriarch of Constantinople (A.D. 806-815). [5]

By the eleventh century, saints were also being commemorated in the *proskomidia* of the Greco-Byzantine Church, with a corresponding offering of bread. [6] The number of loaves, then, would depend on whether or not any commemorations were made for the dead and/or a saint. About the same time, the Patriarch of Constantinople, Nicolas Grammaticus (1084-1111) prescribed at least four loaves. The first was the "Lamb"; the second commemorated the Blessed Virgin; the third, St. Michael and Gabriel and the other angels; the fourth, the Precursor, the apostles, prophets, and holy pontiffs, the saint of the day, and all the saints. If any commemoration of the living or of the dead were to be made, a loaf was to be offered for each. What is not clear, however, is whether all or only part of these breads were to be consecrated. [7] Such practice was far from uniform, as is evident from the various documents of the times. [8]

---

[4] *Codex Barberini, gr.*, 336 (Brightman, LEW, pp. 309-310).

[5] Cf. Nicephorus I, Canon 11 (PG 100, 856). The necessity of defining that it was no fault to offer only one loaf of bread for three persons proves the custom of offering as many loaves as there were commemorations.

[6] When the question was asked whether or not it was lawful to use only one loaf in celebrating the Divine Liturgy, Peter Chartophylax (c. 1091-1118) answered : "Unless a commemoration of a saint be made or that of a deceased person, there is nothing which would hinder (one from celebrating the Divine Liturgy with only one loaf)" : Ἐρωτήματα in G. A. Rhallis-M. Potli, Σύνταγμα τῶν θείων καὶ ἱερῶν κανόνων, Vol. V, p. 369.

[7] Cf. Nicolas Grammaticus, Περὶ τοῦ πῶς ὀφείλει ποιεῖν ὁ ἱερεὺς τὴν προσκομιδὴν (edit. A. S. Pavlov, *Nomokanon pry bol'shem trebnyku* [Moscow, 1897], pp. 410-412).

[8] E.g., six loaves at least are prescribed in the *Typikon* given by Alexis the Studite, Patriarch of Constantinople, to a monastery he founded (c. 1025-1043); cf. MS. of Synodal Library of Moscow, N. 380 (formerly 330), fol. 228 v, in A. Gorsky-K. Nevostrujev, *Opysanie slavianskikh rukopisej Moskovskoj Synodal'-noj biblioteky*, Vol. III (Moscow, 1859), i, p. 266. Seven are prescribed in the *Typikon* of Irene Augusta (p. 1118), chap. 34 (PG 127, 1056 BC); again, these are in the nature of special obligations imposed on the monastery by the empress

A semblance of uniformity was achieved in the Greco-Byzantine Church in the fourteenth century after promulgation of the *Constitution* of Philotheus. We know, however, that in the thirteenth century another practice was taking root in some places : the large host or " Lamb " was to be cut out of the first *prosphora*, or loaf, and placed on the *diskos*; whether the other loaves were to be offered whole or whether particles were to be cut out from them is unknown. [9] Philotheus, the Patriarch of Constantinople (1351-1378), issued his *Constitution* prescribing five loaves (προσφορά), from which one or more particles could be cut out. This was the origin of the present standard practice. [10]

From all the extant documents dating from the eleventh to the fourteenth centuries, it is evident that the number of loaves depended on the number of commemorations. At first, in addition to the " Lamb, " loaves could also be offered for the living and the dead; when the commemoration of saints was introduced into the *proskomidia*, it was placed before the commemorations of the living and the dead. This order is another indication that the ancient custom of reading the diptychs provided the inspiration for including

who founded it rather than a standard usage in Byzantine churches. Indirectly, however, these prescriptions do indicate the *type* of commemorations which could be made in the Byzantine Church at the time : " Each day seven loaves are (to be) offered in the Divine Liturgy : one, the Lord's (i.e., the " Lamb "); another (in honor) of our Blessed Lady and Mother of God; another (in honor) of the saint of the day; another for the expiation and remission of sins both of my most gracious emperor (i.e., her husband Alexis Comnenus) and my own; another for the deceased monks; another for our deceased parents and the rest of those close to us; another for our living children, relatives and the rest of those close to us. After our death, the aforementioned loaf is to be offered singly for the remission of our sins, and this is to be made in perpetuum. If one of us two dies before the other, one separate loaf is to be immolated for the living, another for the deceased; however, after the death of the one who had outlived the other, one loaf is to be offered for both (of us). " Our translation from the Greek in PG 127, 1056 BC. Another prescription, quoted by A. Dmitrievsky (*Opysanie liturgicheskikh rukopisej khraniaschikhsia v bibliotekakh pravoslavnago vostoka*, Vol. I, *Typika* [Kiev, 1895], p. 768), from the *Typikon* given to the monastery Τῶν ἡλίου βωμῶν (or Τῶν ἐλεγμῶν) by a certain Nicolas the Mystic (written some time between 1143-1179) has : " In all the Liturgies celebrated in the church, one oblation is to be immolated in my name; the same should also be done after my departure to the Lord.... " See also A. Dmitrievsky, *op. cit.*, p. 647.

[9] Cf. A. Dmitrievsky, *op. cit.*, Vol. III, p. 117.

[10] *Constitution* of Philotheus, cf. A. Dmitrievsky, *op. cit.*, Vol. II, *Euchologia* (Kiev, 1901), pp. 820-821. A slightly different usage is recorded in Nicolas Cabasilas (1371), *Liturgiae expositio*, 10 (PG 150, 385 D-387 A).

similar commemorations in the same place in the *proskomidia*. Ancient diptychs contained not only the names of the living and the dead, but also those of the saints, who were mentioned first. It became necessary to categorize the saints in the order of their greatness. The intercessory prayer of the anaphora served as an example.

The Blessed Mother of God headed the list, the Precursor John the Baptist followed, then the Apostles, the saint of the day, etc. (see below, pp. 631). The origin of such a list in the *proskomidia* may traced to the eleventh, twelfth and thirteenth centuries (cf. pp. 280, above). During the next two centuries, although usages still differed in many churches, the series of saints was being enlarged. For instance, after the particle in honor of the Baptist, the thirteenth-century *Euchologion* preserved in MS. 719 of Patmos, adds other particles " in honor of the holy and glorious, all-laudable apostles, of our holy and God-bearing fathers Basil the Great, John Chrysostom, Athanasius, etc. " [11]   A manuscript dated 1306, at the Esphigmenon monastery of Mount Athos, lists the Blessed Mother, St. John the Baptist, the prophets, the apostles, the holy, God-bearing fathers, priest-martyrs, wonder-workers and " unmercenaries " (see p. 295, for meaning), holy men and women, then the living and the dead and, finally, the celebrants of the Liturgy. [12]

A fifteenth-century manuscript inserts, after the commemoration of the apostles, that " of the glorious, holy hierarchs and ecumenical doctors Basil the Great, Gregory the Theologian, John Chrysostom, and all the holy hierarchs, " and continues with commemorations " of the holy, glorious and great martyrs George, Demetrius, Theodore and all the holy martyrs, of our holy fathers filled with

---

[11] Published by A. Dmitrievsky, *op. cit.*, Vol. II, *Euchologia* (Kiev, 1901), pp. 171-172. There is here no mention of the living or the dead.

[12] Cf. A. Dmitrievsky, *op. cit.*, pp. 263-264. Another fourteenth-century manuscript, Grottaferrata Γ.B. iii, immediately after the commemoration of the Mother of God, lists those in honor " of the incorporeal Powers of heaven, of the prophet, forerunner and Baptist John, of the holy, glorious and all-celebrated apostles, of our father among the saints and hierarch Basil, of our father among the saints Chrysostom, of our father among the saints Gregory the Theologian, of our father among the saints Nicholas; and we also remember all the saints through whose intercession may God look down upon us.... " The commemorations of the living and dead follow. Cf. Brightman, LEW, Appendix Q, p. 548. Our translation from the Greek in Brightman.

God, Anthony, Euthymius, Sabbas and all the venerable fathers, of the holy, glorious and great physicians working without fees, Cosmas and Damian and of all the holy unmercenaries, of the holy and just parents of God [Joachim and Anne], and of saint N—— whose memory we keep and of the holy saints through whose intercession may God accept this sacrifice upon his heavenly altar..., " etc. [13] Comparisons between the fifteenth- or sixteenth-century commemorations and those of the twelfth and thirteenth illustrate the growth of such lists. Finally in 1600, when the Venice edition of the *Euchologion* was published, the series was completed and, except for a few minor variations, is identical with that of today.

In the Byzantine-Slav Church, the *proskomidia* had undergone similar evolution and development. At first, the rite of preparation was as simple as in the early Greco-Byzantine Church. The *Liturgikon* of Anthony the Roman (1147), for example, states that the priest is to prepare the first loaf by dividing it into four at the beginning of the Liturgy and merely " offer " the others. [14] The *Liturgikon* of Barlaam of Khutinsk (1102) prescribes the preparation of only one *prosphora*, and this by the deacon. [15] It seems quite certain, however, that the general practice of the Russian Church at the time was the use of more than one *prosphora*. [16] This would also indicate that there may have been commemorations conjoined to the *prosphory*.

Later, the Slav *proskomidia* parallels the growth of the same ritual in the Greco-Byzantine Church. Thus, a thirteenth-century manuscript prescribes the use of five *prosphory* with the following commemorations : the first, was the " Lamb, " the second honored

[13] From the MS. Paris *Graec.*, 2509, fol. 226 v. Our translation from the Greek in Brightman, LEW, Appendix Q, p. 550. Our bracketed material supplied for clearer meaning.

[14] The Synodal Library of Moscow, *Codex* 342; cf. A. Gorsky-K. Nevostrujev, *op. cit.*, Vol. III, i, pp. 1 ff.

[15] The Synodal Library of Moscow, N. 343; cf. A. Gorsky-K. Nevostrujev, *op. cit.*, Vol. III, i, pp. 5 ff.

[16] Cf. Reply of Bishop Niphont of Novgorod (1130-1156) to Kirik, a monk, who had asked if it were permissible to celebrate the Divine Liturgy with only one *prosphora*. He answered that it was not allowed unless it were the only one available; cf. *Vprashanie Kirikovo jerze vprasha Episkopa Novgorodskavo Niphona i inikh, Pamjatniky Rossijskoj Slovenosti XII vika*, p. 194.

the Blessed Virgin, the third was for saints, the fourth for the living and, finally, the fifth for the dead. [17] The Slav churches, with some exceptions, favored the use of five *prosphory* in the fourteenth century. [18] This practice was confirmed by the introduction of the *Constitution* of Philotheus by Metropolitan Cyril of Kiev (1376-1406). [19]

Complete uniformity was not achieved. Some of the fifteenth-century *Liturgika* began to prescribe the use of six *prosphory* and even seven. [20] This lack of uniformity was perhaps greater in the churches of Russia than it was in the churches of the Ukraine. [21] When the Slav edition of the *Nomokanon* was published in 1620 at Pechersk Lavra (Monastery of the Caves) at Kiev, its text fully agreed with its Greek counterpart and prescribed the use of five

[17] *Codex* 524, fol. 4, of Sophia Library; cf. A. Petrovsky, *Histoire de la rédaction slave de la liturgie de S. Jean Chrysostome*, XPYCOCTOMIKA, pp. 873-874; also, Krasnoseltsev, *Materialy dlja istorii chinoposlidovania liturgii sv. Ioanna Zlatoustago* (Kazan, 1889), p. 20.

[18] So *Codex* 522, fols. 9-12, and *Codex* 523, fols. 7-12, of Sophia Library but Codex 526, fols. 4-6, of same Library prescribed only four *prosphory* (of which the second was in honor of the saint of the day, the third for the living, and the fourth for the dead). Three loaves, according to several fourteenth-century MSS. (*Codices* 1053, fol. 28, and 1054, fol. 23, of same Library), were sufficient if the Divine Liturgy was for a sick person. Cf. A. Petrovsky, *op. cit.*, p. 882; and Krasnoseltsev, *op. cit.*, pp. 11-13. The fourteenth-century *Molytovnyk-Sluzhebnyk* (edit. Kowaliv [New York, 1960]), pp. 5-7, also mentions five *prosphory*.

[19] The fourteenth or fifteenth century *Ustav* in Metropolitan Isidore's *Liturgikon* also prescribes five *prosphory*; cf. MS. *Vat. Slav.*, N. 14, pp. 115-119.

[20] Thus, *Codices* 528, fols. 86-90; 529, fols. 36-40; 531, fols. 4-8, etc., of Sophia Library; cf. A. Petrovsky, *op. cit.*, pp. 898-899. When seven loaves were used, the " Lamb " was cut out from the first; the particle in honor of our Blessed Mother, from the second; that in honor of the saints, from the third; that for the bishop, from the fourth; that commemorating the emperor, from the fifth; that for the superior of the monastery and for the living, from the sixth; finally, that for the dead, from the seventh.

[21] One would strongly suspect that lack of uniformity was the principal reason why the Synod of Moscow (1551) did not clearly define the number of *prosphory* to be used in celebrating the Eucharistic Liturgy. Its acts (collected in the *Stoglav*, chap. 9, " *Ukraz borzestvennia slurzby kako dostoit sviaschenniku ili s diakonom slurzititili jedinomu* " [3rd edit., Kazan, 1912], p. 46) states that the large bread, the " Lamb " is to be cut out from the first *prosphora*; the small particle in honor of the Blessed Mother, from the second; that in honor of the Baptist, from the third, and from the " remaining *prosphory* " those for the whole Orthodox episcopate, for the emperor, for the princes, and for all Christians, both living and dead. The various Russian *Liturgika* (missals) printed between 1583 and 1617, however, prescribe seven *prosphory*.

prosphory. [22] The Moscow editions of the same by Patriarchs Joasaphat I (1639) and Joseph (1651, increased the number from five to seven. [23]

Uniformity finally came to the whole Slav Church with the liturgical reform of Patriarch Nikon of Moscow (1652-1658), when the *Nomokanon* was again edited. The use of five loaves was prescribed once more. Thousands of priests and laymen objected to this and other reforms and broke away from the Orthodox Church. They became known as the *Raskolniky* (Schismatics), the *Starovery* (Old Believers) or the *Starobriadtsy* (Old Ritualists). To this day, they use seven loaves.

Such is in brief the history of the *proskomidia* in the Byzantine Church.

For several hundred years, the commemoration of the Mother of God has appropriately come first after the *ahnets*, the " Lamb " itself. In today's rite of preparation, not only does it come first : it is even in a category of its own, since the particle representing her is in a place of honor on the *diskos*—on the right side of the *ahnets* representing the Son of God (at the priest's left). The *Constitution* of Philotheus prescribed that it be on the left of the " Lamb, " not beneath it as other documents placed it. [24] The practice of placing it at the right seems to have originated when the particle was given a distinctive shape and verse 11 of Psalm 44 was introduced. [25] A distinctive triangular shape began to be used in the fifteenth century as a special mark of honor. [26] As Mary was close to Christ at the foot of the cross on Calvary, so now by her honored position on the *diskos* she is taking a more intimate share than the rest of the human race both in the sacrifice of the altar and in her Son's glory in heaven.

[22] Cf. A. Pavlov, *Nomokanon pry bol'shom Trebniku* (Moscow, 1897), pp. 406-407.

[23] This change is attributed to the archpriest Avvakum, a colorful figure in these stormy years of Russian church history. Cf. A. Pavlov, *op. cit.*, pp. 408-409.

[24] Krasnoseltsev, *op. cit.*, pp. 43 ff.

[25] E.g., *Cod. Esphigm.*, N. 120 (Dmitrievsky, *op. cit.*, Vol. II, p. 955) and *Cod.* 525 of the Holy Sepulcher at Constantinople (Dmitrievsky, *op. cit.*, p. 818).

[26] The first document which prescribes a triangular shape for this particle seems to be *Cod.* 425 of the Holy Sepulcher at Constantinople (Dmitrievsky, *op. cit.*, p. 818), though *Cod. Esphig.*, N. 120 of the next century differentiates this particle merely by stating that it should be " large. "

Mary's prerogative as the Mediatrix is expressed in the accompanying words : " through whose prayers accept, O Lord, this sacrifice upon your own altar in heaven. " While placing this particle on the *diskos*, the priest recites the tenth verse of Psalm 44 : " At your right hand stood the Queen dressed in golden vesture, adorned with many colors. " It refers to the Church as the bride of Christ, but is applied here to the Blessed Virgin. In the Latin Rite, Psalm 44 is recited at Matins on feasts of the Blessed Virgin. Verses 10 to 16 are applied to her as the Spouse of the Holy Spirit and the Queen of Heaven.

CHAPTER XXVI

THE COMMEMORATION
OF THE CHURCH TRIUMPHANT

After honoring the Mother of God, glorious above all angels and men, the priest commemorates the Church Triumphant by placing particles for its various categories on the *diskos* to the left of the " Lamb " (the priest's right). In all, nine particles are arranged in three vertical rows of three particles each.

The priest cuts small particles from the third prosphora, *saying :*

(In honor and memory) of the honored, incorporeal powers of heaven.

He places this particle to the left of the " *Lamb* " *(his right) and thus begins the first vertical row.* [1]

This brief commemoration contains the general teaching of the Eastern Fathers about the incorporeity, immateriality, and spirituality of the angels. [2] Chrysostom himself strongly opposed any other opinion. [3] Theologians may not always have agreed about incorporeal beings, but the Eastern Christian lived his simple belief that the angels were servants of God, that they were his protectors, helpers, and companions, ever guiding his faltering steps toward God and heaven. He also believed strongly and vividly in the pervading presence of Satan and his cohorts. To the Byzantine Christian, the devil was no mere imaginary being, distant and uninterested in his fate, but a fiercely, viciously evil creature, ever close, beguiling, enticing the unwary into wicked habits and eternal hell— " a roaring lion, seeking whom he may devour " (I Pet. 5:8). Because

---

[1] The Russian Liturgy does not have this commemoration of the angels, but begins immediately with that of St. John the Baptist : " Of the most honorable and glorious prophet, the Forerunner and Baptist John. "

[2] Basil, *Hom. Quod Deus non sit auctor mali*, 9 (PG 31, 349); Didymus, *De Spirit. Sancto*, 1, 5, 6 (PG 39, 1037); Eusebius Caesar., *Dem. evang.*, 4, 1 (PG 22, 252), etc.

[3] Chrysostom, *In Genes. hom.*, 22, 2 (edit. Montfaucon 4, 196 AC).

the Byzantine Christian keenly appreciated the danger the evil one could be to his soul, his devotion to good angels was fervent and genuine. The iconography of Byzantium no less than its liturgy bears ample witness to this.

The angelic hosts were present at Bethlehem. One of them announced the Good News that the Saviour was born and " suddenly there was with the angel a multitude of the heavenly army, praising God, and saying : Glory to God in the highest : and on earth peace to men of good will " (Luke 2:13-14). Here, in the symbolical Bethlehem of the *proskomidia*, the angelic hosts are represented by a particle in their honor.

The priest then honors the prophets, saying :

(In honor and in memory) of the honorable and glorious prophet, the Forerunner and Baptist, John, and all the holy prophets. [4]

The prophetical Jewish heritage has been well preserved in the Byzantine liturgy. Readings from the prophets dominate in the Vespers and Matins offices of the major feasts. Icons of major and minor prophets are shown in the fourth tier of the Slav iconostas etc. The Old Testament prophet was an intermediary between God and the people. He was, in a sense, God's voice to the people, transmitting to them the messages received from the Almighty. The prophets, therefore, played an extremely important role in the religious and social life of the Jew. He was a defender of the moral law contained in the Ten Commandments—and the thundering voice that condemned disobedience and idolatry. He promoted true religion by preaching, teaching, and explaining God and his Law.

This function of the prophet as a teacher is often overshadowed by his other role as a seer, threatening divine chastisement for immorality and disobedience. Many prophetical sayings were concerned with the coming of the Saviour, the Messiah. For centuries, these Messianic prophecies kept the people in a state of lively expectation.

---

[4] The Russian text reads : " (In honor and in memory) of the holy and glorious prophets Moses and Aaron, Elias and Eliseus, David and Jesse, and the three holy children, and Daniel the prophet and all the holy prophets. "

Besides the four major and twelve minor prophets, there were many others. A few are mentioned by name in Russian texts of the *proskomidia* : Moses, Aaron, Elisha, Jesse, and the three holy children. Aaron, the brother of Moses, for example, although seldom listed as a prophet, fulfills an essential prophetical function by speaking to the people and Pharaoh the divine words suggested by Moses, who, due to a speech defect, was unable to carry out his divine mission (Exod. 4:16; 7:1 ff.).

John the Baptist is set in a different, higher place in the Byzantine Church, which honors him with two major feasts, that of his birth (June 24) and that of his beheading (Aug. 29). He deserved this pre-eminence because Christ himself had said of him : " Amongst those that are born of women, there is not a greater prophet than John the Baptist" (Luke 7:28). Indeed, he is "more than a prophet" (Matt. 11:9; Luke, 7:26).

The priest then commemorates the apostles :

(In honor and in memory) of the holy, glorious and ever praiseworthy apostles Peter and Paul, and all the other holy apostles.

Cutting out the third particle, he places it on the diskos below the second particle, and thus completes the first vertical row.

Of all the apostles, Peter and Paul were the greatest. St. Peter was chosen by Jesus himself as the solid rock upon which to build his Church, against which the very gates of hell should not prevail. As Christ's first vicar on earth, he was given highest authority and the power of binding and loosing, not only on earth but in heaven. Paul, on the other hand, was Christ's chosen instrument for propagating his gospel to the nations. As apostle to the world, he surpassed the others in labors and sufferings, enduring incredible hardships, tribulations, watches, sorrows, hunger and thirst, cold and nakedness, beatings with rods and with stones, shipwrecks, imprisonments, and unending travels. In the Byzantine Liturgy, their names are inseparably linked as the " two pillars of the Church and destroyers of error, " " two trumpets proclaiming things divine and revealing the doctrines of God. " [5] For several centuries not

---

[5] *Synaxarion* of the Byzantine Canonical Office.

only was their feast one of the greatest of the year : it was preceded by a period of fasting similar to the Advent Fast of the Latin Rite. [6]

" All the other holy apostles. " In this commemoration are included all the others of the original Twelve called by Christ to be the leaders of the infant Church : Andrew, James, Bartholomew, John, Thomas, Matthew, Philip, James the Less, Simon and Jude. All sealed their indefatigable preaching with martyrdom (St. John died a natural death, but is considered a martyr for having been thrown into a cauldron of boiling oil during Domitian's reign). After Christ, they are the foundation of the Church; that is why it is called " apostolic. "

The priest proceeds with the next commemoration by saying :

(In honor and in memory) of our fathers among the saints, the hierarchs Basil the Great, Gregory the Theologian, and John Chrysostom; Athanasius and Cyril, Nicholas of Myra; Cyril and Methodius, teachers of the Slavs, the holy priest and martyr Josaphat, and all the holy hierarchs. [7]

The priest places the fourth particle beside the first, and thus begins the second vertical row.

This commemoration honors the general class of *hierarchs*, that is, the prelate saints (patriarchs, archbishops, bishops, etc.) who distinguished themselves by their heroic faith.

BASIL THE GREAT, GREGORY THE THEOLOGIAN and JOHN CHRYSOSTOM, Bishops of the fourth century and Doctors of the Church, were the greatest triumvirate of theologians in the Eastern Church. Their personal admirers occasioned such controversies among the Christians of Constantinople that it was necessary in A.D. 1076 to establish a special feast in honor of all three. This feast is celebrated on January 30. Each also has his own feast.

GREGORY NAZIANZEN (the Theologian) was an intimate friend of Basil's. Both studied at Athens and both entered religious life together. The great St. Jerome boasts that he sat at Gregory's

---

[6] This period lasted two to five weeks, depending upon the date of Easter.

[7] Instead of the last four, the Russian recension has : " Nikita, Bishop of Novgorod, Leonty, Bishop of Rostoff, and all the holy hierarchs. "

feet, and calls him his master in the Holy Scriptures. Gregory Nazianzen was so resolute a champion of the faith, so expert and exact in his teachings, that the Eastern Church calls him Gregory the Theologian.

BASIL THE GREAT, brilliant scholar and defender of the true faith against the Arian and Macedonian heresies, compiled the Liturgy that bears his name or, at any rate, revised the contemporary Liturgy of the Cappadocian Church. Because he authored the well-known Basilian monastic rule, praised and adapted by St. Benedict, he is also known as the Patriarch of Eastern Monks.

JOHN CHRYSOSTOM (the " Golden-Mouthed ") was one of the greatest preachers of all time and one of the Church's greatest scholars. The Church honors him as the " Heavenly Patron of Ecclesiastical Orators. " Much in his sermons is still effective in the twentieth century. He is credited with the compilation of the anaphora which bears his name, the " ordinary " anaphora of the Byzantine Church today.

These three great men lived amid the jealousies, misunderstandings, and enmities that plagued the Church of the fourth century. None of them lived to see the full effects of their labor, but they were God's chief instruments in eliminating Arianism and other heresies. All three were persecuted by civil officials, thwarted and deserted by their brother bishops. They had much in common—most of all, their eminent sanctity.

Another champion of the faith against the Arian heresy which denied that Christ was true God was ST. ATHANASIUS, the " Father of Orthodoxy. " While only a deacon, he had been called by his bishop to go to the Council of Nicaea (A.D. 325), where his great learning and ability attracted much attention. As Patriarch of Alexandria for forty-six years, he, more than any other single man, stemmed the tide of Arianism. Adamant in his defense of the true faith, he was a meek and humble man, truly beloved by his flock. He lived in constant danger of death at the hands of his enemies, who had him banished no less than five times. His feast is celebrated on May 2.

A name usually linked liturgically with Athanasius is that of

CYRIL OF ALEXANDRIA. [8] As Patriarchs of Alexandria, both suffered horribly for their defense of the true doctrine.   Where Athanasius was the defender of orthodoxy against Arius, Cyril was the champion against Nestorius, who denied the unity of the Person in Christ (and denied therefore that Mary was the Mother of God).   Cyril presided over the Third Ecumenical Council at Ephesus in 431. His feast is June 9.

In Lycia in the town of Myra lived a contemporary of Athanasius and Cyril, NICHOLAS.   As abbot of a monastery, he led many souls to God; later, as Archbishop of Myra, he became a special protector of the innocent and the wronged.   Favored by God with the power of miracles, he is popularly called the " Wonder-worker " or " Performer of Miracles. "   Many touching examples of his kindness and generosity toward the poor have been recorded.   His works are commemorated in the modern Santa Claus, whose name is a corruption of St. Nicholas.   He is the patron of Russia.   Many nations honor him on his feast day, December 6.

STS. CYRIL and METHODIUS, because of their great missionary activity among the Slavs, are called " equal to the apostles " by the Canonical Office of the Slav Church.   Brothers by blood and religion, both became important prelates.   Cyril was made Bishop of Catania and the old Slav Cyrillic alphabet is ascribed to him. Methodius became Archbishop of Moravia.   The former died in Rome in 867, the latter in Velehrad in 885.   These great missionaries translated many liturgical books from the Greek into Slavonic. Their feast is celebrated on May 11.

JOSAPHAT KUNSEVICH, Archbishop of Polotsk, has the honor of being the first Oriental to be formally canonized at Rome (1867). His life was spent in a labor of love, the reconciliation of souls with the Church.   He died for his work by having his skull crushed with an ax by the people of Witepsk.   This " thief of souls, " as he is still called, died on November 12, 1623.   His feast day is November 12.

The priest then begins the commemoration of the martyrs :

(In honor and in memory) of the holy apostle, the first

---

[8] A feast common to both is celebrated on January 18.

martyr and archdeacon, Stephen; the holy and great martyrs Demetrius, George, Theodore of Tyre, and all the holy martyred men and women. [9]

The fifth particle which the priest cuts out is placed below the first in the second vertical row.

Martyrs alone are commemorated in the Roman Canon both before and after the consecration (in the *Communicantes* and *Nobis quoque peccatoribus*). There are not as many in the *proskomidia*. This does not indicate any imbalance : martyrs were numerous in both East and West.

ST. STEPHEN leads the brilliant host. Counted among the seventy-two disciples of Christ, he was the first to die. Dragged outside Jerusalem by an angered mob, he was stoned to death for having dared to preach the doctrine of Christ to the Jews (Acts 6-7). His feast day is celebrated in the Eastern Church on December 27; in the Western Church, on December 26.

ST. DEMETRIUS is one of the most popular saints, in the Ukraine and Russia. This third-century martyr of Thessalonica (d. A.D. 306) held the high government office of consul, was imprisoned, tortured, and finally speared to death because he refused to persecute Christians. His feast is October 26.

ST. GEORGE, patron of armies, was a high-ranking Cappadocian army officer (a tribune). When Diocletian published his first edict against the Christians at Nicomedia, George not only resigned his commission but openly rebuked the Emperor for his cruelty. Diocletian submitted him to dreadful torments and finally had him beheaded. The Eastern Liturgy calls him " Great among the Martyrs. " Devotion to St. George as the symbol of successful combat against evil is one of the most ancient in the Church. His feast in both East and West is celebrated on April 23. England, Malta, Barcelona, Valencia, Aragon, and Genoa have chosen him for their patron.

---

[9] The Russian recension continues with listing by name the following women martyrs : " Thecla, Barbara, Kyriaka, Euphemia and Paraskevia, Catherine, and all the holy martyred women. "

THEODORE, surnamed Tyro, is also a soldier-saint and martyr of the early fourth century (he is surnamed thus, not because he was a young recruit, but because for a time he belonged to the Cohors Tyronum). When asked to choose between apostasy and death, he told his commander that he was ready to be cut to pieces and to offer up every limb to God. Given a brief reprieve to think things over, he used his freedom to set fire to the great temple of Cybele. He was condemned to be burned alive. As the flames rose, a fellow Christian is said to have seen his soul go up to heaven like a flash of light. This happened at Amasea in the Pontus, c. A.D. 306 when Galerius Maximian and Maximin ruled the empire. In the East, his feast is celebrated on February 17.

Millions have been martyred in Christ's Church, perhaps millions in our own century. All are honored in this commemoration.

Then the priest says :

(In honor and in memory) of our venerable and God-bearing fathers Anthony, Euthymius, Sabba, Onuphrius, and all venerable fathers and mothers. [10]

After taking out the sixth particle, the priest places it below the second of this row, and thus completes the row.

The literal meaning of *bohonosnyk* is *God-bearing* or *filled with God*. The expression refers to spiritual fathers and mothers, usually superiors of monastic communities.

The first name in this commemoration is that of a founder of cenobitical life, ST. ANTHONY OF EGYPT. Popularly referred to as the Patriarch of Monks, St. Anthony was one of the most ascetic saints in the notably ascetic Eastern Church. Born in Upper Egypt in the middle of the third century, he gave away his vast possessions and became a desert hermit. His only food was bread and water, and these he never tasted before sunset, sometimes only once in two or three days. After he had lived in this way for twenty years,

---

[10] The Russian recension inserts the following list of saints immediately after Onuphrius : " Athanasius of Athos, Anthony and Theodosius of the Caves, Sergius of Radonezh, Barlaam of Khutinsk, and all venerable fathers; and the venerable matrons, Pelagia, Theodosia, Anastasia, Eupraxia, Fevronia, Theodulia, Euphrosyne, Mary of Egypt, and all the holy and venerable matrons. "

many people came to him for direction, and thus a monastery was born—perhaps the first. Anthony's many miracles attracted much attention. He fled once more into solitude and died peacefully at a very old age. His feast in both East and West is celebrated on January 17.

ST. EUTHYMIUS, a fifth century Armenian, was also a hermit and the founder of monasteries. His feast is celebrated on January 20. Chosen as the Superior of a monastery while yet a young man, he heard the call to a higher life and retired into the wilderness about six miles from Jerusalem. Desert caves were the only witnesses of his extreme penitential life during the five years he spent there. Later, he founded a monastery and became its leader, promoting a strictly penitential spirit. When he was ninety, his soul separated from his emaciated, worn-out body and went up to be completely " filled with God. "

ST. SABBA became the Superior General of all the anchorites of Palestine some time before the end of his long ascetical life. That is why he is called the Patriarch of Palestinian Monks. After the death of his master, Euthymius, he went into the wilderness where he lived in a cave near the Kedron brook. Eventually, he founded a new monastery and became a priest at fifty-three. His feast is December 5, the day on which he died at the age of ninety-four.

Another of the greatest hermits of all time, ST. ONUPHRIUS, lived alone for sixty years in the desert of Thebais. He died during the reign of Constantius. Despite his excessive asceticism, he is very popular in the East. In the Ukraine, for example, many men bear his venerable name. His feast is on June 12.

The next commemoration is for a category of saints known in the Byzantine-Slav Rite as *bezsrebrennyky*. The closest that one can come to translating *bezsrebrennyky* would be " unmercenary, " that is, those who worked without money, fees, or pay. More literally, it means " without silver, " but this may give the erroneous impression that they were paupers, which is not true.

The priest says :

(In honor and in memory) of the holy and wonder-working unmercenaries Cosmas and Damian, Cyrus and John,

Panteleimon and Hermolaus, and all the holy unmercenaries.

After cutting out this particle, the priest places it on the diskos *beside the first one of the second row. This begins the third vertical row.*

The first named of these miracle-working *bezsrebrennyky* are COSMAS and DAMIAN. This inseparable pair were brothers, in fact, twins according to some sources. Born in Arabia, both studied in Syria and became well-known physicians. They are called *bezsrebrennyky* because they charged no fees for their medical services. This fact, coupled with their expert skill in medicine, won many converts for Christianity. When the persecution of Diocletian broke out, they were among the first to be singled out as Christians because of their fame and charity. Arrested by order of Lysias, governor of Cilicia, they were tortured and finally put to death. Whether they were decapitated or thrown into the sea with their hands and feet tied is a matter of conjecture, since sources differ. In the East, their feast is celebrated on July 1; in the West, on September 27.

Another team of physicians working without pay was that of CYRUS and JOHN. During the final years of the Roman persecutions, Cyrus was at the height of his fame as a doctor in Alexandria. He worked in the slums and charged no fees. By so doing, he converted many pagans, so many in fact that news of him reached Rome. Escaping arrest, he fled to Arabia and continued to win souls for Christ through free medical practice. He eventually became a monk in order to devote himself entirely to charity. A young Christian soldier from Mesopotamia, John, worked with him. So famous a doctor could not long go unnoticed : persecution soon caught up with Cyrus and John. They neither flinched nor weakened under agonizing torture, even when salt and vinegar were poured into their wounds. They were finally beheaded in A.D. 311 or 292. Their feast day is January 31.

PANTELEIMON was yet another physician saint. He was so expert in his profession that he became the personal physician to Emperor Galerius Maximianus. He was a Christian at the time, but *la dolce vita* of the imperial court proved too much for him, and he apostatized. HERMOLAUS, a zealous priest, won him back to Christ. Knowing that sooner or later Diocletian's persecution would catch up with him, he prepared for it by giving all his wealth to the poor. Hermolaus and two other friends were arrested with him in his own house. All were tortured and condemned to be beheaded. Hermolaus and his friends were martyred first, Panteleimon the following day. That is why St. Panteleimon's feast is celebrated on July 27, the day after that of St. Hermolaus and his two companions. St. Panteleimon is the patron saint of physicians.

The priest proceeds with the next commemoration :

(In honor and in memory) of the holy and just forefathers of God, Joachim and Anne. [11]

After cutting out the eighth particle, the priest places it on the diskos below the preceding one.

JOACHIM and ANNE, sometimes called " the forefathers of God, " were the grandparents of Christ, since they were the parents of his Mother Mary. Almost nothing is known about their lives. Those whom God finds useful for his plans (especially if the work done through them is important) must remain in obscurity, for it is he and not they who must be glorified and remembered. The Eastern Church celebrates their feast on September 9, the day after the birthday of their sinless daughter.

The ninth and final commemoration of the Church Triumphant is made with the words :

(In honor and in memory) of Saints N—— and N—— (the patron of the church and the saint of the day) and all the saints through whose prayers, O God, protect us. [12]

---

[11] After St. Joachim and St. Anne, the Russian recension commemorates the patron saint of the church, the saint of the day (mentioning both by name); *the holy and equal to the Apostles, Methodius and Cyril, teachers of the Slavs, the holy and equal to the Apostles, the great prince Vladimir, and all the saints through whose prayers, O God, visit us.*

[12] In the Russian Liturgy, this commemoration was made in connection with the preceding particle. At this point, another commemoration is made : *(In honor and memory) of our father among the saints John, Archbishop of Constantinople, the Golden-mouthed.*

After cutting out the ninth particle, the priest places it on the diskos *immediately below the preceding one, and thus completes the third and final vertical row.*

Besides the patron saint of the church and the saint of day, all the saints of heaven are commemorated in this petition; thus the whole Church Triumphant is honored. And so ends testimony to the ancient belief in the communion of saints, a doctrine as old as the Apostles' Creed itself.

CHAPTER XXVII

THE COMMEMORATION
OF THE CHURCH
MILITANT AND SUFFERING

The Church on Earth

The Church on earth is at all times militant. If it is to fulfill its divine destiny, it must be. Christ said that he came not to bring peace, but a sword (cf. Matt. 10:34). The peace the Church brings, like that of its Founder, is not necessarily between man and man, as the world may give it. Christ's doctrine, to which the Church is ever faithful, is a sword, dividing its members from the rest of the world. At times, it will cause a brother to deliver his brother to death, and a father, his son; or it will make children rise up against their parents and cause their death (cf. Matt. 10:21). With its supernatural edge, this sword divides haters from the hated, persecutors from the persecuted, scourgers from those who are scourged. Since the very beginning, there was war between Christ's Church and its enemies, forever intent on enslaving, perverting and destroying it. That is why the Church of Christ must be militant.

The priest takes the fourth prosphora *in his hands and intercedes with God :*

Remember, Lord, Lover of mankind, His Holiness our universal Pontiff N——, Pope of Rome; and our Most Reverend Archbishop and Metropolitan N——, our God-loving Bishop N——, and every bishop of the orthodox faith, the honorable priests, the deacons in Christ, and all the clergy *(if in a monastery :* **our Very Reverend Father Protoarchimandrite N——, Archimandrite N——, Protohegumenos N——, and Hegumenos N——),** **our brothers and co-celebrants, priests and deacons, and all our brothers**

whom you have called into your communion, through your tenderness of heart, O all-gracious Lord. [1]

After cutting out a particle, the priest places it on the diskos *below the holy bread, or* ahnets. *This particle is the first in the horizontal row for the petitions of the Church militant.*

The *Ecclesia* is strong and invincible only insofar as God will help and protect it. The gates of hell will never prevail against it, but God never promised to take away weariness or suffering. Generally speaking, God governs and protects his Church through the pope, the bishops, and the priests. The general fruit of the Eucharistic Sacrifice is shared more abundantly by those members of Christ's body who contribute more copiously to its welfare. The Holy Father ranks first, for he is the visible head, the vicar of Christ on earth, the father of all Christians. This is but the first of six prayers in which he is mentioned by name in the course of the Divine Liturgy.

As in the diptychs of old, most *proskomidia* petitions for the living and the dead begin with " Remember, Lord.... " If these simple words had the power to gain heaven itself for the repentant Thief (Luke 23:42-43), they should be no less efficacious in obtaining blessings and grace for the friends of God who have dedicated their lives to his work. The hierarchy and clergy, from archbishop and metropolitan down to the most humble cleric in minor orders, participate in the work of feeding the flock of Christ; hence, the prayer includes every rank from archbishop to priest. [2]

The word *orthodox*, coming from the Greek (ὀρθός, true or right, and δόξα, opinion, belief) means " those of the true faith. " The Slavonic equivalent is *pravoslavnej*. The faithful of the One, Holy, Catholic and Apostolic Church are the only ones who in all humility can rightly claim this title of true believers. Byzantine Christians

---

[1] The Russian Catholic recension has a slight variation in the first part of this prayer : " Remember, Lord, Lover of men, every true bishop, our lord His Holiness, the universal Pontiff N., Pope of Rome, and our Holy Patriarch N., (our Metropolitan N., or our Archbishop N., or our Bishop N.), etc. "

[2] If a priest-monk celebrates the Liturgy, then he inserts into the prayer the names of his superiors : the *protoarchimandrite*, *archimandrite*, *protohegumenos*, *hegumenos*, Byzantine equivalents for superior general, provincial, superior, etc.

among others earned themselves this title during the Monophysite heresy of Eutyches. After the General Council of Chalcedon (A.D. 451) they willingly accepted its definitions of the dogma of two natures in Christ; hence, they were called the " true " or " orthodox " Christians. In 1054, however, most of these true Christians of the East broke away from Rome and its jurisdiction. Even after the break, they retained their title of " true " or " orthodox. " [3] And not without reason : " The Orthodox Church has no other origin than that of the Catholic Church : she is purely and simply the Christian Church of the Eastern part of the Roman Empire. " [4] The Catholic Church has a perfect claim to the same title, *orthodox*, since it has preserved all the truths entrusted to it by Christ.

At the Last Supper, Christ prayed : " And not for them only do I pray, but for them also who through their word shall believe in Me, that they all may be one, as Thou, Father, in Me, and I in Thee; that they also may be one in Us " (John 17:20-21). Together with the hierarchical shepherds and leaders, all the baptized faithful who have not cut themselves off from the *Ecclesia* are members of the body of Christ. " The Church, " said Cyprian, " is the people united to the bishop, the flock clinging to its shepherd. The bishop is in the Church and the Church in the bishop. " [5] All are one in Christ, all make up his body. The Church is Christ with us. Or as Ignatius of Antioch put it some sixty or seventy years after Jesus' death, " Where Christ is, there is the Catholic Church. " [6] The whole *Ecclesia* is therefore included in the commemoration : " And all our brothers whom you have called into your communion. "

All of them benefit from the sacrifice. Each of them is made holier, more divine, more Godlike because each is drawn into closer union with Christ. Because Christ loved his Church, he delivered himself up for it. In every Eucharistic Sacrifice he delivers himself up anew for it, " that he might sanctify it... that he might present

---

[3] The term *schismatic* (meaning *split up*, from the Greek verb σχίζειν, " to split, " the inference being that they have split from Rome), since it is offensive, should never be used. Less offensive is *dissident* (from Latin *dissidere*, " to sit apart, " " to disagree "), because they disagree with Rome.

[4] Dom Gregory Bainbridge, " L'Orthodoxie, " *Lumière et Vie*, 19 (1955).

[5] Cyprian, *Epist.*, 69 (PL 4, 418 C-419 A).

[6] Ignatius of Antioch, *To the Smyrnaeans*, 8, 2 (edit. ANF, Vol. I, p. 90).

it to himself a glorious Church, not having spot or wrinkle or any such thing but that it should be holy and without blemish" (Eph. 5:27). The priest-celebrant, as Christ's instrument, represents the whole *Ecclesia*; but as a sharer in the sacrifice, he does more than that; he brings it with him. The particle he places for it on the *diskos* spiritually contains the reality of all those human lives that are truly offering themselves in faith and love.

Then the priest intercedes :

Remember, Lord, N——. [7]

Here, the priest prays for any living person he wishes, cutting out a bread particle, and placing it on the *diskos* next to the previous one. If he wishes to pray for more than one person, he mentions each by name and puts a particle on the *diskos* for each. The first of these is usually the intention for which the sacrifice will be offered. It may be, for instance, for the health of Pavlova, for the success of Ivan in his studies, or for gentle rain over a parched land. [8] For each intention, the priest adds a particle on the *diskos*. The *proskomidia* resembles the ancient offertory practices of " offering an oblation for each name" and reading the diptychs (see p. 518 ff.).

Commemorating the Church Suffering

As soon as the priest has completed the intercessions for the living, he begins those for the dead. Taking the fifth prosphora *into his hand, he says :*

In blessed memory and for the forgiveness of sins of the

---

[7] In the Russian recension there is a special petition for the government : " Remember, Lord, our government and all the armed forces " (*or* " Remember, Lord, our God-fearing sovereign, Emperor N., or King N., and all the armed forces ").

[8] It seems that the priest may include unbelievers, heretics, and excommunicates because the rubrics clearly state *any of these he wishes* (*Ordo celebrationis*, n. 112, 113) and because he recites these names to himself. On the other hand, since these silent commemorations are a liturgical prayer of the Church and correspond to the earlier public reading of names from the diptychs, the mind of the Church may be that the priest name only those in communion with it.

blessed founders of this holy church [*if in a monastery :* **of this holy monastery**]. [9]

The priest begins the second horizontal row of particles, for the faithful departed, immediately below the row for the living.

Those who have helped in founding and building their parish church are remembered in every Eucharistic Sacrifice that shall ever be offered there. When they are departed from this world, a year may pass, two, three, ten, a hundred. Their children and their children's children may have forgotten about them; no trace may be left of their tomb : yet a particle of bread will be offered in their name in every sacrifice, to be made the Eucharist. Countless congregations will intercede for their soul! A beautiful and wholesome thought even if it were only imagined, but it is real, the sheer, tremendous reality constituting this commemoration.

Praying for the forgiveness of sins in this petition admits of more than one interpretation. We know that once a person dies with grave sin on his soul, there is no more forgiveness. Such final impenitence is irrevocable; there is no return from hell. Obviously, then, it is not for the forgiveness of unconfessed, unrepented, grievous sin that this prayer is said. There is here a dramatic transfer of time from the present to the past in petitions regarding matters already settled by God in the Particular Judgment. The phrase "for the forgiveness of sins," therefore, should be interpretde in this light.

Temporal punishment is due to forgiven sins. Much of it is suffered by the penitent during his lifetime, through *epitimia* (expiating works assigned by the confessor), reception of the sacraments, good works, suffering, etc. After death, any temporal punishment still due is expiated by suffering in a temporary place of cleansing, usually called purgatory. This suffering may be lessened through prayer. [10] That is why the Church has prayed for the departed from

---

[9] The Russian recension of this commemoration reads : " In memory and for the forgiveness of sins of the holy patriarchs, of the orthodox and God-fearing tsars and God-fearing tsarinas, of the blessed founder of this holy church " (*if in a monastery* : "of this holy monastery").

[10] Both Catholics and Orthodox believe that Christians here on earth have a duty to pray for the departed, and they are confident that the souls of the departed are helped by such prayers. The liturgical services for the dead and the prayers

its earliest days, especially during the Eucharistic Sacrifice (see
p. 518 ff.).   When Cyril of Jerusalem wrote, " Then we remember
also those who have fallen asleep before us... because we believe
that those souls benefit very greatly for whom supplication is made
while the holy and tremendous sacrifice lies before us, " [11] he was
describing a practice of long standing.

*Having prayed for the founders of the Church, the priest
commemorates by name the bishop who ordained him (if he is dead) and
any other deceased persons for whom he wishes to pray.   He cuts out
a particle in the name of each, places all of them in line on the* diskos,
and says for each one :

**Remember, Lord, the soul of your departed servant
N———.** [12]

Then he makes the last commemoration for the departed :

**And all our orthodox fathers and brothers who have
fallen asleep in the hope of resurrection, eternal life and
communion with you, O Lord, the Lover of mankind.**

*And he also cuts out a particle for this last intention and places it on
the* diskos.

The naming of the dead is a close parallel to the ancient custom
of reading the diptychs.   Even today in Byzantine-Slav churches,
both Ukrainian and Russian, the people who wish to have the
Liturgy celebrated for their departed relatives and friends sometimes
bring their diptych-booklet and give it to the priest so that he can
mention all the names it contains.   The first to be remembered is
the ordaining bishop of the celebrant.   Every priest is grateful to
the bishop who ordained him, for through him he not only received
the official call into the Lord's service but also the great gift of the

they contain are, after all, the same in both Churches.   Precisely why the souls
need our prayers and how they are helped by them is not entirely clear in Orthodox
theology : the answers have varied somewhat at different times.   Today, the
majority of Orthodox theologians are inclined to the belief that the faithful do not
suffer at all.   Others again hold that perhaps they suffer but, if so, their suffering
is purificatory, not expiatory.   A third group prefers to leave the whole question
open and avoids detailed formulations.

[11] Cyril of Jerusalem, *Cat. mystag.*, V, 9 (Quasten, *Mon.*, 102).

[12] The Russian recension has : " Remember, Lord, N. "

priesthood itself. Through the bishop's hands the celebrant received the very power of God, the power to forgive the sins of man, to call down upon the altar the Son of God himself in the Eucharist.

In the last part of the commemoration, the priest prays for all the departed faithful : *And all our orthodox fathers and brothers.* The word *orthodox* (see above, pp. 300 f.) here means those who have departed this earthly life in the true faith, as members of the true Church. Death is called a "falling asleep." The imagery covers more than the natural resemblance of death to sleep : it is scriptural. [13] The idea that death is but a sleep is implied in the English word *cemetery,* which, like the Latin, *coemeterium,* derives from the Greek κοιμητήριον, meaning a *place of slumber,* a *chamber of sleep*—a term by which the Church has designated her places of burial from the earliest days. The biblical presentation of eternal happiness as sabbatic rest was especially fitting in the ancient world where masses of people were condemned by economic circumstances to a life of unending, hard labor. With relatively few exceptions, ancient man could scarcely imagine greater bliss than unending rest or slumber. For those who died in the love of God, death is a sleep of peace, far removed from all suffering, sweat, and toil. But it is more than that. The "inheritance which is imperishable, undefiled, and unfading, kept in heaven for you" (I Pet. 1:4) is described in Holy Writ as something "that eye hath not seen, nor ear heard : neither hath it entered into the heart of man, what things God hath prepared for them that love Him" (I Cor. 2:9). Even the body will joyously awake in the glorious resurrection of the dead to share in never-ending bliss : "I am the resurrection and the life; he who believes in me, though he die, yet shall he live, and whoever lives and believes in me shall never die" (John 11:25-26). Yes, the people of God wept at death. So did the Lord (John 11:35). They wept with one another even as they rejoiced, even as we weep and rejoice today. Through their tears, the people of God can see salvation and reunion with their beloved ones. For them, death is truly a "falling asleep" with the joyous hope and expectation of awakening to eternal life, a

[13] E.g., Job 3:13; 19:25-27; Ps. 12:4; Isa. 26:19; Dan. 12:2; Ecclus. 30:17; II Macc. 12:45; I Cor. 15:18, 34; Rev. 14:13; etc.

life of complete union with Love, a life of bliss which will never end.

Death does not, nor can it, sever the bond of mutual love linking the members of the *Ecclesia*. In God and in his Church, no division separates the living and the departed : all are one in the love of the Father. In life, the members of the *plebs sancta Dei* pray for each other and ask for each other's prayers. They pray also for the faithful departed and ask the faithful departed to pray for them, thus bearing each other's burden.

The Final Commemoration

The last particle is that for the celebrant himself and for the forgiveness of his sins. [14] *Before placing it on the* diskos, *the priest says :*

Lord, according to your great mercy, remember my unworthiness, and forgive me all my sins, both voluntary and involuntary. [15]

The repenting humility of man shines through this petition for forgiveness. Typically Byzantine, it begs forgiveness for all voluntary and involuntary sins. The Western mind may be disconcerted by the notion of involuntary sin, but it makes good ascetical sense. No one but God knows the measure of personal guilt involved in any faulty act. Who but God can judge the whole complex of objectively sinful actions whose subjective guilt is lessened or totally vitiated by involuntariness due to varying degrees of lack of realization, consent or freedom of the will? Is all guilt eliminated even in the case of extreme extenuating circumstances? Who knows his own mind and will in some acts? Who can unravel his motives? How much personal guilt is there in collective guilt? If my country sends the Jews to the gas-chanbers, or is unjust to any minority on account of race, color, or creed, what is my share of its guilt? When is there no sin at all in merely material sins? How much guilt is there in what Western theologians call imper-

---

[14] Other particles, however, can still be added for the living or the dead until the Great Entrance.

[15] The Russian recension omits the phrase " according to your great mercy. "

fections, both positive and negative? [16] Praying for ten minutes is good but if one has the opportunity, praying for an hour is better, a greater perfection. Why did I pray less? Was it laziness, negligence? Was a grace squandered?

Byzantine theologians generally are less prone to excuse from all guilt such so-called imperfections. By his self-accusation of voluntary and involuntary sins, the Byzantine Christian is all-inclusive. For him, including every taint of personal guilt, even of actions whose voluntariness is not immediately apparent, is a means toward achieving greater purification.

"*After completing all the commemorations, the priest gathers together the particles on the diskos so that none of them will be in danger of falling off.*" This rubric is a necessary precaution for the Great Entrance when the *diskos* is carried in procession to the main altar. The precaution is taken at this point so that it will not be forgotten later.

Now that all the particles are on the *diskos* around the holy bread, the *ahnets*, the symbolism of Bethlehem is complete. At Bethlehem, the Son of God came to dwell among us mortals and was surrounded by his chosen, loved ones; on the *diskos*, he is now symbolically by present and surrounded by his beloved elect, the members of the Church Triumphant, Militant, and Suffering. In the manger, God the Son was hypostatically united to his carnal body; symbolically, on the *diskos* he is mystically united to his members, for the *ahnets* touches and is surrounded by small particles—except on the upper side. The whole pattern is a graphic representation of the mystical body with Christ as its Head.

The disposition of the particles on the *diskos* around the large host is a relatively late development. A thirteenth-century document is one of the earliest sources to prescribe any set order of particles, restricting the categories of saints to nine. A single particle was to commemorate each category, and all were to be placed in three rows on the *diskos*. [17] In the next century, the *Constitution* of

---

[16] " Negative imperfection " is usually defined as a mere lack of greater perfection in a human act, while a " positive " one may be (a) an involuntary violation of a less important law, or (b) an action or omission that is contrary to a mere counsel.

[17] This is *Cod.* N. 421 of St. Panteleimon Monastery; cf. Krasnoseltsev, *Materialy dlja istorii chinoposlidovania liturgii sv. Ioanna Zlatoustago* (Kazan, 1889), p. 46.

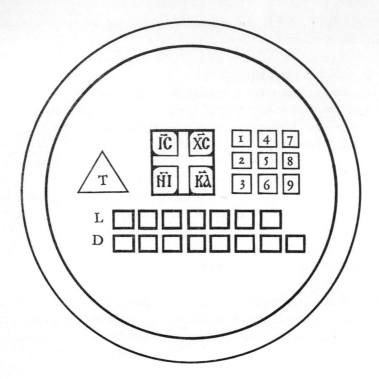

Philotheus prescribed that the particle honoring the Mother of God
and those commemorating the saints be placed to the left of the
" Lamb, " or large host, while the rest of the particles (for the living
and the dead) be placed below the " Lamb. " [18]   This and subsequent
legislation on the matter still left unanswered the question of what
was to be considered " the right side " or " left side " of the principal
host.   This occasioned one of the most celebrated controversies in
the annals of the Byzantine Church. [19]   No longer is there any doubt
about the respective sides today : they are denominated logically
enough from the viewpoint of the " Lamb, " and not from that of
the onlooker.

[18] Cf. Krasnoseltsev, *op. cit.*, pp. 43 ff.
[19] For details, cf. S. Pétrides, *Echos d'Orient*, Vol. III, pp. 75-77.

CHAPTER XXVIII

THE INCENSING
AND COVERING OF THE GIFTS : I

Continuing the rite of proskomidia, *the deacon takes the censer, puts incense into it, and says to the priest :*

Bless the incense, sir.

And immediately he adds :

Let us pray to the Lord.

The priest blesses the incense in the censer with a sign of the cross, and says :

We offer incense to you, Christ, our God, as an odor of spiritual fragrance; receive it on your altar in heaven above, and send down upon us in return the grace of your most Holy Spirit.

From time immemorial, incense has been used in religious ceremonies. The Jews used it in the Temple. The pagans used it in their holy places.

Because it was " holy to the Lord, " incense was to be burned and offered only to Yahweh. As far back as the time of the exodus, God expressly directed how it was to be prepared, and also where, when and how it was to be burned (Exod. 30). The altar of incense stood in the sanctuary in a place of honor, between the seven-branched candlestick and the loaves of proposition. On this altar, a special incense offering was to be made to the Lord twice a day, at nine in the morning and at three in the afternoon, but the incense itself was to burn continually. The preparation and storing of incense was a function reserved to the Levites. [1]

The custom of burning spices after the evening meal was common in all Mediterranean countries, but in the Jewish *chabûrah* supper, spices were brought in, blessed, and burned with a religious intent

---

[1] For the use of incense on the day of atonement, see Lev. 16:12-14.

during the ceremonial of the lamp, [2] except on Fridays, because of the Sabbath.

The first Judeo-Christians probably maintained this practice. There is no trace of opposition to it in the New Testament. On the contrary, the use of incense is mentioned as part of the ideal worship of heaven (Apocalyse, 8:3-4). The apostles and their disciples, being Jewish, were familiar with the hallowed use of incense in the Temple.

Aversion to incense developed during the persecution of the churches founded by Gentile converts, because of its intimate connection with pagan worship. The burning of incense before idols constituted a kind of sacrifice in the Greco-Roman world. Every Roman family, for example, offered incense to the household gods *(lares familiares)* on the *calends, nones,* and *ides* of every month and on all important family occasions. Near the entrance to every temple stood an altar of burnt offerings, and inside the temple stood one or more smaller altars *(foculus, arula, craticula)* for incense offerings.

During the persecutions, burning incense before the idols or the deified emperor was regarded as a sign of apostasy which, until A.D. 252, resulted in exclusion from the *Ecclesia* for life. *Turificati*, "incense-burners," was the term used to qualify the apostates. [3] That is why Christian writers and apologists argued against the practice of using incense in their own services. [4] Hence, it was not used during liturgical functions in the pre-Nicene, persecuted Church.

After the Peace of Constantine, the burning of perfumes or spices in churches was resumed, probably for olfactory reasons.

---

[2] During the first century *A.D.*, the order of the respective blessings was disputed by the rabbinical schools : the school of Shammai taught that the lamp was to be blessed, the " thanksgiving " said, then the spices blessed and burned, in that order; the school of Hillel, on the other hand, held that the " thanksgiving " was to be said after the blessing of the lamp and that of the spices. Cf. *Berakoth, Mishnah* viii, 5, *Tosefta,* vi, 6 (pp. 68-69).

[3] Cyprian, *Epist. ad Cornelli Papae,* X (PL 3, 788 A). Pudentius (405) even gives them a more derogatory name, *turifer grex,* the incense-burning crowd.

[4] Eusebius, *Praep. Evangelica,* iv, 10, where he cites Porphyry (PG 13, 786-787 [*Series graeca*]), and iv, 13, citing Apollonius (PG 13, 788 [*Series graeca*]); Origen, *Contra Celsum,* viii, 17 (PG 8, 840 C-843 [*Series graeca*]), etc.

During the next century, it became widespread in Jerusalem, Antioch, and some of the cities in Italy, [5] again probably as a fumigation, without liturgical purpose. In the predominantly semitic churches of East Syria, incense-burning was regarded as a means of propitiation or atonement for sin (a thoroughly Jewish idea) as early as A.D. 363. [6]

In Jerusalem, in the fourth century, incense was burned as a mark of honor. Etheria describes this ceremonial as occurring in the Office of Lauds, immediately before the reading of the Gospel by the bishop : " Behold, censers are brought in. . . so that the whole basilica is filled with fragrance. " [7] It is impossible to determine whether the incense was a mark of respect for the bishop or for the Holy Gospel. Incense, like torches, had been borrowed from secular practice. [8] From honorific to liturgical use, there was but a step. Incense was widely used by all the Churches of Christendom from the fifth to the eighth centuries. [9] In the Rite of Constantinople, one of the first references to its liturgical use comes from the sixth century when it was customary to incense the whole church at the beginning of the paschal office. [10] This incensing, however, may have been proper to the paschal office only or to some liturgical function other than the Mass. The first certain reference regarding the use of incense during the Divine Liturgy is contained in an early recension of the *Commentary* of St. Germanus (715-729) when he

[5] Chrysostom, *In Matt. hom.*, 88, 4 (edit. Montfaucon 7, 830 DE); Etheria, *Peregrinatio*, chap. 24, 10 (CSEL XXXIX, 73); Ambrose, *Exp. Evang. Lucae*, i, 28 (PL 15, 1545); *de Cain et Abel*, i, 19 (PL 14, 344 D); Paulinus of Nola, *Carmina*, 14, 100 (PL 61, 467 B) and 26, 410 (PL 61, 647 A).

[6] St. Ephraem wrote in his *Carmina Nisibena* (xvii) : " Thy burning of incense is our propitiation : praised be God who has hallowed thine offering. " Cf. Lietzmann, *Messe und Herrenmahl, Eine Studie zur Geschichte der Liturgie*, 9 (Bonn, 1926), p. 86.

[7] Etheria, *Peregrinatio* (edit. L. Duchesne), *Origines du culte chrétien*, p. 515. A similar use of incense is described in the *Apostolic Constitutions*, II, 26, 8 (edit. Funk, I, p. 105).

[8] Cf. Atchley, *A History of the Use of Incense in Divine Worship* (London, 1909), pp. 51-56.

[9] E.g., Ps.-Dionysius, *De ecclesiastica hierarchia*, chap. 3, § 2 (PG 3, 425 B); also chap. 3, § 3 (PG 3, 428 D); James of Edessa (703), *De sacris mysteriis* (Rahmani, *I fasti della chiesa patriarcale Antiochena* [Rome, 1920], p. xx). So also the ancient Greek Liturgy of St. James (Brightman, LEW, p. 32, 2-14; p. 32, 27-32; p. 36, 6-13; p. 41, 10-32, etc.).

[10] Eustratius of Constantinople, *In vita S. Eutychii* (PG 86, 2377 C).

explains the Alleluia chant.[11]   The ninth-century Anastasian
version of the same *Commentary* also mentions that there is to be
incensing at the end of the *proskomidia*.[12]

By the eleventh century, in certain dioceses, there were three
instances of incensing during the Liturgy of St. John Chrysostom :
at the covering of the Gifts in the *proskomidia*, at the Great Entrance,
and before the Communion of the faithful.[13]   The first of these is
described thus : " ...the deacon, when he accepts the thurible,
says to the priest : ' Bless, O Lord, this incense. '   And the priest
says : ' We offer incense to Thee, O Christ God, for an odor of
spiritual fragrance.   Send us the grace of the Holy Spirit, now and
always.   Amen. ' "[14]   This prayer is similar to the present formula,
although shorter.   This first incensing at the covering of the Gifts
in the *proskomidia* is found in most manuscripts of the Greco-
Byzantine Liturgy from the twelfth to the fifteenth centuries.[15]
Incensing in its present form was established only after the twelfth
century.[16]

The Slav Church seems to have followed its mother Rite as

---

[11] N. 30 of said *Commentary* (edit. N. Borgia, *Il commentario liturgico di s.
Germano Patriarcha Constantinopolitano e la versione latina di Anastasio Bibliotecario*
[Grottaferrata, 1912], p. 25).

[12] Edit. N. Borgia, p. 21.

[13] The Liturgy of S. John Chrysostom, trans. by Leo Thuscus, *Liturgiae sive
missae sanctorum patrum : Jacobi apostoli et fratris Domini, Basilii magni e vetusto
codice latinae translationis, Ioannis Chrysostomi, interprete Leone Thusco, De ritu
missae et eucharistia* (Paris, 1560), pp. 52-53, 57-58, 73.

[14] *Ibid.*, pp. 52-53.

[15] E.g. the twelfth-century *Cod. Rossanensis* (*Vat. gr.*, 1970), edit. C. A. Swainson,
The Greek Liturgies Chiefly from Original Authorities (London, 1884), pp. 191 and
192, col. 1 : only two incensings, however, are given in the whole Liturgy, this and
another at the Lesser Elevation.   The Erasmian edition of the Liturgy (I. Goar,
Euchologion, p. 104) has the same arrangement.   Though the *Typikon* of S. Sabba
in the thirteenth-century *Cod. Athono-Protat.*, 72 (A. Dmitrievsky, *Opysanie liturgicheskikh rukopisej khraniaschikhsia v bibliotekakh pravoslavnago vostoka*, Vol. III
[St. Petersburg, 1917], pp. 119, 120, etc.) gives three incensings during the Divine
Liturgy, none is at the *proskomidia* : they are at the *Alleluia* chant, before the
Great Entrance, and at the end of the Great Entrance when the Gifts are deposited
on the altar.   Nicolas Cabasilas (1371), on the other hand, does mention this
first incensing at the covering of the Gifts in the *proskomidia* (*Liturgiae expositio*,
chap. 11 [PG 150, 389 CD]).

[16] A history of this development is found in Dom Placide de Meester, O.S.B.,
Les origines et les développements du texte grec de la liturgie de S. Jean Chrysostome,
XPYCOCTOMIKA, pp. 308, 313-314, 331, 333.

regards this first incensing, but the accompanying prayer is different. The twelfth-century *Liturgikon of Barlaam of Khutinsk*, for example, already prescribes incensing of the Gifts at the *proskomidia*. [17]

Today, the Byzantine-Slav Rite, no less than the Greek, glories in the abundant use of incense during its liturgical functions; it is indeed an integral part of their ceremonial.

Frequent and abundant incensing is pleasing to the senses : fragrant smoke rises in clouds. There is here a prodigal spending, for God's sake, as the sign of an outpouring of irrepressible love. It has come to symbolize many things. Mostly, the fragrant smoke signifies prayer going up to God. The basis for this symbolism is found in Sacred Scripture : " ...and the four and twenty ancients fell down before the Lamb, having every one of them harps and golden vials full of odors which are the prayers of the saints " (Apoc. 5:8). Again, " And another angel came and stood before the altar, having a golden censer : and there was given to him much incense, that he should offer up the prayers of all saints, upon the golden altar which is before the throne of God. And the smoke of the incense of the prayers of the saints ascended up before God from the hand of the angel " (Apoc. 8:3-4).

In the *proskomidia*, the deacon puts the incense into the censer while the priest blesses it. It then becomes a sacramental, an object dedicated to the Lord, possessing supernatural efficacy by reason of an official blessing and prayer of the Church. As a sacramental, it becomes a means of obtaining blessings from God. In this case, the blessing requested is the grace of the Holy Spirit, as is evident from the final words of the Prayer of Incense : " and send down upon us in return the grace of your most Holy Spirit. "

The expression " on your altar in heaven above " (or " on your heavenly altar ") is not contained in the eleventh-century Liturgy of Chrysostom (cf. p. 312, above). It must have been interpolated later, but the liturgical use of the expression itself is quite ancient. In the East, it dates back to about A.D. 300; in the West, certainly

---

[17] MS. of Moscow Synodal Library, N. 343 (A. Petrovsky, *Histoire de la rédaction slave de la liturgie de S. Jean Chrysostome*, XPYCOCTOMIKA, p. 864); the fourteenth or fifteenth century *Molytovnyk-Sluzhebnyk* (edit. Kowaliv), p. 6 of its text; the fourteenth or fifteenth century *Liturgikon* of Isidore, Metropolitan of Kiev, in its *Ustav* (MS. *Vat. Slav.* N. 14, p. 122).

to St. Ambrose, since his text of the Canon contains it.   The various
Eastern Liturgies refer to it frequently since the fourth century.   In
the preparation for Communion of the *Apostolic Constitutions*
(Book VIII, 13, 3), the divine acceptance of the *Gift* is said to be
" on God's heavenly altar. "   The Liturgy of St. Mark uses it
several times; [18] so do the Greek St. James, [19] the West Syrian
anaphoras of Timothy and Severus; [20] also the Byzantine Liturgy
at this and other points.   In the West, medieval commentators
offered various interpretations, often unfounded. [21]   In comparing
parallel passages in the Oriental Liturgies where the expression is
used, there is no reason for assuming any other meaning than the
natural sense of the word.   The heavenly altar is but a figure,
probably stemming from the passage in Apocalyse (8:3-5) quoted
above.

The Prayer of Incense contains three elements : the offering to
God, the hope that he will receive it in heaven, and the request
for grace.

The Star (Asteriskos in Greek)

The *star* is a sacred utensil consisting of two pieces of bent metal,
gold-plated, joined in the center, with a small star suspended from
the intersecting point.   Its purpose is practical : to prevent the
particles from being touched by the veils that will cover them.

*After the priest has blessed the incense and said the Prayer of Incense,
the deacon says :*

Let us pray to the Lord.

The priest incenses the star *by holding it over the censer.   He
places it over the particles and says :*

**And the star came and stood over the place where the
Child was** (Matt. 2:9).

When the star is positioned over the paten, it hangs directly over
the large host, or *Lamb*.   It represents the star of Bethlehem,

---

[18] Cf. Brightman, LEW, 115, 118, 122, 123 f.
[19] Brightman, LEW, 36, 41, 47, 58 f.
[20] Cf. *Anaphorae Syricae* (Rome, 1934-1944), 23, 71.
[21] E.g., Remigius of Auxerre, *Expositio* (PL 101, 1262 f.); Isaac of Stella, *Ep. de
off. missae* (PL 194, 1889-1896); Paschasius Radbertus, *De corp. et sang. Domini*,
VIII, 1-6 (PL 120, 1286-1292); etc.

shining over the manger where the Child Jesus lay on the first Christmas night. The star itself is not the usual five-pointed figure of Christmas decorations, but the six-pointed one of the Jews, the Star of David. It is perhaps a more appropriate representation of the Bethlehem star than the five-pointed one : Jesus, according to his human nature, was a descendant of the House of David.

The symbolism of Bethlehem becomes clear precisely at this point when the star is placed over the Lamb : the star appears over the place where the Child lay. [22] The large host, or Lamb, lies on the *diskos*, or paten; in Bethlehem, the Christ Child lay in the manger. Around the large host, representing Christ, lie the small particles in honor of the Mother of God, the angels, the saints, the living and the dead; around the manger in Bethlehem were his Mother, the angelic hosts, and the chosen shepherds who were privileged to be summoned to the side of Christ. The shepherds were the chosen ones at Bethlehem; now, the chosen are the members of Christ's Church, militant, triumphant, and suffering. In Bethlehem, a star shone over the stable; in the *proskomidia*, a star hangs over the paten.

In the Byzantine Rite, the *star* is referred to as early as the last half of the eleventh century, although liturgical books, both Greek [23] and Slav, [24] do not mention it before the fourteenth century. It seems to have fulfilled originally a practical function only—to keep the veils from touching the hosts—rather than a liturgical need. Later, the *star* was given a beautiful liturgical symbolism, which writers and commentators of the late fourteenth and early fifteenth centuries were careful to explain. [25]

[22] " And the star came and stood over the place where the Child was " is taken from Matthew's account of what happened at Bethlehem (2:9).

[23] The star is mentioned in the *ordo* of the Liturgy contained in the *Typikon* of S. Sabba in the *Cod. Petroburgensis*, 585 (cf. A. Dmitrievsky, *op. cit.*, III, p. 185); also in the *Constitution* of Philotheus (Dmitrievsky, *op. cit.*, II, *Euchologia*, p. 821. Cf. also S. Pétridès, *Astérisque* (DAL, I, 3003).

[24] MS. N. 274, fol. 3, of Count Tolstoy Library and MS. of Moscow Synodal Library, N. 345 (Gorsky-Nevotrujev, *Opysanie slavianskikh rukopisej Moskovskoj Synodal'noj biblioteky*, Vol. III [Moscow, 1859], 1, 21); also the fourteenth or fifteenth century *Liturgikon* of Isidore, Metropolitan of Kiev, in its *Ustav*, MS. *Vat. Slav.* N. 14, fol. 121.

[25] E.g., Nicolas Cabasilas (1371), *Liturgiae expositio*, chap. 11 (PG 150, 389 C); Ps.-Sophronius of Jerusalem, *Commentarius liturgicus*, 3 (PG 87, 3985 BC); and Simeon of Thessalonica (1429), *Dialogus*, chap. 96 (PG 155, 285 D).

CHAPTER XXIX

THE INCENSING AND COVERING
OF THE GIFTS : II

*B*efore the gifts are covered with the veils, the deacon again says :
Let us pray to the Lord.

The priest incenses the first of the small veils (by holding it over the censer) and covers the paten and the particles while he says Psalm 92 :

The Lord has reigned, he is clothed with beauty : the Lord is clothed with power and he has girded himself. For he has established the world, which will not be moved. Your throne is prepared from of old; you are from eternity. The floods rise, O Lord, the floods have lifted up their voices; the floods lift up their waves with the sound of many waters. Wonderful are the surges of the sea : wonderful is the Lord on high. Your testimonies are become exceedingly credible. Holiness befits your house, O Lord, unto the length of days (Psalm 92).

The deacon prays :

Let us pray to the Lord. Cover (it), sir.

The priest incenses the second of the small veils in the same way as the first. He covers the holy chalice with it and says :

Your virtue, O Christ, has covered the heavens, and the earth is full of your praises.

Again the deacon :

Let us pray to the Lord. Cover (it), sir.

The priest takes the third veil, the aer, *and incenses it as the others. Then he covers both the paten and the chalice with it while he says :*

Cover us with the shadow of your wings; drive away from us every enemy and foe. Make our life peaceful, Lord, have mercy on us and on your world, and save our souls because you are good and the Lover of mankind.

In the Latin rite, only one veil is used to cover the chalice and paten. In the Byzantine, there are three : a small veil for the paten; another small veil for the chalice, and a larger veil to cover both. The two smaller veils are usually called *pokrovtsi* in Slavonic (meaning " small coverings, small veils. ") The third veil, since it is larger than the others, is called *pokrov* but it is known also as the *aër* (ἀήρ, meaning " air "), because during the recitation of the Creed the priest waves it over the Holy Gifts and thereby " stirs the air. "

These veils or coverings protect the Holy Gifts from dust, insects, etc. This practical function was soon overshadowed by what they were thought to represent : the swaddling clothes with which the Infant Jesus was wrapped. [1]

While covering the holy bread and paten, the priest contemplates the mystery of Bethlehem : the beauty and power of almighty Yahweh, King of heaven and earth, hidden under the helplessness of a Babe! Wonder and praise for divine beauty and might are summed up in the words of Psalm 92. God's beauty and majestic power reveal themselves in nature. His works of creation are like a beautiful robe. He is the Lord of the world he has made, Master of the rushing waters and breaking waves. He has established not only the natural order, but also the moral. He is wonderful in both; beauty is becoming to his house forever. This juxtaposition of the physical and moral orders is found in many passages of the Old Testament.

In the prayer for covering the chalice, the priest praises the newborn Babe for his limitless good works. All the earth praises and exults with him. The benefits to man of his coming into the world are certainly incalculable, so immense that they " cover the heavens. " As a result, the whole earth is " full of his praise. "

In the final prayer of covering, the priest asks the newborn King for protection : " Cover us with the shadow of your wings, make our life peaceful, Lord. " If our enemies are driven away, vanquished, we will be safe, peaceful. The plea for mercy and salvation is tempered with hope : " because you are good and the

---

[1] Later, as the drama of the Divine Liturgy progresses, they take on a different meaning : the winding sheets with which the body of Christ was wrapped for burial.

Lover of mankind. " The reason is childlike, Godlike, in its simplicity, humility, and truth. No better theological reason can be given. *Chelovikoljubets*, Christ the *Lover of man* (or *mankind*), is an expression containing a world of meaning and has become one of the distinguishing marks of Slav spirituality.

The Slavs seem to have been naturally attracted to the love that was in the heart of Christ, for not long after they adopted Christianity, they felt drawn to Christ as the Lover of man rather than to the original Byzantine concept of Christ as the *Pantocrator*, the *emperor (tsar)*, *all-powerful ruler*, the *severe judge*. In the beginning, the Kievan Slavs accepted this severe, awesome concept of Christ the emperor and austere judge as part of their Byzantine heritage. This aspect of Christ's formidable justice and might was burned into their conscience. But little by little, the Slav heart felt attracted by Christ's all-embracing love, charity, and compassion.

Just as no one can truly appreciate the boundless, burning love of Christ without deep awareness of the sufferings endured by him in consequence of that love, so the Slavs were irrevocably, indelibly impressed by Christ's Passion, his utter humiliation, and his final supreme act of love, death by crucifixion.

The ideal of Christ as the meek, humiliated, gentle Lover of man appears in the earliest Slav writings; it is reflected in the lives of their greatest saints, St. Theodosius and St. Sergius. It is expressed in the countless icons of the Saviour holding the open Gospel Book with the words recorded by St. John : " A new commandment I give unto you; that you love one another.... " The love expressed in the Western devotion to the Sacred Heart is the very same that has drawn so many Slavs to Christ. [2]

Since the whole rite of *proskomidia* represents the mystery of Bethlehem, the beginning of the hidden life of Christ while " He grew in wisdom and grace before God and men " (Luke 2:52), there is nothing which expresses this idea better than " hiding " the Holy Gifts (representing Christ, the Blessed Mother, etc.) with veils.

Though not actually of recent origin, the covering of the gifts is

---

[2] In Russian and Ukrainian iconography, the heart of Jesus is never exposed, for it is too sacred for man's unworthy gaze.

definitely one of the last additions to the ceremonial of the Divine Liturgy. Insofar as is known, none of the most ancient Greek texts mentions anything about it, neither do the most ancient commentaries. [3] It it only between the twelfth and the fourteenth centuries that the rituals of incensing the veils (by holding them over the censer) and of covering the gifts became established, together with the corresponding prayers. At first, the ritual was simpler, [4] but during the latter part of the fourteenth century it was finally standardized almost as it is today. [5] Likewise, in the Slav branch of the Byzantine Rite, the gifts were being covered with veils in the late twelfth century. [6] Again, the ceremony at first was

[3] E.g., nothing is mentioned regarding this in the *Commentary* of S. Germanus of Constantinople (715-729), nor in the ninth or tenth century manuscript of Grottaferrata Γ. B. VII, nor in the eleventh century *Constitution* (Διάταξις τῆς προσκομιδῆς) in *Ad Paulum Hypopsephium Gallipolitanum* (edit. Mai), NPB, X, ii, pp. 167-169, nor in the eleventh century Cod. Burdett-Couts. III, 42 (cf. C. A. Swainson, *The Greek Liturgies Chiefly from Original Authorities* [London, 1884], p. 108).

[4] The ceremonial in the Liturgy of St. John Chrysostom as translated into the Latin by Leo Thuscus (fl. 1200) is still undeveloped : the accompanying prayers are brief and probably only two veils were used. As given in that Liturgy, the rubrics state : " While the deacon holds the thurible, the priest unfolds over the thurible the sacred corporals that are to be put over the holy chalice; while these are being saturated with the odor of smoke, he says, ' The Lord hath reigned; he is clothed with beauty : the Lord is clothed with power and he hath girded himself. Thy throne is prepared now and always and forever. ' Then he covers the chalice and adds, ' His virtue hath covered the heavens, and the earth is full of his praise, now and always and forever ' " (Our translation from the Latin in *Liturgiae sive missae sanctorum patrum : Jacobi apostoli et fratris Domini, Basilii magni e vetusto codice latinae translationis, Ioannis Chrysostomi, interprete Leone Thusco, De ritu missae et eucharistia* [Paris, 1560], p. 52). The Erasmian recension of the same Liturgy had prescribed three veils but the accompanying prayers were still brief : " For the *diskos* : ' (His virtue) hath covered the heavens. . . . ' For the chalice : ' The Lord hath reigned; he is clothed with beauty, ' etc. In putting on the large veil : ' And bright clouds have covered them. By the word of the Lord the heavens have been made firm, ' etc. " (Our translation, from the Greek in Goar, *Euchologion*, p. 104).

[5] The entire rite of covering the Gifts, for example, in the fourteenth century *Constitution* of the Mass *ordo* in the *Typikon* of S. Sabba, *Cod. Petroburgensis*, 585 (A. Dmitrievsky, *op. cit.*, III, p. 185) is very similar to that of today described above; so also in the *Constitution* of Philotheus (1345-1376); cf. A. Dmitrievsky, *op. cit.*, II, *Euchologia*, p. 821.

[6] The covering of the Gifts with veils is mentioned in the *Liturgikon* of Barlaam of Khutinsk (1192) in these words : " And he (the deacon) covers the Gifts while he says : ' The Lord hath reigned. . . . ' In covering the chalice : ' The Lord is clothed with power. ' " Our translation from the Slavonic in Gorsky-Nevostrujev, *op. cit.*, III, p. 6.

simple, and even during the thirteenth century only two veils were used. [7] In the fourteenth century three veils were used, as today, but the accompanying prayers were changed somewhat from those used in the Greco-Byzantine Rite. [8] Today's ritual dates from the introduction of the *Constitution* of Philotheus into the churches of the Ukraine and Russia in the late fourteenth century, though some texts of the next two centuries still contained the earlier forms. [9] Final uniformity in this matter was achieved by the reform of Patriarch Nikon (1654).

Incensing of the Prothesis and the Prayer of Offering

When he has covered the gifts, the priest takes the censer and incenses the whole oblation while saying :

Blessed is our God who is thus well pleased. [10]

And the deacon adds :

At all times, now and always and for ever and ever. [11]

In saying the foregoing prayer, both the priest and the deacon reverently make a small bow. [12] *The priest returns the censer to the deacon (or he may do so after the Prayer of Offering). Then the deacon says :*

For the oblation of precious gifts, let us pray to the Lord.

The priest takes the censer and, without making any sign of blessing, says the Prayer of Offering :

O God, our God, you have sent Jesus Christ, our Lord and God, to be our Saviour, Redeemer, and Benefactor through

[7] Cf. A. Petrovsky, *op. cit.*, pp. 874, 881.

[8] For the covering of the paten and chalice, the same prayers were said as in the previous century, but for the final covering of the Gifts with the large veil, the following was said : " Sanctity becomes thy house. " This, at any rate, is prescribed in *Cod. Tolstoianus*, 274, p. 3; also in *Cod.* 345 of the Moscow Synodal Library. Cf. Gorsky-Nevostrujev, *op. cit.*, III, i, p. 21.

[9] E.g., MS. of Solovetzky Library N. 1023, p. 75; N. 1025, p. 87, etc. (A. Petrovsky, *op. cit.*, p. 919); also the *Liturgikon* of Metropolitan Isidore, MS. *Vat. Slav.*, 14, fol. 122.

[10] " Glory be to You " is added to this exclamation in the Russian recension; also, the prayer is said three times.

[11] In the Russian recension, since the priest says his part three times, the deacon answers three times.

[12] In Russian churches, three bows are made because the prayer is said three times.

**whom you bless and sanctify us; you sent him to become the
bread from heaven and food for the whole world. Bless
this oblation yourself and accept it on your altar in heaven.
Since you are good and love mankind, remember those
who have offered it and those for whom it is offered and
preserve us from all fault in celebrating your divine mysteries. For hallowed and glorified is the majesty of your
most honored name, Father, Son and Holy Spirit, now and
always and for ever and ever. Amen.**

During the incensing, both priest and deacon bow before the
gifts just as the shepherds and Magi bowed in adoration before the
newborn Babe in Bethlehem. The incensing itself is to remind
the faithful of the Magi's gifts to Christ, one of which was
frankincense, an important incense resin. It is not the gifts, as
Irenaeus carefully points out, but the inner intention, the offering
of the heart that is decisive before God and pleasing to him. [13]
Within the natural gifts of bread and wine is implied the internal
oblation, the heart of every offerer; it rises heavenward like the
clouds of incense. *Thus is our God well pleased.*

Then the priest formally presents these gifts to God in the *Prayer
of the Proskomidia.* Its essence is the petition that God bless and
accept the oblation on his altar in heaven; in return, that he " remember " those who offer it as well as those for whom it is offered.
Its first phrase, " O God, our God, " is filled with strong feeling.
Acts of faith follow, faith in the incarnation, redemption, and true
Presence : " You have sent Jesus Christ, our Lord and God, to be
our Saviour, Redeemer, and Benefactor.... You sent him to
become the bread from heaven and food for the whole world. "
Through him in all these attributes man is blessed and sanctified.

Sanctification means " to make holy " as God is holy; hence, to
make man like God. The Eastern Fathers boldly developed the concept of sanctification to its fullest degree, " theosis, " " divinization, "
or " deification. " This process begun on earth will be completed
in heaven and is the final goal of every Christian ". Man's redemption, sanctification, and salvation mean his deification. Basil

---

[13] Irenaeus, *Adv. haer.*, IV, 18, 1 (PG 7, 1024 f.); *ibid.*, IV, 18, 3 (PG 7, 1026 f.).

describes man as a creature who has received the order to become God. [14] Athanasius teaches that God became man that man might become God. [15] The Byzantine Liturgy carried the same idea : " In my Kingdom, said Christ, I shall be God with you as Gods. " [16] St. Maximus wrote : " We remain creatures while becoming God by grace, as Christ remained God when becoming man by the Incarnation. " [17] Since man is composed of both body and soul and since Christ has saved and redeemed the whole man, deification involves the body also : " Man's body is deified at the same time as his soul. " [18] The complete, full deification of the body, however, must wait until the Last Day. The doctrine of deification has a solid biblical foundation; it is the constant theme of John's Gospel, the Epistles of Paul, and recurs in II Peter : " Through these promises you may become partakers of the divine nature. " [19]

The offertory nature of this prayer is obvious from its text. The bread and wine have been formally prepared and are now being presentend to God by the priest in the name of all the offerers. The first stage of offering is being completed (cf. pp. 509 f.). The bread is still only bread, the wine only wine, but they have become offerings; they have acquired a new characteristic : dedication to God (a sacramental in the Western sense).

" Bless this oblation yourself and accept it on your altar in heaven. " Again, there can be no question of a real altar in heaven, for, strictly speaking, an altar is a place for offering sacrifice—and a real sacrifice such as we have here on earth does not exist in heaven. True, Christ in heaven is the High Priest and the Mediator for us before God. He presents his bloody death to God in order to apply to us the

[14] Basil, *De Sancto Spiritu*, IX, 23 (PG 32, 109); the expression he uses is Θεὸν γενέσθαι.

[15] Athanasius, *De incar.*, 54 (PG 15, 958 C [*Series graeca*]); cf. also *De decretis*, 14 (PG 15, 1081 [*Series graeca*]); Gregory Nazianzen, *Or.*, xxx, 14 (PG 20, 784 D [*Series graeca*]).

[16] *Canon* for Matins of Holy Thursday, Ode 4, Tropar 3.

[17] St. Maximus, *Gnostic Centuries*, 11, 88 (PG 90, 1168 A).

[18] *Ibid.*, 11, 88 (PG 90, 1168 A).

[19] While the Eastern Fathers and writers spoke of deification, they did it in the light of the distinction between God's essence and his energies; thus they avoid all forms of pantheism. *Theosis* means union with the divine energies, not with the divine essence. Man does not become God by essence, but is merely a " created God, " a God by grace or by status.

fruits of the redemption.   From the Apocalypse (5:10; 20:6), we know that the blessed in heaven also are priests of God.   Through Christ and in union with him, they offer unceasingly the sacrifice of praise, homage, and thanksgiving to the triune God.   The most common interpretation of the heavenly altar here is that it symbolizes this heavenly sacrifice of praise and thanksgiving.   Accordingly, in this prayer God is asked to bless our earthly oblation and to unite it with the heavenly oblation of the blessed.   Since the latter, the sacrifice of the Church Triumphant, is always in God's presence and is entirely pleasing to him, so will our oblation be agreeably received by him if united with the all-pleasing sacrifice of the blessed in heaven.   How this union of sacrifices is possible and takes places is a mystery.

The *Prayer of the Proskomidia* is the oldest prayer in the whole rite of preparation.   It is the only one included in the texts of the eighth and ninth centuries. [20]   The form then in use for the Liturgy of St. John Chrysostom, however, was different from that of today. The present prayer, originally contained in the Liturgy of St. Basil the Great, was substituted for it.   In the Byzantine-Slav Rite, the *Euchologia* of the eleventh century already contain the Basilian formula of this prayer for the Liturgy of St. John Chrysostom, [21] but it was said just before the covering of the Gifts instead of after, as it is today.   This was the nucleus around which the rest of the *proskomidia* was built.

The Proskomidia *Dismissal*

Standing where he is by the proskomidia table, the priest begins the dismissal with these words :

Glory be to you, Christ God, glory be to you.

Deacon : **Glory be to the Father and to the Son, and to the Holy Spirit, now and always, and for ever and ever.   Amen. Lord, have mercy** [*thrice*]**. Bless.**

[20] Cf. *Codex Barberini, gr.,* 336 (Brightman, LEW, p. 309).

[21] The first to have this Basilian formula in the Liturgy of Chrysostom was the *Liturgikon* of Barlaam of Khutinsk (twelfth century), MS. of Moscow Synodal Library, N. 343 (Gorsky-Nevostrujev, *op. cit.,* III, p. 6.

Then the priest pronounces the dismissal itself :

May Christ, our true God, through the prayers of his most pure Mother, through those of our father among the saints, John Chrysostom, Archbishop of Constantinople, and through the prayers of all the saints, have mercy on us and save us, for he is good and loves mankind. [22]

Deacon : **Amen.**

This standard dismissal marks the end of the *proskomidia* or rite of preparation. A similar dismissal ends all Byzantine liturgical services. With the exception of a slight addition prefixed for Sundays, the dismissal of the Byzantine *proskomidia* never varies according to feasts or seasons as do the dismassals for the Divine Liturgy itself, the Vesper Service, Matins, etc. The *proskomidia*, the official rite of preparation for the Divine Liturgy, is now ended (see pp. 459 ff. for Dismissals).

Even in the earliest centuries, Christian assemblies ended with a dismissal of some sort. Yet, the dismissal of the *proskomidia* is one of the very latest additions to the rite of preparation. It is possibly that of the Canonical Hour of Sext as used in the fourteenth or fifteenth century. [23] Since the Hour of Sext was to be recited before the Divine Liturgy as a kind of preliminary preparation for it, it would have been natural also to have its dismissal end the rite of preparation, or the *proskomidia*. At any rate, some time during or after the fifteenth century the present dismissal formula became the standard ending.

---

[22] On Sundays, the priest prefaces the dismissal with : " May Christ our true God, who is risen from the dead...., " etc. In the Russian recension of the dismissal, the text reads slightly differently : instead of, " of our father among the saints John Chrysostom, Archbishop of Constantinople..., " it has " of our father among the saints, John, Archbishop of Constantinople, the Golden-mouthed. "

[23] *Cod. Vat. gr.* N. 573 (Krasnoseltsev, *Materialy dlja istorii chinoposlidovania liturgii sv. Ioanna Zlatoustago* [Kazan, 1889], p. 102). The fourteenth or fifteenth century *Liturgikon* of Metropolitan Isidore, in its *Ustav*, prescribes a dismissal (*vidpust*) without specifying its kind; cf. MS. *Vat. Slav.* N. 14, fol. 123.

LITURGY
OF THE CATECHUMENS :
INTRODUCTION

CHAPTER XXX

THE TRANSITIONAL RITUAL

I f they wished to become Christians, pagans had to learn the
doctrines of the Church by attending the catechetical synaxis, the
Liturgy of the Catechumens. The two essential things to learn
before baptism were : (1) the proper methods of prayer and (2) the
major teachings of Christ—including the duties and dignity of the
baptized. In this " instruction-and-prayer service " he was taught
to pray, by taking part in the congregational singing of the psalms,
etc. He was also given an understanding of the truths of revelation
and the duties resultant therefrom, by hearing the Sacred Scriptures
read and explained.

The origin and early evolution of this service we have examined
in some detail above (pp. 30 ff.), but it is well to stress here its
underlying purpose : *instruction and prayer*, for the benefit both of
the catechumens and the baptized, who had to be reminded of their
duties and of the truths of their religion. Hence, even after whole
populations had become Christian and very few catechumens were
left, the Church kept the Liturgy of the Catechumens. The process
of learning about the Incarnation, the Redemption, and the dignity
and duties of a true Christian, does not cease with baptism or with
the rudimentary catechetical instructions preceding it, but continues
throughout one's whole life.

The Liturgy of the Catechumens performed another function :
to create an atmosphere of faith before beginning the great *Mysterium*

fidei, the celebration of the Eucharist. Until the fifth century, the Liturgy of the Catechumens, or fore-Mass, began rather abruptly with the reading of the lessons, introduced by a brief " greeting " of the celebrant to the congregation. [1] Later, other prayers, hymns and ceremonies were introduced into the service to enhance the atmosphere of faith before the reading of the lessons, which in turn prepared those present for a more devout attitude at later stages. Originally, there was a simple introduction; then, there was added a preliminary to the preliminary, and so forth.

The Oriental preliminary ceremonial far surpasses in extent that of the Western or Roman Liturgy. Among all the Oriental Liturgies, the Byzantine has the most complicated introductory ritual. It includes not only the preparatory prayers of the priest before the inconostas (pp. 218-220), his entrance into the sanctuary (pp. 220-221), the vesting, the prothesis, or *proskomidia*, but also everything up to the actual reading of the lessons, i.e. the *Opening* or ἔναρξις, consisting in the *ektenia* or litany of peace, the three antiphons (each with their own oration said by the priest and a shorter litany sung by the deacon), the Little Entrance, followed by different hymns *(tropars, kondaks)* and, finally, the lofty trisagion.

The Liturgy of the Catechumens, present in all Rites, varies according to the " spirit " of the people, Greek or Roman, Gentile or Jew, Slav or Arab. Hence, there is unity in variety.

Initial Incensing

Immediately after the proskomidia *dismissal, the priest goes to the holy table while the deacon incenses the prothesis three times. Then he goes to the holy table and incenses it crosswise from all four sides,*

---

[1] There is ample evidence of this in the Orient and it must have been no less true of the West if we are to judge from a rather unusual incident in the life of St. Augustine. Just before the service began on a certain Easter Sunday, a man was instantaneously cured. The cure caused much excitement among the people in church. Augustine, who was about to make his entrance for the service, was still in the sacristy when this happened. After the excitement died down, the service finally began—with a greeting by the celebrant and the reading of the lessons. We have here, therefore, evidence from the West, c. A.D. 426 that the fore-Mass began with a mere greeting of the bishop, followed immediately by the lessons. Cf. *Civ. Dei* 22, 8 (CSEL XL, 2, p. 611, 1.7).

*beginning with the front (west), then proceeding to the south, the east
and the north.*

While thus incensing, he silently recites :

**While you were in the tomb with your body, in hell with
your soul, and in Paradise with the thief, you were also on
the throne with the Father and Holy Spirit, O Christ, permeating all things, O unlimited One.**

*Then, while reciting the Psalm of Repentance, Psalm 50, the deacon
incenses the icon behind the altar and other images in the sanctuary.
Leaving the sanctuary through the north door, he bows before the
royal doors, and incenses the images on the south side of the iconostas,
beginning with the icon of the Saviour; then those on the north side,
beginning with that of the Mother of God. Next, he incenses the right
and left choirs and, then the people—either from the solea or, depending
upon local custom, by going through the church to the vestibule. After
returning to the sanctuary through the south door, he again incenses the
holy table three times. Finally, he incenses the celebrant three times.*

The interval between the *proskomidia* and the beginning of the
Divine Liturgy proper is taken up with incensing. The deacon
meditates on what happened during the interval between the first
Good Friday and Easter Sunday. The short prayer " While you
were in the tomb " refers to those dramatic truths. In the darkness
of the tomb, Christ's body of flesh escaped corruption. After Jesus
exhaled his final cry, his soul did not rise up to the Father. Released
from the body, it " descended into hell, " or Hades, the gathering
place of the souls of the just who had died before the gates of heaven
opened on the day of Christ's Ascension. Christ appeared to them
and announced the good news that the hour of their entry into heaven
was at hand. The Good Thief had asked Jesus to remember him
when he came into his Kingdom. In reward for that simple petition
and good will, Jesus had told him : " This day thou shalt be with
me in paradise " (Luke 23:43). " Paradise " (the LXX rendering
of " garden " in Eden) signified an abode or dwelling-place for the
blessed.

While Christ's body was in the tomb and his soul in the Kingdom
of the dead, Christ as true God, the second Person of the Trinity,

was also enthroned, and reigned in heaven with the Father and the
Holy Spirit. As God, he was (and is) omnipresent and infinite.

This prayer is attributed to St. John Damascene, although it was
borrowed from the Holy Week services and placed at this point
only in the fourteenth century, [2] that is, after the altar had assumed
the symbolism of the Lord's tomb, and the placing of the holy gifts
upon it was seen as expressing the burial of Christ.

The deacon further prepares himself for the coming sacrifice by
reciting Psalm 50, which is an act of contrition, confession, and
supplication. Rubrics requiring the recitation of either Psalm 50
or Psalm 25 appeared between the thirteenth and sixteenth centuries.[3]
Psalm 25 was also fitting, since it is David's prayer to God that he
be delivered from his distress and that he may come to worship
him in his tabernacle. The pentitential spirit of the East, however,
settled for Psalm 50.

The ancient Eastern custom of greeting every guest and offering
him ablutions and perfumes upon entering the house is enacted at
the beginning of the heavenly banquet, the Divine Liturgy. Incensing and bowing to all, the rich and the poor alike, the deacon
salutes them as guests of the Lord. Instead of earthly perfumes
and ablutions, he offers them incense, symbolizing the all-powerful
grace of the Mystical Supper.

Dionysius the Pseudo-Areopagite, writing about A.D. 485, seems
to offer the first description of incensing as a preliminary to a liturgical function, a practice soon adopted in most of the Greco-Syrian
churches, and finally throughout most of Christendom : " After
ending a sacred prayer before the divine altar, the hierarch begins
by censing there and goes throughout the whole enclosure of the

---

[2] The *Constitution* of Philotheus seems to be the first document to place it in
this position. In the Slav Church the fourteenth or fifteenth century *Liturgikon*
of Metropolitan Isidore has it in its *Ustav* (cf. MS. *Vat. Slav.*, N. 14, fol. 123).

[3] E.g., *Cod Pant.* (Krasnoseltsev, *Materialy dlja istorii chinoposlidovania liturgii
sv. Ioanna Zlatoustago* [Kazan, 1889], p. 14) and *Cod. Esphigm.* of year 1306
(Dmitrievsky, *Opysanie liturgicheskikh rukopisej khraniaschikhsia v bibliotekakh
pravoslavnago vostoka*, Vol. II [Kiev, 1901], p. 265).   In the Slav Church. Ps. 50 is
prescribed in MS. 523 of the Sophia Library, p. 14, but it is said during the kissing
of the altar by the priest and deacon (Petrovsky, *Histoire de la rédaction slave de
la liturgie de S. Jean Chrysostome*, XPYCOCTOMIKA, Rome, 1908, p. 882);
the *Liturgikon* of Metropolitan Isidore prescribes Ps. 50 during the actual incensing
as it is done today (cf. MS. *Vat. Slav.*, N. 14, fol. 123).

sacred edifice. After returning once again to the holy altar, he begins the sacred melody of the psalms. " [4]

What had begun as a purely Syrian [5] liturgical practice soon found its way into Byzantium. Incensing the whole church at the beginning of some liturgical functions was an established custom at Constantinople toward the end of the sixth century [6]. While incensing is mentioned in other parts of the Byzantine Liturgy prior to the thirteenth century [7] none of the earlier manuscripts refer to it at the beginning of the Liturgy. From the thirteenth century on, evidence of this initial incensing abounds, although some documents have it performed by the priest, [8] others by the deacon. [9] It is a fair inference, therefore, that this initial incensing became widespread in the Byzantine Liturgy some time during the thirteenth century or in the latter part of the twelfth. It would then be one of the latest additions.

---

[4] Ps.-Dionysius, De eccl. hierarch., iii, 2 (Quasten, Mon., 294).

[5] Curiously enough, the present East Syrian Rite has no preliminary incensing, though it has retained the psalmody before the lessons which seems to have been introduced about the same time. Two explanations are generally given for this : (1) the psalmody had been prefixed to the readings before the use of incense had been adopted in liturgical functions; (2) the preliminary censing had been discarded with the adoption of the Byzantine preliminaries, i.e., the formal preparation of the Gifts, the preparatory prayers of the celebrant, etc.

[6] Cf. Eustratius of Constantinople, Vita S. Eutychii (PG 86, 2377 C).

[7] E.g., S. Germanus of Constantinople (A.D. 715-729) in his Commentarii liturgici (no. 30, edit. N. Borgia, Il commentario liturgico di s. Germano Patriarca Constantinopolitano e la versione latina di Anastasio Bibliotecario [Grottaferrata, 1912], p. 25) explains the use of incense only at the Alleluia chant and the ninth-century Anastasian version of the Commentarii (edit. op. cit., p. 21) tells us of the incensing done at the end of the proskomidia. The eleventh-century Liturgy of St. John Chrysostom, translated by Leo Thuscus (Liturgiae sive missae sanctorum patrum : Jacobi apostoli et fratris Domini, Basilii magni e vetusto codice latinae translationis, Ioannis Chrysostomi, interprete Leone Thusco, De ritu missae et eucharistia [Paris, 1560], pp. 52-53) has three incensings : at the end of the proskomidia, at the Great Entrance, and just before the Communion of the faithful. The Erasmian recension, on the other hand, has two : at the covering of the Gifts in the proskomidia and before the Small Elevation at the " Holy Things to holy people " (I. Goar, Euchologion, pp. 104, 107), etc.

[8] E.g., the thirteenth century Cod. Patm. N. 719 (Dmitrievsky, op. cit., Vol. II, p. 173); Cod. Esphigm. of year 1306 (ibid., p. 265); the thirteenth century Cod. Pantel. (Krasnoseltsev, op. cit., p. 14) and the fifteenth century MS. of Patr. of Jerusalem (ibid., p. 88).

[9] The Typikon of Vatop. in the fourteenth century Cod. of Moscow Synodal Library, N. 381 (Krasnoseltsev, op. cit., p. 22); the Constitution of Philotheus (op. cit., p. 48); the fifteenth century Cod. Sin., N. 986 (Dmitrievsky, op. cit., p. 606) and the fourteenth or fifteenth century Cod. Vat. gr., N. 573 (Krasnoseltsev, op. cit., p. 102).

CHAPTER XXXI

THE PRAYER TO THE HOLY SPIRIT : DIALOGUE

*A*fter returning the censer to the server, the deacon goes to the right side of the priest. Standing together before the altar, they say :

Heavenly King, Consoler, Spirit of truth, everywhere present and permeating all things, Treasury of blessings and Giver of life, come and dwell within us, and cleanse us from every stain and save our souls, O gracious One.

Then making three small bows :

Glory to God in the highest and on earth peace, and divine favor toward men [*twice*].

Lord, open my lips, and my mouth shall declare your praise (Ps. 50:17).

Comparable to the " Come, Holy Spirit " of the Latin Rite, the prayer " Heavenly King " is primarily theological. Being God, equal to the Father and the Son, the Holy Spirit is King of Heaven, King of All. Towards the end of his life, Christ spoke of the Holy Spirit as the Paraclete (John 14:16, 26; 15:26; 16:7). This Greek word means literally " one called in, " as helper, pleader, defender, advocate. Some versions of the Scriptures retain the Greek word " Paraclete " in their texts. [1] Others, including the Slavonic, render it as " Consoler. " [2] This is satisfactory only if the word is understood to include the assistance, protection, advice, and intercession required to sustain and increase spirituality or deification.

---

[1] E.g., Syriac Peshitta, Coptic, Ethiopic, Gothic and the Vulgate (Sixtine-Clementine edition).

[2] E.g., Syro-Palestinian, Armenian and Georgian. The Slavonic Version was translated from the Greek in the ninth century by SS. Cyril and Methodius, the " Apostles of the Slavs, " probably from the Antiochene text then used in Constantinople. Many scholars maintain that the earlier codices differ from the later in that they present many Hesychian and Caesarean readings. Gennadius of Novgorod completed the Slavonic text on the basis of the Vulgate in the fifteenth century.

St. John, who offers in his Gospel the fullest theology of the Holy Spirit, quotes Jesus as calling the Holy Spirit " the Spirit of Truth " who " will teach you all things " (John 14:17, 26). The prayer " Heavenly King " is directly inspired by a later text from St. John : " But when the Paraclete cometh, whom I will send you from the Father, the Spirit of truth, who proceedeth from the Father, shall give testimony of me " (John 15:26). The expression " Spirit of Truth " is neuter in Greek, but it is immediately followed by the masculine personal pronoun " he " (ἐκεῖνος), which has a strongly determinative sense : " this particular one. " This clearly indicates that the Spirit is a person. Furthermore, the Spirit of Truth is addressed in this prayer as a person, and divine attributes are ascribed to him, making him the equal of the Father and the Son.

The divine attributes and external works are common to all three Persons. Each one possesses the divine nature, and each one operates in virtue of infinite wisdom, power, goodness, etc. Yet, certain attributes and works are appropriated *ad extra* to each Person individually.

To the Holy Spirit are attributed the works of love. Since love is especially manifested in doing good, to him is ascribed the giving of every good gift. This is shown by the fact that he is addressed here as the " Treasury of blessings. " The greatest work of love, however, is the sanctification of souls by grace. First and foremost is the gift of sanctifying grace which gives supernatural life, the very beginning of the life of God in the soul; hence, the Holy Spirit is addressed also as the " Giver of Life, " as in the so-called Nicene Creed.

The Holy Spirit, the immediate author of sanctifying grace, is communicated to the soul in the form of justification. [3] " Come and dwell within us, " we plead in this prayer.

The doctrine of the indwelling of the Holy Spirit in our souls is developed by St. Paul in his Epistle to the Corinthians : " Know you not that you are the temple of God and that the Spirit of God dwelleth in you? " (I Cor. 3:16; cf. I Cor. 6:19). The relation of the Holy Spirit to the soul of the just is that of an indweller. It is

---

[3] " The charity of God is poured forth in our hearts, by the Holy Spirit *who is given to us* " (Rom. 5:5). Our italics.

not the same as the substantial union of body and soul in man, nor as the hypostatic union of the eternal Word with the human nature in Christ, for the Holy Spirit is not united with the just soul as one person with himself. Man remains an independent person after his sanctification or deification by the presence of the Holy Spirit, and the Holy Spirit remains distinct from the just man.

The Church Fathers strongly rejected the doctrine of Nestorius, who maintained that the union between the eternal Word and the humanity of Christ was the same as that existing between the Holy Spirit and the souls of the just. Christ as man is the true Son of God because he is one and the same divine person as the eternal Word, while the just man is merely an adopted son of God because he does not become one person with the Holy Spirit dwelling in his soul. Yet, the union between the Holy Spirit and the soul of the just man is real, in a literal sense, as the Fathers have always maintained.

" Cleanse us from every stain and save our souls. " The forgiveness of grave sins is an essential part of justification and, hence, also of eternal salvation. Justification is a spiritual renewal and regeneration; it means that sin is really destroyed, but not necessarily every stain or effect of sin. The plea in this prayer is for a cleansing of " every stain " so that nothing remains to mar the supernatural beauty of the soul. The desire is for perfect purification.

This incomparable prayer to the Holy Spirit, which is used at the beginning of almost every Byzantine service, was introduced into the Divine Liturgy some time during the thirteenth century. [4]

After praying for the indwelling of the Holy Spirit and for perfect purification, the priest and deacon repeat twice the hymn of praise which the angels sang at Bethlehem to announce the great news of the Messiah's birth. Recited here at the beginning of the Divine

---

[4] MS. of Library of Patmos, N. 719 (Dmitrievsky, *Opysanie liturgicheskikh rukopisej khraniaschikhsia v bibliotekakh pravoslavnago vostoka*, Vol. II, *Euchologia* [Kiev, 1901], p. 173); also the fourteenth century MS. of Sophia Library, N. 523 (Krasnoseltsev, *Materialy dlja istorii chinoposlidovania liturgii sv. Ioanna Zlatoustago* [Kazan, 1889], p. 14); MS. N. 274 of Count Tolstoy's Library, p. 3 (Petrovsky, *Histoire de la rédaction slave de la liturgie de S. Jean Chrysostome*, XPYCOCTOMIKA, p. 882, n. 4); *Liturgikon* of Isidore, Metropolitan of Kiev, in its *Ustav*; cf. MS. *Vat. Slav.*, N. 14, fols. 123-124.

Liturgy, after the Bethlehem symbol offered by the *proskomidia*, this angelic hymn announces the same glad tidings. Christ will come to dwell among us on the altar in the Divine Liturgy with his real Eucharistic presence.

The text of the hymn (Luke 2:14) is somewhat different from that of the Douay Version (which follows the Vulgate rendering). The text here is that commonly used by the Greek Fathers, with εὐδοχία (good will) in the nominative case, though the manuscript evidence favors the genitive εὐδοχίας (of good will), as the Vulgate has it. [5] Luther and the King James Bible follow the common Greek version of the text. What is this good will? Some scholars translate εὐδοχία as the perfection of the desire for God. Others maintain that εὐδοχία (good will) is " divine favor, " " divine good will " or " pleasure. " This seems the closest to the original Greek. If we accept this meaning, it makes little essential difference whether εὐδοχια is in the nominative or the genitive. The word refers to a proclamation of God's good will toward man, the mercy which moved the Father to send his Son to redeem the world, God's desire to save all men.

The first words of the hymn " Glory to God in the highest " are an expression of the angelic recognition and praise for the greatest work of God. An angel speaking to man about God must speak in terms that man's intellect can understand : the phrase " in the highest " praises God by fixing his throne in the highest heaven, since the Jewish mind had long before formed the idea of God's excellence by placing his throne above the heaven of the stars.

With Christ's birth, honor is restored to God, peace (the fullness of supernatural, salutary goods) is restored to the world, and the perfection of God's favor is restored to man. At the altar of sacrifice this joyful message of the angels has its perfect fulfillment; the highest glory is rendered to God, since an infinite Person, Jesus Christ, sacrifices himself to his praise and glory; true peace, divine favor, pardon and reconciliation are granted to man.

Finally, verse seventeen of Psalm 50 is recited : by accommodation,

---

[5] The text would then read : " Glory to God in the highest; and on earth peace to men of good will. " There is still another possible rendering of the text : " Glory to God in the highest and on earth; peace to men of good will. "

it becomes a prayer to God that he open the lips of the celebrants, that they may render praise in performing the divine mysteries.

Blessing and Sending Forth the Deacon

Priest and deacon go to the holy table, where the priest kisses the Gospel Book and the deacon the holy table itself.

Inclining his head toward the priest and holding the orar *with three fingers of his right hand, the deacon says :*

It is time to sacrifice unto the Lord.   Bless, sir.

The priest blesses him, saying :

Blessed is our God at all times, now and always and for ever and ever.
Deacon : **Pray for me, sir.** [6]

Priest : **May the Lord direct your steps.**
Deacon : **Remember me, holy sir.**

Priest : **May the Lord remember you in his kingdom, at all times, now and always and for ever and ever.**
Deacon : **Amen.**

The deacon then makes a small bow and, while holding the orar *with the first three fingers of his right hand, leaves the sanctuary through the north door, since the royal doors are not opened until the little Entrance.* [7]   *He takes his place before the royal doors and reverently makes three small bows.   With each bow, he says in a low voice :*

O Lord, open my lips, and my mouth shall declare your praise (Ps. 50:17).

Like the reverent kissing of icons, the kissing of the Gospel Book and the holy table by priest and deacon shows the love mingled with awe due to holy things.   The Gospel is holy because it contains the words and life of our Saviour, the holy table because the same Saviour will come to offer himself upon it for our sins.   But there

---

[6] The Russian recension has : " Pray for me, holy sir. "

[7] In many Catholic Ukrainian churches, the royal doors are opened by the priest before he goes to the holy table, just at the end of the *proskomidia* while the deacon is incensing.   They remain open until the end of the Liturgy.

is deeper meaning than the mere kissing of two objects intimately connected with the Divine Liturgy. Since the Gospel Book represents Christ and the altar his throne, kissing them really expresses the love and awe which is in the heart of the celebrants for Christ himself; the kiss, then, is a *greeting* of love and peace. The deacon, since he has lesser Orders than the priest, dares to kiss only the throne (altar).

This ritual was borrowed from pagan antiquity : custom dictated the kissing of the temple threshold when one entered it. The pagan altar was honored with a kiss, [8] also the family table at the beginning of a meal. The kiss served to show reverence for something that had had a formal religious dedication pronounced over it. With the coming of Christianity, the practice served a Christian purpose. Kissing the altar seems to have been adopted into the Syrian Liturgy before the end of the fourth century; from Syria, the practice quickly spread to its dependent Churches and thence to the West.

The short dialogue between priest and deacon is moving. Like a child going away from its parents for a while, the deacon simply says, " It is time to go, pray for me, " and finally, " remember me. " The words establish a perfect understanding of the hearts.

At the Divine Liturgy, the deacon always represents the angel of the Lord. His office consists in ministering and " flying " from the holy table to the people of God, and from the people to the holy table. He knows he is unworthy : that is why he humbly asks the priest for prayers. The priest sends him out with a blessing and a prayer that the Lord direct his steps and remember him in his Kingdom.

The lips of the deacon, being human, are powerless, dumb before the glory of God's work of love, the Eucharistic Sacrifice. God himself must open those human lips and give them power in order that the deacon may worthily perform his task. That is why he prays : " O Lord, open my lips, and my mouth shall declare your praise. "

---

[8] Similarly, the images of the gods were greeted by a kiss or even by a kiss thrown to them from a distance, e.g., Minucius Felix tells us of Caecilius throwing a kiss of greeting to the statue of Serapis when he passed it (*Octavius*, 2, 4 [CSEL, II, 4, 1. 22]). The Italians still " blow " kisses at statues.

When Leo Thuscus, relying on documents of the eleventh and twelfth centuries, translated the Liturgy of Chrysostom into Latin about A.D. 1180, he included a dialogue between priest and deacon identical to the present one except for one sentence. [9] This does not mean that at the time this form of the ritual was accepted throughout the Byzantine Church. Slight differences appear in most of the thirteenth and fourteenth century sources. Some, for example, have the priest and the deacon merely making three bows before the altar after the " O Heavenly King " prayer, the deacon saying, " Bless, sir, " and the priest blessing him. [10] Other sources have both the priest and the deacon kissing the altar, the deacon saying " It is time to sacrifice, Father, to the Lord, " and both reciting Psalm 50. [11] The fourteenth or fifteenth century *Liturgikon* of Metropolitan Isidore, however, has the priest kissing the Gospel Book and the deacon, the altar. Then the deacon bows his head before the priest and, while holding the *orar* with three fingers of his right hand, says to the priest : " It is time to serve the Lord, sir, bless (me). " The rest of the dialogue is identical with today's. [12]

---

[9] Instead of the priest answering " May the Lord direct your steps, " his translation reads : *Prosperos faciat Dominus Deus gressus nostros sua gratia, nunc, et semper et in saecula saeculorum* (" May the Lord God direct our steps favorably by his grace, now and always and for ever and ever "). F. Claudius de Santes, *Liturgiae Sive Missae Sanctorum Patrum Iacobi Apostoli et fratris Domini, Basilii Magni, e vetusto codice Latinae translationis, Ioannis Chrysostomi, Interprete Leone Thusco* (Antwerp, 1562).

[10] MS. of Sophia Library, N. 523 (Krasnoseltsev, *op. cit.*, p. 14); also MSS. of the Roumiantsev Museum, Nos. 398, 399 (cf. A. Petrovsky, *op. cit.*, p. 882). Almost identical rubrics are found in the MS. of Sophia Library, N. 526 (Krasnoseltsev, *op. cit.*, p. 7) and th MS. of the Library of Count Tolstoy, N. 274 (*op. cit.* p. 4).

[11] MS. of Sophia Library, N. 523 (*op. cit.*, p. 14); cf. also MS. of Moscow Synodal Library, N. 381 (Krasnoseltsev, *op. cit.*, p. 22).

[12] *Liturgikon* of Metropolitan Isidore, its *Ustav* (cf. MS. *Vat. Slav.*, N. 14, fol. 124).

CHAPTER XXXII

THE OPENING SIGN OF THE CROSS

tanding before the royal doors, the deacon sings in a loud clear voice :

Bless, Sir.

The priest, standing in the center before the holy table, and making the sign of the cross over it with the Gospel Book, begins loudly and solemnly :

Blessed is the Kingdom of the Father, and of the Son, and of the Holy Spirit, now and always and for ever and ever.

The choir (and/or the people) :

Amen.

In the Latin Rite, the sign of the cross with which the priest begins the prayers at the foot of the altar is generally considered as the beginning of the Mass of the Catechumens. In the Byzantine Rite, it is the petition of the deacon, and the priest's sign of the cross with the Gospel Book, while he says " Blessed is the Kingdom.... " In both Rites, the proceedings began originally with the Entrance Rite, when the bishop-celebrant solemnly entered the church in procession. This corresponds with the Latin *Introit* and the Byzantine *Little Entrance*. The *enarksis* (ἔναρξις, beginning), up to the Little Entrance, was not an original part of the Liturgy of the Catechumens. Like the *proskomidia*, it was added as an introductory rite some time between the fifth and the ninth centuries. [1]

The deacon's petition, " Bless, Sir, " refers to the whole congregation, whose place the deacon takes in formally presenting their requests to God. That is why the deacon stands before the royal doors, that is, with the people. The people themselves directly

---

[1] The early eighth century Armenian version of Chrysostom's Liturgy already contains the *enarksis* (ἔναρξις) in a form almost identical with the present one (cf. Aucher, *La versione armena della liturgia di S. Giovanni Crisostomo, fatta sul principio dell'VIII secolo*, XPYCOCTOMIKA [Rome, 1908], pp. 373-378). The Armenians had probably received it in that form from the Byzantines prior to A.D. 693, when the Byzantine occupation of Armenia ended.

participate in the Liturgy by singing the responses, etc., but it is the deacon who voices their requests.

In making the sign of the cross with the holy Gospel Book over the altar, the priest uses a formula which is exclusive to the opening of the Divine Liturgy. Solemn liturgical rites in the Byzantine Churches always begin with some trinitarian invocation, but this one is uniquely reserved for the Eucharistic sacrifice. [2] Actually, the words are non-essential, since the sign of the cross is often made silently. The important element is the sign itself.

The sign of the cross, made with the thumb or index on the forehead, was used in some liturgical functions as early as the second century, although it appears in the Eucharistic Liturgy only in the fourth century. [3] It was made by the celebrant at the beginning of the *anaphora*, the Eucharistic prayer.

The " Tractate Berakoth " gives a long list of blessings for all occasions of Jewish life. Many of its shorter invocations provided early Christians with expressions for their liturgical services. In the East, actual Jewish texts have been preserved in some instances. The opening blessing of the Divine Liturgy reveals the " Berakoth " style, while its trinitarian amplification is obviously Christian. It carefully avoids using the divine name by substituting such terms as *malkouth*, the " reign, " " kingdom, " or more in keeping with modern terminology, the " majesty " of God. The formula is based on a Syrian antecedent, and on Mark 11:10 : " Blessed be the kingdom of the father David that cometh..., " the song of the Jewish throngs that accompanied Jesus on his triumphal entry into Jerusalem.

The chief purpose of the Liturgy is the glorification of the Trinity. Beginning with a trinitarian formula, the priest exalts a fundamental dogma of the New Law. Professing belief in one God is common to both Laws, but believing in the Father, the Son, and the Holy Spirit pertains only to the New.

Another mystery distinguishing the Christian faith from that of the Jews is the redemption. The ritual sign of the cross, whatever

---

[2] The lesser Byzantine liturgical functions begin with the thoroughly Jewish " Blessed is our God, now and always, and for ever and ever. "

[3] *Apostolic Constitutions*, Book VIII; cf. p. 124.

its form, is the sign of Christ crucified, the sign of our redemption. As the priest makes it over the altar with the Gospel Book, the faithful also cross themselves. By ancient Christian tradition, the sign of the cross was to be made before any important undertaking. As the re-enactment of Calvary, the Eucharistic Liturgy, the " Christian act, " is one such undertaking.

In the course of the Divine Liturgy, the faithful make the sign of the cross thirty-six times—at every blessing and doxology, and whenever the three Persons of the Trinity are mentioned. Anyone wishing to place emphasis on a particular prayer or litany will also cross himself. Eastern Slavs, Russians, Ukrainians and White Russians have carried the practice into their daily living. They sign themselves when leaving on a trip, when going to work or returning from it, when beginning their work or ending it. They make a reverent sign of the cross on passing a church, on hearing of a death, accident or other bad news, on meeting a funeral procession. They make it in fear, danger, temptation, or as a sign of fervent entreaty; or again, on passing a roadside cross or an icon-shrine, or before the " icon-corner " in any home. They make it before and after meals. When a mother is putting her child to sleep, she traces the sign of the cross over it. " The father's blessing establisheth the houses of the children " (Ecclesiasticus 3:11) is for them no mere abstract statement from the Scriptures : it is lived daily in their actions and traditions. At weddings, the young couple's fathers and mothers bless their children at the doorstep before they depart for the nuptials in the church. Any important event, even the most mundane, is sanctified with this truly Christian practice.

The sign of the cross of the Byzantines is different from that of the Latins. The thumb and first two fingers of the right hand are joined at the tips; the fourth and fifth fingers are folded over the palm. The two fingers and thumb signify the three Divine Persons of the Trinity, while the other two fingers symbolize the two natures in Jesus Christ. With the fingers so joined, the forehead is touched first (" In the name of the Father "), then the breast (" and of the Son "), the right shoulder (" and of the Holy..."), and finally the left shoulder ("...Spirit. Amen. "). Meanwhile, the head and shoulders are slightly bowed as a sign of submission to the Godhead.

The right shoulder is touched first, not the left as in the Latin Rite. Prior to the end of the twelfth century, Christians of both East and West made the sign of the cross from the right to the left. [4] Latin Catholics began making it with all the fingers extended, and from the left shoulder to the right, at the time of Pope Innocent III (1198-1216). Supposedly, this meant that Jesus came from the Father to earth by becoming man, then descended into the left side, i.e., into hell, by his Passion and thence into his Father's right side, by his ascension. Another explanation was that making the sign from the left, the weak side, the side of sin, to the right, the side of salvation, would symbolize the death of Christ on the cross, and our being carried by it from the left to the right side, to salvation.

The earlier, more ancient way of making the sign of the cross, as it is still done in the Byzantine Church, from the right to the left, is understood to mean that salvation passed from the Jews, who were at the right side of God (the side of honor, belonging to the chosen people) to the Gentiles, who were at his left. [5] Touching the right shoulder first also expresses the Christian hope to be put among the righteous on the right hand of Christ, the Judge at the Final Judgment. [6]

The Amen

To this formula of praise, the faithful answer : " Amen. " The Amen is indeed, as St. Jerome put it, the " seal of prayer. " Originally coming from the Hebrew root 'MN, meaning " steadfast, " " fixed, " " settled" and, hence, " true, " Amen can be translated as " truly, " " verily, " or " so be it. " These words, however, do not express its full meaning, a meaning which is really untranslatable.

---

[4] In the Latin Rite the priest, when imparting a blessing, still makes the sign of the cross from the right to the left.

[5] The ancient Christians derived their idea of the right side as being the side of righteousness, the side of honor, from the Scriptures : e.g., the Queen of heaven " stood on the right hand, clothed in a vesture wrought with gold and diverse colors " (Ps. 44:10); Jesus " sitteth at the right hand of the Father " (Rom. 8:34), etc.

[6] In general, the complete sign of the cross was and is made to acknowledge that all our faculties (mind, heart, and soul) and all our strength (shoulders) are being dedicated to the service of God through the cross of Christ, the sign of our redemption.

That is why, after the first century, "Amen" was left in its original Hebrew. The closest we can come to its exact meaning is to borrow the expression used by the Jews when they translated the Old Testament into Greek : "Would that it might be so," an expression that is at once a wish and an affirmation. In Old Testament times, the time of fear and punishment, this word was usually used for the affirmation of curses, anathemas, and public pronouncements against evildoers. In the New Testament era, the time of forgiveness and love, it is used as the solemn affirmation of a blessing. It is found over forty times in the New Testament. Liturgically, it is a solemn ratification of prayer. The Amen was already in liturgical use during the lifetime of the Apostles, as we know from St. Paul's Letter to the Corinthians : "Else, if thou shalt bless with the spirit, how shall he that holdeth the place of the unlearned say Amen to thy blessing?" (I Cor. 14:16).

CHAPTER XXXIII

THE GREAT *EKTENIA* OR LITANY
OF PEACE

From his place, facing the royal doors, the deacon sings the Great *Ektenia; at every petition, the deacon raises the end of his* orar *with three fingers of his right hand.*

Deacon : **In peace let us pray to the Lord.**

People : **Lord, have mercy.**

Deacon : **For peace from on high and for the salvation of our souls, let us pray to the Lord.**

People : **Lord, have mercy.**

Deacon : **For the peace of the whole world, for the well-being of the holy churches of God, and for the unity of all, let us pray to the Lord.**

People : **Lord, have mercy.**

Deacon : **For this holy church, and for those who enter it with faith, reverence and the fear of God, let us pray to the Lord.**

People : **Lord, have mercy.**

Deacon : **For His Holiness, our Universal Pontiff N——, Pope of Rome, let us pray to the Lord.** [1]

People : **Lord, have mercy.**

Deacon : **For our Most Reverend Archbishop and Metropolitan N——, for our God-loving Bishop N——, for the reverend priests, the deacons in Christ, for all the clergy and people, let us pray to the Lord.**

People : **Lord, have mercy.**

---

[1] In the Russian Catholic recension, the next petition of the deacon is joined to this one; hence, after the words " Pope of Rome " it goes on, " and for our Most Reverend Metropolitan (*or* Archbishop, *or* Bishop) N., for the venerable order of priests, the deacons in Christ, and all the clergy and people, let us pray to the Lord. "

Deacon : **For our sovereign authorities and for all the armed forces, let us pray to the Lord.** [2]

People : **Lord, have mercy.**

Deacon : **For this city [or for this village, or for this holy monastery], for every city and country, and for the faithful who live in them, let us pray to the Lord.**

People : **Lord, have mercy.**

Deacon : **For good weather, for abundant fruits of the earth, and for peaceful times, let us pray to the Lord.**

People : **Lord, have mercy.**

Deacon : **For those traveling by land and sea, for the sick, the suffering, the imprisoned, and for their salvation, let us pray to the Lord.**

People : **Lord, have mercy.**

[*In the Ruthenian recension the universal commemoration or petitions for the dead are inserted here.*]

Deacon : **For our deliverance from all affliction, wrath and need, let us pray to the Lord.**

People : **Lord, have mercy.**

Deacon : **Help us, save us, have mercy on us, and protect us, O God, by your grace.**

People : **Lord, have mercy.**

Deacon : **As we remember our all-holy, immaculate, most blessed and glorious Lady, the Mother of God and ever-virgin Mary together with all the saints, let us commend ourselves and one another and our whole life to Christ God.**

People : **To you, O Lord.**

Until a few years ago, the " Kyrie eleison " was the only remnant of Greek in the Latin Mass. It was not, as sometimes supposed, a survival from the time the Mass was said in Greek, but a fifth or early sixth century transplant from the *ektenias* of the Byzantine

---

[2] This petition may also be : " For our God-protected Emperor (or King) N—, etc. " depending on the type of government in a given country.

Liturgy.   Originally, the Kyrie was an acclamation in the Latin Church by the people or by the priest and people together; only later did it come to be recited by the priest alone.

In the Byzantine-Slav Rite this litany is called *Velyka(ya) Ektenia,* " the Great Ektenia, " or *Myrna(ya) Ektenia,* " the Ektenia of Peace. "   These names come from the Greek ἡ μεγάλη ἐκτενή (ς), great, intense prayer (also ἡ μεγάλη συναπτή, the great collection of petitions), or εἰρηνικά, litany of peace, a name derived from its opening petitions for peace, e.g., " In peace, let us pray... for peace from on high... for peace of the whole world, " etc.   Sometimes called ἡ καθολικὴ συναπτή, the universal collection of petitions, it corresponds to the litany of the same name in the Liturgy of St. James.   With each petition the deacon, representing the angel of the Lord, raises his *orar,* the symbol of the angel's wing, as a sign to the people that they should lift up their hearts and minds as they pray for each blessing.

" In peace let us pray to the Lord. "   The quieting of turbulent passions, putting away all earthly troubles and worries, external as well as internal peace, calm, and a clean, clear conscience are the ideal dispositions for good prayer.   A man who is discontented with his lot in life cannot have peace within him, but only he who is grateful and " in everything gives thanks " (I Thess. 5:18). [3]   Only in that spirit of peace can a man rightly approach God in prayer. Peace with one's brother is presupposed, for the Master himself told us that if our brother has anything against us, we must leave our offering before the altar and become reconciled with him before offering it (cf. Matt. 5:23-24).

" For peace from on high. "   Peace from God, the peace which the Saviour himself gives : " Peace I leave with you; my peace I give unto you : not as the world giveth, do I give unto you.   Let not your heart be troubled : nor let it be afraid " (John 14:27).   It is the peace in which we can take our rest at the end of a day because our burdens, no matter what they be, are not so heavy when our conscience is clean.   It is " the peace of God, which surpasseth all understanding " (Phil. 4:7).

[3] Cabasilas, *Commentary,* trans. J. M. Hussey and P. A. McNulty (London, S.P.C.K., 1960), p. 44.

Peace is the sign of God's Kingdom, "for the Kingdom of God is not meat and drink : but justice and peace and joy in the Holy Spirit" (Rom. 14:17).

Being disposed to the things that are of peace, of God's Kingdom, the deacon urges prayer for peace in every form, not only for the faithful themselves but also for the whole world.

The Slav, eternally yearning for peace, for peace of conscience, peace with God, peace in every form, with every fiber of his being, understands and loves this Syro-Byzantine petition. Centuries of war have left their heavy imprint on his sensitive soul.

" Now, the church had peace throughout all Judea and Galilee and Samaria : and was edified, walking in the fear of the Lord : and was filled with the consolation of the Holy Spirit" (Acts 9:31). Only when the various nations and races of the world are at peace with each other can the Church of God grow.

" For the well-being of the holy churches of God and for the unity of all. " " The holy churches of God " do not mean that more than one church or religion has been established by God, nor does " the unity of all " mean that we are praying for the union of the various non-Catholic Churches with Rome. The expression " the holy churches of God " means the various local churches or congregations of the one true Church, as St. Paul and the early Christians used to refer to them, i.e., the Churches of Antioch, Rome, Corinth, Ephesus, etc. [4] None of the various non-Catholic Churches or denominations was yet in existence when this petition was formulated in the early centuries of the Church. The fourth-century *Apostolic Constitutions* has : " Let us pray for the peace and stability of the world and of the holy churches...." [5] The unity referred to in the Byzantine petition is the oneness, peace, love, and harmony that these various local churches should live in, without strife, quarrel, or envy.

" For this holy church, and for those who enter it with faith, reverence and the fear of God. " The *Apostolic Constitutions* has

---

[4] Col. 4:16; Rom. 16:16; I Cor. 1:2; I Thess. 1:1; II Thess. 1:1; I Pet. 5:13, etc.

[5] *Apostolic Constitutions*, Book VIII, cf. above, p. 118.

" for this holy parish, " [6] and that is what the petition essentially means.

The *Memento, Domine* of the Latin Canon expresses the same notion when it asks the Lord to remember " all here present, whose faith and devotion are known unto thee.... "

In the next two petitions, the *ektenia* enumerates the Holy Father, the Metropolitan Archbishop, then the bishop, the priests, the deacons, all the clergy (such as those with minor orders), and finally the faithful. This is the Kingdom of God upon the earth hierarchically organized. Their needs are many, their wants varied. In their intercessions, whence the present petitions are derived, the early Christians were specific in their requests. For the bishops they asked " that they rightly dispense the word of truth, " [7] and " that the compassionate God let them continue in his holy churches in health, honor, and long life and that he grant them an honorable old age in piety and righteousness "; [8] for the priests, " that the Lord deliver them from every improper and wicked action and that he grant them both a sound and an honorable ministry "; [9] for the deacons and other clergy, " that the Lord grant them a blameless ministration. " [10] Prayers for the faithful included almost every need. [11]

" For our sovereign authorities and for all the armed forces. " The early Christians prayed " for the kings and rulers, " [12] " for the princes who lead a pious life, " [13] the Byzantines and Slavs for their " God-protected Emperor or Tsar "; today under the democracies we pray for legitimately constituted governing bodies. Praying " for kings and for all that are in high station " is every Christian's duty; it always has been since Paul wrote to Timothy (cf. I Tim. 2:1-2).

The protectors of a nation's freedom and sovereignty, the armed

---

[6] *Ibid.*, cf. above, p. 119.

[7] Chrysostom, *De prophet. obscurit.*, 2, 5 (edit. Montfaucon 6, 188 A).

[8] *Apostolic Constitutions*, Book VIII, cf. above, p. 119.

[9] *Ibid.*, cf. above, p. 119.

[10] *Ibid.*, cf. above, p. 119.

[11] *Ibid.*, cf. above, p. 119-121.

[12] Chrysostom, In II Cor. ii, 8 (edit. Montfaucon, 10, 441 AB).

[13] *Apostolic Constitutions*, Book VIII, cf. above, p. 120.

forces, are associated with the governing bodies. Theirs must be a moral as well as a physical courage.

" For this city (or village or monastery), for every city and country, and for the faithful who live in them. " From the national government, the *ektenia* goes to the community, large city or simple village. If the Liturgy is celebrated in a monastery, then the monastery is mentioned instead. In the Ukraine or Russia, cities would often boast of a monastery in the neighboring countryside where the people would gather for the Sunday Eucharist. The charity of the *Great Ektenia* is not limited to any one country : it includes every city and country of the world, and especially the faithful who live in them, wherever they be. It discerns neither Jew nor Gentile, Greek nor Roman, Slav nor Teuton. It has been thus since the days of Chrysostom, when the Christians prayed " for all who are here and everywhere. " [14]

" For good weather, for abundant fruits of the earth, and for peaceful times. " The *ektenia* does not omit the simple things of life. The humblest peasant knows well that, if God who sends down the rains and makes the sun to shine does not bless his crops, all his labor will be in vain. In Chrysostom's time, the Antiochene Christians prayed " for the weather, " [15] as had the Christians of Thmuis a generation or two earlier. In the *Prayer for Fruitfulness*, which Sarapion gives, they prayed that God " grant the rains most full and most fertilizing; cause the earth also to bear fruit and to produce in great abundance. " [16]

" For those traveling by land and sea, for the sick, the suffering, the imprisoned, and for their salvation. " In ancient or modern times, no traveler is ever certain of reaching his destination unhurt in soul or body. [17] Then as now, nature and fallible humanity combine to threaten the most cautious traveler. Death, or injury

[14] Chrysostom, *De prophet. obscurit.*, ii, 5 (6, 188 A).

[15] *In II Cor.*, ii, 8 (edit. Montfaucon, 10, 441 B).

[16] Sarapion, *Euchologion*, 23 (edit. J. Wordsworth, *Bishop Serapion's Prayerbook* [London, 1910], p. 84). Prayers for rain are connected with petitions for the rising of the Nile in both the Liturgy of St. Mark (Brightman, LEW, pp. 119, 127) and the Liturgy of the Coptic Jacobites (Brightman, LEW, pp. 159, 168).

[17] *Apostolic Constitutions*, Book VIII (see above, p. 120) had an identical petition : " Let us pray for those who travel by sea or by land. "

still come as a thief. Only the hand of God can stay these perils of road, sea, or air. For those who shall not reach their journey's end on earth, salvation is asked (" and for their salvation ").

The sick and the suffering are ever in need of prayer. The Christians realized it when they prayed sixteen hundred years ago " for our brothers who are tried with sickness, that the Lord deliver them from every sickness and disease and that he restore them in health to his holy Church. " [18] Prayer will deliver them, give them the gentle balm of patience and the light to see the finger of God in their suffering and pain. Hour by hour they stand on the threshold of eternity. If God beckons, prayer will give them the key of supernatural love to unlock the gates of the other Jerusalem where there is no more pain, sorrow, or tears.

The petition for the imprisoned probably originated during the persecutions with prayers for those condemned " for the name of the Lord. " The *Apostolic Constitutions,* which provides so much detailed information about the early Liturgy, gives this petition as : " Let us pray for those who are in the mines, in banishment, in prisons, and in chains for the name of the Lord. " [19] But even after the persecutions ended, the Christians kept praying for the imprisoned in accordance with Gospel precept. They must have realized that praying for the imprisoned took them one step closer to hearing those blessed words : " Come, ye blessed of my Father, possess you the Kingdom prepared for you from the foundation of the world " (Matt. 25). Praying for those in prison does indeed belong to the same virtue of mercy as visiting them there. Christ is in them as he is in the beggar or the widow. We have his word for it, " I was in prison. . ." (Matt. 25:34-46).

" For our deliverance from all affliction, wrath and need. " This group of pleas is almost as general as the *libera nos a malo* of the Lord's Prayer : deliverence from all affliction, whatever it be, from all wrath and want of soul and body.

---

[18] *Ibid.,* cf. above, p. 120. Chrysostom also tells us they prayed " for those in sickness. " Cf. *De incompr. Dei nat.,* iii, 6 (edit. Montfaucon 1, 468 E).

[19] *Ibid.,* cf. above, p. 120. Chrysostom merely gives " for those. . . in the mines, for those in bitter servitude. " Cf. *De incompr. Dei nat.,* iii, 6 (edit. Montfaucon 1, 468 E).

" Help us, save us, have mercy on us, and protect us, O God, by your grace. "

Though God will never allow us to be tempted beyond that which we can endure (I Cor. 10:13), we need his help, his grace, for " without me you can do nothing " (John 15:5), " for it is God who worketh in you, both to will and to accomplish, according to his good will " (Phil. 2:13). Without his help and his grace, we are not even " sufficient to think anything of ourselves, as of ourselves : but our sufficiency is from God " (II Cor. 3:5). Grace is indeed needed for salvation, for eternal life. Since it is supernatural, of a higher order, the means required to obtain it must be supernatural, must belong to the same order. The man who, like Pelagius, denies or does not recognize the utter necessity of grace, would not plead to God for his help.

Grace is a free gift of God, absolutely gratuitous, given purely out of God's goodness and mercy. Man can neither merit grace nor obtain it by his own natural resources or power : " And if by grace, it is not now by works : otherwise grace is no more grace " (Rom. 11:6). Implicit in this petition is the doctrine of the absolute gratuity of grace. Only when a man realizes that he has absolutely no right to something, no just claim to it through merit or title, will he throw himself on someone's mercy. If there were just claim, there would be no reason to ask for mercy.

CHAPTER XXXIV

THE FINAL COMMENDATION
OF THE *EKTENIA*

As we remember our all-holy, immaculate, most blessed and glorious Lady, the Mother of God and ever-virgin Mary together with all the saints, let us commend ourselves and one another and our whole life to Christ God.

The absolute surrender of mortal man by himself into the hands of God demands great boldness and must be founded on a clear conscience. When such words of surrender are uttered by a just man, he gives himself to the love of God who will accept him. But when said by a sinner, he gives himself over completely to divine justice and anger, without any assurance that God will accept him. That is why Cabasilas could write :

> It is not given to all to commend themselves to God and to place themselves in his care. For the words of commendation are not in themselves enough; it is necessary that God should accept us. It is essential that we have assurance (of this acceptance), and that only comes from a clear conscience; such a conscience as we have when our own heart does not reproach us, when we concern ourselves with the things of God, when, in order to care for his interests, we do not hesitate to neglect our own. For then we abandon all anxiety for our own affairs, confidently committing them into God's hands, in the sure and certain faith that he will accept our trust and will preserve it.
>
> Since this matter requires so much wisdom and thought, we do not make this commendation until we have first summoned to our aid the all-holy Mother of God and the choir of all the saints. [1]

That is why such a bold surrender of ourselves to God is made through the help of his Mother whose every action was motivated

---

[1] Cabasilas, *Commentary on the Divine Liturgy*, trans. by J. M. Hussey and P. A. McNulty (London, S.P.C.K., 1960), p. 49.

by pure love for him. [2]   It is made also with all the saints, God's proven friends, beloved by him.   The faithful assent to this total surrender of themselves to God by answering : " To you, O Lord. " While in the primitive Church Christ was being preached from the housetops, his Mother remained hidden in the Church's tradition until several centuries later.   Hence, the ancient commendation was made through Christ, not through his Mother : " Let us earnestly pray and commend ourselves and one another to the living God, through his Christ. " [3]

The glorification of Mary came not so much to honor her apart from her Son, but to safeguard the right doctrines of Christ's person. The implications inherent in defense of orthodox dogmas concerning Christ redounded to her glory and honor because of her relationship to him.   The more clearly defined the theology of Christ became, the more apparent was Mary's position of honor.   Her titles in this commendation, " all-holy, immaculate, most blessed and glorious Lady, Mother of God, every-virgin Mary, " were not imaginary epithets coined by some pious monk, but theological truths with a depth of meaning deriving from doctrinal clarification of her Son's humanity and divinity, of his one person and twofold nature, etc. Thus, during the first three centuries, when Gnostics, Docetae, Valentinians, and others attacked the humanity of Christ, several writers and Fathers of the Church strongly defended true doctrine by insisting on the facts that the Son of God was truly incarnate, with a real body like ours, and that he was born of Mary. [1]   As a result, Mary's maternity was brought to the fore.   By giving birth to Christ, the Incarnate God, she is entitled in the strictest sense of the word to be called the Mother of God.

---

[2] This giving over of ourselves and our whole life to God is tantamount to a perfect renewal of the vows and promises of Holy Baptism, a perfect consecration of ourselves to Christ through (the help of) Mary.   Devotees of St. Louis de Montfort will easily recognize its similarity to the kernel of his *True Devotion*. Compare especially chap. 1 of Part. II, *Treatise on the True Devotion to the Blessed Virgin*.

[3] *Apostolic Constitutions*, Book VIII; cf. above, p. 121.

[4] E.g., Ignatius of Antioch, *Ad Ephes.*, 7 (PG 3, 648 A [*Series graeca*]); *Ad Smyrn.*, 2-6 (PG 3, 687-689 [*Series graeca*]); Irenaeus, *Ad. haeres.*, III, 16, 6 f.; III, 18, 7; III, 21, 10 (PG 7, 925, 937 f., 955)); Tertullian, *De carne Christi*, 17 (PL 2, 781); Origen, *In Luc. homil.*, VIII; *Cont. Celsum*, I, 35 (PG 13, 1817, 1818, 1821).

The term *Theotokos* (Mother of God) was specially coined for her, [5] and from the beginning of the fourth century it became her most frequent title.   Mary's divine maternity came under attack in the fifth century because the doctrine of the one person in Jesus Christ was attacked by Nestorius and his followers, who maintained that in Christ two persons were joined together, namely, God the Son (the Word) and the man Jesus.   Since Mary gave birth only to the man Jesus, she could not be called Theotokos.   In A.D. 431, to the great jubilation of the people, the Council of Ephesus defined Mary's divine maternity as a dogma of faith, condemned the doctrine of Nestorius, and specifically assigned to her the title Theotokos. [6] The divine person who took flesh and was born of Mary had two natures, the divine and the human.   He was both God and man. Now, as God suffered and died only in his human nature, it is true that he was born of Mary although he took only his human nature from her.   Denying this would amount to subverting the doctrine of the redemption and the plan of salvation, since God alone could redeem us through an adequate satisfaction.

The name *Theotokos* is of particular importance for understanding the Eastern Church's intense devotion to Mary.   Byzantine liturgical services often mention her name, usually by giving her full title, as in the commendation we are discussing.   The veneration, honor, and reverence shown to her, far from eclipsing the worship of God, have exactly the opposite effect : the higher the faithful's esteem of the Mother of God, the deeper their appreciation of her Son's majesty, for they venerate the Mother on account of the Son. [7]   Those who

---

[5] By Origen, according to Socrates (*Hist. eccl.*, VII, 32 [PG 67, 812]), but some attribute it to Hippolytus of Rome (cf. H. Rahner, *Hyppolyt von Rom als Zeuge für den Ausdruck "Theotokos"* in Z.K.T. 59 [1935], pp. 73-81).

[6] Able defenders of Mary's maternity were not lacking before or after Ephesus. Besides Origen, we have : Peter of Alexandria (*Fragm.* [PG 18, 517]); Athanasius (*Contra Arianos* [PG 26, 349, 996, 1025]); Didymus of Alexandria (*De Trinitate* [PG 39, 422, 481, 484]); Cyril of Alexandria (*Anath.*, I [PG 76, 393], *Hom. pasch.* [PG 77, 778]; Basil (*Hom. in sanctal Christm generationem* [PG 31, 1460]); Gregory Nazianzen (*Epist.*, 101 [PG 37, 177]); Gregory of Nyssa (*Epist.*, 3 [PG 46, 1024]); etc.

[7] Byzantine theology, like the Latin, clearly marks the distinction between the worship due to God alone and the veneration due to the Mother of God : in precise theological terms it distinguishes λατρεία reserved for the worship of God from ὑπερδουλεία, προσκύνησις, the veneration of the *Theotokos*, which is on an entirely different plane.

do not believe in the Incarnation and redemption often refuse to honor Many. This is as true today as it was in the early centuries of Christianity.

Prysnodiva Maria (ever-virgin Mary), "Always-a-virgin," is the exact meaning of *prysnodiva* and its Greek counterpart ἀειπαρθένος. Coined by the Greek Fathers, this term is more precise than the Latin *virgo Maria* or the English *Virgin Mary*, for it contains in itself the clear and unequivocal meaning that Mary was a virgin *before, during, and after* the birth of Christ. Christians, of course, believed this from the beginning, [8] but the Church made it an article of faith in A.D. 553 at the Fifth Ecumentical Council (II Constantinople).

The doctrine of Mary's perpetual virginity is in no way contradicted by the Scriptures, which speak of the brothers and sisters of Jesus (Mark 3:31). The Greek word is a translation of the Aramaic *ach*, which expresses consanguinity in varying degrees, such as half-brother, nephew, or cousin. [9] Though not exactly parallel, the Ukrainian words *brat*, " brother," and *sestra*, " sister," are sometimes used for cousin; however, usually the Ukrainians will add to them the prefixes *dvoyuridnej* and *dvoyuridna* to indicate " first " cousins.

Nor does the passage Joseph " knew her not till she brought forth her firstborn" (Matt. 1:25) give any reason for doubting the perpetual virginity of Mary. The Greek ἕως, " till," and the Semitic word

---

[8] Cf. Aristides, *Apol.* (PG 96, 1121); Justin, *I Apol.*, I, 22, 32, 33; *Dial. cum Tryph.*, 66, 75, 76, 100 (PG 6, 363, 380, 627, 651, 710); Irenaeus, *Adv. haeres.*, III, 19, 1-3 (PG 7, 938, 941, 953); Tertullian, *De carne Christi*, 23 (PL 2, 790); Origen, *Homil.* 14 *in Luc.* (PG 13, 1834); Jerome, *De perpetua virginitate B. Mariae adv. Helvidium* (PL 23); Gregory the Wonderworker, *Sermo in Nativ. Christi*, 13-15 (PG 10, 301-392); Ambrose, *Epist.*, 42, n. 3 f. (PL 16, 1124); Augustine, *Sermo 3 in Natali Domini*, n. 1 (PL 38, 995); Didymus, *De Trinit.*, 3, 4 (PG 39, 832); etc.

[9] Aside from solid tradition that Mary had no other children than Jesus, many instances in Sacred Scripture can be cited where the word " brother " is used in this broad sense to indicate nephew or cousin, e.g., Lot in Gen. 14:14 as " brother " of his uncle, Abraham; Jacob as " brother " of his uncle, Laban, in Gen. 29:15; the sons of Cis in I Chron. 23:21-22 as brethren of their cousins, the daughters of Eleazar. Neither the Hebrew language nor the Aramaic had any specific term to signify " cousin "; they either had to resort to " brother " or to the rather clumsy circumlocutions, " son of (paternal) uncle " or " son of the brother of the mother. " If one accepts the " brethren of the Lord " in the strict sense of blood-brothers, one will encounter many difficulties in the other parts of the New Testament.

represented by ἕως, merely deny the action for the period of time preceding the verb " brought forth " without implying anything for the period of time following it.   There is simply no implication as to the future : this use of " till " in the Scriptures can be seen clearly in many other passages. [10]   The sacred writer wished to say that Joseph did not participate in any way in the conception of Jesus.

Neither does the word " firstborn " in Luke 2:7 imply any younger brothers or sisters.   It is a literal translation of the Greek πρωτότοκος, which is the equivalent of the Hebrew *b*ʿ*kor*, a term always used in an absolute sense for " that which openeth the womb " (Exod. 13:2; Num. 3:12; etc.) without implying any " second " child.   The first male child, even if no other children were born later to the same parents, was always called the " firstborn. "   Πρωτότοκος, like its Hebrew equivalent, merely indicated the fact that there were no male children born before that one.   This has been corroborated by modern archaeological discoveries. [11]

Mary's other titles derive from her position as Mother of God. Her eminent holiness, for example.   The Byzantine Church calls her παναγία, " the all-holy one, " [12] because she is the supreme example of *synergy*, the cooperation between God's will and man's freedom.   Forever respecting the free will of man, God became incarnate through the free consent of the person he chose as his Mother.   She could have refused, but she did not.   " So the knot of Eve's disobedience was loosed through the obedience of Mary, " says Irenaeus, " for what Eve, a virgin, had bound through her

[10] E.g., in I Tim. 4:13, St. Paul exhorts Timothy to attend to the reading, exhortation, and doctrine " till " he comes, without implying that Timothy can neglect these things in the future after Paul's visit.   In II Kings 6:23, Michol, the daughter of Saul, had no child " till " the day of her death; the passage certainly does not imply that she had children then or afterwards.   Another passage (I Macc. 5:54), in speaking of the Maccabees offering thanksgiving sacrifices, " because not one of them was slain till they had returned in peace " does not imply that one of them was slain after their return.   Thus also Gen. 8:7, Deut. 34:6; etc.

[11] In 1922, for example, in Tell el Yaheoudieh, Egypt, an ancient stele (dating probably to a time immediately preceding the birth of Christ) was discovered; its Greek inscription states that a woman, Arsinoe, died in bringing her " firstborn " into the world.   She could not have given birth to any other children.

[12] Origen may have been the first to call her παναγία (cf. I. Ortiz de Urbina, *La Mariologia nella Patrologia Orientale*, O.C.P. 6 [1940], p. 59).

unbelief, Mary, a virgin, unloosed through her faith. " [13] Jerome puts it more succinctly : " Death by Eve, life by Mary. " [14] And Cabasilas : " The Incarnation was not only the work of the Father, of his Power and his Spirit... but also that of the will and faith of the Virgin.... Just as God became incarnate voluntarily, so he wished that his Mother should bear him freely and with her full consent. " [15]

Also, from end to end of the Byzantine world, both Catholic and Orthodox greet the Mother of God as ἄχραντος, " the immaculate, spotless one, " no less than eight times in the Divine Liturgy alone. But especially on the feast of her conception (December 9 in the Byzantine Church) is her immaculateness stressed : " This day, O faithful, from saintly parents begins to take being the spotless lamb, the most pure tabernacle, Mary... "; [16] " She is conceived... the only immaculate one "; [17] or " Having conceived the most pure dove, Anne filled...." [18] No sin, no fault, not even the slightest, ever marred the perfect sanctity of this masterpiece of God's creation. For hundreds of years, the Byzantine Church has believed this, prayed and honored Mary in this way. Centuries of sacred tradition stand behind this title. [19] Even during the twelfth and thirteenth centuries, when some Western theologians doubted or denied the truth of her immaculate conception, Byzantine Catholic and Orthodox theologians unanimously taught it. [20] Two of Thomas Aquinas'

[13] Irenaeus, *Ad. haeres.*, III, 22, 4 (PG 7, 959).

[14] Jerome, *Epist.*, 22, 21 (PL 22, 408).

[15] Cabasilas, *On the Annunciation*, 4-5 (PO 19, p. 488).

[16] From the Office of Matins, the Third Ode of the Canon for the feast.

[17] From the Office of Matins, the Stanzas during the Seating, for the same feast.

[18] From the Office of Matins, the Sixth Ode of the Canon for the same feast.

[19] The very vastness of available testimony precludes listing. Two excellent surveys may be consulted : A. Ballerini, *Sylloge monumentorum ad mysterium conceptionis immaculatae virginis deiparae spectantium* (Rome, 1854-1855), and C. Passaglia, *De immaculato deiparae semper virginis conceptu commentarius* (Rome, 1854-1855).

[20] Among the better known ninth to thirteenth century Byzantine theologians : Patriarch Photius in his homilies *De Annuntiatione* and *De Nativitate Deiparae* (S. Aristarchis, Φωτίου λόγοι καὶ ὁμιλίαι,, Vol. II [Constantinople, 1900], pp. 230-245, 368-380); George of Nicomedia in his homilies (PG 100, 1336-1504), especially *Conceptione deiparae* and *Praesentatione Mariae virginis*; Michael Psellos in the recently discovered and edited homily *De Annuntiatione* (PO 16, pp. 517-525); John Phurnensis, *Oratione de Dormitione* (G. Palamas, Θεοφανοῦς τοῦ κεραμέως

most ardent disciples among the Greeks disagreed with him on one point only, his failure to admit the immaculate conception of the Mother of God. [21] Demetrios Kydonios (fourteenth century) translated some of Aquinas' works into Greek, but vehemently opposed Thomas' views on the immaculate conception. [22] No less did the other great Thomist, Georgios Scholarios (fifteenth century), in his synopsis of the immaculate conception. [23]

The Greek Orthodox Church's belief in the immaculate conception continued unanimously until the fifteenth century, then many Greek theologians began to adopt the idea that Mary had been made immaculate at the moment of the Annunciation. [24] Among the Eastern Slavs, belief in the immaculate conception went undisturbed until the seventeenth century, when the Skrizhal (Book of Laws) appeared in Russia, [25] and proposed what the Slavs considered the " novel " doctrine of the Greeks. The views proposed in the Skrizhal

ὁμιλίαι, [Jerusalem, 1860], append., pp. 271-276); Michael Glykas, *Annales*, III (PG 158, 439-442); Germanus II, Patriarch of Constantinople, *In annuntiationem* (edit. Ballerini, *op. cit.*, Vol. II, pp. 283-382); Theognostos the Monk, *In dormitionem* (PO 16, pp. 457-562); Nicetas David, *In nativitatem B.M.V.* (PG 105, 16-28); Leo the Wise, *In dormitionem* and *In praesentationem* (PG 107, 12-21); Patriarch Euthymius of Constantinople, *In conceptionem Annae* (PO 16, pp. 499-505); Bishop Peter Argorum, *In conceptionem B. Annae* (PG 104, 1352-1365); John Mauropos, *In dormitionem* (PG 120, 1075-1114); James the Monk, *In nativitatem et in praesentationem* B.M.V. (PO 16, pp. 528-538). Cf. Jugie, *L' Immaculée Conception dans l'Ecriture Sainte et dans la tradition orientale* [Rome, 1952], pp. 164-307, for others.

[21] Aquinas seems to have been in error on this point, cf. *Summa Theologica*, III, q. XXVII.

[22] Demetrios Kydonios, *Hom. in annuntiationem deiparae*, contained in *Cod. Paris gr.*, 1213 (cf. Jugie, *op. cit.*, pp. 276-279).

[23] Georgios Scholarios, *In dormitionem* (PO 16, p. 577); cf. Petit-Siderides-Jugie, *Œuvres complètes de Georges Scholarios*, Vol. I [Paris, 1928], pp. 202-203; also Petit-Siderides-Jugie, *op. cit.*, I, p. 501; also Jugie, *Georges Scholarios et l'Immaculée Conception*, Echos d'Orient (Paris-Istanbul, 17 [1915], pp. 527-530).

[24] Nicephorus Callixtus, however, expressed doubt during the fourteenth century (cf. Jugie *L' Immaculée Conception dans l'Ecriture Sainte et dans la tradition orientale*, p. 213), but the great Cabasilas' (1371) teaching on the immaculate conception (*In nativitatem* [PO 19, pp. 468-482]; *In dormitionem* [PO 19, pp. 498-504]) still had great influence in the subsequent centuries. Perhaps even more influential was Patriarch Gregory Palamas (1446-1452) whose homilies on the Mother of God are second to none even today (*De hypapante ; De annuntiatione ; De dormitione* [PG 151]; also *In Christi genealogiam* and *In praesentationem* [edit. K. Sophocles, Τοῦ ἐν ἁγίοις πατρὸς ἡμῶν Γρεγορίου τοῦ Παλαμᾶ ὁμιλίαι κβ', Athens, 1861]).

[25] The *Skrizhal* is the Russian version of John Nathaniel's Ἡ θεῖα λειτουργία.

were branded as blasphemous, especially among the *Staroviery* (Old Believers), who maintained the ancient customs and beliefs, however small or inconsequential. [26] This reaction confirms the ancient Byzantine and Slav tradition of the immaculate conception. Only after Pope Pius IX defined the dogma in 1854 did opposition to the doctrine solidify among most Orthodox theologians. [27] The Orthodox Church, however, has never made any definitive pronouncement on the matter. Its official position is rather a suspension of judgment than a true objection. When Patriarch Anthimos VII, for example, wrote his reply to Pope Leo XIII's letter in 1895, and listed what he believed to be the errors of the Latins, he found no fault with their belief in the immaculate conception, but objected to the fact that the Pope had defined it. [28]

Ὑπερευλογημένη, " the one most blessed beyond all others, " is another way of saying what Elizabeth told Mary at her visitation : " Blessed art thou among women. " Of all God's creatures, Mary is indeed the most blessed with grace, beauty of soul and perfection. The inspired Greek words, recorded by St. Luke (1:28), which the angel Gabriel spoke on the day of the annunciation, were : Χαῖρε, κεχαριτωμένη, " Hail! Full of grace! " The Greek perfect participle refers not so much to time or tense but, rather, to the kind of action, namely, perfected, fully completed. If the sacred author had wished merely to indicate past time, he would have used the aorist participle. The word κεχαριτωμένη, therefore, is more precisely translated here as " completely graced, perfectly graced " rather than simply " having been graced. " Indeed Mary was perfectly blessed, for she was perfectly graced. In the history of mankind, no woman is better known, loved, and venerated than the " all-holy, immaculate, most blessed and glorious Lady, the Mother of God and ever-virgin Mary.

To every petition of the *Great Ektenia* the faithful respond, " Lord, have mercy. " " Have mercy on me, O Lord, thou son of David, " cried the woman of Canaan who sought the cure of her daughter

---

[26] Cf. N. Subbotin, *Materialy dlja istorii Roskola*, Vol. IV (Moscow, 1878), pp. 39-50, 229, and Vol. I (Moscow, 1874), p. 457.

[27] Most of them seem to have objected on the grounds that it was unnecessary to define it.

[28] Ἐκκλησιαστικὴ Ἀλήθεια (Constantinople, 1880-1923, Vol. 15 (1895), p. 244.

(Matt. 15:22). "O Lord, thou son of David, have mercy on us," pleaded the two blind men on the road from Jericho (Matt. 20:30). "Jesus, Master, have mercy on us," called out the ten lepers as they stood afar off (Luke 17:13). Jesus heard their humble prayers and granted their petitions. "Lord, have mercy," cry the people in the Divine Liturgy to the same Christ who walked the byways of Palestine nearly two thousand years ago.

The expression "have mercy" must be taken in its total scriptural sense. The Greek word ἐλέησον, used in the Gospels and early Liturgies, is popularly translated as "have mercy," but this does not convey the whole meaning. 'Ελέησον has the same root form as ἐλαίον (referring to olive oil or to the tree from which it comes). Homer uses the word ἐλαίον almost exclusively as anointing oil. Oil is poured out to soothe and heal, as in the parable of the good Samaritan. In the Old Testament, it is poured on the heads of kings and priests as the image of God's grace which comes down and flows on them (Ps. 133:2), empowering them to transcend mere human capability.

The original idea is contained in the olive tree of Genesis (8:6-21). Of the several birds sent out by Noah to find dry land, only the gentle dove returns with an olive twig. This is a sign from God that his wrath is ended, that he is giving man another chance. The olive tree and its oil indicate primarily the end of God's wrath, an offering of peace to sinners who have turned against him. It speaks, moreover, of God's healing grace abundantly poured upon us in order that we may live according to his will, and receive an increase in power. A hand, wounded and festering, is unable to work, but a healed one can. By our own power, we can do nothing, but with the grace of God we can work miracles.

The Slavonic *milost* and *pomyluj* go back to the Greek ἐλέησον in that they, too, express the end of God's wrath toward us and the healing oil of his grace, but they bring out especially his loving-kindness. Their root-form expresses endearing tenderness; hence, when we pray, "Have mercy on us" *(pomyluj)*, we are not merely asking God to save us from his wrath, to heal us, but we are also asking for his love. Knowing the power of perseverance in prayer, the faithful reiterate this cry fifty-nine times during the Divine

Liturgy (excluding the rite of preparation). The cry is sent up to God after each petition, because in hearing and granting each petition, God will show his mercy-love toward his people. The people never tire of calling for it, because they know that as sinners they have no right to it. But God will hear the mournful cry of his people and will show them his mercy, for "not by the works of justice which we have done, but according to his mercy" (Tit. 3:5) does he save us. The people of God know that his "mercy exalteth itself above judgment" (James 2:13).

CHAPTER XXXV

THE HISTORY OF THE *EKTENIA*

Essentially the *ektenia* is a litanic, supplicatory prayer of the entire congregation, the *ecclesia*, voiced through the deacon or priest, and united to the prayers of the celebrant. " I desire therefore, first of all, that supplications, prayers, intercessions, and thanksgivings be made for all men : for kings and for all that are in high station : that we may lead a quiet and a peaceable life in all piety and chastity," wrote Paul to Timothy (I Tim. 2:1-2). In the *Great Ektenia*, there are intercessions for the rulers of the country, for those in high governmental offices, etc. Undoubtedly, St. Paul taught the people those very things which he asks Timothy to do. Just as surely, Timothy listened to the voice of Paul. This may well be the original form of the *ektenia*.

The petition " eleison," or the more formal " Kyrie eleison," directed at any one of the gods, can be traced to pre-Christian times and, hence, must have been very familiar to the early converts. [1] Pre-Christian Jews were also familiar with this petition as addressed to the true God, for Holy Scriptures abound in examples of its use (e.g., Pss. 6:3; 40:5, 11). With proper changes, it was only natural that the Christians should adopt such practices in their own prayers.

All this, of course, does not prove that some form of litanic, supplicatory prayer was used in the very early Christian liturgical services, although it probably was. A careful study of Clement's letter to the recalcitrant Corinthians suggests such a possibility (see above, pp. 35-36). Hints of it appear also in Justin's *Apology* when he tells of saying " earnest prayers in common for ourselves, for the newly baptized, and for all others all over the world." [2] Ultimately, this great Prayer of Intercession can be traced

---

[1] How strongly this habit must have been entrenched among the people is witnessed by a fifth century Alexandrian preacher denouncing the practice of many Christians who had kept bowing to the rising sun and crying out, ἐλέησον ἡμᾶς (" Have mercy on us "). Cf. Dölger, *Sol salutis, Gebet und Gesang im christlichen Altertum* [Münster im W., 1920], pp. 61-63.

[2] Justin, *First Apology*, chap. 65.

to the Jewish Liturgy. [3] In the early evolution of this type of prayer in the Christian assemblies, the petitions were probably made by the celebrant (the bishop, or the priest as his substitute), while the laity's part may have been limited to a moment of silent prayer after each petition. It is not known precisely when the congregation began expressing its union with the celebrant by saying " Amen, " or " Kyrie eleison. " It was probably very early. [4] The actual content of these early supplications is also unknown, but from the fourth century on, many references indicate a surprising similarity.

In the Egyptian Church, for example, astonishing resemblances appear in the various prayers (22-30) of Sarapion's *Euchologion* (c. A.D. 353-360), especially in the " Prayer for the People " (27) : In that petitions are prayers for the well-being of the faithful, the peace of the state, the tranquillity of the Church, the slaves, the poor, the aged, travelers, the sick, etc.; we can say the same of the prayer for the bishop and the various members of the Church (25), which included priests, deacons, subdeacons, lectors, etc.   These, we must remember, were the bishop's prayers. While the bishop prayed, the deacon made similar petitions. [5]

[3] Cf. A. Baumstark, *Comparative Liturgy* (Westminster, Md., 1958), p. 45.

[4] Cf. *ibid.*, pp. 45-46.

[5] Another set of Alexandrian intercessions or slightly revised versions of them, which may even antedate the *Euchologion* of Sarapion are still used at several points in the Liturgy of the Coptic Rite :

" *Deacon :* Pray for the peace of the One Holy Catholic and Apostolic Orthodox Church of God. *The people bow deeply and say :* Lord, have mercy.

" *Celebrant :* We pray and beseech thy goodness, O Lover of mankind : remember, O Lord, the peace of thine only Holy Catholic and Apostolic Church which is from one end of the world to the other : bless all the peoples and all the lands : the peace that is from heaven grant in all our hearts, but also graciously bestow upon us the peace of this life.   The emperor, the armies, the magistrates, the councillors, the people, our neighbors, our comings-in and our goings-out, order them all in thy peace.   O King of peace, grant us peace, for thou hast given us all things : possess us, O God, for beside thee we know none other : we make mention of thy holy name.   Let all our souls live through thy Holy Spirit, and let not the death of sin have dominion over us or over all thy people; through thine only-begotten Son, Jesus Christ, by whom glory and might be unto thee in the Holy Spirit now and throughout all ages.

" *Deacon :* Pray for our Patriarch, the Pope, and Father N—, Lord Archbishop of the great city of Alexandria. *The people bow deeply and say :* Lord, have mercy.

" *Celebrant :* We pray and beseech thy goodness, O Lover of mankind : remember, O Lord, our Patriarch, our honored Father N———.   Preserve him to us in safety many years in peaceful times, fulfilling that holy pontificate which thou thyself hast committed unto him according to thy holy and blessed will,

From the Church at Jerusalem, *c.* A.D. 390, Etheria tells how one of the deacons would read a list of petitions and " as he spoke each of the names, a crowd of boys stood there and answered him each time, ' Kyrie eleison, ' as we say, ' Lord, have mercy.... ' " [6] If this was done at Vespers, more cogent reasons would have dictated the same at the Eucharistic Liturgy.

About the same time or a little before (*c.* A.D. 370), we meet the fully developed litanic form in the Antiochene Church, as offered by the compiler of the *Apostolic Constitutions* in Book VIII, along with a wealth of rubrical prescriptions. One such rubric is : " *At each of these petitions which the deacon pronounces, the people should say,* Kyrie eleison, *especially the children* " (see above, p. 111). The petitions themselves referred to a series of classes (catechumens, those possessed of evil spirits, those in the last stages of preparation for baptism, the penitents, etc.). Over each class, the deacon proclaimed a lengthy series of petitions to which the people responded, " Kyrie eleison, " and the bishop imparted his blessing in the form of a prayer. Although the compiler may have expanded the series, he has preserved faithfully the Antiochene practice : direct evidence for this is found in Chrysostom's homilies preached in Antioch (see above, pp. 109-121). The same may be said for the "prayers of the faithful, the intercessory petitions for the world at large, " etc., as even a cursory study of these sources will reveal. No less astonishing is the resemblance between these fourth-century forms and the present *ektenias* in the various Byzantine liturgical services. [7] It is understood, of course, that the position of these litanic forms was not at

---

rightly distributing the word of truth, feeding thy people in holiness and righteousness; and with him, all the orthodox bishops and presbyters and deacons, and all the fullness of thine One Holy Catholic and Apostolic Church. Bestow on him with us peace and safety from all quarters; and his prayer which he maketh on our behalf and on behalf of all thy people—and ours as well on his behalf, do thou accept on thy spiritual altar in heaven for a sweet-smelling savor. And all his enemies visible and invisible do thou bruise and humble shortly under his feet, but himself do thou keep in peace and righteousness in thy holy Church.

" *Deacon :* Pray for this holy *ecclesia* and our meetings. *The people bow deeply and say :* Lord, have mercy; etc. "

[6] *Aetheriae peregrinatio*, chap. 24 (CSEL, XXXIX, 72).

[7] The student of the Liturgy will also want to include the petitions mentioned by Basil (A.D. 379) in his letters : *Epist.*, 155 (PG 32, 612); *Epist.*, 97 (PG 32, 493); *Epist.*, 148, 2 to end (PG 32, 581 AB); etc.

the beginning of the service, but after the lessons just before the various dismissals ending the Liturgy of the Catechumens.

By the eighth century, not only were all the *ektenias* of the Byzantine-Armenian Liturgy of St. John Chrysostom substantially the same as they are today in the Byzantine Liturgy, but also nearly all their petitions or supplications, as regard their text, their order and their division. [8] The only difference of any importance is in the *ektenia* that now follows the Gospel reading. [9] The Byzantine system may have been imposed upon Armenia during the military occupation between A.D. 630 and 693.

Why was this litanic prayer, originally found at the closing of the synaxis, shifted to different parts of the Divine Liturgy? What is now called the enarksis (ἔναρξις) was originally a separate prayer service, akin to one of the canonical hours. Performed in the narthex of the church, it consisted in the veneration of the images of Christ, of the Mother of God, and of the saints adorning the church doors. It is essentially litanic, consisting in a threefold *ektenia* and a threefold antiphon. It may have been performed occasionally before the Liturgy of the Catechumens (probably while the people were waiting for the entrance of the bishop). By the seventh century, it had become a habit, so much so that it came to be seen as an actual part of the Liturgy. [10] The modified position of the other *ektenias* is probably due to other but similar reasons.

Some authors hold that when the Eucharistic Prayer and later most of the celebrant's prayers began to be recited silently, and when the veil screen (iconostas) was set up—excluding the laity from their traditionally intimate participation in the divine services—the ektenias began to be recited because the people had nothing else to do. [11] Others explain that the celebrant, occupied with his own part

---

[8] Cf. Catergian-Dasian, *Die Liturgien bei den Armeniern*, TU (Wien, 1897), pp. 182 ff.; also G. Aucher, *La versione armena della liturgia di S. Giovanni Crisostom*, ΧΡΥΣΟΣΤΟΜΙΚΑ, pp. 373 ff.

[9] Cf. Catergian-Dasian, *op. cit.*, pp. 189-190; Aucher, *op. cit.*, pp. 380-381.

[10] In the early eighth century Armenian version of Chrysostom's Liturgy, the whole *enarksis* is considered part of the Divine Liturgy. Cf. Aucher, *op. cit.*, pp. 373-377.

[11] E.g., Dom Gregory Dix in his otherwise superb book, *Shape of the Liturgy* (London : Dacre Press, 1960), pp. 482-483.

of the Liturgy, let the deacon conduct what was going on outside the sanctuary. The priest could then prepare himself for the sacrifice with silent prayers, etc. [12]

It should be clear, however, even to the student uninitiated into the intricacies of the Byzantine Liturgy, that the silent recitation of the Eucharistic Prayer had nothing to do with bringing in the *ektenias* as if they were to occupy the attention of the congregation while the liturgical action, the Eucharist proper, proceeded apart from them behind the screen. The reason is that no *ektenia* occurs during the Byzantine Eucharistic Prayer, or for that matter during any priestly action in the course of the whole Divine Liturgy! In fact, the people sing enough responses to keep them busy during any liturgical service, without resorting to the *ektenia*. As for the veil, and later, the screen, they created little if any difficulty for the celebrant. In fact, without a deacon, he can do his part and also intone the *ektenias*.

The popularity of the *ektenias* can be explained to a great extent on merely psychological grounds. Their petitions are vivid expressions of the people's ordinary needs; their content is all-inclusive; their language, brief, and concrete. By repeating the words mentally or whispering them after the deacon, the uninitiated could pray for their uncomplicated needs in words they understood. The ektenias put them in the midst of a fundamental evangelical atmosphere because the petitions are full of the evangelical spirit. The invariable responses were suited to the uneducated who constituted the mass of the converts after the fourth century. Even today, the first things a visitor learns at any Byzantine service are these short, unchanging responses of the people : *Hospody, pomyluj*, Κύριε ἐλέησον, " Lord, have mercy. "

As services became longer, an attempt for more brevity was made by having the celebrant pray some of his prayers silently while the deacon was still repeating with the people the *ektenias* originally intended as introductions to these same prayers.

[12] *Ibid.*

CHAPTER XXXVI

THE ANTIPHONS,
THEIR PRAYERS AND *EKTENIAS*

W*hen the deacon and people are singing the last part of the* Great
Ektenia, *the priest recites the Prayer of the First Antiphon
silently :*

O Lord, our God, whose power is indescribable, whose
glory is incomprehensible, whose mercy is measureless and
whose love for man is beyond words : in your kindness, Lord,
look down upon us and upon this holy Church, and grant
to us and to those who are praying with us the riches of your
mercy and compassion.

*As soon as the deacon has finished the final ektenia-commendation,
the priest sings the following doxology, which forms the conclusion to
both the* Great Ektenia *and the Prayer of the First Antiphon :*

For to you, Father, Son, and Holy Spirit, is due all glory,
honor, and adoration, now and always and for ever and ever.

People : Amen.

*Then the deacon makes a small bow, leaves his place, stands before
the icon of Christ and holds his* orar *with three fingers of his right hand,
while the cantors (and/or the people) sing the First Antiphon, or
the typica :* [1]

---

[1] Here we give the First Antiphon which is used for all ordinary Sundays of
the year according to Ruthenian usage. It consists of Ps. 65:1-4, interspersed with
a versicle invoking Our Lady's intercession, as given above. On ordinary weekdays
verses 2, 3, and 16 of Ps. 91 are sung, interspersed with the same versicle. On
major feasts, both the verses from the psalms and the versicle are proper to the
feast. For details, cf. I. Dolnysky, *Typik tserky ruskokatolycheskiya* (Lvov, 1899),
pp. 57, 97, 101 f., 106, 110, 113, 115, 120 f.

In the Russian recension of the Liturgy, the First Antiphon for ordinary
Sundays consists of Ps. 103 and ends with the minor doxology, " Glory be to the
Father, " etc. (In the Douay Version this is Ps. 102). For ordinary weekdays,
it is the same as the Ruthenian recension, including the same versicle, except that
the Russian usage inserts also the versicle after the first half of the minor doxology.
For major feasts, they are proper to the given feast. For details, cf. K. Nikolsky,
Posobie k izucheniu Ustava Bogosluzhenia pravoslavnoi tserkvy (St. Petersburg,
1907), pp. 374-384.

**Shout joyfully to the Lord, all the earth : sing to his name;
give glory to his praise.**

**Through the prayers of the Mother of God, O Saviour,
save us!**

**Say to God : how terrible are your deeds; in the multitude
of your strength, your enemies shall lie to you.**

**Through the prayers of the Mother of God, O Saviour,
save us!**

**Let all the earth adore you and sing to you : let it sing to
your name, O Most High One.**

**Through the prayers of the Mother of God, O Saviour,
save us!**

**Glory be to the Father and to the Son, and to the Holy
Spirit, now and always, and for ever and ever.   Amen
(Ps. 65:1-4).**

**Through the prayers of the Mother of God, O Saviour,
save us!**

This is the first of the three antiphons of the Divine Liturgy. It consists in quotations from the psalms, concluding with a doxology
and a refrain-acclamation repeated after each verse.   Each of the
antiphons includes a silent prayer recited by the celebrant, and a
small *ektenia*.   When originally introduced into the Liturgy, the
psalms were chanted in full.   Later, they were shortened to three
or four verses.   The responsorial-antiphonal style of singing gives
the cantors a moment of rest and allows the congregation to participate actively without any preparation or written text.

The first four verses of Psalm 65, in the first antiphon for the
ordinary Sunday, are an invitation for all nations to worship God
because of his mighty works, a fitting prayer for the opening of the
Divine Liturgy.   The second selection, used on ordinary weekdays
and on the feasts of the Blessed Mother and the saints, is no less
fitting.   The themes of the antiphons for the major feasts of Christ
correspond to the particular mystery of each feast.   There are eight
such major holy days which have their own proper festive antiphons :
the Exaltation of the Holy Cross, Christmas, Epiphany, Palm Sunday,
Easter, the Ascension, Pentecost, and the Transfiguration.

Although called " antiphons, " these chants are not to be confused with the Latin Rite's antiphonal singing : two choruses alternating verse by verse. The Byzantine technique is closer to the older responsorial method which dominated the field until the fourth century. A soloist chanted the psalm verse by verse. After each verse, the people repeated the same refrain or *responsum*. [2] The primitive Church inherited this style of singing from the Jewish people, who followed it in the singing, not only of the psalms, but also of the other scriptural books. The Jewish refrain was an interpolated phrase. The Christian refrain was taken either from the first verse of the psalm or from the context. Since they were repeated after each verse, they became familiar to the whole congregation. Chrysostom often refers to them as starting points for deeper study of the psalms themselves. [3]

About this time, there was an independent prayer service, resembling the present canonical hours, which Etheria calls " the first morning service on Sundays. " She witnessed it in Jerusalem c. A.D. 390, and tells us that after the entrance of the bishop into the church of the Anastas, psalms were intoned by a priest, by a deacon, and by another cleric, each in turn; to each verse of these psalms, the people responded with a refrain; a prayer followed each psalm. The same plan is found in the Byzantine ἔναρξις, but at the time it had nothing to do with the Eucharistic Liturgy.

In the middle of the fourth century, the responses were sung differently in Antioch : either two choirs, or one choir and the congregation, alternated (whence the name *antiphonal* — " answering voice "). The choir began with a short verse, the refrain, and gave the tune (now called the *antiphon* in the Latin Rite), and then sang the first verse of the psalm. The congregation responded by repeating the introductory verse. The choir then sang the second verse, and the congregation repeated the introductory verse, and so on, until the end. Two monks, Flavian and Diodore, who were later to become bishops, introduced this style of singing when they organ-

---

[2] *Apostolic Constitutions*, Book II, 57 (Quasten, *Mon.* 182).
[3] E.g., *In Ps.* 117, esp. 1 (edit. Montfaucon 5, 317-318); *In Ps.* 144, 1 (edit. cit., 5, 466 E-467); etc.

zed an anti-Arian lay movement in Antioch. [4] This developed eventually into the *canon* of the Byzantine office (see pp. 396 ff., below). The *Prokeimenon*, which comes before the Epistle, is another variant of Antiochene antiphonal singing (see pp. 413 ff.). Antiphonal singing became immediately popular in large congregations in the great fourth-century churches. Besides the advantages already indicated, the attendance no longer had to strain to hear the voice of a single singer. Large city cathedrals soon formed special singing groups, the *schola cantorum*.

In the fifth century, the trinitarian doxology, " Glory be to the Father...," was added at the end of the psalms.

Antiphonal singing spread throughout Christendom in both the East and the West. Caesarea was using it, as St. Basil tells us, by A.D. 379; Milan adopted it probably at the instance of St. Ambrose (A.D. 389), and finally Rome. It is said that Pope Celestine I (A.D. 422-432) ordered antiphonal singing at the entrance ceremony. [5] Perhaps Rome set a precedent in the Liturgy by prescribing that the entrance of the celebrant be accompanied by antiphonal singing. [6]

Such at any rate was the origin of the Latin *introit* chant. When singing was introduced into the Syro-Byzantine processional entrance, however, it was not the antiphonal singing of the psalms, but special entrance chants, the *eisodika* (εἰσοδικα), essentially *troparia*

---

[4] Cf. Theodoret, *Hist. eccl.*, IV, 22-24 (PG 42, 1420 C-1422 C [*Series graeca*]).

[5] *Liber pont. Vita Caelestini* (edit. Duchesne, *Liber pont.*, I, 20). This account unfortunately is not reliable, but at least we know that antiphony was used at the Entrance ceremony when this section of the book was written, *ergo*, prior to the middle of the sixth century; cf. Batiffol, *Leçons sur la Messe* (Paris, 1920), p. 105.

[6] Paulinus of Nola makes no mention of any singing in the description of the processional entrance in *Carmina*, xiv (PL 61, 464-468), c. A.D. 400; nor does there seem to be any introit in the Rite of Africa. In the East, the processional entrance of the bishop is known at Laodicea by the middle of the fourth century, but there is no evidence of singing. In the homilies preached at Antioch (c. A.D. 390) and at Constantinople a few years later, Chrysostom refers to a formal entrance but mentions no accompanying chant. In fact, if we are to take the " silence " of the offertory procession, so emphasized by Theodore of Mopsuestia (cf. edit. Mingana, in *Woodbrook Studies* Vol. VI, p. 84) as meaningful, it seems that the Eastern Christians at this time found silent processions most impressive. Etheria, however, does mention " hymns " during the bishop's procession from one church to another in Jerusalem; whether these " hymns " continued once the bishop entered the church, she does not say (cf. *Aetheriae peregrinatio*, chaps. 24, 25 (CSEL XXXIX, 71 ff., 74 ff.).

taken from the *canon* of the Byzantine Office. Indirectly, they do have a common origin with the antiphonal singing of Antioch, since the canons evolved from it (see, p. 391).

The responsorial singing of the psalms, that is, the three antiphons, may have been placed at the beginning of the Liturgy to occupy the people while they themselves were waiting for the bishop-celebrant's formal entrance. What had begun as a semi-independent practice would then have become part of the Liturgy. There is, however, insufficient documentation on these centuries (fifth to eighth) to indicate with certainty how the evolution actually occurred. [7]

The three antiphons first appear in the eighth century texts of the Byzantine Liturgy, and it would seem that they had no connection with the entrance rite. [8] Isidore Pyromal's redaction of the Liturgy of St. Basil, for example, merely has the office of the antiphons performed *before* the entrance of the bishop. [9] The *Commentary* of St. Germanus of Constantinople (715-729) fails to mention any link between the antiphons and the entrance rite when it explains the mystical meaning of the antiphons as a preparation for the coming of the Son of God. [10] It is the same with the eighth-century Codex Barberini, which contains the three antiphons, complete with their respective prayers of the celebrant almost as they are today. [11] The antiphons seem never to have been used as entrance chants, as were the Latin *introits*: the poetical *eisodika (troparia)* performed that function. Surprisingly, the Latin *introits* and the Byzantine anti-

---

[7] There may be an indication of the original function of the psalm-antiphons in the 97th Canon of St. Basil the Great, describing the beginning of the Coptic-Alexandrian Liturgy : " When they commence to celebrate the Mysteries... they do not begin before all the people gather together and recite the psalms until they enter. After the people have congregated, they read from the Epistles, then from the Acts of the Apostles and from the Gospel " (*Canons of St. Basil the Great*, edit. I. E. Rahmani, *I fasti della chiesa patriarcale Antiochena* [Rome, 1920], p. xiv).

[8] *Codex Barberini, gr.* 336, cf. Brightman, LEW, pp. 310-312; for the eighth century Armenian version of Chrysostom's Liturgy, cf. Aucher, *La versione armena della liturgia di S. Giovanni Crisostomo*, XPYCOCTOMIKA, pp. 375-377.

[9] Goar, *Euchologion*, pp. 153-154.

[10] Edit. N. Borgia, *Il commentario liturgico di s. Germano Patriarca Constantinopolitano e la versione latina de Anastasio Bibliotecario* [Grottaferrata, 1912], p. 21.

[11] Brightman, LEW, pp. 310-312; so does the early eighth century Armenian version of Chrysostom's Liturgy, cf. Aucher, *op. cit.*, pp. 375-377.

phons, despite their structural similarity and common origin in the
ancient responsorial-antiphonal chanting of the psalms, are not
functionally parallel in the Mass; while the *introits* and the *eisodika*,
although exactly parallel, differ in both structure and origin. [12]

" I heard this Psalm *(Come, let us adore)* sung at the beginning
of Mass in the Church of Hagia Sophia at Constantinople, " writes
Amalarius of Metz in A.D. 833. [13] Even at this late date in some
churches, the " office of the antiphons " still seems to have been an
independent service before the Divine Liturgy. The ninth-century
Typikon of the Church of Hagia Sophia at Constantinople even
mentions that it may be omitted on those days when the Office of
the Midnight Vigil is celebrated (i.e., before major feasts). [14]

In the tenth century, however, the " office of the three antiphons "
had become established as an invariable feature of the Divine Liturgy
as it is today. Pseudo-Germanus, Pseudo-Sophronius, Theodore of
Andida, and others bear ample witness to this. [15]

There seems to have remained some doubt as to the exact place
of the priest's silent prayers. A thirteenth century document
prescribes their precise position : the prayer of the first antiphon,
before the doxology of the *Ektenia of Peace* (the *Great Ektenia*);
the prayer of the second antiphon, before the first *Little Ektenia*;
that of the third antiphon, before the second *Little Ektenia*. [16]

In some churches of the fourteenth century, a second series of
antiphon prayers was used in parallel with the first, [17] only to disappear later.

---

[12] They do have a remote common origin in the Antiochene antiphonal singing
of psalms, but the *eisodika* trace their immediate origin to the *Canon* of the Byzantine Office... which in turn, developed from the antiphonal technique! See p. 397.

[13] Amalarius of Metz, *Ord. Antiph.* C. XXXI (PL 105, 1243-1316).

[14] Krasnoseltsev, *Typik tserkvy Sv. Sofii v Konstantinopoli*, Litopys (Odessa,
1892), p. 227.

[15] Migne (PG 98, 401-405; 87, 3994; 140, 401-412).

[16] MS. of Sophia Library, N. 524, p. 7-8 (Petrovsky, *Histoire de la rédaction
slave de la liturgie de S. Jean Chrysostome*, XPYCOCTOMIKA, p. 875. Cf. also
Euchologion, p. 101).

[17] MS. of Sophia Library, N. 522, pp. 15-16 (Petrovsky, *op. cit.*, p. 883);
compare also fourteenth century MS. of Moscow Synodal Library, N. 279 in
Krasnoseltsev, *Svidinia o nikotorikh liturgicheskikh rukopis'akh Vatikanskoi biblioteki*
(Kazan, 1885), p. 298. Cf. also MS. of Esphygmenon Library of year 1306 contained in Dmitrievsky, *Opysanie liturgicheskikh rukopisej khraniaschikhsia v bibliotekakh pravoslanago vostoka*, Vol. II, *Euchologia* [Kiev, 1901], p. 265.

Second Antiphon and the Monogenes

After the First Antiphon, the deacon returns to his usual place (before the royal doors), makes a small bow, and sings :

Again and again in peace let us pray to the Lord.

People : **Lord, have mercy.**

Deacon : **Help us, save us, have mercy on us, and protect us, O God, by your grace.**

People : **Lord, have mercy.**

Deacon : **As we remember our all-holy, immaculate, most blessed and glorious Lady, the Mother of God and ever-virgin Mary, together with all the saints, let us commend ourselves and one another and our whole life to Christ our God.**

People : **To you, O Lord.**

In the meantime, the priest recites silently the Prayer of the Second Antiphon :

O Lord our God, save your people and bless your inheritance. Guard the fullness of your Church. Sanctify those who love the beauty of your house; bring them to glory by your divine power. And do not forsake us who trust in you.

Then the priest sings the doxology, concluding both the Prayer of the Second Antiphon and the Little Ektenia :

For yours is the majesty, and yours is the Kingdom and the power and the glory, Father, Son, and Holy Spirit, now and always and for ever and ever.

People : **Amen.**

After making a bow, the deacon leaves his place before the royal doors and stands before the icon of the Mother of God while the cantors (and/or the people) sing the Second Antiphon, or the Typika :

O God, be generous to us, and bless us; make the light of your countenance shine upon us and have mercy on us.

O Son of God, risen from the dead, save us who sing to you : alleluia.

That we may know your way upon the earth, your salvation among all the nations.

O Son of God, risen from the dead, save us who sing to you : alleluia.

Let people confess to you, O God, let all the people give praise to you.

O Son of God, risen from the dead, save us who sing to you : alleluia. [18]

After these verses of the Second Antiphon, the cantors (and/or the people) sing the doxology and the Monogenes hymn.

Glory be to the Father and to the Son, and to the Holy Spirit, now and always, and for ever and ever.   Amen.

O only-begotten Son and Word of God, though immortal, you deigned for our salvation to take flesh of the holy Mother of God and ever-virgin Mary; and, without undergoing change, you became man.   You were crucified, O Christ God, and by your death you trampled down death, you who are one of the Holy Trinity and are glorified with the Father and the Holy Spirit : save us!

Repeated many times in the various liturgical services of the Byzantine Church, the *Little Ektenia,* so called because of its brevity, consists in the opening invocation of the *Great Ektenia,* its petition for God's protection, commemoration of the Blessed Mother, and doxology in honor of the Holy Trinity.   Here, as in many other instances, the doxology ending the *ektenia* also concludes the silent prayer of the priest.   Besides keeping the people occupied during the priest's silent prayer, the *Small Ektenia* emphasizes the urgency of these final entreaties.

The " fullness of the Church, " mentioned in the Prayer of the Second Antiphon, refers to those who make up the fullness of Christ's Church, all the members of the mystical body of Christ, so that not one of them be lost.

As a preparation to the coming of the Son of God in the Euchar-

---

[18] Since Vatican II, the Second Antiphon with its *ektenia* has been omitted by the Ruthenians.

istic Sacrifice, the antiphon for ordinary Sundays admirably accommodates the meaning of the original verses of Psalm 66, used as a harvest hymn by the Jews. After the Incarnation and redemption, the harvest was Messianic : in the Old Law it was a prayer that God bless Israel, the chosen people, so that the Gentiles would be led to recognize him; in the New Law it is a prayer that God bless his chosen ones, the members of his Church, so that the whole world may acknowledge and revere him as the one true God. The refrain " O Son of God, risen from the dead " is the theme of Sunday, the day specially dedicated to the resurrection of Christ. It is both a profession of faith in the greatest proof of Christ's divinity, and a plea for salvation.

Composed as an entrance chant *(eisodikon)*, the celebrated *Monogenes* Hymn (ὁ μονογενής) is attributed by the Byzantines to Emperor Justinian I, [19] and is said to have been written in A.D. 528 when Patriarch Severus of Antioch was his guest. The Syrian Jacobites ascribe it to Severus himself and give the date A.D. 512-518. Justinian certainly ordered its adoption into Byzantine liturgical use in A.D. 528. [20] The Byzantine and Syrian texts of this hymn differ somewhat. [21]

From Constantinople, the *Monogenes* spread to the other Churches of the East, but not without reservation. Because of persecution by Justinian, the Jacobite (Monophysite) Churches of Syria and Egypt never adopted it. The royalist Greek churches of Antioch and Alexandria found it desirable, both on account of its doctrinal content and because of Justinian's reputed authorship. The Armenian Church which had repudiated the Council of Chalcedon (and, hence, supposedly identified itself with Monophysitism) did accept the *Monogenes* hymn when it adopted a revised version of the Byzantine *enarksis*. The Slav Church, on the other hand, because

[19] His name is also prefixed to it in some codices, e.g., *Codex Pal.*, *gr.* 367, fol. 23 (P. de Meester, *Les origines et les développements du texte grec de la liturgie de S. Jean Chrysostome*, XPYCOCTOMIKA, p. 321, n. 2.

[20] Theophanes (ninth century), *Chronographia* (PG 108, 477 B); cf. also Georgius Cedrenus (eleventh century), *Historiarum compendium* (PG 121, 729 B).

[21] See Brightman, LEW, pp. 365 f., and p. 33, for comparison; also J. Puyade, O.S.B., " Le tropaire ' O Monogenes, ' " in *Revue de l'Orient Chrétien*, xvii (1912), pp. 253-255).

of its Byzantine origin, accepted the whole Byzantine *enarksis* and with it the *Monogenes* hymn, as is evidenced from the earliest documents. [22] Since the *Monogenes* hymn is also specifically anti-Nestorian, the Nestorian Churches do not have it.

The *Monogenes* hymn was used originally as an entrance chant. It has survived to this day in that capacity in the Syro-Antiochene, Alexandrian (Liturgy of St. Mark), and Armenian Churches. [23] Just when it was changed from its place as an entrance chant to its present position is unknown, but apparently it was some time after the ninth century. [24]

The strongly anti-Nestorian doctrinal content of the hymn can leave no doubt that it was written to vindicate Christ's consubstantiality with God the Father and the Holy Spirit. Nestorius, Bishop of Constantinople and former disciple of Theodore of Mopsuestia in the Antiochian School, taught that Christ being a perfect man, his human nature had its own subsistence, its own autonomy and, therefore, its own personality; that the Son of God dwelt in the body of Christ as in a temple or as God dwells in the just. Hence, the union of the Son of God and his human nature were *moral* only, and Christ, one in appearance, was really *two persons*. Wherefore Mary should not be called the Mother of God *(theotokos)*, but the Mother of the man Christ.

The author of the *Monogenes* hymn calls Christ " the only-begotten Son and Word of God. " The Son of God, the Word, did not dwell in the body of Christ as in a temple : Christ *was* the Son of God; he *was* the Word of God, as St. John clearly attests, " . . . and the Word was God " (John 1:1). Being God, he was immortal, but because of our salvation, he took upon himself mortal flesh from the virgin Mother. This is an echo of the Constantinopolitan Creed : " For

[22] Cf. A. Petrovsky, *op. cit.*, p. 866.

[23] So also in the twelfth century Italo-Greek Liturgy of St. Peter, as seen in the *Codex Rossanensis (Vat. gr.*, 1970).

[24] Some authors suggest that the original function of the *Monogenes* was in the canonical office. Some time during the seventh or eighth century when the antiphons became an integral part of the Liturgy of the Catechumens, the *Monogenes* was included. E.g., de Meester, *Dict. d'Archéol.* (col. 1613). This theory could be supported if it could be proved that the Second Antiphon had once been used as the Third Antiphon just before the Entrance, in which case the *Monogenes* could still have been used as an *eisodikon*.

us men and for our salvation he came down from heaven, took flesh of the Virgin Mary and was made man. " The Son of God became *man* by the Incarnation, by taking human nature. If a mere " moral " union existed between him and his human nature, we could not truly say that *he* became incarnate, that *he* became *man*. For it would certainly be incorrect to say that God *becomes* the temple in which he dwells or that he *becomes* the just man he elevates through sanctifying grace. The union between the Son of God and his human nature is certainly closer than that suggested by Nestorius.

The *Monogenes* hymn also clearly states that Christ became incarnate, " took flesh of the holy Mother of God and ever-virgin Mary, " thereby clearly contradicting the Nestorian heresy. The hymn emphatically calls Mary the *Mother of God (Theotokos)*; yet, she never ceased being a virgin.

The hymn then stresses the fact that Christ, when he became man, was indeed still God : " Without undergoing change. " His becoming incarnate did not change his divinity. He did not cease being God by becoming man. If Christ were not one person, and that a divine one, he would not be God, nor would God have died for us, but only the man Christ. Such an assumption would subvert the doctrine of the redemption and the whole scheme of salvation, because God alone could redeem us adequately. But the Son of God, Christ, is indeed only one, a divine person. All his actions, human or divine, are those of one subject, the Son of God. As if to dispel even the smallest doubt, the *Monogenes* uses the direct address, " O Christ God, " then continues, " you who are one of the Holy Trinity. " As such, he is to be " glorified with the Father and the Holy Spirit. "

In the first and second centuries, the *Docetae* claimed that Christ had assumed only an apparent body. For them, all matter was evil, the product of an evil principle. The Church has always taught that the Son of God assumed a human nature in reality, not merely in appearance. When St. John (1:14) says that " the Word was made flesh and dwelt among us, " the word " flesh " signifies, as in other scriptural passages (e.g., Gen. 6:12), the entire nature of man. The term " flesh " is used to indicate that which is visible and lowest, as it were, in human nature, in order to emphasize the reality of the

Incarnation and the condescension of the Son of God. The *Mono-genes* hymn teaches this same truth when it says that the only-begotten Son of God, the Word, deigned to take flesh of the Holy Mother of God and ever-virgin Mary. If Christ had had only an apparent body, our redemption and Christ's death would also have been merely apparent. Denying the reality of Christ's body is to deny the Incarnation and redemption, because without a true body, Christ would not have been man, nor could he have redeemed us. The *Monogenes* hymn proclaims that the Son of God " became man " and that " by his crucifixion and death he trampled down death "—another way of saying what Paul said to Timothy : " . . . who hath destroyed death and hath brought to light life and incorruption. . . " (II Tim. 1:10). The reality of Christ's human nature is shown beyond all doubt by the sufferings and death he endured for us.

The *Monogenes* hymn also attacks Monophysitism or Eutychi-anism. Eutyches, Archimandrite of Constantinople, opposed Nesto-rianism by defending the substantial unity of Christ to the point of assigning to him, not only oneness of the Person, but also oneness of nature (Monophysitism). Eutyches taught that before the Incar-nation there were two natures, the divine and human, but after the Incarnation, only one remained. His disciples, attempting to explain his doctrine, often speak of the " mixture " of the two natures, of " absorption " of one in the other, of a " formal union, " similar to that of body and soul.

Scripture, the Fathers, and the Church, teach that Christ is true God and true man—and so does the *Monogenes* hymn. Christ can be true God only if his divine nature remains intact, unchanged; he is true man only if his humanity remains unchanged. Christ cannot rightly be called true God or true man unless his divinity and humanity retain essentially and truly a divine and a human nature. The words of the hymn, " without undergoing change, " further elucidate the true doctrine of the Church. If Christ's humanity were absorbed by his divinity, he would not be true man, neither would his divinity remain unchanged. If both natures were blended or mixed together like two different liquids in a container, his divinity would lose its simplicity and would therefore be changed. The resulting blend would be neither a divine nor a human nature, neither God nor man. Finally, if the two natures *completed each other through formal union,* the result would again be neither God nor man but a compound of both, for the divine nature would have received from the human nature a complement similar to that which the soul receives from the body.

The rich doctrinal content of the *Monogenes* hymn leads to as many corollaries as there are major doctrinal propositions. Because of the union of the attributes of both natures in the one divine person *(communicatio idiomatum),* Christ as man is the Son of God and has a right to supreme worship, etc. Some writers see in the *Monogenes* hymn a summary of the teachings of St. Athanasius, St. Basil, and the two Gregorys.

The hymn contains two parts : the praise and glorification of the God-man with the Father and the Holy Spirit, and a brief petition for salvation, "save us." The first part represents a direction upward, a movement from us to God. We give something. We give praise and glory to the incarnate God and to the Holy Trinity. Then we ask for something, salvation. This second part moves as it were from heaven to earth. From heaven comes the salvation of us all. Every prayer should follow this pattern, exemplified in the *Our Father.* Prayer unites man and God; it is an exchange between earth and heaven. Prayer goes back and forth between time and eternity, over the bridge built by the Incarnation. It is by means of this bridge and only by this bridge that the heavens are again opened for man. This is the *good news* which is the Holy Gospel, the news of great joy which gladdened the angels so on the first Christmas morn.

Christ is to be glorified together with the Father and the Holy Spirit, but this glorification rests on *love,* not on the servile fear that prompted the worship of God in the Old Dispensation. The summons to the glorification of God in the New Dispensation rests on the fact of the Incarnation : the only-begotten Son of God became man and died for us out of love for us. The call for the glorification of God in the Old Law was based on the tradition of the Jewish race, which looked upon the majesty of God as it did on the sovereign power of an Eastern emperor or king. To the Jewish race, the Lord Almighty was enthroned above the seraphim and spoke to his people from a pillar of fire, the all-powerful King who ruled with a righteous hand. He was invisible to every eye, but saw all and punished quickly and severely; he was the severe Judge, unsparing, seated on a red throne, glittering with gold and precious stones, costly incense streaming forth from jeweled censers. The heavens were his throne and the earth his footstool. Trembling with fear, the faithful were to bow before his infinite majesty. The Eastern Christian, because he believed in the Dispensation of Love, dared to beseech his God for salvation despite his deep feeling of guilt and sin, despite the psychology of fear and despotism that had been impressed upon him by the heavy hand of untold centuries.

Up to this point, the Introduction Rite still symbolizes the hidden life of Jesus in Nazareth. The *Monogenes* hymn symbolizes the baptism of Jesus in the river Jordan by John the Baptist, when the heavens were opened and the Spirit of God descended upon him as a dove, and a voice from heaven said : " This is my beloved Son, in whom I am well pleased " (Matt. 3:16-17).

The Third Antiphon, Its Prayer and Ektenia

When the singing of the Monogenes *is finished, the deacon returns to his usual place before the royal doors and sings the Little Ektenia :*

Again and again in peace let us pray to the Lord.

People : **Lord, have mercy.**

Deacon : **Help us, save us, have mercy on us, and protect us, O God, by your grace.**

People : **Lord, have mercy.**

Deacon : **As we remember our all-holy, immaculate, most blessed and glorious Lady, the Mother of God and ever-virgin Mary, together with all the saints, let us commend ourselves and one another and our whole life to Christ our God.**

People : **To you, O Lord.**

While the deacon is chanting the ektenia, *the priest secretly says the Prayer of the Third Antiphon :*

You gave us grace for these common and united prayers, and promised to grant the petitions of two or three gathered together in your name : fulfill now the petitions of your servants for their good, granting us the knowledge of your truth in this world and life everlasting in the world to come.

Then the priest sings the doxology ending the prayer and the Little Ektenia :

For you are a good God and the Lover of mankind, and we give glory to you, Father, Son and Holy Spirit, now and always and for ever and ever.

People : **Amen.**

The deacon returns to the sanctuary through the south door, and the royal doors are opened. The cantors (and/or the people) sing the Third Antiphon or the Beatitudes (on Sunday, where this is customary) :

Come, let us rejoice in the Lord; let us shout with joy to God our Saviour.

O Son of God, risen from the dead, save us who sing to you : alleluia.

Let us come before his presence with praises; and let us shout with joy to him with psalms.

O Son of God, risen from the dead, save us who sing to you : alleluia.

For the Lord is a great God, and a great King over all the earth.

O Son of God, risen from the dead, save us who sing to you : alleluia.

The Byzantine Rite glories in repetitions as a lesson of perseverance : " Again and again, let us pray to the Lord. " If we ask what we should request of God, the Byzantine Church answers that God help us, save us, have mercy on us, and protect us by his grace. We pray for salvation. What should we do to attain it? Pray again and again and give our whole life to Christ through the mediation of the Blessed Virgin Mary, our " glorious Lady. "

The *Monogenes* Hymn, which had told us of the limitless love of God manifested through Christ's incarnation and crucifixion, has just been sung. We now ask once more for divine assistance and protection in order to attain salvation; we ask for the very life which pulsed in Christ and runs from him to us.

In the Prayer of the Third Antiphon, the priest reminds Christ the God-man of his promise when he said : "...if two of you shall consent upon earth concerning anything whatsoever they shall ask, it shall be done to them by my Father who is in heaven; for where there are two or three gathered together in my name, there am I in the midst of them" (Matt. 18:19-20); (see p. 582 f.). In the celebration of the Divine Liturgy, there are always two or more gathered in his name, and so their prayers warrant answering, nay, must be answered in some way, for God has so promised.

In the doxology, the priest gives additional reasons why God should answer the prayers of his people : " because you are a good God and the Lover of mankind. " Again, the simplicity of the doxology defies verbal embellishment. As is the case with many prayers of the Byzantine Liturgy, one has the feeling that the expressions are the nearest that human words can come to God's beauty and simplicity. In simplicity there is beauty. In beauty there is simplicity. God is both in one!

As the majesty of the Liturgy moves slowly on, the royal doors are opened in preparation for the *Little Entrance* and the Third Antiphon is sung. On Sundays, this consists of Psalm 94:1-3—an invitation to praise the Lord God with joy. Joyless praise is no praise at all. Psalm 94 exudes joy in the praise of Yahweh, the great God and King. The phrase " over all the earth " in verse 3 is a change from the original " above all gods. " The meaning, however, remains the same.

LITURGY
OF THE CATECHUMENS:
THE SERVICE OF READINGS

CHAPTER XXXVII

THE LITTLE ENTRANCE

When the cantors (and/or the people) come to the doxology of the Third Antiphon, the priest and deacon, still standing before the altar, make three small bows. The priest takes the Holy Gospel Book from the altar and gives it to the deacon. Preceded by candlebearers and beginning from the right-hand side, both go around the altar and through the north door into the church proper. As soon as they come to the royal doors, the candlebearers stand opposite each other, one near the icon of the Mother of God and the other near the icon of the Saviour; the priest stands in the middle and the deacon a little in front of him and to his right.

They both bow their heads as the deacon says in a subdued voice:

Let us pray to the Lord.

The priest says the Prayer of the Entrance silently:

Master and Lord, our God, who have established in heaven the orders and armies of angels and archangels to minister unto your majesty: grant that with our entrance may enter the holy angels who serve with us and glorify your goodness.

For all glory, honor, and adoration belong to you, Father, Son, and Holy Spirit, now and always and for ever and ever. Amen.

Then, the deacon, holding the orar *with three fingers and pointing eastward (i.e., toward the sanctuary) with his right hand, says to the priest in a low voice :*

Sir, bless the holy entrance.

The priest blesses toward the East as he says :

Blessed be the entrance of your saints, at all times, now and always and for ever and ever.

Deacon : **Amen.**

The deacon then offers the Holy Gospel to the priest, who kisses it. After the third verse of the Third Antiphon (or the Beatitudes) is sung, the deacon proceeds to the center and stands before the priest; raising his arms a little and showing the Holy Gospel, the deacon sings in a loud voice :

Wisdom! Let us stand straight.

Both make a small bow and go into the sanctuary through the royal doors; first the deacon, then the priest. The deacon, when he reaches the altar, puts the Holy Gospel on it. The candlebearers make a bow together before the royal doors and return to their places.

Then the cantors (and/or the people) sing :

Come, let us worship and bow down to Christ.

O Son of God, risen from the dead, save us who sing to you : alleluia.

The *Little Entrance* is a remnant of the ancient entrance rite introduced into the Eastern synaxis soon after the persecutions had ended. The bishop-celebrant and his concelebrants would gather at some prearranged place, go to the church, vest at the entrance, then enter the church in procession. In a small church, without a vestibule, the celebrants would vest at the altar. A bishop still vests at the altar in both the Byzantine and Latin Rites. In either case, their processional march into the church was fully ceremonial, as befitted the dignity of a bishop.

The first detailed description of such an entrance is given in the writings of Etheria. [1] During her vist to Jerusalem *c.* A.D. 390, she describes the entrance of the bishop into the church of the Resur-

---

[1] *Aetheriae peregrinatio,* chap. 25 [CSEL XXXIX, 74 f.].

rection—an entrance purposely delayed until all the people were in place, in order that he might enter the church in procession through their midst. The occasion is not actually an Eucharistic service, but one of the daily offices. We may infer that a similar processional entrance preceded the synaxis. [2] The Canons of Laodicea in Asia Minor about A.D. 363 indicate that presbyters may not enter and take their seats in the *bema* (in the apse) before the bishop has made his formal entrance : they are to enter with him. [3] Chrysostom, in his homilies in Antioch *c.* A.D. 390, and Constantinople shortly after A.D. 400 also speaks of a formal entrance. [4] The Clementine Liturgy of the *Apostolic Constitutions*, on the other hand, mentions no entrance procession, but begins immediately with the readings. [5] There could have been no formal entrance procession in the pre-Nicene days of the persecutions. The simple buildings of primitive Christianity would not have been suitable for the elaborate ceremonial. The ancient entrance rite must then have been introduced shortly after Nicaea.

In the original entrance ceremony, the Gospel Book was not carried in procession. This is obvious from the Prayer of the Entrance, which today is the same as that in an ancient formulary of the Liturgy of St. Basil, in which the priest prays, "...grant that with *our* entrance may enter the holy angels who serve with us...." In other words, the entrance is that of the sacred ministers (" our " entrance) and not the entrance of the Gospel Book or of Christ as symbolized by the Gospel. [6]

---

[2] *Op. cit.*, chap. 24 (CSEL XXXIX, 73).

[3] Canon 56, NPNF, Series II, Vol. XIV, p. 157.

[4] Chrysostom, at Antioch, *Adv. Jud.*, 3, 6 (edit. Montfaucon 1, 614 C); *In Matt.*, 32, 6 (edit. Montfaucon 7, 374 A); at Constantinople, *In Col.*, 3, 3 (edit. Montfaucon 11, 348 C).

[5] *Apostolic Constitutions*, Book VIII; cf. above, p. 108.

[6] This is substantiated by the Byzantine Armenian Liturgy of Basil of the early eighth century which mentions nothing about carrying the Gospel Book in its ceremonial of the Little Entrance (cf. Catergian-Dasian, *Die Liturgien bei den Armeniern*, Fünfzehn. Texte und Untersuchungen [Vienna, 1897], pp. 186 f.). On the other hand, the early eighth-century Armenian version of Chrysostom's Liturgy may have had the entrance with the Gospel : after the Prayer of Entrance, it has the rubric, " Then the priest salutes the Gospel by making three bows and goes to the altar. " (Cf. Aucher, *La versione armena della liturgia di S. Giovanni Crisostomo*, XPYCOCTOMIKA, p. 378).

In the *Codex Barberini* of the eighth or ninth century, the Liturgy of Chrysostom still had its own formula for the Prayer of Entrance; later, the present formula—from the Liturgy of St. Basil, in the same *Codex*—was used instead. [7]

The ancient papal processions at the Stational Churches in Rome are familiar to many. [8] The ceremonial concerning the Gospel Book is worthy of note. An acolyte takes up the Gospel Book in the folds of his chasuble *(planeta)* and, preceded by a subdeacon, brings it to the altar. All arise as a mark of respect. [9] The subdeacon takes the Gospel from the acolyte and places it reverently on the altar. [10]

In the eighth-century Byzantine Church, the entrance is also made with the Gospel Book : " The entrance of the Gospel indicates the presence and entrance of the Son of God into this world. " [11] The stational services probably had inspired the idea of introducing the Gospel into the Byzantine entrance procession. After the *pro-*

---

[7] Cf. Brightman, LEW, p. 312. The early eighth century Armenian version of Chrysostom's Liturgy, however, does have a prayer of entrance as it is today (cf. Aucher, *op. cit.*, pp. 377-378). On the other hand, the ninth or tenth century *Cod.* 226 of the Imperial Library of St. Petersburg has the same dual form of the prayer as *Cod. Barberini* (cf. Krasnoseltsev, *Svidinia o nikotorikh liturgicheskikh rukopis'akh Vatikanskoi biblioteki* [Kazan, 1885], p. 285). Some fifteenth century MSS. show a curious innovation : in passing the *prothesis* table, the deacon addresses the priest, " Bless, sir, the *prothesis,* " to which the priest responds, " Blessed be the *prothesis* of your holy mysteries " (e.g., MS. 530, p. 35, MS. 536, p. 18, and MS. 542, p. 15 of the Sophia Library). The fourteenth or fifteenth century MS. N. 573 of Vat. Library exhibits the same peculiarity (cf. Krasnoseltsev, *Materialy dlja istorii chinoposlidovania liturgii sv. Ioanna Zlatoustago* [Kazan, 1889], p. 108).

[8] The clearest and best-known of all the Roman *Ordines* is the *Ordo Romanus* I, first published by J. Mabillon (*Museum Italicum,* II [Paris, 1689]) and included by Migne in PL 78, 937-1372; M. Andrieu published a new critical edition in 1931, *Les Ordines Romani du haut moyen-âge,* Vol. I (Louvain). Another *Ordo* which gives an excellent description of the Roman stational services is that of St. Amand (Duchesne, *Christian Worship,* pp. 455-480).

[9] The *Ordo* of St. Amand, eighth century, has " ...*non praesumat sedere quisquam quando cum (subdiaconum) viderit praetereuntem.* "

[10] *Ordo Romanus,* I, 3, 5 (PL 78, 938 C, 940 A); etc. There is still a trace of this ceremonial in a pontifical Mass in the Latin Rite when, according to the Ceremonial of Bishops (III, 8, 25), a subdeacon should carry the closed Gospel Book in the procession in which the pontiff is led to the altar. Even in the Latin Low Mass, the priest should be preceded to the altar by an acolyte carrying the missal (*Rit. ser.,* 2, i.).

[11] Cf. *Liturgical Commentary* of S. Germanus of Constantinople (A.D. 715-729), 24 (edit. N. Borgia, *Il commentario liturgico di s. Germano Patriarca Constantinopolitano e la versione latina di Anastasio Bibliotecario* [Grottaferrata, 1912], p. 21).

thesis and *enarksis* had been prefixed to the synaxis, the old entrance rite could no longer be conveniently made, unless some circuitous route was deliberately introduced (the celebrant and his assistants would have to go from the sacristy or sanctuary to the entrance of the church and then go in procession back to the sanctuary). Unless a new element were interjected, the whole process would be artificial and superfluous. The Gospel Book, therefore, was taken for the veneration of the faithful. This put meaning back into the procession, and the Little Entrance, as we know it today, was born. Its purpose : the veneration of the Gospel by the faithful. [12]

In the Prayer of the Entrance, the priest begs God, who created the angels for his glory, to grant that these angels make the entrance with him, and that, together with him, they serve God and glorify him. He asks that the angels and archangels be at his side when he performs his official duties. Is this presumption? No. The priest asks God to send his angels to help him in fulfilling his altar functions, precisely because he considers himself unworthy. The angels will make up with their holiness what is lacking in him.

The royal doors are opened in preparation for the Little Entrance, revealing the resplendent altar, the dwelling place of God's glory, the supreme source of revelation contained in the Sacred Scripture. In the first stage of the Little Entrance, the Gospel Book (signifying God's revelation to us), is carried from the sanctuary (symbolizing

---

[12] Some hold the opinion that the Gospel Book was introduced into the entrance-procession to represent the bishop who, in turn, represented Christ. According to this theory, primitive Christians regarded the bishop as Christ's representative and, since the ordinary celebrant of the pre-Nicene Eucharist was the bishop (each parish had a bishop as its pastor), they considered his entrance as that of Christ the High Priest. After the rise of dioceses, most parishes had to be served, not by bishops, but by priests (as is the case today). Without a bishop, the old entrance rite no longer had the same meaning, i.e., it was not the " entrance of Christ, the High Priest. " The Gospel Book (symbolizing Christ), therefore, was introduced into the entrance ritual. Such a theory is not plausible : (1) after the change, the Little Entrance with the Gospel was and is made at pontifical Liturgies where the bishop is present; thereby, no symbolic representation is needed; (2) the priest was and is regarded as the bishop's and Christ's representative to the people in a very real way; hence, another " symbolic representation " was not necessary; (3) the change, if made for this reason, would have come several hundred years earlier. The rise of dioceses or eparchies (where many parishes " belonged " to one bishop) had taken place in the first two centuries following Nicaea, c. A.D. 325-500, and the change in the entrance rite was made during the seventh or eighth century.

heaven) into the church of the faithful (signifying the people on earth).

During the entrance procession, the deacon raises the Holy Gospel to his forehead, the seat of knowledge in man, in order to represent divine wisdom which leads to eternal happiness. This idea is emphasized when he stands before the royal doors, lifts up the Gospel and calls out, " Wisdom! " He immediately adds : " Let us stand straight. " By standing straight, the congregation becomes more attentive, more alert to heed the dictates of divine wisdom.

The Gospel Book, expressing the word of God, came to be seen as the symbol of Christ. Its entrance symbolized that of Jesus at the beginning of his public life. The procession—out of the sanctuary, into the church, up to the royal doors, and back into the sanctuary—signifies the travels of Jesus as he went from place to place preaching to the people. The candlebearers, preceding the deacon with the Gospel, represent St. John the Baptist, the precursor, who prepared the way for the coming of the Saviour. The Saviour was the Light of the World. John was a lesser light, announcing to many the one who was to come. The burning candles are signs of his divine wisdom lighting the way for men on their life-journey to eternity. The Baptist faded from the scene when Christ came and began his preaching; likewise, the candlebearers (representing the precursor) retire by remaining outside the iconostas when the priest and deacon make their solemn entrance into the sanctuary.

Psalm 94:6 (modified for liturgical use) expresses adoration for Christ, the Incarnate Word, who came down from heaven to save us.

CHAPTER XXXVIII

THE VARIABLE HYMNS :
TROPARIA AND *KONTAKIA*

The cantors then intone the hymns of the day : troparion, kontakion, *and sometimes the* theotokion. [1]

On ordinary Sundays, one of the eight series of resurrectional troparia, kontakia, etc., is sung, in one of the eight proper modes, or tones. The present text is that of the first series, sung in the first mode or tone :

Troparion : **Though the stone was sealed by the Jews, and soldiers guarded your most pure body, you did rise on the third day, O Saviour, granting life to the world. For this reason the heavenly Powers cried out to you, O Giver of Life : glory to your resurrection, O Christ, glory to your Kingdom. Glory to your providence, O only Lover of mankind.**

Glory be to the Father and to the Son, and to the Holy Spirit, now and always, and for ever and ever. Amen.

Kontakion : **As God, you did rise from the tomb in glory and did restore the world to life with yourself, and the human race sings praises to you as God. And death has vanished. Adam exults, O Master. Eve, now delivered from her bonds, rejoices, crying : " You, O Christ, are the one who gives resurrection to all. "**

Troparia and *kontakia* may be proper to any of the following :

1. *The patron of the church,* the Lord, the Blessed Mother, or one or several saints.

2. *The day of the week,* Every day of the week commemorates a different mystery or saint : Sunday, the Resurrection; Monday, the angels; Tuesday, St. John the Baptist; Wednesday, the Holy Mother

---

[1] The proper Slavonic terms for these hymns are *tropar, kondak,* and *bohorodychen*; however, their Greek names are better known.

of God and the holy cross; Thursday, the Apostles and St. Nicholas; Friday, the holy cross; Saturday, all the saints and the dead.

3. *The saint of the day.* The Byzantine Church dedicates each day of the year to a particular saint or mystery.

4. *The dead*; while the *troparia* and *kontakia* for the dead do not vary with the day of the week, the Epistle and Gospel readings do.

5. *A special intention*; besides the general intention " for every kind of petition, " there are propers for some of the more frequent intentions, e.g., in time of war, for peace, in time of storms, for abundant crops, etc.

Several sets of propers must often be combined. For example, if a major feast falls on a Sunday, the Sunday propers are said with those of the given feast. Precise regulations concerning the order of precedence (and therefore the resultant combinations) for the different classes of feasts, etc., are carefully set down in the *Ustav* or *Typikon* (a book comparable to the *Ordo*). These regulations are far too detailed to be included here. We are giving merely certain general norms which govern the order of the *troparia* and the *kontakia*:

a. The *troparia* come before the *kontakia*. If there is a *theotokion*, it is the last.

b. *Troparia* in honor of our Lord come before those commemorating the Blessed Virgin; those of the Blessed Virgin, before those of the saints, etc.

c. *Kontakia* will generally follow the same order as the *troparia* (*b*) but with many more exceptions.

Most eparchies (dioceses) issue a yearly *ustav (ordo)*, so that the parish priest and cantors will know just what *troparia* and *kontakia* are to be used on any given day, and what is their order of precedence.

The *troparia* and *kontakia* are essentially hymns. The origin and idea of Christian hymnody, especially in the East, point more to Hebrew than to Gentile sources. The inspired hymnal of the Old Testament, known as the Psalter, was taken over by the infant Church both as Sacred Writ and as a hymnal. [2]

---

[2] The Lord used it in prayer, made quotations from it, and explained it to his followers (cf. Matt. 5:4; 7:23; 21:16, 42; 26:30; 27:46; Luke 24:44; etc.). The Apostles followed this example (cf. Acts 1:20; 2:25-28, 30, 34; 4:11, 25; etc.).

The word ψαλμός, " psalm, " used by the Septuagint as a generic
designation and its derivative verb ψάλλειν were accepted by the
first Christians as referring to both hymns and psalms. The Septuagint used the word ᾠδή, " ode, " or " song, " in the same sense, and
so did the first Christians. In the New Testament, for example,
the evangelists (Matt. 26:30; Mark 14:26) write of ὑμνήσαντες,
" singing a hymn, " at the end of the Last Supper (probably referring
to the *Hallel*, composed of psalms). St. Paul and Silas did the same,
ὕμνουν τὸν Θεόν, in their prison at Philippi (Acts 16:25). St. Paul
likewise recommended singing ἐν ψαλμοῖς καὶ ὕμνοις καὶ ᾠδαῖς
πνευματικαῖς, in " psalms and hymns and spiritual songs " in his
letter to the Ephesians (5:19). Here obviously it was the singing not
only of psalms properly speaking, but also of other compositions
of sacred music. In writing to the Corinthians (I Cor. 14:26),
St. Paul also says that each of them has his own psalm (ἕκαστος
ψαλμὸν ἔχει). In the very beginning, Christian hymns tended to
be modeled on familiar Jewish patterns. [3] As the number of Gentile
converts increased, Christianity came into close contact with pagan
culture, and new types of hymns modeled on Hellenistic poetry
began to appear. The practice of singing hymns (or psalms?) in
Bithynian churches at the beginning of the second century is known
from the famous letter of Pliny to Trajan. [4]

Philo's account of new hymns composed by the first-century
Egyptian ascetics is quoted by Eusebius : "...they also compose
songs and hymns to God in every variety of meter and melody,
though they divide them, of course, into measures of more than
common solemnity. [5] Whether these ascetics, the Therapeutae,
were Christians or not is irrelevant. The important thing is that
Eusebius considered Philo's account an allusion to Christian practice, to " the first heralds of the Gospel and the customs handed
down from the beginning by the Apostles. " [6]

---

[3] E.g., the first-century " Odes of Solomon, " discovered in 1909, are a collection
of Syriac hymns reminiscent of their Hebrew prototypes, the Psalter, the Sapiential
Books, and Isaiah. Cf. R. Harris and A. Mingana, *The Odes and Psalms of Solomon*
(1920), II, 59.

[4] Pliny, *Ep. ad Trajanum*, X, 96 (see Kirch, *Enchiridion fontium hist. eccl.* [5th
edit., Freiburg, 1941]).

[5] *Eccl. hist.*, II, 17, 13 (PG 13, 78 C [*Series graeca*]).

[6] *Ibid.*, II, 17, 24 (PG 13, 80 A [*Series graeca*]).

In describing the agape of his day, Tertullian tells us that each man was invited to come forward and sing to God's praise, using either a scriptural text or one of his own composition. [7]   In the third century, Origen states : " For we sing hymns to the Most High alone, and his only-begotten... and we praise his only-begotten Son. " [8] In the first two centuries, the Church favored the free composition of hymns and sacred song as an element of worship consonant with the spirit of the times.   Early in the third century, however, original compositions were discouraged, because of the introduction of heretical ideas and also because of the danger of their taking a preponderant place in corporate spiritual life.   The danger of heresy was especially menacing from the Gnostic camp.   Hymns composed by such authors as Basilides, Valentinus, Bardesanes, and other Gnostics although inconsistent with Christian dogma, became extremely popular, and most effective as a means of propagating heretical beliefs.   In the last half of the fourth century, the Church became definitely hostile to the private composition of sacred song in its Liturgy.   About A.D. 363, for example, the Council of Laodicea forbade the singing of private (ἰδιωτικούς) " psalms " in churches and admitted only " the book of the hundred and fifty psalms. " [9] Apparently, the habit of expressing private religious feeling in hymns died hard, for in 563 the Council of Braga renewed the prohibition. [10] If a hymn were not based on some scriptural passage, it was excluded from liturgical use.

After the third century biblical psalms were used with increasing frequency, as the antiphonal technique came to be developed (see above, p. 367).   Both the Latin and the Byzantine Rites have preserved some instance of antiphonal psalmody : the former, in the recitation of Psalm 94, *Venite exsultemus*, at the Office of Matins on Epiphany; [11] the latter, at the antiphons of the Divine Liturgy, at

[7] Tertullian, *Apol.*, chap. 39 (PL I, 468) : " *ut quisque de Sacris Scripturis vel proprio ingenio potest.* "

[8] Origen, *Contra Celsum*, VIII, 67 (ANF, IV, 665).

[9] Can. 59, Mansi, *Sacrorum conciliorum nova et amplissima collectio*, Vol. II (Florence, 1759), 574 C.

[10] Can. 12, Mansi, *op. cit.*, Vol. IX, 778 C-D.

[11] We may also cite the example of the canticle *Nunc dimittis* alternating with its antiphon *Lumen ad revelationem gentium* on February 2, during the distribution of the candles.

Vespers of Epiphany (Psalms 66 and 92), at Vespers of Christmas
(Psalms 86 and 92), on Holy Saturday during the Liturgy of St. Basil
" combined with Vespers " in " Bless ye all the works of the Lord "
(Benedicite omnia opera Domini Domino), etc. [12]   In the Latin Rite,
the antiphon was reduced to the first and last lines of a psalm.   In the
Byzantine Rite, these refrains gradually expanded into a complete
stanza or *troparion*.   Since, however, the constant repetition of a
long and invariable text would prove monotonous, hymnographers
prepared a series of different textual stanzas, to be sung according
to the melody of the first stanza, the *hirmos*.   These *troparia* were
composed by monks and clergy well versed in theological orthodoxy.
A complete series of such stanzas (now called an *Ode* in the Byzantine
Rite) entwined around the psalm or canticle like an ivy-vine around
a trellis.   Rome adopted this practice in some instances, e.g., in the
recitation of the scriptural Canticles *Benedictus* and *Magnificat*
whenever the ancient rubric *Hodie antiphonamus* appears. [13]   The
Byzantine Office has many examples.

The next step in the evolution was to drop most of the psalm,
and to retain only enough of the original text to correspond with the
troparia or stanzas.   Finally, these few remains of the biblical
canticles disappeared completely and were replaced by new, short
and invariable *stikhoi*.   In this way, the poetical *canon* (see below,
p. 396 f.), now independent of the scriptural canticles, became one
of the predominant features of the Byzantine Office, since it was
introduced into almost every liturgical function, including those in
which the canticles had never been recited.

Some of the evolution can be traced to second-century Syria, at
which time Bardesanes, and his son Harmonius, wrote hymns em-
bodying Gnostic doctrines and set them to agreeable melodies which
became extremely popular.   St. Ephraem, fearing that some of the
faithful might be misled, composed many hymns in the Syriac
language, principally in tetrasyllabic, pentasyllabic, and heptasyllabic

---

[12] Other examples may be found in the Byzantine Office, but they do not
concern the Psalms.

[13] The Antiphonary of St. Corneille of Compiègne also has an example of this
for Holy Saturday in a series of antiphons to the Magnificat drawn from Matt.
28:1-7, which is similar to the *Diatessaron* of Tatian.   Cf. A. Baumstark, *Tatia-
nismen im romischen Antiphonar*, in O.C., Series 3, V (1930), pp. 165-174.

meters, divided into stanzas of four, twelve, sixteen, or twenty lines, thus imitating Bardesanes while teaching orthodox theology. [14] Many of his hymns still exist and may be identified with Byzantine *kontakia*, especially as interpreted by the great melodist of the later fifth century, Romanos the Melode. The ancient Syriac tradition of the *Mâdrâšê* and of the *Sôghîtê* (of which St. Ephraem is the peerless master) is continued in Romanos and his followers.

Characteristic of Syriac hymns is the *ephymnium* : in a five-line stanza, the fifth line generally had a complete meaning—prayer, invocation, doxology, etc. It could be sung either by the full choir or by a separate section of it. Such a " fifth line " was called an *ephymnium*. As subject-matter for these hymns, Ephraem used major Christian truths concerning death, judgment, resurrection, etc., which he exposed in simple and tender language. [15]

About the time of Ephraem, or somewhat later, other hymnographers composed Greek hymns more or less along classical lines— anapaestic, Ionic, iambic, hexametric and pentametric, etc., with the anacreontic as a favorite. This represented an attempt by educated Christians to preserve the Greek civilization in the Church. The better known authors include Methodius, Bishop of Olympus (ex. A.D. 311); Synesius, Bishop of Ptolemais in Cyrenaica (A.D. 420); Gregory Nazianzen, Patriarch of Constantinople (A.D. 380-381). Other hymns of the same kind were written in later centuries. Sophronius, Patriarch of Jerusalem, (seventh century) wrote at least seven anacreontic hymns, and John Damascene—better known for his writings in a different school (the Melodoi)—authored several lengthy compositions in trimeter iambic.

The short prayer-hymns written in poetic verse and inserted after each verse of a psalm were called *troparia*. As early as the fifth century, they were composed in strophic form and became much longer than their prototypes. These then were sung between the last three, four, five, or six verses of a psalm. Even today we have a similar arrangement in the Byzantine Canonical Office at Vespers

[14] Sozomen, *Hist. eccles.*, 3, 6 (PG 25, 1223-1224 [*Series graeca*]).

[15] Theodoret says that the hymns of Ephraem were sweet and profitable, adding much to the brightness of the commemorations of martyrs in the Syrian Church.

and Matins of even the most ordinary Sundays. [16] One of the earliest and most revealing reports on the *troparia* and their position in the Canonical Hours of the Eastern Church dates from the sixth century : the description of a visit by Abbots John and Sophronius to Nilus, Abbot of Mount Sinai. [17] Arriving at the hour of Sunday Vespers, Abbot Nilus began with the Doxology, Psalm 1 (Μακάριος) and Psalm 140 (Κύριε, ἐκέκραξα), but without singing the customary *troparia* (χωρὶς τῶν τροπαρίων); then he went on to the prayer " O gladsome Light " (Φῶς ἱλαρόν) and " Deign, O Lord, to keep us this evening without sin " (Καταξίωσον, Κύριε, ἐν τῇ ἑσπέρα); he concluded the service with Simeon's prayer. After a meal, Matins was recited, part of which consisted in the nine *Odes*, but again without *troparia*. Likewise, for Lauds they recited Psalms 148, 149, and 150 but without *troparia*. If John and Sophronius were not scandalized, they were certainly astonished by these omissions, for they asked Nilus why he did not follow the practice of the " Catholic and Apostolic Church. " Nilus tried to convince them that he did. It is evident, however, that the liturgical Office at Mount Sinai followed, not the general practice of the Eastern Church, but the rule of the fourth-and fifth-century solitaries.

The first authors of *troparia* in the Byzantine Church to be mentioned by name are Anthimus the Poet and Timocles the Monophysite, who had a large following in Constantinople about the middle of the fifth century. [18] None of their compositions has survived. The introduction of the " All-night Vigils " into the Byzantine Liturgy is attributed to Anthimus. [19] The only *troparia* from fifth-century Byzantine hymnography to have come down to us seem to be those of Auxentius, preserved in his *Vita*. [20] They are inspired by Hebrew poetry in both form and style. [21]

[16] At Vespers, cf. K. Nikolsky, *Posobie k izucheniu Ustava Bogosluzhenia pravoslavnoi tserkvy* (St. Petersburg, 1907), pp. 197-205, 218-224; for Matins, *ibid.*, pp. 323 f.

[17] Cf. I. B. Pitra, *Iuris ecclesiastici Graeci historia et monumenta* (Paris, 1868), ii. 220, and Christ-Paranikas, *Anthologia graeca carminum christianorum* (Leipzig, 1871), pp. xxx-xxxii.

[18] Cedrenus, *Compendium historiarum*, I, 612 (C.S.H.B.).

[19] Theodore the Lector, *Excerpta ex eccl. hist.* (PG 86, 173-175).

[20] *Vita S. Auxentii* (PG 114, 1412).

[21] This is pointed out by T. M. Wehofer, " Untersuchungen zum Lied des Romanos auf die Wiederkunft des Herrn, " *Sitzungsber. d. Ak. d. Wiss. in Wien,*

What is more pertinent to our study is the use to which these *troparia* were put by Auxentius. From his *Vita*, we learn that he would teach pilgrims *troparia* composed of two or three phrases. All would chant them together, sometimes for hours. Then they would sing the " Song of the Three Holy Children, " Auxentius singing the first hemistich of each *troparion* and the people responding with the second, and so forth. The *Vita* also tells us that these *troparia* consisted in a short prayer, that they were interspersed in his sermons, and that he taught the people to sing them in their proper order (κατὰ τάξιν).

By far the most famous schools of Greek hymnology, however, were that of the original *Melodoi*—Anastasius, Kyriakos, and most of all, Romanos—extending from the sixth to the seventh centuries, and that of the later *Melodoi*, beginning with the eighth-century iconoclastic controversies and extending over later centuries. Some elements of earlier date were incorporated into the compositions of these two schools.

The original school of Romanos—of which Anatolius, Patriarch of Constantinople was a fifth-century precursor—produced dramatic and animated hymns; those of the later school consisted mainly in the graver, more solemn chant still found in Byzantine service books. [22]

The foremost contribution of the first school of *Melodoi* to Byzantine hymnography was the developement of a new poetical form of hymn, the *kontakion*, [23] consisting in eighteen, thirty, or even more structurally similar stanzas, generally less dependent upon scriptures than earlier Byzantine hymns. Each stanza, also called a *troparion*,

---

Phil.-Hist. Kl., cliv, Part 5 (1907), pp. 11-15. In publishing the hymn, Wehofer accordingly has the form showing the correspondence of stanzas 2, 6, and 7 as antistrophes to 1, 4, and 5. The third stanza has two verses which are of equal length but are not antistrophic.

[22] Most of the hymns of the Romanos school, contained in the various *Tropologia*, went out of use before the tenth century. A few of these, or parts of them, are still extant in MS. form in the libraries of Moscow, Rome, and Turin.

[23] Not to be confused with the *kontakion* of later hymnography, a liturgical term still in use to designate the *troparion* at the end of the sixth Ode in a Canon and constructed according to a *hirmos* differing from that of the Ode itself (see below, p. 397).

varied from three to thirteen lines. [24] Since the rise of the *kontakion* is linked to the name of Romanos, we may assume that it was used in the Byzantine Liturgy some time during the first decades of the sixth century, [25] although the name *kontakion* first occurs only in ninth century writings. [26]

Scholars such as C. Emereau, Baumstark, and P. Maas, as well as H. Grimme and W. Meyer before them, have ably defended the hypothesis of the *kontakion*'s Syrian origin, that is, that its essential features derive from the main forms of fourth- and fifth-century Syriac poetry, viz., *Memrâ, Mâdrâšê* and *Sôghîtê*. [27] Byzantine tradition and hagiographers, however, consider Romanos as the inventor of the *kontakion*; in fact, no *kontakia* earlier than his time have ever been discovered in Byzantine liturgical manuscripts. Some elements of the *kontakion* may have originated in Syriac liturgical poetry, but Romanos adapted them to the spirit of Byzantine hymnody and introduced them into the Constantinopolitan Liturgy. This is all the more probable since he was of Syrian origin. [28]

[24] Such *troparia* were composed according to strict rules and were built on the pattern of a model stanza, the *hirmos,* either specially composed for it or a *hirmos* already used for another *kontakion.* Other terms commonly used and associated with the *kontakion* are the *prooemium,* which is a short *troparion* metrically and melodically independent of the *kontakion;* the *ephymnium,* which is a refrain linking the *prooemium* and *kontakion.* All the stanzas end with this refrain and with the musical mode, or *ikhos.* Usually the choir or people would sing the refrain and a soloist would sing the *kontakia.*

[25] The *Vita* of Romanos, contained in the *Menologion* of Emperor Basil II (*Cod. Vat.,* 1613), states that he lived during the time of Emperor Anastasius. There were two emperors of that name, Anastasius I (491-518) and Anastasius II (713-716); it has now been established that Romanos lived during the days of Anastasius I. Papadopoulos-Kerameus proved this in 1905 from a MS. containing the life of St. Artemius, which mentioned that the hymns of Romanos were sung during the time of Heraclius, i.e., A.D. 610-641. P. Maas also came to the same conclusion from a study of references within the hymns themselves to events of the sixth century (cf. P. Maas, " Die Chronologie der Hymnen des Romanus, " in B.Z., 1906, pp. 1-44).

[26] Cf. E. Mioni, *Romano il Melode* (Turin, 1937), p. 10.

[27] Cf. C. Émereau, *Saint Éphrem le Syrien* (Paris, 1919), pp. 97 ff.; A. Baumstark, " Festbrevier u. Kirchenjahr der syrischen Jakobiten, " *Studien z. Geschichte u. Kultur des Altertums,* iii (1910); P. Maas, " Das Kontakion, " B.Z. (1910), pp. 290 ff.; H. Grimme, " Der Strophhenbau in den Gedichten Ephraems des Syrers, " *Collect. Friburg.,* ii (Fribourg, 1893); W. Meyer, " Anfang u. Ursprung der lat. u. griech. rythm. Dichtung, " *Abhandlungen der bayrischen Akademie der Wissenschaften, philos.-philol. Classe,* XVII, 2 (1884), pp. 267-450.

[28] Romanos was a Jew, born at Emesa on the Orontes, who became a deacon at Berytus in northern Phoenicia before he went to Constantinople.

The last half of the seventh century marks the beginning of the third period of Byzantine hymnography, the later school of the *Melodoi*. Ushered in by such giants of hymn-writing as Andrew of Crete, [29] John Damascene, and his foster-brother Cosmas of Jerusalem, [30] the period did much to establish the system of hymnody used today in the Byzantine Church. Some of the better-known hymnographers of this period are : Joseph of Thessalonica and his brother, the famous Hegumen Theodore; Theophanes (759-c. 842) and Theodorus (called the " Branded Ones "); St. Methodius, Patriarch of Constantinople († 846); Joseph of the Studium († 883); Metrophanes († c. 910); the emperors Leo VI (886-912) and Constantine Porphyrogenetus (913-959); the nun Kasia (or Icasia, mentioned by Gibbon), who probably also wrote the music for the compositions of Byzantius, Georgius, and Cyprianus; and last but not least, John Mauropus, Metropolitan of Euchaita. Also, many important compositions were written by unknown, unheralded monks at the great monasteries of the Studium in Constantinople and St. Sabbas in Palestine.

The chief contribution of this later school of the *Melodoi* is the *Canon* and its introduction into the *Orthros* or Morning Office. [31] Basically, the Canon consists of nine Odes or songs, [32] each of which

---

[29] Born at Damascus, c. A.D. 600, Andrew of Crete is credited with the invention of the *Canon*, the new, complex poetical form for which the period is known. His most famous work is the peintential masterpiece, the " Great Canon " of mid-Lent week. He died as the Bishop of Crete, c. A.D. 740.

[30] The compositions of John Damascene and Cosmas of Jerusalem are considered matchless (cf. G. Papadopoulos, Συμβολαὶ εἰς τὴν ἱστορίαν τῆς παρ'ἡμῖν ἐκκλησιαστικῆς μουσικῆς [Athens, 1890], pp. 154-162). Damacene's *Canon* for Easter Day, called the " Queen of Canons, " is the most famous.

[31] The importance of hymnody, especially that of the *Canons*, in the various services of the Byzantine Church is incalculable. The wealth of material available in Byzantine liturgical books alone is breathtaking. Hymnody, according to Neale, who made a partial study of it, includes about four-fifths of all the material (about 5,000 pages) in the liturgical books of the Byzantine Church. The history of the individual *Canons* and Odes (hymns) must be dealt with separately—a vast field of research for an inquiring scholar.

[32] The second Ode in the *Canon* is suppressed. Originally, the second Ode was modeled on the canticle " Hear, O ye heavens " (Deut. 32:1-43), but, because of its mournful character, it was used only in Lent. As a result, later *Canons* (destined for the ecclesiastical year outside of Lent) were composed without the second One.

is made up of several similar troparia or stanzas. [33] The first troparion of each Ode, called the *hirmos*, sets the style and regulates the following troparia or stanzas in regard to syllabic measure, the periodic series of accents, the rhythms, etc.; thus, each suceeding troparion of the same Ode contains not only the same number of verses but also the same number of syllables in each verse with the accents on either the same or equivalent syllables. Depending on their position in the Ode, and the position of the Ode in the Canon, other troparia are called by different names—*kontakion, ikhos, katabasia*, etc. [34] Regardless of their name, they are all troparia.

Some of these troparia were taken from the Divine Office and incorporated as variables into the Divine Liturgy. The original position of the troparia and kontakia, therefore, was not in the Divine Liturgy but in the Divine Office, especially in the highly complex system, the Canon. This is important for ascertaining the dates of the various compositions. If we read in some authors that the troparia, kontakia, etc., are a later addition to the Divine Liturgy, and in others, that these same troparia and kontakia were written by authors dating back to the fifth and sixth centuries, we may begin to doubt the veracity of such sources unless we remember that these hymns, when originally written, were intended for use in the canonical hours and only later were incorporated into the Divine Liturgy. What is more, if the composition of a given troparion or kontakion

---

[33] Originally, each Ode consisted of six to nine stanzas *(troparia)* but after the introduction of a number of additional monostrophic stanzas, only three to each Ode were generally used in the service. All nine Odes were modeled on the pattern of the Nine Scriptural Canticles.

[34] I.e., the (1) *kontakion* is merely a troparion found at the end of the sixth Ode (but is built upon a *hirmos* differing from that of the Ode);

(2) *ikhos* is the stanza following a *kontakion* at the end of the sixth Ode (structurally, it is almost the same as the *kontakion* except for its greater length);

(3) the *katabasia* is merely the term used for the *hirmos* that is repeated at the end of the Ode (it gets its name from the fact that two groups of singers descend [καταβαίνουσι] from their seats and sing it together in the center of the choir);

(4) *kathisma* is a troparion sung while the congregation remains seated;

(5) *theotokion* is the name given to a troparion in honor of the Mother of God (and follows each Ode of a Canon); this same name is used for the whole ninth Ode of the Canon (because the whole Ode is dedicated to the Blessed Mother);

(6) *staurotheotokion* is a troparion in honor of the Blessed Mother at the cross;

(7) *hypakoe* is a troparion sung after the third Ode of the Canon (originally the term was used only for the troparion after Psalm 118 of the Morning Office).

has been traditionally attributed to the pen of, say, John Damascene or even Gregory Nazianzen, such an affirmation is probably true, although proof has been obscured or even completely lost.   The *troparia* and *kontakia* were introduced into the Divine Liturgy probably to instruct the faithful and to urge them to imitate the virtues of Christ, his Mother, or the saint whose excellence is described.

These Byzantine hymns, especially those of the later *Melodoi* school, did as much in molding the dogmatic theology of the Byzantine Church as they did in " fixing " its system of hymnody.   With their polished language, economy of words, poetic and literary form, some of them are not only literary gems but excellent expressions of religious feeling.   The later *Melodoi* were no mere poets dreaming of impossibly beautiful seas : they were, pre-eminently, theologians expressing dogmatic truth in poetic form.   In the *Canons*, the mood is often exultant and eschatological, but the dogmatic content is superbly expressed.   The technique of repeating the same ideas in varied ways tends to produce in the listeners a religious mood intensified by both the solemn ritual and the visual richness of the many icons found in every Byzantine church.

These liturgical chants came to the Slavs from Byzantium.   They were brought by the Greek monks who Christianized them.   Though the system itself and the traditional Greek patterns were preserved, [35] the Slavs soon began to adapt the music of the Greek Church to their own requirements or composed their own tunes.   Church music and hymnody became a prominent feature of Ukrainian and Russian life.   Until the revolution of 1917, singing was the medium through which the Ukrainian and Russian peoples learned the catechism, Holy Scripture, and mystical theology.   Many of these traditional chants, whose words were translated from Greek into Slavonic (the old vernacular of the Slavs), acquired in the translation a dramatic, colorful freshness that is strikingly beautiful.

---

[35] In the Slav Church, the system is the same as far as the general structure of the Canon is concerned; whether the Slav translators managed to fulfill all the original rules governing the structure of the Ode (syllabic measure, periodic series of accents, rhythm of its component troparia, etc.) is another question.

CHAPTER XXXIX

THE TRISAGION

*W*hile *the cantors are singing the* troparia *and* kontakia *proper to the day, the priest stands before the center of the holy table and recites the* Prayer of the Trisagion *in a low voice :*

O Holy God who rest among the saints, whose praises are sung by the seraphim with the Trisagion Hymn and are glorified by the cherubim and adored by all the Powers of heaven : you brought all things into being out of nothingness and created man according to your image and likeness and adorned him with your every gift; you give to him that asks wisdom and understanding; you do not despise the sinner but offer him repentance for his salvation; you allowed us, your lowly and unworthy servants, to stand even at this moment before the glory of your holy altar and to offer the worship and honor due to you : accept, O selfsame Lord, even from the mouths of us sinners the hymn of the Trisagion, and in your goodness look down upon us. Forgive us every offense, whether voluntary or involuntary; sanctify our souls and bodies, and grant that we may serve you in holiness all the days of our life, through the prayers of the holy Mother of God and all the saints who have pleased you throughout the ages.

When the cantors begin chanting the final troparion, *the deacon inclines his head toward the priest and, holding the* orar *with three fingers, says to the priest :*

Bless, master, the time of the thrice-holy hymn.

As he blesses the deacon, the priest sings the doxology of the Trisagion Prayer :

For you are holy, our God, and to you we give glory, to the Father, and to the Son, and to the Holy Spirit, now and always.

The deacon goes near the royal doors, turns toward the congregation and, raising the orar *with three fingers of his right hand, concludes the above doxology by singing its final words :*

And for ever and ever.

People : **Amen.**

And immediately after, the people also sing the Trisagion :

Holy God, Holy Mighty One, Holy Immortal One, have mercy on us.

Holy God, Holy Mighty One, Holy Immortal One, have mercy on us.

Holy God, Holy Mighty One, Holy Immortal One, have mercy on us.

Glory be to the Father, and to the Son, and to the Holy Spirit, now and always and for ever and ever. Amen.

Holy Immortal One, have mercy on us.

Holy God, Holy Mighty One, Holy Immortal One, have mercy on us. [1]

An Eastern prayer always expresses the profound humility of the sinner, but also hopeful trust in God's mercy. In his deep contemplation, the Eastern Christian realizes his own utter sinfulness and misery, but he is even more vividly aware that God's justice is tempered with mercy, that in God's feelings for us sinners there is pity, tenderness, and love.

A Russian or Ukrainian peasant at prayer will fall on his knees,

---

[1] The Greek forms ("Αγιος ὁ θεὸς, ἅγιος ἰσχυρὸς, ἅγιος ἀθάνατος) are in the nominative case (hence, the translation would read : " Holy is God, Holy the Mighty One, Holy the Immortal One ") but Greek grammatical usage has the nominative sometimes used in exclamations, and even in other expressions, where the vocative is more common (cf. W. Goodwin, *A Greek Grammar* [Boston, 1892], p. 223). The Slavonic translators, who were very much at home with the Greek, accordingly used the vocative case (i.e., *Sviatej Bozhe,* not *Boh,* etc.). Our translation follows the Slavonic.

On Christmas, Epiphany, the Vigil of Palm Sunday, Holy Saturday, Easter Sunday, and all the days of the Easter Octave and Pentecost, the Trisagion is replaced by : " For as many of you as have been baptized in Christ have put on Christ " (Gal. 3:27). Alleluia. " This is repeated in the very same way in which the Trisagion is sung.

The Trisagion is also replaced on the Feast of the Exaltation of the Cross and on the third Sunday of Lent by : " Before your cross we bow in worship, O Master, and we glorify your holy resurrection. " This is repeated in the same way.

press his forehead against the ground, and remain there, his brow in the dust, with a kind of life-giving humility, his face streaked with tears of sorrow. [2]

Many kernels of dogmatic truth are embedded in the *Trisagion Prayer*, but two doctrines are emphasized : universal creation and the creation of man in God's image and likeness.

To create, according to the Scholastic concept, is to produce a thing which in no way previously existed, either in itself or in the potentiality of a subject *(ex nihilo sui et subjecti)*. Aside from the technical language, the Scholastics could not improve on the definition of creation contained in this prayer : " O Holy God... You brought all things into being out of nothingness. " The phrase " all things " includes everything finite, both visible and invisible; the creative act is exclusively attributed to God, " who brought all things into being "; it excludes the use of any pre-existing matter, whereby true creation is denoted, not mere formation : " out of nothingness. " The Fathers, of course, from the very first centuries, have developed and defended the doctrine of universal creation, including primitive matter itself, against such adversaries as the Neoplatonists, the Gnostics, the Manicheans, etc. The concept of creation contained in the foregoing prayer is equally opposed to any theory of self-existent primitive matter from which all things either are made or are evolved (evolutionism, materialism, naturalism, etc.).

" O Holy God... you... created man according to your image and likeness and adorned him with your every gift. " Creating man to his own image and likeness means that God endowed man with prerogatives which give man a resemblance, however imperfect, to God. This resemblance to God, in man, includes many things supernatural and natural : the natural endowments of the soul, i.e., its spirituality, freedom, and immortality; the absolutely supernatural endowment of sanctifying grace (*re.* first parents), including the

---

[2] Tears of repentance and of prayer were a much-appreciated charismata since the end of the fourth century, especially in Egypt and Syria. Byzantium and the Kievan Slavs inherited this idea from Syria and generalized it to the point where it was considered an element necessary to any sincere prayer. Pseudo-Gennadius even gives practical suggestions for acquiring this grace of tears : " If you have no tears, do not despair; sigh frequently and heavily from all the heart : for tears are the gift of God, and by and by, with sighs and prayers, you will obtain them from God... " (50). " Having found tears, preserve them with all your strength " (51).

virtues of faith, hope, charity, justice, kindness, etc., infused into
the soul with sanctifying grace; also, the relatively supernatural or
preternatural gifts, such as infused, extraordinary knowledge,
exemption from concupiscence and from suffering, and even immortality of the body.   Though not enumerated, these endowments
and gifts are implicit in the prayer, for they are what makes man
most like God.

The text of the *Trisagion Prayer* can be traced back to the beginning of the eighth century in the Armenian version of Chrysostom's Liturgy; [3] hence, its origin probably goes back at least to the
seventh century.

The liturgical Trisagion (τρίς = thrice, ἅγιος = holy), to be
distinguished from the biblical Trisagion (the *sanctus* hymn) in the
anaphora, is found in all the Offices of the Byzantine Church.   In
the other Oriental Rites, it is used frequently.   In the Latin Rite,
it is confined to the *preces* of *Prime* and the *Adoratio crucis* on Good
Friday. [4]   The liturgical Trisagion was already common to the whole
East, including the Monophysite and Nestorian Churches, before
the end of the fifth century, but almost nothing is known about its
origin.   The earliest evidence of its use is found in a series of acclamations at the Council of Chalcedon (A.D. 451). [5]

Byzantine historians generally accept the tradition that the Trisagion was divinely inspired.   The most common interpretation is
that during a severe earthquake at Constantinople, while the patriarch, St. Proclus (A.D. 434-446), was leading the people in prayer,
a boy was " lifted up into the air " and heard the angels singing the
Trisagion.   This account is based chiefly on two sources : the *Letter
to Peter the Fuller* (Monophysite Patriarch of Antioch), ascribed to

[3] Cf. G. Aucher, *La versione armena della liturgia di S. Giovanni Crisostomo*,
XPYCOCTOMIKA, pp. 378-379.   In the eighth or ninth century *Codex Barberini*,
gr. 336, however, this identical prayer appears in the Liturgy of St. Basil, while
another, a different prayer, appears in the Liturgy of Chrysostom. Cf. Brightman,
LEW, pp. 313-314.

[4] Since the famous amplification " Who was crucified for us " had not been
added to the Trisagion in the Passion ceremonies of the Latin Church, it seems
that the Trisagion was incorporated into these ceremonies at Rome prior to any
of the lengthy controversies regarding the legitimacy of this amplification.   Cf.
A. Baumstark's article, " Der Orient und die Gesange der Adoratio Crucis, " in
Jb. Lw., II (1922), 1-17.

[5] Cf. I. D. Mansi, *Sacrorum conciliorum nova et amplissima collectio*, 6, 936 C.

Acacius, Archbishop of Constantinople (A.D. 471-489); [6] and the testimony of St. John Damascene (A.D. 749), based on different historical sources, in his *De fide orthodoxa*. [7]

The main trouble with this account is that there is no record of any earthquake at Constantinople between A.D. 434 and 446, under the patriarchate of Proclus. [8]

The account of the Trisagion's origin offered by Iesuiabus I, Katholikos of the Chaldeans (A.D. 581-596) is substantially the same as the Byzantine version although it differs in several details. [9] An angel is said to have appeared to a certain pious priest of Constantinople, while the city was being racked with great earthquakes because of its wickedness. The angel told the priest to go into the church to praise God with these words : " Holy God, Holy Mighty One, Holy Immortal One, have mercy on us. " The earthquakes ceased (temporarily at least), but no one believed the priest's vision. On the third night, angels appeared to him again, told him not to be afraid of entering the ravaged city, and instructed him to do whatever they did. With a few brave souls, he went back into the same church, where they saw the angels standing before the altar, praising God and saying, " Holy God, Holy Mighty One, Holy Immortal One, have mercy on us. " They all began singing the hymn, and when they had sung it three times, the earthquakes ceased completely. The great city was spared further destruction.

The *Liber Heraclidis* (A.D. 451-539) gives yet another and com-

---

[6] *Ep. ad Petrum Fullonem* (Mansi, *op. cit.*, 7, 1121 D).

[7] St. John Damascene, *De fide orthodoxa*, 1, III, chap. 10 (PG 94, 1021 AB). Substantially the same account about the origin of this hymn is given in the spurious letters of Pope Felix III (A.D. 483-492), *Ad Petrum Fullonem*, supposedly written at the Synod of Rome, A.D. 485, and *Ad Zenonem* (Mansi, *op. cit.*, 7, 1037-1054).

[8] Of the three earthquakes during the reign of Emperor Honorius II, the first occurred in A.D. 422, according to the *Chronicon Paschale* (PG 92, 797 A) and Philostorgius (fifth century), *Hist. eccl.*, XII, 8-9 (PG 65, 617 A-C). The second, in A.D. 447, is recorded by Marcellinus Comes, *Chronicon* (PL 51, 927), and in *Chronicon Paschale* (PG 92, 805-808 [cf. also Evagrius, *Hist. eccl.*, I, 17; PG 86, 2467-2470]). According to the *Chronicon Paschale* (PG 92, 809 C-812 A), the third happened in A.D. 450.

[9] Iesuiabus I, *Commentarius de trisagio* (edit. G. Furlani, " Il trattato di Yeso'yabh d'Arzon sul Trisagion, " *Revista degli studi orientali*, VII [1916-1918], pp. 691-693).

pletely different version. [10] The only common point is its attribution to divine revelation (at least indirectly) and its date, some time before A.D. 448-449. According to this narrative, the hymn originated as a refutation of the Monophysite doctrine : that in Christ there is only one nature, the divine, and therefore that God himself suffered and died in the Passion of Christ. The Monophysites directly opposed any formula of praise in which God was extolled as " mighty " (ἰσχυρὸς = incapable of suffering?) and " immortal " (ἀθάνατος) even in Christ's Passion and death. [11]

The original meaning of the Trisagion definitely insists on God's " immortality, " an attribute not found in Sacred Scripture, nor in any of the ancient formulae of prayer. The fact that the Council of Chalcedon used the very same words confirms the idea of a refutation of Monophysitism. It seems, then, that the Trisagion was originally a purely Christological hymn, which explains its use in the Latin Church to honor Christ's Passion and death. In later controversies, the Byzantines addressed it to the Blessed Trinity, in order to avert any suspicion of heresy. [12]

Whatever its origin and the reasons for its use, the Trisagion appears to have been incorporated into the Byzantine Liturgy at

[10] Cf. F. Nau, *Nestorius, Le livre d'Héraclide de Damas*, pp. 318-323.

[11] There is nothing contradictory to the above account in the explanation of the Trisagion's origin and meaning by a certain Jewish convert to Christianity, given in Iobius Monachus, *De Verbo incarnato commentarius*, I, VI, chap. 25 (contained in Nestorius, *Bibliotheca cod.* 222 [PG 103, 772]); a similar explanation, but without reference to supernatural revelation, is given of the hymn by the great Byzantine liturgist of the fourteenth century, Nicolas Cabasilas, *Liturgiae expositio*, chap. 20 (PG 150, 412-414).

[12] The Byzantine Church has managed to preserve the Trisagion in its original form without the interpolation " Immortal One, *Who was crucified for us* " by the Monophysite Patriarch of Antioch, Peter the Fuller (A.D. 468-470), who thus succeeded in making it a proclamation of Monophysite doctrine. The Syrian and Coptic Monophysites adopted the interpolation in their Liturgy. The Emperor Anastasius I (A.D. 491-518) tried to incorporate it into the hymn at Constantinople, and seditions resulted. See Marcellinus Comes (fl. c. A.D. 550), *Chronicum* for the year 512 (PL 51, 937 C-938 B); also Evagrius Scholasticus (sixth century), *Hist. eccl.*, I, III, chap. 44 (PG 86, 2697 B). The Trisagion with the said insertion, if addressed to the Blessed Trinity, would mean that not only God the Son but also the Father (heresy of Patripassianism) and the Holy Spirit suffered death on the cross; or it would deny the distinction between the three Persons in the Trinity (heresy of Sabellianism). If, however, the hymn with the insertion were directed only to the Incarnate Word, it would be dogmatically acceptable. Cf. M. Jugie, *Monophysisme*, IV, *Le theopaschitisme*, DTC, X, 2237-2241.

Constantinople some time between A.D. 430 and 450. This we have
on the contemporary testimony of a predecessor of Patriarch Proclus, the banished and heretical Nestorius. [13] Its use in the Byzantine
Eucharistic Liturgy was without doubt already an established custom
during the time of Marcellinus Comes (fl. A.D. 550). [14] Its position
in the Liturgy was certainly fixed by the eighth century. [15]

[13] Cf. Nestorius, *Bazaar of Heraclides* (edit. Bedjan, p. 499).

[14] Cf. Marcellinus Comes, *Chronicum* for year 512 (PL 51, 937 C-938 B).

[15] This we know from St. Germanus of Constantinople (715-729), *Liturgical
Commentary*, n. 25 (edit. N. Borgia, *Il commentario di s. Germano Patriarca Constan-
tinopolitano e la versione latina di Anastasio Bibliotecario* [Grottaferrata, 1912], p. 22).
It is confirmed by the *Cod. Barberini* (*gr.* 336); cf. Brigthman, LEW, app. 313-314.

CHAPTER XL

THE BLESSING AND *PROKEIMENON*

While the Trisagion is being sung by the cantors and the people, it is recited by the priest and deacon. As they say it, both make three small bows together before the altar. Then the deacon says to the priest :

Command, sir.

While both proceed to the apsidal throne, the priest says :
Blessed is he that comes in the name of the Lord (John 12:13).

Deacon : **Bless, sir, the seat on high.**

Priest : **Blessed are you on the throne of glory in your Kingdom, sitting among the cherubim, at all times, now and always and for ever and ever.**

The priest blesses the throne and sits on the seat to the south of it.
When the singing of the Trisagion hymn is finished, the deacon comes to the royal doors, lifts his orar *with three fingers of his right hand and says :*
Let us be attentive!

From his place behind the altar, the priest blesses the people, saying aloud :
Peace be to all.

Deacon : **Wisdom! Let us be attentive.** [1]

The deacon returns to the priest behind the altar. The cantors then intone the Prokeimenon *which, like the* troparia, *is proper to the day and is sung according to one of the eight tones. The resurrectional* Prokeimenon *(for Sundays) of the first tone is :*

Let your mercy, O Lord, be upon us, according as we have hoped in you (Ps. 32:22).

---

[1] In the Russian recension, the people answer " And to your spirit " before the deacon proclaims " Wisdom. " The deacon does not say " Let us be attentive " after " Wisdom. "

Verse : **Rejoice in the Lord, you just; praise befits the righteous.**

In every Byzantine church, there is an apsidal throne, an ornamented, seat behind the altar, facing the people. The seats for the celebrants other than the bishop are on its right and left. Such an arrangement dates back to the days when the bishop was the ordinary celebrant of the Eucharist, to pre-Nicene times when the Liturgy was still celebrated in private homes. The *Didascalia* states that the presbyters' seats are found " in that part of the house which is turned to the East, with the bishop's throne in the midst of them. [2] There is reason to believe that this accommodation already existed in the second century. St. Ignatius speaks of the bishop as " enthroned as the type of God, and the presbyters as that of the college of Apostles, and the deacons entrusted with the deaconship of Jesus Christ. " [3] This is what the throne still symbolizes today : the throne of the King of Glory, whom the bishop represents. The formula used by the celebrant in blessing the throne even alludes to this symbolism, " Blessed are you on the throne of glory in your Kingdom.... " Perhaps the first Byzantine Codex, that has a formula of blessing the throne is the eighth-century *Codex Barberini.* [4] The great respect commanded by this " throne of the King of Glory " is evident from the ancient Byzantine custom, still preserved, which dictates that no one but the bishop may ever sit on it. The priest-celebrant, even if he celebrates alone, always sits on the seat beside

---

[2] Later fourth-century evidence abounds, e.g., Canon 56 of the Council of Laodicea (c. A.D. 363), NPNF, Series II, Vol. XIV, p. 157; *Testamentum Domini*, i, 19 (Rahmani, *Testamentum Domini Nostri Jesu Christi* [Mainz, 1899], 23; Quasten, *Monumenta eucharistica et liturgia vetustissima* [Bonn, 1935-1937], 237); Basil, *Ep.*, 183 (PG 18, 1252 A [*Series graeca*]); etc. The ancient Church of St. Clement in Rome has the bishop's throne behind the altar.

[3] Ignatius, *Ep. ad Magnesios*, 6, 1 (PG 3, 659 AB [*Series graeca*]).

[4] *Cod. Barberini, gr.* 336, Brightman, LEW, p. 314, lines 16-20. The prayer could not have been adopted universally, however; as late as the fourteenth and fifteenth centuries, practice differed. In the fourteenth century, for example, MS. 522, p. 19, and MS. 523, p. 20, of the Sophia Library contain a different form of the throne prayer. The fifteenth century MS. 527, p. 25, of the same Library contains no prayer for blessing the throne, while other fifteenth century *Liturgika* revert to the older form of the prayer, e.g., MS. 540, p. 33, and MS. 553, p. 26, both of the Sophia Library. Absolutely identical with today's throne prayer is that contained in the fifteenth century *Liturgikon* of Isidore, Metropolitan of Kiev; cf. *Cod. Vat. Slav.*, No. 14, rubrics of its *Ustav*, fol. 128.

it, " as Christ does beside his Father, as the Apostles did beside Christ. "

The greeting " Peace be to all, " now given in the form of a blessing by the celebrant, also reaches back into early Christian days. [5] This is merely a slight revision of the original " Peace be to you, " and really means the same. This greeting marks the beginning of the Liturgy of the Catechumens, consisting originally in the opening greeting, the lections, the intermediate psalms, the Gospel, and the dismissals (see above, p. 60). In the Latin Mass, this greeting occurs just before the collect in the form of the *Dominus vobiscum*, " The Lord be with you, " and its response, " And with your spirit. " [6] In the Russian recension of the Byzantine Liturgy, the lector answers also, " And with your spirit. "

Both forms of greeting, " The Lord be with you (all) " and " Peace be to you (*or* to all), " are ancient. From time immemorial, the Jewish people greeted one another with " Shalom " (Peace be to you), and for thousands of years, the customary Oriental greeting has been " Salaam, " meaning the same. [7] In Christian times, this greeting took on a special, beautiful significance, for it was the first greeting of the Risen Christ to his own (John 20:19). In fact, it seems to have been Christ's favorite greeting after the resurrection (cf. Luke 24:36; John 20:27; etc.). During his public life, when sending his disciples to the cities and towns of Israel, Jesus instructed them : " Into whatsoever house you enter, first say, ' Peace be to this house ' " (Luke 10:5; Matt. 10:12). The recurrent greeting of St. Paul in writing to his converts was always, " Grace to you and peace " (Rom. 1:7; I Cor. 1:3; II Cor. 1:2; Gal. 1:3; Eph. 1:2; Phil. 1:2; Col. 1:3; I Thess. 1:2) or, " Grace, mercy and peace " (I Tim. 1:2; II Tim. 1:2) or merely " Grace and peace " (Tit. 1:4; Philem. 1:3).

---

[5] The Greek-Byzantine Liturgy omits it. Cf. Brightman, LEW, p. 370, lines 35 ff.

[6] This form of greeting, slightly revised to read " The Lord be with you all, " is also found in the Egyptian Church in the Liturgy of St. Mark (cf. Brightman, LEW, p. 125, etc.) and in *Const. eccl. aegypt.* (cf. Funk, *Didascalia et Constitutiones Apostolorum* [Paderborn, 1905], Vol. II, 99, 102).

[7] Even today in Syria, for example, " Peace be to you " is the everyday salutation; its answer is, " The Lord be with your spirit " or " Blessed is he that comes. "

Hundreds of years before the Incarnation, Isaiah (736-700 B.C.) acclaimed Christ as ' the Prince of Peace ' (Isa. 9:6); at his birth, the angels sang of peace; and peace is *the* great message of his Gospel (Rom. 10:15). It was peace together with his Eucharist that Jesus gave to his chosen ones as his last gift : " Peace is my bequest to you, and the peace which I give you is mine to give; I do not give peace as the world gives it " (John 14:27). The early Christians valued, cherished, and used this greeting, " Peace be to you, " which they always interpreted in the christological sense. In this same sense, they greeted one another, and they engraved the same words on the walls of the catacombs.

While the formula, " The Lord be with you, " was originally favored, all the Eastern Churches except Egypt had come to use " Peace be to you " by the fourth century. For the early rite of Constantinople, there is the testimony of Chrysostom : " When he who presides over the *ecclesia* enters the church, he immediately says, ' Peace be to all. ' " [8] For the Pontic Church there are Gregory Nazianzen, [9] and the Liturgy of St. James (Greek). [10] St. Maximus (A.D. 662) indirectly confirms this when he says that the salutation of peace was made before each reading. [11] Originally, the salutation was made when the celebrant entered the church, immediately before the lessons. Later, it became separated from the entrance by the Trisagion hymn and its prayer. Its position in the present Byzantine-Slav Liturgy differs from the original only in that the Trisagion hymn and prayer intervene. The modern Greek Liturgy no longer has a blessing at this point, although formerly it had one [12]. In this

[8] At Constantinople c. A.D. 407; cf. Chrysostom, *In ep. ad Colossenses homil.*, III, 4 (PG 62, 322-323; edit. Montfaucon 11, 347 E); at Antioch, *Homil. adv. Iud.*, III, 6 (PG 48, 870; edit. Montfacon 1, 614 C).

[9] Gregory Nazianzen, *Oratio XXII*, 1 (PG 35, 1131 A), but this passage could also refer to the salutation immediately before the Gospel reading.

[10] *Cod. Vat., gr.* 2282 (edit. A. Rocchi, in A. Mai, PNB, X, ii, p. 42); cf. also Brightman, LEW, p. 32.

[11] Maximus, *Mystagogia*, chap. 12 (PG 91, 689 D); *Quaestiones et dubia*, 68 (PG 90, 841 D-849 A).

[12] E.g., the eighth century Byzantine-Armenian Liturgy of St. Basil (Catergian-Dasian, *Lie Liturgien bei den Armeniern* [Vienna, 1897], pp. 189, 197, 212); the eighth or ninth century Liturgy of Chrysostom contained in *Cod. Barberini, gr.* 336 (Brightman, LEW, pp. 314, 320); the tenth or eleventh century Liturgy of St. Basil in the *Codex* of Isidore Pyromal (Goar, *Euchologion*, pp. 181-182); the eleventh

instance, the ancient practice is better preserved by the daughter
Slav Rite than by its Greek-Byzantine mother. Both Rites, however,
have the same greeting before the reading of the Gospel.

In the Western Church, the formula *Pax vobis(cum)* was widely
used in the beginning, but later came to be reserved to the bishop,
the direct representative of Christ. [13] For the last nine hundred
years, the lower clergy in the Latin Church were restricted to the
Dominus vobiscum, " The Lord be with you. " This, too, has its
origin in pre-Christian times. In the book of Ruth (2:4), we read
of Boaz greeting his reapers with, " The Lord be with you. " It
must have been a frequent, if not daily, salutation among the Jews,
for it is found several times in Sacred Writ, e.g., Judg. 6:12; Tobias
7:15; II Chron. 15:2; Luke 1:28; II Thess. 3:16; etc. From the
Talmud, we know that this same greeting " was used when a man
would recall his companions to remembrance of the Law. " [14] In
this light, the greeting, " The Lord be with you, " could be a vestige
of the Church's Jewish heritage, since in the early Christian synaxis

century Liturgy of John Chrysostom in *Cod. Burdett-Coutts*, III, 42 (edit.
C. A. Swainson, *The Greek Liturgies Chiefly from Original Authorities* [London,
1884], p. 116 b); the fourteenth century order of the Divine Liturgy in the rotulo
of *Esphigmenon* of the year 1306 (edit. A. Dmitrievsky, *Opysanie liturgicheskikh
rukopisej khraniaschikhsia v bibliotekakh pravoslavnago vostoka*, Vol. II; *Euchologia*
[Kiev, 1901], pp. 266, 267; etc.); the same also in the *Cod.* 381 of the Moscow
Synodal Library, fourteenth century; (edit. N. Krasnoseltsev, *Materialy dlja
istorii chinoposlidovania liturgii sv. Ioanna Zlatoustago* [Kazan, 1889], pp. 24, 26,
28); also the *Ustav* in the *Liturgikon* of Metropolitan Isidore, cf. fourteenth or
fifteenth century *Cod. Vat. Slav.*, No. 14, fol. 128.

[13] In the Latin Church whenever the *Gloria in excelsis* is said in the Pontifical
Mass, the bishop greets the people with *Pax vobis* (" Peace be to you "). But in
imparting the greeting the Latin bishop, unlike the Byzantine-Slav priest who
blesses the people, merely turns toward the congregation and stretches out his
hands—a gesture signifying the desire to be united with the people and to draw
them together into the prayer that is just beginning. In sixth century Spain,
the *Pax vobis* began to supersede the *Dominus vobiscum* in the Mass until it was
forbidden by the Synod of Braga (A.D. 563) even to bishops. The present rule
for the *Pax vobis* and its relationship with the *Gloria in excelsis* seems to have
been stabilized after the reply of Pope Leo VII in A.D. 937 to the bishops of Gaul
and Germany : " On Sundays, the principal solemnities and the feasts of saints,
we say the *Gloria in excelsis* and *Pax vobis*. On other days in Lent, the Ember
Seasons, the vigils of saints and fast days, we say only *Dominus vobiscum* (PL 132,
1068). Pope Innocent III (1178-1180) again remarks that the *Pax vobis* is suitable
only for bishops who are vicars of Christ (*De s. altaris mysterio*, ii, 24 [PL 217,
812]).

[14] Tractate *Berakoth, Tos.*, vii. 23.

the first lessons after the greeting were taken from the Law and the Prophets. The salutation is less definitely christological than the *Pax vobis*, for *Dominus* originally meant God. While in the Latin Liturgy, the word *Dominus* remains indeterminate, the implicit understanding is that the Lord God does come to us in Christ, who is our Emmanuel. Christ assured his followers that " Where two or three are gathered in my name, I am there in the midst of them " (Matt. 18:20), a condition fulfilled in the Mass. Furthermore, he promised to be with his Church till the end of time : " And behold I am with you all days, even to the consummation of the world " (Matt. 28:20).

The reply of the *ecclesia* in the Russian and Latin Rites, " And with your spirit" *(Et cum spiritu tuo)* also suggests a Jewish origin because of its Semitic parallelism. There are similar instances in St. Paul. [15] The Semitic expression for " your spirit, " meaning " your person, " can be rendered, " And with you too. " It seems, however, that even in the early centuries the expression was already being interpreted in a more Christian sense. Chrysostom, for example, sees in the phrase " your spirit " the indwelling of the Holy Spirit, [16] or the special grace of the Holy Spirit received by the celebrant at his ordination. [17]

After the greeting, the Latin Rite summons its people to attention for prayer with *Oremus* (Let us pray). The Byzantine-Slav Rite uses the direct appeal, " Let us be attentive. " It does this not only here before the *Prokeimenon*, but also before the Epistle and before the Gospel, besides the first time, immediately before the greeting. The repetition of this exhortation stresses the special attention the people must give to Sacred Scripture—the *Prokeimenon*, the Epistle, and the Gospel—containing the very wisdom of God. That is why the word *Wisdom* is added to the call for special attention in the last three instances.

[15] Cf. II Tim. 4:22; Gal. 6:18; Phil. 4:23; etc.

[16] Chrysostom, *In II Tim. homil.*, 10, 3 (PG 62, 659 f. or edit. Montfaucon 11, 725 A).

[17] Chrysostom, *Prima de Pent.*, n. 4 (PG 50, 458 f. or edit. Montfaucon 2, 463 BC). Likewise, Theodore of Mopsuestia, *Catecheses*, vi (edit. Minganga, *Commentary of Theodore of Mopsuestia on the Lord's Prayer and on the Sacraments of Baptism and the Eucharist* [Cambridge, 1933], p. 91).

The call of the deacon for attention (πρόσχωμεν) before the readings is ancient; it probably began as a rubric and later was incorporated into the text of the Liturgy. Chrysostom places it before the first reading (from the Prophets) in the early fifth-century Liturgy at Constantinople. [18] In the early eighth-century Armenian version of Chrysostom's Liturgy, the immediate setting of each scriptural reading was expanded to include the phrase " With wisdom " and the blessing " Peace be to all. " [19] The admonition, warning the people to pay attention, was even more explicit in the ninth-century Syrian Liturgy : before the first lesson, the deacon cried out " Sit down and be quiet! " and " Be quiet, " before all the other lessons. [20]

The Latin Rite summons, *Oremus*, has a closer Byzantine parallel in the *ektenias*, when the deacon announces the petitions, " Let us pray, " " In peace let us pray, " etc. The *Oremus* could be an abbreviation of a longer form. On Good Friday, for example, the bidding is very similar to the Eastern *ektenia* :

Oremus, dilectissimi nobis, pro Ecclesia sancta Dei : ut eam Deus et Dominus noster pacificare, adunare et custodire dignetur toto orbe terrarum... detque nobis quietam et transquillam vitam degentibus... etc.	Let us pray, dearly beloved, for the holy Church of God, that our Lord and God will deign to give her peace, to preserve her unity, and to guard her throughout the world ... and that he will suffer us to lead a peaceful and quiet life. Etc.

Especially worthy of note is that which followed this bidding : the deacon calls, *Flectamus genua.* The faithful kneel and pray in silence for a while. The deacon signals, *Levate*, and so forth. An identical ceremonial is found in one of the most ancient Eastern *ektenias.* [21]

---

[18] Chrysostom, *In Act. Ap.*, xix, 5 (edit. Montfaucon 9, 159 E).

[19] Cf. Aucher, *La versione armena della liturgia di S. Giovanni Crisostomo fatta sul principio dell'VIII secolo*, XPYCOCTOMIKA (Rome, 1908), pp. 379-380. There is no blessing for the Gospel however.

[20] Cf. Ps.-George of Arbela, *Explicatio off. eccl.*, iv, 4 ff. (edit. R. H. Connolly-W. Corrington, *Two Commentaries on the Jacobite Liturgy by George Bishop of the Arab Tribes, and Moses Bar Kepha* [London, 1913], pp. 9-11 [12-13]).

[21] In the Alexandrian Liturgy; cf. Brightman, LEW, p. 159.

In this light, the medieval explanation for the word *collecta* as meaning the collection of the various private prayers with which the priest " gathers and concludes the petitions of all " becomes clear. [22]

Prokeimenon means " placed before " or " prelude. " It comes before the reading of the scriptural pericopes and consists in a verse or two from the psalms or the prophets, accommodated to the theme of the feast or saint of the day. [23]   The term itself was coined sometime before the eighth century, since we meet it for the first time in the *Liturgical Commentary* of St. Germanus of Constantinople (A.D. 715-729). [24]

The Sabbath Morning Service of the Jewish synagogue, on which the Mass of the Catechumens is modeled, was developed after the destruction of Jerusalem, yet its origin can be traced to earlier times. It contains a twofold blessing.   The first opening the synagogue assembly, imparted by the presiding leader with the words *Barku el* (Bless the Lord), and the second, the *Shema* itself, consisting in several blessings and excerpts from the Pentateuch, [25] after which the lections were made.   Likewise, in the Byzantine-Slav Liturgy there are a blessing (" Peace be to all ") and the *Prokeimenon*, consisting in excerpts from the Psalms or the Prophets.   Yet, they do not correspond to the *Shema* of the Jewish service.   The origin of the *Prokeimenon* is found, rather, in the singing of the Psalms of David after (and between?) the first two pericopes of Scripture to which the *Apostolic Constitutions* (Book II) refers : After the readings from the Law and the Prophets, " when the two lessons have been read individually, some other persons should sing the hymns of

[22] Thus, Bernold of Constance (1100), *Micrologus*, 3 (PL 151, 979); also Walafrid of Strabo, *De eccl. rer. exord. et increm.*, 22 (PL 114, 945); etc.

[23] Technically there are two kinds of *prokeimena* : the " *prokeimenon* of the day " and " the Epistle *prokeimenon*, " depending on whether it expresses a closer relationship to the proper for the day (*prokeimenon* of the day) or to the Epistle lection (*prokeimenon* of the Epistle).   Cf. J. Pelesh, *Pastyrskoe Bohoslovie* [Vienna, 1885], p. 487, n. 2; also K. Nikolsky, *Posobie k izucheniu Ustava Bogosluzhenia Pravoslavnoi Tserkvy* [St. Petersburg, 1907], p. 211.

[24] *Commentarium liturgicum*, 28 (edit. N. Borgia, *Il commentario di s. Germano Patriarca Constantinopolitano e la versione latina di Anastasio Bibliotecario* [Grottaferrata, 1912], p. 25).

[25] From Deut. 6:4-9; 11:13-21; Num. 15:37-41.

David and the people should join in at the conclusion of the verses. " [26] This evidently derived from the singing of the psalms in the synagogue when the scrolls were being put away (see above, p. 32). At some point in time, the readings from the Old Testament were dropped in the Syro-Byzantine Church, [27] but the blessing and excerpts from the Psalms remained.

The Latin counterpart of the Byzantine *Prokeimenon* is the *Gradual*, though it now comes after the Epistle reading. But this was not always so; in the fragments of a Roman Mass book from southern Italy, the *Gradual* invariably follows the first of its three lessons, and the Alleluia chant follows the second. [28] Even prior to 1970, when the Latin Rite had three lections on a few occasions each year, one of the chants followed the first reading and the other the second. [29]

Both the Byzantine *Prokeimenon* and the Latin *Gradual* were originally sung from the ambo. Long after the ambo disappeared from Latin churches, the idea remained of singing the *Gradual* from a high place. [30] Now, however, both Rites have abandoned this custom, just as both have shortened the Psalm to a mere fraction of its original length. This was probably done some time during the fifth or sixth century. Even so, the way in which the *Prokeimenon* is sung today is still reminiscent of that described in the *Apostolic*

[26] *Apostolic Constitutions*, Book II; cf. above, p. 145, for the English, and Brightman, LEW, p. 29, for the Greek.

[27] This happened during the eighth or ninth century in the Byzantine Church, for the ninth century recension of the Divine Liturgy by Anastasius Bibliothecarius (edit. N. Borgia, *op. cit.*, 25 ff.) does not refer to the reading of the prophets, though it does mention the *Prokeimenon*, the epistle, and the Alleluia.

[28] Cf. A. Dold, *Die Zürcher und Peterlinger Messbuchfragmente aus der Zet des ersten Jahrtausends im Bari-Schrifttyp* (*Texte und Arbeiten*, I, 25 [Beuron, 1934], p. XXX).

[29] Thus the *Psalmellus* of the Milan Liturgy comes after the first of three lections and the Alleluia chant after the second.

[30] Cf. Durandus, *Rationale*, iv. 16, John Beleth, *Div. offic. explic.*, 38 (PL 202, 46); etc. In fact, its very name *Graduale* (*gradus*=step) in the Latin Rite derives from the lower part or step of the ambo where it was read together with the epistle. Ambos were built in Latin churches until the thirteenth century. They are still in use at Milan. For the Byzantine Rite, or rather its antecedents, we have the testimony of the Council of Laodicea, Canon 15 (Mansi, *Sacrorum conciliorum nova et amplissima collectio*, Vol. II, 567); *Apostolic Constitutions*, Book II, 57, 5 (cf. above, p. 145, or Quasten, *Monumenta euchristica et liturgia vetustissima*, [Bonn, 1935-1937], 182).

Constitutions : [31] the *Prokeimenon* proper (an antiphon-type verse) is sung first by the lector, and then is repeated by the choir (or people); then the *stikh* (which takes the place of the once complete psalm) is chanted by the lector; the choir repeats the *Prokeimenon* by way of refrain; finally, the lector sings the first half of the same *Prokeimenon* and the choir the last half. [32] Prior to the late Middle Ages, the Latin *graduale* was sung in an almost identical manner. Durandus, for example, describes it in his time : The cantor intoned the first verse, the choir repeated it; the cantor intoned the second and the choir repeated the first; then the cantor intoned the first again in a higher tone and the choir repeated it. [33]

[31] Book II; cf. above, p. 145.

[32] The Ruthenians, however, abbreviate this procedure : the choir (or people) sing the *Prokeimenon*, the lector the *stikh*, and the choir repeats the *Prokeimenon* (in some localities the *Prokeimenon* is again repeated, with the lector singing the first half and the choir the second).

[33] Durandus, *Rationale*, iv, 19, § 8; cf. also *Ordo Rom.*, II, 7 (PL 78, 974). This ancient tradition was restored by St. Pius X in 1907 in the *Graduale Romanum* (*De ritibus servandis in cantu Missae*, 4) : *Finita epistola aut lectione ab uno vel a duobus inchoatur responsorium, quod dicitur graduale, usque ad signum *, et cuncti, aut saltem cantores designati, prosequuntur debita cum attentione. Duo dicunt versum gradualis, quem ab asterisco circa finem totus chorus absolvit ; aut juxta ritum responsorialem, quando magis id videtur opportunum, post versum a solis cantoribus aut a cantore expletum, cuncti repetunt primam partem responsorii usque ad versum.*

CHAPTER XLI

THE READING OF THE EPISTLE

Immediately after the Prokeimenon, *the deacon proclaims :*
Wisdom!

The lector, vested in the stikhar, *stands before the* solea *in the center of the church and chants the title of the Epistle :*

The reading of the Epistle of the holy Apostle Paul to the N——.

Deacon : **Let us be attentive.**

The lector intones the Epistle proper to the day or occasion, beginning with the word :

Brothers...

When the Epistle reading is finished, the priest says in a low voice :

Peace be to you.

And the deacon answers, also in a low voice :

Wisdom.   Let us be attentive. [1]

The heart of the Liturgy of the Catechumens, the synaxis, is the reading of the Holy Scriptures.   The origin of this service is found in the Liturgy of the synagogue (see above, p. 31). The highlights of this rite were the *Parascha* and the *Haftara*, readings from the *Law* and from the *Prophets* respectively. [2]   Since they were Jews, the very first Christians were familiar with this ritual and continued to frequent both the Temple and the synagogue services.   After the final breach with Judaism, when they held their own somewhat modified service, the Christians retained the readings from Sacred Writ as its most

---

[1] The Russian recension has the cantor answering, " And to your spirit. "

[2] E. Schürer, *Geschichte des judischen Volkes im Zeitalter Jesu Christi* (4th edit.; Leipzig, 1907), Vol. II, pp. 497-544.

prominent feature. They naturally added selections from the writings of the Apostles and from the Gospels. St. Paul himself instructed his converts to have his letters read in their new assemblies : " When this letter has been read out to you, see that it is read out in the Laodicean church too, and that you read the letter they have received at Laodicea " (Col. 4:16; cf. also I Thess. 5:27).

Paul went out to the far corners of the then known world, gained converts, and founded churches to continue the work begun there. When a church had been firmly established and a bishop or priest had been ordained to care for the increasing flock, the Apostle would move on to the next city. He would write to people in his earlier foundations, give them advice, instruction and admonition. These letters were read to the faithful at the Sunday synaxis. The bishop or priest would say in effect : " We have received a letter from the Apostle Paul; now if you will all listen, it shall be read to you. " This is precisely what happens even now in the Liturgy of the Catechumens, but in a much more formal way. " Let us be attentive " is simply a more solemn way of saying, " Listen carefully. "

Any bishop to whom such a letter was sent had copies forwarded to other churches. In this way, all of St. Paul's letters, or Epistles, and those of St. John, St. Peter, etc., were circulated in the primitive Christian communities. At first, they were read and reread quite frequently, for the simple reason that they were only few. Besides, the divinely inspired wisdom they contained would benefit the Christians, no matter how often they were repeated.

In early days, there was no set pattern for the readings. They were read from beginning to end, or until the bishop signaled the reader to stop. During Justin's time, for instance, they were read " as long as the time allows. " [3] The next time the Christians assembled, the reader would continue with the passage where he had left off before.

In some places at least, in addition to the Epistles, letters from other bishops were read. Such as the *Gesta* of St. Ignatius of Antioch, of St. Clement, and of St. Cyprian, and the Acts of the

[3] Justin, *First Apology*, chap. 67; above, p. 42.

Martyrs. Great interest was aroused by such letters—especially those written by Christians awaiting execution for their faith. [4] Many such letters described the unflinching loyalty of those who had already gone out into the arena to be torn by wild beasts, nailed to crosses and set afire, etc. The thought of dying for the faith was never far from the mind of even the most ordinary Christian in those days. Most realized that they would eventually be arrested, but the essential question was whether they could go through with it or would become apostates. Letters of exhortation and encouragement from others preparing for the supreme trial would be sources of special interest and inspiration. With the end of the persecutions, this practice was gradually discontinued in most places and the readings were restricted to selections from the Scriptures. [5]

The readings were always in the vernacular. If the Christian communities had groups of people speaking different languages, special provision was made to have special assemblies for each language group. As late as the end of the fourth century, for example, Etheria tells us that at Jerusalem the readings were in Greek, but for those who could not understand Greek, in Syrian. [6]

Gradually, the initial freedom regarding the amount of reading diminished, and more or less equal portions were assigned for each service. Such portions were marked off in the margin of the Scriptures and thus a new term was born : *pericope* (from the Greek

---

[4] The first testimony of such readings from martyrs at the synaxis is contained in the second-century *Acts* of Apollonius (n. 47, *Bibliothek der Kirchevӓter*, XIV, pp. 327 f.). The Third Council of Carthage (A.D. 397) in its 36th Canon (Mansi, *Sacrorum conciliorum nova et amplissima collectio*, III, 924), expressly sanctioned such a practice for Masses celebrated on their individual feasts. Augustine attested to the practice in his day (Roetzer, *Des hl. Augustinus Schriften als liturgie-geschichtliche Quelle* [Munich, 1930], 62 f., 107 f.).

[5] In some Churches, the custom died hard. At Milan, such a practice was still observed in the year 1024, as is evident from the letter of Paul and Gebhart, two clerics from Regensburg (J. Mabillon, *Museum Italicum* [Paris, 1724], 2, p. 97). For Gaul, see Gregory of Tours, *De gloria mart.*, I, 86 (PL 71, 781) and *De mirac. S. Martini*, II, 29; 49 (PL 71, 954, 963); also, cf. *Expositio ant. liturgiae gallicanae Germano Parisiensi ascripta* (edit. J. Quasten, [*Opuscula et Textus, ser. liturg.*, 3; Münster, 1934], 13 f.) and Lectionary of Luxeuil (edit. P. Salmon, *Le lectionnaire de Luxeuil* [Rome, 1944], 27 ff., 181 f.).

[6] *Aetheriae Peregrinatio*, chap. 47 (CSEL, XXXIX, 99). Epiphanius, in fact, mentions the office of translator of lections and homilies (*Expositio fid.*, chap. 21 [PG 41, 825]).

περικοπή, " a portion cut off. " [7]   Since books were not paged, and the Bible had not been divided into verses, an index giving the first and last words of each pericope was made.   Such indexes, called *synaxaria* in Greek, are known from the fourth century. [8]   The next development consisted in giving not only the headings but also the whole text of the lessons; a complete book arranged thus would then be called the *Apostolos, Euaggelion, Synaxarion*, etc., depending on whether it contained the Epistles, Gospels, or other readings.   The Byzantine Church still uses this system; so do most of the other Eastern Churches.

The only uniformity regarding the number of readings in the first few centuries seemed to be that every synaxis should have at least two, the last of which was to be the Gospel as the " crown of all the holy Scriptures. " [9]

Gradually, however, the number of lessons became fixed in each Church.   Perhaps the most common arrangement consisted in two readings from the Old Testament, a direct inheritance from the synagogue service, followed by two readings from New Testament. This ancient practice is clearly indicated in the *Apostolic Constitutions*, in both Book II and Book VIII (see above, pp. 145 and 108 f. respectively), and traces of it can still be found in the Syrian Jacobite Rite. [10]   The Chaldaic Rite, which has faithfully preserved so many Semitic traits, has also kept the two lessons from the Old Testament (the first always from the Pentateuch) before its Epistle and Gospel. [11] By the fourth century, however, liturgical development in most Churches had reduced the two Old Testament pericopes to one. The direct Syro-Antiochene antecedents of the Byzantine Rite and the Rite of Constantinople itself were no exceptions; as both Basil and Chrysostom testify, each had three lessons : (*a*) the Prophets,

---

[7] From about the time of the Talmud, the Jews had a fixed cycle with definitely outlined passages *(parashoth)* arranged for each Sabbath.   Cf. I. Elbogen, *Der jüdische Gottesdienst in seiner geschichtlichen Entwicklung* (2nd edit. Frankfurt, 1924), pp. 159-162.

[8] In the Western Church, similar arrangements of the lessons were made in the *comes, libri comites*, or *libri comici*.

[9] Origen, *In Ioann.*, i, 4 (PG 14, 26).

[10] Cf. A. Baumstark, *Nichtevangelische syrische Perikopenordnung des ersten Jahrtausends* (Munster i. W., 1921), pp. 16-19.

[11] Baumstark, *op. cit.*, pp. 16-19; Brightman, LEW, 256, 1.25.

(b) the Epistle, and (c) the Gospel. [12]   The Armenian Rite, derived
from the ancient Rite of Constantinople, still has three lections, the
first of which is always from the Old Testament Prophets. [13]   Traces
of this practice are also found in the Western Church.   The Latin
Rite, for example, has three lessons on Wednesday and Friday of
Holy Week, Ember Wednesday, and on Wednesday of the fourth
week of Lent; the old Gallican Rite had three; [14] so also the Rite of
Toledo. [15]   The suppression of the Old Testament pericopes took
a different form in the Coptic and Ethiopian Liturgies, where the
two Old Testament lections were replaced by two more New Testament lections, bringing their number to four : (1) Epistles of St. Paul,
(2) the Catholic Epistles, (3) the Acts, and (4) the Gospels. [16]

The final step in the evolution of the Byzantine and Roman Rites
was the total suppression of the Old Testament reading : only the
Epistle and the Gospel were left in the Mass.   Other Byzantine
liturgical services have kept the Old Testament readings, e.g.,
Vespers, Matins, etc.   In the Latin Mass, the Old Testament reading
was reinstated in 1970.   It is unknown just when this final suppression took place in the Byzantine Liturgy; certainly by the ninth
century, as we know from Anastasius Bibliothecarius. [17] but evidence
prior to the eighth century is far from certain. [18]   Mostly because of

[12] For the Cappadocian Church, cf. Basil, *In sanctum baptisma*, 1 (PG 31,
425 AB); also *In psalmum*, 28, 7 (PG 29, 304).   For the Antiochene Church,
cf. Chrysostom, *In Rom.*, xxiv, 3 (edit. Montfaucon 9, 697 E), *De baptismo Christi*,
2 (*edit. cit.*, 2, 369 C), and *Cur in Pentecoste*, 5 (*edit. cit.*, 3, 89), for the reading of
the Prophets and Epistle : for the reading of the Gospel, cf. *In Matt.*, i, 6 (*edit.
cit.*, 7, 13 B).   For the Church at Constantinople, cf. Chrysostom, *In ep. ad He-
braeos homil.*, *VIII*, 4 (*edit. cit.*, 12, 91 BC, or PG 60, 217); *In Actus apost. homil.*,
XXIX, 3 (*edit. cit.*, 9, 229, or PG 60, 217) and *In II ad Thess, homil.*, III, 4 (*edit.
cit.*, 11, 527-528 or PG 62, 485); etc.; also cf. Theodore Sykeota (d. A.D. 613),
n. 16, *Acts SS. Apr.*, III, 37.

[13] Brightman, LEW, pp. 371-372.

[14] Duchesne, *Origines du culte chrétien* (Paris, 1909), p. 185.

[15] PL 85, 109-111, etc.

[16] Brightman, LEW, pp. 76-78, 152-154, 255-258, 212-215.

[17] C. 879 (edit. N. Borgia, *Il commentario liturgico di s. Germano Patriarco
Constantinopolitano e la versione latina di Anastasio Bibliotecario* [Grottaferrata,
1912], pp. 25 ff.).   Here, the Epistle is given between the Prokeimenon and the
Alleluia chant, but no mention is made of the reading from the Prophets.

[18] E.g., St. Germanus I of Constantinople in his *Commentarius liturgicus*, nn.
28 ff. (edit. N. Borgia, *op. cit.*, pp. 25 ff.), does not mention the reading of the

Byzantine influence, the Greek Liturgies of St. James and St. Mark have also entirely deleted the lections from the Old Testament since the eleventh century and now have only two lessons, the Epistle and the Gospel. [19]

The Scriptural pericopes in the original synaxis followed through from one service to another in an unbroken, continual series, the *lectio continua*. The voluminous commentaries of the Fathers in both the Eastern and the Western Churches on the Old and New Testaments are in fact preached after such scriptural readings. With the introduction of the great feast days into the Liturgy, the continuity was broken, for on those days lessons were chosen which were more properly accommodated to the given feast. This system still prevails in the Byzantine Church as regards both the Epistle and the Gospel.

The cycle of Epistle and Gospel readings begins, not with the liturgical year on September 1, but with Easter Sunday, and continues daily until Palm Sunday of the following year—a system of Byzantine invention which cannot be traced back beyond the eighth century. There are exceptions to the continuous reading of the Epistle cycle, but the order is clearly discernible. [20]

Prophets, but then neither does he mention the Epistle. Cf. however, J. A. Jungmann, *Mass of the Roman Rite*, Vol. I (New York : Benziger, 1951), p. 395.

[19] Cf. Brightman, LEW, pp. 36 ff., 118 f.

[20] See schema of the Byzantine-Slav cycle of Epistle readings on p. 443. Besides the interruptions for the great feast days already mentioned, the most notable disruption of order occurs when a new Epistle is begun : thus, while the weekdays begin and continue the reading of the new Epistle, the next several Saturdays and Sundays still continue with the final chapter of the preceding one.

Another notable disruption of order is the " interpolated weeks. " The pre-fast period of the *Triodion* always begins on the 10th Sunday before Easter and the same Epistles and Gospels recur each year not only during Lent but also during the pre-fast *Triodion* period. Easter, however, does not occur on a fixed date each year. When Easter is late in a given year and the period between it and that of the previous year is more than fifty-two weeks, one or more weeks of lections must be "interpolated" before the beginning of the pre-fast *Triodion* period (i.e., before the 10th Sunday before Easter). If there is only one extra week, the Epistles of the 29th week are repeated for that extra week. When two weeks must be interpolated, then the Epistles for the 29th and 17th weeks are repeated; when three extra weeks have to be taken care of, then the Epistles for the 29th, 31st, and 17th weeks are repeated for these extra weeks just before the *Triodion* period. If the interpolated limit of four weeks occurs, then we have the following arrangement : the Epistles for the 29th and 31st weeks are repeated; this is followed by Epistles of the 32nd week; lastly, the Epistles for the 17th week are repeated just before the pre-fast *Triodion* period.

ANNUAL CYCLE OF THE GOSPELS

Week	Mon.	Tues.	Wed.	Thurs.	Fri.	Sat.	Sun.	
EASTER							John	
St. Thomas	John	Luke	John	John	John	John	John	
Myrrh-bearing Women	″	John	″	″	″	″	Mark	
Paralytic	″	″	″	″	″	″	John	
Samaritan Woman	″	″	″	″	″	″	″	
Blind Man	″	″	″	″	″	″	″	
Fathers of Council	″	″	″	Luke	″	″	″	
PENTECOST	″	″	″	John	″	″	″	
1st after Pentecost	Matt.	Matt.	Matt.	Matt.	Matt.	Matt.	Matt.	
2nd ″ ″	″	″	″	″	″	″	″	
3rd ″ ″	″	″	″	″	″	″	″	
4th ″ ″	″	″	″	″	″	″	″	
5th ″ ″	″	″	″	″	″	″	″	
6th ″ ″	″	″	″	″	″	″	″	
7th ″ ″	″	″	″	″	″	″	″	
8th ″ ″	″	″	″	″	″	″	″	
9th ″ ″	″	″	″	″	″	″	″	
10th ″ ″	″	″	″	″	″	″	″	
11th ″ ″	″	″	″	″	″	″	″	
12th ″ ″	Mark	Mark	Mark	Mark	Mark	Matt.	Matt.	
13th ″ ″	″	″	″	″	″	″	″	
14th ″ ″	″	″	″	″	″	″	″	
15th ″ ″	″	″	″	″	″	″	″	
16th ″ ″	″	″	″	″	″	″	″	
17th ″ ″	″	″	″	″	″	″	″	
18th ″ ″	Luke	Luke	Luke	Luke	Luke	Luke	Luke	
19th ″ ″	″	″	″	″	″	″	″	
20th ″ ″	″	″	″	″	″	″	″	
21st ″ ″	″	″	″	″	″	″	″	
22nd ″ ″	″	″	″	″	″	″	″	
23rd ″ ″	″	″	″	″	″	″	″	
24th ″ ″	″	″	″	″	″	″	″	
25th ″ ″	″	″	″	″	″	″	″	
26th ″ ″	″	″	″	″	″	″	″	
27th ″ ″	″	″	″	″	″	″	″	
28th ″ ″	″	″	″	″	″	″	″	
29th ″ ″	″	″	″	″	″	″	″	
30th ″ ″	Mark	Mark	Mark	Mark	Mark	″	″	
31st ″ ″	″	″	″	″	″	″	″	= Also Sunday of
32nd ″ ″	″	″	″	″	″	″	″	Publican &
33rd ″ ″	″	″	″	″	″	″	″	Pharisee
34th ″ ″	″	″	″	″	″	″	″	= Prodigal Son
35th ″ ″	″	″	″	″	″	″	Matt.	= Meat Fast
Cheese Fast Week	Luke	Luke	a-lit.	Luke	a-lit.	Matt.	Matt.	= Cheese Fast
First Week of Lent	a-lit.	a-lit.	Pre-sanct.	a-lit.	Pre-sanct.	Mark	John.	
2nd ″ ″ ″	″	″	sanct.	″	sanct.	″	Mark	
3rd ″ ″ ″	″	″	″	″	″	″	″	
4th ″ ″ ″	″	″	″	″	″	″	″	
5th ″ ″ ″	″	″	″	″	″	″	″	
6th ″ ″ ″	″	″	″	″	″	John	John	= Palm Sun,
Holy Week	Matt.	Matt.	John	Matt.	a-lit.	Matt.		

In nearly all the Eastern Churches, the lector chants the Epistle; [21] the Byzantine is no exception. This has been the unbroken tradition of the Church from the very early centuries of Christianity. In the middle of the second century, Justin Martyr mentions that the " commentaries of the Apostles " and the " writings of the Prophets " are read by the " reader. " [22] Abundant evidence since then is not wanting. Even in the Latin Rite, the reading of the Epistle was reserved to the lector in the first seven or eight centuries. [23] Whether or not this was consciously copied from Jewish practice is unknown, but we do know that in the synagogue liturgy the lessons were read by special readers who had been trained to read Hebrew. It is obvious that in the Christian Church the reader always had to have a certain amount of education for his office. Another unbroken tradition is the vesture of the lector. Whenever the lector performed his service he was vested in the *stikhar(ion)*; this probably dates back to the beginning when the *linea* was the standard garment worn in daily life. When secular fashions changed in the fourth century, the Church kept the *linea* (now known as the *stikhar(ion)* in the Byzantine Church).

Like the Jewish synagogue which had a tribune, [24] the early Christian church in both East and West had an elevated place on which stood a small, movable reading desk; this was called the *ambo*, [25]

[21] The exceptions are the Maronite Rite, which has been Latinized, and the Chaldaic since the seventh century; cf. Abraham bar Lipheh, *Interpretatio officiorum eccl.* (edit. R. H. Connolly, p. 172); cf. also Ps. George of Arbela, *Expositio officiorum eccles.*, IV, chap. 6 (edit. R. H. Connolly, p. 15).

[22] Justin, *First Apology*, chap. 67, cf. above, p. 42.

[23] One of the first references designating the subdeacon as the reader of the Epistle in the Latin Church was the *Ordo Rom.*, I, n. 10 (PL 78, 942). Amalarius (850) still opposed the newly introduced practice, since neither the ordination of the subdeacon nor ecclesiastical legislation till then had assigned this duty to him (*De eccl. off.*, II, 11 [PL 105, 1086]). Bernold of Constance (1100) still speaks of this practice as being based on custom only (*Micrologus*, c. 8 [PL 151, 982]). Though the ceremony of giving the subdeacon the book of Epistles at ordination dates back to the thirteenth century (cf. de Puniet, *Das römische Pontifikale*, I, 174), the Latin missal still permitted the lector to read the Epistle at Mass when no subdeacon was present (cf. *Ritus celebr.*, VI). Vatican II changed this and reverted to the ancient practice of having a " reader " read the Epistle.

[24] As Ezra did, in Neh. 8:4.

[25] Cyprian, *Ep.* 38, 2 (CSEL, III, 580 f.); 39, 4 (583 f.); Canon 15 of Council of Laodicea (Mansi, *op. cit.*, II, 567); *Apostolic Constitutions*, Book II, 57, 5 (Quasten, *Monumenta eucharistica et liturgia vetustissima* [Bonn, 1935-1937], 182).

from the Greek ἀναβαίνειν (to walk up). The term *ambo* first appears in the Council of Laodicea. [26] But either with or without the desk, this was the place from which the lector read the lessons. Probably most early ambos were made of wood, but some of the later models were of costly marble, often enormous in size and decorated with mosaics, reliefs, gilt, etc. [27] That of St. Sophia at Constantinople was large enough and rich enough to be used for the coronation ceremonial of emperors. [28] Most Greek churches still have the early form of ambo, usually placed at the side. All that remains of the ancient ambo in Byzantine-Slav churches is the semicircular extension before the iconostas on which is placed the *analoj*, or lectern for reading the Gospel; it is still called the *ambon*, or *amvon*. In addition to this, the Ruthenian Church has preserved another vestige of the ancient ambo in the form of the *tetrapod*, a desklike table on which are placed the crucifix, candles and, an icon; at the *tetrapod* (which stands before the ambo) baptisms, confirmations, and marriages are performed as well as certain other services either in whole or in part. [29] For the chanting of the Epistle, however, the lector no longer ascends the ambo nor uses the *tetrapod*; he stands on the floor in the middle of the church before them. In the Byzantine-Slav Liturgy, the Epistle, or "Apostle," as it is commonly called, [30] is always chanted *recto tono*, but with certain cadences or melodic figures to indicate the various punctuation marks, etc. It can best be described as speech-song. The Church probably borrowed this method from the culture of antiquity. [31] It avoids two extremes. On the one hand, it obviates any semblance of passionate

---

[26] Mansi, *op. cit.*, II, 567.

[27] Cf. H. Leclercq, "Ambon," DACL, I, 1330-1347.

[28] Some of the churches of Rome have fine examples of ambos in marble. Perhaps the oldest is that in S. Clemente (reconstructed in the twelfth century); the best known of the later models, enriched with marble mosaics or Cosmati work, are in S. Maria in Ara Coeli and S. Maria in Cosmedin. Ravenna and several churches in southern Italy have other fine examples of early ambos.

[29] E.g., the *Parastas*, a service for the dead; some of the "All-Night Vigil" services, etc.

[30] In the West, the Epistle was also often called *Apostolus*, e.g., in the Gregorian Sacramentary; cf. PL 78, 25.

[31] For literary references, see O. Casel, *Das Gedächtnis des Herrn in der altchristlichen Liturgie* (*Ecclesia Orans*, 2; Freiburg, 1918), 14, n. 1.

speech whereby the lector could inject his own sentiments, mood or emotion into the sacred text. On the other hand, it avoids the monotony of the severe *tonus rectus*, unbroken by any cadence whatever, which is not appropriate for festive occasions. The speech-song's only object is the congregation's practical understanding of the text.

CHAPTER XLII

THE ALLELUIA CHANT
AND PRE-GOSPEL PRAYER

After the Epistle, the choir and people begin the Alleluia *chant and the verses from the Psalms that are proper to the given day. Here we shall give those of the first resurrectional tone :*

Alleluia, alleluia, alleluia.

Verse : **God who gives me vengeance and subdues the people under me** (Psalm. 17:48).

Alleluia, alleluia, alleluia.

Verse : **You who honor the king with deliverance and show mercy to David his anointed, and to his seed for ever** (Ps. 17:51).

Alleluia, alleluia, alleluia.

While the Alleluia is being sung, the deacon takes the censer, puts incense into it, approaches the priest, and says :

Bless, sir.

The priest imparts his blessing with the words :

Blessed be our God, now and always, and for ever and ever. Amen.

After receiving the blessing, the deacon begins the incensing : first, the holy table from all four sides, then the entire sanctuary and the celebrant. Leaving the sanctuary through the north door, he incenses the icons of the iconostas, both choirs and the people. In the meantime the priest stands before the holy table and silently recites the prayer before the Gospel.

O Master and Lover of mankind, make the spotless light of your divine wisdom shine in our hearts and open the eyes of our mind to an understanding of the things you teach in the Gospel. Instill in us also a fear of your blessed command-

ments, so that trampling upon all the desires of the flesh, we may begin to lead a spiritual life, both thinking and doing all that is pleasing to you. For you are the enlightenment of our souls and bodies, Christ our God, and we give glory to you, together with your eternal Father and your all-holy, gracious and life-giving Spirit, now and always and for ever and ever. Amen.

After completing the incensing, the deacon returns to the sanctuary through the south door and puts back the censer in its place.

Alleluia! Praise ye Yahweh! This Old Testament doxology, like certain other words from the Hebrew (Amen, Hosanna, etc.) is left untranslated in the Liturgy. Originally belonging to the Hallel, the Psalms of Praise, the *Alleluia* was placed at the close of these psalms in the Massoretic text, [1] while the Septuagint places it at the head of each psalm, as does the Vulgate. As used by the Jews, it was an acclamation, a cry of praise and joy to God. [2] This same sense of praise and joy is clearly apparent in the saints' use of the *Alleluia* in St. John's Apocalypse when they glorify God for his judgments on the great harlot (Rev. 19:1-15).

In Christian usage, as we see it in the agape outlined by Hippolytus of Rome but modified by some Eastern source, the *Alleluia* was to be a response by the people during the recitation of the Hallel Psalms (see above, p. 50). This was evidently an adaptation of the Hallel to the responsorial method employed in the synagogue, where the signal for the people's refrain was the cantor's cry, " Halleluyah." [3] When was the *Alleluia* inserted as a refrain into the psalms at the Liturgy of the Catechumens? No one really knows for certain, but it must have been in the early centuries. The *Alleluia* chant is found in all the present Liturgies, except the Ethiopic, in more or less the same place before the Gospel and in almost the same form. [4]

---

[1] So also the *Novum Psalterium* (Pontificii Instituti Biblici).

[2] Cf. DAL I, 1226-1246.

[3] Cf. I. Elbogen, *Der jüdische Gottesdienst in seiner geschtlichen Enwicklung* (2nd edit., Frankfurt, 1924), 496.

[4] For the Armenian, cf. Brightman, LEW, p. 426, lines 1-4; the Syrian, Brightman, LEW, p. 79, lines 1-10; Chaldean, Brightman, LEW, p. 258, line 29, p. 259, line 3; Coptic, Brightman, LEW, p. 156, lines 16-21. The Ethiopic Rite

Yet, ancient Oriental sources are strangely silent on the point. This can be explained only if the *Alleluia* was so intimately connected with the pre-Gospel psalm chant that it was not specifically distinguished, was not even considered separate.

The first Byzantine source to mention the *Alleluia* before the Gospel is the *Liturgical Commentary* of St. Germanus I of Constantinople, dating from the beginning of the eighth century. [5] Yet, we know from Pope St. Gregory that it was already an established Byzantine custom a full century earlier. In his letter to John of Syracuse, Pope Gregory mentions that the *Alleluia* was brought to Rome from Jerusalem by St. Jerome in the time of Pope St. Damascus (366-384), and that Rome does not sing it *as do the Byzantines* but restricts its use. [6] Thus, we have proof of the *Alleluia* being sung in the Byzantine Church a full hundred years before any Byzantine evidence comes to light. By Pope St. Gregory's time, the use of the *Alleluia* was being restricted in the West, [7] although the original practice there did not limit its use to seasons of joy. [8] This difference between Byzantine and Roman Churches—where the *Alleluia* is excluded from seasons of penance and sorrow—is still clear today. The only exception to the universal use of the *Alleluia* in Byzantine Churches is that it is not sung on Holy Saturday in the Liturgy of St. Basil.

The method of singing the *Alleluia* chant is the responsorial-antiphonal of the Syro-Antiochene Church (see pp. 367 ff., above).

---

has found a kind of substitute for the Alleluia chant, but this is of recent origin, cf. S. A. B. Mercer, *The Ethiopic Liturgy, its Sources, Development and Present Form* (London, 1915), p. 338, and Brightman, LEW, p. 220, line 20.

[5] Germanus I of Constantinople, *Commentarius liturgicus*, n. 29 (edit. N. Borgia, *Il commentario liturgico di s. Germano Patriarca Constantinopolitano e la versione latina di Anastasio Bibliotecario*, p. 25).

[6] " ...*magis in hac re consuetudinem amputavimus quae hic a Graecis fuerat tradita* "; cf. *Ep.* 9, 11 (PL 77, 955-958):

[7] About the middle of the fifth century, Sozomen is even under the impression that at Rome the Alleluia was originally sung only on Easter Sunday (*Hist. eccl.*, VII, 19 [PG 67, 1476]); for reliability of the report, see Cabrol (DACL, I, 1236). Rome probably removed the Alleluia from Quadragesima, as had Spain and Africa at the time of St. Isidore (*De eccl. off.*, I, 13, 3 [PL 83, 750 f.]). Gregory the Great seems to have restricted its use further, by eliminating it from Septuagesima (cf. Callewaert, *Sacris erudiri*, 650, 652 f.).

[8] As late as c. A.D. 400, the Alleluia was still sung at sorrowful solemnities even at Rome, e.g., at the burial of Fabiola; Jerome, *Ep.* 77, 12 (CSEL, 55, 48, l. 12).

First the *Alleluia* is sung three times by the choir or people; then a verse of the psalm is intoned by the cantor (or cantors); the *Alleluia* is repeated three times by the people. If there is another verse from the psalm, it is taken by the cantor (or cantors), and finally the *Alleluia* is again sung three times by the people. This verse from the psalm is called an *alleluiarion* or if more than one, *alleluiaria* (or merely the Alleluia). Like the psalm verses of the *prokeimenon* before the Epistle, the *alleluiaria* consisted originally in whole psalms. They are now reduced to a mere verse or two. Like the *prokeimena*, they are accommodated to the given day, feast, or saint. Since they are variable in the Liturgy, the proper *alleluiaria* are given in the *Ustav (ordo)*. The rubrical prescriptions applying to them are too complicated to be given here.

Although the Alleluia is sung in the Byzantine Rite during times of mourning and penitential seasons, it is still a cry of praise to God, overflowing with joy and thanksgiving; it is the cry of a soul rejoicing because it will soon hear the Lord, the Master himself, speaking through the Gospel. This joy of hearing the Master's words outweighs all considerations of mourning and penance; that is why the Alleluia is sung in the Byzantine Rite even at funeral Masses.

The incensing, like the Alleluia during which it is done, is also a preparation for listening to the reading of the Holy Gospel and is designed to draw the thoughts of the faithful heavenward. It is a sign of prayerful reverence and homage to the Gospel of Christ. It is that and more : the smoke diffusing into every corner of the church symbolizes the grace of the Holy Spirit, which spreads throughout the world through the Gospel and the good tidings it brings. This symbolism reaches back at least eleven centuries, for St. Germanus of Constantinople explains it in essentially the same way when writing at the beginning of the eighth century about the pre-Gospel incensing. [9] Apparently, this incensing before the Gospel was not a universal practice in the Greek Church, for, aside from St. Germanus and a few others, most Byzantine sources up to the

---

[9] Germanus I of Constantinople, *Commentarius liturgicus*, n. 30 (edit. N. Borgia, *op. cit.*, p. 25).

fourteenth century do not mention it. [10]   It is notknown when the
Slavs adopted this incensing in their Liturgy, but it was probably
during the early fifteenth century, after the *Constitution* of Philotheus
had been introduced into the Ukraine and Russia. [11]

The pre-Gospel prayer, " O Master and Lover of mankind, "
differs from its seeming counterpart in the Latin Mass, the *Munda
cor meum*, in that the latter is a personal prayer of the priest for
worthily proclaiming the Gospel, while the former is a prayer for
and in the name of the people (note the first-person-plural forms)
for enlightenment and understanding Christ's truth contained in the
Gospel as well as for the grace to do whatever his word teaches.   The
reason for this is obvious : in the Byzantine Rite the office of deacon
is still a vital, living part of the Liturgy, and one of its practical
functions is the reading of the Gospel; in the Latin Rite, on the
other hand, the reading of the Gospel for the most part falls to the
priest, since the office of deacon has become a transitory, temporary
state, a stage preparatory for the priesthood. [12]   Much closer in
meaning and context to the *Munda cor meum* is the prayer of the
priest while blessing and sending forth the deacon : " May God...
grant you the power of announcing his word with great strength," etc.

The prayer " O Master and Lover of mankind " seems to have
been borrowed by the Byzantine Church from the Greek Liturgy of
St. James, where it is found in tenth-century texts. [13]   It must have
become part of the Byzantine Liturgy about the same time. [14]   In

---

[10] Thus, the Liturgy of St. John Chrysostom translated by Leo Thuscus
(c. 1200) does not; nor does the Erasmian recension of it, contained in Goar,
Euchologion; and neither does the great Greek liturgist of the fourteenth century,
Nicolas Cabasilas (1371).   On the other hand, the *Constitution* of the Liturgy in
the thirteenth century *Typikon* of S. Sabba, *Cod. Athono-Protat.*, 72 (A. Dmitrievsky, *Opysanie liturgicheskikh rukopisej khraniaschikhv bibliotekakh pravoslavnago
vostoka*, Vol. III, *Tipika* [St. Petersburg, 1917], p. 119) does mention it at the
Alleluia chant; also Theodore of Andida in the thirteenth century (PG 140, 440 D).

[11] E.g., the early fifteenth-century *Liturgikon* of Isidore, Metropolitan of Kiev,
has this incensing; its rubrics are those of Philotheus (cf. *Cod. Vat. Slav.* N. 14,
fol. 128).

[12] Since Vatican II the diaconate may again become a permanent state.

[13] The Greek Liturgy of St. James, Vatican *rotulo* 2282 (edit. A. Rocchi, in
A. Mai, NPB, X, ii, p. 47).

[14] It is found in the eleventh century Liturgy of St. John Chrysostom in *Codex
Burdett-Coutts* III, 42 (edit. C. A. Swainson, *The Greek Liturgies Chiefly from
Original Authorities* [London, 1884], p. 117).

many churches of the Byzantine Rite, however, there was no prayer before the Gospel till the fourteenth century. [15] But in many places where, during these centuries a pre-Gospel prayer was said, it was this same one; [16] in others, it differed. [17]

The Slav recensions show a similar diversity from the twelfth to the fourteenth centuries. [18] The Bulgarian version of the *Constitution* of Philotheus has the prayer as it is today, while its Greek original, as already noted, does not. However, the Kievan version of the same *Constitution* omits it as does the Greek original. [19]

Moments like the *Alleluia* chant represent the ultimate in liturgical participation. With everyone actively taking part—the priest saying

[15] Cf. *Codex Barberini*, gr. 336 (Brightman, LEW, p. 314); the Liturgy of Chrysostom trans. by Leo Thuscus, *Liturgiae Sive Missae SS. Patrum Iacobi Apostoli et fratris Domini, Basilii Magni, e vetusto codice Latinae translationis, Ioannis Chrysostomi, Interprete Leone Thusco* (Antwerp, 1562), p. 55; the Erasmian recension of the same Liturgy (twelfth century) in Goar, *Euchologion*, p. 105; the twelfth century MS. *Burdett-Coutts*, I, 10 (Swainson, *op. cit.*, p. 148; the *Ordo* of the Liturgy in Cod. 381 of Moscow Synodal Library (Krasnoseltsev, *Materialy dlja istorii chinopslidovania liturgii sv. Ioanna Zlatoustago* [Kazan, 1889], p. 24); also the *Constitution* of Philotheus, Patriarch of Constantinople (1354-1376), edit. N. Krasnoseltsev, *op. cit.*, p. 56.

[16] In the thirteenth century Liturgy contained in MS. N. 719 of Patmos Library (Dmitrievsky, *op. cit.*, Vol. II, *Euchologia* [Kiev, 1901], p. 173); in the *Typikon* of S. Sabba, *Cod. Ahono-Protat.*, N. 72 (Dmitrievsky, *op. cit.*, II, p. 266, and III, p. 120). Thus the Liturgy of St. Basil trans. into Latin by Nicolas Hydruntinus (edit. F. J. Mone, *Lateinische und griechische Messen aus dem 2.-6. Jh.* [Frankfurt, 1850], p. 139), though here this prayer is found at the beginning of the Liturgy together with some other prayers, perhaps a sign that such a prayer was elective.

[17] E.g., the thirteenth or fourteenth century MS. of Esphigmenon Library (Dmitrievsky, *op. cit.*, II, p. 266), and the fourteenth century MS. N. 345 of Moscow Synodal Library (Gorsky-Nevostrujev, *Opysanie slavianskikh rukopisej Moskovskoj Synodal'noj biblioteky*, Vol. III [Moscow, 1859], I, p. 21).

[18] Compare, for example, the fourteenth century MS. N. 347 of Moscow Synodal Library (Gorsky-Nevostrujev, *op. cit.*, III, 1, 14) and the fifteenth century MS. N. 530, p. 37, MS. N. 533, p. 26 of Sophia Library (Petrovsky, *Histoire de la rédaction slave de la liturgie de S. Jean Chrysostome*, XPYCOCTOMIKA [Rome, 1908], p. 902) with MS. N. 529, p. 48, MS. N. 574, p. 58 of Sophia Library (Petrosvky, *op. cit.*, p. 902) and the thirteenth century MS. *Vat. Slav.* No. 9 (O. Horbatsch, *De tribus textibus Liturgicis Linguae Ecclesiasticae (Palaeo) Slavicae in Manuscriptis Vaticanis* [Rome, 1966], p. 129).

[19] For the Bulgarian version, prepared by Archbishop Euthymius of Tirnovo (1375), cf. Krasnoseltsev, *op. cit.*, p. 55, n. 1. The Kievan version is contained in the *Liturgikon* of Patriarch Cyprian (1380-1407) preserved in Codex N. 344 of Moscow Synodal Library (Krasnoseltsev, *op. cit.*, p. 55.) Nor is a pre-Gospel prayer contained in the fourteenth or fifteenth century *Liturgikon* of Isidore, Metropolitan of Kiev, cf. MS. Vat. Slav. N. 14, fol. 8.

the pre-Gospel prayer, the deacon incensing, the cantors singing the verses from the psalms while the people sing the Alleluia as a refrain—all are joined together in one collective act of worship, in one mighty crescendo of harmonious, united adoration of the Almighty.   Almost nineteen hundred years ago, Clement of Rome had written to the Corinthians: ". . . we are obliged to carry out in fullest detail what the Master has commanded us to do. . . . He has ordered the sacrifices to be offered and the services to be held, and this not in a random and irregular fashion, but at definite times and seasons. He has, moreover, himself, by his sovereign will determined where and by whom he wants them to be carried out. . . . Special functions are assigned to the high priest; a special office is imposed upon the priests; and special ministrations fall to the Levites.   The layman is bound by the rules laid down for the laity. . . . " [20]   The Byzantine Church has, indeed, learned its lesson well.

---

[20] Pope St. Clement, *The Epistle to the Corinthians* (chap. 96), from *The Epistles of St. Clement of Rome and St. Ignatius of Antioch*, trans. by James A. Kleist, (*Ancient Christian Writers*, Vol. I [Westminster, Md. : 1946], 40).

CHAPTER XLIII

THE READING OF THE GOSPEL
AND THE HOMILY

The deacon approaches the priest, bows toward him and, holding his orar with his fingertips and pointing to the Gospel Book, intones :

Master, bless the one who goes to announce the Gospel of the holy Apostle and Evangelist N——.

While he blesses the deacon, the priest intones :

May God, through the prayers of the holy, glorious, and most praiseworthy Apostle and Evangelist N——, grant you the power of announcing his word with great strength for fulfilling your office of singing the Gospel of his well-beloved Son, our Lord Jesus Christ.

After showing reverence for the Holy Gospel with a small bow, the deacon takes it and, preceded by candlebearers who go out of the sanctuary through the side doors of the iconostas, goes through the royal doors to stand at the ambo (or before the royal doors) for the reading of the Gospel. He places the Gospel Book on the analoj *(lectern) and stands facing the people. The priest, who is standing before the holy table but facing the congregation, intones :*

Wisdom! Let us stand straight to listen to the Holy Gospel. Peace be to all!

People : **And to your spirit.**

Deacon : **The reading of the Holy Gospel according to N——.**

People : **Glory be to you, O Lord, glory be to you** *(they cross themselves).*

Priest : **Let us be attentive.**

The deacon then chants the Holy Gospel. When the Gospel reading is finished, the priest says to the deacon :

Peace be to you, who have announced the good tidings.

And the people sing the response :

Glory be to you, O Lord, glory be to you *(they cross themselves).*

The deacon returns to the sanctuary through the royal doors and gives the closed Gospel Book to the priest, who kisses it and places it either in the center or on the right side of the holy table.

All the Churches of Christendom have always shown great reverence for the Gospel of Christ, but the Syro-Byzantine family has given it exceptional honor.   Christian antiquity took special pains to copy the Gospel Book with all possible splendor, not infrequently doing it entirely in gold or silver script on purple vellum and binding it in costly covers of gold or silver metalwork or carved ivory, adorned with jewels.   This tradition is preserved in the Byzantine Rite where the Holy Gospel Book, one of the most beautiful objects in the church, is carried in solemn procession at the Little Entrance during every Liturgy. [1]   It is still regarded as the symbol of Christ himself.   At synods and councils, it was placed on a throne or on the altar. [2]

Likewise, in Byzantine churches, it is in the place of honor, the front center of the altar (which in turn is the symbol of Christ's throne in heaven), the very place where his most precious body and blood repose during the Divine Sacrifice.   For nine hundred years, the only things permitted on the altar, even in the Latin Rite, were the Blessed Sacrament and the Holy Gospel Book. [3]   At present, in the Byzantine Rite, nothing may be placed on the altar except what is necessary for the Divine Liturgy.   Candlesticks are excluded in those churches where the seven-pronged candelabrum is placed *behind the altar*.   No flowers, artificial or natural, are permitted. Since Vatican II, the Latin Church is reverting to this ancient practice.

The liturgy itself bears all the marks of special reverence due to the Holy Gospel.   In processions, the clergy highest in rank should come last.   Likewise, the Gospel is the final reading in every Rite,

---

[1] Also at Solemn Matins, at the solemn procession around the church on the feast of the parish patron, etc.

[2] E.g., Cyril of Alexandria († 444), speaking of the third Ecumenical Council of Ephesus, says that when " the holy synod met together at the church, it conferred on Christ, as it were, the position of member and president of the council. Indeed the venerable Gospel was placed upon a sacred throne " (*Apol. ad Theodos. imper.* [PG 76, 471]).   Since Cyril's time this has become the customary practice.

[3] Cf. Leo IV († 855), PL 115, 677.

a custom probably dating back to Apostolic times. When Augustine said, " We should listen to the Gospel as though God himself spoke to us, " he expressed the opinion of all Christendom.

The Gospel, like the other lessons, was read originally by the lector. [5] Cyprian (A.D. 258), explaining his reason for conferring the order of lector on Celerinus, a man who had been tortured for the faith and still bore the scars of his ordeal, said : " Should he not be placed in full view on the ambo... so that, raised up on this higher place and shown to the people in honor of his fame, he may read the precepts and Gospel of the Lord, which he has always observed with courage and fidelity? May the voice that has confessed the Lord be heard speaking every day the things the Lord has said.... No one is better able to read the Gospel to his brethren than a confessor, because all who hear him can set forth his faith as an example to themselves...." [6]

Gradually, however, this sense of the Gospel's importance led to the idea that its reading should be reserved to the higher ministers. By the beginning of the fifth century, in most places it had become the deacon's prerogative. [7] In the Latin Church, at the ordination of a deacon, this privilege had not been expressed during the first ten centuries, nor is it in any of the Eastern ordination rites today. Yet, the tradition is wholly in accord with the deep reverence shown to the Gospel in all the Church's Rites. In fact, it could not have been long after the deacons assumed the duty of reading the Gospel that other members of the higher clergy began doing so. Sozomen (fl. 439-450), for example, tells us that in Constantinople the bishop read the Gospel on Easter day; in Alexandria, the archdeacon; and " in other places, deacons read the Gospel, in many churches priests only. " [8] In Jerusalem, at least, on Sundays, the function was reserved to the bishop. [9] An interesting custom arose in the Western

---

[4] *Tract 30 in Joan.* (PL 35, 1633).

[5] Justin, *First Apology*, chap. 67.

[6] Cyprian, *Ep.* 34 (PL 4, 323).

[7] Thus, the *Apostolic Constitutions* (Book II, lvii, 7, see p. 145); St. Jerome (*Ep.* 147, § 6 [PL 22, 1200]); *Testamentum Domini* (1. I, 27, edit. I. E. Rahmani, *Testamentum Domini Nostri Jesu Christi* : Mainz, 1899, p. 58 [59]), etc.

[8] *Hist. eccl.*, VII, 19 (PG 67, 1477 A). During Chrysostom's time at Constantinople it seems that the Gospel was read by the celebrant; cf. Socrates, *Hist. eccl.*, VII, 5 (PG 67, 745 CD).

Church at the Christmas midnight Mass when the Roman emperor stood in full regalia to sing the Gospel. This was probably inspired by the first line of the Gospel of this Mass : " At that time, there went forth a decree from Caesar Augustus. . ." [10]

Another mark of honor shown directly to the Gospel Book is the practice of bearing lighted tapers, or candles, before it (indirectly this mark of honor is shown to Christ himself, whom the Gospel Book symbolizes). As soon as the Gospel Book is taken by the deacon and carried to the *analoj*, the candlebearers march out through the side doors of the iconostas and take their place at his right and left. Many of the faithful also stand with lighted candles during the Gospel reading. This practice reaches back into Christian antiquity, for in the fourth century, St. Jerome testified that such a custom was common to all the Oriental Churches even on the brightest day. [11] Besides honoring the word of God, it gives an air of joy to the whole proceedings, a joy expressed more palpably to the senses while all listen to the " glad tidings. " This liturgical usage was no doubt borrowed from secular custom. Lighted torches were an honor especially reserved to the emperor under the Antonines; from imperial honors, this privilege passed to other officials of the empire, more specifically, to judges when exercising their duties. [12] Since Constantine's time, bishops were authorized to give judgment in certain cases; such authority was confirmed in A.D. 408. A bishop, therefore, going to court (the basilica) to sit in judgment was preceded by servants carrying the *liber mandatorum* (book of law) and four lighted torches or candles. Gradually, perhaps imperceptibly at first, these privileges passed from the judicial sphere to the liturgical. The book of the Gospels was substituted for the *liber mandatorum*. It was then but a step to transfer the honors from the person of the bishop to the Gospel Book itself and to the Supreme Judge whom the book symbolized.

[9] *Aetheriae Peregrinatio*, chap. 24, 10 (CSEL, XXXIX, 73 f.).

[10] E.g., thus, Emperor Charles IV at Basle in 1347, at Mainz in 1353, and at Cambrai in 1377; Emperor Sigismund at Constance in 1414; Frederick III at Rome in the presence of Pope Paul II, etc.; see L. Biehl, *Das liturgische Gebet für Kaiser und Reich.* pp. 100 f.

[11] Jerome, *Contra Vigilantium*, chap. 7 (PL 23, 346).

[12] Cf. E. G. C. Atchley, *A History of the Use of Incense in Divine Worship* (London, 1909), pp. 55 f.

The Gospel of Christ was held in such high esteem that some time before the Council of Orange in A.D. 441, the idea arose that the Gospel was too sacred to be heard by ears other than those of the faithful, for this council decreed that catechumens were not to be excluded, implying that a contrary custom had arisen. [13] Similar attempts must have been made later, for the Roman baptismal rite as revised in the sixth century puts the Gospel in the same category as the sharing of the confession of faith and the Lord's Prayer, traditionally withheld from the uninitiated by the *disciplina arcani*. There seems to have been no such extreme in any of the Eastern Churches. The traditional rule of the Church from the earliest times certainly was to the follow Lord's advice : " Go ye into the whole world and preach the gospel to every creature. He that believeth and is baptized shall be saved " (Mark 16:15-16). This idea is vividly expressed in the Byzantine-Slav Rite, during the Easter Sunday Liturgy, when the Gospel is sung in several languages, usually five or six.

The deacon seeks a blessing from the celebrant to perform his mission : " Master, bless the one who goes to announce the Gospel of the holy Apostle and Evangelist N——. " In the Byzantine Church, this custom dates back at least to the twelfth or thirteenth century, since it occurs in the manuscripts of this period. [14]

The celebrant invests the deacon with the mission of proclaiming the Holy Gospel, not only by blessing him but also by giving him the

---

[13] Canon 18 (Mansi, *Sacrorum conciliorum nova et amplissima collectio*, Vol. VI, 439). Later councils enacted similar legislation.

[14] Cf. A. Dmitrievsky, *Opysanie liturgicheskikh rukopisej khraniaschikhsia v bibliotekakh pravoslavnago vostoka*, Vol. II, *Euchologia* (Kiev, 1901), p. 141; Goar, *Euchologion*, pp. 102, 105; also Krasnoseltsev, *Materialy dlja istorii chinopslidovania liturgii sv. Ioanna Zlatoustago* (Kazan, 1889), pp. 24-25, 44.

In the Slav Church, the fourteenth or fifteenth century *Liturgikon* of Metropolitan Isidore has the blessing in very simple form : after the deacon asks for it, the priest says : " May God, through the prayers of the holy Apostle, Evangelist N—— grant you the power of announcing with great strength " while he imparts the blessing to the deacon; cf. MS. *Vat. Slav.* No. 14, fols. 128-129. The blessing of the deacon is similar in the fourteenth century *Cod. Vat. Slav.* No. 9 : " May the Lord, King of (his) beloved (Son's) powers, grant to those who are announcing the power of announcing with great strength, through the prayers of the holy Apostles and Evangelists, Matthew, Mark, Luke, John, and all the other holy Apostles. " Cf. O. Harbatsch, *De tribus textibus Liturgicis Linguae Ecclesiasticae (Palaeo) Slavicae in Manuscriptis Vaticanis* (Rome, 1966), p. 130.

book of the Gospels. The priest prays that the deacon announce the good tidings with great strength as the Apostles did, referring to Acts 4:33. This sending forth of the deacon by the celebrant is the literal answer to St. Paul's question : " How can there be preachers unless preachers are sent on their errand? " (Rom. 10:15).

A hushed reverence for the words of the Gospel is enjoined by the acclamations and the celebrant's exhortation as he turns to the congregation and says : " Wisdom! Let us stand straight to listen to the Holy Gospel. "

It is not known precisely when these words were introduced into the Byzantine Liturgy, but they may have originated in fourth-century Syria. Among the directions given by the author of the *Apostolic Constitutions*, Book II, is the rubric : " While the Gospel is being read, all the priests, deacons, and people should stand up in great silence for it is written, ' Be silent and hear, O Israel, ' and ' But do thou stand there and hear. ' " [15] From rubrical direction to textual incorporation is but a step. [16] The early eighth-century Armenian version of Chrysostom's Liturgy has nearly identical words : " Wisdom. Let us stand straight. Listen to the Holy Gospel with fear. " [17] The pre-Gospel blessing, " Peace be to all, " may also reach back to fourth-century Syria. Brightman's reconstruction of the Liturgy at Antioch from Chrysostom's writings puts such a blessing before the homily. [18] This was done in Constantinople certainly before the middle of the seventh century. Maximus indicates its position there at the time. [19]

Standing for the Gospel reading was not the only mark of respect

---

[15] *Apostolic Constitutions*, Book II; cf. above, p. 145.

[16] E.g., the acclamation " The Doors, the doors "; see below, p. 537.

[17] Cf. Catergian-Dasian, *Die Liturgien bei den Armeniern* (Vienna, 1897), pp. 362-363; also the Erasmian recension of Chrysostom's Liturgy (Goar, *Euchologion*, p. 105) and that translated by Leo Thuscus (c. 1200, Paris edit. pp. 55 ff.). Silence and attention was enjoined before the Gospel in the Latin Mass up to the seventh and eighth centuries with the words, *State cum silentio audientes attente*, or with some similar formula; cf. Atchley, *Ordi Romanus Primus* (London, 1905), 76.

[18] Cf. Brightman, LEW, p. 470; for the Pontic Liturgy, see Gregory Nazianzen, *Or.* XXII, I (PG 35, 1131 A).

[19] Maximus, *Quaestiones et dubia*, 68 (PG 90, 849 A) and *Mystagogia*, 12 (PG 91, 689 D). Still, it seems not to have been general practice in the whole Byzantine Church, for many later sources omit it.

accorded to the words of Christ; everyone stood bareheaded; [20] even the emperor took off his crown, [21] and bishops their miters (a practice still observed in the Byzantine Rite).

The responses of the faithful, " Glory to Thee, O Lord, Glory to Thee, " before and after the Gospel are related to the idea that the Gospel Book represents Christ. They are also cries of joy and praise to the Master, who has revealed himself to mankind. This formula dates back to the eighth century and is often found in later codices. [22] The server's reply in the Latin Mass, *Gloria tibi, Domine* (Glory to Thee, O Lord) and *Laus tibi, Christe* (Praise to Thee, O Christ), are the Western parallels to the Byzantine pre-and post-Gospel acclamations; they have been added to the Latin Mass rather late and could be due to Byzantine influence, since the older answers in the Latin Church were *Amen*, [23] *Deo gratias*, and even *Benedictus qui venit in nomine Domini*. [24]

After the Gospel is read, the deacon closes the Gospel Book and takes it to the celebrant to be kissed. [25] This is to indicate how precious and sweet the contents of the Gospels are. It is an act expressing in deed the thought of the psalmist : " More to be desired

---

[20] *Apostolic Constitutions*, Book II, 57 (Quasten, *Monumenta eucharistica et liturgia vetustissima* [Bonn, 1935-1937], 182); Sozomen, *Hist. eccl.*, VII, 19 (PG 67, 1477 A); Philostorgius, *Hist. eccl.*, III, 5 (PG 65, 485 AB).

[21] In the West this was paralleled by the kings and queens of France who took off their crowns.

[22] E.g., the eighth century Byzantine Armenian Liturgy of St. John Chrysostom (Catergian-Dasian, *op. cit.*, p. 363); the Erasmian recension of the same Liturgy (Goar, *Euchologion*, p. 105); the same Liturgy translated by Leo Thuscus (c. 1200; Paris edit., p. 56); the *Constitution* of Philotheus (edit. Krasnoseltsev, *op. cit.*, p. 56); etc.

[23] Beleth, *Rationale*, 39 (PL 202, 48); Durandus, *Rationale*, IV, 24, § 30; St. Benedict's Rule, XI.

[24] Durandus, *op. cit.*

[25] If any higher prelates, e.g., bishops, are present, custom dictates that the Gospel Book be taken to them also to be kissed. The Latin Rite has a parallel practice. The Latin practice of taking the Gospel Book to the people to be kissed, recounted by *Ordo Rom.* II, n. 8 (PL 78, 972 B), and popular for a time, especially in the countries of the North, was forbidden by Honorius III in 1221 and was restricted only to those anointed as priests, bishops, and kings (A. Potthast, *Regesta pont. Rom.*, I [Berlin, 1874], p. 573). A similar practice was prevalent in most of the Ruthenian churches (and still is in many), though not after the Gospel reading but during the Little Entrance. The " new " rubrics for the Divine Liturgy issued during the liturgical reform of 1944 are silent on the point but their very silence would seem to intimate that such a practice is to be abolished.

than gold and many precious stones (are the words of the Lord) and sweeter than honey and the honeycomb " (Ps. 18:11).

The history of the Gospel lections and their arrangement is almost the same as that of the Epistle readings (see pp. 418f., 421, above). The present cycle of Gospel pericopes certainly dates back to the eighth century and probably earlier. With a few exceptions, all four Gospels are read through completely at least once during the liturgical year at the Divine Liturgy; the exceptions mostly consist in Gospel pericopes for the great holy days and those describing the passion and death of the Lord (these latter, however, are read during the *Service of the Holy and Redeeming Sufferings of Our Lord Jesus Christ*, the special Matins for Good Friday). Beginning with Easter Sunday, the Gospel of St. John is read until Pentecost Sunday : the remaining chapters are read (*a*) during the Divine Liturgy on Lazarus Saturday (Saturday before Palm Sunday) and on Palm Sunday itself, (*b*) during the Service of the Holy and Redeeming Sufferings of Our Lord, i.e., Matins for Good Friday, and (*c*) during those times when any of the last five of the eleven regular resurrectional Gospels for Sunday Matins is read. The outline below illustrates not only how the whole Gospel of St. John is read during the year but also when its component pericopes are used (the numbers in parentheses indicate the order for continuous reading) :

Period	Pericope	Period	Pericope
(1) Easter Sunday John .	1:1-17	(18) Wednesday	6:35-40
(2) Easter Monday . . .	1:18-28	(19) Thursday	6:40-44
Easter Tuesday-exception		(20) Friday	6:48-55
(3) Wednesday	1:29-51	(45) Saturday . . 15:12-27, 16:1-2	
(6) Thursday	3:1-15	(11) 4th Sunday, after Easter,	
(5) Friday	2:12-22	i.e., Sun. of the Paralytic	
(8) Saturday	3:22-36	Man	5:1-15
(55) ⌠2nd Sunday, after Easter, i.e.,		(21) Monday	6:57-70
⌡St. Thomas Sunday .	20:10-31	(22) Tuesday	7:1-13
(4) Monday	2:1-11	(23) Wednesday	7:14-44
(7) Tuesday	3:16-21	(25) Thursday	8:12-20
(12) Wednesday	5:17-24	(26) Friday	8:21-30
(13) Thursday	5:25-30	(27) Saturday	8:31-42
(14) Friday . . . 5:30-47, 6:1-2		(9) 5th Sunday after Easter,	
(16) Saturday	6:14-27	i.e., Sunday of Samar-	
3rd Sunday after Easter, exception i.e., Ointment-bearing Women		itan Woman	4:5-42
		(28) Monday	8:42-51
(10) Monday	4:46-54	(29) Tuesday	8:51-59
(17) Tuesday	6:27-33	(15) Wednesday	6:5-14

Period	Pericope	Period	Pericope
(31) Thursday . .	9:39-41, 10:1-9	(34) Saturday before Palm	
(32) Friday	10:17-28	Sunday	11:1-45
(33) Saturday	10:27-38	(36) Palm Sunday . . .	12:1-18
(30) 6th Sunday after Easter,		(39, 40) Holy Thursday at	
i.e., Sunday of Man		Liturgy	13:3-17
Born Blind	9:1-39	Good Friday Matins	
(35) Monday	11:47-56		
(37) Tuesday	12:19-36	(41) First Gospel John .	13:31-50
(38) Wednesday . . .	12:36-47	(42, 43, 44) First Gospel	14 complete
Ascension exception		(45) First Gospel . .	15 complete
(42) Friday	14:1-11	(46, 47, 48) First Gospel	16 complete
(43) Saturday	14:10-21	(49, 50) First Gospel .	17 complete
(49) 7th Sunday after Easter		(51) First Gospel	18:1
i.e., Sunday of the Holy		(51) Second Gospel . . .	18:1-28
Fathers	17:1-13	(52) Fourth Gospel 18:28-40, 19:1-16	
(44) Monday . . .	14:27-31, 15:1	(53) Ninth Gospel . . .	19:25-37
(46) Tuesday	16:2-13	(54) Eleventh Gospel . .	19:38-42
(47) Wednesday	16:15-23	Sunday Matins, Eleven Resurrectional	
(48) Thursday	16:23-33	Gospels	
(50) Friday	17:1, 18-26	(55) Seventh Gospel John .	20:1-10
(58) Saturday	21:15-25	(56) Eighth Gospel John	20:11-18
(24) Pentecost Sunday . .	7:37-52	(57) Ninth Gospel . . .	20:19-31
(37, 38) Wednesday before		(58) Tenth Gospel . . .	21:1-14
Palm Sunday	12:17-50	(59) Eleventh Gospel . .	21:15-25

Aside from an occasional final verse of a chapter, only a few passages from the entire Gospel are unaccounted for, namely, John 8:1-12, 13:18-30, and 19:17-24. Several Gospel passages, however, are duplicated (e.g., those indicated above by nos. 37-38, 42-51, 55, 58). The Gospels of the other evangelists are read in a similar way. Without going into detail, we may mention that from Pentecost to Palm Sunday the entire Gospels of Matthew, Luke, and Mark are read in more or less this sequence : from Pentecost Monday to the Monday of the week preceding the twelfth Sunday after Pentecost, St. Matthew's Gospel (also on Saturdays and Sundays of the following six weeks); from Monday of the week preceding the Twelfth Sunday after Pentecost to the Monday of the week preceding the eighteenth Sunday after Pentecost, the Gospel of St. Mark during all weekdays (i.e., except Saturdays and Sundays); from the Monday of the week preceding the eighteenth Sunday after Pentecost to the Monday of the week preceding the thirtieth Sunday after Pentecost (and on Saturdays and Sundays of the following five weeks); from the Monday of the week preceding the thirtieth Sunday after Pentecost to Cheese Fare Week, i.e., the week preceding Lent, St. Mark's Gospel again on all weekdays (except on Saturdays and Sunday). The remaining passages of these three Gospels are read during Cheese Fare Week and Lent until Palm Sunday, as well as during the Good Friday Matins and those times when any of the first six of the regular eleven Resurrectional Gospels are read. Like the Gospel of St. John, the other three are read through completely during the liturgical year in a more or less continuous order (see table, p. 422).

The Ukrainian or Russian peasant, even if illiterate, knew the contents of the Bible by the truly remarkable use of the Scriptures in his parish church—not only the New Testament, but also the Law (the Pentateuch) and the Prophets, read during solemn Vespers and Matins on Sundays and holy days. These latter services were known and loved by lay people no less than by monks, as is evident even today in the immigrants who without any special training or ability can sing almost all of these services from memory! The word of God is indeed a seed of life, which brings forth the fruits of salvation a hundredfold. Like the Eucharist, so the Gospel words are " the spirit and the life " (John 6:64). Jesus never spoke abstractly, nor did he present doctrinal definitions to the ordinary people of his day. He always spoke in parables, he told them stories illustrating his revolutionary doctrines. He told them of the merciful, charitable Samaritan and his Jewish enemy, or he contrasted the poor, humble publican with the haughty, race-proud Pharisee. Instead of speaking abstractly of repentance, he told them the story of the forgiving, loving Father and his prodigal but repentant son. That is why he could capture the attention of his audience and they would listen enthralled, understand his lessons and forget little. He does no less today through his Liturgy.

The Homily

The sermon preached after the Gospel lesson is no more an interpolation than are the lessons themselves, for it reaches back to the Jewish Sabbath service of the synagogue where there was always an explanation of the Scriptures just read. The Lord himself took

ANNUAL CYCLE OF EPISTLES

	Week	Monday	Tuesday	Wednesday	Thursday	Friday	Saturday	Sunday	
								Acts	Easter
PASCHALTIDE	1st	Acts	Acts	Acts	Acts	Acts	Acts	"	
	2nd	"	"	"	"	"	"	"	
	3rd	"	"	"	"	"	"	"	
	4th	"	"	"	"	"	"	"	
	5th	"	"	"	"	"	"	"	
	6th	"	"	"	"	"	"	"	
	7th	"	"	"	"	"	"	"	Pentec.
TIME AFTER PENTECOST	1st	Eph.	Rom.	Rom.	Rom.	Rom.	Rom.	Hebr.	
	2nd	Rom.	"	"	"	"	"	Rom.	
	3rd	"	"	"	"	"	"	"	
	4th	"	"	"	"	"	"	"	
	5th	"	"	"	"	"	"	"	
	6th	"	I Cor.	I Cor.	I Cor.	I Cor.	"	"	
	7th	I Cor.	"	"	"	"	"	"	
	8th	"	"	"	. "	"	"	I Cor.	
	9th	"	"	"	"	"	"	"	
	10th	"	"	"	II Cor.	II Cor.	"	"	
	11th	II Cor.	II Cor.	II Cor.	"	"	I Cor.	"	
	12th	"	"	"	"	"	"	"	
	13th	"	"	"	"	"	"	"	
	14th	"	"	"	Gal.	Gal.	"	II Cor.	
	15th	Gal.	Gal.	Gal.	"	"	"	"	
	16th	"	"	"	Eph.	Eph.	"	"	
	17th	Eph.	Eph.	Eph.	"	"	"	"	
	18th	"	"	"	"	"	"	"	
	19th	Phil.	Phil.	Phil.	Phil.	Phil.	"	"	
	20th	"	"	"	"	"	II Cor.	Gal.	
	21st	"	Col.	Col.	Col.	Col.	"	"	
	22nd	Col.	"	"	"	"	"	"	
	23rd	I Thess.	I Thess.	I Thess.	I Thess.	I Thess.	"	Eph.	
	24th	"	"	"	"	"	"	"	
	25th	II Thess.	II Thess.	II Thess.	II Thess.	II Thess	Gal.	"	
	26th	I Tim.	I Tim.	I Tim.	I Tim.	I Tim.	"	"	
	27th	"	"	"	"	II Tim.	"	"	
	28th	II Tim.	II Tim.	II Tim.	I Tit.	I Tit.	Eph.	Col.	
	29th	Heb.	Heb.	Heb.	Heb.	Heb.	"	"	
	30th	"	"	"	"	"	"	"	
	31st	"	"	James	James	James	Col.	I Tim.	
	32nd	James	James	"	"	I Pet.	I Thess.	"	
PRE-FAST	33rd	I Pet.	I Pet.	I Pet.	I Pet.	II Pet.	II Tim.	II Tim.	
	34th	II Pet.	II Pet.	II Pet.	I John	I John	"	I Cor.	
	35th	I John	I John	I John	"	II John	I Cor.	"	
	36th	III John	Jude	a-lit.	Jude	a-lit.	Rom.	Rom.	
LENT	1st	a-lit.	a-lit.	Pre sanct.	a-lit.	Pre sanct.	Heb.	Heb.	
	2nd	"	"	"	"	"	"	"	
	3rd	"	"	"	"	"	"	"	
	4th	"	"	"	"	"	"	"	
	5th	"	"	"	"	"	"	"	
	6th	"	"	"	"	"	"	Phil.	Palm Sunday
Holy	Week	Presanctified		Gifts	I Cor.	a-lit.	Rom.		

such an opportunity to preach to the people at Nazareth (Luke 4: 16-30; Mark 6:2-4); Paul and Barnabas similarly preached after the lessons in the synagogue at Antioch in Pisidia (Acts 13:14-47).   In the primitive Christian assemblies, Justin tells us, on Sundays after the reader finished the lections, " the one presiding gives a speech in which he admonishes and exhorts (all) to imitate these beautiful teachings. " [26]   In his sermons Origen constantly says : " Let us attend to what has been read, " [27] and the very contents of his homilies prove that the sermons followed the lessons. [28]   The great Augustine indicated the same in one of his sermons when he said : " First we have heard the lesson from the Apostle.... After that the lesson from the Gospel showed us the ten lepers healed. " [29] Others—for example, Clement of Alexandria, Tertullian, the author of the *Apostolic Constitutions* (Book II), and Cyprian—leave no doubt whatever that the sermon followed the readings in the early Christian synaxis. [30]   In short, all early evidence indicates that the bishop's sermon was indeed an integral part of the synaxis; in fact, without it the service was considered liturgically incomplete.   Pre-Nicene Christians everywhere believed that the bishop received a special gift *(charisma)* at his consecration to fulfill his office of preacher. Preaching sermons was regarded as much a bishop's " special liturgy" as was his offering of the Eucharistic Sacrifice.   In the third century, at a synaxis in Caesarea, Origen scandalized the faithful because he was not a bishop and yet dared to preach! [31] That he did so at the invitation of the local bishop seems to have made no difference.   In Hippo, in North Africa, as late as the close of the fourth century, the people were indignant because their aged bishop had delegated the faculty to preach at the synaxis to St. Augustine who was not then a bishop.   After the downfall of Arius,

[26] Justin Martyr, *First Apology*, chap. 67.

[27] E.g., *In Gen. homil.*, I, 17 (PG 12, 160).

[28] *In Gen. homil.*, x, 1 (PG 12, 215); *In ex. homil.*, VII, 8 (PG 12, 349); *In Lev. homil.*, IV, 9 (PG 12, 444), etc.

[29] *Sermo clxxvi*, I (PL 38, 950).

[30] Clement of Alexandria, *Strom.*, 6, 14 (PG 9, 337); Tertullian, *De praescript.*, 36 (PL 2, 49); *Apostolic Constitutions*, Book II (cf. above, p. 145); Cyprian, *De mortalitate*, 1 (Hartel 1, 297).

[31] Cf. O. Bardenhewer, *Geschichte der altkirchlichen Literatur* (2nd edit.; Freiburg, 1914), II, pp. 108 f.

priests were forbidden to preach in Alexandria and North Africa. [32]
This condition prevailed until the beginning of the fifth century.
For a long time, Rome and Italy had similar regulations. [33] We
should remember that almost every town was a bishopric at the time.
Such restrictive measures prove the strong conviction of the people
regarding the bishop's gifts in fulfilling his "special liturgy" of
preaching. In the Eastern Church, it showed itself in a different
way : while the practice of having more than one preacher at the
Sunday synaxis was common by the fourth century, the bishop
always spoke last because he was seen as the voice of authentic
teaching in matters of faith. This liturgical teaching authority, or
office, was even more vividly expressed in another custom : the
bishop always preached from his *cathedra*, his seat of authority. [34]
There was a rule in the Egyptian Church that the bishop, while
preaching, was to hold the Gospel Book in his hand—another sign
of his special authority. Judging from ancient Byzantine icons of
holy bishops and confessors, it seems that such a practice was not
limited to Egypt. [35]

Everywhere in the ancient Church the sermon was considered as
much a part of the service as were the readings. The sermon's
proper liturgical place is immediately after the Gospel. In the Latin
rite, many regarded the sermon as an interpolation rather than an
integral part of the Liturgy. This may be due to the pre-Vatican II
tendency to regard as non-liturgical anything in the vernacular, any
more or less extemporaneous text, anything that was not standard
and invariable. In the primitive Church, however, even the anaphora, the canon of the Mass, was more or less extemporaneous, and
certainly far from "standardized" (see above, p. 55).

[32] Socrates, *Hist. eccl.*, V, 22 (PG 67, 640); Sozomen, *Hist. eccl.*, VII, 19 (PG 67, 1476 f.).

[33] This is evident from the letter of disapproval sent from Rome to the bishops of Provence, where priests were beginning to preach (Celestine I, *Ep.* 21, 2 (PL 50, 528-530).

[34] This, of course, was true of both the Eastern and the Western Church. Chrysostom, however, preached from the ambo, a course of action dictated more by practical considerations than by any other. Similar considerations probably induced the present practice of bishops preaching from the *amvon*.

[35] In modern times, Byzantine bishops hold the pastoral staff (crozier) while they preach. This, again, is a sign of authority.

CHAPTER XLIV

THE INSISTENT *EKTENIA*

fter the sermon, the royal doors are closed. [1] *Going out of the sanctuary, the deacon takes his usual place before the royal doors, and begins the Insistent Ektenia :*

Let us all say with our whole soul and with our whole mind, let us say :

People : **Lord, have mercy.**

Deacon : **Lord almighty, God of our fathers, we beseech you, hear us and have mercy.**

People : **Lord, have mercy.**

Deacon : **Have mercy on us, O God, according to the greatness of your mercy; we beseech you, hear us and have mercy.**

People : **Lord, have mercy. Lord, have mercy. Lord, have mercy.**

In the meantime the priest recites the following prayer in a low voice :

O Lord, our God, accept this earnestly repeated supplication from your servants, and have mercy on us according to the greatness of your mercy. Send your compassion upon us and upon all your people who are expecting from you the riches of your mercy.

The deacon continues :

Again let us pray for His Holiness, our Universal Pontiff N——, Pope of Rome, for our Most Reverend Archbishop and Metropolitan N——, for our God-loving Bishop N——, for those who labor and serve in this holy church, for our spiritual fathers and all our brothers in Christ. [2]

---

[1] In many of the Ruthenian churches, however, the royal doors are not closed at this point.

[2] When the Divine Liturgy is celebrated in monasteries, the foregoing petition reads : " Again let us pray for His Holiness, our Universal Pontiff N——, Pope of Rome, for our Most Reverend Archbishop and Metropolitan N——, for our God-loving Bishop N——, for our Very Reverend Fathers, the Protoarchimandrite N——, the Archimandrite N——, the Protohegumenos N——, and the Hegumenos N——, for those who labor and serve..., etc. "

People : **Lord, have mercy. Lord, have mercy. Lord, have mercy.**

Deacon : **Let us pray for our sovereign authorities and for all the armed forces.** [3]

People : **Lord, have mercy. Lord, have mercy. Lord, have mercy.**

Deacon : **Again let us pray for the people here present who expect from you great and abundant mercy, for those who have given us offerings and for all orthodox Christians.**

People : **Lord, have mercy. Lord, have mercy. Lord, have mercy.**

Priest : **For you are a merciful God and the Lover of mankind, and we give glory to you, Father, Son, and Holy Spirit, now and always and for ever and ever.**

People : **Amen.** [4]

Translating the Greek ἐκτενὴς δέησις (or ἐκτενὴς ἱκεσία) or the Slavonic *suhuba ektenia* as *double* or *twofold ektenia* could induce a wholly erroneous concept of this beautiful chain of petitions. Rendering them as *redoubled ektenia*, in the sense of repeating or re-echoing, would be much more desirable and correct in that, after the first two petitions, all the responses " Lord, have mercy" are repeated three times. Such a rendering would also have the added

---

[3] This petition may also be : " For our God-protected Emperor (*or* King) N—— " etc., depending on the type of government in a given country.

[4] After the first three petitions, the Russian Catholic recension of the *Insistent Ektenia* varies considerably : while the responses of the faithful are the same, the deacon's petitions are as follows :

" Again let us pray for His Holiness, our Universal Pontiff N——, Pope of Rome, for our Most Reverend Archbishop (*or* bishop) N——, and for all our brothers in Christ.

" Again let us pray for our sovereign authorities and for all the armed forces (*or* For our God-protected Emperor——).

" Again let us pray for our brother priests and monks, and for all our brothers in Christ.

" Again let us pray for the blessed and ever-remembered founders of this holy church (*or* monastery), and for all our orthodox fathers and brothers who are gone before us and who are laid to rest here or elsewhere.

" Again let us pray for our benefactors, for those who bring offerings to this holy and venerable church, for those who labor in its service, the singers and the people present here who expect from you great and abundant mercy. "

The doxology is the same as that of the Ruthenian recension.

merit of suggesting the redoubled fervor urged on the congregation
by the exhortations of the deacon. That may be the reason why
this *ektenia* is also known as the *Ektenia of Fervent Supplication*.
We have translated the title of this *ektenia* as *insistent* because its
introductory petitions do indeed express persistence, urgency, and
pressing need. The threefold responses are a sign of this insistent
intensity designed to compel divine attention. The first three supplications introduce the rest of the petitions with a magnificent
crescendo of insistence, urgency, and desperation which culminates
in the threefold cry for mercy by the people or *ecclesia*.

In the first supplication, the deacon urges the people to pray with
their whole soul and mind, that is, with their whole being. There
is, however, deeper meaning in the words " soul and mind. " One
of the main ascetic principles of the early Byzantine era must be
taken into consideration : intense inner discipline was required of
every person in the struggle against the passions, a struggle which
numbered among the inner foes all " cogitations, both sinful and
neutral, " i.e., the whole contents of the " psychic " against the
" pneumatic " life of thought and heart. In short, spirit against soul.
The deacon's exhortation urges all to pray with their whole " har-
monized inner being, " that is, with their whole consciousness
emptied of all extraneous contents, even " neutral cogitations. " The
second petition is a direct appeal to the Omnipotent Lord. The God
who spoke to Moses, the transcendent, almighty God, whose worship
early Byzantine piety borrowed from Judaism.

The expression " God of our fathers " is typically Judaic. [5] The
early Byzantine Christian oscillated between fear and hope, between
the God of Mercy and the God of Justice, as this petition shows.
The third introductory supplication also reveals its Jewish character
in that it repeats the purely Judaic expression, *O God, according to
the greatness of your mercy.* [6]

---

[5] E.g., the beginning of Jewish *Berakha* in the Prayer of the Eighteen Benedictions : " Blessed be thou, O Lord God of our Fathers. "

[6] In the *Morning Service*, in the prayers on entering the synagogue, Adler
translates it, " O God in the multitude of thy mercy, " a translation much more
akin to the original Slavonic and Greek expressions. In fact, the Greek and
Slavonic are literal translations of the Hebrew. Cf. Adler, *Service of the Synagogue*,
New Year (New York : Hebrew Publishing Co.) p. 25, for original.

The celebrant's prayer, prayed silently during the recital of the *Insistent Ektenia,* appears to be a type of the ancient prayer-collect in that it is a summary of the preceding intercessions by the deacon and people. Judaic influence shows itself here as it did in the introductory supplications, especially in phrases like " O Lord, our God. . . ; according to the greatness of your mercy; the riches of your mercy, " etc. Though the actual date of its composition is an open question, both the prayer-collect form and its Judaic expressions would suggest a date hundreds of years before it first appears in the Barberini text of the eighth century, perhaps as early as the pre-Nicene era. This introduction, revealing as it does Judaic and early Byzantine characteristics, can without doubt be numbered among the oldest parts of the ancient " common prayers " after the readings in the Christian service (see, pp. 41 f., 63).

The introduction itself is lengthy when compared to the small number of petitions which follow : there are today three introductory supplications and three petitions comprising the *Insistent Ektenia.* This lengthy introduction alone suggests how truncated the present *ektenia* has become. Its former length, aside from historical evidence, can be deduced by combining all the *ektenias* found now in the other parts of the Divine Liturgy and inserting them here, which was their original place, or perhaps more correctly after the Ektenia of the Catechumens and their dismissal. The Dismissals and prayers of the *Apostolic Constitutions* (Book VIII) are representative of the fullest development of these post-Gospel intercessions and, as a mediate antecedent, they also serve to illustrate what this *ektenia* had been before most of its petitions were shifted to the other parts of the Divine Liturgy. The actual length and content of the universal prayer of intercession (and of its dismissal) in the primitive Church are unknown, but there can be little doubt that even the earliest Christian synaxis ended with it [7] as the Jewish synagogue

---

[7] Besides Justin Martyr (chaps. 65 and 67 of his *First Apology,* cf. above, 41 f.), Hippolytus refers to it (*Trad. Apost.,* edit. Dix, pp. 29, 60), Cyprian indicates it (*communis oratio, De dom. or.,* chap. 8, in CSEL, III, 271), as well as Origen ("let us arise and pray, " *In Num. homil.,* xx., 5 [PG 9, 660 A : *Series graeca*]); likewise the sermon in the African Church during Augustine's time often ended with " Turn to the Lord, " i.e., to the East, for a prayer (*Ep. 55,* 18, 34 [CSEL, XXXIV, 209]); also Sarapion, *Euchologion,* which has a prayer " after the rising up from the sermon " (n. 20, cf. above, p. 91); etc.

service, on which the Christian synaxis was modeled, ended with the *Shemoneh Esreh* and the final prayer-blessing (cf. above, p. 32).

When Justin mentions this prayer of intercession in the 67th chapter of his *First Apology*, he merely states : " We all then stand up together and recite a prayer " without giving a hint of its content. In the 65th chapter, he gives but slightly more information : "... (we) say earnest prayers in common for ourselves, for the newly-baptized, and for all others all over the world, so that we who have come to the knowledge of the truth may also by the grace of God be found worthy to live a good life by deed and to observe the commandments by which we may gain eternal life. " Since he calls these prayers χοινάς, or " common, " this seems to indicate that either the entire community said the same formula in unison or that it took up, phrase by phrase, the prayer which was being said by the celebrant. No other second-century writer sheds any light on the matter. As already seen, Clement's famous prayer (chaps. 59 and 61 of his *Epistle to the Corinthians*) may have been just such a common prayer at the end of the Christian synaxis (see above, p. 34 ff.).

It is believed that, before the invention of the *ektenia* in the fourth century, the subject or petition of this " common prayer " was announced by the celebrant and that the congregation was invited to pray at a signal from the deacon (probably, " Let us bend the knee "). The people would then kneel and pray in silence. After a moment's prayer, the deacon or subdeacon would tell the congregation to rise and the celebrant would announce another petition, and so on. Such a practice is still found in the Roman Liturgy in the prayers of Good Friday (see above, p. 412). Later, the invitation to prayer and the " bidding " passed from the celebrant to the deacon. These prayers are very ancient : Not only are they found in the oldest Sacramentaries : they also name the *confessores* after the clergy—which indicates that they belong to the time of persecutions, when witnesses to the faith enjoyed the rights and privileges of clerics. [8] These prayers, though probably dating from the fourth or fifth century in their present form, could be similar

---

[8] Hippolytus, *Apostolic Tradition* (edit. Dix, 18 f.) and Baumstark, *Missale Romanum. Seine Entwicklung, ihre wichtigsten Urkunden und Probleme* (Eindhoven-Nijmegen, 1929), p. 20.

to those used in the third century. They begin with a petition for the Church, " that our Lord and God be pleased to keep her in peace, unity and safety throughout all the world. " The next petition is for the Pope, the bishop, the clergy and rulers, for the catechumens, for all who are in danger and tribulation. The last are for heretics and schismatics, for the Jewish people and pagans.

We already have had occasion to point out another instance which is thought to contain elements of the pre-Nicene common intercessions; this is the very ancient litanic (prelitanic?) form of prayer in the Alexandrian Liturgy (see above, p. 361 n. 5). Both the Roman Good Friday Prayers and the Alexandrian are similar in form and, to a certain extent, in content also. Both may serve as examples of what these common intercessory prayers in the synaxis may have been before the very full developments of the fourth-century Syrian Church and the invention of the present form of the *ektenia*. The similarity between the Roman and Alexandrian prayers seems to indicate that the pre-Nicene petitions were substantially the same in both East and West. Their position in the Divine Liturgy did not vary either. One of their characteristics was that they were offered by the whole *ecclesia* as a corporate act, with each " order, " the celebrant (bishop or priest), the deacon, and the laity actively discharging their distinctive function.

Before the end of the fourth century, the different Churches began to use different variants in their intercessory prayers. The transference of the petitions themselves from their position after the sermon to the anaphora (i.e. of those parts of the petitions which are now embodied in the text of the anaphora) as well as the development of the *ektenia* as such in the Antiochene Church, certainly played the most important, if unwitting, part. [9]

By the end of the fourth century, there had already developed an elaborate system of dismissals in which the more recent form of intercessory prayer, the *ektenia*, played a vital role. According to the *Apostolic Constitutions* (Book VIII), this system consisted in four sets of dismissals, set up according to definite, plans (see above, pp. 109-118). The first set of dismissals, for example, begins with the

[9] The veil screening off the sanctuary from the sight of the congregation may also have played an indirect part.

deacon bidding the catechumens to kneel; then he announces a series of petitions for their intention; in answer to each petition the congregation prays, " Lord, have mercy. " Besides answering this, the catechumens took no active part. When the *ektenia* is finished, the deacon bids them to bow for the bishop's blessing (a rather lengthy prayer), and finally they are told to depart. A similar plan is followed for other categories of people : those possessed of evil spirits, those who have almost finished their preparation for baptism, and the penitents. Because of the elaborateness of such a system, we may be inclined to believe that the compiler of the *Apostolic Constitutions* imagined most of it. Such a practice, however, obtained in the Antiochene Church and probably also in the Cappadocian Church. Chrysostom, in homilies he preached in Antioch, leaves little doubt, at least as regards the first half of the petitions. Neither do the Canons of the Council of Laodicea (*c.* A.D. 363) referring to the Church of Asia. [10] In the Cappadocian Church (*c.* A.D. 270-275), after the sermon, it was the ἀκροώμενοι, " hearers, " who were first dismissed but without a prayer, [11] then the catechumens, the χειμαζόμενοι, " energumens "; [12] finally, the ὑποπίπτοντες, " kneelers, " were told to depart after a prayer. [13] After that, came the prayers of the faithful, followed by the " bidding " of the deacon. [14]

There was a subtle difference between the older form of intercession and the newer. The former had the people praying in silence, the latter has them answering, " Lord, have mercy, " aloud. While originally the celebrant offered a summary prayer or collect after each petition, he now does so only after or during a series of

---

[10] From Canon 19, we know that the sermon was followed by a prayer for the catechumens and their departure; this in turn was followed by a prayer for the penitents, who received a blessing before their departure; finally, the three Prayers of the Faithful were recited (NPNF, Series, II, Vol. XIV, p. 136).

[11] Gregory the Wonderworker, *Ep. can.*, 11 (PG 10, 1048 AB).

[12] In Canon 17 of the Council of Ancyra, the dismissal of the *energumens*, though not specifically mentioned, can safely be assumed, since the Canon mentions their presence at the service before this; cf. NPNF, Series II, Vol. XIV, p. 70.

[13] Gregory the Wonderworker, *loc. cit.*; though he does not tell us the relative order of the dismissals, See also St. Basil, *Ep.* 217, 56, 75 (PG 32, 697 A, 804 AC); Gregory of Nyssa, *De bapt. Christi* (PG 46, 421 C).

[14] Cf. Canon 2 of the Council of Ancyra, which states that one of the duties of a deacon is " to make proclamations " (Κηρύσσειν), lit. " to act the herald "; cf. NPNF, Series II, Vol. XIV, p. 63.

petitions. While the celebrant prayed *with* those who had been interceding, he now offers a single prayer-collect *for* them. Thus the *ektenia* was born. [15]

The *ektenia* never was a dialogue between the deacon and the people, nor is it today. The deacon for the most part speaks to the people (by proclaiming the subject for which to pray), while the people answer, not the deacon, but God.

In the old form of the petitions, the deacon's role was never that of an active intercessor (that was reserved to the celebrant and the people), whereas in the new form, the deacon does sometimes assume that role, for instance, in the first petition and the one near the end, " Help us, save us.... "

In the Ruthenian recension of the Byzantine-Slav Liturgy, only a few of the many original petitions remain. Those for the Church hierarchy and civil authorities have been left in at this point, while similar petitions for the hierarchy and civil rulers have been inserted in three other places.

Early Christians, despite the afflictions, sufferings, and tortures inflicted upon them by the state, always managed to embrace their civil rulers in the charity of their prayers. For hundreds of years, the Byzantine Christian held that the *basileus* was the model of devotion, and his palace, the focal point, not only of civil and social action, but also of ecclesiastical devotion. Praying for temporal and spiritual authorities was equally indispensable. Cabasilas writes : " And what prayer could be more fitting for all, after the Gospel, than one for those who keep the Gospel, who imitate the goodness and generosity of Christ, the shepherds of the people, those who govern the state. These, if they are faithful to the precepts of the Gospel, as the Apostle says, ' achieve after Christ that which is lacking in Christ, ' in governing his flock as he would wish.... " [16]

The divine origin of the princely power, based on biblical and patristic traditions, endowed the prince with great dignity and implied obedience to him as to a " minister of God " (Rom. 13:14).

---

[15] This is somewhat different, of course, from the intercessions inserted in the anaphora.

[16] Nicolas Cabasilas, *A Commentary on the Divine Liturgy*, chap. 23, trans. by J. M. Hussey and P. A. McNulty (London, 1960), p. 63.

Yet, the Byzantine political doctrine of sacred autocracy was not preached in early Kievan Russia-Ukraine, even by the Greek clergy. Political circumstances in the Slav state prevented any real " deification " of power. The *kniazy* or princes (translated by the Greeks as ἄρχοντες, rulers, commanders, governors—high officers of imperial administration) who ruled the Kievan lands enjoyed no such prerogative. Unlimited or autocratic power for the Russian tsar came much later.

The early Kievan Church demanded of temporal rulers obedience to religious and moral law; in fact, Kievan religious literature— what little there is left of it—is more concerned with having the princes obey the law than with having the people obey the princes. [17]

After spiritual and civil rulers, the same petition goes on to intercede " for those who labor and serve in this holy church. " [18] Cabasilas explains this as applying to " those who in any way contribute to the common good of the Church and of religion. " [19] Besides lectors and cantors (holding minor orders in the Byzantine Church), singers are included, and also all those who keep the churches clean and in good repair. In the Byzantine-Slav Church, such tasks are assigned to lay people, called *starshi bratia* (older brothers) and *starshi sestrychki* (older sisters). Their duties in addition to cleaning, include replacing burned-out candles, washing altar linens, polishing the metal utensils, etc. In earlier days, the *starshej brat* would also light the stove before the services. [20]

However, in many churches of the Ukraine and Russia there was

[17] Kievan chroniclers in general are very outspoken about the sins and vices of their princes. Some would even consider a revolt of citizens against their princes as an act of God's will, as the chastening providence of the Almighty (*Lavr.*, 1068). Perhaps the constitutional place of the *veche*, the people's assembly in the Kievan state, influenced this justification.

[18] The Russian recension has " for those who labor in its [the church's] service, the singers, " etc. (*Sluzhebnyk*, Rome, 1942, p. 225).

[19] *Op. cit.*, p. 63.

[20] An eighty-year old *starshej brat* in a country parish in eastern Saskatchewan used to walk five miles to church even during forty-five degree below-zero weather to perform his duties! A truly monumental feat when we remember that he had to get up at four-thirty in the morning in order to get to church two hours before the Liturgy began. When forbidden to do this during the severe winter weather (for fear of his freezing to death), he went off quietly by himself and wept.

no heating of any kind, even in the coldest winter weather. Bearing the cold was regarded as a form of penance. The *starshej brat* and *starsha sestra* parallel the faithful attendants who " served in the temple " at Jerusalem, such as Simeon and Anna, mentioned in the Gospel.

The petition goes on to pray " for our spiritual fathers. " The term " spiritual fathers " is unique to the Ruthenian recension. The Greek and Russian recensions have " for all our orthodox fathers, " which may not mean the same. The Ruthenian *ottets dukhovnej*, " spiritual father, " refers to anyone who has exercised the office of father confessor, although not necessarily to one with the power of sacramental absolution. An *ottets dukhovnej* could be a monk without sacred orders, to whom the laity went for spiritual direction and advice. Since all the known pre-Mongolian Eastern Slav monasteries were built in the immediate outskirts of towns, it seems that their primary role was religious guidance. [21] The Eastern Slav always seems to have unburdened his soul to a monk in preference to a secular priest. The inspiration for this sincere trust in the monk is epitomized by Dostoevsky in the remark of Father Zossima, the *staretz* of Alyosha Karamazov, who talked to the peasants, to the poor and forsaken : " The Russian monk has always been on the side of the people. " Deeper than that, however, reverence and filial trust for the monks was engendered by the various authors of early Russian-Ukrainian " admonition literature. " The *Admonition of the Father to His Son*, for example, exhorts :

> " My son... have recourse to them [the monks] and they will comfort you; shed your sorrows before them and you will be gladdened; for they are sons of sorrowlessness and know how to comfort you, sorrowing one.
>
> "...seek a God-fearing man... and serve him with all your strength. After finding such a man, you need grieve no more; you have found the key to the Kingdom of Heaven; adhere to him with soul and body; observe his life, his walking, sitting, looking, eating, and examine all his habits; first of all, my son, keep his words, do not let any of them fall to the

---

[21] Later when the totally contemplative spirit was developed in Russia and the Ukraine, monks did seek isolation from the world in forests, in underground cells, etc., far from the turmoil of the world.

ground; they are more precious than pearls... the words of the saints. " [22]

Simple Slav people took such advice eagerly to heart, and accepted the monk as " spiritual father. "

The petition continues, " For all our brothers in Christ. " Inherited from the Byzantine Liturgy (which in turn had obtained it from earlier Christian sources), this phrase is colored with a special meaning for the Ukrainian and Russian, embracing all fellow Christians and ultimately all fellow men in kinship. This sense of common origin or common blood imparts a certain warmth, a certain family tenderness in human relationship. Kinship names are continually on the lips of the Russian and Ukrainian peasants, even in addressing strangers. The appellations " father, " " grandfather, " " uncle, " " brother " (and the corresponding feminine designations) are chosen in accordance with the age or degree of moral and social importance of the person addressed. In this light, all social life can be said to have been shaped as the extension of family life, and raised to the level of blood kinship. This gens-ethic stems back to the pre-Christian Kievan era when the *rod* (*gens*, or even Celtic *clan*) was a vital social reality related to the worship of the minor gods, the dead. The founder of the *rod*, the ancestral chief, was always a special patron of the house and as such was called " house-spirit " (*Domovoi*). [23] Another manifestation of this feeling for the *rod* is found among the Russian and Balkan Slavs in that they have preserved the use of patronymic names. Of the two personal names which every Russian has, for example, the second is a derivative from his father's; i.e., if my father's name was Ivan and mine was Vladimir, I would be called Vladimir Ivanovich. In the gens-ethic of the *rod*, Christianity had fertile soil for its doctrine of brotherhood in Christ.

Between this petition and the next, the celebrant may, if he wishes, insert the *ektenia of special petitions*; that is, a group of supplications for special intentions.

---

[22] Translation from G. P. Fedotov, *The Russian Religious Mind* (New York : Harper Torchbook edit., 1960), p. 215.

[23] Remains of the pagan belief in the *Domovoi* could still be found among the Russian peasants of the last century.

Then comes the general petition for the attendance : " Again let us pray for the people here present who expect from you great and abundant mercy, for those who have given us offerings. "

The meaning of this petition is obvious. The Slav caritative ideal is perhaps best seen in the very word *mylostynia* (giving of offerings, almsgiving), the root of which is *myslost* (love). *Mylostynia*, in fact, literally means a manifestation of love, kindness. In addition to the offerings or charitable acts, there must be also inner love, a feeling of tender compassion for the recipient. The " love duties " so frequently stressed in the early religious literature of ancient Kiev are very clear on this point. The author of the *Hundred Chapters*, for example, after urging his readers to feed the hungry, to visit the sick and imprisoned, adds " and sigh as you witness their distress. " After reminding them to care for the sick, he emphasizes that " when he (the sick man) is moaning with pain, you must shed tears of compassion " (chap. 61).

CHAPTER XLV

THE DISMISSAL
OF THE CATECHUMENS : ITS ORIGIN

*D*eacon : **Catechumens, pray to the Lord.**
People : **Lord, have mercy.**
Deacon : **Let us, the faithful, pray for the catechumens, that the Lord have mercy on them.**
People : **Lord, have mercy.**
Deacon : **That he instruct them in the word of truth.**
People : **Lord, have mercy.**
Deacon : **That he reveal to them the Gospel of righteousness.**
People : **Lord, have mercy.**
Deacon : **That he unite them to his holy, catholic, and apostolic Church.**
People : **Lord, have mercy.**
Deacon : **Save them, have mercy on them, help and protect them, O God, by your grace.**
People : **Lord, have mercy.**
Deacon : **Catechumens, bow your heads to the Lord.**
People : **To you, O Lord.**

While the deacon and people sing the Ektenia *of the Catechumens, the priest says the Prayer for the Catechumens :*

O Lord, our God, you who dwell on high and still look upon the lowly; who sent forth your only-begotten Son, our Lord and God, Jesus Christ, as the salvation of mankind : look down upon your servants, the catechumens, who bow their heads before you. In due time make them worthy of the waters of regeneration, the forgiveness of their sins, and the robe of immortality. Unite them to your holy, catholic, and apostolic Church, and number them among your chosen flock.

Then he continues aloud :

That with us they also may glorify your most honorable and magnificent name, Father, Son, and Holy Spirit, now and always and for ever and ever.

People : **Amen.**

The deacon finally pronounces the dismissal :

All catechumens, go out! Catechumens, go out! All catechumens, go out! Let not one of the catechumens remain![1]

How did the various dismissals originate? Probably when the Liturgy of the Word, the synaxis, was still an independent entity and usually separated from the Eucharist, the whole proceedings ended with the common, intercessory prayers. Later, however, when the synaxis was often if not always joined to the Eucharistic celebration, attended by the faithful, the *ecclesia* alone, the problem arose as to whether those who were not full members of the *ecclesia* (those not baptized or those who could not receive Communion) should be allowed to participate actively in the formal prayers of the faithful.[2] This question was raised not so much because of the *disciplina arcani* which arose in the third century and lasted only a comparatively short while, but because of the sound Christian feeling that the most sacred things of the *ecclesia* should not be heard by profane ears nor seen by profane eyes. One of these sacred things was the common intercessory prayer of the faithful. The idea won out that those not entitled to full membership be dismissed before it,[3] although in some Eastern Churches the catechumens apparently were allowed to remain for it.[4]

---

[1] Since Vatican II, the whole *ektenia* of the catechumens and its prayer (together with their dismissal) are omitted by the Ruthenians.

[2] Distinguished from non-supplicatory types of prayers, such as singing of the psalms, glorification of God, etc.

[3] In the Pontic Church of the third and fourth centuries, for example, not only the catechumens but also the penitents were dismissed; cf. Gregory the Wonder-Worker, *Ep. can.*, 11 (PG 10, 1048 AB); Basil, *Ep.* 217, 56, 75 (PG 32, 697 A, 804 C); Gregory of Nyssa, *De baptismo Christi* (PG 46, 421 C). Other Churches had similar dismissals, but the Syrian had the most developed form (cf. *Apostolic Constitutions*, Book VIII; see above, p. 109-118).

[4] See Sahidic *Canones*, c. 64 f. (Brightman, LEW, p. 462; cf. *ibid.*, p. 461); also the *Canones Basilii*, c. 97 (edit. Rahmani, *I fasti della chiesa patriarcale Antiochena* [Rome, 1920], p. xv).

The beginnings of the formal dismissals consisted in a prayer and blessing by the celebrant—sometimes in the form of a "laying of the hand" on each person individually, [5] but mostly on a group. [6] Outside the area of Syrian influence, the dismissals affected only the catechumens and the penitents, [7] or the catechumens alone, as in the West, where penitents were generally allowed to remain in silence during the Eucharistic Liturgy. [8]

The catechumenate and the public penitential system, [9] in the third and fourth centuries, were responsible for the embellished forms of dismissals in the Syrian Church—and they were elaborate (see above, pp. 109-118). They survived the changes brought about by Chrysostom's predecessor, Patriarch Nectarius, in A.D. 391, [10] and lasted as late as A.D. 520. The Syriac documents published by Nau bear ample proof that the dismissal of penitents continued in Syria and Constantinople even after A.D. 530. [11]

In most Churches, the dismissal-formula of the catechumens survived long after the disappearance of the catechumenate, and have lasted even to this day in the Byzantine Liturgy (except, as noted,

[5] E.g., Canon 19 of Council of Laodicea (NPNF, Series II, Vol. XIV, p. 136). The catechumens are to go "under the hand" (ὑπὸ χεῖρα) of the bishop, after the prayer offered for them (cf. Brightman, LEW, p. 518).

[6] E.g., Sarapion, *Euchologion*, no. 21 f. (edit. Funk, *Didascalia et Constitutiones Apostolorum* [Paderborn, 1905], Vol. II, pp. 158 ff.).

[7] In fourth century Asia Minor, Council of Laodicea, Canon 19 (NPNF, Series II, Vol. XIV, p. 136).

[8] Cf. H. Koch, "Die Büsserentlassung in der alten abendländischen Kirche," (*Theol. Quartalschr.*, LXXXII [1900], pp. 481-534). The only exception for the West seems to be Canon 29 of the Epaon synod which legislates that penitents were to leave with the catechumens (Mansi, *Sacrorum conciliorum nova et amplissima collectio*, VIII, 562).

[9] The Church historian, Socrates states that the penitential system was established in the Church during the Novatianist controversy of the third century; its object was to direct penitents regarding the exercises required of them when they repented (*Hist. eccl.*, V, 19 [PG 67, 614]); also Sozomen, *Hist. eccl.*, VII, 16 (PG 67, 1457).

[10] According to Sozomen, Nectarius abolished the penitential system and "bishops everywhere followed his example." Cf. *Hist. eccl.*, VII, 16 (PG 67, 1457).

[11] F. Nau, "Littérature canonique syriaque inédite," in *Revue de l'Orient chrétien*, XIV (1909), 46-68. In the sixth century in the West, the *Dialogues* (ii, 23) of Gregory the Great contain what appears to be a vestige of a dismissal for penitents : " if there be anyone who does not communicate, let him depart " (*si quis non communicet, det locum*).

in the Ruthenian Rite since Vatican II). At the other extreme, in Rome, the dismissal formula and its prayer vanished completely from the Mass at a very early period, perhaps immediately after the disappearance of the catechumenate. [12]

After the sixth century, probably few catechumens remained in Byzantium. Their dismissal would then have ceased to have any real importance. Yet, St. Maximus the Confessor (A.D. 662) mentions the practice of dismissal and expulsion, not only of the catechumens, but also of all the other people who were unworthy to attend the Eucharist. [13] Historical sources show that they obeyed. [14]

Today's formula of dismissal can be traced back to the eighth-century Byzantine-Armenian Liturgies of Sts. Basil and Chrysostom.[15] The eleventh-century formula, similar to that of today, contain no dismissals of penitents or of any other class except the catechumens. [16] At that time, however, there could hardly have been question of any actual departure of anyone, even the catechumens. Present day *Liturgika*, both Greco-Byzantine and Byzantine-Slav, contain the complete, unabridged formula of the dismissal for the catechumens, but such a dismissal is an anachronistic formality. The Greeks often omit it, especially on weekdays, but the Slavs have kept it, [17] with the exception noted above.

If the dismissal may be done away with, the prayers for the catechumens should be maintained. Not only does the need to pray for candidates to the Church remain unchanged, but the prayers themselves are far from anachronistic.

[12] Elsewhere in the West, i.e., in Gaul, Spain, North Africa, and Milan, the dismissals survived longer. The seventh century *Expositio* of the Gallican Liturgy still has a litany-like prayer and collect for the catechumens as well as their dismissal.

[13] *Mystagogia*, chap. 14 (PG 91, 692 D-693 B).

[14] *Ibid.*, chaps. 13, 15, 23, 24 (PG 91, 692 B, 693 BC, 700 B, 704 B). From his *Scholia in Ecclesiasticam Hierarchiam* (chap. III, iii, iii [PG 4, 141 C]), however, we must conclude that all of them were *collectively* dismissed and not each class individually.

[15] Catergian-Dasian, *Die Liturgien bei den Armeniern* (Vienna, 1897), pp. 192, 365; cf. also G. Aucher, *La versione armena della liturgia di S. Giovanni Crisostomo, fatta sul principio dell'VIII secolo*, XPYCOCTOMIKA, p. 382.

[16] The Liturgy of St. John Chrysostom, contained in *Codex Burdett-Couttss* III, 42 (edit. C. A. Swainson, *The Greek Liturgies Chiefly from Original Authoritie*, London, 1884), p. 120).

[17] Cf. A. Kyprian, *Evkharistia* (Paris, 1947), p. 189; A. King, *The Rite of Eastern Christendom* (Rome, 1948), p. 178.

In the *ektenia,* the deacon first exhorts the catechumens to prayer : " Catechumens, pray to the Lord. " This is good theology and expert psychology. Without prayer, no one can be saved, much less experience true conversion. He who prays much with sincerity is psychologically disposed to receive it. Presumably, the catechumens are to pray silently, since the rest of the *ektenia* applies to the faithful alone, as indicated in the *Apostolic Constitutions,* Book VIII (cf. above, p. 109). The present Byzantine dismissals have borrowed from the fourth-century Syrian Liturgy, not only their form, [18] but also the petitions of the *ektenia,* although they are fewer than in the *Apostolic Constitutions.*

Present Form of the Ektenia	*Excerpts from the Apostolic Constitutions*
Catechumens, pray to the Lord.	Ye catechumens, pray.
Let us, the faithful, pray for the catechumens, that the Lord have mercy on them.	Let us all earnestly pray to God that he who is good and the lover of mankind will mercifully hear their prayers and supplications.
That he instruct them in the word of truth.	That he may instruct and teach them wisdom.
That he reveal to them the Gospel of righteousness.	That he reveal to them the Gospel of his Christ.
That he unite them to his holy, catholic, and apostolic Church.	That he unite and number them with his holy flock.

The celebrant's prayer for the catechumens differs, but contains a number of identical ideas and phrases.

Present Form of the Prayer	*Excerpts from the Apostolic Constitutions*
O Lord, our God... you who sent forth your only-begotten Son ... Jesus Christ, as the salvation of mankind, look down	O almighty God... God the Father of your Christ, your only-begotten Son... who through Christ didst appoint

---

[18] I.e., exhorting the catechumens to pray (which they do in silence), the *ektenia* of the catechumens (the deacon announces the petitions and the faithful answer " Lord, have mercy "), the celebrant's prayer for them, and the actual words of dismissal.

upon your servants, the catechumens, who bow their heads
before you. In due time make
them worthy of the waters of
regeneration....

your disciples to be the teachers
of piety, do you now also look
down upon your servants who
are being instructed in the
Gospel of your Christ, and give
them a new heart and renew
within their bowels a right
spirit....

Unite them to your holy,
catholic, and apostolic Church
and number them among your
chosen flock.

Grant them a holy admission
and unite them to your holy
Church, and make them partakers of your divine mysteries....

In both Liturgies, the prayer is addressed, not to Christ, but to
God the Father, and both contain prayer-blessings before the
actual dismissal. Another prayer that closely parallels the present
Byzantine prayer for the catechumens is that of the *Apostolic
Constitutions* for those to be illumined (see above, p. 114 f.).
Both classes were preparing for baptism, and the same scriptural
texts were used.

After exhorting the faithful to pray for the catechumens, that God
instruct them in the word of truth and reveal to them the gospel of
righteousness, the deacon begs them to pray that God unite them
to his holy, catholic, and apostolic Church. It not enough for
salvation to have the mind enlightened and to learn the truth, for
as St. James says, "...faith without works is dead" (James 2:26).
Additional grace is needed to move the will to act, to receive baptism.

The catechumens are told to bow their heads to the Lord and the
celebrant recites the prayer-blessing over them. Reciting verses five
and six from Psalm 112, he implores God the Father who looks down
upon the lowly to look down upon the catechumens who have their
heads bowed to him. God gives grace more abundantly to the
humble and lowly than to the proud and exalted. The grace be-
seeched again is the waters of regeneration, that is, baptism and all
that it implies, forgiveness of sins, the robe of immortality or sanctifying grace, and membership in Christ's Church. The four marks
of the true Church are mentioned specifically. The faithful are *united*
in the *holy, catholic* and *apostolic Church*. God's chosen flock is *one*,
for a flock cannot be said to be one flock if the members composing

it differ in faith, worship or government.   Only that Church can be called *holy* which teaches a holy doctrine in faith and morals, has a founder who is holy and enables its members to lead a holy life. Only that Church is *catholic* which is truly universal in time, place, and doctrine.   Finally, only that Church is *apostolic* which is histori- cally joined to the apostles and has maintained the doctrine, sacra- ments, and tradition they had established or kept.   It is to this Church, the only true one bearing the four marks, that the celebrant begs God unite the catechumens.

At present, the words of dismissal must be understood spiritually. Recalling Christ who drove out the disorderly, dishonest vendors from the Temple, everyone should drive out sinful, shameful, or excessive cravings, thoughts, and desires from the temple of his soul. In this sense, the words of the dismissal could be understood to mean, " All evil spirits go out (of my soul); evil spirits go out, all evil spirits go out; let not one of the evil desires remain. "   With his own temple emptied of evil, the man of faith is prepared to participate in the sacred acts which are about to begin, the Liturgy of the Faithful.   In ancient times, the *energumens* (those afflicted with an unclean spirit) were formally expelled.   Today, when hearing the words of the dismissal, we should expel all evil thoughts from our soul.

While pronouncing the dismissal, the celebrant unfolds the *iliton*. [19]   On this *iliton* the holy gifts will be placed, that is, the bread and wine after the Great Entrance (see, p. 491).

Liturgical texts place the rubric concerning the unfolding of the *iliton* immediately before the dismissal of the catechumens.   Logic- ally and historically, it belongs to the Liturgy of the Faithful, for it is essentially the " spreading of the tablecloth. "   As such, it is traceable not only to the pre-Nicene days of the Church, but to the very Apostolic era when the Eucharist was celebrated during the common meal.   In the early days, the tablecloth covered the whole table. [20]   When the people ceased to bring their offerings to church,

---

[19] The Greek *eileton*.   This is a square of linen serving, in the Byzantine Rite, the same purpose as a corporal in the Latin.

[20] E.g., in Africa, c. A.D. 360, cf. Optatus of Mileve, *De schismate Donatistarum*, VI, 2 (PL 11, 1068 A).

and the number of communicants began to fall, there was no longer any need for a large cloth. The smaller Eucharistic particles probably also resulted in the use of smaller cloths. In the West, the size of the corporal—the Latin counterpart of the *iliton*—was reduced only in the late Middle Ages : in the year 1000, it still covered the entire mensa. [21] At solemn papal Masses, it still covers the whole width of the altar. [22] The present *iliton* (Greek, είλετον) is nearly the same size as the corporal. The date of its reduction in size probably approximates that of the Latin. [23]

The unfolding of the *iliton* is an example of those many liturgical acts, practical in origin, and symbolical by later attribution. Theodore of Mopsuestia is the first to have seen here anything more than a tablecloth : he explains it as " the figure of the linen cloths at the burial of Christ. " [24] So does Pseudo-Germanus. [25] This meaning was accepted later by all liturgical commentators, even though the size of the cloth was reduced to such an extent that it can no longer be compared to a shroud.

[21] Cf. J. Braun, *Die liturgischen Paramente in Gegenwart und Vergangenheit. Ein Handbuch der Paramentik* (2nd edit., Freiburg, 1924), p. 206.

[22] It is spread out over the altar by the (Cardinal) deacon and subdeacon at the beginning of the offering of the gifts. Cf. Brinktrine, *Die feierliche Papstmesse*, p. 18.

[23] It is difficult to be precise regarding the dates. The process could have begun just before the eighth century, immediately after the prothesis rite had been transferred to the beginning of the Divine Liturgy and after the communion particles were being cut out of the *prosphoras*—there would no longer be any need for a large *eileton* on the holy table (altar). On the other hand, the regal ritual and great number of concelebrants at Hagia Sophia in Constantinople would not have been conducive to a significant reduction in the size of the *eileton* there until much later. This may have influenced the other Byzantine churches to keep the larger cloth, " as was done at the great Hagia Sophia, " longer than was necessary.

[24] *Catecheses*, V (edit. Mingana, *Commentary of Theodore of Mopsuestia on the Lord's Prayer and on the Sacraments of Baptism and the Eucharist* [Cambridge, 1933], p. 86).

[25] Migne, PG 98, 417.

LITURGY OF THE FAITHFUL : THE PRE-ANAPHORAL RITUAL

CHAPTER XLVI

THE INTERCESSORY PRAYERS OF THE FAITHFUL

The heart of the Liturgy of the Faithful is the Eucharistic Sacrifice, the greatest act of divine love that mankind has been privileged to witness, an act uniquely divine, which mortal mind can never adequately grasp because the boundless love which prompted it can never be understood completely.

The essence of the Liturgy of the Faithful—the offertory, transubstantiation, and communion—was instituted by Christ himself. Whatever has been added was an attempt by man, not to improve his perfect Sacrifice, but to adapt its meaning and reality to their own particular culture. The variety of cultures and races, the succeeding generations within them, are represented by the variety of Rites and by the differences of ritual within each Rite. Several major civilizations and empires, and countless lesser social groups that arose, flourished, and disappeared since the first Eucharistic Supper, have left their mark, but the essence, the meaning of the Eucharistic Sacrifice, remains the same for all people throughout the ages. The Eucharistic Sacrifice, like Christ himself, was and is all things to the *holy people of God*.

The Rites and rituals adorning the Eucharistic Liturgy are the form in which man's love for God is expressed in every way devised by human genius. In the Byzantine-Slav Liturgy, the evocative rituals of Antioch, Palestine, Cappadocia, Asia, and the Pontus are present with the incomparable richness of Byzantium. The Slavs have imprinted their spirit on that Liturgy by adding to it the beauty of their chants.

To the people of Russia and the Ukraine, the Eucharistic Liturgy is indeed " the Passover revealed; the Passover new and holy; the Passover mystical; the Passover all-august, Christ, the Passover and the Atonement; the spotless Passover; the great Passover; the Passover of the faithful; the Passover which openeth unto them the gates of Paradise; the Passover which sanctifieth all the faithful. " [1]   Indeed the Passover of infinite Love!

The deacon calls the faithful to prayer :

Deacon : **All we faithful, again and again in peace let us pray to the Lord.**

People : **Lord, have mercy.**

In the meantime the priest silently recites the First Prayer of the Faithful :

We thank you, Lord God of Powers, for having allowed us to stand now at your holy table and to fall down before your compassionate self for our sins and the errors of the people. Accept, O God, our supplication; make us worthy to offer you prayers and entreaties as well as the unbloody sacrifice for all your people.   By the power of your Holy Spirit, enable us, whom you have appointed to this your holy ministry, to call upon you without blame or offense and with our conscience as a clear witness at all times and in all places, so that in hearing us you may have mercy on us according to the abundance of your kindness.

Deacon : **Help us, save us, have mercy on us, and protect us, O God, by your grace.**

People : **Lord, have mercy.**

Deacon : **Wisdom!**

Priest : **For to you are due all glory, honor and adoration, to the Father, and to the Son, and to the Holy Spirit, now and always and for ever and ever.**

People : **Amen.**

---

[1] From Easter Matins, the first *tropar* or the Canticles (tone V).

Deacon : **Again and again in peace let us pray to the Lord.** [2]

People : **Lord, have mercy.**

The priest silently recites the Second Prayer of the Faithful :

Often and again we fall down before you and we beseech you, gracious Lover of mankind, that you regard our entreaty and cleanse our souls and bodies from all defilement of flesh and spirit. Grant us the grace to stand before your holy table without any blame or offense. God, grant also to those who are praying with us a betterment of life, faith, and spiritual understanding. Grant that they may always serve you with fear and love and that they may share in your holy mysteries without blame or condemnation and become worthy of your heavenly Kingdom.

Deacon : **Help us, save us, have mercy on us, and protect us, O God, by your grace.** [3]

People : **Lord, have mercy.**

Deacon : **Wisdom!**

Priest : **So that, ever protected by your might, we may give glory to you, Father, Son, and Holy Spirit, now and always and for ever and ever.**

People : **Amen.**

While the priest sings the doxology, the deacon bows and goes into the sanctuary through the north door.

There is no break between the Liturgy of the Catechumens and the Liturgy of the Faithful so that most liturgical books (*Sluzheb-*

---

[2] Since Vatican II, the Ruthenians omit everything between the two Prayers of the Faithful.

In the Russian recension, the deacon continues with the following *ektenia :*

" For peace from on high and the salvation of our souls, let us pray to the Lord.

" For the peace of the whole world, for the well-being of the holy churches of God and for the union of all, let us pray to the Lord.

" For this holy church, and for those who enter it with faith, reverence and the fear of God, let us pray to the Lord.

" For our deliverance from all affliction, wrath, and need, let us pray to the Lord. "

The people answer, " Lord, have mercy, " to each of these petitions. This *ektenia* is omitted if the Russian priest is celebrating without a deacon.

[3] Since Vatican II, the Ruthenians omit this petition and its response.

nyki, Liturgika) join the exhortation or " bidding, " " All we faithful again and again in peace let us pray to the Lord, " with the dismissal of the catechumens. If the exhortation is considered part of the dismissal formula, it loses all meaning and the original plan of the general intercessory prayers is distorted. Future editions of the official *Liturgikon* or *Sluzhebnyk* should make it clearly part of the Liturgy of the Faithful.

The original plan both of the dismissals and of the intercessory prayers of the faithful was as follows :

a. " Bidding " : " Let us pray to the Lord. "

b. Response : " Lord, have mercy. "

c. *Ektenia* or various petitions (to each of which the response was " Lord, have mercy). "

d. Prayer-blessing.

e. Dismissal formula (except for the faithful).

This plan can still be seen in the prayers of the faithful :

a. Bidding : " All we faithful, again and again in peace let us pray to the Lord. "

b. Response : " Lord, have mercy. "

c. Petition : " Help us, save us, have mercy on us, " etc.

d. Prayer of the priest (now prayed silently) and its concluding doxology.

When the priest celebrates without a deacon, this plan is less discernible, in that he recites the silent prayer *before* the *ektenia*-petition. When celebrating with a deacon, he recites the prayer assigned to him while the deacon intones the petitions of the *ektenia* (or what is left of them in the case of the Ruthenian Liturgy).

" All we faithful, again and again in peace let us pray to the Lord. " At this point in the ancient Liturgy, only the faithful, the members of Christ's body, were left in church, so the deacon bade them to renewed corporate prayer " in peace. " Peace was a prerequisite to the Holy Sacrifice : peace between its members, without rancor, without dispute, a harmonious unity of hearts and minds. The early Christian appreciation of the Church's unity as the body of Christ was intense; this explains the never-ceasing plea for peace of soul, peace among its members, peace among the Churches. Centuries of Christianization have not lessened the urgency of such a plea.

The first silent prayer, " We thank you, Lord God of Powers, " is said for the celebrating clergy. It is fundamentally a prayer of gratitude to God for two great privileges : that of allowing them to pray to God, and that of offering for the people the most holy Sacrifice—a privilege not accorded even to the greatest potentates on earth, but only to the ordained priest. This prayer is also one of sincere entreaty to make the celebrants worthy of what they are about to do.

Apocalypse 11:17 tells us of the four-and-twenty ancients who fell on their faces and adored God, saying, " We give thee thanks, O Lord God Almighty. " The influence of this passage on the first sentence of the prayers is clear : " Lord God Almighty " becomes the " God of Powers "; the four-and-twenty ancients falling on their faces before God correspond to " falling down before God's compassionate Self " the Slavonic has, " before his Compassions. " The sentence ends with the reason why the priest offers his prayer and sacrifice at the altar : " for our sins and the errors of the people. " This is the very reason why the high priest of the Old Dispensation offered sacrifice on the great Day of Atonement (Heb. 9:7). The comparison is significant. The emphasis is on the holiness of the ministry to be performed. Although priests of the Old Dispensation entered the Holy Place twice daily to offer incense, and at other times to perform the blood-ritual, change the shew-bread, etc., the high priest alone entered the Holy of Holies—and this only once a year—to sprinkle the propitiatory and sanctuary with the blood of the bull and goat which had been offered for his own errors (ignorances) and sins as well as for those of the people. [4] In contrast, priests of the New Dispensation are permitted to offer an infinitely more holy sacrifice, not that of blood but an unbloody one, the Sacrifice of the Son of God himself! That is why the first sentiments expressed by the clergy at the beginning of this Liturgy are those of profound gratitude.

After gratitude, their immediate concern is that God, by the power

---

[4] See below, p. 516, for Slav interpretation of ignorance.

of his Holy Spirit, make them worthy to perform this supremely holy office at all times and places without blame or offense, and, in the words of Paul to Timothy, " with a pure conscience " (I Tim. 3:9).

In the second prayer, similar but more urgent pleas are presented. " Regard our entreaty " is a phrase borrowed from Solomon's inaugural address at the dedication of the Temple (III Kings 8:28). Also borrowed is Paul's exhortation to the Corinthians that they cleanse " their being from all defilement of the flesh and the spirit " (II Cor. 7:1). Western theologians usually hold that sin defiles the soul alone. Western biblical scholars accordingly interpret Paul's cleansing from all defilement of flesh and spirit as implying guilt for participating in pagan worship and unchastity at Corinth. [5] Interpreted in the light of early Byzantine thought, the phrase in the liturgical text includes all kinds of sin which defile both soul and body. Much of the early Byzantine moral theology which the pre-Mongolian Novgorodian Church adopted was based on the old Jewish religio-physical principle : many sins defile the body as well as the soul, and therefore render the person unacceptable or unclean for sacred functions. Accordingly, the soul was cleansed when the moral fault was forgiven, but for the body's ritual uncleanness to be removed, ablutions were necessary, the prescribed time limits observed, etc. In this way the whole man was cleansed. Ritual uncleanness in the ancient Byzantine Church could also be incurred without moral fault. A mother, for example, giving birth to a child, a married priest engaging in legitimate marital relations, etc., would become ritually unclean. Such " defilement of the flesh " would entail no personal sin or moral fault; however, moral guilt or sin would be imputed to the person if he performed certain sacred actions or functions without first removing his ritual uncleanness. Many such religio-physical prescriptions and regulations date back to apostolic times and to the Jewish heritage. Their similarity is too great to be explained in any other way. If the meaning of Paul's cleansing from all defilement of flesh and spirit were not the same as that held by the early Byzantine Church, it could not have been

---

[5] *A Catholic Commentary on Holy Scripture* (New York : Thomas Nelson and Sons, 1960); " I and II Corinthians, " by W. Rees, p. 1105.

long before such an interpretation was adopted, certainly by the time this prayer was penned.

In the phrase, " those who are praying with us, " the priest clearly emphasizes his unity with the faithful, the people of God. Since the faithful will offer the divine Sacrifice together with the priest, they too must be accounted worthy to stand at God's holy altar. The holiness and worthiness of the Church depends to a large degree upon the holiness and worthiness of its members. The holier the Church, both clergy and faithful, the more pleasing to God will be their act of offering the Eucharistic Sacrifice; the greater their perfection and fervor, the more truly acceptable to God will their act of offering become. The object offered in this divine Sacrifice, Christ himself in the Eucharist, is infinite and therefore infinitely pleasing in itself to God, but the measure in which this Sacrifice by the priest and people will be acceptable to God will depend upon their personal holiness and fervor. The greater the saints and the greater their number in the militant Church which offers the Eucharistic Sacrifice, the more pleasing to God their act of offering. Many faithful seem to have lost sight of a great truth : a single Christian soul, the most humble child in the state of sanctifying grace will increase the Church's holiness and have an immediate influence on every Divine Liturgy celebrated throughout the world. That is why the priest prays in the name of the people for the grace of being cleansed from all defilement, of standing before God's altar without blame or offense, and for growth in spiritual understanding and faith. In becoming worthy to share in God's holy mysteries, in his Sacrifice, priest and people will become worthy of his heavenly Kingdom. Paul told the Thessalonians that, since their " faith groweth exceedingly and the charity of every one... towards each other aboundeth, " it is a clear indication of the " just judgment of God, " that is, that they will be judged " worthy of the Kingdom of God " (II Thess. 1:3-5).

In their present form, the Prayers of the Faithful are remnants of a lengthy series of intercessions, some of which found their way into other parts of the Divine Liturgy after the fourth century. Their history and development is traced in other chapters of this work (see above, pp. 360-364). To recapitulate : the starting point

was the original common prayer of the faithful after the lessons and
homily noted in Justin's account of the Sunday service, the earnest
prayers in common for ourselves, for the newly baptized, and for
all others throughout the world. [6]   In the West, Hippolytus clearly
indicated these intercessory prayers no less than Cyprian. [7]   Third
or fourth century Egypt has such a prayer " after the delivery of the
homily. " [8]   Such a prayer was recited antiphonally by the celebrant
and the people, that is, the celebrant would invite the people to
prayer, say his part, and the people would respond.   As time went
on, the deacon began to take a more prominent part, not only by
taking over the invitation to pray, but also by announcing the special
intentions.   Thus, the original bidding form of the intercessory
prayer crystallized into the *ektenia*, first probably in the Antiochene
Church, and then it spread to the other Churches of Christendom.
In conjunction with the *ektenia*-form, the lengthy dismissals of the
various categories were developed.   The next step, at least in the
Byzantine Church and its kindred Rites, was the shifting of most of
these *ektenia*-petitions to other parts of the Divine Liturgy.   Thus,
we find the early fifth-century Antiochene Church inserting some
ektenia-petitions between the fraction of the host and the *Sancta
sanctis* at the Small Elevation, and so do the Liturgy of Mopsuestia
and the so-called Clementine Liturgy. [9]

By the eighth century, the position and division of nearly all the
ektenias in the Byzantine-Armenian Liturgy of St. John Chrysostom
were the same as those we find later throughout the Byzantine Church
(see above, p. 363).   In the Byzantine Church itself, the process of
shifting petitions lasted for several centuries, both before and after
the eighth century.   At the end of the eighth century, for example,
the Liturgy in the *Codex Barberini* already has the *Great Ektenia*
at the beginning of the *enarksis*, and the *ektenia* before the *Our
Father*—but not the one before the Creed. [10]

---

[6] Justin Martyr, *First Apology*, chaps. 65 and 67.

[7] Cf. J. Jungmann, *The Mass of the Roman Rite : Its Origins and Development*
(New York : Benziger Bros., 1955), p. 480.

[8] Sarapion, *Euchologion*, cf. above, p. 91.

[9] Cf. A. Raes, *Introductio in Liturgiam Orientalem* (Rome, 1947), pp. 52-59,
for schemata.

[10] Brightman, LEW, pp. 310, 338, 319-320.

The petitions of the Roman Good Friday prayers are almost the same as those in the "common prayers" of the Roman Rite recited after the homily since the third century and possibly too as early as the first (see above, p. 412 f.). These are grouped roughly into nine categories. While the "common prayers" of the faithful in other Liturgies correspond more or less to such a grouping, most of the Eastern Liturgies include numerous other petitions. These, however, do usually lend themselves to a threefold series, with the corresponding prayer of the celebrant for each series. In Canon 19 of the Synod of Laodicea (A.D. 343-381), for example, we read : "After the sermons of the bishops, the prayer for the catechumens is to be said by itself first; when the catechumens have gone out, the prayer for those who are doing penance; and after these have passed under the hand (of the bishop) and have departed, there should then be offered the *three prayers of the faithful*, the first in silence (διὰ σιωπῆς), the second and third called out (διὰ προσφωνήσεως)." [11]

Some of the Eastern Liturgies, such as the Greek Liturgy of St. James, the Armenian Liturgy and the Liturgy of the West Syrian Jacobites, have by a process of retrogressive evolution retained only one such prayer-form, consisting in the deacon's *ektenia* and the celebrant's prayer. In Egypt, the only portion to survive retains the name of "the three" (αἱ τρεῖς). [12] The Byzantine Liturgy has two, the First and the Second Prayer of the Faithful, but as early as the ninth century their content had already been changed into what it is today, i.e., merely pleading for personal worthiness for service at the altar. [13] Despite the personal, almost private, character of these prayers after the eighth century, the Slav Byzantine Church preserved something of the original universal quality of the old intercessory prayers : until the thirteenth or fourteenth century they maintained the *Greak Ektenia* at this point—except when the priest celebrated without a deacon. Most of the petitions of the

---

[11] Our translation and italics (from Mansi, II, 567). That is, the petitions of the second and third prayers were to be "called out" by the deacon to the people, a process very similar to if not identical with the *ektenias* (cf. Brightman, LEW, pp. 519 ff.).

[12] Brightman, LEW, pp. 121 f., 160 f., 223 ff.

[13] Brightman, LEW, pp. 316 f., 375 f.

Great Ektenia, now found at the beginning of the Liturgy of the Catechumens, were originally to be said by the deacon immediately after the invitation, " All we faithful again and again in peace let us pray to the Lord. " [14] As many petitions of the *Great Ektenia* were to be recited as were necessary to give time to the celebrant to say his two silent prayers. The deacon would then interrupt the petitions with the word, " Wisdom, " and the celebrant would intone the concluding doxology. [15] This practice is confirmed by many other sources. [16] All indications point to the conclusion that this was the original position of the *Great Ektenia.*

[14] *Constitution* of Philotheus (Krasnoseltsev, *Materialy dlja istorii chinoposli-dovania liturgii sv. Ioanna Zlatoustago* [Kazan, 1889], pp. 58, 107).

[15] *Ibid.* In effect, this is still carried out in the Russian recension of the Liturgy, celebrated with the assistance of a deacon, when he makes the petitions mentioned above (p. 469, n. 2). These are from the *Great Ektenia.*

[16] E.g., the twelfth or thirteenth century Liturgy of St. Basil (*Cod. Sin.,* N. 1020, edit. A. Dmitrievsky, *Opysanie liturgicheskikh rukopisej khraniaschikhsia v biblio-tekakh pravoslanago vostoka,* Vol. II, *Euchologia* [Keiv, 1901], p. 141); the Liturgy of Chrysostom edit. by Demetrius Duca in 1526 (C. A. Swainson, *The Greek Liturgies Chiefly from Original Authorities* [London, 1884], p. 121); Morel's edition of the Liturgy (Paris, 1560), pp. 88-89; also a tenth century Arabic version of Chrysostom's Liturgy (edit. C. Bacha, *Notions générales sur les versions arabes de de la liturgie de S. Jean Chrysostome suivies d'une ancienne version inédite,* XPY-COCTOMIKA, pp. 425, 455); the Liturgy of Chrysostom in the fourteenth century Serbian MS. of Vatican Library, *Cod. bombycinus Slavo* No. 9 (edit. O. Horbatsch, *De tribus textibus Liturgicis Linguae Ecclesiasticae (Palaeo) Slavicae in Manuscriptis Vaticanis* [Rome, 1966], pp. 133-134).

CHAPTER XLVII

THE *CHERUBIKON*
AND CORRESPONDING PRAYER

*I*mmediately after responding *Amen, the people slowly and solemnly begin singing the first part of the* Cherubikon, *or Cherubic Hymn :*

Let us who mystically represent the cherubim and sing the thrice-holy hymn to the life-giving Trinity—let us now lay aside every earthly care.

When the people begin singing the Cherubikon, *the deacon puts incense into the censer, brings it to the priest, and asks for the blessing with the usual words. After the incense is blessed by the priest, the deacon recites Psalm 50 while he incenses the holy table from all sides, the apsidal icon, the Prothesis, the icons of the iconostas, both choirs, and the people. Then he returns to the sanctuary through the south door and incenses the priest.*

Meanwhile, the priest lifts up his hands and silently prays the Prayer of the Cherubikon :

No one bound by the desires and pleasures of the flesh is worthy to come to you, or to draw near to you, or to serve you, O King of Glory; for serving you is something great and awe-inspiring even for the heavenly powers themselves. Yet, through your indescribable and boundless love for mankind, you became man without change or loss; you became our High Priest and, as Master of all, you granted to us the priestly ministry of offering both this liturgy and the bloodless sacrifice. For you alone, O Lord our God, rule over all in heaven and on earth, you alone are borne upon the throne of the cherubim, you are the Lord of the seraphim and the King of Israel. You alone are holy and rest among the holy. I therefore make my prayer to you who alone are good and ready to hear me : look at me, a sinner and your unprofitable servant, and cleanse my soul and heart from any thought of evil; since I am endowed

with the grace of priesthood, make me worthy by the power
of the Holy Spirit to stand before this your holy table and
to perform the sacrifice of your sacred and immaculate body
and precious blood. It is to you, then, that I come with my
head bowed low and implore you not to turn away your face
from me, nor to reject me from among your children, but
instead graciously permit these gifts to be offered to you by
me, a sinner and your unworthy servant. For it is really
you, Christ our God, who offer and are offered; it is you who
receive and are received yourself, and it is to you that we
give glory together with your eternal Father, and with your
most holy, good, and life-giving Spirit, now and always and
for ever and ever. Amen.

*After incensing, the deacon takes his place at the priest's right and
holds the censer with the ring finger of his left hand. As soon as the
priest ends the prayer above, both he and the deacon, with hands lifted
up, say the Cherubic Hymn three times :*

Let us who mystically represent the cherubim and sing
the thrice-holy hymn to the life-giving Trinity—let us now
lay aside every earthly care.

So that we may welcome the King of all, who comes invisibly, borne aloft by armies of angels. Alleluia, alleluia,
alleluia.

*After each recitation of the hymn both the priest and deacon lower
their hands and make a small bow; then both kiss the holy table if
such is the custom and, if they wish, the hand-cross.*

Unlike nearly all the other silent prayers of the celebrant during
the Divine Liturgy, the Prayer of the Cherubikon is strictly personal.
It is, as some of the oldest texts denominate it, " the prayer which
the priest recites in behalf of himself during the singing of the
Cherubikon. " [1] Its primary characteristic is the first-person singular.

A masterpiece of composition, it is a prayer for priestly worthi-

---

[1] E.g., *Cod. Barberini* (Brightman, LEW, p. 318); cf. also Dmitrievsky, *Opysanie
liturgicheskikh rukopisej khraniaschikhsia V bibliotekakh pravoslavnago vostoka,*
Vol. II, *Euchologia* (Kiev, 1901), pp. 19, 65, 141, 142, for both *Cod. Barberini*
and *Cod. Sebastianov.*

ness, an entreaty for acceptance, and the plea of a weak, human mortal for that angelic purity required of one who would perform the sacrifice of the New Law. Its directness is piercing, yet veiled with words of delicate subtleness. It possesses the lovable quality of every truly repentant sinner—gentle meekness—yet it has the boldness of the tested saint. It is the prayer par excellence of the *sacerdos Dei* who must bridge the infinite abyss between the holiness of Yahweh and the sinfulness of man.

Literally translated, the first sentence would read : " No one tied up with the desires and pleasures of the flesh is worthy to come to you "; that is, no one who has the habit of giving in to the desires and pleasures of the flesh is worthy to come before the almighty " King of Glory " (an expression borrowed from Ps. 23:7), for even the angels tremble with awe and wonder in merely serving Him. Why does the priest, then, dare to offer the bloodless sacrifice of the cross? The answer is in the next sentence : because of God's boundless love for man, his Son became man like us and our High Priest. As the absolute Master of all things, he deigned to give to mere man this tremendous, this divine power of bringing down himself on the altar at man's request.

The next few lines, introductory to the next petition for worthiness, exalt and glorify God. Yahweh alone is God, he rules over all things, he is borne on the cherubic throne, he is the Lord of the seraphim and King of Israel. Then comes a second appeal for cleansing, to be effected by the Holy Spirit, in order that the sacrificial act may be performed worthily. This petition is a personal *epiclesis*, a beseeching of the Holy Spirit to come down upon the person of the celebrant. The same plea is repeated : " It is to you then that I come with my head bowed low and implore you not to turn away your face from me nor reject me from among your children. " Like the psalmist of old, from whom the expression " turn not away your face from me " (Ps. 112:7) is borrowed, the priest prays for clemency. " Nor reject me from among your children, " taken verbatim from the book of Wisdom (9:4), is another scriptural expression of God's disfavor.

A sinful and unworthy servant, the priest prays once more that he be allowed to offer the Sacrifice, " for it is really you, Christ our God, who offer and are offered; it is you who receive and are received yourself. " These few lines, the apex of the whole prayer, contain profound Eucharistic doctrine : that the primary offerer of the Eucharistic Sacrifice is Christ himself, the same Christ who offered the sacrifice of the cross, and that the priest is merely the instrumental minister, Christ's representative. Centuries after this line was penned, the encyclical *Mediator Dei* of Pius XII taught : " The priest, then, is the same : Jesus Christ, whose sacred person is represented by his minister... and therefore when he [the priest] exercises his priestly power he, as it were, ' lends Christ his tongue and gives him the use of his hand. ' " [2] The prayer also shows Christ, the victim of the cross, as the same victim that is offered in the Eucharistic Sacrifice. In the Eucharistic Sacrifice, however Christ the victim is not in his natural state, but in a sacramental state, that is, under the accidents of bread and wine, as Thomas Aquinas pointed out carefully hundreds of years later. [3] Finally, that Christ is the one who receives the sacrifice and the one who is received. In the Eucharistic Sacrifice, Christ offers himself to the Father and to the Holy Spirit and is received by them. But since he is God, consubstantial with them, he is also received by himself, being one of the Holy Trinity. He then both receives himself and is received by himself. This mystery is akin to the mystery of the Incarnation : for as he became man for the sake of our salvation without ceasing to be God, so he offers himself anew in the Eucharistic Sacrifice.

This point occasioned a major theological controversy in the Byzantine Church during the twelfth century. One school of thought held that if the words " *it is you who receive and are received yourself* " refer to Christ, they are heretical because Christ is the offerer only, while the sacrifice is received by God the Father and the Holy Spirit, since the Eucharistic Sacrifice cannot be offered to Christ but only to them. This view, originally proposed by a mere deacon, counted among its proponents some of the most famous Eastern bishops : Soterichus Panteugenus, Patriarch-elect of Antioch, Eustachius of Dyrrachium (modern Durazzo), and Michael of Salonika.

[2] *Mediator Dei*, 73 (Catholic Truth Society, London, 1947).
[3] *Sum. Th.*, III, q. 64, a. 5 ad I.

The question was settled on January 26, 1156, at the Synod of Constantinople (called by Patriarch Luke Chrysoberges), which affirmed that these words referred to Christ, and forbade their omission. [4]

This prayer is sometimes attributed to St. Basil. But his authorship is improbable since the prayer first appears in the text of his Liturgy only in the eighth or ninth century *Codex Barberini*, and the tenth or eleventh century *Codex Sebastianov*. [5] Even then, it was not used universally in the Byzantine Church, since other codices of the same centuries do not have it. [6] It seems, therefore, that it was introduced into the Liturgy of St. Basil during the seventh century, or toward the end of the sixth. Judging from the text itself, which assumes that the Gifts are already on the altar, it must have been written when the rite of preparation was still linked with the Great Entrance. [7] Since this rite was transferred to the beginning of the Divine Liturgy during the seventh century, the prayer must have been introduced earlier.

Because this prayer appears much later in the Liturgy of St. John Chrysostom, [8] it was probably borrowed from that of St. Basil. This probably happened during the eleventh century, since twelfth-century codices of Chrysostom's Liturgy contain it. Furthermore, it must have been used extensively at the time, since it occasioned the twelfth century controversy mentioned above. [9]

This prayer is found also in the Liturgy of St. James, the Armenian Liturgy, and the Alexandrian Liturgy of St. Gregory the Theologian.

---

[4] Cf. Mai, *Specilegium Romanum*, Vol. X (Rome, 1844), pp. 16-93, and Jugie, *Theologia Dogmatica Christianorum Orientalium ab Ecclesia Catholica dissidentium*, Vol. III (Paris, 1930), pp. 317-320, for a fuller treatment of the question.

[5] Dmitrievsky, *op. cit.*, pp. 19, 65, 141, 142, 147.

[6] E.g., *Cod. Porphyr.* and *Ross*; cf. de Meester, *Les développements du texte grec de la Liturgie de S. Jean Chrysostome*, ΧΡΥϹΟΣΤΟΜΙΚΑ, p. 330, n. 3.

[7] The line in question reads : " ...graciously permit *these* gifts to be offered to you by me. "

[8] Though it does appear in the early eighth century Armenian version of Chrysostom's Liturgy; cf. Aucher, *La versione armena della liturgia di S. Giovanni Crisostomo, fatta sul principio dell'VIII secolo*, ΧΡΥϹΟΣΤΟΜΙΚΑ, pp. 384-385.

[9] The prayer is included in the Arabic Liturgy of St. John Chrysostom, which dates back to the tenth century (edit. Bacha, *op. cit.*, pp. 426-428 (Arabic) and pp. 456-457 (French trans.).

Nothing certain is known about which of these Liturgies borrowed from which. [10]

The Cherubikon

This solemn, beautiful hymn with its elaborate chant was originally used during the procession of the Great Entrance. At present, it is divided into two parts : the first is sung by the people before the celebrant begins the procession with the Gifts, and the second, immediately after the celebrant has completed the commemorations.

The *Cherubikon* is so intimately linked with the symbolic or mystic meaning of the Great Entrance that it would be difficult, if not impossible to understand its words in their true sense independently of this symbolism.

In ancient Rome, the newly elected emperor was customarily carried out to the people by his legionnaires, on a shield raised aloft on spears and canopied by a forest of inclined spears and standards. The people cried out, " Long live the emperor! " In the Great Entrance, the *pantocrator*, the king, the almighty King of all, God himself, comes invisibly borne aloft by the cherubim and armies of angels. The *Cherubikon* has the *plebs sancta Dei*, the holy people of God, representing the cherubim; like them, the people must worship God with an undivided heart, " laying aside every earthly care. " Excessive concern for the things of earth draws the mind away, distracts it from God and his coming. According to the Scriptures, the Lord of all is praised by the cherubim with the Alleluia. Correspondingly, the people welcome him with the thrice-holy cherubic exclamation.

Cedrenus, writing in the eleventh century, dates the *Cherubikon* to the ninth year of Justin II's reign, that is, A.D. 574. [11] He does not say, however, whether Justin II personally composed the hymn,

---

[10] In the Greek St. James, this prayer dates back at least to the tenth century, since it is found in the *Vat. Rotulus*, 2282 (edit. A. Rocchi, in Mai, NPB, X, ii, pp. 52 f.) where it is called the prayer of the " divine Basil. " For the Armenian Liturgy, see above, p. 481, n. 8. For the Alexandrian Liturgy of St. Gregory the Theologian, cf. Renaudot, LOC, I, p. 88.

[11] Cf. Cedrenus, *Historiarum compendium* (PG 121, 748 B). Justin II reigned from A.D. 565 to 578.

or commissioned someone else to do it. There are valid grounds for ascribing an earlier date to the hymn. Dionysius the Pseudo-Areopagite refers to the Great Entrance and to a hymn in the Syrian Church about A.D. 500, indicating that it was sung before the Kiss of Peace. [12] He does not give the text, and so positive identification with the *Cherubikon* is impossible. Since he tells us that the Creed was also recited before the kiss of peace, he was obviously writing after the insertion of the Creed into the Liturgy, about A.D. 416. From other internal evidence of his work, we know that he must have written after the publication of the *Henoticon* by Emperor Zeno (A.D. 482). [13]

Yet, this hymn probably was the *Cherubikon*, for somewhat later, Eutychius, Patriarch of Constantinople (A.D. 552-565), disapproved of the Great Entrance and the hymn, because the people were being taught to sing as if they were indeed bearing the King of Glory—an obvious allusion to the *Cherubikon*. [14]

Emperor Justin II may have ordered that the hymn be sung in all the churches of his dominion, but credit can hardly be given him for having composed or introduced.

Although general incensing usually preceded all important liturgical functions, it seems to have been one of the latest additions in the rite of the Great Entrance. It may have coincided with the introduction of the Great Entrance itself—at which ceremony the censers were carried in the procession—but the incensing of the Gifts at the table of preparation and at the time of their deposition on the altar are much later practices. This was being gradually introduced into the rite during the thirteenth century and probably continued into the fourteenth. [15] In the Slav Church, even during the fourteenth or fifteenth century, there was only one incensing after the Great Entrance, when the priest had placed the Holy Gifts

[12] Ps.-Dionysius, *De eccles. hier.*, chap. 3 (PG 3, 428 A).

[13] The *Henotikon*, meaning " unification, " was a formula drawn up by Acacius of Constantinople for settling the controversy between the true Church and the Monophysites.

[14] Eutychius, *Sermo de paschate et ss. eucharistia*, 8 (PG 86, 2400-2401).

[15] Cf. Dmitrievsky, *op. cit.*, II, pp. 141, 173, 205, and Krasnoseltsev, *Materialy dlja istorii chinoposlidovania liturgii sv. Ioanna Zlatoustago* (Kazan, 1889), pp. 25, 107.

on the altar. [16]   Only during the latter part of the fourteenth century was there a general incensing of the sanctuary and of the people. [17]

The first references to the recitation of a psalm in the Great Entrance dates from the thirteenth or fourteenth century.   The psalm was selected according to local usage, although most churches seem to have chosen Psalm 23. [18]   Others had Psalm 50, which is now in use. [19]   In some churches, the psalm was recited before the Great Entrance; [20] in others, it was recited in a low voice by the priest as he carried the Gifts to the altar during the Great Entrance. [21]

[16] While incensing the Gifts, the priest would recite : " Holy, holy, holy, Lord God of Hosts, " and then the " O heavenly King. "   For the whole rite of Entrance, cf. MS. N. 520, pp. 19, 13, and MS. N. 526, pp. 15, 15, of Sophia Library, and MS. N. 345 of Moscow Synodal Library (Gorsky-Nevostrujev, *Opysanie slavians-kikh rukopisej Moskovskoj Synodal'noj biblioteky*, Vol. III [Moscow, 1859], p. 21; also MS. N. 522, p. 26, MS. N. 523, p. 29, of Sophia Library, MS. N. 274, p. 24, of Count Tolstoy's Library, etc.

[17] In the Greek Church, the *Constitution* of Philotheus (cf. Krasnoseltsev, *op. cit.*, p. 58).   The Slav Church followed suit with its translation of the same *Constitution*; cf. *Liturgikon* of Metropolitan Isidore, *Cod. Vat. Slav.*, N. 14, fols. 131-132.   Even then, the people were not incensed but only the altar from all sides, and the priest.   After the recitation of the Cherubikon Prayer, the deacon went to the *Prothesis* and incensed the Gifts.

[18] Cf. de Meester, *op. cit.*, p. 332.

[19] E.g., *Cod. Patmos*, N. 709 (of year 1260), the fifteenth century *Cod.*, N. 8 (182) of Met. Library of H. Sepulcher of Constantinople, and fifteenth century MS. 986 of Sinai Libraty, the MS. 120 of Esphigmenon (year 1602), etc.; cf. Dmitrievsky, *op. cit.*, II, pp. 157, 475, 609, 959, etc.

[20] E.g., the thirteenth century MS. 518, p. 25, and MS. 524, p. 20, of Sophia Library; cf. Petrovsky, *Histoire de la rédaction slave de la liturgie de S. Jean Chrys-ostome*, XPYCOCTOMIKA, p. 875, n. 4.

[21] E.g., MS. of year 1306 of Esphigmenon Library (cf. Dmitrievsky, *op. cit.*, II, p. 266); the fifteenth century MSS. of Sophia Library, N. 533, p. 42, N. 540, p. 46, and N. 839, p. 4 (cf. Petrovsky, *op. cit.*, p. 904).

CHAPTER XLVIII

THE PRIMITIVE OFFERTORY

It is quite inaccurate to consider the stages of preparation of the gifts—the bread and wine—as constituting the *offertory*. A better understanding will be obtained from a study of some of the original aspects of the rite.

At the dawn of the Christian era, the Eucharistic Sacrifice was celebrated during the common meal (see above, pp. 18-29). When the faithful brought their gifts or provisions from home and set them on the common table, they were " offering " them, donating them to God and to the Church in the true sense of the word—yet this was not the formal or ritual offertory without which the Eucharistic Sacrifice would have been essentially incomplete. This offering of the faithful was not the same as that of the bishop. Toward the end of the first century, Clement of Rome indicated that the " bishop's office " was " to offer the gifts " (προσφέρειν τὰ δῶρα). [1] Justin, a little more than a half-century later, calls this the προσφορά, the *offering* or *oblation* in the service. [2] By way of explanation, he continues : " We refer to the sacrifices which we Gentiles offer to him everywhere, the Eucharistic bread and the Eucharistic chalice. " [3] But before this formal oblation of the bishop, there was a stage of offering pertaining to the deacons. Justin describes this too : " After completing the prayers, we greet each other with a kiss. Then bread, and a cup of mixed wine and water is offered, προσφέρεται, perhaps better translated here as *brought forth* or *presented* to the one presiding over the brethren. " [4] The same function is described by Hippolytus in the *Apostolic Tradition* (c. A.D. 210) : " Then let the deacons bring up the oblation (προσφορά) to (the bishop). " [5] This offering or presentation differs from that of the faithful and from that of the bishop; it was a liturgy proper to the deacons.

---

[1] I Clem. 44.
[2] Justin Martyr, *Dialogue with Trypho*, chap. 41 (edit. Otto, pp. 134-135).
[3] *Ibid.*
[4] Justin Martyr, *First Aplogy*, chap. 65; see above, p. 41.
[5] Hippolytus, *Apostolic Tradition*, iii, 4; see above, p. 51.

The parts to be played by the deacon and the bishop are even more clearly distinguished by Hippolytus in his version of the ordination prayer of a deacon : the office of deacon is " to bring up (ἀναφέρειν) that which is offered (προσφέρεται) to you by your ordained high-priest. " [6] This passage confirms the notion that the formal, ritual offertory is the proper service of the bishop.

The Canons of the Council of Ancyra, c. A.D. 314, define the three " liturgies " or services even more specifically : that of the bishop is " to offer " (προσφέρειν) the oblation (τὰ προσφορά), that of the deacon is " to bring it up " or " present it " (ἀναφέρειν), and the faithful, the communicants, are " to bring " (προσενέγκειν) it to the church or to the deacons. [7]

These distinctions are a key to the understanding of the early Liturgy. They also help us understand the whole offertory rite and its different phases.

In the Byzantine-Slav Liturgy, these phases have specific names : (1) the " gathering in " of the gifts formerly brought by the faithful; (2) the " laying out " of the gifts on the altar after the Great Entrance or presentation of the gifts to the bishop or celebrant by the deacons; (3) the formal " offering up " of the gifts to God, by the bishop or celebrant during the Eucharistic Sacrifice.

In treating of the *proskomidia*, we have had occasion to point out the vivid consciousness which the early Christian had of his part in the whole rite as a true corporate offering by the Church in its organic, hierarchic unity (see above, p. 255). Each member appreciated his proper part in the collective offering. The bishop through his consecration, the priest through his ordination, the deacon through his sacred orders, and the faithful through the holy character of baptism were indeed partakers, each in his own special way, of the Church's genuine, official oblation. The various stages of liturgical prayer and action of the Byzantine offertory bring this vividly to mind even today.

During the first two centuries, the acts of offering—by faithful, deacons, presbyters or bishops—were simple and unceremonious.

---

[6] *Ibid.*, ix, 11; edit. Dix, 17-18 for full prayer.
[7] Council of Ancyra, Canons 1, 2, 3; cf. Mansi, *Sacrorum conciliorum nova et amplissima collectio*, II, 513 ff.; or NPNF, Series II, Vol. XIV, pp. 63-64.

Perhaps the early Christians sought to make their offerings in a manner that would distinguish them from pagan and Jewish sacrificial practices. The infant Church preferred to emphasize the spiritual character of the offerings, the tremendous reality of the *Eucharistia*, the Gift from heaven itself.

Soon, however, danger threatened from other sources : Gnosticism, —a complex Greco-Oriental belief in the essential antithesis of matter and spirit—and Docetism—an exaggeration of the spiritual nature of Christianity going so far as to deny the reality of Christ's human nature. As an immediate reaction, the Church stressed the value of material creation and the goodness of earthly gifts. A corresponding approach may be detected in the Liturgy : the idea that the presentation and offering of material gifts to God is in reality the offering of the " first-fruits of his creation. " This, Irenaeus points out, is not only part of the Mosaic Law—" as Moses says, ' Thou shalt not appear in the presence of the Lord thy God empty ' (Deut. 16:16)—but also an expression of gratitude to God which sanctifies the creature. " [8] He continues : " But our opinion is in accordance with the Eucharist and the Eucharist in turn establishes our opinion. For we offer to him his own, " that is, his own creatures of bread and wine. [9] The Gnostic contention that created things have their origin in some inferior or malignant power leads him to answer the question : How can one believe that the bread over which thanks has been given is the body of the Lord and the cup his blood if it is the creation of this malignant power? [10]

This restoration of the earthly value of the offerings resulted in the elaboration of proper liturgies for the different categories of members of the *ecclesia* : the faithful, the deacons, the presbyters, and the bishop.

From the principle that the material gifts of bread and wine could be offered to God, there arose another, closely related to it : that other material offerings could be offered also, and that, in fact, every gift to the church or to the poor was actually a gift to God. Since the very beginning of Christianity, the offerings for the needs of the

[8] Irenaeus, *Adv. haer.*, Book IV, chap. 18, 1-6 (edit. ANF, Vol. I, pp. 484-486).
[9] *Ibid.*, Book IV, chap. 18, 5 (*edit. cit.*, p. 486).
[10] *Ibid.*

Church and its poor seem to have been made mostly on the occasion of liturgical services. These were now more closely joined to the Eucharistic celebration itself. Cyprian proves the point in his castigation of a wealthy matron. " Anoint your eyes, not with the make-up of the devil, but with Christ's eye-salve, that you may be able to begin to see God... both by good works and by character, for your eyes do not see the needy and poor. You are wealthy and rich, and do you think that you celebrate the Lord's Supper, if you do not even consider the offering? You come to the Lord's Supper without an offering, and yet you dare to take part in the sacrifice which the poor man has offered! " [11]   He could remonstrate thus only if the layman was obliged at the time to contribute bread and wine for the sacrifice and money to the community poor box, the corban.

Origen speaks of praying to God, " that we may be worthy to offer him gifts, which he may restore to us, and bestow upon us in Christ Jesus heavenly things in exchange for earthly. " [12]   Close parallels may be found in the deacon's *ektenia* of the *Apostolic Constitutions* and in the intercessions of the Preface in St. Mark's Liturgy. In fact, the practice is scriptural and commonplace in Christian thought. By the fourth century, offering gifts in one form or another was almost universal in the Church.

The articles offered varied from church to church. Oil was popular and so were wax and candles. The oil was generally used in church lamps. A mosaic from the church floor at Aquileia, dating from the era of Constantine, shows an offertory procession in which people bring bread, wine, grapes, flowers, and even a bird. [13]

A few overzealous ministers started the practice of " offering " gifts other than bread and wine, so that the matter had to be covered by law. In A.D. 393, for example, a synod in Hippo stated emphatically : " At the Sacrament of the body and blood of Christ, nothing is to be offered except bread and wine mixed with water. " [14]

---

[11] Cyprian, *De opere et eleemos.*, chap. 15 (CSEL, III, 384).

[12] Origen, *In Luc. homil.*, xxxix (PG 13, 1901-1902).

[13] See illustration in Righetti, *Manuale di storia liturgica*, II (Milan-Genoa, 1945), 29.

[14] Can. 23 (edit. Mansi, *op. cit.*, III, 922). It permits, however, the offering of milk and honey at the Easter Baptism, the first grapes of the season, and grain.

The *Apostolic Canons* are even more severe : " If any bishop or presbyter, contrary to what our Lord has ordained regarding the sacrifice, offers up something else at the altar of God, such as honey, milk, or a strong brew instead of wine... fowls or animals or vegetables in opposition to the ordinance, he should be deposed. Aside from ears of new corn or wheat and bunches of grapes in season and oil for the holy lamp and incense, nothing should be brought to the altar at the time of the divine oblation. All other fruits should be sent to the bishop at his house as first-fruits to him and to the presbyters and not to the altar. Naturally the bishop and presbyters are to distribute them to the deacons and to the other clergy. " [15]

[15] *Canones Apostolorum*, 2-4 (*Apostolic Constitutions*, Book VIII, 2-4), in Funk, *Didascalia et Constitutiones Apostolorum* (Paderborn, 1905), I, 564. Our translation into English.

CHAPTER XLIX

THE GREAT ENTRANCE :
PROCESSION OF THE OFFERTORY

After reciting the Cherubikon, *the priest and deacon go to the* proskomidia *table. The priest takes the censer and incenses the holy gifts of bread and wine three times, saying in a low voice :*

O God, be merciful to me a sinner.

He returns the censer to the deacon, who holds it with one finger of his right hand. Then the deacon says to the priest :

Take, sir.

The priest takes the large veil, the aër, *folds it, and puts it on the deacon's left shoulder as he says to him :*

Lift up your hands unto holy things and bless the Lord.

The priest then takes the diskos, *which is covered with its veil, and with great attention and reverence, places it on the head of the deacon. The deacon, while holding the end of the orarion with his left hand and the censer with his right, holds the* diskos *to his forehead with both hands. The priest himself takes the holy chalice, covered with a small veil, and holds it before his chest. Preceded by the candlebearers, both go out through the north door. As he goes out, the deacon exclaims :*

May the Lord God remember in his Kingdom all you orthodox Christians, at all times, now and always, and for ever and ever.

The deacon proceeds through the royal doors into the sanctuary, where he waits for the priest on the right side. As soon as the deacon has completed his commemoration, the priest proceeds through the north door and intones :

May the Lord God remember in his Kingdom His Holiness, our Supreme Pontiff N——, Pope of Rome, our Most Reverend Archbishop and Metropolitan N——, our God-loving Bishop N——, all the priests, religious clergy, our sovereign

authorities, all the armed forces, the noble and ever remembered founders and benefactors of this holy church *(and as he comes before the royal doors, he turns toward the people and continues)* and all you orthodox Christians, at all times, now and always and for ever and ever. [1]

People : Amen. So that we may welcome the King of all, who comes invisibly borne aloft by armies of angels. Alleluia, alleluia, alleluia.

The priest goes into the sanctuary through the royal doors. When he reaches the altar, he places the chalice on it. Taking the holy diskos *from the deacon, he places it on the altar to the left of the chalice. He removes the small veils from the* diskos *and chalice and lays them on one side of the altar; then he takes the large veil, the* aër, *from the shoulder of the deacon, incenses it by holding it over the censer, and covers the holy gifts with it. As he does this, he says :*

The noble Joseph, after taking down your immaculate body from the cross, wrapped it in a clean shroud with sweet spices and sorrowfully laid it in a new grave. [2]

---

[1] When the Divine Liturgy is celebrated by religious in monasteries, the following is inserted immediately after the commemoration of the bishop : " our Most Reverend Fathers Protoarchimandrite N——, Archimandrite N——, Protohegumenos N——, and Hegumenos N——". Also, the phrase " of this holy chapel " is substituted for " of this holy church. "

The Russian recension has a slightly different arrangement in its commemorations. The following are some of the more usual :

Deacon : " May the Lord God remember in his Kingdom His Holiness, the Supreme Pontiff ——, Pope of Rome, always, now and forever, and through all eternity. "

Priest : " May the Lord God remember in his Kingdom our Most Reverend Archbishop (*or* Bishop) N—— always, now and forever, and through all eternity. "

Deacon : " May the Lord God remember in his Kingdom our sovereign authorities, always, now and forever, and through all eternity. "

Priest : " May the Lord God remember in his Kingdom all you orthodox Christians, always, now and forever, and through all eternity. "

[2] This rite varies slightly in the Russian recension. After the priest and the deacon enter the sanctuary, the royal doors are closed and the curtain is drawn. While taking the *diskos* from the deacon, the priest says the *tropar* : " The noble Joseph, " and adds :

" While you were in the tomb with your body, in hell with your soul, and in Paradise with the Thief, you were also on the throne with the Father and the Holy Spirit, O Christ, permeating all things, O unlimited One.

" Because it gives life, because it is more beautiful than Paradise itself, your

Receiving the censer from the hands of the deacon, the priest incenses the holy gifts three times, saying :

Deal kindly, O Lord, with Sion in your good will, so that the walls of Jerusalem may be rebuilt; then shall you be pleased with the sacrifice of righteousness, with offerings and holocausts; then shall they lay bullocks on your altar (Ps. 50:20-21).

In the meantime, the royal doors are closed, if customary. The candlebearers who have been standing on each side bow to the sanctuary and return to their place.

At the Jewish *chabûrah*, conforming to a strict rule, the participants placed their contribution to the meal on a sideboard as they entered the house. The first Christians probably did the same. We know, for instance, that a similar practice existed in Syria in the third century. [3] By the fourth or fifth century, the faithful in the West (except in the Gallo-Frankish Church) kept their gifts until the offertory, [4] at which time they brought them processionally to the deacon who placed them on the altar. In the East, the faithful generally made their offerings before the beginning of the service, placing them either on special tables in the church itself, or in a side-room, the *diakonikon*. A document indicates that in the fifth century, in Syria, " the *diakonikon* should be to the right of the entrance... so that the Eucharistic offerings may be examined. " [5] But this is an exception since it generally came to be placed close to the sanc-

---

tomb is truly more resplendent than any kingly palace, O Christ; it is the fountain from which springs our resurrection. "

Then, as the priest covers the *diskos* and chalice with the large veil, he again says the *tropar* : " The noble Joseph. "

[3] Cf. Didascalia ii, 27 (edit. Connolly, *Didascalia Apostolorum* [Oxford, 1929], p. 120).

[4] The Gallo-Frankish Church seems to have followed the Eastern custom whereby the faithful made their offering before the beginning of the service in a room set aside for the purpose (cf. G. Nickl, *Der Anteil des Volkes an der Mess-liturgie im Frankenreiche* [Innsbruck, 1930], pp. 36 ff.).

[5] *Testamentum Domini*, I, 19 (Rahmani, *Testamentum Domini Nostri Jesu Christi*, Mainz, 1899, p. 23 or Quasten, *Monumenta eucharistica et liturgia vetustissima* [Bonn, 1935-1937], 237). There seem to be vestiges of this in the traditional " shopping corner " of Russian Orthodox churches near the entrance door where loaves and candles are sold and whence they are sent with the family diptych-books to the priest at the *proskomidia*-table.

tuary, as may be seen in the fourth-century *Apostolic Constitutions*. [6]

Whatever the place provided for the gifts, the offerings had to be transferred to the altar : "...the deacons should bring the gifts to the bishop at the altar." [7] This simple act is the nucleus around which the elaborate Great Entrance ceremony was built, beginning in the fifth or sixth century. One of the first to mention any development was Pseudo-Dionysius, writing early in the sixth century. [8] By the middle of that century, however, the splendor of the procession had become excessive, for Eutychius, Patriarch of Constantinople (A.D. 552-565), vigorously opposed its glamour because it gave the impression that the King of Glory himself was being borne. [9] Also, the lavish procession attracted all the attention, while the offering itself seemed incidental. The magnitude of the procession at Hagia Sophia, as early as in the days of Justinian, may be inferred from his decree of A.D. 535, ordering that the clergy of Hagia Sophia and the three churches annexed to it number no more than four hundred and twenty-five. [10] This included sixty priests, one hundred deacons, forty deaconesses, ninety subdeacons, one hundred and thirty-five lectors and cantors. Furthermore, the doorkeepers were to be no more than one hundred.

The order of the procession, as we know from later sources, was : first a subdeacon with a lighted candle, then the archdeacon who bore on his head the veiled *diskos* with the altar bread; behind him came other deacons bearing any number of empty *diskoi*; these were followed by an archpriest carrying the chalice with the wine; then other priests with empty chalices. Behind these came a priest with the liturgical lance and another with the spoon for administering Holy Communion. Bringing up the rear of the procession came yet other deacons who carried liturgical books, the crucifix, the sponge (for cleansing the sacred vessels), the liturgical

---

[6] It corresponds to one of the two παστοφόρια mentioned in Book II, 57 (Quasten, *op. cit.*, 181).

[7] *Ibid.*, Book VIII (see above, p. 124). Hippolytus uses almost identical words : "To (the bishop) then let the deacons bring up the oblation (προσφορά)." See above, p. 485.

[8] Ps.-Dionysius, *Eccl. hierarch.*, III, 2 (Quasten, *op. cit.*, 294).

[9] Eutychius, *Sermo de paschate et ss. eucharistia*, 8 (PG 86, 2400-2401).

[10] *Novellae*, 3, 1 (edit. Z. v. Lingenthal, I, p. 71).

fans, relics, banners, etc.   Last of all came the deacon bearing the *omophorion* (the episcopal stole or *pallium*) of the bishop celebrant, who himself awaited the procession at the main altar.   Perhaps the procession was not quite as elaborate in all detail during Eutychius' time, but how else explain the formidable array of clergy during Justinian's era?   If anything, the number of clergy serving Hagia Sophia must have increased, for we know from the decree of Heraclius (A.D. 610-641) that the influx of clergy from the provinces in fact was not stopped.   The new decree " reduced " the number of clergy to eighty priests, one hundred and fifty deacons, forty deaconesses, seventy subdeacons, and one hundred and eighty-five lectors and cantors. [11]

A serious misinterpretation of the rite came from the region of Antioch not long after Chrysostom's time—even before the Great Entrance reached its gigantic size.   It is found in the *Catecheses* (A.D. 410) of Theodore of Mopsuestia.

> We must therefore think of the deacons who (at the offertory) carry the Eucharistic bread and bring it out for the Sacrifice as representing the invisible hosts of ministry (the angels) but with this difference : that through this ministry of theirs and through these memorials they do not send Christ our Lord to his salvific passion (i.e., as the angel did in Gethsemane). When they bring up (the oblation at the offertory) they place it on the altar in order to complete the representation of the Passion so that we may think of him on the altar as if he were placed in the sepulcher after enduring his passion.   This is why by spreading the linens on the altar the deacons portray (to us) the figure of the linen cloths at the burial....   They stand on both sides and fan all the air above the holy body with fans.... by this they show the greatness of the body which is lying there, for it is customary when the corpse of the great ones of this world is carried in a bier that some should fan the air above it.... the same is done with the holy, awe-inspiring body lying on the altar, a body which is far from all corruption and which will very shortly rise to an immortal being.
>
> It is in remembrance of the angels who kept coming to the passion and death of our Lord that the deacons stand in a

[11] J. Pargoire, *L'Église byzantine de 527 à 847* (Paris, 1905), pp. 60-61.

circle, fan the air, and offer honor and adoration to the sacred, awe-inspiring body which is lying there.... They do this to show that, since the body lying there through its union with the divine nature is the high, dreadful, holy and true Lord, it must be seen and kept with great fear.

These things take place while all are silent before the Liturgy begins, for with quiet and reverent fear, with silent and noiseless prayer, all must watch the bringing up and spreading forth before God of such a great and wonderful object. When our Lord died, the Apostles went home and remained there in great silence and immense fear.... When we see the oblation (placed) on the table, which denotes that it is being placed in a kind of sepulcher after its death, great silence falls on those present.... They must look at it with a quiet and reverential fear because it is necessary for Christ our Lord to rise again in the awe-inspiring Liturgy.... [12]

After reading this, one understands Eutychius! Why all this fear and adoration in the presence of unconsecrated elements? Theodore's explanation of the rite has been a source of embarrassment to Eastern theologians and liturgists for centuries. Two possible explanations have been offered for the awe and reverence : that the " reserved sacrament " was carried around—but this practice of the Gallic Church was unknown in the East; and that this was the " fermentum, " the bringing to a parish church of the species consecrated at the bishop's Liturgy—but the " fermentum " had been abandoned in the fourth century. Besides, the Great Entrance was even more elaborate at the bishop's Liturgy than at that of a parish church.

The conclusion is unavoidable that Theodore taught a novel doctrine.

The authentic Byzantine tradition of preparing the gifts at the *proskomidia* does represent Christ's passion and death. It serves as an anticipation of the unbloody death of Christ which is to come later in the Eucharistic Sacrifice, a time of preparation for the great mystical, sacrificial act of Christ's redemptive death. It matters little whether the *proskomedia* takes place before the Divine Liturgy

[12] Theodore of Mopsuestia, *Catecheses*, chaps. V and VI (edit. A. Rücker, *Ritus Baptismi et Missae, quem descripsit Theodorus ep. Mopsuestenus in sermonibus catecheticis* [Münster, 1933], 21 ff.) Our translation into English.

of the Word or immediately before the Eucharistic Sacrifice, as it did before the eighth century : in the *proskomedia*, the bread and wine are merely symbols of the body and blood—which they are to *become* in reality at the transubstantiation. Even as symbols, they are worthy of reverence. That is why almost all of Theodore's symbolism has survived in the Byzantine Church : the bearers of the sacred gifts symbolizing the angels; the deacons with their fans representing the angels hovering over the cross; the metal *ripidia* in the form of seraphs; the altar seen as the tomb of Christ and the linens, as the winding sheet in which his body was wrapped, etc. As all of these are merely representations, symbols or " images " of the reality, so also are the bread and wine. The authentic tradition of the Byzantine Church has always implied mere symbolism. [13] This is evident from the wording of the liturgical prayers : " Bless this oblation..., " [14] " For the precious gifts that have been brought forth..., " [15] " Permit us to offer you these gifts.... " [16] On the other hand, after the consecration and epiclesis, the prayers clearly and unmistakably identify the body and blood of the Eucharistic Christ. [17]

Maximus the Confessor (A.D. 662) intreprets the entrance as a *figure* or *representation*, though not of the dead body of Christ, but of the incarnation and beginning of our redemption, when he asks the question, " What does the entrance with the holy mysteries signify ? " [18] He distinctly uses the word *signify* (σημαίνει) without a hint of anything else.

In the eighth century, Germanus I of Constantinople (A.D. 715-

---

[13] Theodore's idea that the offertory " preconsecrates the sacrament " in some sense is also found in the Nestorian Church (cf. Brightman, LEW, p. 267, lines 11, 30 ff.); this was introduced into that Church apparently by Narsai of Edessa in the latter part of the fifth century. Narsai in turn avowedly accepted the whole idea from Theodore (cf. *Liturgical Homilies of Narsai*, edit. Connolly, p. 3, also pp. 14, 16). The Armenians borrowed the same idea directly from Theodore's adherents in Byzantium.

[14] *Prayer of Offering* in the *proskomidia*.

[15] *Ektenia of the Offertory*.

[16] *Prayer of the Offertory*.

[17] E.g., the prayer of administration : " The servant of God, N——, is receiving the precious, holy and pure body and blood of our Lord, God and Saviour Jesus Christ.... "

[18] Maximus the Confessor, *Mystagogia*, chap. 16 (PG 91, 693 CD).

725) also explains the Great Entrance symbolically in his *Liturgical Commentary* : " Carried by material hands, Christ makes his entry with the Holy Spirit in order to be symbolically immolated; all this is perceived by the mind (νοερῶς). " [19] According to his interpretation, the placing of the gifts upon the altar also signifies the burial of Christ by Nicodemus. [20] Identical symbolism is given to this ritual act also by Pseudo-Sophronius and by Simeon of Salonika. [21]

Almost the same interpretation is given at the beginning of the sixth century by Narsai, for the Chaldean Church, when he explains the entrance rite as *representing* Christ led to his passion and death, the bread on the *diskos* and the wine in the chalice, as the *symbols* of his death, and the placing of the gifts on the altar as *expressing* his burial. [22] In another *Homily*, explaining the entrance with the gifts, Narsai is even more specific : "...and he brings up, he sets thereon the bread and wine as a corpse. The burial day of the King he transacts mystically, and he sets soldiers on guard by a representation. Two deacons he places like a rank (of soldiers) on this side and that, that they may be guarding the dread Mystery of the King of Kings. Awe and love lie upon the faculties of their minds while they look intently upon the bread and wine as upon the King. " [23] Here, however, he says : " he sets thereon the *bread and wine* as a corpse " and not " he sets thereon *the corpse* of Christ "; no less significantly in the last sentence, " they look intently upon the *bread and wine* as upon the King. "

Later, some Byzantine clerics were influenced by Theodore's interpretation of the Great Entrance, and the faithful in some churches prostrated themselves in adoration before the gifts because they believed them to be the body and blood of Christ. Those who did were mistaken in their understanding of the rite and its authentic

---

[19] Germanus I of Constantinople, *Commentarius liturgicus*, 37 (edit. Borgia *Il commentario liturgico di s. Germano Patriarca Constantinopolitano e la versione latina di Anastasio Bibliotecario* [Grottaferrata, 1912], pp. 29-31). Our translation.

[20] *Ibid.*

[21] For Ps.-Sophronius, see PG 87, 4001; for Simeon of Salonika, see PG 155, 728.

[22] Narsai, *Expositio mysteriorum*, Homil. XVII (edit. Mingana, I, p. 272).

[23] Narsai, *Homily XXI* (edit. R. H. Connolly, *Liturgical Homilies of Narsai* [Cambridge, 1909], p. 55); see also edit. Mingana, I, p. 350.

tradition.   This was discussed at length in 1371 by Nicholas Cabasilas in his *Commentary on the Divine Liturgy*.   In this commentary, he also gives the underlying reasons for the liturgical acts :

> This is done, no doubt, for practical reasons; it was necessary to bring the offerings which are to be sacrificed to the altar and set them down there, and to do this with all reverence and devotion.   This is the way in which the kings of old brought their gifts to God; they did not allow others to do it for them, but brought their offerings themselves, wearing their crowns.   Also this ceremony signifies the last manifestation of Christ, which aroused the hatred of the Jews, when he embarked on the journey from his native country to Jerusalem, where he was to be sacrificed; then he rode into the Holy City on the back of an ass, escorted by a cheering crowd.
>
> ...If any of those who prostrate themselves thus before the priest who is carrying the offerings adores them as if they were the Body and Blood of Christ, and prays to them as such, he is led into error; he is confusing this ceremony with that of " the Entry of the Presanctified, " not recognizing the differences between them.   In this entry of the offerings, the gifts are not yet consecrated for the sacrifice; in the Liturgy of the Presanctified they are consecrated and sanctified, the true Body and Blood of Christ. [24]

Two important points stand out in these passages.   Cabasilas states unequivocally that those who believe they are adoring the body and blood of Christ at the Great Entrance are in error, that they are confusing this ceremony with " the Entry of the Presanctified, " where the sacred elements are indeed the body and blood of Christ consecrated at a previous Liturgy. [25]   Like Pseudo-Germanus and Theodore of Andida before him, [26] Cabasilas interprets the Great Entrance as representing the triumphal entry of Christ

[24] N. Cabasilas, *A Commentary on the Divine Liturgy*, trans. by J. M. Hussey and P. A. McNulty (London, 1960), pp. 65-66.

[25] It would be pointless, we believe, to delve into later controversies concerning the Great Entrance, such as that occasioned by Gabriel Severus, Metropolitan of Philadelphia (A.D. 1616), who distinguished three types of adoration which can be given to the gifts.   A fiery denunciation of these arguments was given by Peter Arcudius in 1633.   A saner approach, more consonant with reality, was made by Goar in his *Euchologion* of 1647 (n. 110, pp. 131-132).

[26] Cf. Migne, PG 98, 419, for former, and PG 140, 441-444, for latter.

into Jerusalem on Passion Sunday. Such symbolism naturally leads to increased pomp and ceremony, which are justified by what is represented, and not by the presence of the unconsecrated elements. In fact the extreme pomp and ceremony surrounding the Great Entrance may well have induced the symbolism of Christ's triumphal entrance into Jerusalem in the first place. This symbolism in turn certainly induced the insertion of the scriptural words, *Blessed is he who comes in the name of the Lord*, into the Great Entrance during the fourteenth century. [27]

The Accompanying Ritual

Until the thirteenth or fourteenth century, the deacon and priest would wash their hands before the Great Entrance; [28] this is still done by the bishop in a Pontifical Liturgy. Before the eighth century, when the rite of preparing the gifts was performed immediately before the Great Entrance, this was the natural time to wash the hands. After sorting, handling, and preparing the gifts, washing

[27] Though later discontinued, this prayer is found in some fourteenth and fifteenth century texts of the Liturgy (cf. Krasnoseltsev, *Materialy dlja istorii chinoposlidovania liturgii sv. Ioanna Zlatoustago* [Kazan, 1889], pp. 61, 108). Not all Greek texts of these centuries have " Blessed is he who comes in the name of the Lord, " for some sources have " Open, ye princes, your doors, open ye the eternal doors, " (cf. Krasnoseltsev, *op. cit.*, p. 60, and MS. N. 719 of Patmos Library, edit. Dmitrievsky, *Opysanie liturgicheskikh rukopisej khraniaschikhsia v bibliotekakh pravoslavnago vostoka*, II, *Euchologia* [Kiev, 1901], p. 173). Both prayers are still found in the Slav Liturgy of the fifteenth century, e.g., MSS. N. 531, p. 30, N. 534, p. 18, and N. 535, p. 27 of Sophia Library (Petrovsky, *Histoire de la rédaction slave de la liturgie de S. Jean Chrysostome*, XPYCOCTOMIKA, pp. 905-906); the *Liturgikon* of Metropolitan Isidore, in its *Ustav*, has only the first prayer; cf. MS. *Vat Slav.*, N. 14, fol. 133. These prayers probably were suppressed because of the greater number of commemorations, " May the Lord remember in his Kingdom, " which were being introduced into the Great Entrance rite during the sixteenth century; cf. MSS. N. 1020, p. 58, N. 1021, p. 57, N. 1025, p. 103, and N. 1029, p. 131, of Solovetsky Library, Theological Academy of Kazan (Petrovsky, *op. cit.*, p. 920).

[28] E.g., the early eighth century Armenian version of Chrysostom's Liturgy (Aucher, *La versione armena della liturgia di S. Giovanni Crisostomo, fatta sul principio dell'VIII secolo*, XPYCOCTOMIKA, p. 385); the ninth or tenth-century *Cod. Porphyrios*, etc. (for details, cf. Krasnoseltsev, *op. cit.*, pp. 102, 107, 288, and Dmitrievsky, *op. cit.*, II, p. 141). For the Slav Church, cf. thirteenth century MSS. N. 518, p. 25, N. 524, p. 20, of Sophia Library (Petrosvky, *op. cit.*, p. 875) and the fourteenth century MSS. 520, N. 522, N. 523, N. 526, of Sophia Library (Petrovsky, *op. cit.*, p. 883), and MS. N. 345 of Moscow Synodal Library (Gorsky-Nevostrujev, *Opysanie slavianskikh rukopisej Moskovskoj Synodal'noj biblioteky*, Vol. III [Moscow, 1859], p. 21), etc.

the hands was dictated by sheer utility. When the preparation of the gifts was shifted to the beginning of the Liturgy of the Word, the custom of washing the hands still survived for several centuries, although the necessity for it had disappeared. Had the washing of hands occurred after the Great Entrance, which implied handling various utensils and vessels, it could have some purpose. Such a prescription does appear in some Slav missals of the twelfth century.[29]

When in the thirteenth and fourteenth centuries more and more Byzantine churches were introducing the practice of washing the hands immediately after vesting, before the beginning of the Divine Liturgy, they discontinued the washing before the Great Entrance. By the sixteenth century, the practice was universally adopted in the Byzantine and Syrian Churches. All the other Oriental Rites have the washing of the hands both at the offertory and before the beginning of the Divine Liturgy.

The custom of placing the large veil, the *aër*, on the deacon's shoulder seems to have originated in the fourteenth century, but at the time it was placed on the right shoulder and not on the left, as it is today. [30] The priest now says : *Lift up your hands unto holy things and bless the Lord*, an adaptation of Psalm 133, verse two. Introduced probably in the latter part of the fourteenth century, this verse was to be said first by the deacon and then by the priest, or only by the deacon. [31]

Another new practice of the fourteenth century was the commemoration " May the Lord God remember all of you in his Kingdom. " When first introduced, it consisted of one simple invocation,

---

[29] E.g., the *Liturgikon* of Anthony the Roman and that of Barlaam of Khutinsk; cf. MSS. N. 342 and N. 343 of Moscow Synodal Library (Gorsky-Nevostrijev, *op. cit.*, III, 1, 2, 6); so does the fourteenth century MS. *Vat. Slav.*, No. 9; cf. O. Horbatsch, *De tribus textibus Liturgicis Linguae Ecclesiasticae (Palaeo) Slavicae in Manuscriptis Vaticanis* (Rome, 1966), p. 136.

[30] Cf. Petrovsky, *op. cit.*, p. 888. The fourteenth or fifteenth century *Liturgikon* of Metropolitan Isidore, however, has the priest placing the veil on the deacon's left shoulder; cf. MS. *Vat. Slav.*, No. 14, fol. 132.

[31] E.g., MSS. N. 534, p. 32, N. 836, p. 32, of Sophia Library (cf. Petrovsky, *op. cit.*, p. 904). Compare also MS. 984 of Sinai Library and MS. Vat. 573 (Dmitrievsky, *op. cit.*, p. 909, and Krasnoseltsev, *op. cit.*, pp. 89, 108). The Kievan fourteenth or fifteenth century *Liturgikon* of Metropolitan Isidore has the priest alone saying the verse; cf. MS. *Vat. Slav.*, No. 14, fol. 132.

as is the case in the Greek recension of the Liturgy today. [32] The fourteenth-fifteenth century Kievan *Liturgikon* of Metropolitan Isidore, for example, still has, *May the Lord God remember all of you in his Kingdom, always, now and forever and ever.* [33]

The Slav Church soon added other commemorations to the original brief invocation. In the fifteenth century, we find several : " May the Lord God remember in his Kingdom your nobility; may the Lord God remember in his Kingdom your episcopacy; may the Lord God remember in his Kingdom your humility and patience. " [34]

In the sixteenth century, commemorations of the monasteries, towns, villages and their inhabitants, the archbishop, the sovereign and his household, etc. were inserted. [35] Some local usages survived until the seventeenth century, but by then most of the Slav Church had attained uniformity. The Ukrainian or Ruthenian Church, for example, finally evolved a formula more or less uniform, if we except the difference between Catholic and Orthodox usage regarding the commemoration of the Holy Father. [36] The Greek Church still uses the old short form; so do the Russian Old Believers.

By contrast, the Russian Synodal Church has the greatest number of commemorations and the greatest variety of local customs. As late as the nineteenth century, names of individual members of the royal family were mentioned. [37]

As long as everything was being said in a low voice by the sacred ministers during the Great Entrance, the singing of the *Cherubikon* remained uninterrupted, but when the commemorations began to be

---

[32] Cf. Petrovsky, *op. cit.*, p. 888.

[33] MS. *Vat. Slav.*, No. 14, fols. 132-133. Thus also the fifteenth century MSS. N. 562, p. 30, N. 559, p. 35, N. 564, p. 71, N. 972, p. 38, etc., of Sophia Library (except that the invocation was recited three times); cf. Petrovsky, *op. cit.*, p. 905, n. 1.

[34] MSS. of Sophia Library, N. 530, p. 42, N. 532, p. 4, N. 546, p. 90; cf. Petrovsky, *op. cit.*, p. 905.

[35] MS. of Sophia Library, N. 567, pp. 17-18, and MS. N. 1029, p. 131, of Solovetsky Library (Petrovsky, *op. cit.*, pp. 907, 920).

[36] The Catholic practice was firmly established by the *Sluzhebnyk*, or missal, of Metropolitan Cyprian Zochowsky, published in Vilno, 1692 (p. 90) and the Synod of Zamosc, 1720 (Sess. III, Tit. I).

[37] Archimandrite Kyprian, *Evcharistia* (Paris : YMCA Press, 1947), p. 199.

chanted in the fifteenth century, the *Cherubikon* was cut in two parts. The first was sung before the commemorations of the Great Entrance, and the second, after their completion. This is still the practice.

The symbolism of Christ's passion and death continues after the Great Entrance. The taking of the *diskos* from the head of the deacon symbolizes the taking of Christ's body from the cross; the placing of the gifts on the altar represents the burial, while the incensing recalls the anointing of Christ's body by Nicodemus. The placing of the large veil over the gifts symbolizes the stone rolled before the entrance of the tomb. It is accompanied by the recitation of the beautiful *troparion* " Noble Joseph, " which recalls the events of the burial in poetic form. It is taken from the Vesper Service of Holy Friday, in which the burial of Christ is portrayed in an entirely different though no less effective manner. This *troparion* was inserted during the fourteenth century, at the time of the publication of the *Constitution* of Philotheus. [38] This is one of the few instances in which symbolism induced a liturgical change. The final two verses of Psalm 50, which accompany the *troparion*, were also added at about the same time. [39]

Psalm 50 is a psalm of repentance. The final two verses—a Jewish addition qualifying true repentance probably introduced after the destruction of Jerusalem in 586 B.C.—must be taken with the rest : external ritual without inward contrition will not satisfy God. By accommodation, the priest prays that God himself build up and protect his own chosen ones and the souls of all the offerers together with the walls of Jerusalem, so that nothing may vitiate this inner penitence; only then will they be able to offer external ritual that will please God.

Psalm 50 was recited originally by the ministers during the actual entrance. [40] Later, it was said only by the deacon during the general

[38] Cf. Krasnoseltsev, *op. cit.*, pp. 60-63; also the fourteenth or fifteenth century *Ustav* in the *Liturgikon* of Metropolitan Isidore; cf. MS. *Vat. Slav.*, No. 14, fol. 133.

[39] Cf. Dmitrievsky, *op. cit.*, II, p. 618, n. 8 and p. 959; also the fourteenth or fifteenth century *Ustav* of Metropolitan Isidore's *Liturgikon*; cf. MS. *Vat. Slav.*, No. 14, fols. 133-134.

[40] Dmitrievsky, *op. cit.*, II, pp. 157, 475, 609, 959; see above, p. 484.

incensing (as it is today). The original purpose of the psalm at this point is further spiritual purification of the sacred ministers through sorrow and contrition. The final two verses said by the celebrant after the deposition of the gifts on the holy table obtain here an accommodated meaning : that God will be satisfied by the Divine Holocaust of the Eucharistic Sacrifice.

CHAPTER L

THE PRE-ANAPHORAL DIALOGUE OF PRIEST AND DEACON

After returning the censer, the priest unfolds his felon. Bowing his head, he says to the deacon :

Remember me, brother and fellow minister.

The deacon bows his head, holds his orar *with three fingers, and says to the priest :*

May the Lord God remember your priesthood in his Kingdom.

Priest : **Pray for me, my fellow minister.**

Again, the deacon bows his head, holds his orar *with three fingers and says to the priest :*

May the Holy Spirit come upon you and the power of the Most High overshadow you.

Priest : **May the same Holy Spirit minister with us all the days of our life.**

Deacon : **Remember me, Reverend Sir.**

Priest : **May the Lord God remember you in his Kingdom, at all times, now and always and for ever and ever.**

Deacon : **Amen.**

This prayerful encounter between priest and deacon is more than a dialogue : it is also an expression of brotherly love in preparation for the Sacrifice.

The priest initiates this exchange by asking the deacon to remember him. In answer, the deacon prays that God remember him as a priest—" remember " in the sense that Christ " remembered " the good thief on that first Holy Friday. Again, the priest makes a simple, straightforward plea that the deacon pray for him. If the humble simplicity of the plea is touching, the fact that a higher minister asks a lower one to pray for him is even more touching. The deacon's response is taken almost word for word from Luke 1:35 : " May the

Holy Spirit come upon you and the power of the Most High over-shadow you, " a personal epiclesis.

The overshadowing cloud is the traditional symbol of divine presence and mysterious action. [1] In the Old Testament, the Spirit of God intervenes when things are to be brought to life or when a special power from God is to be given for the fulfillment of some divine purpose, [2] such as the Incarnation. A similar action takes place at the moment of the transubstantiation in the Divine Liturgy.

The priest begs the Holy Spirit to minister with them for as long as they live. The deacon, in turn, asks the priest to pray for him. This the priest does with almost the same prayer as that of the deacon at the beginning of the dialogue. The whole is reminiscent of an early Christian practice : imploring one another for prayers before important undertakings, a dangerous journey, imprisonment, or martyrdom.

The post-entrance, pre-anaphoral dialogue appeared in the Byzantine Liturgy during the eleventh or twelfth century. Leo Thuscus has it in his Latin version [3] In the Slav churches, a similar dialogue was in use in the twelfth century : [4]

> *First Concelebrant :* Bless, Reverend Sir.
>
> *Celebrant :* Unto many years, Father, may the Holy Spirit come upon you and the power of the Most High overshadow you, and pray for me, virtuous Father.
>
> *First Concelebrant :* May the Lord remember you in his Kingdom.
>
> *Celebrant :* May it be done according to your word.

A slightly different order was observed by the priest and deacon in some churches during the fourteenth century : [5]

---

[1] Cf. Exod. 19:9, 16; 13:21; III Kings 8:10-12; Isa. 6:4; Luke 9:34; Acts 1:9; etc.

[2] Cf. Gen. 1:2; Num. 24:2; Judg. 3:10, 6:34; I Kings 10:6; Ps. 103:30; Isa 11:2; etc.

[3] Cf. de Meester, *Les origines et les développements du texte grec de la liturgie de S. Jean Chrysostome,* XPYCOCTOMIKA (Rome, 1908), p. 331; also Dmitrevsky, *Opysanie liturgicheskikh rukopisej khraniaschikhsia v bibliotekakh pravoslavnago vostoka,* Vol. II, *Euchologia* (Kiev, 1901), p. 206, for a similar usage.

[4] MSS. of Synodal Library of Moscow, N. 342, N. 343; cf. Gorsky-Nevostrujev, *Opysanie slavianskikh rukopisej Moskovskoj Synodal'noj biblioteky,* Vol. III (Moscow, 1859), i, 2, 6.

[5] Krasnoseltsev, *Materialy dlja istorii chinoposlidovania liturgii sv. Ioanna Zlatoustago* (Kazan, 1889), pp. 62-69.

Priest : Bless, O holy one.

Deacon : May the Holy Spirit descend upon you and the power of the Most High overshadow you. Remember me, holy Sir.

Priest : May the Lord remember you in his Kingdom, now and always, and for ever and ever.

A parallel is found in West Syrian and East Syrian Liturgies. In the Syrian Jacobite Liturgy, the celebrant calls on the people : " My brethren and my masters, pray for me that my sacrifice may be accepted. " [6] The Nestorian Liturgy has a much longer dialogue :

Priest : Bless, O my Lord, my brethren; pray for me that this offering be accomplished at my hands.

People : God, the Lord of all, strengthen thee to fulfill his will and receive thine offering and be well pleased with thy sacrifice for us and for thyself and for the four corners of the world by the grace of his compassion for ever. Amen.

Priest (repeats a long prayer) : Glory to thee, the finder of the lost *(etc. Then he concludes with)* : Bless, O my Lord. Pray for me, my brethren and my beloved, that I be accounted worthy to offer before our Lord Christ this sacrifice living and holy for myself and for all the body of the holy church by the grace of his compassion for ever. Amen.

People : God the Lord of all, be well pleased with thy sacrifice and receive thine offering, which thou offerest for us and for thyself by his grace and mercy for ever. Amen. [7]

Since these two practices are common to both Syrian Liturgies, they are probably quite ancient, certainly antedating the Byzantine dialogue by centuries.

The *Orate fratres* of the Latin Mass, later than the Syrian prayer but earlier than the Byzantine, is essentially the same. It appears at the same point, that is, after the presentation and arrangement of the gifts on the altar. Its oldest text, the eighth-century Roman pontifical rite as adapted to Frankish circumstances, has the celebrant address his petition to the other priests. [8] Later, according to

[6] Brightman, LEW, p. 83, lines 1-2.

[7] *Ibid.*, pp. 272-273.

[8] Cf. *Breviarium eccl. ord.* (edit. Silva-Tarouca, *Giovanni " Archicantor " de S. Pietro a Roma e l'ordo Romanus da lui composto* [Atti della Pont. Accademia Romana di archeologia, Memorie : Rome, 1923], 198).

Amalar, the petition is addressed to the people. [9] Both the early Latin and the Byzantine forms were personal : *Orate pro me,* [10] *orate pro me, fratres,* [11] and *orate pro me peccatore.* [12] The personal element is even more evident in *Obsecro vos, fratres, orate pro me.* [13] Another petition generally follows, that the priest's sacrifice be acceptable to God. A few of the older Latin missals have the same verse, Luke 1:35, transformed into a blessing, like that of the Byzantine Rite : " May the Holy Spirit come upon you and the power of the Most High overshadow you. " [14] A common origin is probable. The Latin practice seems to antedate the Byzantine, but other considerations preclude final judgment as to the order of derivation.

[9] Amalar, *De eccl. off.*, III, 19 (PL 105, 1132); also Remigius of Auxerre, *Expositio* (PL 101, 1252).

[10] *Ordo Rom.*, VI, n. 10 (PL 78, 993 B).

[11] Sacramentary of the papal chapel about A.D. 1290; cf. Brinktrine, *Eph. liturg.* (1937), 203.

[12] *Sacramentary of Lorsch,* tenth century, cf. Ebner, 247; *Missa Illyrica,* cf. Martène, 1, 4, IV (I, 512 A). Also see Ebner, 301, 306, 327, for the Italian Mass orders since the eleventh century.

[13] *Sacramentary of Moissac,* cf. Martène, 1, 4, VIII (I, 539 D). Other examples can be found in Martène, 1, 4, 7, 4 (I, 396). The Missal from S. Pol de Léon has, *Orate pro me, fratres et sorores, et ego orabo pro vobis*; cf. Martène, 1, 4, XXXIV (I, 644 D).

[14] The Prayer Book of Charles the Bald, written about A.D. 870, as well as the older Missal of Fécamp (Martène, 1, 4, 7, 4 [I, 386 A]), and in the Missal of Beauvais, (Martène, 1, 4, 7, 4 [I 396 A]), and the two Sarum MSS. of the fourteenth century; cf. Legg, *The Sarum Missal,* 219, n. 7.

THE OFFERTORY *EKTENIA*
AND PRAYER

When the dialogue is completed, the deacon bows to the priest, goes out through the north door and, after taking his usual place in front of the royal doors, begins the following ektenia :

Let us complete our prayer to the Lord.

People : **Lord, have mercy.**

Deacon : **For the precious gifts that have been brought forth, let us pray to the Lord.**

People : **Lord, have mercy.**

Deacon : **For this holy church, and for those who enter it with faith, reverence, and the fear of God, let us pray to the Lord.**

People : **Lord, have mercy.**

Deacon : **For our deliverance from all affliction, wrath, and need, let us pray to the Lord.**

People : **Lord, have mercy.**

While the deacon is singing the ektenia, *the priest recites the* Prayer of Offering, *silently :*

Lord, almighty God, you alone are holy; since you accept the sacrifice of praise from those who call upon you with their whole heart, accept also the prayer of us sinners and take it to your holy altar. Make us worthy of offering you gifts and spiritual sacrifices for our sins and for the errors of the people. Grant that we may find kindness before you and that our sacrifice may be acceptable to you. May the good spirit of your grace rest upon us and these gifts that have been set forth, and upon all your people.

Deacon : **Help us, save us, have mercy on us and protect us, O God, by your grace.**

People : **Lord, have mercy.**

Deacon : **Let us ask the Lord that this whole day be perfect, holy, peaceful, and sinless.**

People : **Grant it, O Lord.**

Deacon : **Let us ask the Lord for an angel of peace, a faithful guide and guardian of our souls and bodies.**

People : **Grant it, O Lord.**

Deacon : **Let us ask the Lord for the pardon and forgiveness of our sins and offenses.**

People : **Grant it, O Lord.**

Deacon : **Let us ask the Lord for whatever is good and profitable to our souls and for peace in the world.**

People : **Grant it, O Lord.**

Deacon : **Let us ask the Lord that we may spend the rest of our lives in peace and repentance.**

People : **Grant it, O Lord.**

Deacon : **Let us ask the Lord for a Christian and peaceful end to our lives, without pain or blame, and for a good defense before the dread judgment-seat of Christ.**

People : **Grant it, O Lord.**

Deacon : **As we remember our all-holy, immaculate, most blessed and glorious Lady, the Mother of God and ever-virgin Mary, together with all the saints, let us commend ourselves and one another and our whole life to Christ, our God.** [1]

People : **To you, O Lord.**

Priest : **Through the mercy of your only-begotten Son, together with your all-holy, good and life-giving Spirit, may you be blessed now and always and for ever and ever.**

People : **Amen.**

The offertory prayer, accompanied by an *ektenia,* continues and completes the series originated in the *proskomidia* and the Great Entrance.   The first oblation of the bread and wine with its con-

---

[1] Since Vatican II the final eight proclamations of this *ektenia* are omitted by the Ruthenians.

current symbolism occurs in the *proskomidia,* where the sacred elements are presented as the image (icon) of Christ and his passion. The actual bearing these elements to the altar of God during the Great Entrance is also part of the offertory rite. Its completion is formally introduced with the deacon's request : " Let us complete our prayer to the Lord. " This can be interpreted either as an act of the anaphora through which the Victim of the Sacrifice is offered to God, or in the Western sense, as the completion of the offering of the material bread and wine. Both senses may be read into the proclamation of the deacon found in the *Apostolic Constitutions* : " Let us stand straight before the Lord with fear and trembling to offer (the oblation). " [2]

Then comes a prayer by the deacon, the people, and the celebrant : the deacon announcing the petitions, the people responding, and the priest reciting the prayers of offering in the name of all.

As generally printed, the *ektenia* is divided into two parts, with the priests's prayer between. In fact, the *ektenia* is a continuous whole. [3]

There is considerable difference between this *ektenia* and the *Great Ektenia* found at the beginning of the Divine Liturgy. The petitions of the *Great Ektenia* are concerned mainly with temporal, earthly blessings; these, with spiritual benefits. The reason seems to be the proximity of the moment of sacrifice. The general theme is expressed in one of the petitions of the *Apostolic Constitutions,* " that (God) grant... eternal goods in exchange for the temporal; heavenly goods in exchange for the earthly. " [4]

" For the precious gifts that have been brought forth. " In commenting on this petition, Cabasilas interprets it as a prayer " for that which is about to take place; that these gifts may be consecrated, and that what we offer at the beginning may achieve its end. " [5] Another interpretation is based on historical antecedents : the

[2] *Apostolic Constitutions,* Book VIII; see above, p. 124.

[3] I.e., when the Divine Liturgy is celebrated with the assistance of a deacon. If the priest celebrates alone, he divides the *ektenia* as it is given in the texts.

[4] *Apostolic Constitutions,* Book VIII, see above, p. 120.

[5] N. Cabasilas, *A Commentary on the Divine Liturgy,* trans. by J. M. Hussey and P. A. McNulty (London, 1960), p. 66. For the original Greek text see PG 150.

ektenia, replacing the diptychs, is actually intended for those who offer the gifts. [6] These interpretations are not mutually exclusive. The Divine Sacrifice is indeed offered for some particular intention or person, in addition to its other purposes. The rest of the *ektenia* tends to confirm the historical interpretation, since it intercedes for the spiritual welfare of the offerers—and those who attended were offerers. In the fourth century, as we have seen, these petitions were part of the intercessory prayers of the faithful. In fact, if we excluded the later additions to the Liturgy—the Great Entrance and its ceremonial—we would notice that this ektenia is a continuation of these prayers. [7]

" Help us, save us, have mercy on us and protect us, O God, by your grace. " This seems to be an abbreviated version of the petition found in the *Apostolic Constitutions* : " Let us pray for one another, that the Lord keep us and guard us by his grace till the end and deliver us from the evil one and from all the scandals of those that work iniquity, and save us for his heavenly Kingdom. " [8]

" That this whole day may be perfect, holy, peaceful and sinless. " The *Apostolic Constitutions*, from which this petition is taken almost word for word, has : " That this day and the whole of your life may be peaceful and sinless. " [9] Chrysostom has a slightly different form : " Beseech that your present day and all the days of your life may be peaceful. " [10]

" For an angel of peace, the faithful guide and guardian of our souls and bodies. " " What are they, all of them, but spirits apt for service, whom he sends out when the destined heirs of eternal salvation have need of them ? " (Heb. 1:14). From the very beginning

---

[6] See below, pp. 518-527, for comprehensive treatment of this problem.

[7] In the fourth century the gifts were selected and prepared probably while one of the deacons was occupied with announcing the last of the petitions for the faithful. According to the *Apostolic Constitutions*, the subdeacon brought water for washing the priest's hands *after* the final call that none of the catechumens, hearers, unbelievers or heretics remain (each group had been dismissed before the prayers of the faithful). Then the gifts were brought to the altar by the deacons (cf. *Apost. Const.*, Book VIII, see above, p. 124). The offertory followed. Could it be that the offertory prayer was merely the final prayer of the whole series?

[8] *Apostolic Constitutions*, Book VIII, see above, p. 121.

[9] *Ibid.*, see above, p. 111.

[10] Chrysostom, *In II Cor.* ii, 10 (edit. Montfaucon, 10, 440).

Christians believed that in their struggle against evil they were assisted by angel guardians, for Christ himself, warning against giving scandal to little ones, said, " I tell you, they have angels of their own in heaven, that behold the face of my heavenly Father continually " (Matt. 18:10). The angel is not omnipresent, but, owing to his spiritual nature, he is not tied to any particular place and can exercise his influence wherever he acts while still remaining in heaven. Though it is impossible to tell precisely in what way and at what given moment the action of our angel is making itself felt in our soul, yet, according to the most ancient tradition and Holy Scripture, angels are always present in our life to protect us and guide our steps to heaven. God gives us an angel to walk by our side through the whole journey of life, as he gave Raphael to accompany Tobias. This angel makes use of our instinct of self-preservation to warn us of danger and he encourages us to live according to the will and law of God. Imbued with God's own loving-kindness, he shares his wisdom with us when our own fails. In a word, he is indeed the faithful guide and guardian of our souls and bodies. In the days of Chrysostom, the petition was simply : " Let us pray for an angel of peace. " [11]

" For the pardon and forgiveness of our sins and offenses. " This is a slight embellishment of the original petition found in the *Apostolic Constitutions* : " Beseech the forgiveness of your transgressions, " [12]— an indirect appeal for sanctifying grace. Without that grace, or charity, diffused in our hearts by the Holy Spirit, our sins would not be remitted.

" For whatever is good and profitable to our souls. " What is good and profitable to our souls? Certainly, justification, that internal, inherent gift, conferred by sanctifying grace, by which we are born anew to a supernatural life. Together with it, we receive the virtues of faith, hope, and charity—the supernatural habits of these virtues. Here, the Holy Spirit, the immediate author of sanctifying grace, is communicated to the soul : " The charity of God is poured forth in our hearts by the Holy Spirit, who is given to us " (Rom. 5:5). Eminently profitable and good for our souls

[11] *Ibid.* (edit. Montfaucon 10, 440).
[12] *Apostolic Constitutions*, Book, VIII; see above, p. 111.

are good works, the actual exercise of of all the virtues, especially the virtues of faith, hope, and charity, all of which lead to eternal beatitude.

In the days of Chrysostom, the petition was simply : " Pray for that which is good and salutary. " [13]

" That we may spend the rest of our life in peace and repentance. " Oscillating between fear and hope, man lives in the presence of the God of mercy and the God of fear. Byzantinism distinguished itself from Western Christianity by emphasis on this dualism. Fear is the fountainhead of repentance. Repentance in all its nuances was one of the mightiest forces of Russian-Kievan devotion, even as it was in Syro-Byzantine Christianity. Repentance begets hope and, with hope, trust and peace of soul.

Chrysostom cites the petition as : " Pray that your present day and all the days of your life be peaceful. " Repentance is presupposed, for without repentance there can be no true peace of soul.

" For a Christian and peaceful end to our life, without pain or blame, and for a good defense before the dread judgment seat of Christ. " The Old Testament offers a pessimistic view of death and life beyond the grave. The good and evil that man did were repaid here on earth; beyond the grave, the chosen people seemed to believe in a dismal existence of the soul in some deeply hidden abyss called Sheol. The bitter words of Job reflect their general thought : " Brief, brief, is my span of days—to find some comfort in my misery. Soon I must go to a land whence there is no returning, a land of darkness, death's shadow over it; a land of gloomy night, where death's shadow lies over all, and no peace haunts it, only everlasting dread " (Job 10:20-22). Man's one hope was for a long life on earth. In those days, no one seems to have prayed for a happy death.

During the last few centuries before Christ, the idea of a blissful life after death began to grow. " But the souls of the just are in God's hands, and no torment, in death itself, has power to reach them. Dead? Fools think so; think their end loss, their leaving us, annihilation; but all is well with them..." (Wisdom 3:1-2).

---

[13] *Ibid.* (edit. Montfaucon 10, 440).

With the coming of Christ, the prospect of a morbid, meaningless and hopeless existence vanished.   What contrasting comfort, what glorious hope the Son of God held out for his followers : " I am the resurrection and life; he who believes in me, though he is dead, will live on; and whoever has life, and has faith in me, to all eternity cannot die " (John 11:25-26).   Being a Christian to the end brought with it the prospect of an eternally happy future.

The thought of death still shakes the Christian, for it will settle his destiny forever.   The last moments of life on earth are extremely perilous : not only does Satan use all the wiles at his command to lure the soul away from God, but sometimes wracking pain and anguish leave man powerless for fervent prayer, unable to think about God and the state of his soul.   Final perseverance is a special grace from God, but the good Christian trusts that God in his loving-kindness will grant this grace to the just man in answer to his earnest and constant prayer.   What better moment to pray for this grace of a Christian, peaceful end to our life, without pain or blame, than at the very Sacrifice of the Son of God?

Both Chrysostom and the *Apostolic Constitutions* have a shorter petition : " (Pray for) a Christian end (to your life). " [14]

The scriptural foundation of the petition's final words is evident. " We shall all stand, one day, before the judgment seat of Christ... and so each of us will have to give an account of himself before God, " writes Paul to the Romans (14:10-12).   He enlarges upon this when writings to the Corinthians : " All of us have a scrutiny to undergo before Christ's judgment seat, for each to reap what his mortal life has earned, good or ill, according to his deeds " (II Cor. 5:10).

Society surrounded human judgment with fitting ceremony.   Even Pilate, when he " sent for water and washed his hands in full sight of the multitude, " was acting out a very ancient custom.   It is cited in Deuteronomy 21:6-7; Virgil and Ovid also mention it.   The judgment seat itself is another ceremonial element.   St. Paul and the author of this petition reflect a mode of thinking still current with us.   At the particular judgment, however, there is no question

---

[14] *Ibid.* (edit. Montfaucon 10, 440); also, *Apostolic Constitutions*, Book VIII, see above, p. 111.

of a judge making his appearance and assessing the value of a life after listening to charges and defense. [15] This judgment is a purely spiritual event: the meeting of God and the soul. Englightenment will pierce the soul, and in a flash it will clearly grasp the import of all its acts, good and evil. This judgment has no duration in time : it takes place wordlessly in the silence of eternity.

"As we remember our all-holy, immaculate...." We have already commented on this commemoration to the Mother of God (see above, pp. 350-357). Here, we shall merely point out the appropriateness of commending ourselves and our whole life to God at the very moment of the liturgical offertory. At the very time when our gifts are being offered to God through his appointed representative, we the faithful are dedicating our whole being and life to him through the hands of Mary and the saints. The priest-celebrant, officially representing the whole mystical body and each of its members, offers the gifts to God, while the faithful offer themselves as vital parts of the mystical body with Christ as their head. This idea was not quite developed in the fourth-century Syrian Church, which had a similar "dedication" in the dismissal prayers of the catechumens. Chrysostom gives it as : "Commend yourselves to the living God and to his Christ," [16] while the *Apostolic Constitutions* has, "Commend yourselves to the only-begotten God through his Christ." [17] Since this litany was recited at the dismissal of the catechumens and not at the offertory or even as part of the prayers of the faithful, it had an entirely different meaning from what it has today.

The precise time when these petitions and the offertory prayer assumed their final place and form in the Byzantine Liturgy is unknown, but it was probably during the seventh century. They are found in the Armenian version of Chrysostom's Liturgy in the early part of the eighth century. [18]

The *Codex Barberini* (*gr.* 336) does not contain the ektenia at this point, but then, neither does it list any of the deacon's *ektenias* any-

---

[15] Many ascetical works, especially Syrian, Byzantine, and Russian, do, however, employ just such imagery in describing the particular judgment.

[16] Chrysostom, *In II Cor.*, ii, 10 (edit. Montfaucon 10, 440).

[17] *Apostolic Constitutions*, Book VIII; see above, p. 111.

[18] Aucher, *La versione armena della liturgia di S. Giovanni Crisostomo, fatta sul principio dell'VIII secolo*, XPYCOCTOMIKA (Rome, 1908), 385-386.

where else.   Since it does include the present offertory prayer, it was
probably combined with an *ektenia*, for by that time " enclosing "
the celebrant's prayer within an *ektenia* had been standard procedure
for centuries in the Syro-Byzantine family of Liturgies—with the
doxology ending both the prayer of the priest and the *ektenia* of the
deacon.   Probably in the seventh century, when the reading of the
diptychs was shifted to the intercessions after the consecration and
to the *proskomidia* at the beginning of the Liturgy, the *ektenia*
replaced these older practices.   In fact, the prayer is still called the
Prayer of the Proskomidia [19] in the *Codex Barberini* (*gr.* 336).   In
later texts, this prayer is entitled the " Prayer of Setting Forth after
the Sacred Gifts have been placed on the Altar. "

   As is evident from this title, its original purpose was somewhat
different from that of today.   Its essential meaning, however, is the
same : dedicating gifts, offering them to God, and asking him to
receive them.   These gifts are not only material : they include our
labor, toil, and sweat, which procure our survival, and also " all our
spiritual sacrifices, " obviously the products of our minds and souls.
Through these gifts, our entire life is included in this offering " for
our sins and for the errors of the people. "   More literally, this last
would read " and for the people's *unawareness*. "   Byzantine asceticism has always had a deep sense of penitence even for imperfections,
both culpable and inculpable.   Invincible ignorance excuses from
moral guilt, but how much ignorance is guiltless?   In many cases,
this question cannot be answered.   The ancient Byzantine-Slav
penitential discipline gave ignorance another dimension : it was
considered " worse than sin. "   For the author of the *Preface to
Repentance*, for example, " ignorance is worse than sin because the
sinners who repent sincerely are saved, but the senseless, falling into
heresies, are damned. " [20]   It is a valid ascetical principle, therefore,
to have our sorrow and penitence embrace all our " ignorances " in
the hope that God will absolve even the smallest guilt from our

---

[19] Brightman, LEW, pp. 319-321.
[20] Cited by G. P. Fedotov, *The Russian Religious Mind* (New York, 1960),
p. 235.   This idea of ignorance is one of the chief reasons why the *Preface* puts
such emphasis on the wisdom, experience, and moral rectitude of the priest-
confessor.   It bluntly tells the layman, " If the priest is rude, or ignorant, a drunk-
ard or a proud man, he will make you wicked, negligent, loose and lazy. "   Cf.
Fedotov, *ibid*.

souls. The perfection of penitence includes sorrow for not having attained perfection in something despite our complete lack of guilt.

There is a great similarity between the next sentence and the *In spiritu humilitatis* of the Latin offertory (prior to Vatican II).

Byzantine	Latin
Grant that we may find kindness before you and that our sacrifice may be acceptable to you.	Accept us, O Lord, in the spirit of humility and contrition of heart; and grant that the sacrifice we offer this day in your sight may be pleasing to you, O Lord God.

Both express the more profound meaning of external oblation, the offering and personal surrender of oneself to God, and both express the desire that this sacrifice may be acceptable and pleasing to him. There is also a clear parallelism between the pleas addressed to the Spirit in both Rites : [21]

Byzantine	Latin
May the good Spirit of your grace rest upon us and these gifts that have been set forth and upon all your people.	Come, almighty and eternal God, Sanctifier, and bless this sacrifice, prepared for the glory of your holy name.

Since both formularies are preparatory to the anaphora, they cannot be called true epicleses. The ceremonies of the offertory are related to the central rite of the transubstantiation. The true offering of the holy Sacrifice is accomplished only in the Eucharistic anaphora. The Byzantine formula is older, but there can hardly be any question of borrowing. Common theological considerations are perhaps the best explanation for the similarity of content. Both Churches had ritual blessings for products of nature and objects of human use. The sacred gifts would then be blessed quite naturally.

---

[21] The Latin prayer does not necessarily refer to the Holy Spirit, but its meaning was seldom understood otherwise in the Middle Ages. In the Mozarabic Liturgy, this prayer is explicitly addressed to the Holy Spirit : *Veni, sancte Spiritus sanctificator, sanctifica hoc sacrificium de manibus meis praeparatum.* In some parts of the Western Church, an expanded version was used : *Veni sanctificator omnium, Sancte Spiritus, et sanctifica hoc praesens sacrificium ab indignis manibus praeparatum et descende in hanc hostiam invisibiliter, sicut in patrum hostias visibiliter descendisti.* Cf. eleventh or twelfth century Missal of Monte Cassino (Ebner, 310, 328); Missal of St. Vincent-on-Volturno (Fiala, 205); also a Minorite missal (Ebner, 314).

CHAPTER LII

THE DIPTYCHS

The Eastern diptychs (δίπτυχα) consisted of two hinged (δίπτυχον — twofold) tablets with the names of those who were to be remembered in the Eucharistic Sacrifice. The δίπτυχα τῶν ςώντων listed the names of the living, the δίπτυχα τῶν νεκρῶν (or δίπτυχα τῶν κεκοιμημένων), those of the dead—that is, of the saints to be commemorated and deceased persons commended to the official prayers of the Church. The original place of the diptychs in the Eucharistic Liturgy is still a matter of doubt. Did the reading of the lists first take place at the offertory or at the intercessions after the consecration? No one knows.

The first evidence of individuals being mentioned by name comes from the African Church in the middle of the third century. Shortly before dying, Bishop Geminius Victor had made the priest Faustinus his executor—contrary to the rulings of the Carthaginian Council of bishops. Cyprian, to whom the case was referred, enforced the Council's decision : " No offering (oblation at the offertory) should be made for him, nor any sacrifice be celebrated for his repose. For he does not deserve to be *named* at the altar of God in the prayer of the priest.... " [1] We can deduce from this that at least at Requiem Masses, the custom of making an offering (an oblation at the offertory) for a dead person had been established and the deceased probably were being named during the Eucharistic prayer around A.D. 249.

About five years later, when Cyprian sent a huge sum of money to the Numidian bishops for ransoming their brethren from barbarian captivity, he asked the bishops to " present them [i.e., their benefactors and contributors] in your sacrifices and prayers " and adds, " I have added the names of each one and also those of my colleagues and fellow-priests... all of whom, in conformity with the claims of faith and charity, you ought to remember in your supplications and

---

[1] Cyprian, *Ep.* LXV, 2 (edit. ANF, V, p. 367; Oxford edit., Ep. I); our italics and parenthesis.

prayers. " [2]   This passage refers to a list of names; otherwise, why would Cyprian have been so careful to " add " the names of contributors and benefactors ?   At this time, therefore, the African Church also had some kind of Diptych of the Living.   This conclusion is further strengthened by another *Epistle*, in which Cyprian deplores the abuse of having an oblation offered in the name of the lapsed. [3] The abuse proves the rule.   If an oblation were offered in the name of the lapsed, a fortiori it must also have been made in the name of those in good standing.

About fifty years later (*c.* A.D. 305), the 29th Canon of the Council of Elvira ruled that the names of energumens—those possessed by evil spirits—could not " be recited at the altar with the oblation. " [4] Whatever the contemporary standard for judging who was possessed, such people, although they did not receive Communion, sometimes offered their *prosphora* and were mentioned by name—an abuse which the Council sought to rectify.   In this instance, the " naming " of the living took place just before the offertory as each one presented his oblation. [5]   In the Spanish Church, since energumens were sometimes mentioned by name, people in good standing were certainly mentioned as a matter of standard procedure.

Later practice in the Mozarabic Church is even more explicit, since some of its prayers include the names of the *offerentium et pausantium*, that is, of the living offerers and the departed.   Judging from both Cyprian and the Spanish custom, the relatives or friends of the deceased could and did offer in " the name of " the departed who had died in communion with the Church.   The point at which the naming was done was the same in both Churches : at the offertory.   The African Church may have had the dead named also in the anaphora, after the consecration.

In the *Sacramentary* of Sarapion (c. A.D. 353-360), the recital of names occurs after the consecration and the equivalent of an epi-

[2] Cyprian, Ep. LIX, 4 (edit. ANF, V, p. 356; Oxford edit., *Ep.* lxii).

[3] " *Offertur nomine eorum,* " *Ep.* IX, 2 (CSEL 3, 519; edit. ANF, V, p. 290).

[4] Can. 29; cf. Heffele-Leclercq, *Histoire des conciles d'après les documents originaux*, Vol. I (Paris, 1907), 237.

[5] The Spanish offertory prayers are called the " prayers *ad nomina,* " i.e., at the names.

clesis.   The text at this point reads : " We intercede also on behalf of all those who have been laid at rest, whose memorial we are making. "   There follows a rubric : *After the recitation of the names.* Then the text continues : " Sanctify these souls..." etc. (see above, p. 95).   Judging from internal evidence, E. Bishop argues that the recitation of the names of the departed and the intercession for them may have been an import from Jerusalem. [6]

Were the names of the people mentioned also when their oblation was brought to the altar?   There is nothing to disprove it.   Sarapion's description did not include the offertory so we cannot say what the practice was.   Could the wealth of prayers contained in Sarapion—for the sick, for the local church, for the bishop and various members of the church, priests, deacons—and the *Prayer of the Bending of the Knee* dealing with names inscribed in the *Book of Life* have been connected with the offertory?   It is possible, especially the last-mentioned prayer, although most authors believe they were used as *Prayers of the Faithful.*

Cyril's *Mystagogic Catecheses* indicates that in Jerusalem the dead were commemorated after the consecration : " Then, we remember also those who have fallen asleep before us, first the patriarchs, prophets, apostles, martyrs... then the Holy Fathers and bishops... and in a word all who in past years have fallen asleep among us, because we believe that those souls benefit very greatly for whom supplication is made while the holy and tremendous sacrifice lies before us. " [7]   This, however, proves only that categories of persons were mentioned and provides no clue concerning individual names. Immediately afterward, Cyril deals with objections to the practice. Basing their opinion on the form which these objections take, some authors argue that individual names were mentioned here. [8]   This, however, is far from being proved.   Since the practice had caused discussion at Jerusalem, we may suppose it was an innovation.

Before turning our attention to the Byzantine Church, let us examine the evidence from the East Syrian Church.   The ancient

---

[6] E. Bishop, *J. Th. St.*, XIV, 36 ff.

[7] Cyril of Jerusalem, *Cat. Mystag.*, V, 9 (Quasten, *Monumenta eucharistica et liturgia vetustissima* [Bonn, 1935-37], 102).

[8] E.g., E. Bishop, *J. Th. St.*, XIV, 34.

Liturgy of Addai and Mari mentions " the book of the living and the dead. " This is read during the offertory before the kiss of peace. [9] While it names the patriarch and the local bishop, the book of the living is brief, listing only categories of people. The book of the dead, on the other hand, is a long catalogue of proper names, including the names of major saints of the Old and New Testaments, a list of succession of the (Nestorian) patriarchs of Mesopotamia, the names of local bishops, hermits and anchorites. Many are described lovingly and colorfully. Details vary from one manuscript to another. Examples may be quoted from Brightman : " For the poor woman and her two sons, famous martyrs "; " the founders of the godly congregation of the Monastery of Bith Quqa "; " ...the sons of Gregory who are laid in this blessed village "; " the illustrious among athletes and providers of churches and monasteries, generous in alms, sustainers of orphans and widows, Emir Matthew and Emir Hassan "; etc. [10] The series includes " presbyters and deacons and scholars who have departed from this church. " It ends with a beautiful epitaph reminiscent of those found on the crosses of unknown soldiers : " All them that in a true faith departed from this world of whom our Lord alone knoweth the names. " [11] The Liturgy of Addai and Mari does not contain any such listing of names in the anaphora after the consecration. Since it is one of the oldest Liturgies, its evidence lends considerable weight to the thesis that names were listed originally at the offertory, and not in the intercessions of the anaphora.

Narsai provides some indication that the East Syrian Rite had both diptychs in essentially their present state at the beginning of the sixth century, " While the kiss of peace is being given one to another in church, the book of the two lists of names, the living and the dead, is recited. " Then he gives the prayers the people recited after each diptych, " On behalf of all orders deceased from this holy church, and for those who are deemed worthy of the reception of

[9] Brightman, LEW, pp. 275-281.

[10] *Ibid.*

[11] In American military cemeteries, the inscription generally reads : " Here lies a comrade in arms known only to God. " The *Apostolic Constitutions*, Book VIII (see above, p. 137), has in the same spirit, " And all whose names thou thyself knowest. "

this oblation; on behalf of these and of thy servants in every place : receive, Lord, this oblation. "[12]   But some authors argue that the prayer suggests that originally it did not follow any diptych of the living, but was followed merely by the "naming" of the dead, headed by a succession-list of the patriarchs.[13]   The argument cannot be settled definitely.[14]

At any rate, by Narsai's time, the East Syrian Liturgy has the diptychs at the offertory immediately before or during the kiss of peace.   In spite of Greek modifications elsewhere, the ancient tradition prevailed as regards the placing of intercessions in the East Syrian Liturgy.

In the early part of the fifth century, some Italian churches must have named individuals before the offertory, since it warranted Pope Innocent I's rebuke (c. A.D. 415) : " Your own wisdom will show how superfluous it is to pronounce the name of a man whose oblation you have not yet offered to God [through the offertory prayer]. . . . So, one should first commend the offerings and afterward name those who have made them.   One should name them during the divine mysteries, and not in the part of the rite which precedes, so that the mysteries themselves lead up to the prayers to be offered. "[15]   But this papal opinion seems to be an exception, since in and about Rome, the priest probably did " first commend the offerings and afterwards name those who have made them, " soon after the offertory and early in the Canon.[16]   Milan and northern Italy also had " prayers. . . for kings, for the people, and the others " soon after the offertory but still within the Canon.[17]

Aside from the East Syrian evidence, we have been considering the diptychs in their rather primitive form, basically lists of names

[12] See Connolly, *The Liturgical Homilies of Narsai* (Cambridge, 1909), pp. 10-11, for complete text.

[13] E.g., G. Dix, *The Shape of the Liturgy* (2nd edit. London, 1945), p. 506.

[14] See Connolly, *J. Th. St.*, XIII, 592 ff.

[15] Innocent I, *Ep.* 25 (PL 20, 553 ff.).   Our brackets.

[16] See. E. Bishop, *Liturgica historica* (Oxford, 1918), pp. 96 ff., for the involved history of the commemoration of the dead within the Roman canon.   It was a peculiarity of funerals and Requiem Masses, akin to the " proper " preface for feast days.

[17] Cf. Ambrose, *De sacramentis*, IV, 4, 14 (Quasten, *op. cit.*, 158).

of the living and of the dead. In Constantinople, however, the word *diptychs* came to mean technically that combination of lists of eminent living and dead authorities, officially established and amended by ecclesiastical experts whenever necessary. When the diptychs came into prominence at Constantinople, each such official list was arranged in the order of ecclesiastical precedence : first the bishops, then the other clergy, and lastly the laity. The diptych of the dead included a succession-list of past bishops of Constantinople; when it came to the laity, it enumerated deceased emperors before anyone else. That much we know from the official correspondence between Constantinople and the Churches of Alexandria and Antioch concerning the insertion of John Chrysostom in the Diptych of the Dead.

Chrysostom, Bishop of Constantinople, had been deposed and had died in exile in A.D. 407. Ecclesiastical politics at that time were especially fiery. Accusations and counteraccusations of heresy were numerous : the insertion or erasure of names from the diptychs depended on them, so that they actually constituted an index of the current political situation—especially reflecting the fight between Monophysites and " orthodox. " Chrysostom's name was included in the Diptych of the Dead in Constantinople. Alexandria and Antioch were urged to do likewise. It is clear, then, that these Churches had official lists.

At the time of their original introduction into the Liturgy, at least at Constantinople and Antioch, the Diptychs of the Dead were clearly parochial. From the writings of Cyril and Chrysostom, it appears that, besides past bishops of the local see, they included only those personally known, loved and mourned by the members of the congregation. Later, as shown by much bickering, they came to be officially compiled. In the midst of power politics, the local dead seem to have been forgotten. The country parishes probably kept a sense of proportion as they still do, but not the eminent cathedral parishes, and least of all, the " Great Church " of Hagia Sophia.

At what point in the Liturgy were the Byzantine diptychs read? The question is still far from closed. Brightman, in interpreting Chrysostom's reference (*In Act. Ap.* xxi, 4 [edit. Montfaucon 9,

176 A]) after some hesitation, places the reading of the diptychs in the Liturgy immediately before the anaphora, after the pax and the Creed. [18]   But in his reconstruction of the Byzantine Liturgy of the seventh century, he places it immediately after the Great Entrance, " at the bringing up (of the gifts), " before the pax and Creed. [19] Bishop, on the other hand, argues that Brightman must be corrected on this, and that the diptych reading must be placed at the intercessions after the consecration in both the Constantinopolitan and Antiochene Churches. [20]   Dix agrees with this opinion. [21]

Shortly after the time of Cyril and Chrysostom, the Liturgy in Mopsuestia of Cilicia was described in detail, in the *Catecheses* written in A.D. 410 by Theodore of Mopsuestia. [22]   Theodore, a lifelong friend of Chrysostom, was Bishop of Mopsuestia for thirty-six years (A.D. 392-428).   His description of the Liturgy, as it appears in the last two lectures, is clearly of the same type as that of the North Syrian Rite, contained in the *Apostolic Constitutions* (Book VIII).   As such, it is a modification of that of Jerusalem.

Important for our purpose at hand is the position of the diptych reading.   After the Great Entrance and a preparatory prayer by the priest, there came the greeting and the kiss of peace.   Then the deacon asked the congregation to stand for the diptych reading. When the diptychs were completed the anaphora began.   Equally important for our consideration is the mention of the departed at the beginning of the intercessions, after the consecration and invocation.

The same general position of the diptych reading is also given by Pseudo-Dionysius, *c.* A.D. 485.   Writing from the borderland of North Syria, Mesopotamia, and Asia Minor, he tells us clearly that

---

[18] Brightman, LEW, p. 528; also pp. 523-533.

[19] Brightman, LEW, pp. 535-536. His source is *Relatio motionis inter Maximum et principes* 5, *in opp. S. Max.*, i, p. xxxiv : *Schol.*, in E. H., iii. 2, p. 306.
Holding a similar opinion are A. Petrovsky (*Chry. Chtenie*, LXXXIV [March, 1904], p. 414) and de Meester (*Eastern Churches Quarterly*, " The Byzantine Liturgy, " III [July, 1938], p. 132, as well as DACL 1611, 1615).

[20] E. Bishop, *Appendix* to *Narsai*, pp. 109-111; also, *J. Th. St.*, XII (1911), pp. 319-328; *ibid.*, pp. 400 ff.

[21] G. Dix, *op. cit.*, p. 503.

[22] Edit. Rücker, *Ritus Baptismi et Missae, quem descripsit Theodorus ep. Mopsuestenus in sermonibus catecheticis* (Münster, 1933); edit. Mingana, *Commentary of Theodore of Mopsuestia on the Lord's Prayer and on the Sacraments of Baptism and the Eucharist* (Cambridge, 1933).

" when all salute one another, the mystic recitation of the holy diptychs relating to the mysteries is performed. " [23]

All this does not prove conclusively that the diptych reading in the Byzantine Liturgy occurred at this point, but it is a good indication. An evaluation of all the available evidence is necessary to form a reasonable opinion.

To avoid confusing issues it may be well to point out and distinguish clearly between the intercessions at the end of the synaxis, the intercessions in the anaphora after the consecration, and the diptychs. Those at the synaxis were made for categories of persons, except for the local bishop and the emperor, who were generally mentioned by name. Their oldest form consisted of a bidding and a collect, with a pause for silent prayer between. During the fourth century, and later, these intercessions were transferred from the end of the synaxis to the anaphora after the consecration, where they still retained the name *intercessions*. Their original place at the end of the synaxis was taken by the newer Antiochene form of *ektenias*, or litanies. But the listing of names always was distinct from the intercessions. It originated in the pre-Nicene Church, and evolved into the diptych readings of the post-Nicene era.

By evaluating the evidence available both before and after Nicaea, we may, with some reservations, form the conclusion that the original position of the listing of names was *at the offertory*. Yet we cannot exclude the possibility that it may have occurred both at the offertory and in the anaphora after the consecration.

At the Offertory	In Intercessions after the Consecration

1. *Cyprian*

Certain	*Probable*
Offering made for dead persons, and in the name of the living.	Dead named in anaphora, " the prayer of priests. "

2. *Council of Elvira*

Certain	
Names of the living recited at altar with the oblation.	

---

[23] Ps.-Dionysius, the Areopagite, *De hierarchia eccl.*, chap. 3, ii (PG 3, 425).

3. Spanish Church

Certain
Prayers *ad nomina.*

4. Mozarabic Church

Certain
Names of *offerentium et pau-santium.*

5. Sarapion

Certain
Recitation of names.

6. Cyril of Jerusalem

Certain
Dead remembered " while the holy and tremendous sacrifice lies before us. "

Possible
Dead mentioned by name.

7. Liturgy of Addai and Mari

Certain
" Book of the living and the dead. "

8. Narsai

Certain
Book of two lists of names of both living and dead.

9. Theodore of Mopsuestia

Certain
Diptychs read at offertory.

Certain
Departed mentioned at beginning of the intercessions.

Possible
Departed mentioned by name.

10. *Pseudo-Dionysius the Areopagite*

Certain
Diptychs read.

11. *Italy*

Probable
Rome : in funeral and requiem Masses only, soon *after* the offertory early in the Canon.

Certain
Divergent custom : names before the offertory.

To sum up, the weight of evidence favors the offertory as the original position for the listing of names. Somewhat later, when the intercessions were shifted from the end of the synaxis to the anaphora after the consecration, individual names began to be mentioned also at this point. Up to the seventh and eighth centuries, the practice of the Byzantine Church seems to have been the same. The placing of the general categories of persons and individual names of the living and the dead at the *proskomidia* rite seems to be a direct vestige of such practice. The *proskomidia*, we must remember, originally occurred immediately before the offertory and was shifted to the beginning of the Divine Liturgy not very long before the eighth or ninth century. This is also the time when we have definite proof that the reading of the diptychs occurred no longer at the offertory, but at the intercessions after the consecration—although the intercessions themselves had already been part of the Byzantine anaphora for centuries. [24]

---

[24] The *Cod. Barberini, gr.* 336, gives the diptychs of the dead and the living in the anaphoral intercessions of the Byzantine Liturgy of St. Basil (cf. Brightman, LEW, pp. 331, 336). So does the early eighth century Armenian version of Chrysostom's Liturgy (cf. Aucher, *La versione armena della liturgia di S. Giovanni Crisostomo, fatta sul principio dell'VIII secolo,* XPYCOCTOMIKA, p. 391).

CHAPTER LIII

THE KISS OF PEACE

After the concluding Doxology and Amen, the priest turns to bless the people :

Peace be to all.

People : **And to your spirit.**

Deacon : **Let us love one another, that with one mind we may confess.**

People : **The Father, Son, and Holy Spirit, the consubstantial and undivided Trinity.**

Bowing three times, the priest kisses the holy gifts, which are still covered : first, the diskos, *then the holy chalice, and finally the edge of the holy table before him ; while making these bows, he says in a low voice each time :*

I will love you, O Lord, my strength; the Lord is my might and my refuge.

If there is more than one priest celebrating, each kisses these holy objects ; each concelebrant also turns to the celebrant and they exchange the kiss of peace by kissing each other's shoulder. In doing this, the celebrant says :

Let Christ be among us.
He is, and he will be.

Remaining in the same place, the deacon makes three bows, kisses the image of the cross on his orar, *and intones :*

The doors! (Guard) the doors! In wisdom let us be attentive!

All the Oriental Liturgies have the kiss of peace at some point before the anaphora. The Latin Rite stands alone in having the kiss of peace before Holy Communion. [1] Even in the Latin Mass,

---

[1] Its transference dates back at least to the time of Augustine of Hippo (A.D. 396-430); cf. *Sermo* 227 (PL 38, 1101); also Pope Innocent I, *Ep.* 25 (PL 20, 553).

however, it is introduced with *Pax Domini sit semper vobiscum*, an expression similar to the Byzantine " Peace be to all. " The response is identical, " And with your spirit. "

Among the Jewish people, the kiss of peace as a sign of respect or friendship predates by many years Jacob's reconciliation with Esau. During Christ's time, the kiss was one of the preliminary courtesies to any ceremonial meal : its omission caused our Lord's rebuke to Simon (Luke 7:45). The early Church made use of it as a matter of course. The numerous references by Paul leave no doubt that the kiss of peace as a token of Christian communion and fellowship was an accepted practice at that very early date. It probably was used at the apostolic Eucharistic celebrations, although there is no direct proof for it. [2]

The kiss of peace was given originally between the prayers of the faithful and the beginning of the Eucharistic celebration. Justin shows it in that position. [3] It probably belonged to the common prayers of the faithful at the end of the synaxis, rather than to the Eucharistic Sacrifice. Reflecting the opinion of the times, Tertullian calls it the *signaculum orationis* with which the faithful conclude the prayer in common. [4] The uninitiated, the catechumen, was not permitted to exchange the kiss of peace with any of the faithful until he was baptized, for he did not yet belong to the " communion " of the Holy Spirit, the Church. [5] The kiss was given for the first time to each new Christian by the bishop after he had also conferred on him the gift of the Holy Spirit by signing him on the forehead with chrism, i.e., after confirmation. [6]

When the catechetical synaxis was joined to the celebration of the Eucharist, the kiss in fact concluded the common prayers of the faithful and initiated the Eucharistic proceedings as a kind of preliminary to the offertory. The Council of Laodicea (*c.* A.D. 363),

[2] See Lietzmann, *Messe und Herrenmahl* (Bonn, 1926), p. 229.

[3] Justin Martyr, *First Apology*, chap. 65, see above, p. 41.

[4] Tertullian, *De or.* 18 (CSEL, 20, 191). Origen also seems to link the kiss with the prayers of the faithful rather than with the offertory when he states that the brethren greet each other with a kiss " after the prayers. " Cf. *In Rom. homil.*, X, 33 (PG 14, 1282-1283).

[5] Hippolytus, *Apostolic Tradition*, xviii, 3.

[6] *Ibid.*, xxii, 3.

for example, prescribes without comment the order to be followed :
" . . . there should then be offered the three prayers of the faithful . . .
and then the [kiss of] peace is to be given. And after the presbyters
have given the [kiss of] peace to the bishop, then the laity are to give
it [to one another], and so the Holy Oblation is to be completed. " [7]

As the years went by, the kiss was related more and more closely
to the oblation, and to the proper dispositions of the one who made
it. The biblical admonition (Matt. 5:22) regarding reconciliation
with one's brother before " bringing one's gift to the altar " undoubtedly influenced this change of emphasis. As early as the end of the
first century, the *Didache* insists on the reconciliation of fellow
Christians before they can attend the Eucharistic celebration, " that
your sacrifice may not be profaned. " [8] Beginning in the latter part
of the second century, the kiss of peace was generally a preliminary
to the oblation. [9] We have Hippolytus placing it in this position,
Chrysostom doing so for Antioch, and the *Apostolic Constitutions*
also placing it here. [10] Toward the middle of the fourth century,
however, Jerusalem seems to have led the way in changing the
position of the kiss from before to after the offertory. [11] While
Chrysostom in the Church of Antioch still places the kiss (*c.* A.D. 390),
before the offertory, [12] fifth-century Syria adopted the Jerusalem
custom. [13] It must have spread further north by the fifth century,
since the Rite of Mopsuestia in southern Asia Minor also had the
kiss after the offertory during the time of Theodore (*c.* A.D. 410). [14]

---

[7] Council of Laodicea, Canon 19 (Mansi, *Sacrorum conciliorum nova et amplissima collectio*, Vol. II, 567).

[8] *Didache*, xiv, 2 (ANF, Vol. VII, p. 381).

[9] Cf. Hippolytus, *Apostolic Tradition*, iv, I (Dix, *The Treatise on the Apostolic Tradition of St. Hippolytus of Rome* [London, 1937], 29); *Apostolic Constitutions*, Book VIII, 11, 7-9 (edit. Funk, p. 494); see above, p. 123.

[10] Hippolytus, *Apostolic Tradition*, iv, I (Dix, *ibid.*); Chrysostom, *De compunctione*, i, 3 (edit. Montfaucon I, 127 AB or PG 47, 382); *Apostolic Constitutions*, Book VIII, 11, 7-9 (edit. Funk, p. 494).

[11] Cyril of Jerusalem, *Cat.*, xxiii, 3 (NPNF, Series II, Vol. VII, p. 153).

[12] *De compunctione*, i, 3 (edit. Montfaucon I, 127 AB or PG 47, 382); also *In II ad Cor. orat.*, xviii, 3 (edit. Montfaucon 10, 568 or PG 51, 527).

[13] Ps.-Dionysius, the Areopagite, *De hierarchia eccl.*, chaps. 2 and 3; cf. Brightman, LEW, Appendix E, p. 488.

[14] Theodore of Mopsuestia, *Catecheses*, v (edit. Mingana, *Commentary of Theodore of Mopsuestia on the Lord's Prayer and on the Sacraments of Baptism and the Eucharist* [Cambridge, 1933], p. 92.

Spreading still further northward, the practice must have been adopted by Constantinople some time during the fifth or sixth century. The tremendous influence of the Byzantine Church caused its adoption in that position in most of the other Eastern Churches. [15]

Rome, on the other hand, followed the African Church in changing the kiss to its present place before Holy Communion. This change must have come to Rome at the very beginning of the fifth century, for in A.D. 416, Pope Innocent I wrote to Bishop Decentius of Gubbio, insisting that the kiss was not to be exchanged until after the completion of the entire sacrifice. Here, Pope Innocent draws attention to its function as a seal and guarantee upon everything that has been done. " By the kiss of peace, the people affirm their assent to all that has been done in the celebration of the mysteries. " [16] A curious reason indeed, especially since Augustine had given a more convincing one long before, i.e., that the kiss of charity is a good preparation for Holy Communion. Augustine's idea, of course, had won out in the Western Church. Certainly, since the time of Gregory the Great, the kiss was regarded as a natural preparation for Communion. [17] Some time before the ninth century, the Ambrosian Rite of Milan followed Rome in transferring the kiss from its original position to its present place before Holy Communion; however, it still kept the early invitation to it—*Pacem habete*—in the ancient position. [18]

The Greeting

The original greeting of the celebrant as he gave the kiss of peace must have been closely related to the action, the conferring of peace and unity to the members of Christ's body. It was probably simple : " Peace be to all, " " Peace be to you, " or some such uncomplicated expression. The answer was probably the standard : " And with

---

[15] In the West, probably as the result of the temporary occupation of Spain by Byzantine forces under Emperor Justinian during the sixth century, the Mozarabic Rite adopted the Byzantine position of the kiss in its Mass.

[16] Innocent I, *Ep.* 25, 1 (PG 20, 553).

[17] Gregory the Great, *Dial.*, III, 36 (PL 77, 307 C) and *In ev.*, II, 37, 9 (PL 76, 1281 A). Cf. also Sophronius, *Vita s. Marieae Aeg.*, chap. 22 (PL 73, 87 B),

[18] Cf. *Missale Ambrosianum Duplex*, p. 236, where it is found immediately after the Gospel.

your spirit. " The universality of this formula in the various Churches, as borne out by later evidence, suggests such a common origin. Augustine, one of the first to give us a formula connected with giving the kiss, has : " Peace be to you " and the response, " And with your spirit. " [19] The *Apostolic Constitutions* has a similar formula for introducing the kiss : " The peace of God be with you all, " and the response : " And with your spirit. " [20]

We have already noted the *Didache*'s insistence on reconciliation before anyone receives the Eucharist (see above, p. 530). Far from being a formality, the kiss of peace had real meaning and purpose in the early centuries of the Church. It was an expression of interior charity (presupposing reconciliation) among the members of the *ecclesia* before the Eucharist. Up to the fourth century, it still did not degenerate into a mere formality : while it was being exchanged, the deacon called out : " Is there anyone that keeps aught against his fellowman? " not as a stereotyped rubric, but because even at this last moment the bishop might make peace between them. [21] Cyril of Jerusalem, explaining the rubric of his day, " *Embrace one another and let us salute each other*, " states that " the kiss is a sign that our souls are united and that we banish all remembrance of injury. " [22]

During the fourth century, when many liturgical details tended to become stereotyped, it was necessary to reiterate the original meaning of the kiss; hence, in some Eastern Churches the deacon warns the faithful : " Let no one have anything against another, let no one be (given the kiss) in hypocrisy. " [23] This warning survived

---

[19] Augustine, *Sermo* 227 (PL 38, 1101), and *Enarr. in ps.* 124, 10 (PL 37, 1656).

[20] After this, the deacon summons the people to exchange the kiss with the words of I Cor. 16:20 : " Greet one another with the holy kiss " (*Apostolic Constitutions*, Book VIII, see above, p. 123).

[21] *Didascalia Apostolorum* (edit. Connolly [Oxford, 1929], p. 117). At that time, the bishop and the presbyters mediated in all such disputes between the faithful of their own church at regular sessions of " Christian courts "; cf. *ibid.*, ii. 45 (*edit. cit.*, p. 111). Holding such church courts precluded the faithful from suing each other before courts of a pagan state. Another reason for such Christian courts was to make it easier for the church's members to be reconciled before the Sunday Eucharist.

[22] Cyril of Jerusalem, *Cat.*, xxiii, 3 (PG 33, 1112 AB).

[23] *Apostolic Constitutions*, Book II (cf. above, p. 146). These directives are based on the *Didascalia*.

in the Liturgy of some Eastern Churches for centuries even after they had abandoned the actual giving of the kiss among the faithful.

In the Byzantine Churches, after the celebrant's blessing and the people's response, there is a characteristic addition : the deacon emphasizes the necessity of mutual love and unity by exhorting : " Let us love one another so that with one mind we may glorify, " and the people complete the sentence : " The Father and the Son and the Holy Spirit...", etc. By breaking into the deacon's exhortation, as it were, the people indicate their eagerness to be one in harmony and love : without unity and mutual love as one spiritual family the faithful cannot " with one mind " confess the Triune God.

The deacon's exhortation, " Let us love one another " is undoubtedly much older than the eighth or ninth century manuscript in which it first appears. [24] It may be a modification of a similar prayer in the Liturgy of St. James. [25] The *Constitution* of Philotheus sanctioned its use. [26] The latter part of the exhortation (" so that with one mind we may glorify ") and the people's response date back at least to the twelfth century in a slightly different form. What is now the response of the people was then said by the priest after the exhortation, " Let us love one another. " The kiss was given, accompanied by the words, " The peace of Christ (be given) to your priesthood "; then again the priest would repeat what is now the response, " The Father, the Son, and the Holy Spirit, " etc. [27]

Brotherly love goes hand in hand with the love of God. To show this, the priest recites verses two and three of Psalm 17. [28] To

[24] *Cod. Barberini*, gr. 336 (Brightman, LEW, p. 320).

[25] In the Liturgy of St. James, the " prayer of peace " just before the kiss of peace reads : " O God and Lord of all, make these our unworthy selves worthy of this salvation, O thou Lover of mankind, that cleansed from all guile and all hypocrisy, we may salute one another with a holy and divine kiss, united with the bond of love and peace. " etc.

[26] Cf. Krasnoseltsev, *Materialy dlja istorii chinoposlidovania liturgii sv. Ioanna Zlatoustago* (Kazan, 1889), p. 62.

[27] MS. of the Synodal Library of Moscow, N. 342, N. 343 (cf. Gorsky-Nevostrujev, *Opysanie slavianskikh rukopisej Moskovskoj Synodal'noj biblioteky*, Vol. III [Moscow, 1859], 1, 3, 6; also Krasnoseltsev, *Svidinia o nikotorikh liturgicheskikh rukopis'akh Vatikanskoi biblioteki* [Kazan, 1885], p. 154).

[28] These verses must have been introduced during the last half of the fourteenth century, for the *Liturgikon* of Metropolitan Isidore has them (cf. MS. *Vat. Slav.*, N. 14, fol. 135); also the fifteenth century MS. N. 836, p. 27, of Sophia Library

indicate even more plainly the source from which peace and love are to be derived, the priest kisses the holy gifts. The same sentiment apparently prompted the kissing of the altar in the Latin Mass before the pax during the Middle Ages. [29] From this arose the Western practice of kissing the sacred host before offering the kiss of peace to the deacon. [30] During the thirteenth century in England, and apparently in certain parts of France, a custom similar to the present Byzantine practice was adopted : the priest would kiss the brim of the chalice and often also the paten or the corporal. [31] The practice of kissing the gifts came later to the Byzantine Church. Ordinarily this would be a sign of " borrowing, " but the less than cordial relations existing between the two Churches at the time would preclude any such interchange of liturgical usages. The Byzantine-Slav Church seems to have adopted the custom during the fourteenth or fifteenth century [32]; many sixteenth-century sources specifically prescribe the kissing of the *diskos* brim, the chalice and the edge of

(cf. Petrovsky, *Histoire de la rédaction slave de la liturgie de S. Jean Chrysostome*, XPYCOCTOMIKA [Rome, 1908], p. 907) and MS. N. 986 of Sinai Library (Dmitrievsky, *Opysanie liturgicheskikh rukopisej khraniaschikhsia v bibliotekakh pravoslavnago vostoka*, Vol. II, *Euchologia* [Kiev, 1901], p. 611), except that these last two sources also add the next verse of Ps. 17 : " and deliverer, my God and my helper, in Him I will put my trust. "

[29] *Osculato altari dat pacem astanti*, Bernold, *Micrologus*, chap. 23 (PL 151, 995). The same prescription is given in a Sacramentary of the eleventh century from Arezzo (cf. Ebner 4) and in the Pontifical of Mainz of the twelfth century (Martène, I, 4, xvii [I, 602 C].

[30] For France, cf. John Beleth, *Explic.*, chap. 48 (PL 202, 54) and Herbert von Sassari, *De miraculis* (A.D. 1171), I, 21 (PL 185, 1298 A); for Italy, about A.D. 1100, *Cod. Casant.*, 614 (cf. Ebner, 330). England also had this custom, though it was discontinued at the beginning of the thirteenth century; cf. decree of Bishop Richard of Salisbury, 1217 (Slöch, *Hugo*, 131).

[31] *Ordo* of Sarum; cf. Legg, *Tracts*, 265, and Legg, *The Sarum Missal*, 226, n. 5; *Missale* of York; cf. Simmons, 112 f.

[32] The *Ustav* of the fourteenth or fifteenth century Kievan *Liturgikon* of Metropolitan Isidore gives specific instructions for the celebrant to kiss the holy gifts thus : " First (the covering) over the holy *diskos*, then (the covering) over the holy chalice and, finally, the holy altar before him. " Cf. MS. *Vat. Slav.*, N. 14, fol. 135. Some celebrants " kiss the holy altar only " (instead of kissing the *diskos*, chalice, and altar), " giving as an excuse " that this is " done at the great Hagia Sophia where we have seen and learned it " (cf. MS. *Vat. Slav.*, N. 14, fol. 135). A curious observation indeed in view of the Slavs' eternal insistence on preserving and faithfully imitating the venerable tradition of Hagia Sophia. The text then insists, not on what was done at Hagia Sophia, but on its own prescription.

the altar; [33] this was to be done by the celebrant during the exhortation, " Let us love one another. "

Today, the kissing of the holy vessels and of the altar is the only remnant of the ancient kiss of peace in the Byzantine Liturgy when it is celebrated by one priest. When it is celebrated by more than one priest, the celebrant and concelebrants kiss each others' shoulder. In giving the kiss, the celebrant says : " Let Christ be among us. " The concelebrant answers, " He is and he will be. " The deacon merely kisses the cross on his *orar*. Like the Byzantine Church, the other Eastern Churches have long discontinued the actual kiss of peace among the faithful and have retained only a symbolic gesture. The East Syrians merely clasp and kiss their neighbor's hands, while the Maronites clasp and kiss their neighbors' fingers. The Copts bow to their neighbors and touch their hand. In the Armenian Church, the faithful merely bow to one another.

From the very beginning, there was fear of abuse. Several of the early Fathers urge great reserve and modesty. Clement of Alexandria reports that " there are those who do nothing but make the churches resound with the kiss, not having love itself within. For this very thing, the shameless use of a kiss, which ought to be mystic, occasions foul suspicions and evil gossip. The Apostle calls the kiss holy. " [34] As a remedy, he even urges a symbolical greeting, "...we are also to greet symbolically our neighbor whom we are commanded to love second only to God. " [35] Origen admonishes that " The very name (holy kiss) teaches that the kisses given in the churches should be chaste.... " [36] The rule of the *Apostolic Constitutions*, that " men should exchange the kiss of peace only with men and women with women " was a reiteration of an earlier one in the *Apostolic Tradition* : " The baptized should greet each other, men greeting men and women, women, but the men should not

---

[33] E.g., MS. of Solovetsky, N. 1019, p. 21; N. 1020, p. 61; N. 1021, p. 61; also MS. of Synodal Library of Moscow, N. 615, p. 62; N. 617, p. 75, of same Library; MS. of Volokholansk, N. 83, p. 100; cf. Petrovsky, *op. cit.*, pp. 920-921.

[34] Clement of Alexandria, *Paedagogus*, III, 11, 81, 2-82 (edit. Stählin, GCS, I, 281, 5-19).

[35] *Ibid.*

[36] Origen, *In Rom. homil.*, X, 33 (PG 14, 1282-1283).

greet the women." [37]   This prescription was not too difficult to
observe when the custom prevailed of separating the sexes, the men
on one side of the church, the women on the other.   Many of the
Byzantine-Slav churches observe this practice even today.

The danger of abuse was probably the greatest single reason for
discontinuing the actual kiss of peace among the faithful.   In the
Byzantine Church, it was maintained for several centuries.   Just
when the kiss among the faithful was abandoned is a matter of
conjecture.   Judging from Maximus the Confessor, it would seem
that the practice was discontinued by his time (A.D. 662). [38]   On the
other hand, the early eighth-century Armenian version of Chrysostom's Liturgy contains the deacon's announcement : *" Greet one
another with the kiss of holiness "*; however, the validity of the argument is doubtful because of the next rubric : *" And they kiss the
altar and one another, "* [39] which may indicate that the kiss was
exchanged only between members of the clergy.   The eighth or
ninth century Byzantine Liturgy contained in the *Codex Barberini*
has the formula " Let us love one another. "   Here also the matter
is left unsettled because of the next rubrics. [40]   Perhaps the faithful
no longer exchanged the kiss of peace, and the formula represents
a modification taking this into account.   It could apply, anyway, to
such restrained practices as those of present-day East Syrians and
Armenians, so that there is insufficient evidence for a final solution
of the question.

" The doors!   (Guard) the doors! "   While these exclamations
are no longer in their original place—after the dismissals—they are
definitely a remnant of the primitive *disciplina arcani*.   In the
chabûrah, latecomers were excluded (see above, p. 21) : in the
Eucharist, only members of the *ecclesia*, the baptized in good
standing, were permitted to participate.   Guarding the doors of the

---

[37] Hippolytus, *Apostolic Tradition*, iv (Dix, 29).

[38] Maximus the Confessor, *Mystagogia*, chap. 17 (PG 91, 693 D); also, chap. 13,
op. cit. (PG 91, 692 C); chap. 23, *op. cit.* (PG 91, 700 C), and chap. 24, *op. cit.*
(PG 91, 708 C).   The total silence regarding the kiss in Germanus, Patriarch of
Constantinople (A.D. 715-729), may also be significant.

[39] Aucher, *La versione armena della liturgia di S. Giovanni Crisostomo, fatta sul
principio dell'VIII secolo*, ΧΡΥΣΟΣΤΟΜΙΚΑ, p. 387.

[40] Cf. Brightman, LEW, p. 320.

church against the intrusion of the uninitiated was a matter of strict
obligation. Tertullian makes this clear when he contrasts the heretical indiscriminate admission of all to their sacred rites with the
true Christian custom of absolute separateness : " Alike they approach,
alike they hear, alike they pray, even the heathen if they come upon
the scene; they will cast that which is holy to the dogs, and pearls,
though they be only false ones, before swine. " [41] Chrysostom
explains it somewhat more mildly : " We too celebrate the mysteries
with closed doors and keep out the uninitiated, not that we have
convicted our rites of any weakness, but that many are still imperfectly prepared for them. " [42]

Accepted originally as an unwritten law, the principle of excluding
outsiders was then incorporated into the rubrics, for instance, in the
Apostolic Constitutions : " Deacons should also stand at the doors of
the men and subdeacons at the doors of the women, so that no one
goes out and no door is opened, even for any of the faithful, during
the sacrifice. " [43]

The next stage of development came when the rubric was made
part of the text of the Liturgy, as occurred in the ancient Liturgy of
St. James, [44] after the dismissal of the catechumens, then before the
recitation of the Creed—but in the second instance, the exclamations
refer, not to the doors of the church, but to the royal doors of the
iconostas. [45] This seems to show the actual transition : the catechumenate has been abolished, and a second set of exclamations
inserted before the Creed is explained as referring to the royal
doors. The Byzantines probably had this dual set of exclamations
but eliminated the first some time before the eighth century and
kept only the second before the Creed. [46] The Byzantine, exclamations refer, not to the closing of the doors—they were closed after
the Great Entrance—but to guarding them, that is, preventing any

---

[41] Tertullian, *De praescr.*, 41 (PL 2, 68 A).

[42] Chrysostom, *In Matt.*, xxiii, 3 (edit. Montfaucon 7, 288 C).

[43] *Apostolic Constitutions*, Book VIII; see above, p. 123.

[44] Brightman, LEW, pp. 41-42.

[45] As proof of this we have the rubric contained in the Latin version of Leo
Thuscus : *Et post datum pacis osculum, innuit archidiaconus extra stanti diacono,
ut introitus cancellorum ianuas claudat et dicit : Januas . . .* (cf. *Cod. Pal. gr.*, 367).

[46] Aucher, *op. cit.*, p. 387; Brightman, LEW, p. 321.

unauthorized person from entering. The Creed, which embodies many of the major Christian truths, came under the *disciplina arcani* as much as the Eucharistic mysteries themselves. Both are about to begin. The transfer of the exclamations to a position just before the Creed preserves at least a symbol of its former meaning. Many pious but imaginary interpretations have been attached to this liturgical text, for instance, by Nicholas Cabasilas in his *Commentary* : " It is in this wisdom (in the Creed) that the priest asks us to open all the doors... that is, our mouths and ears. Open the doors in this wisdom, he says, proclaiming and listening to these high teachings constantly. " [47] But this interpretation contradicts the text which commands, not the opening of the doors, but their guarding against intruders.

[47] Our parenthesis. N. Cabasilas, *A Commentary on the Divine Liturgy*, trans. by J. M. Hussey and P. A. McNulty (London, 1960), p. 67.

CHAPTER LIV

THE CREED

The priest lifts the large veil, the aër, *and holds it over the holy gifts as he says the Creed together with the people :* [1]

I believe in one God, the Father almighty, maker of heaven and earth, and of all things visible and invisible. And (I believe) in one Lord, Jesus Christ, the only-begotten Son of God, born of the Father before all ages. God of God, Light of light, true God of true God; begotten, not made, of one substance with the Father, by whom all things were made; who for us men and for our salvation came down from heaven, and became flesh by the Holy Spirit, of the Virgin Mary, and was made man. He was also crucified for us, suffered under Pontius Pilate, and was buried. And on the third day he rose again, according to the Scriptures. And he ascended into heaven and sits at the right hand of the Father; he will come again in glory to judge the living and the dead, and to his kingdom there will be no end. And (I believe) in the Holy Spirit, the Lord and Giver of life, who proceeds from the Father (and the Son); who together with the Father and the Son is adored and glorified; who spoke through the prophets. (I believe) in one, holy, catholic and Apostolic Church. I confess one baptism for the forgiveness of sins. I await the resurrection of the dead; and the life of the world to come. Amen.

When the Profession of Faith is completed, the priest folds the large veil, kisses it and lays it aside on the altar.

Unlike the Latin Church, which prescribes the recitation of the Creed only on Sundays and certain feastdays, the Byzantine Church recites it at every Liturgy, including those celebrated for the dead. In the Byzantine-Slav Liturgy, it is not recited by the priest alone,

---

[1] When there is concelebration, the assistant priests gently wave the veil over the holy gifts.

but sung by the people, or chanted by the cantor as their representative.   Unlike most of the other Eastern Liturgies, the Byzantine uses
the singular form in the Creed. [2]   The personal expression of belief
is thus preserved, but the communion of the faithful is expressed
by having all the people sing.

The origins of a formal profession of faith reach back to the earliest
days of Christianity.   Before a convert could be received into the
Church by baptism, he had to repent and accept the beliefs of the
Church.   In the New Testament, there is an indication of a " form
of doctrine " (Rom. 6:17), involving not only sincere belief, but
" with the mouth, confession made unto salvation " (Rom. 10:8-10).

Any affirmative answer given by a catechumen to his instructor
may be seen as the foundation of a creed.   Jewish converts, who
believed in the one true God and all the tenets of Jewish monotheism,
may have been asked no more than to declare their belief that Jesus
Christ was indeed the Messiah.   Gentiles, with their background
of polytheism, were certainly expected to make more detailed decla-
rations.

Early in the second century, an explicit affirmation of belief in
the three Persons of the Holy Trinity was a prerequisite for baptism. [3]
It consisted in answering three formal questions in the affirmative.
In the second half of the second century, opposition to Gnosticism
led to further elaboration, for instance, in the writings of Hippolytus. [4]
The Gnostic denied the goodness of creation.   The Christian
neophyte affirms that " God the Father " is the " Maker of heaven
and earth, " meaning that creation is essentially good since it is an
act of the good Father.   The Gnostic denied the reality of Christ's
manhood.   The Christian neophyte declares that Jesus is not only
the Son of God, but also the Son of Man, conceived and born of a
human virgin mother; that he truly suffered at a precise time in
history—under (the governorship) of Pontius Pilate.   The Gnostic
taught that Christ was assumed into heaven from the cross—or
even before he was crucified.   The Christian neophyte declares that

---

[2] Of all the Eastern Liturgies, only the Byzantine and the Jacobite use the
singular form.

[3] *Didache*, VII, 2 (ANF, Vol. VII, p. 379).

[4] Hippolytus, *Apostolic Tradition*, xxi, 12 ff. (Dix, 36, v. 11-18).

he died as all humans die, and that his dead body was buried. The Gnostics were self-constituted cliques. The Christian neophyte declares that the Holy Spirit is in the Holy Church.

About A.D. 200 we find an even more developed " rule " of faith in Tertullian :

> . . . the belief that there is one only God, and that He is none other than the Creator of the world, who produced all things out of nothing through His own Word, first of all sent forth; that this Word is called His Son, and under the name of God, was seen " in diverse manners " by the patriarchs, heard at all times in the prophets, at last brought down by the Spirit and Power of the Father into the Virgin Mary, was made flesh in her womb, and, being born of her, went forth as Jesus Christ; thenceforth He preached the new law and the new promise of the kingdom of heaven, worked miracles; having been crucified, He rose again the third day; (then) having ascended into the heavens, He sat at the right hand of the Father; sent instead of Himself the Power of the Holy Ghost to lead such as believe; will come with glory to take the saints to the enjoyment of everlasting life and of the heavenly promises, and to condemn the wicked to everlasting fire, after the resurrection of both these classes shall have happened, together with the restoration of their flesh. [5]

Tertullian is quoting from the Creed of his day. Like Irenaeus, he insists that this " rule " was instituted by Christ and delivered to us by the Apostles. [6]

Be that as it may, the important fact is that there was a rule of faith which was to be professed by the early Christian. The contents of such a profession probably differed from place to place. As in the Eucharistic Prayer, the main ideas or doctrines were the same but the expression differed. No early text of the Creed was preserved since it came under the law of secrecy : it was to be learned by heart, and never consigned to writing. Whatever is known of the earliest creeds is gleaned from indirect references, and they are few in the East.

[5] Tertullian, *De praescr.*, xiii (PL 2, 26). English trans. from ANF, Vol. IV, p. 249.

[6] *Ibid.* (PL 2, 26, 27, 33, 50).

The so-called Niceno-Constantinopolitan Creed was not composed for the Divine Liturgy, but as a declaration of faith before
baptism.   Later, misbelief and heresy affected the laity, clergy, and
even the hierarchy, so that the Creed became a test, a profession of
faith for all true believers.   The ancient baptismal creeds, simple
and forthright as they were, proved too imprecise for an age of
theological controversy with its attendant minutiae of technicality
and opinion.   An Arian, for example, could accept them with perfect
honesty and yet be a heretic.   The Nicene or Niceno-Constantinopolitan Creed—a more elaborate theological profession—first appeared in the acts of the Council of Chalcedon (A.D. 451). [7]   The part
of the Council was not formulation, but approval and confirmation
of the text.   The Council of Chalcedon openly describes it as the
profession of "the 150 Holy Fathers assembled in Constantinople." [8]
The acts of the Council of Constantinople (A.D. 381) contain no
Creed, and until Chalcedon, there is no source indicating that any
symbol was formulated there, but from the documents of Chalcedon
it seems that the teachings on the Holy Spirit were elaborated at the
synod of Constantinople. [9]

The Council of Nicaea (A.D. 325) did indeed draw up a profession
of faith, the basis of which appears to have been the ancient baptismal
Creed of Jerusalem. [10]   The section dealing with Christ, the Son
of God, was expanded into a carefully worded anti-Arian formula :
" God of God, Light of Light, very God of very God, begotten not
made, being of one substance (ὁμοούσιον) with the Father. " [11]   It
ends with the words " And in the Holy Spirit " followed by an
anathema.   The profession of faith drawn up at Nicaea does not

[7] Mansi, *Sacrorum conciliorum nova et amplissima collectio*, Vol. VI, 957 and
Vol. VII, 112.   For critical edition of text, see E. Schwartz, *Acta conciliorum
oecum.*, II, 1, 2 (Berlin, 1933), 128.

[8] Cf. E. Schwartz, *ibid.*, and "Das Nicaenum und das Constantinopolitanum
auf der Synode von Chalkedon," *Zeitschrift, f. d. neutest. Wissenschaft*, XXV
(1926), 38-88.

[9] Cf. J. Lebon, "Les anciens symboles dans la définition de Chalcédoine,"
Revue d'hist. eccl., XXXII (1936), pp. 860, 870.

[10] Cf. F. Kattenbusch, *Das Apolostische Symbol* (Leipzig, 1894), Vol. I, pp. 233-
244.

[11] All the other statements regarding the divinity of Christ are contained in
the various baptismal creeds.

coincide exactly with the Creed now known as Nicene (or Niceno-Constantinopolitan), which is an expanded version.

After Nicaea, its " confession " was enlarged by various additions in the different Eastern Churches and episcopal Sees. One of these versions was proposed by the representatives of the imperial court and adopted at Chalcedon. In fact the expanded version approved by Chalcedon is found nearly complete in Epiphanius (*c.* A.D. 374) [12] and in Cyril of Jerusalem (*c.* A.D. 350). [13] Without the additions made by these writers and rejected at Chalcedon, the older drafts stand out clearly in this comparative schema :

Niceno-Constantinopolitan Creed

(Small capitals indicate text as it appears in Epiphanius : italics, the parts found in Cyril. Additions, other than Epiphanius and Cyril, are in parentheses. Items in Epiphanius and Cyril, which have not survived in the received version, are not given here).

Nicene Creed

We believe in one God, the Father Almighty, Maker of all things visible and invisible and in one Lord, Jesus Christ, the only-begotten of the Father, that is of one substance with the Father, through whom all things were made both in heaven and on earth,

Who for us men and for our salvation descended, was incarnate, and was made man,

I BELIEVE IN ONE GOD, THE FATHER ALMIGHTY, MAKER OF HEAVEN AND EARTH, AND OF ALL THINGS VISIBLE AND INVISIBLE.

AND IN ONE LORD, JESUS CHRIST, THE ONLY-BEGOTTEN SON OF GOD, BORN OF THE FATHER BEFORE ALL AGES.

(God of God), *Light of Light, true God of true God, begotten, not made, of one substance with the Father,* BY WHOM ALL THINGS WERE MADE.

Who for us men and for our salvation came down from heaven; and became flesh by the Holy Spirit, of the Virgin Mary

[12] Epiphanius, *Ancoratus*, chap. 118 (Lietzmann, *Symbole der alten Kirche* [4th edit.; Berlin, 1935], 19 f.).

[13] Cyril of Jerusalem, *Catecheses*, VII-XVIII (Lietzmann, *op. cit.*, 19).

	AND WAS MADE MAN. HE WAS
suffered	*also* CRUCIFIED *for us, suffered*
and rose again the third day,	*under Pontius Pilate and was*
ascended into heaven	*buried.* And ON THE THIRD DAY
	HE ROSE AGAIN, *according to the*
	Scriptures, AND HE ASCENDED
	INTO HEAVEN AND SITS AT THE
	RIGHT HAND OF THE FATHER
and cometh to judge the living	AND HE WILL COME AGAIN IN
and dead.	GLORY TO JUDGE THE LIVING AND
	THE DEAD, OF WHOSE KINGDOM
	THERE WILL BE NO END.
And in the Holy Spirit.	AND IN THE HOLY SPIRIT, *the*
(The anathema follows).	*Lord and Giver of life, who*
	proceeds from the Father (and
	the Son); *who together with the*
	Father and the Son is adored and
	glorified;
	WHO SPOKE THROUGH THE
	PROPHETS.
	And IN ONE, HOLY, CATHOLIC
	and apostolic CHURCH.
	I confess ONE BAPTISM FOR THE
	FORGIVENESS OF SINS.
	(And) *I await* THE RESURRECTION
	of the dead; AND THE LIFE *of the*
	world to come. Amen.

The most noteworthy fourth-century additions to the Creed were those concerning the divinity of the Holy Spirit. These were occasioned by the struggles against the Macedonian heresy. [14] Macedonius and his followers denied the divinity of the Holy Spirit; this heresy was first condemned in A.D. 360 at a Synod of Constantinople and later by the Council of Constantinople in A.D. 381.

Antioch seems to have been the first to introduce the Creed into its Liturgy which it did around A.D. 500. Pseudo-Dionysius speaks of a Creed before the gifts were placed on the altar. [15]

---

[14] The older baptismal creeds at most contained only one qualifying statement regarding the Holy Spirit : " Who spoke through the prophets. "

[15] Ps.-Dionysius, *De eccl. hierarchia*, III, 3, 7 (Quasten, *Monumenta eucharistica et liturgia vetustissima* [Bonn, 1935-1937], 305 f.).

According to Theodore the Lector (*fl. c.* A.D. 528), the Monophysite Patriarch of Antioch, Peter the Fuller (A.D. 476-488), was the first to have used the Nicene Creed a generation earlier [16]—but this seems to be a later interpolation. [17]

During the Monophysite troubles following the Council of Chalcedon, the policy of the federalist (Monophysite) party had been precisely to slight this council as being that of the emperor and to reject its conclusions through a pretended but ostentatious zeal for the Council of Nicaea. The actual reason for their introducing the Nicene Creed into the Liturgy was this same pretended deference toward the teachings of the venerable Council of Nicaea, which the Monophysites claimed Chalcedon had abandoned.

In Constantinople, the Creed was introduced into the Liturgy under the same pretext. When the Monophysite Emperor Anastasius deposed and banished the unfortunate Patriarch Macedonius II, he installed Timothy (A.D. 511-517)—who immediately imposed the Monophysite practice of reciting the Nicene Creed at the Liturgy. [18] Timothy was seeking in this way to obtain political support from both the Monophysite emperor and the federalist party.

After the See of Constantinople was restored to the true Church, it seemed imprudent to eliminate the Creed, since this would have appeared as an attack on Nicaea. Later, Emperor Justin II (A.D. 567-578) ordered the recitation of the Niceno-Constantinopolitan Creed instead of the Nicene. [19] All the other Eastern Churches, except the East Syrian and Ethiopian, followed the example of Constantinople. The East Syrian uses an ancient baptismal creed cited by Theodore of Mopsuestia, [20] while the Ethiopian uses a unique variant of the Niceno-Constantinopolitan.

Spain, whose coast was under Byzantine domination, was the first

[16] Theodore the Lector, *Hist. eccl. fragm.*, II, 48 (PG 86, 209).

[17] Cf. B. Capelle, " Le Credo," *Cours et Conférences*, VI (Louvain, 1928), pp. 174 ff.

[18] Theodore the Lector, *Hist. eccl. fragm.*, II, 32 (PG 86, 201 A).

[19] John of Biclaro, *Chronicon* (PL 72, 863 B). Placing the Creed just before the Lord's Prayer in the Byzantine Liturgy was obviously a mistake on John's part; he was probably influenced by this position of the Creed in the Spanish Mass.

[20] Cf. Rücker, *Ritus baptismi et missae quem descripsit Theodorus ep. Mopsuestenus* (Münster, 1933), pp. 43 ff.

in the Western Church to order the Creed to be recited "after the fashion of the Eastern Fathers" in its Mass "for the fortifying of our people's recent conversion" from Arianism. [21] Certain parts of France followed suit about two centuries later. [22] The custom, however, spread slowly, for as late as the ninth century many Carolingian sources seem to know little if anything about it. [23] Northern Europe adopted the practice in the tenth century. While Italy, outside of Rome, had long since accepted the custom, [24] Rome itself, out of sheer conservatism or because of distaste for the custom's heretical origin, did not introduce it until 1014, and this under pressure from Emperor Henry II. [25]

The Filioque

The *Filioque* added to the Creed—affirming the procession of the Holy Spirit from both the Father "and the Son" as from one Principle—is probably the most controverted phrase in all liturgical history. It was first used in Spain in the fifth and sixth centuries after the conversion of the Goths. From there it spread, but not without difficulties, to the rest of the Western Church. Because of the violent opposition it aroused, Pope Leo III advised its omission, but the practice was retained in the Latin Church. It gained a foothold in Rome itself, probably during the reign of Pope Bene-

[21] Quotations from the Council of Toledo, Canon 2 (Mansi, *op. cit.*, IX, 993). This was in A.D. 589 after King Reccared and his Visigoths renounced Arianism. The Creed here, however, was inserted into the Mass just before the *Pater noster* where it is found in the present Mozarabic Mass; cf. *Missale mixtum* (PL 85, 556 ff.).

[22] Probably first by Emperor Charlemagne in his palace chapel at Aachen (cf. Capelle, *op. cit.*, pp. 178 f.), and also generally as a reaction against the Christological error of Adoptionism.

[23] Cf. Capelle, *op. cit.*, pp. 180 ff.

[24] E.g., the eighth century rite of Beneventum had it (R. J. Hesbert, " L'Antiphonale Missarum de l'ancien rite bénéventain, " in *Ephemerides Liturgicae*, LII (1938), p. 36 ff.), and Aquileia at the end of that century; there it was introduced by Bishop Paulinus (B. Capelle, " L'Origine antiadoptianiste de notre texte du Symbole, " in *Recherches de théologie ancienne et médiévale*, I [1929], pp. 19-20).

[25] Under Pope Benedict VIII. When the emperor visited Rome in 1014, he was shocked to find the Credo missing from the Mass. In answer to his astonishment, Roman clerics claimed that the Roman Church had never been disturbed by error and so had no reason to include the Creed in its Mass!

dict VIII when the Creed was added to the Roman Mass. From the eleventh century on, the *Filioque* is found in every Latin text.

The trouble was due, not to the doctrine, but to pastoral concern about adding anything to the Creed. Prudence dictated its omission, in deference to those opposing it, not the least of whom were the Byzantines. Furthermore, the Councils of Ephesus (A.D. 431) and Chalcedon (A.D. 451) had forbidden the introduction of any other " faith " or Creed, and had imposed the penalty of deposition on bishops and clerics, and excommunication on monks and laymen for transgressing this law. On the other hand, the decrees of these Councils were not intended as limitations imposed upon the *Ecclesia Docens*, nor did they prohibit the formulation of the same Creed in better words. In Eastern Catholic Churches, the *Filioque* may be omitted except when scandal would ensue. Most of the Eastern Catholic Rites use it.

Even after Photius had taken the *Filioque* as an issue to break with Rome, the theological differences could have been adjusted, as they were in fact at the Council of Florence (A.D. 1438-1439). Some theologians, both Orthodox and Catholic, claim that there is no longer any problem.

The Slavonic Text

The Slavonic text of the Creed, both in the Russian and in the Ruthenian recensions, has *sobornuyu* as a translation of " catholic. " The literal meaning of the Russian word is somewhat different from " catholic "; it is more akin to " gathered together, " " conciliar, " or " synodal. " Some maintain that the term began to be used during the fourteenth century, when the Russian Church had already adopted a somewhat hostile policy toward the papacy. [26] Orthodox writers disclaim such a motive. And they are probably right. The dissident Greek Church whose antipathy towards the papacy has always been stronger than that of the Russian Church, has not eliminated the word " catholic "—so why would the Russian? This seems to be a matter of philology rather than of doctrine.

[26] E.g., Brian-Chaninov, *The Russian Church* (London, 1931), pp. 147-148.

Uncovering the Gifts

Sound liturgical study must be founded on historical facts.   The Latin commentators of the late Middle Ages were not the only ones to indulge in excessive imagination.   Byzantine commentators reached similar extremes in their " explanations " of the rubric concerning the veil that is waved over the holy gifts during the Creed.

The most common explanation is that it represents the descent of the Holy Spirit upon the holy gifts. [27] A beautiful thought—but far more logical and convincing if it were taking place during the consecration or the epiclesis.   Others maintain that lifting the veil indicates the soaring heights of the truths found in the Creed, and that waving it symbolizes the earthquake on the morning of the resurrection, when the angel rolled back the stone from the tomb— since the veil is the symbol of that stone. [28]   Others see in it the soaring of the Holy Spirit over the primeval abyss at the creation of the world, [29] or as the part played by the Holy Spirit in the events recounted by the Creed. [30]   There are some who hold that the uncovering of the gifts during the Creed signifies the revelation of God's truths to us in the New Testament. [31]   According to yet another explanation, the priest, by holding the veil between his eyes and the holy gifts, signifies his (and the people's) steadfastness in the true faith, hidden from us and incomprehensible to mortal eyes. [32] There are many further interpretations : As the eyes of the people cannot see the gifts because of the veil, so human understanding cannot pierce the mystery of transubstantiation. [33]   The veil repre-

---

[27] P. de Meester, *La divina liturgia del n. P.S.G. Crisostomo* (1925), p. 129.

[28] Cf. K. Nikolsky, *Posobie k izucheniu Ustava Bogosluzhenia pravoslavnoi tserkvy* (St. Petersburg, 1907), p. 428; also I. Dmitrievsky, *Istoricheskoe domaticheskoe i tainstvennoe izyasnenie na bozhestvennoyu liturgiyu* (Moscow, 1804), p. 66.

[29] Cf. I Dmitrievsky, *ibid.*

[30] P. de Meester, " The Byzantine Liturgy, " in *The Eastern Churches Quarterly*, Vol. III (July, 1938), p. 133.

[31] T. Mishkovsky, *Izlozhenie Tsarehradskoi Liturhii sv. Vasyliya V. i sv. Ioanna Zlatousta po yeya drevnemu smyslu i dukhu* (Lvov, 1926), p. 494.

[32] J. Pelesh, *Pastyrskoe Bohoslovie* (Vienna, 1885), p. 321.

[33] Z. Narozniak, in *Sv'ata Liturhija Sluzba Boza sv. Ivana Zolotoustoho* (edit. V. Matvijiv [Ukrainian Greek Catholic Seminary, Castle Hirschberg : Germany, 1946]), p. 108.

sents that with which Moses covered his shining face; likewise, the brilliance of the mystery of Consecration is hidden from us, while the slight shaking of the veil means the moving grace of the Holy Spirit. [34] Equally irrelevant are the different references to Christ's protection over the faithful : that the fluttering veil, like a bird unfolding its wings over its young to protect them, represents Christ guarding his own against danger. [35] This explanation is founded on a text in the *proskomidia*, at the covering of the gifts : " Cover us with the shadow of your wings; drive away from us every enemy and foe. "

History, not imagination, provides a better explanation. The gifts were covered to protect them against dust, insects, etc. Since the anaphora, the Eucharist proper, is about to begin, they must now be uncovered. The waving of the veil seems to have a practical rather than symbolic origin. A rubric in the *Apostolic Constitutions* reads : " Two deacons on each side of the altar should hold a fan, made of small thin membranes or of peacock feathers or *of fine cloth*, and should silently drive away small insects flying about so that they may not come near the chalices. " [36] Today, the rubrics state : " the deacon... takes the *ripidion* and reverently waves it over the Holy Gifts. If no *ripidion* is available then he waves the large veil. " [37] This rubric appears immediately after the priest kisses the veil and lays it to one side following the Creed—the very moment when the uncovering of the gifts occurred prior to the fourteenth and fifteenth centuries. The fourteenth-century *Constitution* of Philotheus, for example, still has the uncovering of the gifts in this position and it mentions nothing about the priest waving the veil over them, for this was the deacon's duty. [38] When the uncovering of the gifts was

---

[34] J. Hanulya, The Eastern Ritual (Cleveland, 1950), p. 46.

[35] Bessarion, *Tolkovanie na bozhestvennuiu liturgiu po chynu sv. Ioanna Zlatoustago i sv. Vasilia Velykago* (Moscow, 1885), p. 210.

[36] *Apostolic Constitutions*, Book VIII; see above, p. 124. Our italics.

[37] *Ordo Celebrationis* (Rome, 1944), No. 133, pp. 67-68.

[38] Though it does say that the priest lifts the veil up a little; cf. Krasnoseltsev, *Materialy dlja istorii chinopslidovania liturgii sv. Ioanna Zlatoustago* (Kazan, 1889), p. 64. The Slav Church faithfully followed the *Constitution* of Philotheus in this, as is evident from the *Sluzhebnyk* of Cyprian, Metropolitan of Kiev (1376-1406); cf. Krasnoseltsev, *op. cit.*, p. 65; also the fourteenth or fifteenth century *Liturgikon* of Metropolitan Isidore; cf. MS. *Vat. Slav.*, N. 14, fol. 135. Here

shifted during the fifteenth century to the beginning of the Creed, [39] the celebrant would evidently hold the veil in his hands until the end of the Creed when he would elevate it a little. [40] It was only one short step to waving the veil over the gifts—a natural thing to do, especially during summer when flies were about. The deacon, standing in his place outside the iconostas until the end of the Creed, could no longer do it.

Later, imaginary interpretations were given, as we have seen.

again the utilitarian aspect is confirmed : the gifts were uncovered after the deacon's acclamation, " Let us stand, " etc.; the short time that it took the deacon to enter the sanctuary and take his position beside the priest to fan the gifts was taken up by holding the veil over the gifts while saying the liturgical Trisagion. The same obtains for the fourteenth century MS. N. 347, p. 26, of Moscow Synodal Library; cf. Petrovsky, *Histoire de la rédaction slave de la liturgie de S. Jean Chrysostome,* XPYCOCTOMIKA (Rome, 1908), p. 889.

[39] The fifteenth century *Ordo* of the Divine Liturgy (edit. Krasnoseltsev, *op. cit.*, p. 90). Another *Ordo* of that century (edit. Krasnoseltsev, *op. cit.*, p. 109) clearly corresponds to the *Constitution* of Philotheus. This suggests the fifteenth century as the period of transition for this rubric.

[40] The same fifteenth century *Ordo* (edit. Krasnoseltsev, *op. cit.*, p. 90).

LITURGY OF THE FAITHFUL : THE ANAPHORA OR EUCHARISTIC PRAYER

CHAPTER LV

THE ORIGIN OF THE CHRISTIAN ANAPHORA

The Eucharistic prayer, or *anaphora*, is the core of the Divine Liturgy. It consists essentially in the act of obeying Christ's command, " Do this in *anamnesis* of me, " that is, do what had been done at the Last Supper. After the separation of the Eucharistic Service from the meal, [1] all that was left was the Christian version of the ancient Jewish blessing—the " Cup of the Blessing, " and the " Breaking of the Bread " being transformed into the consecration. This was accompanied by the narrative of the Institution, which constituted the only actual prayer in the primitive rite. Since such short and simple actions were out of all proportion with the importance and majesty of what was being done, there was an obvious need for an expanded ceremonial. The history of the anaphora corresponds to this progressive development.

Until the third century, the thanksgiving or Eucharistic Prayer was improvised, as Justin and Hippolytus indicate. [2] The important

---

[1] See above, pp. 38, 42, 45, 48 f.

[2] Justin Martyr (*First Apology*, chap. 67) states that the one presiding offers up prayers and likewise thanksgivings " as much as he can. " For full text, see above, pp. 41 f. More specifically, Hippolytus : " It is absolutely not necessary for the bishop to use the exact wording... as if he were learning them by heart for his thanksgiving to God. Rather, each one should pray according to his capability. " For full text, cf. edit. Dix, *The Treatise on the Apostolic Tradition of St. Hippolytus of Rome* (London, 1937), 19.

thing to do, then, is to study, not the wording, but the contents. The central theme was an expression of gratitude, so much so that the very sacrament of the body and blood of Christ is called the Eucharist, from the Greek εὐχαριστεῖν, " to give thanks. "

The celebrant " improvised " on the theme of the Jewish thanksgiving after the meal. Such improvisations were different from church to church. They were probably much longer than the Jewish originals. Justin tells us that, after the presiding one " gives praise and glory to the Father of all in the name of the Son and of the Holy Spirit, " he " gives thanks *at length* because God considered us worthy of these gifts. " [3] He says nothing about the content of these thanksgivings. An interesting passage in his *Dialogue with Trypho*, [4] however, provides an outline of their main themes when Justin explains the meaning of the Eucharistic Sacrifice as the offering " of the bread of the Eucharist, which our Lord Jesus Christ commanded us to offer for the *anamnesis* (remembrance) of the passion that he suffered for men to cleanse their souls from all sin, and that at the same time we should give thanks to God for having created the world and all that is in it for the sake of man, for having delivered us from the wickedness in which we were born, and for the complete destruction of evil powers and principalities by undergoing suffering in accordance with his own will. " [5]

After the thanksgivings, all that remained to be done was to " make the Eucharist " itself. How this was achieved is also explained by Justin in chapter 66 of his *First Apology*. The Christians " made the Eucharist by the prayer of his word... the flesh and blood of that Jesus who was made flesh, " by doing " what Jesus ordered them to do. Having taken bread and given thanks, he said : ' Do this in remembrance of me; this is my body. ' In

[3] Justin Martyr, *First Apology*, chap. 65; see above, p. 41.

[4] An imaginary dialogue with the Jew Trypho (Rabbi Tarphon?), that supposedly occurred at Ephesus shortly after the Jewish uprising against the Romans (c. A.D. 135). In this dialogue—actually composed years later at Rome—Justin attempts to explain that the Jewish ceremonial laws are temporary, that Christ is the true Messiah, and that the Christians are the only heirs of the divine promises.

[5] Justin Martyr, *Dialogue* 41. Our translation into English made from edit. Otto, I, p. 134.

like manner, after taking the cup and giving thanks, he said : ' This is my blood, ' and to them only did he give it. " [6]

If we go back for a moment to the Jewish Blessing, or Benediction (the " grace after meals "), of the *chabûrah* suppers, we shall find a parallel of themes, if not of words. This comparison strengthens the theory of a single primitive type of Eucharistic Prayer, characterized by uniformity of themes (or ideas, not of text), modeled on the Jewish Benediction and adapted to the theological tenets of the Christians : the Jewish prayer was rewritten in terms of the New Testament.

After the introductory dialogue, almost identical in its opening phrase, " Let us give thanks unto the Lord God, " the " thanksgivings " were made :

Jewish Berakah Prayer	*Primitive Eucharistic Prayer*
I. First paragraph of Berakah prayer :	I. Christianized counterpart :
(a) Specific thanksgiving for a meal.	(a) Lacking, irrelevant to the Eucharistic service after its separation from common meal.
(b) " Blessing, " or " Glorifying of the Name. "	(b) The celebrant, after taking the bread and wine, " gives praise and glory to the Father of all in the name of the Son and of the Holy Spirit.... " (Justin, *First Apology*, chap. 65; see above, p. 41).
II. Second paragraph : " We thank thee, O Lord, our God, because thou didst give as an heritage unto our fathers a desirable, good and ample land..."	II. The Christians gave " thanks to God for having created the world and all that is in it, for the sake of man.... " (Justin, *Dialogue with Trypho*, chap. 41; see above, p. 552).
III. The Jews went on to give thanks " because thou didst bring us forth, O Lord our God, from the land of Egypt, and	III. The Christians thanked God, " for having delivered us from the wickedness in which we were born and for the com-

---

[6] Justin Martyr, *First Apology*, chap. 66. Our translation made from edit. Otto, I, p. 180.

didst deliver us from the house of bondage... "

IV. The Jews gave thanks " for thy Covenant which thou hast sealed in our flesh; for thy Law which thou hast taught us; the statutes which thou hast made known unto us; the life, grace and loving-kindness which thou hast bestowed upon us... "

V. The Jews went on to give thanks, " for the food wherewith thou dost constantly feed and sustain us, every day, in every season and at every hour. For all this, O Lord, our God, we thank thee and bless thee. "

plete destruction of evil powers and principalities... " (Justin, *Dial. with Trypho*, chap. 41; see above, p. 552).

IV. The Christians gave thanks for the New Covenant, " thanks at length because he considered us worthy of these gifts. " (Justin, *First Apology*, chap. 65; see above, p. 41).

V. The Christians " made the Eucharist by the prayer of his word and by which our flesh and blood are nourished by assimilation... the flesh and blood of that Jesus who was made flesh... what Jesus ordered them to do; that, having taken bread and given thanks, he said : ' Do this in remembrance of me; this is my body. ' In like manner, after taking the cup and giving thanks, he said : ' This is my blood ' and to them only did he give it. " (Justin, *First Apology*, chap. 66; cf. above, p. 552 f.).

The parallel conclusion of the Jewish prayer, " Blessed be thy name by the mouth of all living, continually and forever, " is not mentioned by Justin, but the Christians must have had an appropriate conclusion since the congregation answered *Amen* (*First Apology*, chap. 67, see above, p. 42). Confirming this, the final " glorifying of the name " assumed great importance and was considered obligatory by Hippolytus in his *Apostolic Tradition* (vi, 4).

The primitive Eucharistic Prayer, or anaphora, is marked by uniformity of *ideas* or *themes*, *not of text*. These themes may have been mentioned briefly or expanded at length, and others may have been added—hence, the great diversity of the later anaphoras, which led so many scholars to reject the traditional theory of a single primitive type of Eucharistic Prayer and even led some to believe in a dual origin. [7]

The single-origin theory is confirmed by the fact that all later anaphoras contain two strata : A) the universal, occupying a fixed place in every anaphora; B) the secondary, sometimes missing or found in different places.

A. UNIVERSAL, FIXED ELEMENTS

I. The *Preface-Dialogue,* found at the beginning of every Eucharistic Prayer, is the invitation " Let us give thanks to the Lord " or some such introductory dialogue. We know from the *Mishnah* that this invitation is a literal translation of that prescribed for the Jewish *chabûrah,* when at least ten people are present. [8]

II. *The Christian counterparts of the Jewish thanksgiving at a meal.* The first part of every Eucharistic Prayer consists in praise, glorification and thanks to God for all his gifts—from creation to deliverance. The emphasis may be placed either on the glorification of the divine name, or on the divine " economy " (the dispensation of salvation in creation and redemption), but both are always mentioned.

The *Sanctus* hymn of Isaiah 6:3, beginning with a listing of the heavenly choirs, has a recognizable parallel in the post-exilic Jewish Morning Prayer, with the solemn *Jôzêr* prayer, blessing God as Creator and listing the celestial choirs and their triple *Sanctus.* The first Christians adopted it, then modified it, probably for use in their catechetical synaxis (cf. Clement of Rome's *Epistle to the Corinthians,* chap. 34), then in their Eucharistic service. [9]

[7] E.g., Edmund Bishop, Ceriani, Lietzmann, etc.

[8] Tractate, *Berâkôth,* vii, 5, see below, pp. 565 f.

[9] Like most of the Eastern Liturgies several centuries later, the 34th chapter of Clement's *Epistle to the Corinthians* contains, not only the hymn itself (from Isa. 6:3), but also the passage from Daniel (7:10) introducing it : " Let us consider the vast multitude of his angels, and see how they stand in readiness to minister to his will. For the Scripture says : ' Ten thousand thousand stood ready before him, and a thousand thousand ministered to him, and cried out : Holy, Holy, Holy is the Lord of Hosts; the whole creation is replete with his splendor. ' And so we too, being dutifully assembled with one accord, should as with one voice

Although absent from the original nucleus of the Eucharistic Prayer, the Christian counterpart of the *Jôzêr* deserves to be mentioned as one of its universal, primary elements. [10]

III. The institution narrative with its consecratory formula is so universal and primary that there is no need to insist on it here. [11]

B. SECONDARY ELEMENTS

The other layers of anaphoric material—used in various parts of the Eucharistic Prayer, and sometimes missing entirely—may have been ancient and venerable, but were mere additions to the original nucleus.

I. *The Prayer for the miraculous conversion of the bread and wine.* This developed from the prayer beseeching God's acceptance of the Eucharistic Sacrifice. It follows the institution narrative in all the Churches of Christendom, except in Rome and Alexandria, where it precedes it. In Spanish and Gallic Masses, it came either before or after the narrative. This prayer is not to be confused with the epiclesis proper, which originated after the definition of the Holy Spirit by the First Council of Constantinople, A.D. 381.

II. *The anamnesis.* When it does appear in the early texts, the *anamnesis* is always found after the institution narrative, but before the epiclesis and intercessions. The Malabarese and Chaldean Rites place it after the intercessions, before the epiclesis.

III. *The anaphoric intercessions.* These generally follow the anamnesis and epiclesis—with some notable exceptions. In the

cry out to him earnestly. . . . " (chap. 34; J. A. Kleist, *The Epistles of St. Clement of Rome and St. Ignatius of Antioch*, Vol. I [Westminster, Md., 1946], p. 30).

Its inclusion in some of the Eucharistic Prayers seems to have resulted in some very awkward fusions of texts (e.g., in the Antiochene family of Liturgies) or else it seems to have displaced several of the original thanksgiving series (e.g., in the Liturgies of Jerusalem, Rome, and St. Mark).

[10] Hippolytus, the "antipope" who constantly accused St. Callistus of innovation, composed the *Apostolic Tradition* along the lines of his penchant for archaism by reverting to the original state before the fusion of the thanksgiving prayer and the Jôzêr.

[11] The East Syrian anaphora of SS. Addai and Mari is the sole exception in that it does not contain this element. For details and explanation, see pp 174-177.

ancient tradition of Alexandria, they appear before the *Sanctus* hymn. In Rome, they were originally placed before the institution narrative and the *Sanctus* hymn; prior to Vatican II, they seem to have been divided by the institution narrative and the three prayers following it. [12] In the Gallo-Spanish territories, some traces of the anaphoric intercessions remain occasionally, but they are more often omitted. Fragments of an ancient East Syrian anaphora show that the intercessions were inserted between the anamnesis and the epiclesis. [13]

Besides variations in their relative positions within the anaphora, there are differences in content, structure, and form.

The Final Stage

The final stage was reached when the Eucharistic Prayers crystallized for each Rite into a rigid, permanent, and official form which could not be altered except by competent authority. Each form became final in its own time and place. By the end of the fourth century, some Churches in the West, concerned about the excesses of celebrants, began curtailing freedom in this matter. The Council of Carthage (A.D. 397), for example, enacted a canon enjoining celebrants to use at the altar only those prayers previously edited by the " brothers. " [14] The rule laid down by the Council of Milevium (A.D. 412) was more severe. [15] Such conservatism came much later in the East, particularly in the West Syrian group of Liturgies with its rich store of anaphoras. In the late Middle Ages, Syrian literature boasts, not of theological *Summae* or commentaries on the *Sentences*, so typical of the Latin writings of the time, but of anaphoric formularies composed by their bishops.

However great the variations of text, the Eucharistic Prayer was always considered one unit and named as such in all the ancient Liturgies. The original name *Eucharistia* soon gave way to other names.

[12] The *Memento* for the dead, however, was probably a relatively recent addition.

[13] Cf. edit. R. H. Connolly, in *Oriens Christianus* (N.S.), xii/xiv (1925), pp. 114-117.

[14] Canon 23, edit. Labbé and Cossart, *Sacrosancta Concilia* (Paris, 1671), 2, 170.

[15] Canon 12. Cf. J. A. Jungmann, *Gewordene Liturgie* (Innsbruck, 1941), p. 70 : *Praefatio und stiller Kanon.*

In the Latin-speaking world, some writers and Fathers called it *prex* [16] or *oratio*, [17] terms which we could translate as " the Prayer " or " the Great Prayer. " Others qualified *prex* with *canonica* or *mystica*. [18] Tertullian and others used *sacrificiorum orationes* and *actio gratiarum*. [19] Nor are *actio* and its corresponding verbal form, *agere*, uncommon in the latter years of Christian antiquity. [20] Ultimately, the West settled on the word *canon*, a term first used in Pope Gregory's letter defending his innovations in A.D. 598. [21]

By contrast, the East still has no universally accepted term, although *anaphora* (from ἀναφέρειν, " to lay upon ") is by far the most commonly used. The West Syrians, for example, generally use the word *Korobho*, reverential " approach " to God, from the verb *kerabh* (to approach) common also to *Kurbono* or *Kurbana* (gift), their usual designation for the whole Liturgy. [22] Semitic language groups frequently use derivatives of *kadosh* " holy "; thus the Catholic Chaldeans and Syrian Nestorians use *quddasha* for the Eucharistic Prayer; the Arabs, *quddas*, and the Ethiopians, *keddase*, although this term is usually reserved for the whole Liturgy.

For some time in the East, the word *prosphora* was used, [23] or even " the Prayer of the Prosphora, " [24]—but this expression was rejected logically enough, since it means in a general way " to bring along. "

The verb ἀναφέρειν is used frequently in the Scripture in the

---

[16] Thus, Gregory the Great, *Ep*. IX, 12 (PL 77, 956); Pope Vigilius, *Ep*. II, 5 (PL 69, 18 D); possibly also Cyprian, *Ep*. XV, 1 (PL 4, 265); *Ep*. LX, 4 (PL 4, 362); and *Ep*. LXVI, 1 (PL 4, 398).

[17] Cyprian, *De dom. orat*., chap. 31 (CSEL, 3, 289, 1, 14).

[18] The former, by Innocent I, *Ep*. XXV (PL 20, 553); the latter, by Augustine, *De trin*., III, 4, 10 (PL 42, 874).

[19] Tertullian, *De orat*., 19 (PL 1, 1181); *Adv. Marc*., 4, 9 (PL 2, 405, B).

[20] *Agere* like the Greek δρᾶν, meaning to sacrifice, Thus, Leo I, in his *Ep*. IX *ad Dioscurum Alex*. (PL 54, 627); cf. also F. J. Dölger, *Antike und Christentum*, Vol. I (1929), pp. 54-65.

[21] PL 77, 956.

[22] James of Edessa (d. 708), however, used *kurobho* and *kurbono* as equivalents; cf. Brightman, LEW, p. 490, line 25.

[23] E.g., Synod of Laodicea, Canon 58 (Mansi, *Sacrorum conciliorum nova et amplissima collectio*, II, 574).

[24] Sarapion, no. 13 (Quasten, *Monumenta eucharistica et liturgia vetustissima* [Bonn, 1935-1937], 59).

sense of " offering a sacrifice. " In Christian usage, both the verb and the noun were used at first in a general sense, [25] then, to designate the whole Liturgy, [26] and finally, the Eucharistic Prayer alone, —a meaning which is still current, especially in the Greek Orient. Some Eastern Churches use it today in a wider sense, embracing also the prayers before Communion or even including the Communion prayers themselves.

Another transient name was θυσία αἰνέσεως, the " thank-offering " derived from the terminology of the Law in the Old Testament, [27] where it denotes the highest form of peace-offering. It passed into general Christian usage from Hebrews 13:15, and later into liturgical parlance, together with the term *anaphora*, to denote the Eucharistic Sacrifice or the Eucharistic formulary used in it. [28]

The word *mystery* or *mysteries* (μυστήριον or μυστήρια) enjoyed more than ephemeral popularity, although it is not clear whether it referred to the whole Eucharistic service or to the Eucharistic formulary alone. [29] It is sometimes used today among the Slavs and the Ethiopians, but generally to designate the whole Divine Liturgy.

The present structure of Eastern anaphoras is threefold : (1) the main formulary, (2) the brief prayers added by the celebrant, the deacon, the choir, or the people, and (3) a few ritual gestures. The Divine Liturgy requires the cooperation and participation of various people, and so does the anaphora. The component parts are complementary.

[25] Heb. 8:27; I Pet. 2:5; Origen, *In Evang. Joh.*, vi, 33, 34.

[26] *Apostolic Constitutions*, Book II, 57-58 (edit. F. X. Funk, *Didascalia et Constitutiones Apostolorum* [Paderborn, 1905], II, pp. 569 ff.); cf. also, Canon 2 of Council of Ancyra (A.D. 314), in Mansi, *op. cit.*, II, 513 B.

[27] Described in Lev. 7:12-15 and 22:29; also, after the reforms of Hezekiah, in II Paralip. 29:31 and Psalm 115:8 (Septuagint).

[28] E.g., Cyril of Alexandria, *De adoratione in spiritu et veritate*, 13 (PG 68, 848 C); Cyril of Jerusalem, *Catecheses* 23, 8-9 (PG 33, 1116 A-1117 A).

[29] Athanasius, *Apologia contra Arianos*, 11 (PG 25, 268 A); also, *Fragm.*, VII (PG 26, 1325 C); Gregory of Nyssa, *In baptismum Christi oratio* (PG 46, 581 C); Epiphanius, *Adv. haer.*, XLII, 3 (PG 41, 700) and XLII, 4 (PG 41, 700-701); Chrysostom, *Contra eos qui subintroductas habent virgines*, 10 (edit. Montfaucon 1, 243 A, or PG 47, 509); and *In epist. I ad Cor. homil.*, XLI, 4 (edit. Montfaucon 10, 393 A, or PG 61, 361); *In Matt. homil.*, XXV, 4 (edit. Montfaucon 7, 310 D, or PG 57, 311); Nilus the Abbot (A.D. 427), *Epist.* (Book I), 44 (PG 79, 104 A); Theodore of Mopsuestia, *In epist. I ad Cor.*, chaps. 10, 11, 3-4 (PG 66, 888 ff.).

In Eastern usage, variations in the Divine Liturgy are generally limited to two areas : the lessons and the chants, proper to time, season, or circumstances. In the Byzantine anaphora, the only allowed variation in chant concerns that in honor of the Mother of God, the *Megalynarion*. The celebrant's part is invariable, although ten times a year the anaphora of St. Basil is used instead of that of John Chrysostom. The ritual acts performed by the celebrants are identical and invariable in both anaphoras. Other Oriental Liturgies are richer in anaphoric formularies, but all follow the same pattern outlined above. A characteristic common to all Eastern anaphoras is the fact that they are not adapted to any festive occasion or mystery, but are merely parallel expressions of an identical theme. Each formulary is conceived as a whole : it continues uninterrupted, despite the participation of various ministers, and of the people themselves. All parts, except those of the celebrant, are chanted. The celebrant recites his inaudibly, except the words of consecration and a few other sentences which are intoned. [30]

The other Oriental anaphoras are generally recited in the same way. The early Church did not pray silently, as is obvious from Justin's description of the Eucharist. [31] The unequivocal testimony of Dionysius of Alexandria also proves it. [32] It was only during the last part of the fifth or the beginning of the sixth century that the practice of saying the anaphora in silence began to take hold. In A.D. 565 Justinian, for example, found it necessary to legislate for the Constantinopolitan Church : " Moreover, we order all bishops and priests... to offer the divine oblation, not silently, but in a voice audible to the faithful...." [33] In the early sixth-century Chaldean Liturgy, on the other hand, Narsai tells us that except for the three " canons " (which are still recited aloud today),

---

[30] I.e., the " prefatory dialogue," the phrase introducing the *Sanctus*, the final words of the *anamnesis*, the commemoration of the Virgin Mary, the intercession for the hierarchy and the doxology concluding the anaphora.

[31] In chap. 67 of *First Apology*, he states that the people joined in with the concluding *Amen*.

[32] Dionysius of Alexandria (d. A.D. 264-265), in Eusebius, *Hist. eccl.*, VII, 9 (PG 20, 656).

[33] Justinian, *Novella*, 137, 6 (edit. R. Schoell and G. Kroll, *Corpus Juris civilis*, III, p. 699). Our translation.

the rest of the anaphora was offered in silence. [34] At about this time, the period of transition in the West Syrian Church was nearly over. This we can infer from the incident first recounted by John Moschus (d. A.D. 619) about some boys being struck by lightning because they had imitated the celebration of the Divine Liturgy as a pastime. How were the words of the sacrifice known? Because " ...in some places the priests make them known in a loud voice, " he complains. " They learned, " he reiterates, " the prayer of the holy sacrifice because it is constantly being declared publicly. " [35]

The practice of saying the Canon silently in the Western Church came at least two centuries later. First apparent in the middle of the eighth century, [36] the transition became widespread within fifty years. [37] The last areas of resistance, however, seem to have endured well into the Middle Ages. [38]

After almost all the Orient had adopted the silent offering of the Eucharistic Prayer, it was inevitable that the custom would prevail in the West. The various reasons adduced for the change are frankly unconvincing. The concepts, for example, that the canon is the Holy of holies into which the priest alone can enter, [39] or that the sacred words must not be profaned lest we call down God's wrath upon ourselves, [40] seem no more than invention. No such reasons can hold true for the Eastern Churches where the custom began, for there the sense of Holy of holies is much more strongly

---

[34] Narsai, Homily XVII, *Expositio mysteriorum* (edit. R. H. Connolly, *The Liturgical Homilies of Narsai* [Cambridge, 1909], pp. 12-23).

[35] John Moschus, *Patrum spirituale*, chap. 196 (PG 87, 3080).

[36] *Ordo Rom.*, I, n. 16 (PL 78, 945); cf. Jungmann, *op. cit.*, 100 ff., for textual criticism of passage.

[37] Florus Diaconus, *De actione miss.*, n. 42 f. (PL 119, 43); Remigius of Auxerre, *Expositio* (PL 101, 1256). See also the commentary " *Quotiens contra se,* " Martène, *De antiquis Ecclesiae ritibus* (2nd edit., Antwerp, 1736-1738), 1, 4, 11 (I, 455 D).

[38] As late as 1217, the Synod of Sarum in England warned that the words of the Canon in the Mass should be pronounced roundly and distinctly (Canon 36, Mansi, *op. cit.*, xxii, 1119); the *Ordo Rom.*, XIV, n. 53 (PL 78, 1165) states that priests must say the Canon in a " lowered " voice, as the deacon and subdeacon did when they recited the Sanctus—but the deacon and subdeacon said the Sanctus in a loud voice!

[39] Cf. Jungmann, *The Mass of the Roman Rite : Its Origins and Development (Missarum Solemnia)*, Vol. II (New York, 1955), p. 104.

[40] Remigius of Auxerre, *Expositio* (PL 101, 1256 D).

conveyed than in the West by the iconostas separating the sanctuary from the faithful, by the curtain drawn during the most sacred moments of the Sacrifice, and so forth.   Furthermore, it is precisely the most sacred words—the words of the Lord consecrating the elements—that are recited aloud.

A simple but much more compelling reason seems to be economy of time. The Divine Liturgy had become immensely long with the many additions and embellishments, the more elaborate chants, dismissals, anaphoric intercessions, and diptychs.   To save time, the celebrant would continue reciting his part in a low voice while the people or deacon continued singing theirs.   Even now, the Divine Liturgy lasts several hours when the complete ritual is followed and the singing is elaborate.

CHAPTER LVI

THE INTRODUCTORY DIALOGUE

Immediately after the Profession of Faith the deacon begins :
Let us stand with dignity, let us stand in awe. Let us be attentive, that we may offer the holy sacrifice in peace.

People : **The mercy of peace, a sacrifice of praise.**

The deacon makes a small bow, enters the sanctuary through the south door, and takes his place at the priest's right. Whenever the need arises, the deacon takes the ripidion and reverently fans the holy gifts. If there is no ripidion at hand, he uses the small, folded veil.

Blessing the people, the priest says :

The grace of our Lord Jesus Christ, the love of God the Father, and the communion of the Holy Spirit be with you all.

People : **And with your spirit.**

After turning around toward the altar, the priest lifts up his hands while intoning :

Let us lift up our hearts.

People : **We have them lifted up to the Lord.**

Priest : **Let us give thanks to the Lord.**

People : **It is fitting and right to adore the Father and the Son and the Holy Spirit, the consubstantial and undivided Trinity.**

Because the holy sacrifice is about to begin, the deacon admonishes the people of God to stand at attention with reverence : " Let us stand with dignity, let us stand in awe.... " Again, what seems to have been a rubric originally has been embodied into the liturgical text. This must have occurred very soon, for the *Apostolic Constitutions* has the deacon proclaiming to the people : " Let mothers take their children in hand.... Let us stand straight before the Lord with fear and trembling to offer (the oblation). "[1] Chrysostom

---

[1] *Apostolic Constitutions*, Book VIII; cf. above, p. 124.

tells us that in Antioch " not in vain does the deacon call out to all,
' Attention, let us stand with dignity ' [more literally, ' Let us
stand upright as is fitting '], in order that we may raise our thoughts
which drag us down to earth, overcome the weaknesses caused by
earthly cares, and stand before God with a just soul. That is why
we are told to stand with dignity [' *upright* as is fitting '], for to
stand with dignity means precisely that a person stand before God
with fear and trembling, with gravity and courageous spirit. " [2]

By the eighth century, the deacon's acclamation was the same as
it is today. [3] In the response, the people accept the deacon's admonition, glorifying the oblation as a pledge of peace and a sacrifice
of praise. As long as the direction for standing straight remained
a mere rubric, it required no response, but after its incorporation
into the liturgical text as an acclamation, some response became
necessary. [4] In the eighth-century *Codex Barberini*, the response is
simple : " Mercy, peace " (ἔλεος εἰρήνη). [5] The early eighth-century
Armenian version of Chrysostom's Liturgy has a slightly more
developed form : " Mercy and peace and the sacrifice of praise. " [6]
That the response was not always understood well is evident from
its varying versions. [7] The present rendition seems to have been

[2] Chrysostom, *De incompr. Dei nat.*, iv, 5 (edit. Montfaucon I, 593 B or PG
48, 734).

[3] E.g., the early eighth century Armenian version of Chrysostom's Liturgy
(cf. Aucher, *La versione armena della liturgia di S. Giovanni Crisostomo, fatta sul
principio dell'VIII secolo*, XPYCOCTOMIKA [Rome, 1908], p. 387); Germanus
of Constantinople, *Commentarius lit.*, 41 (edit. N. Borgia, *Il commentario liturgico
di s. Germano Patriarca Constantinopolitano e la versione latina di Anastasio Bibliotecario* [Grottaferrata, 1912], p. 32). *Cod. Barberini*, however, only gives the
simple Στῶμεν καλῶς, " Let us stand with dignity " (cf. Brightman, LEW, p. 321).
Could the acclamation have been so standard that only an abbreviated form
was necessary ?

[4] Not in all places, however. The tenth or eleventh century *Cod. Sebast.* has
no response, nor does the fourteenth of fifteenth century *Liturgikon* of Metropolitan
Isidore. Cf. MS. *Vat. Slav.*, N. 14, fols. 19-20 of its text, and fol. 135 of its
Ustav (ordo).

[5] Cf. Brightman, LEW, p. 321.

[6] Cf. Aucher, *op. cit.*, p. 387; thus also the fifteenth century MS. *Vat. Slav.*,
N. 10, fol. 51 verso.

[7] It matters little whether the nouns " mercy " and " sacrifice " in the response
appear in the nominative case or in the accusative. If in the nominative, the
response is an entirely independent entity (e.g. ἔλεος εἰρήνη in *Cod. Barberini*,
gr. 336 [Brightman, LEW, p. 321] or Ἔλαιος, εἰρήνη [cf. Krasnoseltsev, *Materialy*

borrowed from the Greek Liturgy of St. James (with the word " peace " in the genitive, i.e., " the mercy of peace "). [8]

As so often happens in liturgical history, what originally had begun as a practical directive was later turned into something symbolic and inspirational. Nothing more was intended than a polite request that the people comport themselves in a way worthy of the august sacrifice. Later interpretations, accommodated to suit the piety of the commentator, sometimes had merit. Cabasilas, for example, gives one of the best—albeit far removed from the original meaning :

> Let us stand firm on this profession of faith... lest we should be thrown off balance by the persuasive arguments of heretics. " Let us stand in fear "; for the danger to those who allow in their minds any doubt or hesitation, concerning matters of faith, is very great.... " Thus standing firm in faith, let our offering to God proceed as is proper. " What does " as is proper " mean ? It means : in peace. Let us take care to offer the holy oblation in peace.... The faithful reply : " Not only do we make our offerings in peace; it is peace itself which we offer as a gift and a second sacrifice...." Now mercy is the child of a strong and true peace. For when the soul is untroubled by passion, there is nothing to hinder it from being filled with mercy and the sacrifice of praise. [9]

At the Jewish *chabûrah*, the *berakah* (the thanksgiving-blessing) was always preceded by a dialogue between the leader and his

dlja istorii chinoposlidovania liturgii sv. Ioanna Zlatoustago, p. 26]). If in the accusative, the response is considered a prolongation of the acclamation (e.g. Ἔλεον... θυσίαν—as in the twelfth century MS. of Sinai Library᾽ N. 973 [cf. Dmitrievsky, *Opysanie liturgicheskikh rukopisej khraniaschikhsia v bibliotekakh pravoslavnago vostoka*, II, p. 84]; Morel's edit. of the Liturgy [cf. Krasnoseltsev, *Svidinia o nikotorikh liturgicheskikh rukopis'akh Vatikanskoi biblioteki*, p. 134; etc.]). The meaning, however, is changed when the word " peace " (εἰρήνη), is put into the genitive case as it is in some versions dating back to the twelfth century (e.g., Ἔλεον εἰρήνης, θυσίαν—in MS. N. 973 of Sinai Library [cf. Dmitrievsky, *Opysanie*, p. 84]; also, in the Liturgy inserted into the works of Chrysostom given in Goar's *Euchologion*, p. 93 [2nd edit.]; also, edit. Morel [cf. Krasnoseltsev, *Svidinia*, p. 134], and of course, in the present renditions of the text).

[8] Cf. A. Rocchi in Mai, NPB, X, ii, pp. 65-66 ,and Swainson, *The Greek Liturgies Chiefly from Original Authorities* (London, 1884), pp. 264-265.

[9] N. Cabasilas, *A Commentary on the Divine Liturgy*, trans. by J. M. Hussey and P. A. McNulty (London, 1960), pp. 67-68.

companions. In a small, intimate gathering, the presiding host
would begin : " Let us give thanks to the Lord. " [10] When at least
a hundred guests were present, the phrase " our God " was added. [11]
" Assent " was given by the gathering immediately afterward, before
the host would proceed with the *berakah*. There can be little doubt
that the Christian dialogue prefatory to the *eucharistia* derived its
inspiration and some of its phrases from the Jewish dialogue.
Hippolytus, writing about the Eucharistic Liturgy as it was celebrated
at the beginning of the third century, quotes it as follows :

> The Lord be with you.
> And with thy spirit.
> Lift up your hearts.
> We have lifted them unto the Lord.
> Let us give thanks to the Lord.
> It is meet and right. [12]

This dialogue, almost identical with the present Latin and
Egyptian rituals, is composed of three parts, each consisting of an
invitation by the celebrant and a response by the people. This same
division is preserved in all of the Liturgies in both the Eastern and
the Western Churches. Only the Chaldean Church adds a short
prayer of supplication " on bended knee. "

The first part, the celebrant's opening greeting and its response,
was probably universal in the primitive Church. Shortly after
Nicaea, in the Syrian Church, it took the form of a blessing adapted
from St. Paul (II Cor. 13:14), and is first encountered in the *Apostolic
Constitutions* : " The grace of almighty God and the love of our
Lord Jesus Christ and the communion of the Holy Spirit be with
you all. " [13] Cyril of Jerusalem does not mention it, but it is found
in the Antiochene Liturgy of St. James and in the East Syrian
Liturgy of Addai and Mari. The present Byzantine form is identical
to that found in the Antiochene writings of Chrysostom, *c.* A.D. 390 :
" The grace of our Lord Jesus Christ and the love of God and

---

[10] In accordance with rabbinical prescription, this formula was to be used
" whenever there are ten in company. "

[11] *Berakoth*, M., vii. 4 and 5.

[12] See above, p. 57.

[13] Book VIII; see above, p. 125.

Father and the communion of the Holy Spirit be with you all. " [14]
We may infer that the substitution took place in Antioch in the
latter part of the fourth century and spread from there to the rest
of the Greco-Syrian Churches. [15] In fact, the innovation spread so
swiftly that some fifty years later Theodoret could say that it was
common to all Churches. [16]

The blessing has lost its original simplicity, but it is still beautiful.
To paraphrase Cabasilas, it procures for us the benefits of the Holy
Trinity, every perfect gift; it asks from each of the Divine Persons
his particular gift : from the Son grace, from the Father love, from
the Spirit communion. For the Son gave himself as Saviour to us
who not only had bestowed nothing upon him but were actually in
his debt. His care of us, then, is truly a gratuity, a grace. The
Father, through the sufferings of his Son, was reconciled to mankind
and showered his love upon his enemies so that indeed his goodness
to us is given the name of love. Finally, the Being replete with
mercy wished to give to his enemies now become his friends the
best of himself. This the Holy Spirit accomplished in descending
upon the apostles. That is why his goodness to men is called
communion—we pray thus in order that we may not lose that which
we have received, but that we may keep it forever. So the priest
does not say : " May these be given to you all, " but " May these be
with you all. " Let not the grace which has been given to you be
taken away. [17]

With slight variations in some liturgical traditions, the second
part, " Let us lift up our hearts, " and its response seem purely
Christian, but their origin is obscure : they may be Hellenic or
Jewish. A formula in the Samaritan liturgy required the hands
to be lifted before certain high points in prayer. [18] Jeremiah urges
in his Lamentations (3:41) : " Let us lift up our hearts with our

---

[14] De s. Pentecoste, i, 4 (edit. Montfaucon 2, 463 B); cf. above, p. 125.

[15] Dom H. Engberding is mistaken when he credits its origin to Constantinople
in his study Der Gruss des Priesters zu Beginn der εὐχαριστία in ostlichen Liturgien,
in JbLw. IX (1929), pp. 138-143.

[16] Ad Ioann. oec. ep., 146 (PG 83, 1393 A) : ἐν πάσις ταῖς ἐκκλησίαις.

[17] Cabasilas, op. cit., pp. 68-69.

[18] Cf. A. Baumstark, " Wege zum Judentum des neutestamentlichen Zeitalters ":
Bonner Zeitschrift f. Theologie u. Seelsorge, IV (1927), 33.

hands to the Lord in the heavens. " In the First Epistle to Timothy (2:28), Paul writes : " I will therefore that men pray in every place, lifting up pure hands.... " In fact, such a practice was common in the early Christian Church. Since the lifting up of the hands was a sign of lifting up the heart to God, it would seem that the *sursum corda* in the Eucharistic Liturgy was merely a directive to the congregation.

The form " Lift up the hearts, " found in Cyprian and Hippolytus, was probably universal in the primitive *Eucharistia*. The Roman and Egyptian Churches have kept it. The Syrian Liturgies have modified it slightly. The Liturgy contained in the *Apostolic Constitutions*, for example, has " Lift up your mind " (see above, p. 125), while Chrysostom has, " Let us lift up our minds and hearts " (see above, p. 125). The Jerusalem formula, given in the *Catecheses* of Cyril and again in the works of Anastasius the Sinaite, is " Lift up your hearts. " [19] The Liturgy of St. James, probably borrowing and enlarging the Jerusalem form, has : " Let us hold the hearts lifted up. " [20] The greatest amplification occurred in the Mozarabic Rite :

Priest : I will go unto the altar of God.

People : Even unto the God of my joy and gladness.

Priest : Lend your ears unto the Lord.

People : We lend them unto the Lord.

Priest : Lift up your hearts, etc.

With the exception of this final example, there is hardly any difference in meaning between the various forms. Cyprian explains the expression as establishing the proper Christian state of mind before prayer, the elimination of fleshly and wordly thoughts, and the concentration upon the Lord. [21] Likewise, Cyril of Jerusalem exhorts his hearers to be rid of " all cares of this life. " [22] About

---

[19] Cyril of Jerusalem, *Catechesis*, xxiii, (*Mystag.*, 4 f.) (PG 33, 1112); Anastasius the Sinaite, *De sacra synaxi* (PG 89, 837 A).

[20] Brightman, LEW, p. 50, line 4.

[21] Cyprian, *De dom. or.*, 31 (CSEL 3, 289).

[22] Cyril of Jerusalem, *Catechesis*, V, (*Mystag.*, 4) (Quasten, *Monumenta eucharistica et liturgia vetustissima* [Bonn, 1935-1937], 99).

two centuries later, the same appeal was incorporated into the cherubic hymn.

" Let us give thanks to the Lord. " As indicated above, similarity with the invitation to the *berakah* of the *chabûrah* and its response point to a Jewish origin. The Byzantine form quotes Hippolytus, who in turn is quoting the rabbinical prescription for a small gathering. The response is a confirmatory acclamation, equivalent to the *Amen* in the *Shema* of the Jewish morning prayer. [23] Historical documents prove that, using some such acclamation, legislative assemblies confirmed important decisions, the taking of office, or λειτουργία and even an election. [24] The acclamation used on such occasions was ἄξιος —which is still used by the Church at ordinations and consecrations. Other expressions, such as, " It is fitting, " " It is right, " were also used. [25] A confirmatory acclamation addressed by the people of God to their official spokesman conforms with history. It was this confirmatory acclamation, more than the final Amen, that induced Chrysostom to write : " The offering of thanksgiving... is common : for it is not the priest alone who completes the thanksgiving but the people with him... when they assent that it is ' meet and right so to do '; only then does he begin the thanksgiving. " [26]

[23] Cf. I. Elbogen, *Der jüdische Gottesdienst in seiner geschichtlichen Entwicklung* (2nd edit., Frankfurt, 1924), pp. 22, 25.
[24] Cf. T. Klauser, " Akklamation, " RAC, Vol. I, pp. 216-233.
[25] Cf. Klauser, *op. cit.*, pp. 227-231, for listing.
[26] *In II Cor. homil.*, xviii, 3 (edit. Montfaucon 10, 568 or PG 61, 527).

CHAPTER LVII

THE PREFACE

W*hile the people are singing the prefatory dialogue's final response, the priest begins the anaphora silently :*

It is proper and right to sing of you, to praise you, to thank you, to adore you in all places of your domain; for you are God ineffable, inconceivable, invisible, incomprehensible, eternally the same, you and your only-begotten Son and your Holy Spirit. You brought us into being out of nothingness and, when we had fallen, you raised us up again. You have not ceased doing everything until you have brought us into heaven and have given us your future Kingdom. For all these things we thank you and your only-begotten Son and your Holy Spirit; we thank you for all benefits, for those of which we know and for those of which we know not, for those bestowed on us openly and in secret. We thank you also for this sacrifice which you deign to receive from our hands, even though there stand before you thousands of archangels and myriads of angels, cherubim and seraphim, six-winged and many-eyed, who soar aloft on their wings, who....

The first part of the anaphora is roughly comparable to the Latin preface, but not in the mistaken sense that it is an " introduction. " The misconception stems from a misunderstanding of the term " preface. " Cyprian (A.D. 258) used the term *praefatio* to designate the first part of the thanksgiving. In the language of the time, *praefari* meant " to utter juridical or ritual formulae. " Technically speaking, the *praefatio*, then, was a prayer which accompanied a sacrifice and was recited by a priest in a loud voice. [1]

Any idea that the preface " introduces " the hymn of victory (the *Sanctus*) or the sacred action itself, or that it is intended to

---

[1] Titus Livy : " *Pontifice maximo praefante carmen...* "; " *Solemne carmen precationis quod praefari solent magistratus...* " (in Batiffol, *Leçons sur la Messe* [7th edit., Paris, 1920], p. 192).

create a reverent atmosphere in which it will take place, is utterly erroneous. The preface is part of the anaphora : in both origin and structure, they are one. The preface gives the anaphora its leading idea : thanksgiving.

The preface is a constant feature in the Byzantine Liturgy, as it is in all the other Eastern Liturgies. There may be different anaphoras, the use of which is determined by rubrics, but each one has its own unchanging opening prayer. In marked contrast, the Latin Rite has made the preface seasonal while the rest of the Eucharistic Prayer was never changed (post-Vatican II developments excepted). The Roman prefaces are alternative ways of beginning the Eucharistic Prayer. The earliest Roman Sacramentary, the *Leonianum*, has two hundred sixty-seven prefaces—one for each feast of the day. But they were so encumbered with detail that they tended to obscure their fundamental purpose. Reform came with Pope Gregory I (*c*. A.D. 600), who seems to have reduced their number to fourteen. [2] The so-called common preface was used for Sundays until the thirteenth century, when the Gallican Church began using instead the preface of the Trinity—a usage adopted by Rome in the eighteenth century.

The earliest forms of the Eucharistic Prayer probably began with a simple " We give thanks, " as in the *Didache* (see above, p. 24 f.) and Hippolytus (see above, p. 57). The early Cappadocian anaphora discovered by Engberding, at any rate, seems to have had such a simple beginning : " We hymn thee, we bless thee, we give thanks to thee, we beseech thee, our God. " [3] In the interest of a smoother transition between the introductory dialogue and the following prayer, the opening phrases were modified in both East and West through the introduction of infinitives dependent upon the preliminary statements, " It is proper and right " : *Vere dignum et iustum est, aequum et salutare, nos tibi semper et ubique gratias agere,* etc.

---

[2] Later, seven of these fell into disuse. Those for Christmas, Epiphany, Easter, Ascension, Pentecost, the Apostles and the Common Preface (for all other saints) remained. By the eleventh century, however, the prefaces of the Holy Trinity, the Cross, Our Lady, and Lent were added. The twentieth century saw another increase in the number of prefaces : for the Dead (1919), St. Joseph (1919), Christ the King (1925), and the Sacred Heart (1928).

[3] P. H. Engberding, *Das eucharistische Hochgebet der Basiliusliturgie* (Münster, 1931), p. 2.

The Byzantine anaphoras—of Chrysostom and Basil—follow the same pattern. The transition from the dialogue to the prayer is short in the Latin Liturgy, longer in Chrysostom, and the longest in Basil :

Chrysostom	*Basil*
	Master, Lord, adorable, almighty Father,
It is proper and right to sing of you, to praise you, to thank you, to adore you. . . .	it is truly proper and right and befitting the greatness of your holiness to praise you, to sing to you, to bless you, to worship you, to thank you, to glorify you, the only true God. . . to offer you. . . .

These opening sentences are characteristic of the rest of the anaphoras : that of Chrysostom is brief, forthright and simple; that of Basil, long, rich, and elaborate. This was clearly recognized in the early Greco-Cappadocian Church, wherein the Liturgy of Basil was used at the ordinary Sunday Eucharist until the ninth or tenth century, while that of Chrysostom only had a secondary role. [4] This was no accident, for in the early Church the preface at a Sunday or feast-day Liturgy was to be more solemn and elaborate that that of less important occasions. [5]

The preface of Basil's anaphora, containing the glorification of God's name, is indeed richer and more elaborate than that of Chrysostom. Yet, when we consider how much more emphasis Basil's anaphora places on the development of the rest of the rite— describing the divine dispensation of salvation, the creation, the redemption, the eucharistic institution, etc—it appears that Chrysostom's shorter blessing of God's name assumes a relatively greater importance when compared to the shorter developments that follow.

This difference has been forgotten by those who claim that one anaphora is an abbreviation of the other. Eastern anaphoras have evolved along two lines : the one stressing the " divine name, " and

---

[4] The *Cod. Barberini*, *gr.* 336, of the eighth or ninth century still accords this position to the Liturgy of Basil.

[5] *Canones Basilii*, 97 (Riedel, 274).

the other, the " divine economy. " The anaphora of Chrysostom
belongs to the first, that of Basil to the second—which seems to
indicate that they are unrelated. Chrysostom's anaphora is not an
abridgment of Basil's.

This conclusion is opposed to that of liturgists who rely on textual
fragments wrongly attributed to Patriarch Proclus (A.D. 434-446),
the " Pseudo-Proclus " [6] This source indicates that Basil shortened
the Liturgy of his time, and that Chrysostom abbreviated that of
Basil, since both wished to shorten the service. Less and less
authority is being given to this source as more light is being shed
by modern scholarship. [7] There is as yet no proof either way, but
all indications lead away from the supposed derivation.

Emphasis on the divine name may be traced to the time when
the *Jôsêr* hymn, together with the *Sanctus* (hymn of victory), of
the Jewish morning service was combined with the thanksgiving
—that is, after the Eucharist had become separated from the meal.
No actual date can be assigned as to the origin of anaphoras stressing
the " divine economy, " yet it seems evident that both lines are
ancient and that they evolved independently.

After the initial giving of praise, the original Eucharistic Prayer
consisted in a series of thanksgivings based on the ancient Jewish
thanksgiving prayer after a meal (see chap. LV, above). The shape
or structure—though not necessarily the content—of these thanksgivings was probably very much akin to those found in the *Didache*,
characterized by a recurrent " We give thanks " (see above, pp. 24-
25). For the content of such a series we turn to Justin's
Dialogue with Trypho, which offers a Christian parallel to the Jewish
custom :

> " ...that at the same time we should give thanks to God
> for having created the world and all that is in it... for having
> delivered us from the wickedness in which we were born,
> for the complete destruction of the evil powers and princi-
> palities by undergoing..., " etc. [8]

The preface of Chrysostom consists likewise in series of thanks-

---

[6] PG 65, 849-852.
[7] E.g., P. H. Engberding, P. de Meester, etc.
[8] Cf. Justin Martyr, *Dialogue with Trypho*, Dial. 41, see above, p. 552.

givings, with a recurrent, " We give thanks.... " Placing the three
texts in opposition will reveal their similarities :

Jewish Thanksgiving	*Justin*	*Chrysostom Preface*
I. Glorification of the divine name.	I. The celebrant " gives praise and glory to the Father of all in the name of the Son and of the Holy Spirit.... " (*First Apology*, chap. 65; see above, p. 41).	I. It is proper and right to sing of you, to praise you, to thank you, to adore you in all the places of your domain; for you are God ineffable, inconceivable, invisible, incomprehensible, eternally the same, you and your only-begotten Son and your Holy Spirit.
II. We thank thee, O Lord our God, because thou didst give as a heritage unto our fathers a desirable, good and ample land.	II. ...thanks to God for having created the world and all that is in it, for the sake of man (*Dialogue with Trypho*, chap. 41; see above, p. 552).	II. You brought us into being out of nothingness (i.e., creation).
III. ...because thou didst bring us forth, O Lord our God, from the land of Egypt, and didst deliver us from the house of bondage.	III. ...for having delivered us from the wickedness in which we were born and for the complete destruction of the evil powers and principalities (*Dialogue*, chap. 41, cf. above, p. 552).	III. And, when we had fallen, you raised us up again.
IV. ...for thy Covenant, which thou has sealed in our flesh; for thy Law, which thou hast taught us; thy statutes which thou hast made known unto us; the life, grace, and loving-kindness which thou hast bestowed upon us.	IV. ...thanks at length because he considered us worthy of these gifts (*First Apology*, chap. 65; see above, p. 41).	IV. You have not ceased doing everything until you have brought us into heaven and have given us your Kingdom. For all these things we thank you ...for all benefits, for those of which we know and for those of which we know not, for those bestowed openly and in secret.
V. ...for the food wherewith thou dost constantly feed and sustain us, every day, in every season and at every hour.	V. ...made the Eucharist by the prayer of his word and by which our flesh and blood are nourished by assimilation (*First Apology*, chap. 66; see above, p. 554).	V. We thank you also for this sacrifice which you deign to receive from our hands....

This similarity, if more than accidental, marks the first part of Chrysostom's anaphora with greater venerability and age than it has been usually credited with. In contrast, Basil's whole preface, is not so much the giving of thanks as a grateful remembrance of all the benefits for which it is fitting and right to praise God, to bless him, etc. The point is that Chrysostom's preface is in every respect so different and independent from that of Basil that it cannot be an abridgment of it. What marks that of Chrysostom with greater venerability and age than that of Basil is its theological content. It is a masterpiece of conciseness and clarity, but clearly lacks the theological development and precision found in Basil. The primitive Christian did not need the theological precision required by orthodox contemporaries of Arius or Nestorius. The theology of the Son and Holy Spirit, for example, in Basil's preface unfolds as a litany of doctrinal truths :

> of our Lord Jesus Christ
> our hope, who is the image of your goodness,
> the seal of your own likeness, showing
> the living Word,
> true God,
> eternal Wisdom,
> Life,
> Sanctification,
> Power,
> the true Light
> through whom the Holy Spirit manifested himself,
> the Spirit of truth,
> the gift of the adoption of sons,
> the pledge of our future inheritance,
> the firstfruits of everlasting blessedness,
> the life-giving power,
> the font of sanctification,
> through whom every creature endowed with reason and understanding is given the power to serve you and send up to you an unending hymn of glory....

By contrast, Chrysostom's preface is simple. It merely names the Son and the Holy Spirit twice, as if there were no need of elaboration. Closely resembling the primitive professions of faith in the *Didache* and Hippolytus, it is more concerned with the affirmation of belief in one God, the three Persons of the Blessed Trinity, and the plain fact of creation and redemption than with developing the corresponding theology. Such fundamental differences are sufficient grounds for questioning the traditional theory that Chrysostom is an abridgment of Basil. Indeed, as we have seen, it would appear that the preface of Chrysostom is the older of the two.

While the first part of Basil's anaphora is the theologian's preface, the first part of that of Chrysostom is everyman's. The basic doctrines contained in it are expressed with simplicity. The doctrine of creation, for example, goes to the heart of the matter : " You brought us into being out of nothingness. " Redemption is explained : " And, when we had fallen, you raised us up again; you have not ceased doing everything until you have brought us into heaven and have given us your future Kingdom. " Not only has redemption come to mankind, but more—in order that this redemption be applied to each person, God does not cease doing everything till we are safe in heaven with him. He obtains this by sending his divine Spirit to dwell with us until the end of time, the Paraclete who by his grace teaches, inspires, draws, and entices us into his divine embrace forever.

In order that the thanksgiving be adequate, all-encompassing, the preface of Chrysostom continues : " We thank you for all benefits, for those of which we know and for those of which we know not, for those bestowed on us openly and in secret. " Nothing really is excluded : the blades of grass and flowers, billions and billions of them; the trees, the animals great and small, millions and millions of them; the rivers, lakes and streams, the mountains and valleys; the rains, the snows to beautify them. Man cannot remember them all, yet thanks are due to God for them. Neither can man estimate the sufferings he has been spared, yet thanks are due for all this too.

Finally, thanks are given to God for the Sacrifice he deigns to receive from our human hands despite the existence of far worthier creatures than we, " even though there stand before you thousands of archangels and myriads of angels, cherubim and seraphim, six-winged and many-eyed, who soar aloft on their wings. " This is the cue for the hymn of victory (the Sanctus). Basil's preface has a similar but much more elaborate transition. The angelic hosts

and their praise are remembered as one only of many benefits. [9]
Both prefaces introduce the Hymn of Victory—yet the angelic
armies are mentioned for completely different reasons : one more
sign, albeit minor, that both prefaces are independent.

Almost every Oriental anaphora mentions the cherubim and the
seraphim, [10] and makes some distinction between the two, usually
based on Ezekiel (10:12) and Isaiah (6:2). Fullest of all anaphoras
are the Byzantine St. Basil, the Syrian St. James, and the Coptic
St. Cyril. [11] The first two also name at least seven orders of angelic
choirs. Basil's anaphoa reads : " For you are praised by the angels,
archangels, thrones and dominations, principalities, powers and
many-eyed cherubim; round about you stand the seraphim, each
with six wings; for with two they cover their faces and with two
their feet, and with two they fly, and they cry one to the other continually with unstilled hymns.... "

Most anaphoras mention the angelic hosts, but in varying descriptions and order. The ordinary anaphora of the Maronite Church
names five, the Coptic of St. Gregory names six. [12] Many follow
Daniel (7:10), mentioning spirits by the " tens of thousands, "
" thousands, " or " myriad. " [13] Chrysostom's anaphora uses
" thousands " and " myriads, " in reference to angels, archangels,
cherubim, and seraphim. Basil, despite his detailed description of
the seraphim, contains no reference to their number or to the number
of any of the other angelic choirs. If Chrysostom's preface had
been an abridgment of Basil's, surely it would not have included any
reference to number.

---

[9] In this it evidently follows the Liturgy of the *Apostolic Constitutions* (Book
VIII) and the Liturgy of St. James, which have an identical arrangment; see
above, p. 132.

[10] The exceptions are the Chaldaic of Theodore the Interpreter, that of
Nestorius, and the Maronite anaphora, which omit the Cherubim; cf. Remaudot,
LOC, II, pp. 612, 622, and Prince Maximilian of Saxony, *Missa syro-maronitica*,
pp. 36-37.

[11] Cf. Brightman, LEW, pp. 402, 86, and 175.

[12] Prince Maximilian of Saxony, *op. cit.*, pp. 36-37, and Renaudot, LOC, I, 27.

[13] E.g., the Chaldaic anaphora of the Apostles (Brightman, LEW, p. 284);
the Coptic of St. Cyril (Brightman, LEW, p. 175); the Ethiopic of the Apostles
(Brightman, LEW, p. 231).

CHAPTER LVIII

THE HYMN OF VICTORY

The deacon goes to the priest's left, takes the asteriskos, *and makes the sign of the cross with it over the* diskos *by touching the upper, lower, left, and right sides; in the meantime, the priest intones :*

Sing, cry out, proclaim and say the triumphal hymn :

People : **Holy, holy, holy, Lord of Sabaoth; heaven and earth are filled with your glory. Hosanna in the highest. Blessed is he who comes in the name of the Lord, Hosanna in the highest.**

After the deacon has made the sign of the cross with the asteriskos, *he kisses it and places it on the altar. Then he goes to the right of the priest and continues to fan the holy gifts with the* ripidion *or the folded veil.*

The first part of the anaphora culminates in what Byzantine liturgists call the " Hymn of Victory "; in the West, it is known as the *Sanctus* or the *Tersanctus*. It is the hymn heard by Isaiah in an ecstatic vision and described by him in the sixth chapter of his prophecies (1-3) :

> I saw the Lord sitting upon a throne high and elevated : and his train [the skirts of his royal robe] filled the temple. Upon it stood the seraphim : the one had six wings, and the other had six wings : with two they covered his face, and with two they covered his feet, and with two they flew. And they cried one to another, and said : Holy, holy, holy, the Lord God of hosts, all the earth is full of his glory. (Douay Version).

From century to century, in one form or another, this hymn has been perpetuated in all the Liturgies of the Church not merely as a commemoration, but rather as a reminder to the faithful that they, the earthly Church, should participate in the heavenly singing. This is done by having all people join in singing the hymn, as expressly stipulated in many Eastern Liturgies. [1] A special rubric to this effect existed in ancient Byzantine texts, [2] but at present it is taken for granted. The idea probably originated at the time of the introduction of this hymn into the Eucharistic Liturgy. Cyril of Jerusalem explains : " Holy, holy, holy is the Lord of Sabaoth. The reason why we recite this confession of God (θεολογίαν) delivered to us from the seraphim, is this : that, with the hosts of the world above, we may be partakers in their hymn of praise. " [3] The testimony for the Cappadocian Church is no less clear. Gregory of Nyssa tells us that the faithful sing the " triumphal hymn... in which the six-winged seraphim join. " [4] Chrysostom extolled community singing more than once, but, regarding the triumphal hymn, he proclaims : " The seraphim above shout the thrice-holy hymn and all mankind below sends it aloft. " [5] Since Chrysostom could say that all mankind sends this hymn aloft, it must have been introduced into the Liturgy long before his time.

There is no *Sanctus* in the Eucharistic Prayer of Hippolytus, but this Roman presbyter had a great love for antiquity. He may have been describing an early form of the Eucharistic service, before its fusion with the catechetical synaxis in which the triple *hagios* from Isaiah had been introduced. [6] Toward the end of the first century, Clement of Rome, describing what was probably part of the Christian community service, cites not only the hymn, but also the introductory verse from Daniel (7:10) precisely as it appears later in most Oriental anaphoras : " Let us consider the vast multitude of his angels, and see how they stand in readiness to minister to his will. For the

---

[1] E.g., West Syrian and Egyptian Liturgies; cf. Brightman, LEW, pp. 50, 86, 132, 176, 231.

[2] Cf. Brightman, LEW, pp. 385, 403, 436; Hanssens, *Institutiones liturgicae de ritibus orientalibus, De Missa rituum orientalium* (Rome, 1932), III, pp. 392 ff., 400.

[3] *Catecheses mystag.*, V, 6 (Quasten, *Monumenta eucharistica et liturgia vetustissima* [Bonn, 1935-1937], 101).

[4] *De bapt.* (PG 46, 421 C).

[5] *In illud, " Vidi Dominum " homil.*, I, 1 (edit. Montfaucon 6, 95 D, or PG 56, 97 f.); also *In II Cor. homil.*, XVIII, 3 (edit. Montfaucon 10, 568 B, or PG 61, 627), and *In Eph. homil.*, XIV, 4 (edit. Montfaucon 11, 108 A, or PG 62, 104).

[6] As we have seen, it was based on the Jewish morning service at the synagogue; cf. above, p. 555.

Scripture says : ' Ten thousand thousand stood ready before him, and a thousand thousand ministered to him, and cried out : Holy, Holy, Holy is the Lord of Hosts; the whole creation is replete with his splendor. ' And so we, too, being dutifully assembled with one accord, should as with one voice, cry out to him earnestly, so that we may participate in his great and glorious promises. " [7]

As mentioned before, the hymn and its prelude from Daniel were soon transferred from the synaxis to the Eucharistic Prayer. They are found in all the known ancient anaphoras later than that of Hippolytus : Sarapion, Deir Balizeh, Addai and Mari, and the *Apostolic Constitutions* (see, pp. 93, 97, 175, 132). As early as A.D. 193, Clement of Alexandria speaks of " giving thanks always to God like the creatures which give glory to God in Isaiah's allegory, " but it is not certain he is referring to the Eucharistic services. [8] References to the hymn in the Liturgy abound in the works of later ecclesiastics. [9]

In Book VII (chaps. 33-88) of the *Apostolic Constitutions*—a super-ficially Christianized collection of Jewish prayers—the *Tersanctus* is seen as a hymn sung by the entire heavenly court of angels, as it was in the synagogue prayer, [10] and as it is in the anaphora of Addai and Mari. In the Coptic anaphora of Basil, and in that of Gregory, only the cherubim and seraphim are said to be singing. In the Byzantine anaphoras of Chrysostom and Basil, it is uncertain whether or not the hymn is attributed to all the angelic choirs or only to the

---

[7] Clement of Rome, *Ad Corinth.*, chap. 34 (J. A. Kleist, *The Epistles of St. Clement of Rome and St. Ignatius of Antioch*, " Ancient Christian Writers, " Vol. I [Westminster, Md., 1946], p. 30).

[8] Clement of Alexandria, *Strom.*, vii, 12 (PG 9, 512).

[9] Chrysostom, *De paenitentia*, 9, 1 (edit. Montfaucon 2, 349, or PG 50, 345); *De baptismo Christi*, 4 (edit. Montfaucon 2, 374, or PG 50, 370); *In illud " Vidi Dominum "* homil., I, 1, 3 (edit. Montfaucon 6, 95, 98 f., or PG 56, 97-98, 100); *In II ad Cor.* homil., XVIII, 3 (edit. Montfaucon 10, 568 B, or PG 61, 627); *In ep. ad Ephes.* homil., XIV, 4 (edit. Montfaucon 11, 108, or PG 62, 105); *In ep. ad Coloss.* homil., IX, 2 (edit. Montfaucon 11, 392, or PG 62, 363 to end); Maximus the Confessor (662), *Mystagogia*, chaps. 19, 24 (PG 91, 696 BC, 704 C); Narsai, Homily XXI (edit. Connolly, *The liturgical Homilies of Narsai* [Cambridge, 1909], p. 57); Homily XXXII (edit. Connolly, *op. cit.*, p. 67); Cyril of Scythopolis, *Vita S. Euthymii*, 78 (Brightman, LEW, p. 385); *Sixth-Ccentury Fragments of an East-Syrian Anaphora*, " Oriens Christianus, " 12-14 (1922-1924), pp. 99-128; etc.

[10] For the Hebrew text of the prayer, cf. W. Staerk, *Altjüdische liturgische Gebete*, 2nd edit.; *Kleine Texte*, 58 (Berlin, 1930).

cherubim and seraphim. The Liturgy of St. James includes not only all the angelic hosts but all of God's creatures, even the inanimate (see above, pp. 151 f.). The other Oriental anaphoras have the faithful joining the angelic choirs. [11]

Text of the Hymn

The hymn itself is slightly different from both the biblical and synagogue texts. Isaiah reads : " Holy, holy, holy, the Lord of Sabaoth, all the earth is full of his glory. " Like almost all Christian Liturgies, the Byzantine has changed the cry into a form of address, by using the second person instead of the third in the possessive : " your glory. " The Syrian and Chaldean Liturgies still have the third person. All the Christian Liturgies have added the word " heaven " : " heaven and earth are filled with your glory, " and eliminated " all " as a modifier of " the earth. " Some Liturgies— but not the Byzantine—have " God " after " Lord, " as in the Vulgate. [12]

In the Byzantine texts, the word *Sabaoth* (armies, hosts, regiments) is untranslated—perhaps to be more widely inclusive, referring not only to the hosts of angels but to the " whole multitude " of beings created by God in the six biblical days. [13] *Sabaoth* is an old Semitic term and may have designated the moon-god. To the Jews, the word *Sabaoth* (hosts) meant the stars, as it does in Genesis, 2:1 and Psalm 32:6. [14]

These changes turn the biblical quotation into a prayer. It is not the angelic hosts alone who cry out to each other : the people

[11] E.g., the Ethiopic anaphora of the Apostles (Brightman, LEW, p. 231); the Armenian anaphora (LEW, p. 436); the anaphora ordinarily used by the Maronite Church (Prince Maximilian of Saxony, *Missa Syro-maronitica*, 36-37). Among the early anaphoras we must include Sarapion, Deir Balizeh, and St. Mark; see above, p. 97.

[12] The Latin, Chaldean, Maronite and Syrian Rites follow this same version. Cf. Baumstark, *Trishagion und Qeduscha*, JbLw, III (1923), p. 28, and P. Sabatier, *Bibliorum sacrorum latinae versiones antiquae*, II (Rheims, 1734), p. 528.

[13] In all the Syrian and Chaldean texts, *sabaoth* is rendered adjectively as " strong, " or " mighty. " The Maronites add the adjectival form to the word *sabaoth*.

[14] Cf. Schrader, *Die Keilinschriften u. das A. Test.* (3rd edit., Berlin, 1903), p. 456.

of God join them in the song of praise. Heaven is not the only place filled with God's glory : so is the earth.

> O marvelous gifts of Christ! On high, the angelic choirs sing glory to the Lord; on earth, through their example, men sing in church the same canticle in choirs. In heaven, the seraphim sing aloud their thrice-holy hymn; on earth, the same canticle resounds from the mouth of the assembled congregation. Thus heaven and earth unite in festive celebration; it is a hymnal celebration of thanksgiving, of praise; it is a choir of common joy, which the ineffable goodness of the Lord organized in his great condescension to us and which the Holy Spirit assembled.... [15]

Perhaps some of the changes were due to a reaction against narrow Jewish nationalism. Christ's Kingdom, the Church, was no longer confined to national boundaries : its worship was extended beyond all borders, to the " four corners " of the earth. The second part of the hymn, different as it is in the Jewish and Christian services, seems to confirm the point. The Jews concluded the *Tersanctus* with Ezekiel 3:12 : " Blessed be the glory of the Lord in the place of his dwelling. " [16] According to Book VII (35) of the *Apostolic Constitutions*, the *Tersanctus* was at first incorporated with that very passage into the Christian Liturgy... but this is not proved. It is certain, however, that the Christians replaced the text of Ezekiel used by the Jews with a cry of victory : the " Hosanna, " and " Blessed is he that cometh in the name of the Lord. "

The substitution reflects a difference in interpretation of the *Shekinah*—the mysterious presence of God with his people. The passage from Ezekiel was merely the praise of this *Shekinah*, localized first in the tabernacle and later in the Temple. According to post-exilic rabbinical teaching (influenced by Ezekiel himself), where two or three were gathered together to read the Scriptures, there in their midst was this special presence of God. Since the Christians accepted Christ as Messiah, as the fulfillment of Israel's eschatological

[15] Chrysostom, *In illud " Vidi Dominum " homil.*, I, 1 (edit. Montfaucon 6, 95 f., or PG 56, 97 f.). Our translation.

[16] This passage refers to the vision of the prophet in which he saw the glory of God borne on the cherubim.

expectation, they replaced the passage from Ezekiel with the acclamation greeting Christ on his triumphal entry into Jerusalem. The Christian idea, paralleling the Jewish, is that Christ himself is the *Shekinah*, the presence of God among his own—especially in the Liturgy. Christ alluded to the rabbinical maxim when he said : " Where two or three are gathered together in my name, there am I in the midst of them " (Matt. 18:20).

Matthew, 21:9 reads " Hosanna to the son of David : Blessed is he that cometh in the name of the Lord : Hosanna in the highest. " In all the Rites, the words " son of David " were replaced by " in the highest. " [17]

" Hosanna " is left in the original Hebrew in all the Rites except the Armenian, which renders it as " glory " or " praise. " [18] The original meaning of " hosanna " is " save, " " help, we pray, " as, for example, in Psalm 117:25. By the time of Christ, however, it had become the equivalent of " hail, " " *vivat*, " or the modern " hurrah. " It was in this sense that the crowd used it on that first Palm Sunday, and the early Christians in their assemblies, as is evident from the *Didache*. [19] The acclamation was borrowed from Psalm 117:25 : " Lord, save me... blessed be he who cometh in the name of the Lord. " Long before the time of Christ, the phrase " he who comes " had become a designation for the promised Messiah. Thus, by shouting this cry to Jesus during his triumphal entry into Jerusalem, the people were recognizing him as King and Messiah. In the Eucharistic Liturgy, the Hosanna became a greeting proclaiming Christ's imminent Eucharistic entrance. Every Eucharistic Sacrifice is a renewed manifestation of Christ, a new entry into the New Jerusalem, a new *parousia*.

No one really knows when this exclamation was annexed to the *Tersanctus*. The first definite evidence comes from Caesarius of

---

[17] Except the Chaldean Rite, which has : " Hosanna in the highest, hosanna to the son of David. " Another change, though it applies only to a few Rites, the Armenian, Syrian, and Chaldean anaphoras as well as the Coptic St. Gregory, have : " who has and will come. " In addition, the Armenian Rite also changed the person from the third to the second : " you who have and will come. " The only anaphoras in which the second part of this hymn is missing entirely are the Coptic of St. Basil and that of St. Cyril.

[18] Hanssens, *op. cit.*, III, p. 394.

[19] Chap. X, 6 (see above, p. 25). ANF, Vol. VII, p. 380.

Arles (d. 540) in the Gallic Church. [20]   Since most of the manuscripts of the Roman Canon have it, it must have been an established practice in the Roman Masses of the time.   In the East, it can be traced only to the eighth century. [21]   The present Byzantine formula is found almost in its entirety for the first time in the interpolated text of Germanus I, Patriarch of Constantinople (A.D. 715-729). [22]   It would seem therefore that the practice originated in the West and spread to the East.   On the other hand, the acclamation is found in the Liturgy of the *Apostolic Constitutions* (Book VIII)—but as a response to *Holy things to the Holy*, before Communion. [23]   It is found in this same position in the *Testamentum Domini*, in the modern Coptic as well as in the Byzantine Rites. [24]   In the *Peregrinatio Aetheriae*, it is used as a responsorial processional chant sung by the people. [25]   How much value can be put on these parallels ? Perhaps the second part of the hymn appeared first in connection with the *Sancta sanctis*, and only later as an addition to the *Tersanctus*.   But if this were the case, why have the Coptic and Byzantine Rites kept it in its original position?   Originally, the acclamation may have been addressed to the celebrant (or to the emperor), later, to Christ in connection with the *Sancta sanctis*, and finally, transferred to the triple Sanctus.   The *Acta* of a council at Constantinople in A.D. 536 speak of the *Benedictus* being sung before the triple Sanctus, after the entrance of the bishop. [26]   Was it related in some manner to the entrance rite?   In fact, in that

---

[20] Caesarius of Arles, *Serm.* 73 (PL 39, 2277).

[21] The Byzantine-Armenian anaphora of St. Basil and the anaphora of Chrysostom; cf. Catergian and Dasian, *Die Liturgien bei den Armeniern* (Fünfzehn Texte und Untersuchungen, Vienna, 1897), pp. 200, 372.

[22] *Comm. liturg.*, 41 (PG 98, 429 D).

[23] Cf. above, p. 141, or Quasten, *Monumenta eucharistica et liturgia vetustissima* (Bonn, 1935-1937), p. 230.   Baumstark argues that the " Hosanna-Benedictus " combination must have been joined to the triple Sanctus at a very early date in Palestine itself as a reaction against the narrowly national Jewish formula or benediction from Ezek. 3:12 : " Blessed be the glory of the Lord in the place of his dwelling "; as such, it was given as a response by the other choirs of angels.

This formula is found in later Jewish services annexed to the triple Sanctus just like the Hosanna-Benedictus in the Christian counterpart after the same triple Sanctus.   Cf. Baumstark, *Trishagion und Qeduscha*, JbLw, III (1923), 23 ff.

[24] Cf. Brightman, LEW, pp. 186, 396 f.

[25] Etheria, *Peregrinatio*, chap. 31 (CSEL, XXX, 83 f.).

[26] Cf. Labbé-Cossart, *Sacrosancta Concilia* (Paris, 1671), v. 1156 D.

instance, it was sung, not by the choir, but by rioters as the climax
of a disturbance of the Eucharistic service. A curious parallel
existed in the fifteenth-century Byzantine Church at the Great
Entrance : the *Sanctus* was recited immediately after the deposition
of the gifts upon the altar, [27] and the *Benedictus* during the entrance
itself. [28] Surely, the Byzantine Church could not have borrowed
the *Benedictus* for this ritual from either the Gallic or the Roman
Church. Many reasons preclude such a possibility.

The words intoned by the celebrant as the deacon makes the
sign of the cross (by touching the four sides of the *diskos*), " Sing,
cry out, proclaim and say the triumphal hymn, " are found in the
earliest texts of both Chrysostom and Basil. [29] They are much older
than the eighth or ninth century, however, for the Liturgy of St.
James has an identical wording (see above, p. 152).

Why are four expressions used to describe the singing of the
seraphim when it would seem that, as in the Clementine Liturgy,
one or two would have done as well? To appreciate the whole
passage, we must go to the source, John's Apocalypse, 4:8 :

> Between the throne and myself was a sea that seemed to be
> made of glass, like crystal. In the centre, grouped round
> the throne itself, were four animals with many eyes, in front
> and behind. The first animal was like a lion, the second
> like a bull, the third animal had a human face, and the fourth
> animal was like a flying eagle. Each of the four animals had
> six wings and had eyes all the way round as well as inside;
> and day and night they never stopped singing : " Holy,
> Holy, Holy, is the Lord God, the Almighty; he was, he is
> and he is to come. " (The Jerusalem Bible).

The imagery of the Liturgies is easier to understand in their
original Greek, and also easier to correlate with the Greek of the
passage above. Almost everything is lost in translations. How can
the Greek ζῷα be rendered? Surely not as " animals. " The

[27] MSS. of Sophia Library, N. 533, p. 42; N. 540, p. 46; N. 839, p. 4. Cf.
Petrovsky, *Histoire de la rédaction slave de la liturgie de S. Jean Chrysostome,*
XPYCOCTOMIKA (Rome, 1908), p. 904.

[28] MSS. of Sophia Library, N. 531, p. 30; N. 534, p. 18; N. 535, p. 27. Cf.
Petrovsky, *op. cit.*, p. 905.

[29] *Cod. Barberini, gr.* 336; cf. Brightman, LEW, p. 385.

Douay-Rheims version has "creatures," which is inadequate and has an unpleasant connotation. "Living beings" is accurate but clumsy. This does not answer the question of who they were. Ezekiel derived his plastic imagery from the composite astronomical figures of the Babylonians. To each of these he gave four faces, —man, lion, bull, and eagle. The description is really of Ezekiel's cherubim, which John simplifies and joins to the seraphim of Isaiah and their triple *Sanctus*. The fourfold verbal expressions which the Liturgies put into the mouth of the angelic choirs correspond to these four living beings and their four faces : *singing* (ἄδοντα) = eagle; *crying out* (βοῶντα) = bull; *shouting* or *proclaiming* (κεκραγόντα) = lion; and *saying* (λέγοντα) = man. Irenaeus is the first person known to have identified them with the four evangelists. [30] His identification remains with us, despite its lack of foundation. Matthew is portrayed as a man, Mark as a lion, Luke as an ox, and John as an eagle. Irenaeus' reasons for identifying the four evangelists with the living beings of John's Apocalypse are curious, to say the least. He reasoned that there are four regions of the earth, four main winds, and, since the Church is scattered throughout the world, it is fitting that God should make his gospel known to us through a fourfold source.

The Liturgies—of Chrysostom Basil or, James—are not following Irenaeus, but alluding to John's description and indicating the varied praise of the angelic choirs. Authentic symbolism sees in these expressions the whole of nature, even inanimate, giving glory to God "after its kind." John's passage is usually interpreted in this sense.

The ceremonial with the *asteriskos*, found in both Byzantine Liturgies, cannot have begun much earlier than the thirteenth century. At that time it was still simple : after the *asteriskos* was lifted over the *diskos*, the deacon wiped it with his fingers or with the *iliton*, kissed it, and laid it aside (usually on one of the veils). [31] Kissing the *asteriskos*, like kissing an icon, was a gesture of piety. Later, the deacon began tracing the sign of the cross over the *diskos*

---

[30] Irenaeus, *Adv. haer.*, III, 11, 8 (PG 5, 797 AB [*Series graeca*]).

[31] Krasnoseltsev, *Materialy dlja istorii chinoposlidovania liturgii sv. Ioanna Zlatoustago* (Kazan, 1889), pp. 26, 64, 110.

and then over himself. [32] Making the sign of the cross with the *asteriskos* over the *diskos* by touching its upper (= east), lower (= west), left (= north), and right (= south) sides is said to symbolize the glory of God extended to the four corners of the world. Since this was introduced at a time when symbolism flourished, perhaps it was done specifically for this symbolical purpose (echoes of Irenaeus?).

[32] Krasnoseltsev, *op. cit.*, p. 110; Dmitrievsky, *Opysanie liturgicheskikh rukopisej khraniaschikhsia v bibliotekakh pravoslavnago vostoka*, Vol. II, *Euchologia* (Kiev, 1901), p. 611.

CHAPTER LIX

THE INSTITUTION:
THE NARRATIVE IN GENERAL

While the people are singing the Hymn of Victory, the priest continues with the Eucharistic Prayer :

With these blessed powers, Lord and Lover of mankind, we too cry out and say : holy and all-holy are you and your only-begotten Son and your Holy Spirit; you are holy and all-holy and majestic is your glory; you have so loved your world that you gave your only-begotten Son in order that whoever believes in him may not perish but may have life everlasting. And after he had come and accomplished for us all that was appointed, on the night that he was betrayed or rather gave himself up for the life of the world, he took bread into his holy, all-pure, and blameless hands, and when he had given thanks and blessed it *(here the priest blesses the bread)*, **sanctified and broken it, he gave it to his holy disciples and apostles, saying :**

(Aloud) TAKE, EAT, THIS IS MY BODY WHICH IS BROKEN FOR YOU FOR THE REMISSION OF SINS.

People : **Amen.**

As the priest pronounces the words of institution, he extends his hand, palm and fingers outstretched, toward the holy gifts. The deacon does likewise with his orar. Then, making the sign of the cross upon themselves, both priest and deacon make a profound bow.

Priest : **In like manner, the chalice** *(he blesses the chalice)*, **after he had supped, saying :**

(Aloud) DRINK OF THIS, ALL OF YOU; THIS IS MY BLOOD OF THE NEW TESTAMENT WHICH IS SHED FOR YOU AND FOR MANY FOR THE REMISSION OF SINS.

People : **Amen.**

Again, in pronouncing the words of institution, the priest bows his head and extends his hand, palm and fingers outstretched, toward the chalice; the deacon does likewise with his orar. *When the people sing* " Amen, " *both priest and deacon cross themselves and make a profound bow.*

The Hymn of Victory, or *Sanctus*, and the anaphoric prayer which follows are welded together by a process similar to that joining the introductory dialogue to the anaphora. This is true of every major Oriental anaphora in use today. [1] The cue in both Byzantine anaphoras is the expression " You are holy, "—although in both anaphoras, it is preceded by a reference to the angelic choirs :

Chrysostom	*Basil*
With these blessed powers, Lord and Lover of mankind, we too cry out and say : holy and all-holy are you....	With these blessed powers, Lord and Lover of mankind, we *sinners* too cry out and say : You are *truly* holy and all-holy.... [2]

Most Oriental, non-Egyptian anaphoras are almost identical. [3] They also take their cue from the word " holy, " [4] one group reinforcing it with the word " truly. " [5] The Byzantine anaphora of Basil belongs to this group. The other group, including the Byzantine anaphora of Chrysostom, has no such qualifier. [6] By

[1] For the Armenian anaphora, cf. Brightman, LEW, p. 436, line 20; Syriac St. James, Brightman, LEW, p. 86, lines 20-24; Maronite anaphora of the Holy Roman Church, *Missale Berytense* (1908), p. 33; Maronite anaphora of St. Peter, E. Renaudot, LOC, II, p. 156, and *Missale Berytense* (1908), p. 42; Chaldaic anaphora of the Holy Apostles, Brightman, LEW, p. 285, lines 20-23; Chaldaic of Theodore, E. Renaudot, LOC, I, pp. 612-613; the anaphora of Nestorius, E. Renaudot, LOC, II, pp. 622-623; the Coptic of St. Basil, E. Renaudot, LOC, I, pp. 13-14; Coptic of St. Gregory, E. Renaudot, LOC, I, pp. 28-29; the Ethiopian of the Holy Apostles, Brightman, LEW, p. 242, lines 3-5. In the Coptic of St. Cyril, however, the epiclesis follows immediately but it is joined to the Sanctus by a few words of transition with the cue " full "; cf. Brightman, LEW, p. 176, lines 15-19.

[2] Italics indicate the only differences between the two anaphoras at this point.

[3] Cf. n. 1, above, for textual reference.

[4] So do the Mozarabic and Gallican Rites of the Western Church.

[5] The Armenian anaphora, the Chaldean of Theodore, the Coptic of St. Basil the Syriac and Greek of St. James; cf. n. 1, above for textual references.

[6] I.e., the Syro-Malabar version of SS. Addai and Mari, the Coptic of St. Gregory Nazianzen, cf. E. Renaudot, LOC, I, pp. 28-29.

contrast, the Egyptian anaphoras, both ancient and modern, instead of using the word " holy " as a cue, have as their starting point the word " full, " the second part of the *Sanctus* hymn. [7]

The minute difference in the words of transition may or may not be interpreted as another sign that Chrysostom's anaphora is not a derivative of Basil's; but what follows is so different that it cannot be disregarded.   In recounting the " divine economy, " the mystery of salvation and redemption, Chrysostom's anaphora is much more sober and shorter than that of Basil.   Among the more profuse anaphoras are those of the *Apostolic Constitutions* (Book VIII), of the *Apostolic Tradition*, of St. James, and their many related Syrian, Armenian, and Ethiopian derivatives.   All these recall at length the major benefits of creation and the many interventions of God in the Old Dispensation, and diverse aspects of the Incarnation and Redemption.   Chrysostom's anaphora omits the creation or any Old Testament intervention.   It begins, immediately after the transitional phrases of praise, with the account of the New Dispensation.

> You have so loved your world that you gave your only-begotten Son in order that whoever believes in him may not perish but may have life eternal.   After he had come and accomplished for us all that was appointed....

The narrative of the institution with the words of consecration follows immediately.

This difference between the two Byzantine anaphoric prayers suggests separate derivation.   If the Chrysostomic prayer were an abbreviation of Basil's, surely something of God's salvific plan in the Old Testament would have survived in it.   The Chrysostom anaphora resembles in its brevity the most ancient formularies known to us, i.e., *Hippolytus, Sarapion, Beir Balizeh,* and *Addai and Mari* (see above, pp. 57, 93, 98).   Obviously the account of God's interventions in the Old Dispensation does not belong to the primitive stratum of any Eucharistic Prayer.   Perhaps it would be rash, on this basis alone, to assign to this part of Chrysostom's anaphora

---

[7] E.g., Deir Balizeh, Sarapion, the Greek St. Mark (cf. above, pp. 97 f.) and the Coptic St. Cyril (cf. Brightman, LEW, p. 176, line 7).

a more primitive date than to the corresponding part in Basil; but there is here an indication of a separate and an equally, if not more, ancient origin.

This tentative conclusion is bolstered further by another consideration. In Chrysostom's anaphora, the grateful remembrance of the New Dispensation and redemption is recounted briefly and with a simplicity reminiscent of the ancient formularies. The corresponding part in Basil's anaphora, though very beautiful, is at least fifteen times longer. The first law of comparative liturgy, in determining textual evolution and the relative age of given formularies, is : *liturgical development proceeds from simplicity to increasing enrichment.* [8] Applying this criterion to the problem at hand, this part of Chrysostom's anaphora must be assigned a more ancient date than the corresponding part of Basil's.

Another law of comparative liturgy, especially valuable in assessing the evolution of texts, is : *the older the text, the less literally does it assimilate biblical passages.* [9] Ancient formularies paraphrase the Bible freely. Chrysostom's text has only one nearly literal passage, the rest is free. The corresponding part of Basil's anaphora contains several almost literal quotations. The second law also indicates the Chrysostom formulary as being older.

The Narrative of the Institution

The core of the *Eucharistia* is the actual narrative of the institution quoting the words said by Jesus over the bread and the wine.

Most Oriental Liturgies, including the most ancient, differ from literal scriptural accounts. The anaphoras of Chrysostom and Basil are no exception. Scholars have often wondered why the core of the Liturgy contained no precise biblical quotations. In fact, it could not have been otherwise. Indeed, the *Eucharistia* had been celebrated long before the evangelists and St. Paul had recorded

---

[8] This is beautifully demonstrated in J. Engberding's, *Das eucharistische Hochgebet der Basiliusliturgie, Testgeschichtliche Untersuchungen und kritische Ausgabe* (Münster, 1931).

[9] Discovered by Fritz Hamm in his excellent study, *Die liturgischen Einsetzungsberichte im Sinne der vergleichender Liturgieforschung untersucht*, L.Q.F., xxiii (Münster, 1928).

for us the details of the Last Supper. Perhaps the later New Testament accounts were actually influenced by the contemporary Eucharistic celebrations which undoubtedly varied in detail. Some interesting and excellent studies have been made of the interrelationship of biblical and the liturgical texts. The most detailed offers seventy-nine instances of textual differences. [10]

From these studies several phases of development are discernible in the liturgical account of the institution. No text has survived prior to that of Hippolytus. Even if it had, it would have represented only a semi-extemporaneous recital by one celebrant for one congregation at one given time (see above, pp. 55 f.).

When the formularies began to crystallize, the first phase consisted in placing the prayers over the bread and the wine in parallel frames —as, for instance, in the Eucharistic Prayer of Hippolytus :

> This is my body which is broken for you.
> This is my blood which is shed for you. [11]

Such parallelism is more developed in the anaphora of Sarapion a century later : the single account has been separated into two independent parallel sections with a prayer between (see above, pp. 94 f.). Though it is difficult to pinpoint the various phases in terms of decades, or even centuries, the first lasted well into the fourth century.

The next stage, characterized by greater parallelism but also by a major amplification of the text, seems to have lasted a little more than a century. It is best exemplified in the Liturgy of the *Apostolic Constitutions* (Book VIII), and to a lesser degree in the basic forms of the anaphoras of St. James, St. Basil, and St. Mark, some time before the middle of the fifth century. [12]

The third phase, or period of accommodation, beginning about

---

[10] P. Cagin, in his incomparable *L'Eucharistia, canon primitif de la messe* (Paris, 1912), compares the four scriptural texts and seventy-six liturgical accounts of the institution and prints them in eighty columns, pp. 225-244. Cf. also F. Hamm, *Die liturgischen Einsetzungsberichte im Sinne vergleichender Liturgieforschung untersucht,* L.Q.F., xxiii (Münster, 1928); also K. J. Merk, *Der Konsekrationstext der römischen Messe* (Rottenburg, 1915).

[11] Cf. above, p. 58.

[12] Here we refer to the *basic* form of these anaphoras, not to their final text.

the middle of the fifth century, is so called because biblical expressions were progressively woven into the traditional liturgical text until there was an almost word-for-word dependence on the scriptural account. This generally ruined symmetry. Perhaps the doctrinal controversies of the times are responsible for it.

The final stage was reached in the sixth century when a reaction set in, and again an attempt was made to render symmetrical the many biblical phrases introduced during the previous period. This was usually done, however, in such a way that certain theological concepts were injected into the account as well as items of current local worship. The purpose of Christ's institution—" for the forgiveness of sins "—was paraphrased in various ways, one example being :

> for the life of the world,
> for eternal life,
> as an atonement of transgressions,
> for those who believe in me. [13]

Such actions attributed to the Lord as raising the eyes to heaven and making the sign of the cross over the gifts may probably be traced to earlier liturgical worship. [14] Even delicate attention to a guest, so characteristic of the East, is evident in the words " tasting " and " mingling " : Christ, being the host, would have partaken of the bread and chalice first, as dictated by Oriental politeness. Adding such details resulted in further amplification of the text. The extensiveness of West Syrian anaphoras, more or less derived from that of St. James, are examples of this final phase.

---

[13] See, Cagin, *op. cit.*, pp. 231 ff., 235 ff.

[14] The detail of Christ's lifting his eyes to heaven is not recorded in the New Testament accounts. From the accounts of Jewish ritual, however, we know that he would have grasped the cup with both hands and raised it up slightly as a gesture of offering to God; it would have been natural for him to have raised his eyes at the same time.

CHAPTER LX

THE INSTITUTION : FOUR PARTS

In the narrative of the institution, four parts are immediately apparent : (1) an introductory passage usually defining the time, (2) a repetition of the action and words of Christ over the bread, (3) a repetition of the action and words of Christ over the wine, and (4) a reminder of the command of Christ to do the same in *anamnesis* of him. These four elements are contained in every Eastern anaphora, except the Nestorian of Addai and Mari. [1]

(1) *The Introductory Passage.* In the introductory formula defining the time of the institution, most of the Oriental anaphoras follow the Pauline expression : " On the night on which he was betrayed. " The exceptions are the Coptic anaphora of St. Basil, and that of the Armenian Church, which relate the institution of the Eucharist to the Passion; [2] the Maronite anaphora of the Holy Roman Church, following the Roman canon : " on the day before he suffered "; [3] the Maronite anaphora of St. Peter, the Chaldean of Nestorius, and that of Theodore the Interpreter, each having its own way of determining the time. [4]

In Chrysostom's anaphora, the introductory formula follows Paul literally, but immediately rewords it to emphasize the fact that Christ's Passion was voluntary. No symmetry is apparent. Basil's account, on the other hand, has a polished, nearly perfect parallelism with an amended version of the Pauline text preceded by an indication of Christ's freedom of choice. Both Byzantine accounts express the purpose of that Passion " for the life of the world " —an expression they have in common with the Liturgy of St. James. [5] Almost all the Oriental Liturgies make it clear that Christ was not so much betrayed as that he gave himself up to death willingly

---

[1] Cf. above, pp. 176 f., or Brightman, LEW, p. 285.
[2] Cf. E. Renaudot, LOC, I, pp. 13-14, and Brightman, LEW, p. 436.
[3] *Missale Berytense* (1908), p. 33.
[4] Cf. E. Renaudot, LOC, II, pp. 15, 623, 613.
[5] The anaphora of St. James has " for the life and salvation of the world "; cf. above, p. 153.

for our salvation. This point must have been considered important at an early stage, since Hippolytus has already : " ...when he was delivered up to voluntary suffering. " [6] Syria and Egypt make no reference to it in their early formularies. [7] The account of Hippolytus expresses the purpose of Christ's Passion in full detail : " that he might abolish death and rend the bonds of the devil and tread down hell and enlighten the righteous and establish that which was decreed and show forth the resurrection " (see above, p. 58). The inclusion of the purpose of the Passion in the institution narrative is more ancient than is generally believed.

(2) *Action of Christ over the Bread.* In describing what Christ did over the bread, the scriptural accounts differ slightly :

Matthew	Mark	Luke	Paul
			...the Lord Jesus Christ the same night in which he was betrayed
1. Jesus took bread	Jesus took bread	And taking bread,	took bread
2.		he gave thanks	And giving thanks
3. blessed	and blessing		
4. and broke	broke	and brake	broke
5. and he gave to his disciples	and gave to them	and gave to them,	
and said :	and said :	saying :	and said :

Five actions are described in the combined texts. Almost every Oriental anaphora, however, names at least six : taking, giving thanks, blessing, sanctifying, breaking, giving. [8] The additional action is sanctifying. Some anaphoras mention yet other actions. The Liturgy of St. James and the Byzantine anaphora of St. Basil for example, have " showing " the bread to the heavenly Father.

---

[6] Cf. above, p. 58. The Roman canon has no such reference today.

[7] Sarapion, Deir Balizeh, St. Mark, the Syrian Liturgy of the *Apostolic Constitutions*, Book VIII. Cf. above, pp. 98, 135.

[8] Sanctifying, however, is omitted in the Ethiopic anaphora of the Holy Apostles (Brightman, LEW, p. 232), in the Armenian (Brightman, LEW, p. 437), in the Chaldaic of Nestorius and that of Theodore the Interpreter (E. Renaudot, LOC, II, pp. 623, 613). The last two also do not contain any reference to giving thanks.

This expression is used even in their basic texts, as indeed in the Syrian tradition generally. [9] The Coptic anaphoras and the ordinary Ethiopian mention that Christ " looked up, " somewhat in the same sense as the Latin, " with his eyes lifted up toward heaven. " This was probably borrowed from other passages in the Gospels (Matt. 14:19; John 11:41, etc.) and became an established formula with early Christians. [10] The Chaldean of Nestorius even speaks of Jesus " eating " the bread. [11]

No biblical account contains any qualifier in reference to Christ's hands, while most of the Oriental Liturgies have some. This was introduced probably in fourth century in Syria. The *Apostolic Constitutions* (Book VIII) and the Byzantine anaphora of Basil have " holy and undefiled. " [12] The anaphoras of Chrysostom, the Chaldean of Nestorius, and the Syriac St. James have these two and add one more, " blameless " ($\check{\alpha}\mu\omega\mu\circ\varsigma$). [13] If the Chrysostom anaphora were an abbreviation of Basil's, the process would have been diametrically opposed. The zenith was reached by the Armenians who have five attributes : " holy, divine, immortal, immaculate and creative "; [14] so do three of the Coptic anaphoras which have, " holy, pure, immaculate, blessed, and vivifying. " [15] Perhaps the Monophysites were trying to emphasize the divinity of Christ.

[9] Cf. Hamm, *Die liturgischen Einsetzungsberichte im Sinne vergleichender Liturgieforschung untersucht*, L.Q.F., xxiii (Münster, 1928), pp. 21, 25, 66 ff. Chrysostom's anaphora has no such expression—another sign pointing away from the theory that it is derived from Basil's anaphora.

[10] Dölger, *Sol salutis, Gebet und Gesang im christlichen Altertum* (Münster, 1920), pp. 301 ff. Also see n. 14, p. 593, above.

[11] E. Renaudot, LOC, II, p. 623.

[12] For *Apostolic Constitutions*, cf. above, p. 135; for Basil, cf. Brightman, LEW, p. 404, lines 29-30.

[13] For the anaphora of Chrysostom (in the Greek), cf. Brightman, LEW, p. 385, lines 25-26; for the Chaldean of Nestorius, cf. E. Renaudot, LOC, II, p. 623; for the Syriac St. James, cf. Brightman, LEW, p. 87, line 2. The Greek St. James lists all these and still another, " immortal " (Dix, *The Shape of the Liturgy* [2nd edit., London, 1945], p. 189). The Ethiopic of the Holy Apostles has : " holy, blessed and immaculate " (Brightman, LEW, p. 232).

[14] Brightman, LEW, pp. 436 f., or Catergian-Dasian, *Die Liturgien bei den Armeniern* (Vienna, 1897), p. 680, lines 881-882. The Catholic Armenians generally omit " immortal " and substitute " venerable " for " creative. "

[15] Cf. Hanssens, *Institutiones liturgicae de ritibus orientalibus*, De Missa rituum orientalium, Vol. III (Rome, 1932), p. 415. Catholic Copts, however, omit " immaculate " and " vivifying. " Cf. Hamm, *op. cit.*, 16, 69 f.

(3) *Words of Christ over the Bread.* The consecratory formula is similar in all the Oriental Churches. [16] That of the two Byzantine anaphoras is identical : TAKE, EAT, THIS IS MY BODY WHICH IS BROKEN FOR YOU FOR THE REMISSION OF SINS. In Paul-Luke, the command to " do this in *anamnesis* of me " comes immediately after the institution over the bread. With the exception of this detail—a mere matter of position—the formula of consecration is purely scriptural.

In most Liturgies, the meaning of the sacred narrative is reinforced by the celebrant's actions. While narrating Christ's actions over the bread and wine, he performs them himself. When he says Christ " took " the bread and chalice, he takes them into his hands, or at least touches them; at the words " he gave thanks, " he bows his head in a gesture of prayerful gratitude; when he says that Christ " blessed, " he makes the sign of the cross over the gifts. Some actions are performed later; the " giving " occurs at Holy Communion, the " breaking, " immediately before Communion. [17] All this serves to emphasize the desire of doing what Christ had done.

The Byzantine Rite has the fewest actions. The priest does not take the Holy Gifts in his hands nor does he touch them in any way during the words of institution : he merely extends his hand, palm and fingers outstretched, toward the bread (or the chalice), pointing

[16] Again, the anaphora of SS. Addai and Mari is the exception, since it omits the entire account of the institution (cf. above, pp. 176 f.). Despite the substantial identity of the consecratory formula in the other Oriental Rites, there are minor differences. Of these the greatest are : (1) the Armenian formula which has, " which is *given* for you *and for many* for the *expiation* and forgiveness of sins " (Brightman, LEW, p. 437); (2) the Maronite Liturgy, which uses the simple Roman formula, " For this is my body "; (3) the Chaldaic of Theodore the Interpreter, which omits, " Take, eat of it, all of you " (Renaudot, LOC, II, p. 613); (4) the Syriac St. James, which has, " . . .which is broken for you and given for the remission of sins " and adds for balance, " and for eternal life " (cf. Hamm, *op. cit.*, pp. 21-23; Brightman, LEW, p. 87); (5) the Coptic, " which is broken for you and is given for many, " finishes with the command, " Do this for an *anamnesis* of me " (Brightman, LEW, 176 f.; the *Euchologion* of Cairo [1898], p. 62 f.); (6) the Ethiopic Liturgies insert the word " bread " into the foruumula, thus : " Take, eat, this *bread* is my body, " (Brightman, LEW, p. 232; also cf. Harden, *The Anaphoras of the ethiopic liturgy* [London, 1928], pp. 35-36).

[17] The West Syrians, Copts, and Ethiopians, however, do crack the bread without separating the parts at the words " He broke, " just before the consecration (cf. Brightman, LEW, pp. 177, 232, and Harden, *op. cit.*, p. 35).

to them at the moment of consecration. [18]   The deacon points to them at the same time with his *orarion*.

Some authors believe that Byzantine priests, even the Orthodox, originally performed the actions of "taking" the sacred elements into their hands and "lifting" them slightly, but they discontinued these practices to stress the exclusive consecratory power of the epiclesis. [19]   This opinion is untenable.   First of all, why did not the Catholic Byzantines continue to perform these actions?   Secondly, the Orthodox have kept the equally meaningful gestures of pointing to the sacred elements—sometimes with added drama.   In addition to pointing with the *orarion*, the deacon may go behind the altar with face and body turned toward the holy gifts. [20]   Such conduct, reminiscent of imperial etiquette, [21] was left unaltered by the Orthodox despite the evident difficulty in explaining away the obvious, that the Eucharistic Christ is present.   Nor was the meaning lost on them, since they found it necessary to attach notes to these texts denying the obvious significance of these gestures. [22]   Still they did not discontinue the practice itself.   Criticisms may be leveled at the Orthodox, but deliberate tampering with liturgical usages cannot be one of them.

The present Byzantine ritual accompanying the words of consecration may go back to early Greco-Caesarean times.   The absence of any action at the consecration seems quite logical, if we remember that the corresponding gestures were made in the ritual preparation of the gifts, in the *proskomidia*.   Until the eighth century, they were much closer to the sacrifice since the preparation occurred immediately before the gifts were brought to the altar.   Every one of the actions is accounted for in the *proskomidia* : the bread is "taken" and "offered" to God in a very real sense; it is "blessed" with the sign of the cross, not once but many times; it is "broken" by the

[18] The Catholics of the Byzantine Rite do bless the bread at the words "He blessed...."

[19] E.g., Hanssens, *op. cit.*, III, p. 446.

[20] Krasnoseltsev, *Svidinia o nikotorikh liturgicheskikh rukopis'akh Vatikanskoi biblioteki* (Kazan, 1885), pp. 26, 100.

[21] Common citizens in the presence of the emperor or the tsar were never to turn their backs to him; in leaving his presence, they were to back away from him.

[22] Brightman, LEW, p. 386.

act of cutting pieces out of the loaves, and the crosswise incision in the main host—which is similar to the West Syrian and Coptic "cracking" of the host without separating the pieces (see above, n. 17, p. 597).

In the anaphoras of James and Basil, even in their basic texts, and in the whole Syrian tradition, the narrative indicates that Christ "showed" the bread to God the Father. [23] In the Syrian Liturgies, the "showing" is done by slightly raising the bread. In those of Basil and Chrysostom, it is done by pointing to the holy gifts with the hand. [24] In his work *On the Holy Spirit*, Basil uses the same expression ἐπὶ τῇ ἀναδείξει, "at the showing" of the Eucharistic bread and the chalice. [25] The meaning of this verb is "to show clearly" or "to point out." Basil's passage has been much discussed and pondered, but surely it can admit of this simple explanation. Pointing to the holy gifts is not done by the Byzantines alone. The Ethiopic anaphora of the Apostles and the Coptic of St. Cyril also has it. [26] This suggests an origin antedating any supposed removal of the other actions from the Byzantine Liturgy.

(4) *Actions of Christ over the Wine.* The narrative regarding the actions of Christ over the wine differ strikingly in the two Byzantine anaphoras. The lines of development appear to be completely separate.

Chrysostom	*Basil*
In like manner, the chalice after he had supped, saying :	In like manner, he also took the cup of the fruit of the vine and, when he had mixed it, and had given thanks, blessed and sanctified it, he gave it to his holy disciples and apostles, saying :

[23] Hamm, *op. cit.*, pp. 21, 25, 66 ff.

[24] The text of Chrysostom, however, does not contain any reference to this action.

[25] Basil of Caesarea, *De spiritu sancto*, chap. 27 (PG 32, 187 B).

[26] In the Ethiopic anaphora of the Apostles, the priest says : "Take, eat (pointing), this bread (bowing) is my body (pointing)." The same gestures are indicated for the chalice. In the *anamnesis* and subsequent "offering" prayer of the same Liturgy—which prayer has remained almost unchanged from the text of Hippolytus—the same gesture is made at the words "and we offer unto

Chrysostom, quoting the simple Paul-Luke account, is the only
one to omit the actions of Christ over the wine, but, like Paul and
Luke, he does specify the time, " after he had supped. " Basil
indicates six actions—and balances them almost perfectly with those
concerning the bread—but he fails to mention the time. In this,
he is following the Matthew-Mark accounts, which indicate three
acts, but not the time. The other Oriental anaphoras resemble Basil
in that they give most if not all of the six actions. [27] Most of the
oldest formularies list at least one or two. Justin, for example, has
two, " took the chalice and gave thanks. " [28] Sarapion, though he
defines the time, has only one action : . . . .Lord Jesus Christ,
taking a cup after supper, said to his own disciples. " [29] Deir
Balizeh has four : " Likewise after supper he took the cup, and when
he had blessed it and had drunk, he gave it to them. . . " (see above,
p. 98). The account in the *Apostolic Constitutions* (Book VIII)
shows the same development :

Apostolic Constitutions (Book VIII)	*Basil*
In like manner also the chalice : he mixed it of wine and water and sanctified it and gave to them, saying. . . .	In like manner, he also took the cup of the fruit of the vine and, when he had mixed it, and had given thanks, blessed and sanctified it, he gave it to his holy disciples and apostles, saying :

thee this bread *(pointing to it)* and this chalice, " etc. Cf. Brightman, LEW,
pp. 233 f. The Coptic anaphora of St. Cyril contains the same gestures of pointing
to the holy gifts immediately after the words of consecration when the priest
recites the Pauline " as often as you shall eat of this bread and drink this
chalice. . . . " Cf. Brightman, LEW, p. 177.

[27] The Ethiopic anaphora of the Holy Apostles, for example, omits " mixed "
(Brightman, LEW, p. 232); the Armenian anaphora omits both " mixed " and
" sanctified, " though it adds " drank " (Brightman, LEW, p. 437); the Chaldaic
of Nestorius omits " gave thanks " and " sanctified " (E. Renaudot, LOC, II,
p. 623); the Coptic of Basil and St. Cyril also interject another act, " tasted, " in
their narrative (Brightman, LEW, p. 177). The only other anaphora which
resembles Chrysostom's in its brevity is the Chaldaic of Theodore the Interpreter,
which has : " In like manner, he gave thanks and gave to them. . . . " (Renaudot,
LOC, II, p. 613).

[28] Justin Martyr, *First Apology*, chap. 66 (see above, p. 552 or edit. Otto, p. 180).

[29] Sarapion, *Euchologion*; cf. above, p. 95.

The only ancient anaphora that parallels Chrysostom is that of Hippolytus, which lists none of the actions of Christ over the wine : " Likewise also the cup, saying... " (see above, p. 58). Unlike Chrysostom, however, Hippolytus does not define the time. In both Hippolytus and Chrysostom, there is a complete lack of parallelism between the narrative regarding the actions of Christ over the bread and those over the wine. This places them in the earliest phase of textual formulation. [30] The same accounts in Basil belong to a later stage characterized by careful parallelism.

Over the Bread	*Over the Wine*
He took bread into his holy and undefiled hands,	In like manner he also took the cup of the fruit of the vine,
he showed it to you, O God and Father,	and when he had mixed it
and gave thanks, blessed,	and had given thanks, blessed
sanctified, broke it,	and sanctified it,
and gave it	he gave it
to his holy disciples and apostles, saying :	to his holy disciples and apostles, saying :

(5) *Words of Christ over the Wine.* The words of Christ over the wine are identical in the two Byzantine anaphoras. This would be significant were it not for the fact that the formula is nearly identical in all the Oriental Liturgies. It seems to be an amalgam of the biblical accounts by Matthew and Mark. In the Byzantine text, the words of Christ over the wine do correspond to his words over the bread, but not as perfectly as in many of the other Rites.

In the Chaldean anaphora of Theodore the Interpreter, the parallelism is almost complete : [31]

Over the Bread	*Over the Wine*
This is my body	This is my blood of the New Testament
which is broken for you for the remission of sins	which is shed for many for the remission of sins. Take, therefore, all of you,
eat of this bread....	and drink of this chalice....

[30] Only as regards the narrative describing the actions of Christ over the bread and the wine, and not the words of institution.

[31] E. Renaudot, LOC, II, p. 623.

No less perfect is the balance in the Syriac St. James :

Over the Bread	*Over the Wine*
Take, eat,	Drink of this, all of you,
this is my body	this is my blood of the New Testament
which is broken	which is shed
for you and for many,	for you and for many,
and given for the remission of sins	and is delivered for the remission of sins
and life everlasting.	and life everlasting.

In the Byzantine text (identical in both Chrysostom and Basil), the balance is only slightly less perfect :

Over the Bread	*Over the Wine*
Take, eat,	Drink of this, all of you :
this is my body	this is my blood of the New Testament
which is broken	which is shed
for you	for you and for many
for the remission of sins.	for the remission of sins.

Historically, then, the words of consecration as they are found in the present Byzantine Liturgy, as well as those in most of the Oriental Liturgies, belong to the phase of well-developed parallelism (see above, p. 592). The early forms had no such balance.

The Two Amens—Corroboration and Affirmation

At the Last Supper, after changing the bread and wine into his body and blood, Christ declared, " Do this in *anamnesis* of me. " If the apostles and their successors are to do what he had done, they must have received from him the power to do it. This power every priest receives at ordination, and he uses it when, pronouncing Christ's words over the bread and wine, he changes them into the body and blood of Chrsit. At the Supper, as on the cross, Christ made his offering personally, while at the Eucharistic Sacrifice he offers himself through the ministry of the priest, who speaks and acts in his name. He must do this if he is to obey the command actually to do what Christ had done at the Last Supper. Gregory of Nyssa appeals to the words of institution, not to the epiclesis, as the authority and historical warrant for believing that the bread and wine are changed into the body and blood of Christ. [32] Chrysostom asserts that "the priest acts as the representative of Christ when he pronounces those words, but the power and grace are God's. ' This is my body, ' he says. These words transform the gifts before him. " [33]

The transformation takes place at this point. That is why the faithful burst into solemn melody immediately after the words of each consecration, singing the corroborative, affirmative " Amen. "

At first, the two "Amens" were said by the deacon. [34] Later, they were taken up by the choir and people, apparently to meet this very need for some form of exterior assent. [35] In the ninth-century West Syrian Church, Moses bar Kepha vainly argued against the practice precisely because he recognized it as an acknowledgment of the completed transubstantiation which seemed to eliminate the need for the epiclesis, which he deemed a requisite. [36] However, the two " Amens " were never dropped, for the West Syrian anaphora of St. James still has them. [37] The Ethiopic and Egyptian Liturgies go even further. The former has the " Amen " repeated *three times* after each consecration, while a beautiful act of faith follows the consecration of the bread : " We believe and confess : we praise thee, our Lord and our God. This is true. " [38] While the two " Amens " are found in the narrative of the acts of Christ in the Coptic Liturgy of St. Basil (" He took bread... and gave thanks. Amen; blessed it, Amen, consecrated it, Amen "), the people respond after each

---

[32] *Or. Cat.*, 37 (PG 24, 752 D [*Series graeca*]).

[33] *De prodit. judae homil.*, i, 6 (edit. Montfaucon 2, 384 B).

[34] Krasnoseltsev, *Svidinia*, p. 110; however, in the early eighth century Armenian version of Chrysostom's Liturgy, the people say the " Amen " (cf. Aucher, *La versione armena della liturgia di S. Giovanni Crisostomo, fatta sul principio dell'VIII secolo*, XPYCOCTOMIKA (Rome, 1908), p. 389). The eighth or ninth century *Cod. Barberini* has no " Amen " after the words of Christ over the bread, only after the consecration of the wine, but it is said by the people (Brightman, LEW, p. 328).

[35] F. Cabrol, DACL, art. " Amen, " I, col. 1559.

[36] Cf. account of Dionysius bar Salibi, edit. Labourt (CSCO, 93), 62, 77.

[37] Cf. Brightman, LEW, p. 52.

[38] Brightman, LEW, pp. 232 f.

consecratory formula with no less explicit an act of faith : " We believe and we confess and we glorify. " [39] In the Coptic Liturgy of St. Gregory Nazianzen, after each consecration the people respond : " It is so in very truth. Amen. " [40] A similar affirmation is found in the ancient East Syrian Church. In the *Seventeenth Homily* attributed to Narsai and written in the early seventh century, the words " in truth, without doubt " are given as part of the formula over the bread. [41] This passage is of more than passing interest, for Narsai is offering here, not only the narrative of the institution, but the formula of consecration as it was used in the Chaldean Liturgy—a Liturgy which supposedly had neither (see above, p. 176) :

> ...He commanded us to perform this Mystery with bread and wine...
> For when the time of the passion of the Lifegiver of all was arrived, he ate the legal passover with his disciples. He took bread and blessed and brake and gave to his disciples, and said, This is my body *in truth, without doubt*. And he took the cup and gave thanks and blessed and gave to his apostles, and said, This is my true blood which is for you.... [42]

Like their counterparts in the other Oriental Rites, the two Byzantine " Amens " express assent to the words of consecration. They are the *ecclesias*'s act of faith in Christ's sacramental presence before the epiclesis. Perhaps this is precisely what was being stressed at the time this custom began, since the epiclesis was being given too much importance in the sixth century.

As regards the time at which the two " Amens " were introduced into the consecration, there is some evidence pointing to the sixth century. The Mozarabic text has them. [43] Now, history indicates that the Arabs blocked Mediterranean commerce prior to the seventh

[39] Brightman, LEW, pp. 176 f.

[40] E. Renaudot, LOC, I, p. 29.

[41] Cf. R. H. Connolly, *The Liturgical Homilies of Narsai* (Cambridge, 1909), p. 16.

[42] *Ibid.*

[43] In the Mozarabic Mass, the *Amen* was said three times : (1) after the command that follows the consecratory formula over the bread, (2) after the formula over the wine, and (3) after the *Quotiescumque manducaveritis* at the end. Cf. *Missale mixtum* (PL 85, 552 f.).

century, so that the custom must have passed from the Syro-Byzantine to the Iberic area before then. [44] Besides the three " Amens, " the Coptic Liturgy of St. Basil has the people responding " We believe and we confess and we glorify. " The fact that these words are in Greek means that this is a tradition from the sixth century at least.

[44] H. Pierenne, *Economic and Social History of Medieval Europe* (6th edit., London, 1958 [translated from the French, *Histoire du Moyen-Age*] Paris, 1931), pp. 40 f.

CHAPTER LXI

THE *ANAMNESIS*

As the people sing the " Amen " after the words of Christ over the wine, the priest says in a low voice :

Remembering therefore this salutary command and all that was done for us : the cross, the sepulchre, the resurrection on the third day, the ascent into heaven, the sitting at the right hand (of the Father), the second and glorious coming. . . .

With his forearms crossed, the deacon takes the diskos *in his right hand and the chalice in his left; then, elevating the vessels slightly, he makes the sign of the cross with them over the altar, as the priest sings in a loud, solemn tone of voice :*

Offering you your own from what is your own, on account of all and through all.

The priest and the deacon then make a profound bow before the sacred species as the following is sung :

We praise you, we bless you, we thank you, Lord, and we pray to you, our God.

When Christ changed the bread and wine into his body and blood, he commanded his apostles to do what he had done in *anamnesis* of him. Obeying the command at the consecration, the priests makes the *anamnesis* of the mysteries in historical sequence : the passion, the cross, the resurrection, the ascension and the second glorious coming of Christ. In most Liturgies, including the Byzantine, this is done immediately after the words of institution. Basil begins by recounting Christ's command (from the Luke-Paul account), while Chrysostom merely alludes to it.

Here, as in so many instances, difficulties of language and translation play an unfortunate role. It is with reason that we have left the word *anamnesis* untranslated : in order to preserve the original meaning. The Douay Version of the Luke-Paul account is not accurate. There is in English no precise equivalent of ἀνάμνησις. The nearest are " memorial, " " commemoration, " " remembrance, " and " memory "—but they connote mental recollection in the absence of the remembered object. In Scriptures, *anamnesis* (and its verbal forms) means recalling or representing before God a past event as presently operative (e.g., III Kings, 17:18; Heb. 10:3-4; etc.). When saying the words, " Remembering therefore this salutary command, " etc., and enumerating the mysteries, the priest is not only recalling them : with the consecratory formula, he has truly brought about the same mystery as had Christ at the Last Supper. That is why Justin was careful to use the verb ἀναμιμνήσκομεν in referring to the Eucharistic Liturgy while he chose a different word, γενομένοι, to describe the Gospels as " memorials. "[1] Also operative in their effects are all the other mysteries which, historically, followed : the cross, the sepulcher, the resurrection, the ascension, the enthronement at the place of honor at the Father's right hand and the second glorious coming of Christ. Every Eucharistic Liturgy is not only the fulfillment of the command to do what Christ had done at the last Supper, but also the renewal of his death and of the concomitant mysteries. This is what Paul meant when he wrote to the Corinthians (I Cor. 11:26) : " For as often as you shall eat this bread and drink the chalice, you shall show the death of the Lord, until he come. "

The *anamnesis* belongs to the secondary strata of anaphoric material.[2] This means that it was probably not part of the original nucleus. But since it is contained in all the ancient texts, it is probably one of the first additions. Even before the appearance of any anaphoric text, Justin was very conscious of the theme, since he said to Trypho, " . . . the Eucharistic Bread, which our Lord Jesus Christ commanded us to offer *in remembrance* of the Passion he endured for all those souls who are cleansed from sin. "[3]

By the time of Hippolytus, the theme of Christ's sacrificial death had been superseded by that of his triumph over death. " Therefore,

---

[1] *First Apology*, chaps., 66, 67 (edit. Otto, *Corpus Apologetarum* (Jena, 1847), I, 181-184).

[2] For the reasons outlined in chap. LV above, p. 556.

[3] *Dialogue with Trypho*, chap. 41 (edit. Otto, I, p. 134).

doing it now in *anamnesis* of his death and resurrection." [4]　In Egypt, the evolution seems to have started later.　Sarapion's anaphora (c. A.D. 353-360) refers only to Christ's sacrificial death. "Wherefore we also making the likeness of the death have offered the bread and beseech thee...." [5]　In the Deir Balizeh fragment, the resurrection is mentioned : "As (often) as ye eat this bread, and drink this cup, ye proclaim my death, ye confess my resurrection. We p(roclaim) thy death, we (confess) thy resurrection and entreat..." (see above, p. 98).　The next stage was reached when the ascension was added.　We find this in the Liturgy of Alexandria during Cyril's time (*c.* A.D. 430) : "Proclaiming the death after the flesh of the only-begotten Son of God... and confessing his return to life from the dead and his assumption into heaven, we celebrate the unbloody sacrifice in our churches...." [6]　Then, finally, the Liturgy of St. Mark has the additional themes of Christ's enthronement at the right hand of the Father and of his Second Coming. [7]

Most of the oriental Rites have undergone a similar evolution in their *anamnesis*.　The *Apostolic Constitutions* (Book VIII) is close to Hippolytus, but has added the ascension, "his return to heaven," and the parousia, "his future Second Coming when he will come to judge the living and the dead and to render to every man according to his works" (see above, p. 135).　In later West Syrian anaphoras, the description sometimes fills a whole page. [8]　The Greek St. James (see above, pp. 145 f.) has a plea for mercy as an outgrowth of the final judgment.　In some later West Syrian anaphoras, the *anamnesis* also describes the various phases of Christ's passion; others, the various events before his public life : his birth, temptation, fasting, and baptism. [9]

None of the anaphoras mention the Pentecost, since only events relating to the God-man would properly be the subject of the

[4] Hippolytus, *Apostolic Tradition*, see above, p. 58.

[5] This is found after the consecration of the bread; another part of the *anamnesis* follows the consecration of the wine : "Wherefore we have also offered the cup, presenting a likeness of the blood"; see above, pp. 94 f.

[6] Cyril of Alexandria, *Ep. oecum. ad Nestor.*, II (edit. Aubert, Vol. 5, 72).

[7] Brightman, LEW, p. 133.

[8] E. Renaudot, LOC, II, pp. 147, 165, 190 f., 205, 216, etc.

[9] Cf. Renaudot, LOC, II, pp. 263, 178, etc.

anamnesis. Besides, reference is made to the Holy Spirit in the epiclesis which follows immediately in most Rites.

In the *anamnesis*, the main difference between the two Byzantine anaphoras is the introduction. Basil begins with Christ's command " Do this, " and combines it with an expanded version of the Pauline formulation (I Cor. 11:26) " For as often as you eat this bread, " which he puts on the lips of Christ. This is matched in one form or another by nearly all the Oriental Liturgies. The exceptions are only three : the *Armenian* and *Chaldean Liturgies*, and the *Byzantine anaphora of Chrysostom*, all of which omit the Pauline formulation. There are, however, fundamental differences between the three. The Chaldeans make the *anamnesis*, not because Christ commanded it but because they " have by tradition received the example for thy Son. " [10] The Armenian anaphora quotes the command of Christ indirectly : " And thine only-begotten Son has commanded us always to do this in memory of him. . . . we therefore, O Lord, obeying this command. . . recall, " etc. [11] Chrysostom mentions a " salutary command, " without explanation. Since this immediately follows the words of institution, the inference is that it is Christ's command, but the fact that this is merely inferred makes this *anamnesis* unique. The differences between the introductory parts of the two Byzantine *anamneses* constitute a further confirmation of their distinct origin. In attempting to assess their relative age, we must once again conclude that the text of Chrysostom is older according to the rule, " The older a text, the less literal its assimilation of biblical passages. " In Basil, the Scriptural quotation is almost literal; in Chrysostom, it is indirect.

The second part of the *anamnesis* is the offering, the sacrifice : " Offering you your own from what is your own, in behalf of all and for all [Slav recension]. " This is identical in the two Byzantine-Slav anaphoras. This second part, despite its brevity, receives the main emphasis. The memorial is recited in a low voice, while the offering is intoned loudly and solemnly. In the Byzantine-Greek

[10] Anaphora of the Apostles (Brightman, LEW, p. 287). Other Chaldean anaphoras express different reasons. See Renaudot, LOC, II, pp. 613-614, for anaphora of Theodore the Interpreter; for the anaphora of Nestorius, LOC, II, p. 624.

[11] Brightman, LEW, p. 438.

text, the grammatical structure makes the stress even more obvious. The memorial part, although longer, is in participial form, while the main verb is the προσφέρομεν, " we offer. " Most of the Eastern Liturgies have the same structure. In the Greek Church, however, this was not always so. Until the eleventh or twelfth century, the offering was also in the participial form (προσφέροντες). [12] The Slav Church follows this older structure, since it received Christianity from Constantinople before the change.

By doing what Christ commanded us to do, we make an *anamnesis* which is both a memorial and an offering-sacrifice—performed, not by the priest alone, but by the priest and the people. In the Roman Mass, this is brought out in the text : *nos servi tui*, and *plebs tua sancta*. In the Byzantine Liturgies, there is no textual reference, but the same meaning is conveyed by the congregation's exclamation : " We praise you, we bless you. " All the Oriental Rites have similar exclamations by which the people ratify and participate in the action of the celebrant.

The object of our offering is τὰ σὰ ἐκ τῶν σῶν, " your own from what is your own). " In other words, what we undertake to offer to God is not something that is ours, but something that is his already : the unbloody sacrifice of his Son. The concept of offering to a deity or God what is his own reaches back to pre-Christian times. The ancient Hebrews learned it from Scriptures : " Who am I, and what is my people, that we should be able to promise thee all these things? All things are thine : and we have given thee what we received of thy hand " (I Chron. 29:14). The same notion is expressed by the *de suo fecit* which pagan Romans carved on their sanctuaries and memorials. In early Christian times, the words " thine of thine own " or their equivalent were often inscribed on foundation stones. [13] When the same inscription was carved on the altar of Hagia Sophia in Constantinople, [14] it had been etched

---

[12] E.g., *Cod. Barberini, gr.* 336 (eighth or ninth century), cf. Brightman, LEW, p. 328 f.; *Cod. Porphyr.* (ninth or tenth century); *Cod. Sebast.* (tenth or eleventh century); Krasnoseltsev, *Materialy dlja istorii chinoposlidovania liturgii sv. Ioanna Zlatoustago* (Kazan, 1889), p. 26.

[13] Cf. H. Leclercq, *Donis Dei (de)*, DACL, IV, 1507-1510.

[14] Cf. Rücker, *Die syrische Jakobusanaphora. Mit dem griechischen Paralleltext* (Münster, 1923), 19 apparatus. The whole inscription reads : " O Christ, your servants Justinian and Theodora offer you your gifts from your own gifts. "

indelibly on the Christian soul, and there is no reason to attribute to Justinian its introduction into the Liturgy. [15] On the contrary, Justinian and Theodora probably borrowed it from the Constantinopolitan Liturgy, just as the Egyptian and Armenian anaphoras had, in almost identical forms. [16] A similar expression, *de tuis donis ac datis*, found in the *Unde et memores* of the Latin Mass, has the same Greco-Roman-Jewish source as the Byzantine.

In the second half of the parallelism, gratitude is indicated as the purpose of the sacrifice : " on account of all and through all. " The perfect balance between the object and the purpose of offering (τὰ σὰ ἐκ τῶν σῶν — κατὰ πάντα καὶ διὰ πάντα) indicates a late phase of development. The economy of words achieves balance and symmetry perhaps at the expense of clarity, for the objects of the prepositions are implied in both the Greek and the Slavonic. Some authors have been misled by the Slavonic " *o vikh i za vsia,* " and have explained this as a petition " for all the people. " [17] True, in the Slavonic the dative plural form *vsikh,* " all, " (as object of preposition " o ") is the same for all genders, but the original Greek is much clearer. The Greek has πάντα, the *neuter* accusative plural (as object of the preposition κατὰ) and not πάντας, the masculine plural or πάσας, the feminine plural accusative : hence, the objects of both prepositions are neuter and cannot be people but inanimate things or actions. Accordingly, if we were to fill in the sentence it would have to read that the priest is offering " you your own from what is your own, on account of all things that you have done for us and through all the things that you have done for us. " i.e., all those things mentioned in the *anamnesis,* the cross, the sepulcher, etc.

The Elevation

When the priest intones the words, " Offering you your own from what is your own, " there is another " showing " of the sacred species. At the consecration, the holy gifts are pointed to, but now they are

[15] As does Neale, *Introduction to the History of the Holy Eastern Church* (London, 1933), Vol. II, pp. 489 f.

[16] Cf. Brightman, LEW, pp. 133, 178, 438.

[17] E.g., J. Pelesh, *Pastyrskoe Bohoslovie* (Vienna, 1885), p. 497.

lifted up. With his forearms crossed, the deacon raises the chalice and *diskos* slightly and makes the sign of the cross with them over the altar. When there is no deacon, the priest does it himself. In the Greek Church, however, the elevation is reserved to the priest. The sign of the cross made over the altar and the crossing of the forearms convey the obvious meaning : that the Eucharistic Sacrifice is the unbloody death of Christ on the cross.

This elevation is comparatively recent, probably not older than several centuries. [18] There is no indication that the elevation was borrowed from the West. Since it is another form of " showing, " it probably has the same origin as the " pointing out " at the consecration. Some manuscripts prescribed only the latter without any other ceremonial at this point. [19]

---

[18] P. de Meester, *Les origines et les développements du texte grec de la liturgie de S. Jean Chrysostome*, ΧΡΥΣΟΣΤΟΜΙΚΑ (Rome, 1908), p. 340. Goar's *Euchologion* (1730) has no rubric in its text of Chrysostom's Liturgy, but the elevation is described in the *Notes* following the text, p. 120, col. 1.

[19] Cf. Dmitrievsky, *Opysanie liturgicheskikh rukopisej khraniaschikhsia v bibliotekakh pravoslavnago vostoka*, Vol. II, *Euchologia* (Kiev, 1901), p. 612; also Krasnoseltsev, *Materialy dlja istorii chinoposlidovania liturgii sv. Ioanna Zlatoustago* (Kazan, 1889), p. 64; also the fourteenth or fifteenth century Kievan *Liturgikon* of Metropolitan Isidore, which has the priest pointing with his hand towards the holy gifts and the deacon with his *orar*; cf. MS. *Vat. Slav.*, N. 14, fol. 137.

CHAPTER LXII

THE EPICLESIS

T*he priest prays the epiclesis inaudibly :*

Moreover, we offer you this bloodless sacrifice of the Word, and we pray and beseech and entreat you : send down your Holy Spirit upon us and upon these gifts set forth here. [1]

The deacon puts down the ripidion *or the veil and approaches the priest. Both make three small bows before the holy table. Then the deacon, bowing his head and pointing with his* orarion *to the holy bread, says in a low voice :*

Sir, bless the holy bread.

The priest blesses the holy bread while he says :

And make this bread the precious body of your Christ.

Deacon : **Amen.**

Again pointing his orarion *to the chalice, the deacon says :*

Sir, bless the holy chalice.

---

[1] In the Russian recension, the following is inserted :

Priest : O Lord, you sent your most Holy Spirit upon your apostles at the third hour; do not take him away from us, O gracious One, but renew us who pray to you.

Deacon : Create in me a clean heart, O God, and renew the right spirit deep within me.

Priest : O Lord, you sent your most Holy Spirit, etc.

Deacon : Drive me not away from your presence, and do not take away your Holy Spirit from me.

Priest : O Lord, you sent your most Holy Spirit, etc.

This *troparion,* together with the versicles from the Byzantine Canonical Office of Sext during Lent, is a twelfth or thirteenth century interpolation (cf. Goar, *Euchologion,* p. 106; also Krasnoseltsev, *Materialy dlja istorii chinoposlidovania liturgii sv. Ioanna Zlatoustago* [Kazan, 1889], p. 64, n. 2). These were suppressed in the 1895 Constantinopolitan edition of the Divine Liturgy. The Russian and Rumanian recensions have retained them, while the Ruthenian has followed the Greek in suppressing them.

The priest blesses it and says :

And that which is in this chalice, the precious blood of your Christ.

Deacon : **Amen.**

Pointing again with his orarion *to both the bread and the wine, the deacon says :*

Sir, bless both of them.

Blessing both the bread and the wine, the priest says :

Having changed them by your Holy Spirit.

Deacon : **Amen, amen, amen.**

The deacon bows toward the priest and returns to his place. He takes the ripidion *and fans the holy elements.*

Meanwhile, the priest continues his prayer in a low voice :

So that for those who partake of them they may serve for a cleansing of the soul, the remission of sins, the fellowship of the Holy Spirit, the fulfillment of the heavenly Kingdom, for confidence in you and not for judgment or damnation.

It is never easy in a translation to convey every nuance of the original meaning. The phrase " bloodless sacrifice of the Word " is a case in point. The original Greek λογικὴν is rendered by the Slavonic *slovesnaya*. The usual translation is " reasonable " or " rational, " but it is incorrect. The Latin *rationabilis*, used by Goar, is no better. The words " spiritual " or " spiritualized " (or even " immaterial ") are closer to the true meaning. The Greek λογικὴν is actually related to λόγος, " word ", i.e., the Word of God, the second Person of the Trinity, in the Johannine and Patristic sense. When Clement of Alexandria applies the corresponding adjective to sheep in one of his hymns, he means not " reasonable " or " logical " sheep, but sheep of the λογος, the Good Shepherd. [2] The Slav translators of the eighth and ninth centuries had an accurate understanding of patristic Greek. To translate λογικὴν, they do not use the word *razumnaya*, " rational, " " reasonable, " but

---

[2] *Paedagog.*, III, cxii; also, Eusebius, *Mart. Palest.*, xii.

slovesnaya, " having a connection with *slovo,* word, " that is, the Word of God. Our translation, " sacrifice of the Word, " is intended to convey this meaning.

There is also some doubt as to whether the Greek participle should be in the present or the aorist—" changing, " or " having changed. " Most manuscripts have μεταβαλών (" having changed "), the aorist participle of μεταβάλλω, [3] though μεταβάλλων (" changing"), the present participle of the same verb, is also found. [4] Even μεταλαβών (" having changed "), which is the aorist participle of μεταλαμβάνω, is found. [5] The old Slavonic translators who, we must remember, were very much at home with the Greek language of their time, have considered the participle as an aorist (past), for they rendered it by *prelojiv.* This is definitely the past participle of the verb *prelogit.* Our translation, based on the Slavonic, has the past tense, " having changed. "

Historical Origins

The epiclesis (from the Greek ἐπικαλεῖν, to call upon, to invoke) is a calling upon God to sanctify something. Its origin may be seen in the Judeo-Christian ritual of the blessing of the bread, and in the *berakah.* These were more than a mere acknowledgment of God's bounty in providing food and drink : the blessing offered them back to God and thus " released " them or made them fit for consumption. It would have been a sacrilege to partake of them without pronouncing the blessing of God's name. It was precisely because of this sense of " offering " connected with the blessing that a pagan, an apostate, or a Samaritan could not take part in the *berakah.* The same idea continued to operate in the Christian blessings. These prayers beginning with a naming of God and

[3] The eighth or ninth century *Cod. Barberini* (Brightman, LEW, p. 330, line 5); the ninth or tenth century *Cod. Porphyrios* (Dmitrievsky, *Opysanie liturgicheskikh rukopisej khraniaschikhsia v bibliotekakh pravoslavnago vostoka,* Vol. II, *Euchologia* [Kiev, 1901], p. 19); the fifteenth century MS. of Sinai Library, N. 986 (Dmitrievsky, *op. cit.,* p. 612); the Liturgies in Goar, *Euchologion,* pp. 62, 81, etc.

[4] Cf. P. de Meester, *Les origines et les développements du texte grec de la liturgie de S. Jean Chrysostome,* ΧΡΥCOCTOMIKA (Rome, 1908), p. 342, n. 6.

[5] E.g., MS. of Esphigmenon Library of the year 1306 (Dmitrievsky, *op. cit.,* p. 267.

ending with a glorification of his name—the doxology—follow this
pre-Christian heritage.   This primitive epiclesis was often used
among early Christians for many different objects—specifically, in
many Churches, for the blessing of the baptismal water. ⁶   In the
Egyptian and kindred Rites, there were several forms of epiclesis
to bless wine, oil, milk, and other produce. ⁷   In this primitive
sense, the whole *Eucharistia* is an epiclesis, a calling of the divine
name upon the material elements.   The blessings, prayers, signs
of the cross, and the words of institution combine to make up one
anaphora, one offering, one transubstantiation and one sacrifice.
It was in this sense that Irenaeus said that the bread receiving " the
invocation of God " was no longer bread. ⁸   Early Christians did
not attempt to determine the exact moment of the transubstantiation.

When calling upon the divine power, they used many terms : the
Spirit of God, the grace of God, his power oɪ blessing, the Word of
God, the wisdom, the Holy Spirit, and sometimes even an angel of
God.   Terminology was far from settled.   In the early Christian
era, the Greek Λόγος and πνεῦμα both appear with the meaning
" spirit. "   This " spirit-Word " terminology, obviously related to
the " Spirit-presence-of-God " is confusing for the modern reader.
Both are probably related to the Jewish notion of the sanctity and
power of the name of God.   In Christian usage, both are founded
on the actual presence of the heavenly Christ as the " quickening
spirit " (cf. I Cor. 15:45).

The pre-Nicene theology of the Incarnation differed from ours.
It was believed to come about through the operation of the Logos
(the Word, Second Person of the Trinity) upon the Virgin Mary and
not as we believe, through the operation of the " Holy Spirit. "
As Athanasius put it, the Logos " formed for himself a body from
the Virgin. " ⁹   Early Christian writers unanimously understood

⁶ Sarapion, *Euchologion*, 7 (edit. Wordsworth, *Bishop Serapion's Prayerbook*
[London, 1910], pp. 68-69]); Tertullian, *De bapt.*, iv (CSEL, 20, 204); Jerome,
Contra Lucif., vi, vii (PL 23, 168 C-171 C); Augustine, *De bapt.*, V, xx (PL 43,
190) in the West, Basil, *De spir. sancto*, xv, 35 (PG 32, 129); Cyril of Jerusalem,
Cat., iii, 3 (PG 33, 1089); and Gregory of Nyssa, *Orat. cat. magn.*, xxxiii (PG 24,
745-746 [*Series graeca*]) in the East.

⁷ Sarapion, *Euchologion*, 5, 7, 17 (edit. Wordsworth, pp. 66, 68, 77-78); *Ethiopic
Church Ordinances* (edit. Brightman, p. 192).

⁸ Irenaeus, *Adv. haer.*, IV, 31, 4 (al. IV, 18, 5; edit. Harvey, II, 205 f.

the Spirit or the " Power of the Most High " to mean the Second, and not the Third Person of the Trinity.." [10] Up to the fourth century, the central theological thought was that God had created and accomplished everything through the *Logos*. That is why the earlier forms of the epiclesis in the *Eucharistia* have the *Logos*, the divine power, changing the bread and wine into the body and blood of Christ. The Liturgy of Addai and Mari, with its Eucharistic Prayer directly addressed to the Son, faithfully reflects this thought, since it postulates transubstantiation by the Son and not by the Holy Spirit. While the early writers clearly had in mind the *Logos*, the Second Person of the Trinity, they applied to him the name " Spirit of God, " " Grace of God, " " Power of God, " " Wisdom of God, " and even " Holy Spirit. " That is why historical documents of the first three centuries are so easily misinterpreted.

After Nicaea, great changes swept the Church. Theological development kept pace with the current progress in liturgical worship and ecclesiastical organization. Clarification, development, and precision were the goals. Fourth century writers attempted to determine the precise moment of transubstantiation and the precise nature of the divine power effecting that change. The consecration had been generally seen as resulting from Christ's words, " This is my body, " etc. This was the opinion of such authors as Ambrose in Milan, Chrysostom in Antioch, Sarapion in Egypt, and Gregory of Nyssa in Asia Minor. [11] But as soon as the Incarnation began to

---

[9] Athanasius, *De incarnatione*, 8 (PG 26, 996).

[10] There are many examples. In commenting on Luke 1:31, Justin states unequivocally : " It is wrong, therefore, to understand the Spirit and the power of God as anything else than the Word, who is also the first-born of God " (*First Apology*, chap. 33, ANF, Vol. I, p. 174). Commenting on the same passage (Luke 1:31), Tertullian also states clearly : " The Spirit of God in this passage must be the same as the Word " (*Against Praxes*, 26, ANF, Vol. III, p. 622); in fact, this whole chapter is built on the thesis that " the Spirit is the Word and the Word is the Spirit. " In writing *Against the Heresy of One Noetus* (chap. 4), Hippolytus teaches no less : " For he was Word, he was Spirit, he was Power " (ANF, Vol. V, p. 225; also chap. 16, ANF, Vol. V, p. 229). Cyprian teaches the same thing in his *Treatise on the Vanity of Idols* (VI, 11) : " He is the power of God, he is the reason, he is his wisdom and glory, he enters into a virgin; being the holy Spirit, he is endued with flesh " (ANF, Vol. V, p. 468).

[11] Cf. Ambrose, *De mysteriis*, ix, 54 (PL 16, 407); Chrysostom, *De Prod. judae*, i, 6 (edit. Montfaucon 2, 453 B); Sarapion, *Eucologion* (cf. above, p. 95); Gregory of Nyssa, *Oratio catechetica*, 37 (PG 45, 96 B-97 B); Augustine, *Sermo*, 227 (PL 38, 1099); *Sermo*, 234, 2 (PL 38, 1116).

be interpreted as the effect of an operation of the Holy Spirit (Third Person of the Trinity), and not of the *Logos*, the theology of the consecration changed also, so that it too came to be seen as being brought about through the Holy Spirit, the Third Person of the Trinity, instead of through the Second. The actual parallel, however, was developed much later by John Damascene. [12] Both changes are based on the theological development and clarification of several doctrines : the office and necessity of God the Holy Spirit, and the Trinity itself.

Cyril of Jerusalem was the first to have the " Holy Ghost Epiclesis " which became typical of Eastern Liturgies, that is, the " calling upon the good God to send the Holy Spirit upon the gifts, so that he may change the bread into the body of Christ and the wine into the blood of Christ... for whatsoever comes in contact with the Holy Spirit is hallowed and transformed. " [13] The wording is derived from the Spirit-presence terminology of Addai and Mari and not from that of the Spirit-Word as in the pre-Nicene Churches outside of Syria. Yet, Cyril refers definitely to the Holy Spirit, the Third Person of the Trinity. [14]

This, then, is the consecratory epiclesis in the strict sense : a plea to God to send the Holy Spirit upon the elements in order to change them into the body and blood of Christ. Cyril had at least one predecessor in his thesis that the consecration was effected by the action of the Holy Spirit : the author of the Syrian *Didascalia* (*c.* A.D. 250), who wrote that " the Eucharist is accepted and sanctified through the Spirit. " [15] The context leaves no doubt that " Spirit " means the Holy Spirit, the third Person of the Trinity. By adopting the novel interpretation of the consecration, Cyril lent it the weight of his authority and thus endowed it with theological respectability.

---

[12] *De fide orthodoxa*, iv, 13 (PG 94, 1141-1152).

[13] *Catecheses*, XXIII, 7 (Quasten, *Monumenta eucharistica et liturgia vetustissima* [Bonn, 1935-1937], 101).

[14] There is some question, however, as to Cyril's authorship of the *Catecheses* (*mystag.*), sometimes attributed to John of Jerusalem (d. A.D. 417). For an excellent treatment of the problem from a historical point of view, see W. J. Swaans, " A propos des Catéchèses Mystagogiques, " *Le Museon*, 55 (Louvain, 1942), 1-43.

[15] Edit. Connolly, p. 244.

All available evidence indicates that in this he was almost alone. The great Church historian and Bishop of Caesarea, Eusebius, never once mentions the new theory in his voluminous works, but clearly confirms the earlier view. [16] Aphraates, an East Syrian bishop and monk, also takes the same for granted. [17] In fact, Syrian liturgical practice was still so firmly permeated with the doctrine of the Eucharistic priesthood of Christ that the Syrian Arians were able to twist it into supporting their heretical view of subordinating the Son to the Father.

After Cyril, the influence of the Jerusalem Rite was swift and far-reaching. Syria was the first to adopt the new epiclesis, soon to be followed by most of the Churches of the East. The Liturgy of St. James asks that the Holy Spirit " make " ($\pi o \iota \tilde{\eta}$) the gifts into Christ's body and blood. The Liturgy of the *Apostolic Constitutions* has " manifest " ($\dot{\alpha}\pi o \varphi \acute{\eta}\nu \eta$); the Byzantine St. Basil has " show " ($\dot{\alpha}\nu \alpha \delta \epsilon \tilde{\iota}\xi \alpha \iota$). [18] Both continue with a prayer that the holy gifts may have a salutary effect on the recipients in Holy Communion. This second part is a Communion Epiclesis, found already in the Eucharistic Liturgy of Hippolytus (see above, p. 58). Since Hippolytus and many of the Oriental Liturgies had it after the institution and *anamnesis*, this is where the consecratory epiclesis was placed. Another reason for this choice was that the space before the words of institution was held by the Christocentric " Thanksgiving. "

The case was somewhat different in the Egyptian Liturgies. In Sarapion, there is a preliminary form of epiclesis immediately after the Sanctus : " Fill also this sacrifice with thy power and thy participation...," [19] which some authors believe to be the only original

[16] *Demonstratio evangelica*, V, iii, 18 (PG 14, 198 A [*Series graeca*]) : " Our Saviour Jesus, the Christ of God, after the manner of Melchizedek, still even now accomplishes by means of his ministers the rites of his priestly work among men. "

[17] *Demonstratio*, xii, 6 (edit. Graffin, *Pat. Syr.*, I, 516-517); also xxi, 9 (edit. Graffin, *Pat. Syr.*, I, 957) and xxi, 10 (edit. Graffin, *Pat. Syr.*, I, 960).

[18] Cf. Brightman, LEW (for Liturgy of St. James), p. 54, line 6; (for *Apostolic Constitutions*, Book VIII) p. 21, line 7; (for Liturgy of St. Basil) p. 329, line 32.

[19] This preliminary epiclesis is also found in Deir Balizeh (Quasten, *op. cit.*, 40) and in the sixth century Coptic anaphora found by L. Lefort in 1940 (cf. Roberts-Capelle, *An Early Euchologium, the Dêr Balyzeh Papyrus* [Louvain, 1949], p. 25, 44 f.).

form. [20] Sarapion, however, has another epiclesis after the words of institution : " O God of Truth, let thy Holy Word come upon this bread, that the bread may become the body of the Word, and upon this cup that the cup may become the blood of the Truth; and make all who communicate to receive a medicine of life for the healing of every sickness, " etc. (see above, p. 95). The plea is for the operation of the Word, the Logos, which corresponds to the older concept. Most of this prayer is a Communion epiclesis, that those communicating may receive " a medicine of life for the healing of every sickness and for the strengthening of all advancement and virtue, not for condemnation... and not for censure and reproach. " This same aspect is reflected in the Liturgies of the Ethiopic Church Order, the *Apostolic Constitutions* (Book VIII), St. Mark, St. James, St. Basil, and St. Chrysostom, but in later Liturgies the consecratory aspect was emphasized. The Syro-Byzantine type of consecratory epiclesis became a distinctive feature throughout the East, despite the fact that it represented the liturgical tradition of only one of the major patriarchates, and originated only in the fourth century.

Even when placed after the words of institution, this consecration-plus-communion epiclesis did not imply any theological opinion regarding the moment of consecration. Scholars still gave little thought to the matter. Had they seen any causal link, they probably would have placed it, not after the words of institution, but before. This would have conformed with the tradition of Alexandria and Rome. Until the eighth century, the Fathers and writers of the Church concerned themselves only incidentally with the question, always attributing consecratory force to the words of institution. [21] One of the most forceful is the declaration of Chrysostom : " The priest stands fulfilling a role (σχῆμα) and saying those words, but the power and grace are of God. ' This is my body, ' he says; this formula (τοῦτο τὸ ῥῆμα) transforms (μεταρρυθμίζει) the elements. " [22]

[20] E.g., Lietzmann (*Messe und Herrenmahl, Eine Studie zur Geschichte der Liturgie* [Bonn, 1926], p. 76); Baumstark (*Comparative Liturgy* [Westminster, Md., 1958], pp. 25 f.).

[21] See Spačil, *Doctrina theologica Orientis separati de SS. Eucharistia*, Vol. II (Rome, 1929, OC 14, 1), pp. 41-58, and Russnak, *Epiklezis* (Prjašev, 1926), pp. 138-154.

[22] *De prod. judae*, i, 6 (edit. Montfaucon 2, 453 B); cf. also ii, 6 (edit. Montfaucon 2, 465 B).

Until John Damascene, references in support of the consecratory power of the epiclesis are ambiguous and equivocal. In the Liturgy of Basil, for example, the holy gifts are called τὰ ἀντίτυπα after the words of institution but just before the epiclesis proper. The word would have been clear enough, were it not for the fact that it is used by the Greek Fathers also in reference to the real body and blood of Christ in the Eucharist. Cyril of Jerusalem uses it in this sense : " Those who taste are not bidden to taste bread and wine, but the ἀντίτυπον of the body and blood of Christ. [23] As long as there is no controversy, such freedom of language is permitted. The author of Basil's Liturgy is in general quite free in his choice of words : for example, he refers not to the body and blood but to the " one bread and chalice " after the epiclesis. Yet, he cannot be accused of denying the real presence.

The case is different, of course, with the eighth century testimony of John Damascene. During the iconoclastic controversy, his opponents held that the Eucharist was the only lawful representation of Christ. To bolster this view, they argued that, between the words of institution and the epiclesis, the Liturgy of Basil referred to the elements as τὰ ἀντίτυπα of the body and blood of Christ. Damascene answered rightly that the Eucharist was not a " representation " of Christ—but then he went on to explain that the word referred to the unconsecrated elements, since the consecration was effected not by the words of institution, but by the epiclesis. As if to remove any doubt, he repeats the point. [24]

The question of the consecratory power of the epiclesis became acute only in the fourteenth century, when Cabasilas and Simeon of Thessalonica used it in the disputes between Latins and Greeks, although the question had been debated before. [25] Both seem to deny the consecratory force of the words of institution used alone,

---

[23] Cyril of Jerusalem, *Catecheses*, XXII (*Mystag.*, IV), 3 (PG 33, 1124); also *antitypa* is used by Gregory Nazianzen, *Or.*, VIII, 18 (PG 20, 508 A, *Series graeca*]; *Apostolic Constitutions* (edit. Funk), V.14, 7; VI.30, 2; VII. 25, 4.

[24] *De fide orthodoxa*, iv, 13 (PG 94, 1141-1152) and *Homil. in Sabb. Sancto*, 35 (PG 96, 637).

[25] E.g., Theodore of Andida (thirteenth century), in A. Mai, NPB, VI (Rome, 1852) and PG 140. Also, Theodore of Melitiniota (1361), *Ethicon*, I, VIII (PG 149, 953).

teaching that they are made fruitful and effective by the epiclesis. [26]
The matter was discussed and agreement was reached at the Council
of Florence (1438), which insisted on the consecratory force of the
words of institution, while allowing that the epiclesis made them
fruitful. [27] This settlement did not last. From the seventeenth
century on, Greek Orthodox theologians have generally advocated
that the epiclesis alone effects the consecration. The Russian
Orthodox generally hold either that both the words of institution
and the epiclesis are necessary, or that the consecration is effected
by the epiclesis alone. [28]

The problem is difficult. If the epiclesis alone effects the transubstantiation, then all Liturgies without one have no transubstantiation,
and hence no Eucharist—which responsible theologians, both
Catholic and Orthodox, find difficult or impossible to believe. All
Eastern Liturgies earlier than the fourth century and all the Masses
ever celebrated by the Latin Church would then have lacked a valid
consecration—which is obviously absurd. Besides, this position
dogmatically, liturgically, and historically goes counter to the
teachings of all the early Fathers and writers of the Church.

How then does one explain the epiclesis without distorting its
meaning or its text?

The Historical Theory. Some have held that the epiclesis underwent a textual evolution : that the original did not contain such
words as " make " or " transform " but only such terms as " show "
or " manifest. " Perhaps there were some changes, as happens so
often in liturgical texts, but the historical evidence is unconvincing.
Textual development generally goes from ambiguity to clarity. In
the liturgical style, the words " show " and " manifest " mean

---

[26] Cabasilas, *Com. Lit.* (PG 150, 429-432); Simeon of Thessalonica (PG 155,
733-737). See also M. Jugie, *Theologica Dogmatica Christianorum Orientalium
ab Ecclesia Catholica dissidentium*, Vol. III, p. 287, and F. K. Lukman, " Nicolaj
Kabasilas in Simeon Solunski o epiclesi, " in *Bogoslovni Vestnik*, Vol. VII (1927),
p. 1-14.

[27] Mark of Ephesus and Isidore of Kiev, however, claimed that the words of
institution and the epiclesis were equally important and necessary.

[28] The most notable exceptions were the reactions in seventeenth century
Russia and the Ukraine, e.g., the first edition of the *Orthodox Confession* of Peter
Moghila, Patriarch of Kiev, which states clearly that the words of institution
consecrate.

essentially " make " and " transform. " Perhaps they were changed precisely because they did not bring out the meaning as clearly as " make " and " transform. " This, however, brings us back to the same position as before.

Fruitful Communion Theory. Those favoring this theory hold that the essential meaning of the prayer is found in its second part : " So that for those who partake of them they may serve as a cleansing of the soul, the remission of sins, " etc. They regard the epiclesis as a petition for the fruitful effects of Communion. This was the basis for agreement at the Council of Florence. It constitutes a perfect explanation of the second part of the epiclesis, but leaves the basic question unanswered : Why does the epiclesis contain a petition for the transformation of the elements?

Liturgical Theory. The external actions of the Trinity result from the cooperation of al three Persons—and the Eucharistic transubstantiation is one such action. The Eucharistic Prayer stresses the work of the Father before the institution narrative, the work of the Son during the account of the institution, and the work of the Holy Spirit after the words of institution in the epiclesis. A liturgical prayer can describe the role of each Person only in succession and by degrees. The same occurs in the other sacraments. In baptism and confirmation, for example, the prayers recited after the " form " ask for graces already conferred when matter and form were joined. Liturgies are celebrated in time and display both dramatic anticipation and retrospections. The epiclesis appears to be only one of many such instances.

CHAPTER LXIII

THE COMMEMORATION
OF THE CHURCH TRIUMPHANT

The priest continues to pray in a low voice :

Moreover, we offer you this sacrifice of the Word for those who have died in the faith, our forefathers, fathers, patriarchs, prophets, apostles, preachers, evangelists, martyrs, confessors, ascetics, and for every just soul that has departed in the faith.

Taking the censer and incensing the holy gifts three times from the front of the altar, the priest intones :

Especially for our all-holy, most pure, most blessed and glorious Lady, the Mother of God and ever-virgin Mary.

He covers the chalice with the small veil or with the lention *(corporal). The choir sings the* Megalynarion.

It is indeed fitting to glorify you, Birthgiver of God, ever-blessed and completely sinless one, Mother of our God. We extol you, since you are higher in honor than the cherubim and incomparably more glorious than the seraphim in being God's Mother by giving birth to the Word of God without violating your virginity.

On major feasts, instead of the Megalynarion *above, the* hirmos *proper to the feast is sung. Meanwhile, the deacon incenses the holy table from all sides and mentions by name all the deceased for whom he wishes to pray. The priest continues with the commemorations :*

(We offer this sacrifice also) for St. John the Prophet, Precursor and Baptist; for the holy, glorious, and most honorable apostles; for St. N——(*the saint whose feast it is*), whose memory we commemorate, and for all your saints through whose prayers may you look kindly upon us, O God.

The original pre-Nicene Eucharistic Prayer or anaphora contained no intercessions. When the Eucharist was celebrated without the synaxis, the absence of all intercessions in this the greatest of prayers occasioned a sense of real loss for the faithful. That is probably why, in the third century, the intercessory " prayers of the faithful " (actually, the closing of the synaxis) came to be used as a preliminary to the Eucharist formula. By the fourth century, the idea of the special efficacy of prayer in the presence of the consecrated species gained ground—as Cyril of Jerusalem explains in his *Catecheses*, " because we believe that those souls benefit very greatly for whom supplication is made while the holy and tremendous sacrifice lies before us."[1] By this time, the intercessions had become part of the indispensable core of the Eucharistic Prayer in Jerusalem, for he continues : " Then, we remember also those who have fallen asleep before us, first the patriarchs, prophets, apostles, martyrs... then the holy fathers and bishops—and, in a word, all who have fallen asleep among us in the past. "[2] Jerusalem probably led the way in this, as it did in many other innovations. The entreaty for communicants towards the close of the Great Prayer seemed the appropriate point at which to include the other entreaties. In " modernizing " its own Liturgy, however, each Church chose to insert the intercessions and commemorations in its own way.

Alexandria and Egypt generally placed the commemorations before the sacrifice, at the opening of the Great Prayer, that is, before the Sanctus. Rome placed the intercessions for the living after the Sanctus, but in the first half of the prayer, and those for the dead, at its close. Edessa placed the intercessions after the Sanctus, in the first half of the prayer before the consecration. The West Syrian Liturgies, which the Byzantine followed, placed them after the epiclesis, before the close of the anaphora. Only the Gallic Liturgies withstood this innovation, leaving the intercessions outside the Great Prayer. As a result, the Mozarabic Mass still has no intercessions within its Canon.

The outline of the commemorations was more or less fixed, but

---

[1] *Catecheses*, XXIII (*mystag.*, V), 9 (Quasten, *Monumenta eucharistica et liturgia vetustissima* [Bonn, 1935-1937], 102).

[2] *Ibid.*

most Churches, particularly the Byzantine, left room for impro-
visation. [3] As late as the ninth or tenth century, the *Codex Porphyrios*
gives no listing, but only the rubric that the celebrant " *may commemorate as many saints and martyrs as he wishes.* " [4] In the eleventh
century, the categories of saints to be commemorated were four. [5]
Later, this number was increased, [6] but depended on local tradition.
The early eighth century Armenian version of Chrysostom's Liturgy
has the same listing and wording as today's Byzantine Liturgy. [7]

In most Churches, the ancient intercessions at the end of the
synaxis remained even when the synaxis and the Eucharist came to
be fused into a single service. As time went on, however, the older
intercessions in the prayers of the faithful disappeared in most
Rites. In the Roman Mass and in the Syriac St. James, the commemorations were eliminated completely. [8] When both commemorations were made, there was duplication not only of ideas but
even of wording, as is evident in the Liturgy of the *Apostolic Constitutions*, where the prototype of the anaphoric intercessions is
unmistakably the deacon's *ektenia* at the end of the synaxis. To
illustrate this, we may compare the more salient petitions :

In the Synaxis	*In the Anaphora*
Let us pray for the holy, catholic and apostolic Church which extends from one end of the earth to the other, that the Lord preserve and keep it stable and free. . . .	We further entreat thee, Lord, for thy Church which extends from one end of the earth to the other. . . that thou preserve and keep it stable till the end of world

[3] Cf. Swainson, *The Greek Liturgies Chiefly from Original Authorities* (London,
1884), p. 132.

[4] P. de Meester, *Les origines et les développements du texte grec de la liturgie de
S. Jean Chrysostome*, XPYCOCTOMIKA (Rome, 1908), p. 344.

[5] *Cod. Burdett-Coutts*, III, 42, of the eleventh century; *Cod. Sin.*, N. 1020, of
the twelfth or thirteenth century.

[6] Cf. Krasnoseltsev, *Svidinia o nikotorikh liturgicheskikh rukopis'akh Vatikanskoi
biblioteki* (Kazan, 1885), p. 292.

[7] Cf. G. Aucher, *La versione armena della liturgia di S. Giovanni Crisostomo,
fatta sul principio dell'VIII secolo*, XPYCOCTOMIKA, p. 390; the eighth or
ninth century *Cod. Barberini* lists all except the forefathers (cf. Brightman, LEW,
p. 331).

[8] The process may have been hastened by the discontinuance of the dismissals
of various categories of penitents, etc.

Let us pray for every bishopric that is under heaven, the bishopric of those who rightly dispense the word of truth.	...and for every bishopric that rightly dispenses the word of truth.
Let us pray for our priests....	
Let us pray for all the deacons and ministers in Christ....	We further entreat thee... for all the priests, for the deacons, and all the clergy....
Let us pray for the princes....	We further beseech thee, Lord, for the king and all those in authority....
Let us pray for the readers, singers, virgins, widows, and orphans.	Moreover we offer to thee... for subdeacons, readers, singers, virgins, widows,...
Let us pray for the married and those in child-bearing.	...for the honorably married and those in child-bearing....
Let us pray for our brothers who are tried with sickness....	...for the sick.
Let us pray for those who are in bitter servitude.	...for those in bitter servitude....
Let us pray for those who are in the mines, in banishment, in prisons, and in chains....	for those in banishment, for those in prison....
Let us pray for those who travel by sea or land.	for those who travel by sea or land. [9]

One element not found in the synaxis *ektenia* was added to the anaphoric intercessions : the commemoration of the saints. We find it already in the *Apostolic Constitutions :*

> " ...for all those holy people who have given thee great satisfaction from the beginning of the world, patriarchs, prophets, just men, apostles, martyrs, confessors, bishops... "
> (see above, p. 137).

It is brief and seemingly least among the petitions, yet it developed into a significant part of the Eucharistic Prayer. It illustrates the doctrine of the communion of saints, that bond which unites the Church Triumphant, Militant and Suffering. The original reason for including the commemoration of saints is expressed clearly in

---

[9] See above, pp. 118-120, 136-137, for full texts.

the Byzantine formula, " that through their prayers and intercessions, God may receive our petition. " The *plebs sancta Dei* in the state of glory are to add their pleas to those of the people of God on earth.

The Commemorations

The Byzantine commemorations read : " Moreover, we offer you this sacrifice of the Word for those who have died in the faith, our forefathers, fathers, patriarchs, prophets, apostles, preachers, evangelists, martyrs, confessors, ascetics, and for every just soul that has departed in the faith. Especially for our all-holy, most pure, most blessed and glorious Lady, the Mother of God and ever-virgin Mary. "

The ancient formula, accidentally left unchanged, may give the impression that the Eucharistic Sacrifice is being offered " for " (ὑπὲρ) the various categories of saints and the Mother of God. Most of the older texts, including the *Apostolic Constitutions* (Book VIII), give just such an impression. [10] The clue to the whole passage in the Byzantine formula is " through whose prayers look down upon us, O Lord. " Most theologians followed Augustine of Hippo : *Iniuria est enim pro martyre orare, cuius nos debemus orationibus commendari,* [11] but there are some notable exceptions. The Armenian Liturgy, for example, contains a formal petition for the saints that God give them " peace "! [12] Simeon of Thessalonica also interpreted this passage in a similar way when he stated that the Church prays here for the saints in order that God may increase their glory and holiness. [13] Obviously, God, through his grace, can increase a person's holiness only while that person is still among the living.

---

[10] Book VIII; see above, p. 137. So also the East Syrian fragment from the sixth century (Brightman, LEW, p. 516), and the Anaphora of St. James (Brightman, LEW, pp. 57, 92 f.), which has " Deign to remember.... " Similarly, the Egyptian Liturgy (Brightman, LEW, p. 128) and the East Syrian (Brightman, LEW, p. 440). For the indefinite meaning of ὑπέρ, " for, " used in this regard, see Jungmann, *Die Stellung Christi*, pp. 234-238.

[11] Augustine, *Sermo* 159, I (PL 38, 868); cf. also *In John. tract.*, 84 ,1 (PL 35, 1847).

[12] Cf. Brightman, LEW, p. 440, line 1.

[13] Simeon of Thessalonica, *Dialogus (de sacra liturgia* [PG 155, 283]).

One's glory in heaven is proportionate to what one has merited while on earth.

Cabasilas explains :

> If the Church were really praying for the saints, she would obviously ask for them those benefits for which she has always prayed. Those things for which she prays on behalf of the dead are these...: the remission of their sins, the inheritance of the kingdom, and rest in Abraham's bosom with the perfect saints. You will not find her asking for anything else on behalf of the faithful departed. Our prayers to God have been fixed within these limits. For it is not permissible to pray for everything which comes into one's head; here too there is a law, and a boundary which cannot be crossed....
>
> Are we to ask for the remission of the sins of the innocent, as if they were guilty and had an account to render? Or pray that the saints may rest with the saints, as if they were not already sanctified? Or ask that the perfect be made perfect, as if they were not so already?
>
> One way or the other they are wrong. Either acknowledging the blessedness and perfection of the saints, they are deliberately jesting with God, and offering vain prayers on their behalf... or they make their prayers in all seriousness, and believe that they can aid the saints, thus denying their glory... and this is an insult not only to them but to God, implying that he does not keep his promises. [14]

In the Byzantine Liturgy of Basil, the reason for introducing the commemorations is completely different : " that we may find mercy and grace together with all the saints who through the ages have been well-pleasing to you : our forefathers, fathers, patriarchs, " etc. Here, the commemorations are made to define in part what *we ask* God to do *for us*, to give us the grace and mercy he has given the saints. Chrysostom, on the other hand, makes the commemorations of the saints in order that God assist us " through their prayers. " If Chrysostom's text were an abridgment of that of Basil, the purpose of the commemorations would have been the same in both. Once again, Chrysostom appears as the oldest, since it

---

[14] Cabasilas, *A Commentary on the Divine Liturgy*, trans. by J. M. Hussey and P. A. McNulty (London, 1960), pp. 108-109.

introduces the commemorations with the simple preposition " for, " as do the most ancient Liturgies. By contrast, Basil weaves the commemorations into the text of the Eucharistic Prayer smoothly, logically and with finesse—almost always a sign of more recent composition.

With the exceptions of the Mother of God and John the Baptist, the lists in both Liturgies contain no names but only categories or classes of saints. Both lists are identical if we equate *teachers* with *ascetics*; an ascetic according to Eastern tradition was by his vocation a " teacher " to those aspiring to the higher life. The order is revealing in that it indicates the types of vocations then regarded as the highest :

Chrysostom	*Basil*
Forefathers in the faith	Forefathers
Fathers	Fathers
Patriarchs	Patriarchs
Prophets	Prophets
Apostles	Apostles
Preachers	Preachers
Evangelists	Evangelists
Martyrs	Martyrs
Confessors	Confessors
Ascetics	Teachers
And for every just soul that has died in the faith	And every just soul made perfect in the faith

As we have seen, the *Apostolic Constitutions* (Book VIII) placed its commemorations of the saints among the intercessions for the living. In Jerusalem, Cyril offers these commemorations at the head of the petitions for the dead—after the intercessions for the living. Both Byzantine Liturgies place them ahead of all the intercessions, presumably to emphasize their place of honor. What surprises students of the Byzantine Liturgy is the fact that the Mother of God does not head the list. This, we must remember, is a list of categories, not of individual names. She does head the latter list (see also, p. 632). The reason why she does not head the list of categories will be explained later (see p. 632). Whatever her position, she is certainly given special honor, for her commemoration is introduced by the word "especially," "in a singular way" (ἐξαιρέτως). The commemoration is sung aloud precisely to show the pre-eminence of Mary among the saints. The incensing is a further mark of honor. The *Megalynarion*, which the people sing to an elaborate musical setting in response to the commemoration, derives its name from the *Magnificat* (μεγαλύνει), which is sung during the Ninth Ode of the Morning Office. On major feast days, the *Megalynarion* is replaced by the proper *hirmos* (initial troparion) of the Ninth Ode.

In the anaphora of Hippolytus, when Mary is mentioned, it is as part of the Christocentric narrative leading to the words of institution. Neither Cyril nor the *Apostolic Constitutions* mention her. The Council of Ephesus (A.D. 431) provided the greatest impetus to Marian devotion in the ancient East, for it gave her the glorious title of *Theotokos (Deipara)*. A separate commemoration in her honor was probably put into the anaphora at this time. The first evidence of it, about seventy years later, seems to be offered by Philoxenus of Mabbogh, who indicates that the diptychs of the saints begin with " her who is to be called blessed and glorified among all generations of the earth, the holy and blessed and ever-virgin Mother of God, Mary. " [15] It seems, however, that real prominence was not given to Mary until several centuries later. As late as the beginning of the eighth century, James of Edessa mentions the commemoration of Mary just before the intercessions for the dead, as the final commemoration in honor of all the saints. [16]

The precise time of origin of the present *Megalynarion* is unknown. It must have been an established practice by the turn of the sixth century. In the early seventh century, the *Chronicon paschale* mentions that, in its stead, certain monasteries would sometimes

[15] Philoxenus of Mabbogh, *Adversus Iulianum Phantasiastam*, in I. E. Rahmani, *Les liturgies Orientales et Occidentales étudiées séparément et comparées entre elles* (Beirut, 1929), p. 223, n. 1. The Monophysite Philoxenus of Mabbogh was born in the Persian province of Beth-Garmai and was murdered at Gangra in Paphlagonia in A.D. 523. He was the Monophysite Bishop of Hierapolis, or Mabbogh, from A.D. 485 to 518.

[16] James of Edessa (A.D. 708), *Commentarius in mysteria* (edit. I. E. Rahmani, *I fasti della chiesa patriarcale Antiochena* [Rome, 1920], pp. xix-xx).

chant another *troparion* of their choice. [17]   This is important, since the last part of the *Megalynarion* (the " More honored than the cherubim... ") has been traditionally attributed to Cosmas the Melodist († 760) while the first part ("Meet it is... ") is said to have been inspired by a vision of a monk of Athos in A.D. 980. [18] The two parts were supposedly ordered into the Divine Liturgy by the patriarch of Constantinople himself.   None of this can be true, since the *Chronicon paschale* refers to this particular *Megalynarion* much earlier.

The practice of singing the *Megalynarion* to an elaborate tune was introduced at this point to fill the void left when the diptychs were no longer read aloud.   Originally, the commemoration of the Mother of God, which now serves to introduce the *Megalynarion*, probably headed the list of the categories of saints as it does in the Syriac St. James anaphora. [19]   Once the public reading of the diptychs was discontinued, her commemoration was shifted to this position in order to introduce the *Megalynarion*.   Though the singing of the *Megalynarion* adds to the unique pre-eminence accorded to the Mother of God, that must have been only a secondary reason for its introduction.

In the parent Greek Rite and most of its branches (not, however, in the Slav Liturgy), the blessing of the *antidoron*, or eulogia, takes place during the singing of the *Megalynarion*, [20] when the priest makes the sign of the cross with the bread over the consecrated elements (sometimes with a short prayer). [21]   This parallels the blessing of natural gifts formerly found at the end of the Canon of Roman Mass. [22]   The Egyptian Liturgy of Sarapion has a petition

[17] PG 92, 989, 1001.

[18] Cf. A. King, *The Rites of Eastern Christendom* (Rome, 1948), II, p. 202.

[19] Cf. Brightman, LEW, pp. 92-93.

[20] Cf. P. de Meester, " The Byzantine Liturgy " in the *Eastern Churches Quarterly*, III (1938), p. 135, and A. King, *op. cit.*, II, pp. 202-203; for the Albanian Church, cf. *Three Liturgies of the Eastern Orthodox Church*, published by the Albanian Orthodox Church in America (Boston, 1955), p. 188.   The Rumanian Church has the blessing of the *antidoron* during the *ektenia* which follows the commemorations.

[21] A. King, *op. cit.*, p. 203.

[22] Cf. J. Jungmann, *Mass of the Roman Rite : Its Origins and Development*, Vol. II (New York, 1955), p. 260.

for donors immediately after the intercessions for the dead. [23] The Egyptian Liturgy today has a similar petition for donors and a recommendation of the gifts offered within the intercessory prayer (though they are not formally blessed). [24] Perhaps the Byzantine Church also blessed at this point natural products other than bread, but there is no proof. Blessings were liturgical creations whose connections with the Eucharistic Sacrifice was only extrinsic. [25] Egypt seems to have been the first to incorporate them into the anaphora. [26] The same phenomenon occurred later in the Latin Liturgy in connection with the blessing of oil, grapes, or new fruits, as mentioned above. The fact that any trace of the Byzantine text of the " short blessing" for the *antidoron* and even the rubric are hard to find seems to indicate that the blessing is para-anaphoric. The Greek Church generally regards the sign of the cross made with the breads over the consecrated elements as a sufficient blessing. The Slav Church considers the *antidoron* particles as already blessed in the rite of *prothesis*, at the time they are cut from the *prosphora*.

During the singing of the *Megalynarion*, the priest continues with the other commemorations. Only two of the saints are mentioned by name : St. John the Baptist and the saint of the day. The Byzantine Church has a tradition of great devotion for the Baptist. It places him in a special category both here and in the *proskomidia*. It rightly honors him as " first among the saints (Matt. 11:11), " a tradition probably inherited from the Syrian Church, for we find evidence that John the Baptist, " messenger and forerunner, " was

[23] *Bishop Serapion's Prayerbook*, trans. by J. Wordsworth (London, 1910), p. 64.

[24] Brightman, LEW, pp. 129, 170 ff., 229.

[25] The *Church Order* of Hippolytus, for example, mentions the current custom of which the blessing of water, milk, and honey was only a later relic; however, after the text of the *Eucharistia*, it includes a rubric concerning the blessing of natural products : to the effect that the bishop should, in case someone brings oil, pronounce a prayer of thanksgiving over it similar to that for the bread and wine (but with the proper changes). The same is to be done with cheese and olives. For both kinds of gifts it suggests a short prayer text (Cf. Dix, *The Treatise on the Apostolic Tradition of St. Hippolytus of Rome* [London, 1937], pp. 10 f.; E. Hauler, *Didascaliae Apostolorum fragmenta Veronensia* [Leipzig, 1900], p. 108).

[26] In the Ethiopian tradition of Hippolytus *Eucharistia* the rubric and text of this prayer of blessing is inserted after Hippolytus' original concluding doxology, but it immediately adds to this the conclusion : " As it was in the beginning, " etc. (Brightman, LEW, p. 190; cf. also p. 233).

included in the anaphoric commemorations of the East Syrian Liturgy as early as A.D. 523. [27] The apostles are named only as a class.

After naming the particular saint of the day, the celebrant commemorates the whole assembly of saints and thus closes the commemorations " of every just soul that has departed in the faith. "

[27] Philoxenus of Mabbogh, *Adversus Iulianum Phantasiastam*, in Rahmani, *Les liturgies orientales*, p. 223. Also mentioned there is St. Stephen, " chief of deacons and first of martyrs "; though not contained in the Byzantine anaphoric commemorations, St. Stephen is commemorated in the *proskomidia* of the Byzantine Liturgy.

CHAPTER LXIV

THE INTERCESSIONS
FOR THE LIVING AND THE DEAD

The priest continues :
Remember also all those who have fallen asleep in the hope of being resurrected to life eternal.

(Here he mentions by name those deceased for whom he wishes to pray.)

And grant them rest where shines the light of your countenance.

Moreover, we pray to you : remember, Lord, all the orthodox bishops who rightly dispense the word of your truth, all the priests, the deacons in Christ, and all the clergy.

We also offer you this sacrifice of the Word for the whole world, for the holy, catholic, and apostolic Church, for all who are living a pure and holy life, for our God-fearing Emperor, N—— (*or* King), and for the whole royal household (*or* for our sovereign authorities) and all the armed forces. Grant them, O Lord, peaceful rule so that we also, sharing their peace, may lead a calm and tranquil life in all piety and honor.

When the people have finished singing the Megalynarion the priest intones :

First of all remember, Lord, His Holiness, the universal Pontiff, N——, Pope of Rome, our Most Reverend Archbishop and Metropolitan N——, our God-loving Bishop N——; preserve them for your churches in peace, safety, honor, health, and length of days as they faithfully dispense the word of your truth.

The deacon mentions the names of all the living for whom he wishes to pray, while the people respond :

And (remember) all (the people) and all (their intentions).

Meanwhile, the priest continues the rest of the intercessions in a low voice :

Remember, Lord, this city in which we live (*or* this village in which we live, *or* this monastery in which we live) and every city and country and all the faithful living there. Remember, Lord, those who travel by sea and land, the sick, the suffering, the imprisoned, and their salvation. Remember, Lord, those who bring offerings and do good in your holy churches and those who are mindful of the poor; send down your mercies upon all of us.

At this point, the priest mentions by name those of the living for whom he wishes to pray. Then he pronounces aloud the final doxology of the anaphora :

And grant that we may with one voice and one heart glorify and praise your most worthy and magnificent name, Father, Son, and Holy Spirit, now and always and for ever and ever.

People : **Amen.**

The intercessions for the dead follow the commemorations of the saints. In many Liturgies, the same formula is used for the commemorations of the saints and of those who died recently—usually, however, in such a way that the saints are distinguished from deceased persons. In the East Syrian anaphoras, there is no distinction. [1] In ancient Christendom the expressions " dying in the faith, " and " the just soul who has departed in the faith, " placed the deceased in the same category as the saints, as may be seen at the end of the list above (see p. 630). This attitude was reflected in het reading of the diptychs with which the anaphoric intercessions have been linked for centuries. Acceptance into the diptychs of the dead (particularly of higher ecclesiastical personages) corresponded more or less to our concept of canonization. This explains why in some post-sixth-century Oriental diptychs the fathers of the first councils, especially the " 318 Orthodox fathers " of Nicaea, are mentioned at the head of the list, along with the " patriarchs, prophets, apostles

---

[1] Hanssens, *Institutiones liturgicae de ritibus orientalibus, De Missa rituum orientalium*, Vol. III (Rome, 1932), pp. 471 f.

and martyrs. " [2]   This may also help to explain why the Orthodox reject the doctrine of purgatory as we understand it.   In practice, however, they still " pray for the dead, " through liturgical services identical with those of the Catholics of the Oriental Rites.

In both Byzantine Liturgies, probably because most of the time had been devoted to the public reading of individual names, the anaphoric intercession for the dead is brief.   When the reading of the diptychs was discontinued, only the introduction and the ending remained : " Remember all those who have died in the hope of rising again to eternal life. . . .   And grant them rest where shines the light of your countenance. "   In between, the priest still offers the names of those dead for whom he wishes to pray, but he does this silently. The Liturgy of Basil also has this beginning and end, but it inserts between what appears to be a petition formula framing the individual name : " for repose and forgiveness for the soul of your servant N——; grant him rest, our God, in a place of light from which grief and mourning have been driven away. "   These are the only direct vestiges of the ancient diptychs for the dead.   For a long time after the diptychs had ceased to be read aloud, the deacon continued to proclaim in a loud voice a bidding for each name remembered silently. [3]

Intercessions for the Living

In both Byzantine Liturgies, the intercessions for the living are much fuller than those for the dead.   They are very similar to the intercessions formerly found at the end of the synaxis from which they were borrowed and adapted.   So much alike are they that they may justly be called a thinly disguised *ektenia*.   The same thing happened in the case of the *Apostolic Constitutions* and the Byzantine *ektenia* of the offertory (see above, pp. 226 f., 510-516).   There is a striking similarity between the anaphoric intercessions of Basil's Liturgy and the prayers of the faithful in the synaxis oft he *Apostolic Constitutions* :

---

[2] E.g., in the Ethiopic anaphora of the Apostles (Brightman, LEW, p. 229); the East Syrian Liturgy (Brightman, LEW, p. 277); also the West Syrian Monophysite Liturgy includes the " three pious and holy and ecumenical synods " (Brightman, LEW, p. 94).

[3] Cf. Krasnoseltsev, *Materialy dlja istorii chinoposlidovania liturgii sv. Ioanna Zlatoustago* (Kazan, 1889), pp. 27, 111.

Anaphoric Intercessions of St. Basil's Liturgy	*Intercessory Prayers of the Faithful : Apostolic Constitutions*
Moreover we pray to you : remember, O Lord, your holy, catholic, and apostolic Church which extends from end to end of the universe; give peace to it ...also preserve this holy church until the end of the world.	Let us pray for the holy, catholic, and apostolic Church which extends from one end of the earth to the other, that the Lord preserve and keep it stable and free from the waves of this life, as built upon a rock until the end of the world.
Remember, O Lord, those who offered you these holy gifts and those through whom and for whom they are offered... those who bring offerings and those who do good work in your holy churches, and those who remember the poor; reward them with your rich and heavenly favors; in place of their earthly, temporal, and perishable gifts, give them heavenly ones, eternal and incorruptible....	Let us pray for those who do good in the holy church and for those who give alms to the poor ...for those who bring offerings and sacrifices to the Lord our God, that God... repay them with his heavenly gifts and give them a hundredfold in this world, and that he grant them eternal goods for those that are temporal, heavenly goods for those that are earthly.
Remember, O Lord, those who are living in virginity, in piety, in asceticism, and those who pursue an honorable way of life.	Let us pray for those who are continent and prudent.
Remember, O Lord, our God-fearing Emperor (*or* King), N——.	Let us pray for the princes who lead a pious life.
Remember, O Lord, the people standing round and those who are absent for honorable reasons, and have mercy on them and on us according to the greatness of your mercy....	Let us pray for the readers, singers, virgins, widows, and orphans.
preserve their marriages in peace and harmony;	Let us pray for the married and those in child-bearing, that the Lord have mercy on them all.

foster the children; guide the young; support the aged; encourage the fainthearted; reunite the separated;

Let us remember the Church's infants, that the Lord may perfect them in his reverence and bring them to maturity.

lead back those who have strayed and join them to your holy, catholic, and apostolic Church;

Let us pray for those who are out (of the Church) and for those who have gone astray, that the Lord convert them.

free those troubled with unclean spirits;

Let us pray for our brothers who are tried with sickness, that the Lord deliver them from every sickness and disease and that he restore them in health to his holy church.

sail with those upon the sea; travel with the travelers; defend the widows; protect the orphans;

Let us pray for those who travel by land or sea.

(Widows and orphans were mentioned with readers and singers above)

deliver those in captivity; heal the sick.

Let us pray for those who are in bitter servitude.

Remember, O Lord, all those who are in tribunals, the mines, exile, and bitter servitude, those in affliction, need, and distress.

Let us pray for those who are in the mines, in banishment, in prisons, and in chains for the name of the Lord.

Remember, O Lord, all those who need your great tenderness of heart; those who love us and those who hate us....

Let us pray for our enemies and for those who hate us. Let us pray for those who persecute us.... [4]

After praying for those whom we have not remembered, because we forgot them, or did not know them or because there were too many names to remember, the anaphoric intercessions of Basil's Liturgy continue : " Deliver, O Lord, this city (village or monastery) and every city and country from famine, plague, earthquake, flood, fire, sword, the attacks of foreign peoples, and from civil war. " This last petition, though not contained in the *Apostolic Constitutions*, still forms part of the *Litiya ektenia* in the *Great Vespers Service with the All-Night Vigil*, and as such we may be assured of its original

[4] See above, pp. 118-121, for their proper order in the *Apostolic Constitutions*.

role as part of an ancient *ektenia*. Intercessions for the hierarchy, comparable to those in the *Apostolic Constitutions*, follow in Basil's anaphora; where the latter entreats God to " preserve them for your churches in peace, safety, honor, health, and length of days as they faithfully dispense the word of your truth, " the former beseeches that the compassionate God " let them continue in his holy churches in health, honor, and long life" and that he "grant them an honorable old age in piety and righteousness. " The *Apostolic Constitutions* universal prayer, " Let us pray for every bishopric that is under heaven, the bishopric of those who rightly dispense the word of truth, " becomes in Basil : " Remember, O Lord, every orthodox bishop who faithfully dispenses the word of your truth." Intercessions for priests, deacons, and the rest of the clergy follow immediately in both cases.

Even the final intercessory pleas of Basil's anaphora are readily identifiable as *ektenia* petitions : " Give us well-tempered and seasonable weather; grant gentle showers to the earth so that it may be fruitful.... Prevent schisms in the Church... quickly destroy the upsurges of heresy by the power of your Holy Spirit. Receive us all into your Kingdom, presenting us as children of light and sons of the day; grant to us your peace and your love, Lord our God, for it is you who have given all things to us. " [5]

No less apparent is the identity of the anaphoric intercessions of Chrysostom's Liturgy with some of the intercessions in the Prayers of the Faithful in the ancient Liturgy of the East Syrians. The following, taken from Brightman's translation of the East Syrian prayers of the faithful, establishes the point : [6]

> For our fathers the bishops let us pray and make request to God, the Lord of all. ℟. That they may stand at the head of all their dioceses : without blame or stain all the days of their life (263, 32-35).
> For orthodox presbyters and deacons and all our brothers in Christ, we beseech thee (262, 32-33).
> For the peace, safety and security of all the world (262, 21).

---

[5] See Appendix A, for full text of the anaphora.

[6] Brightman, LEW, pp. 262-267. We have arranged them in the order of the Byzantine anaphoric intercessions as given in the beginning of this chapter. The numbers in parenthesis after each bidding refer to their relative position in Brightman.

For the holy catholic church here and everywhere... (263, 27).

For the kings who have power in this world... (262, 30).

And especially for the welfare of our holy fathers NN——. R̷. Amen. That he may keep and raise them at the head of all their dioceses; that they may feed and serve and make ready for the Lord a people prepared, zealous of good and fair works (263, 36-37; 264, 1-4).

For this country and them that dwell therein, for this house and them that care for it, for this town (or village) and them that dwell therein... (265, 9-12).

For our land, all lands, and for those who live therein in faith (262, 23-24).

For them that are grievously sick... (265, 24-25).

For the poor and afflicted... the tormented and troubled and grieved in spirit... (265, 30-31).

We ask the mercy and compassion of the Lord continually at all times (266, 22-23).

In the Byzantine Liturgy, as we have seen, most of the petitions have been transferred from their former place at the end of the synaxis to other positions in the Liturgy, becoming the various *ektenias.* The anaphoric intercessions remained in a more or less flexible state for centuries. [7] The present form seems to have been the ordinary formulary into which various petitions and indeed the oft-modified versions of the diptychs could be inserted, for it appears almost intact in the early eighth-century Armenian version of Chrysostom. [8] The commemorations of the *proskomidia,* many of them patterned on these anaphoric intercessions, also took centuries to crystallize. [9] The original position of the diptychs was probably not in the anaphoric intercessions but at the offertory (see above,

---

[7] Compare *Cod. Barberini, gr.* 336 (Brightman, LEW, pp. 332-337), the National Library of Paris *Cod. Gr.,* 2509 (Swainson, *The Greek Liturgies Chiefly from Original Authorities* [London, 1884], pp. 132-133), the Armenian version of the early eighth century (G. Aucher, *La versione armena della liturgia di S. Giovanni Crisostomo, fatta sul principio dell'VIII secolo,* XPYCOCTOMIKA [Rome, 1908], pp. 391-392).

[8] G. Aucher, *op. cit.,* pp. 391-393.

[9] Even the *proskomidia* is mentioned at this point in many manuscripts. Cf. Dmitrievsky, *Opysanie liturgicheskikh rukopisej khraniaschikhsia v bibliotekakh pravoslavnago vostoka,* Vol. II (Kiev, 1901), pp. 84, 824, 960.

pp. 525 ff.).   They must have been moved between the fifth and eighth
centuries, for the eighth or ninth century *Codex Barberini* has them
here. [10]   The intercessions for the individual hierarchs of the Church
(which are sung today) probably come from the diptych-reading, as
indicated by the response : (Μνήσθητι) καὶ πάντων καὶ πασῶν (εὐχῶν),
And (remember) all (of them) and all (their intentions).   The reading
was probably divided into sections, for some manuscripts show that
this response was repeated several times by the cantors. [11]   The
present response, however, probably refers to all the people and
their intentions, since it comes just when the deacon is mentioning
the names of all the living for whom he wishes to pray.   The Slavonic
I vsikh i vsia is much more clear than the original Greek καὶ πάντων
καὶ πασῶν.   It cannot be rendered " and all men and all women " :
the Slavonic would have to read, *I vsikh (muzhej) i vsikh (zhen')*.
In this phrase, the Slavonic *vsia* definitely modifies an inanimate
object, though it is not mentioned; hence, the literal translation reads
" and all (men, people) and everything, " i.e., all the people and all
their intentions (petitions, beseechings).

   The deacon used to read the diptychs aloud, while the priest recited
his part silently.   After the reading was discontinued, the void was
filled with the intercession for the hierarchy and its response.   The
response itself, though verbally brief, was melodiously embellished
to give the celebrant opportunity to complete the silent praying of
the final intercessions.

The Conclusion of the Anaphora

   The ancient rule that every public prayer should close with the
praise of God is respected in the Eastern Liturgies.   As old as the
Didache itself, the rule exemplifies the purpose of prayer : acknowledgment of God's dominion over his creatures.   There is scarcely
any public prayer in the Byzantine Church which does not close with
a solemn doxology.   The anaphoric prayer concludes : " And grant
that we may with one voice and one heart glorify and praise your

---

[10] Brightman, LEW, p. 336.
[11] Krasnoseltsev, *op. cit.*, p. 66; Dmitrievsky, *op. cit.*, II, p. 501.

most worthy and magnificent name, Father, Son, and Holy Spirit, now and always, and for ever and ever. "

The age of this formula cannot be established precisely, [12] however, its hebraism indicates it is ancient. God is praised, not directly, but through his name. When Justin describes this part of the *Eucharistia*, he says that " all the people present cry out in agreement, *Amen.* " [13] The Byzantine anaphora retains the primitive spirit of unity and agreement : " That we may with one voice and one heart glorify and praise.... " Long after most of the anaphoric prayer became silent, this concluding doxology was always sung aloud so that the people could proclaim their ratifying *Amen.* By it, they assert and confirm what the priest has said and done in the Eucharistic Prayer. This apostolic or sub-apostolic custom, continued to be stressed in the ancient Church. [14]

[12] Though it is found in the early eighth century Armenian version of Chrysostom's Liturgy (Aucher, *op. cit.*, p. 392) and in *Cod. Barberini, gr.* 336, of the eighth or ninth century (Brightman, LEW, p. 337).

[13] Justin, *First Apology*, chap. 65; see above, p. 41.

[14] Cf. Dionysius of Alexandria (d. 264/265) in Eusebius, *Hist. eccl.*, VII, 9 (PG 20, 656); Chrysostom, *In I Cor. homil.*, 35, 3 (PG 61, 300, or edit. Montfaucon 10, 325 E).

SECTION VI

LITURGY OF THE FAITHFUL : THE COMMUNION CYCLE

CHAPTER LXV

BEGINNING
OF THE PREPARATORY PRAYERS

After the doxology ending the Eucharistic Prayer, the priest turns toward the people and blesses them while he intones :

And may the mercies of our great God and Saviour Jesus Christ be with all of you.

People : **And with your spirit.**

Taking leave of the priest, the deacon makes a small bow, goes around the holy table, and leaves the sanctuary through the north door. Then, standing in his usual place, he sings the following ektenia :

After commemorating all the saints, again and again in peace let us pray to the Lord.

People : **Lord, have mercy.**

Deacon : **For the precious gifts that have been offered and consecrated, let us pray to the Lord.**

People : **Lord, have mercy.**

Deacon : **Let us pray that our God, the Lover of mankind, after receiving them as a fragrance of spiritual sweetness upon his holy and mystical altar in the highest heaven, may send down upon us in return his divine grace and the gift of the Holy Spirit.**

People : **Lord, have mercy.**

Deacon : **For our deliverance from all affliction, wrath, and need, let us pray to the Lord.**

People : **Lord, have mercy.**

In the meantime, the priest prays silently :

To you, Lord and Lover of mankind, we commend our whole life and hope. We implore you, we pray you, we entreat you : make us worthy, with a pure conscience, to partake of the heavenly and awesome mysteries from this holy and spiritual altar for the remission of sins, the forgiveness of offenses, for the communion of the Holy Spirit, the inheritance of the heavenly Kingdom, for confidence in you and not for judgment or condemnation.

Deacon : **Help us, save us, have mercy on us and protect us, O God, by your grace.**

People : **Lord, have mercy.**

Deacon : **Let us ask the Lord that this whole day be perfect, holy, peaceful, and sinless.**

People : **Grant it, O Lord.**

Deacon : **Let us ask the Lord for an angel of peace, the faithful guide and guardian of our souls and bodies.**

People : **Grant it, O Lord.**

Deacon : **Let us ask the Lord for the pardon and forgiveness of our sins and offenses.**

People : **Grant it, O Lord.**

Deacon : **Let us ask the Lord for whatever is good and profitable to our souls and for peace in the world.**

People : **Grant it, O Lord.**

Deacon : **Let us ask the Lord that we may spend the rest of our life in peace and repentance.**

People : **Grant it, O Lord.**

Deacon : **Let us ask the Lord for a Christian and peaceful end to our life, without pain or blame, and for a good defense before the dread judgment-seat of Christ.**

People : **Grant it, O Lord.**

Deacon : **Having prayed for union of faith, and the indwelling of the Holy Spirit, let us commend ourselves, and one another, and our whole life to Christ God.**

People : **To you, O Lord.**

Priest : **And grant, Master, that with complete confidence and without condemnation we may dare call upon you, God of heaven, as Father and say :**

People : **Our Father, who are in heaven, hallowed be your name; your Kingdom come; your will be done on earth as it is in heaven. Give us this day our daily bread and forgive us our trespasses as we forgive those who trespass against us. And lead us not into temptation, but deliver us from evil.**

Priest : **For yours is the Kingdom, and the power, and the glory, of the Father, and of the Son, and of the Holy Spirit, now and always, and for ever and ever.**

People : **Amen.**

As the Lord's Prayer is being sung, the priest lifts up his hands and keeps them high. At the end, he lowers them.

The oldest accounts of the *Eucharistia* contain no special prayers preceding or following Communion. The immediate preparation for Communion was the Eucharistic Prayer itself, and the reception of Holy Communion formed the conclusion to the service. Biblical texts stressed the fact that the *Eucharistia* was a meal, and it was unthinkable that anyone be present without partaking of the sacrament. Those considered unworthy to receive the sacrament, the unbaptized, the energumens, and the penitents, were excluded at the very beginning of the service, at the dismissals (see above, pp. 63 f.).

Because of the sense of " fear " so evident in fourth-century Syrian writers, the feeling developed that even those considered worthy should prepare themselves for the receiving of Christ. Special prayers were added. What the pre-Nicene Church had expressed merely through actions, the post-Nicene Church began to put into words. [1] After Communion, further prayers were added as a thanks-

---

[1] As the offertory, primarily an action, was supplemented with special prayers.

giving. In a certain sense, then, "communion devotion" was an innovation of the fourth century.

In Egypt, Sarapion gives several prayers before Communion : one that went with the fraction of the bread, and a blessing pronounced over the people with the laying of the hands. A prayer of thanksgiving followed Communion. [2] In the Latin West, the *Our Father* came into the Mass in connection with Communion, as indicated by abundant documents of the late fourth century. [3] Soon afterwards, the Lord's Prayer became part of the preparation for Communion in all the Churches of Christendom.

The first evidence of the *Our Father* between the anaphora and Communion comes from Cyril of Jerusalem; [4] Jerusalem seems to have led the way in this, as in so many innovations. There is no doubt about the *Our Father* being used there as a preparation for Communion, because the author of the *Catecheses* explicitly interprets it in that way. [5] The rite is simple : the Lord's Prayer is introduced with the words, "With a pure conscience we name God as our Father and say... "; after the *Our Father*, there is a proclamation, "Holy things for the holy," with its response, "One is holy, one Lord

---

[2] Sarapion, *Euchologion*, nn. 14-16 (Quasten, *Monumenta eucharistica et liturgia vetustissima* [Bonn, 1935-1937], 64-66). The same pattern is exhibited in the *Egyptian Church Order* (Ethiopian version, cf. Dix, *The Treatise on the Apostolic Tradition of St. Hippolytus of Rome* [London, 1937], pp. 11 f.; Brightman, LEW, pp. 190-193); for the Coptic version, which is actually an Egyptian recension of Hippolytus' *Apostolic Tradition*, cf. Funk, *Didascalia et Constitutiones Apostolorum*, Vol. II (Paderborn, 1905), pp. 101 f., but here the prayer before the blessing is doubled, and after the post-Communion thanksgiving prayer, another laying on of hands in blessing follows.

[3] Optatus of Mileve, *Contra Parm.* (c. A.D. 366), II, 20 (CSEL, 26, 56); Ambrose, *De sacramentis* (c. A.D. 390), V, 4, 24 (Quasten, *op. cit.*, 168); Jerome, *Adv. Pelag.* (c. A.D. 415), III, 15 (PL 23, 585); also, *In Ezech.*, 48, 16 (PL 25, 485), and *In Matt.*, 26, 41 (PL 26, 198); Augustine, *Serm.*, 227 (PL 38, 1101); etc. In Spain, however, the *Pater noster* was not stabilized as part of the Mass until much later. As late as A.D. 633, the Fourth Council of Toledo still had to insist that the *Pater* be said every day at Mass and not merely on Sundays (Canon 10, Mansi, *Sacrorum conciliorum nova et amplissima collectio*, X, 621).

[4] Cyril of Jerusalem, *Catechesis*, XXIII (*Mystag.*, V), 11-18 (PG 33, 1119 A-1123 A). There may be some doubt that Cyril wrote the *Mystagogic Catecheses*, but internal evidence of the time and place at which they were delivered proves that they must have been composed at Jerusalem in the middle of the fourth century (cf. NPNF, Series II, Vol. VII, chap. viii, ix, and xi of the introduction).

[5] The petitions for daily bread and the forgiveness of trespasses are both explained as a preparation for Communion.

Jesus Christ, " Parallels are found in a later, expanded form in the Liturgy of St. James and in the Byzantine Liturgy. During the distribution, a cantor sings Psalm 34, with its refrain, " Taste and see how gracious the Lord is. " As he receives, the communicant responds *Amen.* Finally, the faithful are bidden, " While you wait for the prayer, give thanks to God who has accounted you worthy of such great mysteries. "

The Communion developments are different and much more extensive in the *Apostolic Constitutions* (Book VIII; see above, pp. 139-144). The writings of Chrysostom at Antioch give us additional information about the North Syrian practice, all of which we shall see below in our study of the present Byzantine ritual. This was the nucleus around v hich present Byzantine ceremonial and prayer were built.

The Blessing and Ektenia

True to typical Byzantine form, the pre-Communion proceedings begin with a blessing : " And may the mercies of our great God and Saviour Jesus Christ be with all of you. " This blessing is almost identical in the Byzantine, Armenian, Syrian, and Maronite Rites. Such identity suggests a common origin dating back to a time when intercommunion between these Churches was still intimate. It certainly antedates the earliest available source—the eighth-century Armenian version of the Chrysostom Liturgy. [6] The *Apostolic Constitutions* (Book VIII) has a blessing at this point, with the same response, but the formula is shorter : " May the peace of God be with all of you. " [7] The blessing, if not the wording, stems from this North Syrian original.

The " biddings " by the deacon follow the blessing in the *Apostolic Constitutions*, as they do in the present Byzantine Liturgy. The *Apostolic Constitutions* has no rubric directing the people to answer, " Lord, have mercy, " but this is presupposed. These biddings are somewhat different from those now found in the Byzantine Liturgy, but the first few are very close.

[6] G. Aucher, *La versione armena della liturgia di S. Giovanni Crisostomo, fatta sul principio dell'VIII secolo*, XPYCOCTOMIKA (Rome, 1908), p. 382; also *Cod. Barberini, gr.* 336, of eighth or ninth century (Brightman, LEW, p. 337).

[7] Cf. above, p. 139. Gregory Nazianzen also seems to refer to a blessing at the end of the anaphora (*De or.*, XVIII, 29 [PG 35, 1021]).

Apostolic Constitutions	*Byzantine Liturgy*
Again and again let us pray to God through his Christ.	After commemorating all the saints, again and again in peace let us pray to the Lord.
For the gift that was offered to the Lord God, let us pray.	For the precious gifts that have been offered and consecrated, let us pray to the Lord.
That the good God, through the mediation of Christ, receive it on his heavenly altar as an odor of sweetness.	That our God, the Lover of mankind, in receiving them as a fragrance of sweetness upon his holy and mystical altar in the highest heaven...

From here on, the petitions of the two Liturgies have little in common. Where the *Apostolic Constitutions* repeats the prayers for the Church, the hierarchy, various classes of people, and even good weather, the present Byzantine Liturgy more appropriately asks for gifts of a spiritual nature. The Byzantine *ektenia* at this point is the same as that before the Creed (see above, p. 509).

The petition, " For the precious gifts that have been offered and consecrated, let us pray to the Lord, " is difficult to interpret. There can be no question of praying for the consecrated elements themselves. In his *Catecheses*, Theodore of Mopsuestia interprets the petition (which in his time, *c.* A.D. 410, was said during the fraction) as praying " for those who have brought this holy oblation " and " for those [of us] who have been made worthy of the oblation, that we may be made worthy of looking, standing by its side and partaking thereof"; then he continues, " Through these words, the priest perfects the prayer, asking that the sacrifice may be acceptable to God and that the grace of the Holy Spirit may come upon all so that we may be found worthy of communion with him, and not receive unto punishment that which is exceedingly and infinitely exalted and greater than us. " [8]

It appears from the *Apostolic Constitutions* that this petition and the next were originally one. Together, they are clear : we pray that God receive the gifts on his heavenly altar and give us in return his

---

[8] Theodore of Mopsuestia, *Catecheses*, VI (edit. Mingana, *Commentary of Theodore of Mopsuestia on the Lord's Prayer and on the Sacraments of Baptism and the Eucharist* [Cambridge, 1933], pp. 107-108).

grace and the gift of the Holy Spirit. In the words of Cabasilas, "that they may impart... sanctification to us,... that they may fulfill in us their function, that they be not rendered powerless to produce this grace...." [9] Between the fifth and eighth centuries, this bidding was divided, probably because of its length, with the resulting loss of clarity. The meaning is confirmed by a similar intercession in the Coptic anaphora of St. Mark (or St. Cyril) :

> The sacrifices, the oblations, the thank offering of them that offer honour and glory to thine holy name, receive upon thy reasonable altar in heaven for a sweetsmelling savour, into thy vastnesses in heaven, through the ministry of thine holy angels and archangels : as thou didst accept the gifts of righteous Abel and the sacrifice of our father Abraham.... Give them [the offerers] things incorruptible, heavenly in requital of earthly.... [10]

For a long time in the Christian Church, offerers and communicants were the same. Every communicant, by bringing his gift for the sacrifice, was also an offerer in the ancient sense of the word.

The concept of the heavenly altar is a biblical one : " And there was given to him [the angel] much incense, that he should offer of the prayers of all the saints, upon the golden altar which is before the throne of God (Ap. 8:3-5). " [11] The thought was taken up by early Christian writers, [12] and appeared very soon in the Greek and Latin Liturgies. [13] The expression illustrates the final phase of

[9] Cabasilas, *Commentary on the Divine Liturgy* (trans. by Hussey and McNulty [London, 1960], p. 86).

[10] Brightman, LEW, pp. 170-171. This prayer resembles closely the *Supra quae* and *Supplices* of the Roman Canon.

[11] The gifts offered to God are not visible : they are the prayers of the saints symbolized by incense rising from the altar. This in no way proves or disproves the existence of a sacrifice in heaven. Isaiah (6:6) also alludes to a heavenly altar.

[12] E.g., Hermas, *Pastor* (Commandment X, chap. 2, ANF, Vol. II, p. 27); Irenaeus, *Adv. haer.*, IV, 31, 5 al (edit. Harvey, II, 210); Ambrose, *De sacramentis*, IV, 6 (Quasten, *op. cit.*, 160-162).

[13] Besides the Liturgies of the *Apostolic Constitutions* (Book VIII) and the Byzantine, the Greek St. James and St. Mark use the expression several times (Brightman, LEW, pp. 36, 41, 47, 58 f., 115, 118, 122, 123 f.). The West Syrian anaphora of Timothy and that of Severus, which were originally in Greek, also allude to the heavenly altar (*Anaphorae Syricae* [Rome, 1934-1944], 23, 71). The Latin Mass uses the term in its *Supplices* of the Canon; this can be traced back to Ambrose (*De sacramentis*, IV, 6 [Quasten, *op. cit.*, 160-162]).

human gift-giving : a gift is only fully accepted when it is actually taken into the recipient's possession. [14]

This *ektenia*, transferred from the synaxis at an unknown date, appears in its present position in the eighth century Armenian version of Chrysostom's Liturgy. [15] This seems to indicate that, in the Byzantine Liturgy, it held this place before the end of Byzantium's domination over Armenia in A.D. 695.

A corresponding prayer-collect came with the *ektenia*. [16] This prayer actually " collects " the main petitions and formally presents this summary to God. Since these Byzantine petitions differ fundamentally from those of the *Apostolic Constitutions*, their prayer-collects are also widely different. It had not always been so. We have seen how similar are the first three petitions in the two texts (see above, pp. 649 f.). There is no reason to suppose that originally the rest of the petitions were not similar, at least in content. If so, we would expect to find a closer resemblance between the prayer-collects. There is in fact such a resemblance between the prayer-collect of the *Apostolic Constitutions* and the present Byzantine *Prayer of Inclination* after the *Our Father*—where it even retains its ancient name (see below, pp. 658-661). This is what happened : the Liturgy of the *Apostolic Constitutions* did not have the Lord's Prayer between the biddings and the fraction. When it was incorporated into the Liturgy, it was placed between the biddings and their prayer-collect—and another prayer-collect had to be composed for the *ektenia*. This in turn probably led to a change in the *ektenia* petitions, which were then made suitable as a Communion preparation.

---

[14] Following Apocalypse (8:3-5), several Liturgies have the angels bring the gifts to the altar of heaven, e.g., the Latin Mass in the *Supplices*, the Greek anaphora of St. Mark (Brightman, LEW, p. 129), the Egyptian anaphora of Mark or Cyril (Brightman, LEW, p. 171).

[15] G. Aucher, *op. cit.*, pp. 392-393. All the petitions were identical except for the following minor differences : what is now the final petition had been divided into two separate ones : between these, the standard bidding to the Mother of God was said.

[16] This also appears in the same Armenian version (Aucher, *op. cit.*, p. 393).

The Lord's Prayer

The sentence introducing the *Our Father* is easily detachable from the main body of the *ektenia* : " And grant, Master, that with complete confidence and without condemnation we may dare call upon you, God of heaven, as Father, and say. . . . " Cyril of Jerusalem, introduces the Lord's Prayer with the words, " With a pure conscience, we name God as our Father and say. . . . " [17] The testimony of Cyril is the first we have of the Lord's Prayer being said at the Eucharistic Liturgy. [18] A little later (A.D. 386-398) at Antioch, Chrysostom also mentions the use of the Lord's Prayer at the Eucharistic Liturgy. Commenting on the duty of forgiveness, he refers to it in a way which suggests a similar introduction : " If we do this, we may then with a pure conscience come to this holy and tremendous table and boldly say the words that are contained in that prayer. " [19] The formula seems to have been fairly common since Gregory of Nyssa appears to be acquainted with it. [20] The ancient Liturgies of St. James and St. Mark as well as the Armenian version have similar but longer forms. [21]

The ancients appreciated the fact that it requires great boldness to recite the Lord's Prayer, to call almighty God a Father, even though the prayer was taught to us by Christ himself. [22] What pagan would have dared to call mighty Jupiter or Apollo " my Father " ? We dare to do so only because by baptism we have been made sons of God, partakers of his divine life not only in name but also in fact. It is a prayer proper to the children of God. No neophyte was allowed to say it, as Theodoret tells us before A.D. 458 : " We teach

[17] Cyril of Jerusalem, *Catechesis*, XXIII (*Mystag.*, V), 11-18 (PG 33, 1117).

[18] Let us repeat that there is some doubt that Cyril of Jerusalem actually wrote the *Mystagogic Catecheses*. The *Apostolic Constitutions*, Book VIII, though it represents the Eucharistic Liturgy from almost the same Syrian sphere, does not contain the Lord's Prayer.

[19] Chrysostom, *In Genes.*, XVIII, 8 (edit. Montfaucon 4, 268, or PG 53, 251).

[20] Gregory of Nyssa, *De or. Dom.*, ii (PG 44, 1140 D).

[21] Brightman, LEW, pp. 59, 135 f., 446.

[22] When writing about the Lord's Prayer, the Eastern Fathers frequently refer to the boldness and audacity of mere humans in saying it. Cf. Rousseau, " Le ' Pater ' dans la liturgie de la messe " in *Cours et conférences*, VII (Louvain, 1929), pp. 233 f.

this prayer to none of the uninitiated, only to the faithful. No uninitiated person would dare say : ' Our Father who art in heaven '... before receiving the grace of adoption. " [23]   The prohibition was very real. For years, the text of the Lord's Prayer was not written for fear of profanation. At the end of the fourth century, Ambrose still cautions : " Beware not to divulge carelessly the mysteries of the Creed and the Lord's Prayer.... " [24]   Even in the early times, the *Our Father* seems to have been the first prayer the neophytes said as they joined the faithful. [25]

In ancient Christendom, the Lord's Prayer had a close connection with Communion even outside the Eucharistic Liturgy. In several ancient texts, the petition for daily bread is correlated with the heavenly bread, the Eucharist. [26]   This, in fact, is the interpretation given in two of the oldest commentaries. [27]   It seems, then, that the *Our Father* was recited by the faithful at Communion long before its formal incorporation into the Liturgy. That is probably why it became a permanent part of the formal preparation for Communion in all the Eucharistic Liturgies. Although the *Our Father* is noneucharistic, every phrase may be accommodated to Eucharistic preparation. The daily bread refers actually to " bread that is sufficient for our maintenance and support, " as explained by Theophylactus. [28]

---

[23] Theodoret, *Haereticarum Jablarum compendium*, 5 (PG 83, 399).

[24] " *Cave, ne incaute symboli vel dominicae orationis divulges mysteria...,* " Ambrose, *De Cain*, 11, 35, 37 (PL 14, 353 B). Cf. also Rousseu, *op. cit.*, pp. 235 f.

[25] Cf. Dölger, *Antike u. Christentum*, 2 (1930), pp. 148 ff.; also A. Greiff, *Das älteste Pascha-ritual der Kirche* (Paderborn, 1929), pp. 126-130.

[26] Thus, Tertullian, *De or.*, chap. 6 (PL I, 1262-1263); Cyprian, *De or. Dom.*, chap. 18 (PL 4, 548-549); Juventus, *Ev. hist.*, I, 146 (PL 19, 133 A); Chromatius, *In Matt.*, 14, 5 (PL 20, 361 B) for others, cf. J. P. Bock, *Die Brotbitte des Vaterunsers* (Paderborn, 1911), pp. 110 ff.; also Chase, *The Lord's Prayer in the Early Church* (Cambridge, 1891), pp. 42-53; also J. Lebreton, *La vie et l'enseignement de J.C.N.S.*, II (Paris), pp. 78-80.

[27] In Cyril of Jerusalem's *Catechesis*, XXIII, (*Mystag.*, V, 11-18) (PG 33, 1117 A-1123 A) and Ambrose's *De sacramentis*, V, (Quasten, *op. cit.*, 168-170).

[28] Theophylactus (eleventh or twelfth century), *Enarrat. in Matt.*, 36 (PG 123, 440-441). Etymologically, ἐπιούσιον means either " necessary for subsistence " (from ἐπί + οὐσία) or " for the day that lies before us " (from ἐπί + ἰοῦσα, i.e., belonging to the coming day; cf. Prov. 27:1, LXX). This last rendition, though more probable, seems to make the phrase " this day " redundant. Perhaps the best way to translate the Aramaic idiom which reads literally " of today and the following day " would be " Give us our bread day by day. " Cf. Black, *An Aramaic Approach to the Gospels and Acts* (Oxford, 1946), pp. 149-153.

Such is essentially the interpretation given by Chrysostom, Gregory of Nyssa, Basil, Euthymius, and most modern exegetes. This is not the place to dwell on the exegesis of this great prayer, but we would like to draw attention to the first-person-plural form found from beginning to end. In his own personal communications with the Father, Christ speaks of him as *My Father*; the singular pronoun betokens the incommunicable Sonship of Christ resulting from the act of generation. Our sonship, on the other hand, is not by nature, but through an ineffable adoption brought about by the incarnation and redemption. [29] Through this sonship, all men are brothers and are drawn together as children into one family. The Lord teaches us, through the plural form, to bring all our brothers, all mankind, into our prayer. The form is all the more appropriate for the corporate *ecclesia* whose members are united by bonds closer than adoption. All the baptized are incorporated into one body and nourished by the one bread of heaven.

The version of the Lord's Prayer used in the Greek Byzantine Liturgy is the Koine (K), [30] while the Byzantine-Slav version is based on the *Slavonic Version* of the ninth century, which in turn is translated from the Greek. [31] The later codices of the Slavonic Version show many Hesychian and Caesarean readings; the earlier texts (tenth or eleventh century) seem to have been influenced by the Antiochene text used in Constantinople—but this does not seem to have affected the Lord's Prayer.

The doxology, so familiar to the non-Catholic Anglo-Saxons, is a liturgical addition which has found its way into several editions of Matthew 6:13, e.g., the Peshitta Version. First encountered in the *Didache* (but without the phrase *and the Kingdom*), the addition is probably the direct result of the ancient rule that every public prayer close with praise of God. [32] The Armenian Liturgy still uses the

[29] " For ye have not received the spirit of bondage again to fear but we have received the spirit of adoption, whereby we cry Abba, Father " (Rom. 8:15).

[30] Hanssens, *Institutiones liturgicae de ritibus orientalibus, De Missa rituum orientalium*, Vol. III (Rome, 1932), p. 488.

[31] The Slavonic version was begun by the Slav apostles, SS. Cyril and Methodius, who translated some of the sacred books. It was completed in the fifteenth century by Gennadius of Novgorod.

[32] *Didache*, chap. 8, 2. Cf. Chase, *op. cit.*, pp. 169 ff., or ANF, Vol. VII, p. 379.

exact wording found in the *Didache*. [33] The Byzantine Liturgy had the extended text by the ninth or tenth century. [34] The Greek Liturgies of St. James and St. Mark as well as the East Syrian Liturgy have it also. [35] The Syriac Liturgy of St. James, on the other hand, has the Greek doxology of the fourth century. [36]

Once the Lord's Prayer was formally incorporated into the Liturgy, it was natural that all the faithful should recite it aloud, since it was intended as a prayer of preparation for the Eucharist, and everyone was a communicant in the ancient Church. While all in attendance no longer receive Communion, the Eastern Churches still have this prayer sung by the people or the choir—never by the priest alone. [37] The Byzantine-Slav Liturgy is no exception : usually all the people sing it, though sometimes only the choir or cantors. [38] The present rubrics assign the *Our Father* to the choir, but all the responses in the Byzantine-Slav Rite are for the choir. [39] Older rubrics, however,

---

[33] Brightman, LEW, p. 446.

[34] Brightman, LEW, pp. 339-340. The early eighth century Armenian version of Chrysostom's Liturgy reads : " For yours is the kingdom, and the power, and the glory forever " (Aucher, *op. cit.*, p. 394).

[35] The Greek St. James, however, interjects other prayer-material (an " embolism ") between the Lord's Prayer and the doxology (Brightman, LEW, p. 60). The Lord's Prayer in the East Syrian Liturgy and that in St. Mark ends with the doxology found in the *Didache*—but the latter interpolates other prayer-material between it and the body of the prayer (Brightman, LEW, p. 136), while the former adds other prayer-material and *repeats* the doxology in an expanded form (Brightman, LEW, p. 296).

[36] Brightman, LEW, p. 100, and Rücker, *Die Jakobusanaphora. Mit dem griechischen Paralleltext* (Münster, 1923), p. 49. It too has other prayer-material between the Lord's Prayer and the doxology.

[37] The Armenian Rite has the cantors (Brightman's " clerks, " LEW, p. 446) or the choir singing the Lord's Prayer (cf. Rev. Luke Arakelian, *Armenian Liturgy, with an Outline of Armenian Church History* [Boston, 1951], p. 75; and G. Avedighian, *Liturgia della messa armena* [Venice, 1873], p. 53). A. King, in *The Rites of Eastern Christendom* (Vol. II [Rome, 1948], p. 631) has the choir or the people. On the other hand, Jungmann (*The Mass of the Roman Rite : Its Origins and Development*, Vol. II [New York, 1955], p. 287) and Hanssens, *op. cit.*, Vol. III, p. 489) assign it to " clerics, " but neither gives any sources. Other partial exceptions are the West Syrian and Maronite Rites, where the celebrant begins the first phrase and the people continue (Brightman, LEW, p. 100, and Hanssens, *op. cit.*, Vol. III, p. 489).

[38] Quoting Harnykevitsch (90), Jungmann (*op. cit.*, Vol. II, p. 287, n. 53) says only the director (or chief person) says the Lord's Prayer among the Ukrainians. Among the Ukrainians in Canada and the U.S.A., this is done very seldom.

[39] *Ordo Celebrationis* (Rome, 1944), p. 71, no. 137.

are clearer on this point, assigning the prayer specifically to the people. [40]

In the West, only the ancient Gallican Church followed the East in having the Lord's Prayer chanted by all the people. [41]   The West differed early on this point, perhaps from the very beginning. [42] But now, in the Latin Church, the celebrant says it with the people. In one way or another, therefore, the Lord's Prayer is the people's Communion Prayer in the Universal Church.

[40] E.g., *Cod. Barberini, gr.* 336 of eighth or ninth century (Brightman, LEW, p. 339).

[41] Gregory of Tours (*De mir. s. Martini*, II, 30 [PL 71, 954 f.]) recounts the incident of the mute woman who was miraculously cured at the moment when the *Pater noster* was begun during Sunday Mass.   She then " began to chant the holy prayer with the rest of the people. "   Cf. also Caesarius, *Serm.* 73 (PL 39, 2277).

[42] Cf. Gregory the Great (*Ep.* IX, 12 [PL 77, 957]), who unequivocally states that at Rome, in contrast to the practice of the Greeks, the Lord's Prayer is said by the celebrant alone.   This custom seems to have already been in vogue in the African Church during Augustine's time, since he says that " the Lord's Prayer is said daily at the altar and the faithful hear it " (*Serm.* 58, 10, 12 [PL 38, 299]).

CHAPTER LXVI

THE PRAYER OF INCLINATION, SMALL ELEVATION, AND *KOINONIKON*

The priest turns toward the people and blesses them while he says :
Peace be to all.

People : **And to your spirit.**

Deacon : **Bow your heads to the Lord.**

People : **To you, O Lord.**

We thank you, O King invisible, who formed all things by your infinite power and in the greatness of your mercy brought all things into being out of nothingness. Master, look down from heaven on those who have bowed their heads before you, for they bow not to flesh and blood, but before you, awe-inspiring God. Therefore, O Lord, distribute to all of us for our own good and according to each one's need the offerings set forth here : voyage with those sailing upon the sea, journey with those traveling on land, and cure the sick, O Physician of souls and bodies.

Then aloud : **By the grace, mercies, and love for mankind of your only-begotten Son, with whom you are blessed, together with your all-holy, good, and life-giving Spirit, now and always and for ever and ever.**

People : **Amen.**

Priest, again silently : **Lord Jesus Christ, our God, look down from your holy dwelling place, from the throne of glory in your kingdom; come, make us holy, since you are seated on high with the Father and invisibly present here with us. Deign to give us with your own mighty hand your spotless body and precious blood, and through us to all the people.**

The deacon, standing before the royal doors, wraps his orar *about himself in the form of a cross; that is, if he had not already done so during the Lord's Prayer.   He remains in the same place outside the sanctuary as he makes three small bows with the priest while they both recite each time :*

O God, be merciful to me a sinner. [1]

When the priest uncovers the chalice and extends his hand to take the holy bread, the deacon sings out in a loud voice :

Let us be attentive!

Lifting up the holy bread a little, the priest intones :
Holy things to the holy.

People : **One is holy, one is Lord, Jesus Christ to the glory of God the Father.   Amen.**

Then the Communion hymn proper to the day or feast : the koinonikon *or* prychasten, *ending with a triple Alleluia.*

The series of preparatory acts and prayers for Communion continues.   All this is done, as Theodore of Mopsuestia explains, " so that all of us who are present may receive (Holy Communion). " [2] In the rite described by Theodore, which differed slightly from the Byzantine Liturgy today, there was : (1) a " prayer of gratitude for these great gifts, " (2) a blessing of the people accompanying the fraction, (3) the prayer of the priest, offered after he had prayed for those who presented the gifts, in which he asked " that this sacrifice may be acceptable to God and that the grace of the Holy Spirit may come upon all, so that we may be able to be worthy of its communion, and not receive it to punishment, " and finally, (4) another blessing just before the " Holy things to the holy. " [3]   The North Syrian rite in the days of Chrysostom was the same, except that the Lord's Prayer was added between the two blessings, as we have seen above (p. 139).   The blessing found today in the Byzantine Liturgy immediately after the *Our Father* is the second blessing mentioned by Theodore.

[1] The Russian recension has : " O God, cleanse me a sinner, and have mercy on me. "

[2] Theodore of Mopsuestia, *Catecheses,* VI (edit. Mingana, *Commentary of Theodore of Mopsuestia on the Lord's Prayer and on the Sacraments of Baptism and the Eucharist* [Cambridge, 1933], p. 107).

[3] Mingana, *edit. cit.,* pp. 105, 108.

Prayer of Inclination

The "Prayer of Inclination" which follows the blessing today is the ancient prayer of the "Laying on of Hands," in Sarapion. [4] The form is the same as that in the ancient dismissals. The deacon exclaimed, "Bow down your heads" (Chrysostom), [5] or "Bow down (your heads) and receive the blessing" *(Apostolic Constitutions)*. [6] Whereupon the celebrant would impart a lengthy prayer-blessing. The wording of the prayers differed. King mentions that this particular prayer of inclination dates from the fifth or sixth century, but he gives no source. [7] There are, however, some striking similarities between it and the comparable pre-Communion prayer found in the *Apostolic Constitutions* immediately after the deacon's biddings. [8]

Apostolic Constitutions	*Byzantine Chrysostom*
1. Addressed to " God the Father "	1. Addressed to " God the Father "
2. " great in design "	2. " great in his mercy "
3. " powerful in works "	3. " who formed all things by his infinite power "
4. " Look down upon us and upon this thy flock... "	4. " Look down from heaven upon those who have bowed their heads before you... "
5. " Obtain the good things laid up for us... "	5. " Distribute to all of us for our own good and according to each one's need the offerings set forth... "
6. " ...through thy Christ, with whom glory, honor, praise, acclaim and thanksgiving be to	6. " Through the grace, mercies, and love for men, of your only-begotten Son, with whom,

---

[4] *Bishop Serapion's Prayerbook*, trans. J. Wordsworth (London, 1910), p. 65, no. 3.

[5] Chrysostom, *In II Cor. homil.*, 18, 3 (edit. Montfaucon 10, 568 B).

[6] *Apostolic Constitutions*, Book VIII, see above, pp. 111, 113, etc.

[7] *The Rites of Eastern Christendom* (Rome, 1948), Vol. II, p. 207. No source has been found older than the early eighth century Armenian version of Chrysostom's Liturgy (G. Aucher, *La version armena della liturgia di S. Giovanni Crisostomo, fatta sul principio dell'VIII secolo*, XPYCOCTOMIKA [Rome, 1908], p. 394).

[8] *Apostolic Constitutions*, Book VIII; see above, p. 140.

thee and to the Holy Spirit forever. Amen."	together with your all-holy, good, and life-giving Spirit, you are blessed now and always and for ever and ever. Amen."

This Byzantine prayer-collect came originally after some biddings. This is confirmed by such phrases as "voyage with those sailing upon the sea, journey with those traveling on land, cure the sick"—all of which are easily recognizable as *ektenia* petitions. The material aspects of these petitions make them almost incongruous as a Communion preparation, as indeed they are in their present position. Judging from the *Apostolic Constitutions*, which even included good weather and productive crops in its pre-Communion biddings (see above, p. 140), these petitions were moved, entirely unchanged, from the dismissals to this position.

The prayer seems to have been composed at a time when the ancient pattern was being followed, that is, long before the early eighth century, when it appeared in the Armenian version or in the *Codex Barberini*. [9]

By contrast, the prayer following the doxology shows unmistakable signs of more recent composition. Ancient liturgical prayers were addressed to the Father, while this one is addressed to the Son. The ancient prayers were corporate; this one is individual and personal. Finally, the lack of a doxology is sufficient to attribute it to the early eighth century, when it first appeared in the Liturgy. [10] It may have been introduced as a private devotion, for we have a manuscript from the next century with the rubric, " *and he prays for himself secretly.*" [11] Its place in the Liturgy was still not settled, as is evident from some later texts that either lack this prayer entirely or contain another prayer in its place. [12]

[9] As contained in Aucher, *op. cit.*, p. 394, and Brightman, LEW, p. 340.

[10] In the Armenian version of Chrysostom's Liturgy, cf. Aucher, *op. cit.*, pp. 394-395; cf. also *Cod. Barberini*, Brightman, LEW, p. 341.

[11] *Cod. Grottaf.*, Γ.Β. VII, of ninth or tenth century; cf. Dmitrievsky, *Opysanie liturgicheskikh rukopisej khraniaschikhsia v bibliotekakh pravoslavnago vostoka*, Vol. II, *Euchologia* (Kiev, 1901), p. 158.

[12] The *Cod. Porphyrios*, for example, contains a prayer which seems to be a mutilated version of that found in the Liturgy of St. James and St. Mark; cf. Dmitrievsky, *op. cit.*, II, pp. 824, 828, 950; also Krasnoseltsev, *Svidinia o nikotorikh liturgicheskikh rukopis'akh Vatikanskoi biblioteki* (Kazan, 1885), p. 141.

The same personal, private approach may be seen in the short prayer of the publican : " O God be merciful to me a sinner " (Luke 18:13)—one of the latest additions to the Byzantine Liturgy. It is not in the *Constitutions* of Philotheus, nor in Goar's edition of Basil's Liturgy (1730), but appears in Goar's Liturgy of Chrysostom. [13]   The petition seems, then, to have passed from the Liturgy of Chrysostom to that of Basil.   The Russian recension has a slightly different wording, but this is not surprising since the pre-Communion and Communion ritual in the Slav Church remained unsettled for centuries.

Wrapping the orarion.   The deacon, symbolizing a ministering angel, wraps his orarion around himself crosswise to represent the wings of the cherubim that stand about the throne of God.   The rubric may have had a utilitarian origin : to prevent the flowing vestments from hampering the distribution of Communion.   The symbolism was probably attached to the act during the thirteenth or fourteenth century, at a time when symbolical interpretations were multiplied.

Elevation : " Holy Things to the Holy "

The *Didache*, written toward the end of the first century, is the source of many expressions that later became part of the Eucharistic Liturgies.   There is, for instance : " If anyone is holy, let him come nigh : if anyone is not, let him repent. " [14]   The meaning is close to that of the fourth-century Syrian invitation to Communion : " Holy things to the holy. "   Cyril's rite in Jerusalem and the North Syrian of the *Apostolic Constitutions* have the same formula. [15]   Chrysostom has it also at Antioch. [16]   The *Apostolic Constitutions*, [17] like the present Byzantine ritual, stresses the importance of the invitation by having the deacon call the people to attention.   Jerusalem and

[13] Goar, *Euchologion*, pp. 65, 148.

[14] *Didache*, chap. 10, 6; see above, p. 25.

[15] Cyril of Jerusalem, *Catechesis*, XXIII (*Mystag.*, V), 19 (PG 33, 1124 A); *Apostolic Constitutions*, Book VIII (cf. above, p. 141).

[16] Chrysostom, *In Matt. homil.*, VII, 6 (edit. Montfaucon 7, 114 A, or PG 57, 80 A); cf. also *In Hebr. homil.*, XVII, 4-5 (edit. Montfaucon 12, 169-170, or PG 63, 132-133).

[17] *Apostolic Constitutions*, Book VIII; cf. above, p. 140.

North Syria had the same response, referring to Christ : " One is holy, one is the Lord Jesus Christ.... " [18] Several decades later, the scriptural verses, Luke 2:14 and Matt. 21:9, were added. The Alexandrian Liturgy had it too, as we know from Cyril of Alexandria (A.D. 444) and Didymus (A.D. 313-399?). [19] At present, it is found in all the Oriental Liturgies.

The invitation " Holy things to the holy " cannot be rendered perfectly in English. The Greek ἅγιος, like the Latin *sanctus*, means, not that which is " good " or " holy " in itself, but rather, " that which belongs to God. " St. Paul, for instance, writing to the Corinthians, calls them ἅγιοι despite their quarrels and disssensions. In English, he would not be calling them " *holy ones,* " " *saints,* " yet he called them ἅγιοι —to convey the idea that they " belonged to God, " or that they were " the chosen of God. " A better English translation would read " The things of God for the people of God. " In the ancient Church, the communicants were not " saints " but frail human beings like the rest of us, and they would have been the first to admit it—but they did regard themselves as the people of God, not because of any presumed personal sanctity, but because they were members of the body of Christ, and had been redeemed by the Son of God. We have maintained the traditional translation because it is more familiar.

All the Oriental Liturgies have maintained the same invitation, but only the Byzantine and the Armenian have the original response.[20] The others have changed it almost everywhere into praise of the Holy Trinity. [21] Early evidence of the change appears in Theodore of Mopsuestia who has " One Father is holy, one Son is holy, one Spirit is holy.... " [22] Then he explains, as do later authors, the

---

[18] Cyril of Jerusalem, *Catechesis*, XXIII (*Mystag.*, V), 19 (PG 33, 1124 A); *Apostolic Constitutions*, Book VIII (see above, p. 141), though the scriptural verses Luke 2:14 and Matt. 21:9 were added.

[19] Cyril of Alexandria, *In Ioannem*, IV (PG 73, 700 C), and *In Ioannem*, XII, 20 (PG 74, 695/6 D); Didymus of Alexandria, *De Trinitate*, II, 6 (PG 39, 428 A); III, 13 (PG 39, 861 A), etc.; however, Didymus does not seem to connect it with the Liturgy.

[20] Cf. Brightman, LEW, p. 447, lines 12-14, for the Armenian Liturgy.

[21] Cf. Hanssens, *Institutiones liturgicae de ritibus orientalibus, De Missa rituum orientalium*, Vol. III (Rome, 1932), p. 499.

[22] Theodore of Mopsuestia, *Serm. catech.*, VI (edit. Rücker, *Ritus Baptismi et Missae, quem descripsit Theodorus ep. Mopsuestenus in sermonibus catecheticis* (Münster, 1933), p. 36.

prominence given to the oneness of the divine nature. The development was caused by the theological controversies of the time. In the East Syrian Church, the change seems not to have encountered any difficulties, for evidence of the Trinitarian response is unwavering from the beginning of the sixth century, in Narsai, Abraham bar Lipheh, and Ps.-George of Arbela. [23] In the West Syrian Church however, as late as the eighth century, James of Edessa complains that instead of the trinitarian response, some churches have the christological one, " One is holy, one is Lord, one Jesus Christ to the glory of the Father. Amen. " [24]

Further attention is focused on the body of the Lord through the elevation. In the Byzantine Liturgy, the bread is raised over the *diskos* with the words " Holy things to the holy. " In other Rites, the elevation varies, but always draws attention to the sacrament. In the Coptic Liturgy, for example, the celebrant elevates the host over his head, then makes the sign of the cross with it over the chalice [25]. In the West Syrian Church, the priest takes the paten in both hands, raises it to the level of his eyes, and moves it crosswise from East to West, from North to South, and finally touches his eyes with it. [26] He does the same with the chalice. With the Maronites, the elevation is performed in an almost identical way, [27] The only Oriental Rites which do not have an elevation are the Chaldean and the Ethiopian. [28]

[23] Narsai (A.D. 502-507), *Homily* XVII (edit. R. H. Connolly, *The Liturgical Homilies of Narsai* [Cambridge, 1909], pp. 26-27); Abraham bar Lipheh (eighth century), *Interpretatio officiorum* (edit. Connolly, p. 179); Ps.-George of Arbela (ninth century), *Expositio officiorum ecclesiae*, tr. IV, 25 (edit. Connolly, pp. 75-76).

[24] James of Edessa (A.D. 708), *Epistula ad Thomam presbyteram*, in Dionysius bar Salibi, *Expositio liturgiae*, chap. 3 (edit. H. Labourt, CSCO, 9-10 [38-39, 39]); however, George, Bishop of the Arabs (A.D. 724) in his *Explicatio mysteriorum ecclesiae* (edit. Connolly and Codrington, *Two Commentaries on the Jacobite Liturgy, by George Bishop of the Arab Tribes, and Moses Bar Kepha* [London, 1913], fols. 188 b-189 a, p. 19) and Moses bar Kepha (A.D. 903), *Explanatio mysteriorum oblationis* (edit. Connolly and Codrington, fol. 176 a, pp. 86-87) give the trinitarian response.

[25] Brightman, LEW, p. 184, line 29; J. Bute, *The Coptic Morning Service for the Lord's Day* (London, 1882), pp. 122-123; the *Euchologion of Cairo* (1898), p. 99.

[26] Missal of Sarfeh (1922), pp. 85-86; cf. A. Rücker, *Sie syrische Jakobusanaphora. Mit dem griechischen Paralleltext* (Münster, 1923), p. 72.

[27] C. Missal of Beirut (1908), pp. 40-41; Prince Maximilian of Saxony, *Missa Syro-Maronitica quam ex lingua syriaca in idioma latinum traduxit cum commentario praevio M. pr. S.* (Ratisbon, 1907), pp. 50-51.

[28] Hanssens, *op. cit.*, III, p. 499.

The elevation does not seem to have originated at the same time as the proclamation, " Holy things to the holy. " Neither Cyril of Jerusalem nor the *Apostolic Constitutions* mentions it.   The latter, with its extensive text and rubrics, would have certainly mentioned it, had it been used in the North Syrian Church.

The origin of the elevation may probably be found in a fifth-century practice in Constantinople.   In one of his homilies on *Hebrews*, Chrysostom mentions that the priest " lifted his hand. " [29] According to Cyril of Scythopolis, this same practice was found in the sixth-century Syro-Palestinian Church. [30]   This gesture may have corresponded to the action of a public speaker seeking attention. The practice of raising the holy bread itself must have begun in the Church of Constantinople during the sixth or seventh century, for about the middle of the latter century, Maximus the Confessor writes about it several times. [31]   Another seventh-century author, Anastasius the Sinaite, tells us that the bread was elevated in the Syro-Palestinian Church. [32]   From then on, the practice spread to almost all the Churches of Christendom.

In the Latin Mass, the elevation of the species after the consecration is in a certain sense a counterpart of the Eastern ritual, but it is of comparatively late development. [33]   There is in the Latin Mass a closer parallel in the " showing " of the host during the *Ecce agnus Dei*. . . .   Both the act and the expression *Ecce* have the same purpose as the elevation in the Oriental Liturgies, since they are expressly designed to draw attention to the body of Christ, but they are not derived from the Eastern practice.   The proclamation " Holy things to the holy " and its response, " One is holy " may have been used

[29] Chrysostom, *In Hebr. homil.*, XVII, 4-5 (edit. Montfaucon 12, 169-170, PG 63, 132-133).

[30] Cyril of Scythopolis, *Vita S. Euthymii*, 81 (edit. Cotelier, EGM, II, pp. 268-269).

[31] Maximus the Confessor, *Scholia in Ecclesiasticam Hierarchiam*, c. 3, II (PG 4, 137 A); also *Relatio motionis*, IV (PG 90, 117 B).

[32] Anastasius the Sinaite, *Oratio de sacra synaxi* (PG 89, 844 A).   It could be that Ps.-Dionysius the Areopagite was referring to the same practice in his *De ecclesiastica hierarchia*, III, 2 (PG 3, 424 D); also, *ibid.*, III, 3 (PG 3, 443 C).

[33] Cf. E. Dumoutet, *Le désir de voir l'hostie* (Paris, 1926), for a comprehensive history of the Latin elevation; also, Jungmann, *The Mass of the Roman Rite : Its Origins and Development* (New York, 1955), II, pp. 202-217.

in the West in some isolated instances during the fifth century. [34]
The *Sancta sanctis* corresponds to the sixth-century Roman custom
which had the deacon call out before Communion : *Si quis non com-
municat, det locum.* [35]

The Communion Hym : Koinonikon

To emphasize the sanctity of the moment of the reception of the
sacrament by the celebrating clergy, the royal doors are closed and
the curtain is drawn.   This custom is observed faithfully in Russian
churches, but only occasionally in Ukrainian churches.   Even if done
in an orderly way, the receiving of Communion still entails considerable movement of the concelebrants around the sanctuary.   All this
activity distracts the faithful; hence, it is better to hide it from view.
Later, the practice was given a symbolic meaning : to remind the
faithful of the sanctity of the Upper Room, the holiness of the Last
Supper. [36]

It was natural that the distribution of Holy Communion be
accompanied by song, especially when the number of communicants
was large.   This was the original role of the Communion hymn, or
koinonikon.   In the present Byzantine Liturgy, it accompanies only
the Communion of the clergy.   The *koinonikon*, known usually as
the *prychasten* in the Slav Church, is begun immediately after the
response, " One is holy, one is Lord,... " and must be finished in
time for the invitation to the faithful : "Approach with fear of
God.... "   The *koinonikon* is usually a verse from one of the Psalms,
ending with a triple Alleluia.   It is always proper to the day or
occasion.

The *koinonikon* has changed little since its origin in the fourth
century.   Cyril of Jerusalem is the first to describe it but he does
not make it quite clear whether the psalm was sung during the
distribution of Holy Communion or as a prelude to it : " You hear

---

[34] Cf. G. Morin, *Revue Bénéd.*, 40 (1928), pp. 136 ff., and L. Brou, *Le
' Sancta sanctis ' en Occident*, JThSt, 46 (1945), pp. 160-178 and 47 (1946),
pp. 11-29.

[35] Gregory the Great, *Dial.*, II, 23 (PL 66, 178 f.).   Cf. Jungmann, *op. cit.*,
II, p. 341, n. 4.

[36] K. Nikolsky, *Posobie k izucheniu Ustava Bogosluzhenia pravoslavnoi tserkvy*
(St. Petersburg, 1907), p. 442.

then the voice of the soloist singing the psalms, inviting you with divine melody to partake of the Sacred Mysteries and saying, ' Taste and see that the Lord is good. ' " [37] The "taste and see" was probably the responsory verse (Ps. 33:9) originally intoned by the cantor. Chrysostom reports a little later that in Antioch the *koinonikon* was a responsorial song, that is, one in which the people responded with an unchanging refrain (ὑποψάλλουσιν). At Antioch, Psalm 144 was sung and the responsory verse was, " The eyes of all look hopefully to thee, and thou givest them their food in due time. " [38] Participation by the people is implied in Jerome's remark : " *Quotidie coelesti pane saturati dicimus : Gustate et videte, quam suavis est Dominus.* " [39] Here, Psalm 33 was sung. The same psalm is indicated in the *Apostolic Constitutions* for the North Syrian Rite. [40] The psalm seems to have been chosen freely, but Psalm 33 appears to have been the most popultar. [41] The Byzantine Liturgy has Psalm 33 in its entirety at the distribution of the *antidoron*, or during the cleaning of the sacred vessels (see below, p. 731). The first eleven verses are also used during solemn Vespers, after the blessing of the bread, wheat, oil, and wine.

The early Western Church also had a Communion chant. In Africa, Augustine invites the faithful to Communion several times with the sixth verse of Psalm 33 : " Come ye to him and be enlightened. " [42] Some verses of this psalm, combined with the triple Alleluia, survived in the *antiphona ad accedentes* of the Mozarabic Liturgy. [43] Traces of the same responsorial use of the Alleluia are found in the Armenian, and in the East-and West Syrian Liturgies, [44] also as a finale to the Byzantine *koinonikon*. A similar combination of

---

[37] Cyril of Jerusalem, *Catechesis*, XXIII (*Mystag.*, V), 20 (Quasten, *Monumenta eucharistica et liturgia vetustissima* [Bonn, 1935-1937], 198).

[38] Chrysostom, *In Ps.* 144, *expos.*, 1 (edit. Montfaucon 5, 466 E, or PG 55, 464).

[39] Jerome, *In Isaiam comment.*, II, 5, 20 (PG 24, 86 D).

[40] *Apostolic Constitutions*, Book VIII; cf. above, p. 142. It was chanted responsorially.

[41] Cf. H. Leclercq, " Communion, " DACL, III, 2428-2433.

[42] Augustine, *Serm.*, 225, 4 (PL 38, 1098); *Serm. Denis*, 3, 3 (PL 46, 828).

[43] *Missale mixtum* (PL 85, 564 f.).

[44] Cf. Brightman, LEW, pp. 449-450, 299, 102.

psalm and Alleluia is still used in the Coptic and the Ethiopian Rites.[45]

Different forms of the *koinonika* evolved in both East and West as the years went by. Today, for example, the Byzantine-Slav Church has verses from many psalms. The propers are specified in the *Ustav* or *Typikon*, which also indicates the proper usage in cases of concurrence.[46] The most common *koinonika* are the following :

1. For Sundays, Psalm 148:1 : " Praise ye the Lord from the heavens, praise ye him in the high places. "

2. Holy days in honor of the Mother of God, Psalm 115:13 : " I will take the chalice of salvation, and I will call upon the name of the Lord. "

3. In honor of the Apostles, Psalm 18:5 : " Their sound hath gone forth unto all the earth, and their words unto the ends of the world. "

4. In honor of any saint, Psalm 111:7 : " The just shall be in everlasting remembrance, he shall not fear the evil hearing. "

5. For the dead, Psalm 64:5 and Psalm 101:3 : " Blessed are they whom thou hast chosen and taken to thee, O Lord, and their memory to all generations. "

6. In honor of the Holy Cross, Psalm 4:7 : " The light of thy countenance, O Lord, is signed upon us. "

The triple Alleluia comes at the end.

The Communion of the clergy may take longer than the singing of the *koinonikon*. In most cases, it will be enough to repeat the triple Alleluia. Otherwise, the time may be taken up by singing other hymns, especially Eucharistic hymns. In dissident Slav churches, semi-liturgical Communion prayers are recited; there is a short sermon or even a reading—especially in monasteries or seminaries. Such a reading is usually taken from the Holy Fathers of the Church or from the lives of the saints. This is not a novel practice; it reaches back into the history of ancient Russia and Byzantium. According to the *Ustav*, the six or seven special liturgical readings (*Ustavnykh chtenii*)[47] proper to all major feasts are considered suitable as Communion readings.

[45] I.e., Psalm 150; cf. Brightman, LEW, pp. 185, 240.

[46] Nikolsky, *op. cit.*, pp. 447-448.

[47] Found after the *Kathismata* of the Psalter, after the Third and Sixth Hymn of the Canon, or at the end, before the Canonical Hour of Prime.

CHAPTER LXVII

THE FRACTION AND COMMINGLING

After making a small bow, the deacon enters the sanctuary through the south door and takes his place at the right of the priest.   He makes another small bow and says to the priest :

Sir, break the holy bread.

Reverently, the priest breaks the large host, the ahnets, *into four parts : that is, he first breaks it vertically into two parts; the part which has the inscription XC and KA he holds in his right hand and places on the* diskos; *the part which he holds in his left hand he then divides transversely between the letters IC and NI.   The particle bearing the letters IC he places on the upper part of the* diskos; *the one bearing NI, he puts on the left side of the* diskos.   *Then he takes the unbroken half of the* ahnets *and breaks it transversely between the letters XC and KA.   The particle bearing the letters XC he places on the lower part of the* diskos *and the particle KA he puts on the right side of the* diskos.   *In this way the position of the particles forms the sign of the cross.   While breaking the bread, he recites the following prayer in a low voice :*

Broken and distributed is the Lamb of God, broken but never dismembered, eaten yet never consumed, sanctifying those who receive.

Pointing to the chalice with his orar, *the deacon says to the priest :*

Sir, fill the holy chalice.

The priest takes the particle bearing the letters IC, makes the sign of the cross with it over the chalice, and drops it into the chalice, saying :

The fullness of the Holy Spirit.

Deacon : **Amen.**

After the fraction, the priest wipes his fingers over the holy diskos.

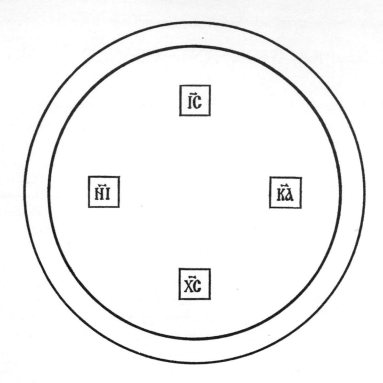

The Fraction

At the Last Supper, Jesus broke the bread before giving it to his
disciples (Matt. 26:26; of also Mark 14:22; Luke 22:19). Obviously,
the bread had to be divided in order to be distributed. But, as at
any Jewish *chabûrah*, the breaking of the bread at the primitive
Eucharist had a deeper meaning : " For we being many are one
bread, one body : all that partake of one bread " (I Cor. 10:17). In
fact, this breaking and the symbolism of unity attached to the bread
were so important that the " Breaking of the Bread " was the oldest
name for the celebration of the Eucharist.

After the Eucharist had been separated from the common meal,
the ceremony of bread-breaking continued to play an important role
in both gatherings (in the agape and in the Eucharistic celebration)
because it was still regarded in the old Jewish sense of imparting
oneness and unity. When congregations became large, however, to
the extent that there were not enough particles for all the commu-

nicants from breaking up the *one loaf* (even a very large one), more than one loaf had to be used by the priest in celebrating the Eucharist. We can get a fairly good idea of how many particles were needed for Communion in any church by the number of clergy attached to it. Some hundred years after Chrysostom, Hagia Sophia in Constantinople (and the three churches belonging to it) had about four hundred twenty-five clerics, with an additional one hundred doorkeepers. [1] In accordance with Eastern custom, most of them would have concelebrated on numerous occasions, and even if some of them did not partake, many did. The additional particles required for the faithful could not have been broken from one loaf. More loaves had to be used. When this happened, the symbolism of oneness was lost. In some localities, the Church flourished; in others, it did not, so that the need for multiple loaves did not arise simultaneously in all churches, but it seems to have started in some congregations as early as the second century. This undoubtedly had some influence on changing the original name from the " breaking of the Bread " to the " Eucharist "—but the symbolism positively had to be changed from that of unity to that of Christ's body being " broken " on the cross. The unity formerly expressed through the " one loaf" was then indicated through the practice of taking the bread for the sacrament from the people's offerings. Small loaves from many " offerers " were " gathered together " for the one sacrifice. [2]

Toward the end of the fourth century, symbolic " explanations " multiply. Chrysostom, commenting on Paul, explains : " But why does he also add ' which we break '? While one may see this being done in the Eucharist, on the cross it was not so, but the very opposite. For ' A bone of him, ' saith someone, ' shall not be broken. ' But what he did not suffer on the cross, he suffers in the sacrifice for your sake and submits himself to being broken, that he

---

[1] Justinian's decree of A.D. 535 limited the clergy to that number. Cf. *Nov.*, 3, para. 1 (*Imp. Iustiniani Novellae*) edit. K. E. Zachariä von Lingenthal, I, p. 71.

[2] Later, this in turn formed the basis for the practice of taking out a particle from each loaf for the sacrifice. Whatever the reasons prompting this later change, it still afforded opportunity for each of the faithful to participate in an intimate way by providing at least a particle from his loaf.

may fill all men. " [3] In the next centuries, many interpretations develop this idea, although there is nothing in the record of the Last Supper suggesting that Christ made any point of the broken bread representing his body to be " broken " on the cross.

According to Theodore of Mopsuestia (*d.* A.D. 423) the breaking was meant to show how the Lord " distributed " his presence among many, as after his resurrection he revealed himself and " distributed his appearance among men, " i.e., the women at the grave, the disciples at Emmaus, the apostles, etc. [4] Narsai gives a similar explanation : " And now, through the receiving of his body, he appears to the sons of the Church; and they believe in him and receive from him the pledge of life. " [5] Eutychius [6] (*d.* A.D. 582) and later authors of the past generally regard the breaking (a violent separation) as a figure of Christ's death on the cross. This meaning was incorporated into the text of many Liturgies—the West Syrian, the Ethiopian, the Byzantine [7] and even the old Gallic Liturgies. [8]

Later, another problem arose. No matter how small the loaves brought by the faithful, not all could be used for the sacrifice because of the danger of consecrating too much bread. Only some could be selected, the surplus being used for the common meal after the Liturgy, given away to the poor, etc. In such an arrangement, however, the yearning to have one's bread used for the sacrifice was unfulfilled for most of the faithful. The Latin Church, for example, when it began using unleavened bread, had individual hosts that were not provided by the faithful. As we have seen, in the Byzantine

---

[3] Chrysostom, *In I Cor. Homil.*, XXIV, 2 (edit. Montfaucon 10, 213 C, or PG 61, 200). Here, of course, the breaking of the Eucharistic bread does not necessarily mean from one loaf. It can be interpreted either way—from one loaf or from several. The meaning given here by Chrysostom may have been suggested much earlier, for we find expanded versions of Paul's I Cor. 11:24 in both Hippolytus and Sarapion. Cf. above, pp. 58, 94.

[4] Theodore of Mopsuestia, *Sermones catech.*, VI (Rücker, *Ritus Baptismi et Missae, quem descripsit Theodorus ep. Mopsuestenus in sermonibus catecheticis* [Münster, 1933], pp. 34 f.).

[5] Narsai, *Hom.*, 17 (edit. Connolly, *The liturgical Homilies of Narsai* [Cambridge, 1909], p. 24).

[6] Eutychius, *De pasch.*, chap. 3 (PG 86, 2396 A).

[7] Brightman, LEW, pp. 62, 97, 98, 239 f., 393, etc.

[8] Cf. Jungmann, *The Mass of the Roman Rite : Its Origins and Development*, Vol. II (New York, 1955), p. 302.

Church, particles were cut from each loaf. For this, the liturgical lance was invented. The present ritual of the *proskomidia* is the final stage of this evolution. It also marks the end of the breaking of the bread for the faithful's Communion. The only remaining trace of it is the ritual fraction of the host by the celebrant. Then came the practice of " commingling, " that is, the placing of a fragment of the broken bread into the chalice, " to show that they are not separable, that they are one in power and that they impart the same grace to those receiving them, " as Theodore of Mopsuestia explains. [9] He is the first to mention it. About a century later, Narsai (*c.* A.D. 502) also explains : " He unites them... the body with the blood, and the blood with the body... that everyone may confess that the body and the blood are one. " [10] Theodore indicates also that the celebrant makes the sign of the cross with the bread over the blood and with the blood over the bread before the commingling. [11] The Byzantines still make the sign of the cross with the bread over the chalice before dropping it into the consecrated wine. The early Latins also made a single sign of the cross with the particle over the chalice before the commingling. [12] Later, the Latin Church universally adopted the threefold sign of the cross, while the Byzantines kept to the one. The Syrian St. James and the Egyptian Liturgies have the priest first dip the particle in the chalice and then make the sign of the cross. The Greek St. James has the sign of the cross made with a bread-particle that has been dipped in consecrated wine, over the undipped particle; then the sign of the cross is made with the undipped particle over the dipped one.

After the fifth century, complicated arrangements of the particles appeared. At first the *prosphora* from which the celebrant and the assisting clergy received Communion were broken into as many pieces as the celebrant wished. As late as the early eighth century,

---

[9] Theodore of Mopsuestia, *Sermones catech.*, VI (edit. Rücker, *op. cit.*, p. 54).

[10] Narsai, *Hom.*, 21 (edit. Connolly, *op. cit.*, p. 59).

[11] Theodore of Mopsuestia, *Sermones catech.*, VI (edit. Rücker, *op. cit.*, p. 54).

[12] E.g., Sacramentary of *Codex Padua* (*Cod. Pad.*, D 47, fol. 11 r-100 r; edit. K. Mohlberg, *Die älteste erreichbare Gestalt der* Liber Sacramentorum Anni Circuli *der römischen Kirche* [Münster, 1927], no. 893); *Ordo* of St. Amand (Duchesne, *Christian Worship : Its Origin and Evolution*, 462); also *Eclogae* (PL 105, 1329). The triple sign of the cross, however, also appears in isolated instances, e.g., *Ordo Rom.*, I, no. 18 f. (PL 78, 945 f.); *Ordo Rom.*, II, no. 13 (PL 78, 975).

Germanus of Constantinople still does not specify the number, but merely states that "the body of the Lord is divided into separate, individual pieces." [13] Perhaps the particles were arranged according to some plan, even before the *proskomidia* had evolved after its transfer to the beginning of the Liturgy. The Syrian Jacobites keep the people occupied while the priest is making the fraction, by having the deacon chant the *kathuliki* (or *brodiki*)—a series of intercessions similar to those found in the Byzantine *proskomidia*. Excluding the later Byzantine addition of the proper names of saints reveals a close similarity :

I. Over the "Lamb"

Byzantine Proskomidia	Syrian Kathuliki
1. You have redeemed us from the curse of the law by your precious blood.... You have bestowed immortality to men.	1. By the blood of his cross he reconciled and united (knit) heavenly things with the things of earth.... And the third day, he rose again from the sepulchre (Brightman, LEW, p. 97, lines 27-34.)
2. The Lamb of God who takes away the sins of the world is being sacrificed for the life and salvation of the world.	2. Thou art the Lamb of God that takest away the sin of the world. Do thou pardon our offenses and forgive our sins and set us on thy right hand. (Brightman, LEW, p. 99, lines 12-17.)
3. One of the soldiers pierced his side with a lance and immediately there came forth blood and water.	3. And he was pierced in his side with a spear and there flowed thereout blood and water. (Brightman, LEW, p. 97, 15-18.)

II. Commemoration of the Mother of God

4. (In honor and in memory) of our most blessed Lady, the Mother of God and ever-virgin	4. My blessed lady Mary, beseech with us thine only-begotten that he be appeased

---

[13] Germanus of Constantinople, *Commentarius liturgicus*, 43 (edit. N. Borgia, *Il commentario liturgico di s. Germano Patriarca Constantinopolitano e la versione latina di Anastasio Bibliotecario* [Grottaferrata, 1912], p. 42).

Mary, through whose prayers, O Lord, accept this sacrifice upon your own altar in heaven. through thy prayers and perform mercy on us all. (Brightman, LEW, p. 98, 11-15.)

III. Commemoration of the Angelic Hosts

5. (In honor and memory) of the honored, incorporeal powers of heaven.

5. Those on high stand in fear and minister it with trembling. (Brightman, LEW, p. 97, 29-31.)

IV. Commemoration of the Prophets and the Apostles

6. (In honor and memory) of ...all the holy Prophets. ...and of all the other holy apostles.

6. ...receive, O Lord, his oblation like those of the prophets and the apostles. (Brightman, LEW, p. 98, 19-21.)

V. Commemoration of the Holy Hierarchs

7. (In honor and memory) of our father among the saints ...and all the holy hierarchs.

7. Remember, O Lord, by thy grace and compassion the fathers and pontiffs : may their prayer be a wall to us. (Brightman, LEW, p. 98, 22-26.)

VI. Intercession for the Church Militant (the Living)

8. Remember, O Lord, ...and every bishop... priests, deacons... all the clergy, our brothers, etc.

8. Remember, O Lord, our fathers and brethren again and our teachers, and us and them account worthy by thy mercy. (Brightman, LEW, p. 98, 27-30.)

VII. Intercessions for the Departed

9. Remember, O Lord, the soul of) N——, and all our orthodox fathers and brothers who have fallen asleep in the hope of resurrection, eternal life and communion with you.

9. ...give rest also to the spirits of the departed and have mercy upon sinners in the day of judgment. The departed who are severed from us and have passed from this world, grant rest, O Christ, to their spirits with the righteous and the just... to lead them to the Kingdom. (Brightman, LEW, pp. 98-99, 34-10.)

Could something like the Syrian *Kathuliki* have taken place during the fraction in the Byzantine Liturgy when the division of particles still took place immediately before Communion? This may have inspired the complicated ritual of the *proskomidia*. The ancient Mozarabic Liturgy, which received much from the Syro-Byzantine, had a parallel arrangement. [14] While the symbolism here is different from the Byzantine, the Mozarabic priest divided the host into nine particles and arranged them in the form of a cross. [15] Nine particles are still used in the Byzantine *proskomidia* for honoring the different categories of saints (the Church Triumphant), and at the fraction, the priest still arranges the fragments in the form of a cross. The seventh century *Expositio*—an early Gallican document—tells the legend of an angel seen cutting the limbs of a smiling child and catching its blood during the fraction of the host! [16] This borrowing of an oriental theme must have occurred before contact with the East was cut off. The Byzantine Liturgy, then, seems to have had some set arrangement of the particles on the *diskos* before the seventh century, yet no written proof of it is available before the eleventh century, at which time the arrangement of four particles on the diskos is described. [17]

The division of the main host, the " Lamb, " into four particles is mentioned for the first time only in the ninth or tenth century, [18] yet we know that the crosswise incisions were being made in the

[14] Cf. A. Baumstark, *Comparative Liturgy* (Westminster, Md., 1958), p. 132.

[15] The Council of Tours, in A.D. 567, gave warning to the priest that the broken particles were to be arranged, not *in imaginario ordine*, but in the form of a cross (Can. 3, Mansi, *Sacrorum conciliorum nova et amplissima collectio*, IX, 793). According to the *Missale mixtum* (PL 85, 557), the particles represented, and were named after, the following mysteries : (1) *corporatio*, (2) *nativitas*, (3) *circumcisio*, (4) *apparitio*, (5) *passio*, (6) *mors*, (7) *resurrectio*, (8) *gloria*, and (9) *regnum*. The first seven composed the cross.

[16] Quasten, *Monumenta eucharistica et liturgia vetustissima* (Bonn, 1935-1937), 21; cf. also *Vitae Patrum*, chap. 6 (Quasten, *ibid.*, n. 4).

[17] Latin version of Leo Thuscus (edit. Antwerp), p. 65; cf. also Krasnoseltsev, *Svidinia o nikotorikh liturgicheskikh rukopis'akh Vatikanskoi biblioteki* (Kazan, 1885), p. 215.

[18] *Cod. Porphyrios*, Krasnoseltsev, *op. cit.*, p. 294; however, the *Cod. Falascae* indicates only three : cf. P. de Meester, *Les origines et les développements du texte grec de la liturgie de S. Jean Chrysostome*, XPYCOCTOMIKA (Rome, 1908), p. 347.

beginning of the ninth [19]—and this is indicated as an established custom so that the host probably was being broken into four parts as early as the eighth century, and yet no writer comments on it for nearly a century and a half.

At present, the particle with the inscription IC is used for commingling, that with XC, for the Communion of the celebrant and other members of the clergy, and those with NI and KA, for the Communion of the faithful. All this is a reminder of the symbolism of union and unity. As we know, early Christians used the *panis quadratus*, which was easily divided into four parts (see above, p. 264).

The Fraction Prayer

The present Byzantine prayer accompanying the fraction has no direct reference to Christ's death on the cross, but concerns Communion. While the eucharistic bread is broken into many parts, the Eucharistic Christ remains undivided, body and blood, soul and divinity, in each fragment The Eucharistic Christ is not limited by time or space. [20]

The Western Rite *Liber pontificalis* indicates that Pope Sergius I (A.D. 687-701) had decreed that " during the time of the fraction of the body of the Lord, the *Agnus Dei qui tollis peccata mundi, miserere nobis*, be chanted by the clergy and people. " [21] Earlier *Ordines* direct the archdeacon to give a signal for the singers to begin the *Agnus Dei* after the distribution of the consecrated bread to the acolytes for the fraction. [22] The *Agnus Dei*, attributed to Sergius I,

---

[19] Gregory of Decapolis, *Sermone historico* (PG 100, 1201 C-1203 C).

[20] The eighth verse of the Latin Rite *Lauda Sion* is similar to the prayer of the fraction. There can hardly be any question of interrelationship, however, since relations between Byzantine and the Latin Churches were anything but conducive to " borrowing. " The similarity is probably due to the great truths of the Eucharist which, of course, both Churches have always held firmly.

[21] *Liber pont.* (edit. Duchesne, I, 376); however, see Silva-Tarouca, *Giovanni " Archicantor " de S. Pietro a Roma e l'ordo Romanus da lui composto*, Atti della Pont. Accad. Rom. di archeologia, I, 1 (Rome, 1923), pp. 183 f.

[22] *Ordo Rom.*, I, n. 19 (PL 78, 946); *Ordo Rom.*, II, 13 (PL 78, 975). The connection of the *Agnus Dei* with the fraction is even clearer in the *Ordo* of S. Amand (cf. Duchesne, *op. cit.*, 461) and the *Capitulare eccl. ord.* (Silva-Tarouca, *op. cit.*, pp. 200, 206)

a Syrian by descent, [23] probably originated after the Eastern territories had been overrun by Islam. [24] The bread had been designated
as the *Lamb of God* in several writings of the Eastern Fathers, [25] and
some of the Syro-Byzantine Liturgies mention the *Lamb of God* who
takes away the sins of the world. The Liturgy of the Syrian Jacobites has, " Thou art the Lamb of God that taketh away the sin of
the world. " [26] This is part of the fraction prayer, and antedates
the conquest by Islam. [27] The Byzantine Liturgy seems also to have
used this expression during the fraction, but when the actual division
of bread-particles for Communion (in essence, part of the fraction)
was transferred to the *proskomidia*, the words naturally would have
been transferred too. [28] At any rate, the expression, " The Lamb
of God who takes away the sin of the world is sacrificed for the life
and salvation of the world, " has been part of the *proskomidia* for
ten centuries (see above, pp. 270 f). After the transference, several
centuries elapsed before another formula was found to accompany
the fraction before Communion (as we know it today). The eighth
or ninth-century *Codex Barberini*, for example, has none; neither
does the eleventh or twelfth century Latin version of Chrysostom's
Liturgy by Leo Thuscus. [29]

Not until the twelfth century do we find any formula accompanying

---

[23] This is disputed. Cf. Silva-Tarouca, *op. cit.*, pp. 183 f.

[24] Cf. Bishop, *Liturgica historica* (Oxford, 1918), pp. 145 f.

[25] E.g., Gregory of Nyssa, (*In Christi resurr. homil.*, I (PG 46, 601 C) : " Isaac,
like Christ, was only-begotten and Lamb at the same time "; Chrysostom (*In
I Cor. homil.*, 41, 4 [edit. Montfaucon 10, 392 E, or PG 61, 361]) : " In the prayer
of petition we approach the Lamb that lies before us "; Origen (*In Joh. homil.*,
X, 12, al (PG 14, 336 B) : " Is this (Eucharist) not the flesh of the Lamb that takes
away the sins of the world? " Also, *Passio Andreae* of the fifth century (Lipsius-
Bonnet, *Acta apost. apocrypha*, II, 1, pp. 13 f.) : " To the almighty, one, and true
God, I offer daily a spotless Lamb that continues unimpaired and alive even after
all the faithful have eaten its flesh and drunk its blood. "

[26] Brightman, LEW, p. 99.

[27] The first manuscript proof goes back only to the ninth century. Cf. Hanssens,
Institutiones liturgicae de ritibus orientalibus, De Missa rituum orientalium, Vol. III
(Rome, 1932), p. 518.

[28] If the *Euchologion* of Sarapion already had the " fraction, and in the fraction
a prayer, " surely the Byzantine Liturgy would have had one prior to the eighth
century, especially since the particles for Communion were still being broken
just before Communion, a task which sometimes took considerable time.

[29] Brightman, LEW, p. 341, and the Latin version of Leo Thuscus (edit.
Antwerp, p. 63).

the fraction—and even then the text varies. " In the breaking of bread the disciples recognized the Lord. Grant, Lord, that we sinners also may recognize you in eternal life. " [30] Various forms of this short prayer are found as late as the sixteenth century, for instance : " The disciples recognized their Lord in the breaking of bread; " [31] or, " In the name of the only-begotten Son of God, our Lord God and Saviour Jesus Christ, they recognized you as the Lord; grant, Lord, that we sinners may recognize you. " [32] Another sixteenth century text is different : " The precious, holy, and pure body of our Lord and Saviour Jesus Christ is being broken; he is giving himself up for the life and the salvation of the world. " [33] There is here an echo of the *proskomidia's* : " The Lamb of God... is sacrificed for the life and salvation of the world. "

The present fraction-prayer is one of the most recent of all the prayers in the whole Liturgy and cannot date back further than the fourteenth or fifteenth century. [34]

The Commingling Formula

The commingling was practiced at the beginning of the fifth century, and possibly earlier. Its formula, however—" The fullness of the Holy Spirit "—first noted in the Armenian version of Chrysostom, is probably not older than this eighth century source. [35] It is found in many later texts, [36] at times with modifications. Some

[30] MS. 518 of the Theological Academy of St. Petersburg (S. Muretoff, *K materialam dlja istorii chinoposlidovania liturgii* [Sergiev Posad, 1895], pp. 93-94, 97, 99). Compare Petrovsky, *Histoire de la rédaction slave de la liturgie de S. Jean Chrysostome*, XPYCOCTOMIKA (Rome, 1908), p. 869.

[31] MS. of Solovetzky, N. 1023, p. 96, and MS. N. 1085, p. 67, of same Library; also MS. N. 267 of Moscow Synodal Library, p. 81. Cf. Petrovsky, *op. cit.*, p. 921.

[32] MS. N. 680 of Moscow Synodal Library, p. 69; also MS. N. 310, p. 228, of same Library. Cf. Petrovsky, *op. cit.*, p. 921-922.

[33] Cf. Petrovsky, *op. cit.*, pp. 921-922.

[34] It is found in the fourteenth or fifteenth century Slav *Ustav* of Metropolitan Isidore's *Liturgikon*; cf. MS. *Vat. Slav.*, N. 14, fols. 140-140 b.

[35] Cf. G. Aucher, *La versione armena della liturgia di S. Giovanni Crisostomo, fatta sul principio dell'VIII secolo*, XPYCOCTOMIKA (Rome, 1908), p. 395.

[36] *Cod. Barberini*, *gr.* 336, Brightman, LEW, p. 341; the twelfth century MS. N. 973 of Sinai Library, Dmitrievsky, *Opysanie liturgicheskikh rukopisej khraniaschikhsia v bibliotekakh pravosloavnago vostoka*, Vol. II, *Euchologia* (Kiev, 1901), p. 85, etc.

twelfth-century Slav documents have : " The union of the holy body
and precious blood of our Lord Jesus Christ, and the fullness of the
Holy Spirit. " [37]   The first part, " The union of the holy body and
precious blood, " may have been taken from the Greek St. James
Liturgy, which had this exact phrase at least two centuries earlier. [38]
This modification lasted in some places until well into the sixteenth
century. [39]   The original Latin formula, *Fiat commixtio et consecratio
corporis et sanguinis D.n.J.C., accipientibus nobis in vitam aeternam.
Amen,* [40] may also have come from the same Syrian source, the Greek
St. James Liturgy, where the act of commingling is simply and
unmistakably designated as a union, a hallowing and consummation. [41]

The present Byzantine formula—" The fullness of the Holy
Spirit, " is brief but obscure.   I. Dmitrievsky suggests an interpretation based on the symbolism of the rite : As Christ's incarnation,
passion and resurrection were wrought through the operation of the
Holy Spirit, so is the mystery of the Eucharist—and in this consists
the fullness of the Holy Spirit. [42]   One of the best-known interpretations, however, is different : The Holy Spirit, through whose opera-

---

[37] Cf. Petrovsky, *op. cit.*, pp. 869-870.

[38] E.g., *Vatican rot.*, 2282 (edit. A. Rocchi, in Mai, NPB, X, ii, pp. 96-97);
cf. also Krasnoseltsev, *op. cit.*, p. 66.   In the twelfth century, another short praye
followed the commingling formula in some Slav MSS. : " Do not reject me, O
Lord my God, on account of the greatness of my sins " (MS. N. 343 of Moscow
Synodal Library, cf. Gorsky-Nevostrujev, *Opysanie slavianskikh rukopisej Moskovskoj Synodal'noj biblioteky*, Vol. III [Moscow, 1859], 1, 7).   Such a prayer is
also found in the Liturgy of St. James (cf. Krasnoseltsev, *op. cit.*, p. 65).

[39] MS. N. 1023 of Solovetzky, p. 96; MS. N. 1029, p. 158, and MS. N. 267 of
Moscow Synodal Library, p. 82.   Cf. Petrovsky, *op. cit.*, p. 922.

[40] Changed to the present reading, *Haec commixtio... fiat accipientibus nobis
in vitam aeternam*, in the reform of the missal at the Council of Trent to forestall
possible misinterpretation on the part of the Protestant Reformers, chiefly the
Utraquists, since the meaning could be : " Let there be a commingling of our Lord's
body and blood, and let it bring the recipients to life everlasting. "   The Utraquists
would have had grounds for arguing that Communion under one species was
insufficient, because they could misconstrue the formula as though the body and
blood of Christ would be united only after the commingling and not at the consecration of the two species.   Cf. *Concilium Tridentinum* (edit. Görres, VIII, 917);
Jedin, " Das Konzil von Trient und die Reform des Römischen Messbuches, "
in *Liturg. Leben* (1939), 46, 58.

[41] Brightman, LEW, p. 62.

[42] I. Dmitrievsky, *Istoricheskoe dogmaticheskoe i tainstvennoe izyasnenie na
bozhestvennoyu liturgiyu* (Moscow, 1804), p. 234.

tion Christ became incarnate, is present and subsists under the species of bread and wine, and is communicated with them to the faithful. This theory, found in Goar, [43] seems to be confirmed by the people's response after their Communion : " We have seen the true light and have received the heavenly Spirit. "

In Holy Communion, the Eucharistic Christ is received—but also the Holy Spirit. The fullness of the Sacrament consists precisely in this, that the Holy Spirit is accomplishing his work, the sanctification of the worthy receiver through divine grace.

[43] *Euchologion,* p. 127, n. 165.

CHAPTER LXVIII

THE *ZEON-TEPLOTA*

Immediately after the commingling comes the rite of the " living water "—the Ζέον or *teplota*. [1]

The deacon offers warm water in a small vessel to the priest, saying :
Bless, sir, the warm water.

Blessing the vessel of warm water, the priest says :
Blessed is the fervor of your saints, now and always, and for ever and ever. Amen.

The deacon pours a little water crosswise into the consecrated wine, saying :
The fervor of faith, full of the Holy Spirit. Amen.

Then he puts the vessel away and stands aside.
This ceremony is proper to the Byzantine Church. The Russians, Catholic and Orthodox, always have it. The Ukrainian Orthodox generally have it, but the Ukrainian Catholics, almost never.

Though the ceremony of *teplota* was being discontinued in some places of the Western Ukraine by the seventeenth century, [2] it was the Catholic Synod of Zamosc (1720) which forbade the practice " for a grave reason " : *Inhibet sancta Synodus gravem ob causam, et abrogat toleratam in Orientali Ecclesia consuetudinem ad consecratas calicis species, aquam tepidam effundendi post consecrationem, ante communionem.* [3] The " grave reason " was not given. It could not have been the danger of diluting the consecrated wine to the extent

---

[1] The warm water and the vessel containing it are sometimes called the ζέον. The vessel itself has several names : θερμάριον, ὀρχιόλιον, and χαδίσκος. Germanus (eight century) and Theodore of Andida (thirteenth century) also refer to it as the λεξητάριον.

[2] As is evident from some of the *Sluzhebnyky* (missals) of the period, e.g., the 1648 edit. of the Sluzhebnyk of Peter Mogila, II, p. 28, etc.; also cf. Odinzov, *Uniatskie bogosluzhenie v XVII i XVIII vv. po rukopisiam Vylenskoj publychnoj biblioteky* (Vilno, 1886), p. 37.

[3] Tit. III, para. 4-a. Cf. *Codificazione Canonica Orientale* (*Fonti, Ius Particulare Ruthenorum*, fasc. XI [Rome, 1933], p. 971).

that it tasted like water, a danger mentioned in the *Sluzebnyk* of Peter Mogila (edit. 1646), for this could easily have been averted by limiting the amount of water. The practice was probably discontinued because of the excessive latinism of some influential members of the Ruthenian clergy. [4] Some fifty years later, " scandalizing the Latins " was given as the explanation of the " grave cause " which prompted the Synod of Zamosc to abrogate the *teplota* for the Catholics. [5]

The *teplota* rite was expressly sanctioned by Pope Benedict XIV some twenty-two years after the synod, yet the prohibition was not rescinded. [6] When Rome published the official *Sluzebnyk* in 1940 as part of the Ruthenian liturgical reform, it included the ceremony but left its practice to the decision of the local ordinary. [7]

History and Meaning

The origin of this practice is shrouded in Christian antiquity. Various origins have been suggested : that the custom is a vestige of ancient secular table practice; [8] that it began in the mountains of

[4] After the liturgical reform of 1944, and at the suggestion of the Holy See, latinizations were expurgated from the Divine Liturgy. Ukrainian Catholic Bishops, however, still wear Latin skullcaps, pectoral crosses, rings, and in some localities, celebrate a hybrid Liturgy (using Latin episcopal thrones, at altars that are more Latin than Byzantine, etc.).

[5] *Bogoslovia pravouchitelnaya*, 3rd edit. published at Pochaiv, 1779, p. 21 : " ...but on account of the fact, although somewhat (sic) invalid, that the Romans would be scandalized, Zamosc ordered this ceremony to be omitted. " Our translation.

[6] The Bull *Etsi Pastoralis* of 1742 for the Italo-Greeks. The zeon rite is included in the official *Euchologion* for the Greco-Byzantine Church, published in Rome, 1754. If there remained any doubt, it should have been dispelled by the Apostolic Constitution *Allatae sunt* (26. VII. 1755) : " *Cumque in congregationibus, quae pro correctione librorum ecclesiasticorum Ecclesiae orientalis habitae fuerunt... diu multumque disputatum fuisset, utrum interdicendus est ritus infundendi in calicem aquam tepidam post consecrationem... responsum fuit die 1. Maji, 1746, nihil esse innovandum, quod rescriptum a nobis deinde confirmatum fuit.* " The ceremony of warm water did cause much *admiratio* among many of the Latin bishops at the Council of Florence (1439), but the Greek theologians, led by Dorotheus, Bishop of Mitylene, eminently satisfied both them and the Pope.

[7] *Sviaschennaya i Bozhestvennaya Liturhia izhe vo ottsa nasheho Ioanna Zlatoustaho* (Rome, 1940), p. 112.

[8] Cf. Hanssens, *Institutiones liturgicae de ritibus orientalibus, De Missa rituum orientalium*, Vol. II (Rome, 1930), p. 235; also C. Daremberg - E. Sagio, *Dictionnaire des antiquités grecques et latines*, V, p. 92.

Cappadocia to prevent the freezing of the wine, [9] etc. The most plausible theory seems to be that of the Aphthartodocetae, favorites of Emperor Justinian (A.D. 527-565)—that the body of Christ remained incorrupt in death and never lost its natural warmth, wherefore warm blood and water issued from it. [10] The union of warm water with the Precious Blood is intended to signify this fact.

Later, in the eleventh century, Niketas Stethatos (Nicetas Pectoratus) suggested that warmth indicated the indwelling of the Holy Spirit, which continued after the death of Christ. [11] This indeed is more in line with the liturgical text of the *teplota* : *The fervor of faith, full of the Holy Spirit.* This may be related also to the commingling rite which precedes : the formulae are similar, and the fact that the *teplota* rite immediately follows the commingling, suggests the warmth of life proceeding from the union of the body and the blood.

Pseudo-Germanus and Theodore of Andida, on the other hand, see in the *zeon* the symbolism and memorial of the blood and water which flowed from the pierced side of Christ on the cross. The rite is performed immediately before Communion to show that our supernatural life also flows out of Christ's side. The three elements—the spirit-life, the blood and the water—are united at this point. [12] Many of the Church Fathers saw in the pierced side of Jesus the origin of the Church, a symbolism expressed in the *proskomidia* when the wine and water are poured into the chalice (see above, pp. 273 f.).

Nicolas Cabasilas (d. 1341) interprets the liturgical formula and sees in it the descent of the Holy Spirit and his communion with the faithful. His explanation deserves to be quoted in full :

[9] D. Attwater, *Catholic Eastern Churches* (Milwaukee : Bruce, 1935), p. 57, n. 18.

[10] See L. H. Grondijs, *L'iconographie byzantine du Crucifié mort sur la croix* (Brussels, 1941), pp. 76 f.; Lebrun, *Explication littérale, historique et dogmatique des prières et des cérémonies de la Messe* (Liège, 1778), pp. 412-413; also see the fine article in ZkTh, 70 (1948), 369-375, by E. Luchesi-Palli.

[11] Niketas Stethatos, *Opusculum contra Latinos* (PG 120, 1011-1022). He is also the first to have tied in the text of I John 5:6-8 with the explanation of the *zeon* rite.

[12] Ps.-Germanus, *Historia eccl. et mystica theoria* (PG 98, 449); Theodore of Andida, *Protheoria* (PG 140, 464),

...he drops into the chalice a little warm water, to symbolize the descent of the Holy Spirit upon the Church. For the Holy Spirit came down when the whole plan of redemption had been completed. And now the descent of the Spirit comes about when the sacrifice has been offered and the holy offerings have reached their perfection; it will be completed in those who communicate worthily.

The whole scheme of Christ's work, as we have seen, is depicted in the host during the liturgy; there we see the symbol of the infant Christ, of Christ led to death, crucified, and pierced with a lance; then we see the bread transformed into the most holy body which actually endured these sufferings, and rose from the dead, and ascended into heaven, where it sits at the right hand of the Father. So it is fitting that the later fulfillment of all these events should be symbolized, that the celebration of the liturgy may be complete, the final effects being added to the work of redemption.

What is the effect and the result of the sufferings and works and teaching of Christ? Considered in relation to ourselves, it is nothing other than the descent of the Holy Spirit upon the Church. So it is fitting that this should be represented after the other mysteries, as it is when the warm water is poured into the chalice.

Since this warm water is not only water, but shares the nature of fire, it signifies the Holy Spirit, who is sometimes represented by water, and who came down upon the apostles in the form of fire. This point of the liturgy represents that moment in time, for the Holy Spirit came down after all things pertaining to Christ had been accomplished. In the same way, when the holy offerings have attained their ultimate perfection, this water is added.

For the mysteries also represent the Church, which is the Body of Christ. It received the Holy Spirit after the ascension of Christ. Now, it receives the gifts of the Holy Spirit after the offerings have been accepted at the heavenly altar. God, who has accepted them, sends us the Holy Spirit in return.... [13]

In the fifteenth century, Simeon of Thessalonica reverted to the thought of Pseudo-Germanus and Theodore of Andida, but devel-

[13] Cabasilas, *A Commentary of the Divine Liturgy*, trans. by Hussey and McNulty (London, 1960), chap. 37, pp. 90-91 (see PG 150, 449-452 for original Greek).

oped it further.   Simeon taught that the warm water mingled with the precious blood shows that the body of Christ, although separated from his soul by death, remained alive because of its perpetual union with his divinity.   The *zeon*, then, is a memorial of the water which flowed from Christ's side and now also symbolizes the fervor of the communicants. [14]

All of these explanations are complementary, each emphasizing a different aspect of the same reality. [15]

At the close of the sixth century, Emperor Maurice (A.D. 582-602), after conquering Persia and much of Armenia, invited the monophysite Katholikos Moses II of Armenia to a conference with the Byzantines in order to bring about a possible reconciliation between the two Churches.   The Katholikos refused, saying : " God forbid that I should cross the (border-) river Aza and be compelled to eat leavened bread and drink hot water with the Byzantines. " [16]   The *zeon* was also known in Syria before the end of the sixth century. Writing about the monks of Syria, a bishop of Ephesus states clearly that " they were accustomed to temper the chalice of the living blood with hot water. " [17]

The practice of the *zeon* is certainly ancient.   How is it, then, that not all the manuscript sources of the Divine Liturgy contain this usage?   Some of the earliest codices, for example, do not even allude to it, e.g., *Codex Barberini* (eighth or ninth century), *Codex Porphyrios* (ninth or tenth century), *Codex Sebastianov* (tenth or eleventh century), etc.   Only one conclusion can be drawn from this lack of uniformity : the rite was not performed everywhere in the Byzantine Church during these centuries. [18]

---

[14] Simeon of Thessalonica, *Lib. de Templo* (PG 155, 742-744).

[15] I Dmitrievsky (*Istoricheskoe dogmaticheskoe i tainstvennoe izyasnenie na bozhestvennoyu liturgiyu* [Moscow, 1804], pp. 235-236), in fact, combines all these various aspects of the *teplota (zeon)* in his explanation of the rite.

[16] PG 132, 1248-1249; cf. also J. Pargoire, *L'Eglise byzantine de 527 à 847* (Paris, 1923), p. 102.

[17] Cf. P. Lagrange, " Un évêque syrien du V°. s, " in *Mélanges d'histoire religieuse* (Paris, 1915), p. 204.

[18] The Slav Church followed the Greek in this : as late as the twelfth century, the *Liturgikon* of Anthony the Roman (1147) and that of Barlaam of Khutinsk (1192) omit it (cf. Petrovsky, *Histoire de la rédaction slave de la liturgie de S. Jean Chrysostome*, XPYCOCTOMIKA [Rome, 1908], p. 870); nor does the fourteenth century *Molytovnyk-Sluzhebnyk,* published by Kowaliv (*Molytovnyk-Sluzhebnyk,*

The original rite of the *zeon* was probably performed in silence. The absence of any accompanying prayer during the first several centuries of its existence as well as the unsettled state of its formulae seem to indicate this. One of the first texts to come down to us is the very general one in the eleventh or twelfth century Latin version of the Liturgy translated by Leo Thuscus.

> *Deacon :* Bless, sir, the warm water.
> *Priest-celebrant :* Blessed is our God always, now and for ever and ever. [19]

In the thirteenth century, when the interpretation of the rite stressing the indwelling of the Holy Spirit (bespeaking warmth) gained more and more ground, the text reflected this accordingly :

> *Deacon :* Bless, sir, the warm water.
> *Priest :* The warmth of the Holy Spirit. [20]

A century later, again probably influenced by the current interpretation of the rite, this was amended to read : " The warmth of the faith of the Holy Spirit. " [21] Both these forms were current in the fifteenth and sixteenth centuries. [22]

A similar diversity of text is found in the Slav Church, which generally imitated the Mother Church in liturgical matters. They did, however, add variations of their own, almost always stressing the role of the Holy Spirit. A thirteenth-century text anticipates by over a century Cabasilas' interpretation of the rite as the descent of the Holy Spirit : " He will descend as rain on a field, and as a drop of rain falling on the ground. " [23] Some fourteenth-century texts,

---

Pamiatka XIV stolittia [New York, 1960], pp. 30-32). Nor was the rite entirely accepted in the Italo-Greek Church as late as the fourteenth century, as is evident from the missals of the twelfth, thirteenth, and fourteenth centuries.

[19] Antwerp edit. of 1562, p. 63.

[20] This formula is identical in the thirteenth century *Cod.* N. 719 of Patmos (Dmitrievsky, *Opysanie liturgicheskikh rukopisej khraniaschikhsia v bibliotekakh pravoslavnago vostoka*, Vol. II, *Euchologia* [Kiev, 1901], p. 170) and *Cod.* N. 709 of Patmos (Dmitrievsky, *op. cit.*, II, p. 158).

[21] MS. of Esphigmenon of year 1306 (Dmitrievsky, *op. cit.*, p. 262).

[22] Cf. Dmitrievsky, *op. cit.*, pp. 612, 475; but although one sixteenth century Codex contains a more elaborate formula : " Blessed and holy is the warmth of the Most Holy Spirit, now and always.... The warmth of the Holy Spirit : the divine laver of regeneration " (Dmitrievsky, *op. cit.*, p. 817).

[23] MS. N. 524 of Sophia Library, pp. 25, 42; cf. Petrovsky, *op. cit.*, p. 876.

on the other hand, read simply : " The fullness of the Holy Spirit, " [24]
a formula identical with that used for the commingling—not an
illogical arrangement since both ritual acts have points of similarity.
The fifteenth-century *Sluzebnyk* of Isidore, Metropolitan of Kiev,
copied the Greek formula :

> *Deacon :* Bless, sir, the warm water.
> *Priest :* The warmth of the Holy Spirit. [25]

Sixteenth century Slav missals have greater diversity than ever.
Some read : " The warmth of the Holy Spirit, always, now and
forever. " [26]   Others : " A laver of divine regeneration through the
Word. " [27]   Still another has a much more elaborate formula :

> *Deacon :* Father, fill this chalice, placing the fullness of the
> Holy Spirit into the chalice.   Bless, Father, the warm water,
> the fervor of the Holy Spirit.
> *Priest :* Change one and the other through the Holy Spirit. [28]

The diversity of forms indicates that the rite was not interpreted
n the same manner in all the localities of the Slav Church.

---

[24] MS. N. 523 of Sophia Library, p. 44 (Petrovsky, *op. cit.*, p. 885) and MS. N.
387 of Moscow Synodal Library (Krasnoseltsev, *Materialy dlja istorii chinoposlidovania liturgii sv. Ioanna Zlatoustago* [Kazan, 1889], p. 28).

[25] Cf. *Cod. Vat. Slav.*, N. 14, fol. 141.

[26] MS. N. 1019 of Solovetzky, p. 27; MS. N. 1021 of Solovetzky, p. 70 (Petrovsky, *op. cit.*, p. 922).

[27] MS. N. 680 of Moscow Synodal Library, p. 70, and MS. N. 1029 of Solovetzky, p . 158 (Petrovsky, *op. cit.*, p. 922).

[28] MS. N. 1023 of Solovetzky, p. 115 (Petrovsky, *op. cit.*, pp. 922-923).

CHAPTER LXIX

THE COMMUNION
OF THE CLERGY : RITE

Before *the deacon receives the eucharistic bread, he goes around the altar and, if necessary, washes the palm of his right hand.*
The priest then says to him :

Deacon, approach.

The deacon comes to the left side of the priest and bows his head, asking forgiveness. The priest breaks the particle XC of the holy bread and offers part of it to the deacon. After kissing the hand of the priest, the deacon prepares to receive the holy bread in the palm of his right hand, placed over his left hand in the form of a cross. Meanwhile, he says :

Give me, sir, the precious and holy body of our Lord, God, and Saviour, Jesus Christ.

Placing the particle in the deacon's right hand, the priest says :

The precious and holy and all-pure body of our Lord, God and Saviour, Jesus Christ is being given to N——, Deacon, for the remission of his sins and for life everlasting.

The deacon goes behind the altar while the priest makes a small bow, takes the other portion of the XC particle, and holds it with the first two fingers of his right hand, saying :

The precious and all-holy body of our Lord, God, and Saviour, Jesus Christ, is being given to me, N——, a priest, for the remission of my sins and for life everlasting. Amen.

With bowed heads, both priest and deacon continue :

Lord, I believe and confess that you are truly Christ, the Son of the living God, come into the world to save sinners, of whom I am the greatest.

O Son of God, receive me this day as a partaker of your Mystical Supper, for I will not reveal this mystery to your enemies, nor will I give you a kiss as did Judas, but like the thief I openly say to you :

Remember me, Lord, when you come into your Kingdom.

Remember me, Master, when you come into your Kingdom.

Remember me, O Holy One, when you come into your Kingdom.

Lord, may the partaking of your holy sacrament be to me not for judgment nor condemnation, but for the healing of my soul and body.

O God, be merciful to me a sinner.

O God, cleanse me of my sins and have mercy on me.

I have sinned very often; forgive me, Lord.

The priest, then the deacon, consume the holy bread with awe and reverence.

Standing up, the priest takes the chalice in his right hand and the lention in his left, holding it under his chin. He drinks from the chalice, saying :

I, N——, a servant of God and priest, am receiving the precious and holy blood of our Lord God and Saviour, Jesus Christ, for the remission of my sins and for life everlasting. Amen.

He wipes his lips and the edge of the chalice with the lention, *and says :*

This has touched my lips and will take away my iniquities and will cleanse my sins.

Then he says to the deacon :
Deacon, approach.

The deacon makes a small bow and says :
Behold, I draw near to our immortal King and God.

Give me, sir, the precious and holy blood of our Lord, God, and Saviour, Jesus Christ.

The priest holds the chalice and lention *in his right hand; with his left, he supports the chalice base. The deacon holds the end of the* lention *under his chin with both his hands as the priest offers the chalice saying :*

The servant of God, N——, deacon, is receiving the precious and holy blood of our Lord, God, and Saviour, Jesus Christ for the remission of his sins and life everlasting.

Then the priest says :

This has touched your lips and will take away your iniquities and will cleanse your sins.

At the Jewish *chabûrah,* the broken bread was received by the guests as they sat or reclined at table. They stood for the recitation of the *berakah,* and to receive the cup of blessing. At the Eucharist, before its separation from the common meal, the Christians probably did the same. When the Eucharist was separated from the meal, however, the distribution of the bread came between the end of the Eucharistic Prayer of Thanksgiving and the passing of the cup. In accordance with their Jewish heritage, the Christians stood for the Thanksgiving Prayer and for the reception of the chalice. Since the bread was received between the prayer and the passing of the chalice, they received it standing too.

The present rite of Communion of the deacon is an example of the ancient rite of Communion of the laity. The bread was given in the hand of the communicant. [1] This is evident from many sources—inscriptions, pictures, drawings and texts. Basil the Great, for example, in his Letter to the Patrician Caesaria (or Caesarius) says clearly : " And even in church, when the priest gives the portion (of bread), the recipient takes it with complete power over it, and so lifts it to his lips with his own hand. " [2] Tertullian, Dionysius of Alexandria, and Pope Cornelius attest to the practice in their respective Churches, [3] but the testimony of Cyril of Jerusalem stands out with its detailed account of the fourth century procedure :

[1] For major proofs concerning the first centuries, see F. J. Dölger, *Ichthys,* Vol. II (Münster, 1922), pp. 513 f, and *Antike u. Christentum,* Vol. 3 (1932), p. 239; Vol. 5 (1936), pp. 236 f. Also F. X. Funk, " Der Kommunion ritus, " *Kirchengeschichtliche Abhandlungen und Untersuchunge,* Vol. I (Paderborn, 1897), pp. 293-308.

[2] Basil, *Ep.* 93 (PG 32, 485-486).

[3] Tertullian, *De idolol.,* chap. 7 (CSEL, 20, 36); Dionysius of Alexandria, in Eusebius, *Hist. eccl.,* VII, 9, 4 (PG 13, 262 C [*Series graeca*]); Pope Cornelius to Fabius, in Eusebius, *op. cit.,* VI, 43, 18 (PG 13, 250 A [*Series graeca*]).

In approaching, come not stretching out your open hands or your fingers spread out, but make your left hand a throne for the right which shall receive the King; then cup your hand and receive the body of Christ, reciting the "Amen." When you have carefully sanctified your eyes by touching (them with) the sacred body, partake of it. But be careful that no particles fall, for what you would lose would be to you as if you lost some of your own members. Tell me, if anyone gave you gold dust, would you not hold it tightly and carefully, and watch lest any of it fall and be lost? Must you not then be even more careful that no particle be lost of that which is more precious than gold and diamonds?

Then, after you have partaken of the body of Christ, approach the chalice of his blood without stretching out your hands; but stand bowed, and in a spirit of worship and reverence repeat the "Amen" and sanctify yourself by partaking of the blood of Christ. And while your lips are still moist, touch them with your hands and sanctify your eyes and your forehead and the other senses. Then tarry in prayer and give thanks to God who has made you worthy of such great mysteries. [4]

The placing of the right hand crosswise over the left is confirmed by Theodore of Mopsuestia and the Trullan Synod. [5] In the sixth century East Syrian Church, the Communion rite was essentially the same. [6]

In most places, the faithful continued to receive the consecrated bread in their hands until well into the eighth century. John Damascene, for example, speaks of it in the eighth century Syrian Church; [7] so does the *Commentary* of Bishop George (probably George " Bishop of the Arabs," a contemporary of James of Edessa)

---

[4] Cyril of Jerusalem, *Catechesis*, XXIII (*Mystag.*, V), 21-22 (Quasten, *Monumenta eucharistica et liturgia vetustissima* [Bonn, 1935-1937], 108-110). Our translation.

[5] Theodore of Mopsuestia, *Sermones catech.*, VI (edit. Rücker, *Ritus Baptismi et Missae, quem descripsit Theodorus ep. Mopsuestenus in sermonibus catecheticis* [Münster, 1933], pp. 36 f.); Trullan Synod (A.D. 692), Can. 101 (Mansi, *Sacrorum conciliorum nova et amplissima collectio*, XI, 985 f.), which also prohibited the use of a golden platter instead of the bare hands.

[6] Can. 3 of *Canonibus ad Iacobum episcopum Insularum*, Darai, in O. Braun, *Das Duch der Synhados nach einer Handschrift des Museo Borgiano* (Stuttgart, 1900), p. 243.

[7] John Damascene, *De fide*, IV, 13 (PG 94, 1149).

in the East Syrian Church. [8] The West generally abandoned the practice in the eighth century, [9] In sixth century Gaul, women were required to cover their hand with a white cloth before receiving the host. [10] Perhaps the change from leavened to unleavened bread in the Western Church also influenced the change in the method of distribution, since the transitions were contemporaneous. The thin, delicate wafers could not be handled easily. But there seems to have been more serious reasons for the change.

When the host was handed to the communicant, there was always the possibility of grave abuse, as proved by the legislation of provincial councils, for instance, Saragossa (A.D. 380) and Toledo (A.D. 400). [11] Later medieval practices certainly lent themselves to such abuse. [12] By our standards, the ancients sometimes seem totally careless. In A.D. 510, in Thessalonica, when persecution was imminent during the conflict with the Monophysites, Bishop Dorotheus of Thessalonica permitted the Eucharist to be distributed in baskets. [13] What led both East and West to change the method of distribution was really the tremendous respect for the sacrament engendered by a deeper appreciation of the mystery.

In both Churches, the sacred bread came to be placed by the priest directly in the mouth of the communicant, but each Rite did it in its own way. The Western Church changed from leavened to unleavened bread, which had the advantage of adhering easily to the tongue. The Byzantine Church placed all the particles into the

[8] He explains that the right hand is held out and supported by the left. Cf. edit. R. H. Connolly and W. Codrington, *Two Commentaries on the Jacobite Liturgy, by George Bishop of the Arab Tribes, and Moses Bar Kepha* (London, 1913), pp. 5-10 (15-20) for description of the whole rite.

[9] Cf. Silva-Tarouca, *Giovanni " Archicantor " de S. Pietro a Roma e l'ordo Romanus da lui composto*, Atti della Pont. Accad. Rom. di archeologia, I, 1 (Rome, 1923), p. 201, *Capitulare eccl. ord.*; also *Hist. eccl.*, IV, 24 (PL 95, 214 D). Later sources are equivocal.

[10] Caesarius of Arles, *Serm.* 227, 5 (PL 39, 2168); also, Synod of Auxerre (A.D. 578 or 585), Can. 36 (Mansi, *op. cit.*, IX, 915).

[11] Council of Saragossa, Can. 3 (Mansi, *op. cit.*, III, 634); Council of Toledo, Can. 14 (Mansi, *op. cit.*, II, 1000).

[12] See Dölger, *Antike u. Christentum*, 5 (1936), 232-247, " Die Eucharistie als Reiseschutz "; also, P. Browe, " Zum Kommunionempfang des Mittelalters, " JbLw, 12 (1934), p. 177.

[13] Cf. Hormisdas, *Ep.* 102 (Thiel, 902); cf. Duchesne, *Christian Worship*, p. 249, n. 3.

consecrated wine and gave them out with a spoon. This permitted communion under both species at a minimum risk. Communion with a spoon eliminated the older usage of imparting the chalice. Some churches seem to have introduced the use of the spoon as early as the eighth century. [14] The Byzantine Church led the way. It took another hundred years before the practice became universal in the East.

Some authors claim that the Communion spoon was introduced by Chrysostom, [15] but nothing proves it. On the contrary, the little available evidence indicates that the spoon could not have been introduced before the eighth century. In A.D. 692, when vessels of gold or other materials were being brought by the faithful for Communion use, the Council in Trullo vigorously condemned the practice. [16] The hands of a living man, made to the image and likeness of God, are still emphatically considered the proper vessel for receiving the body of Christ. Otherwise, it would seem that one would be preferring, " inanimate and inferior matter to the image of God. " [17] Had the spoon been used at the time, it would have received the same condemnation. Communion with the spoon was attacked by Western theologians and writers of the ninth century, [18] showing that by then it was not a widely established custom, even in the East.

The Western Church eventually eliminated the receiving of the chalice by the laity. This was done after other solutions had been tried and rejected, such as drinking from the chalice through a tube *(pugillaris)* [19] or a reed *(calamus* or *fistula),* [20] by having a small amount of consecrated wine poured into a chalice containing non-

[14] Cf. A. Petrovsky, " Istoria china prychaschenia v Vostochnoj i Zapadnoj Tserkvy, " in *Khrystianskoe Chtenie,* I (1900), pp. 368-369.

[15] Among the older writers, Nicephorus Callistus (d. 1341) was of that opinion; according to Goar, so were Arcudius and Ligaridius (Goar, *Euchologion,* p. 130, n. 179 of *Notae*).

[16] Can. 101 (NPNF, Series II, Vol. XIV, p. 408).

[17] *Ibid.*

[18] A. Petrovsky, *op. cit.,* p. 369.

[19] *Ordo Rom.,* I, n. 3; 20 (PL 78, 947); *Ordo sec. Rom.,* no. 14 (PL 78, 976).

[20] Cf. J. Braun, *Das christliche Altargerät in seinem Sein und in seiner Entwicklung* (Munich, 1932), pp. 240-265.

consecrated wine, etc. [21] In some Western churches, the consecrated bread was dipped into the wine *(intinctio)*. The Third Synod of Braga (A.D. 675) disapproved the practice. [22] It continued, however, in many places. [23] This was the method prescribed for administering Communion to the sick, as we know from many sources. [24] The eleventh-twelfth century formula reads : " May the body of our Lord Jesus Christ, tinctured with his blood, conserve, " etc. [25] This was discontinued when the chalice ceased to be given to the laity—that is, after the twelfth century. [26]

The practice of imparting the chalice lingered, though several councils banned it. [27] It was granted to Bohemia in 1433 by popular demand. Later, the Reformers made of ita lmost a symbol of their movement. The pressure continued, and even after the Council of Trent, the issue was brought to the fore : the chalice was reinstated for Germany— but under certain conditions. Both concessions were withdrawn : Bavaria in 1571, Austria and Bohemia, in the general ban of 1621. [28] Requests for Communion under both species have been voiced, in our time, in the spirit of Vatican II. Perhaps the Oriental Rite system will be adopted in the West.

The ancient practice of receiving the sacred bread in the hand is maintained in the Byzantine Church for deacons, subdeacons and, in a Pontifical Liturgy, for the concelebrating priests. At Papal

[21] The seventh century *Ordo Rom.*, I, n. 20 (PL 78, 947 A).

[22] Can. 2 (Mansi, *op. cit.*, XI, 155).

[23] John of Avranches (d. 1079), *De off. eccl.* (PL 147, 37) stresses that the practice continued " not by authority, but because of the extreme fear of spilling the blood of Christ. " Both the *Liber officiorum* of Trier (eleventh century) and Bernold of Constance (*Micrologus*, 19 [PL 151, 989 f.]) argue against it, but testify to its spreading use. It was again censured by the synod of Clermont in 1096 (Can. 38; Mansi, *op. cit.*, XX, 818).

[24] Regino, *De synod. causis*, I, 70 (PL 132, 206); Burchard of Worms (d. 1025), *Decretum*, V, 9 (PL 140, 754); Ivo of Chartres (d. 1116), *Decretum*, II, 19 (PL 161, 165); etc.

[25] Cf. Browe, " Die Sterbekommunion, " in ZkTh (1936), pp. 218 f.; Andrieu, *Immixtio et consecratio* (Paris, 1924), pp. 136 f.

[26] Cf. F. X. Funk, " Der Kommunionritus, " in *Kirchengeschichtliche Abhandlungen und Untersuchunge*, I (Paderborn, 1897), pp. 306-308.

[27] Constance (1414), Sess. 13 (Mansi, *op. cit.*, XXVII, 727 f.); Basle (1437), Sess. 30 (Mansi, *op. cit.*, XXIX, 158); etc.

[28] See, P. J. Toner, " Communion under Both Kinds, " CE, IV, pp. 178-179; also J. Hoffmann, *Geschichte der Laienkommunion bis zum Tridentinum* (Speyer, 1891), pp. 189-209.

Masses of the eighth and ninth centuries, the clergy received the body of the Lord, went to the left side of the altar, placed their hands with the Sacrament on the altar and then consumed it. The deacons did the same on the right side of the altar. [29] The practice was similar in the pontifical Masses of the tenth century. [30] The practice was then abandoned entirely in the West.

Washing of the Hands

In ancient times, communicants were to wash their hands before receiving. Both Chrysostom and Athanasius point this out. [31] The custom of washing the hands before prayer is extremely ancient. [32] Cyril of Jerusalem, in fact, emphasizes its spiritual meaning almost to the exclusion of practical utility, when he remarks, " for we did not come into the *ecclesia* covered with dirt. " [33] The present rubric, directing the deacon to wash the palm of his right hand before Communion, is dictated by practical utility alone. This is clear from the qualifying clause *if need be.* If his hands have become soiled from handling the incense and preparing the censer, etc., the need is there. The ancient, symbolic meaning has been forgotten here.

The Kiss of Peace

The kiss of peace before Communion seems to have originated with the administration of Communion outside the Eucharistic Sacrifice. Sophronius (d. 638), for example, writes about St. Mary of Egypt giving the kiss of peace to an aged monk before receiving Communion from him. [34] Jerome also mentions the *pax* connected with Communion. [35] Gregory the Great writes that a group of monks, on the verge of shipwreck, gave each other the kiss of peace and then received the sacrament (which they carried with them). [36]

---

[29] *Ordo* of S. Amand (Andrieu, *Miscellanea Ehrle,* II [Rome, 1924], 165).

[30] *Ordines,* PL 78, 989; 994.

[31] Chrysostom, *In Eph. homil.,* 3, 4 (edit. Montfaucon 11, 23, or PG 62, 28 f.); Athanasius, *Ep. heort.,* 5, n. 5 (PG 26, 1383 A).

[32] E.g., Hippolytus, *Apostolic Tradition* (cf. Dix, *The Treatise on the Apostolic Tradition of St. Hippolytus of Rome* [London, 1937], pp. 61, 65 f.).

[33] Cyril of Jerusalem, *Catechesis,* XXIII (*Mystag.,* V), 2 (PG 33, 1109).

[34] Sophronius, *Vita S. Mariae Aeg.,* 22 (PL 73, 87 B).

[35] Jerome, *Ep.* 62 al., 82 (PL 22, 737).

[36] Gregory the Great, *Dial.,* III, 36 (PL 77, 307 C); *In ev.,* II, 37, 9 (PL 76, 1281 A).

The giving of the *pax* was especially common in administering Communion to the sick. [37] The practice found its way into the Latin Mass in the tenth century : " And the bishop gives Communion to the priests and deacons with the kiss of peace. " [38] A little more than a century later, we find the same in the Byzantine Liturgy. This seems to be the only time the Byzantine Church borrowed anything from the Latin.

When Leo Thuscus translated the Liturgy of Chrysostom from eleventh and twelfth century sources, he offered detailed directions for the Communion of the clergy—including for the first time the kiss of peace. His description is almost identical with that of the Pontifical Liturgy today :

> If there are more (priest-concelebrants), then after the first receives Communion, he gives it to the others who kiss his hand and cheek. In the same way, one receives from the other. Bowing before the holy altar simultaneously, each eats the flesh of the Lord. In like manner they extend the chalice to one another in order to drink the blood of the Lord. When the priests ... are finished, the archdeacon orders the deacons to approach. When they come up they receive, as the priests have. Then each kisses the cheek of the priest (celebrant). [39]

The kiss of peace at the Communion of the clergy is found in Slav churches of the thirteenth, fourteenth, and fifteenth centuries. [40] Later, the Ukrainians omitted it from all but the pontifical Liturgies. The Russians still have the kiss between celebrant and deacon in all their Liturgies. [41]

The formula for imparting this kiss of peace is different from that

---

[37] Cf. Book of Dimma (c. A.D. 800) for the Celtic Church, in F. E. Warren, *The Liturgy and Ritual of the Celtic Church* (Oxford, 1881), p. 170; also Theodulph of Orleans (d. 812), *Capitulare* (edit. Martène, *De antiquis Ecclesiae ritibus*, I, 7, II [I, 847 C]); the ninth century *Ordo for the Sick*, from Lorsch, edit. C. de Clerq, *Eph. liturg.*, 44 (1930), p. 103; finally, the *Ordo for the Sick* from Narbonne (edit. Martène, *op. cit.*, I, 7, XIII [I, 892 B]).

[38] *Sacramentary* of Ratoldus (PL 78, 245).

[39] Edit. Antwerp (1562), p. 64.

[40] Cf. Petrovsky, *Histoire de la rédaction slave de la liturgie de S. Jean Chrysostome*, XPYCOCTOMIKA (Rome, 1908), pp. 870, 876, 910; the fifteenth century Ukrainian *Molytovnyk-Sluzhebnyk* (edit. Kowaliv, *Molytovnyk-Sluzhebnyk*, *Pamiatka XIV stolittia* [New York, 1960], p. 32).

[41] K. Nikolsky, *Posobie k izucheniu Ustava Bogosluzhenia pravoslavnoi tserkvy* (St. Petersburg, 1907), p. 444.

imparted before the Creed : instead of " Peace be to you, " it is " Christ is among us " and the response, " He is now and will be. " This formula is first encountered during the fourteenth and fifteenth centuries. [42] And so is the response. [43] Since none of the missals prior to the thirteenth century gives any formula for the kiss of peace, the presumption is that it was done in silence before then. The thirteenth century formula was : " Peace in Christ, " and its response, " And with your deaconship. " [44]

Kissing the celebrant's hand before receiving the Eucharistic Bread appears for the first time in the Latin version of Leo Thuscus (1180) (see above, p. 697). In the early eighth-century Armenian version of Chrysostom's Liturgy, the priest kissed the altar before taking the sacred bread in his hand, then he kissed it. [45] In the Kievan Church of the fifteenth century, both priest and deacon kissed the chalice after partaking of it. [46] Kissing the priest's hand that imparts the Eucharistic bread may be an older custom than the eleventh century in the Byzantine Church, for it is found in Egypt about A.D. 500. [47] In some localities of the West, a related custom arose, kissing the priest's foot or the floor. [48]

---

[42] MSS. N. 528 of Sophia Library, p. 132; N. 543, p. 125; N. 530, p. 55; N. 532, p. 63; N. 531, p. 50, of same Library (cf. Krasnoseltsev, *Materialy dlja istorii chinoposlidovania liturgii sv. Ioanna Zlatoustago* [Kazan, 1889], p. 28); also *Liturgikon* of Isidore, Metropolitan of Kiev, in MS. *Vat. Slav.*, N. 14, fol. 144.

[43] MS. N. 986 of Sinai Library; MS. N. 381 of Moscow Synodal Library; MS. N. 573 of Vat.; cf. Krasnoseltsev, *op. cit.*, pp. 28, 113; Dmitrievsky, *Opysanie liturgicheskikh rukopisej khraniaschikhsia v bibliotekakh pravoslavnago vostoka*, Vol. II, *Euchologia* (Kiev, 1901), p. 613; also *Liturgikon* of Isidore, Metropolitan of Kiev, MS. *Vat. Slav.*, N. 14, fol. 144.

[44] Cf. Petrovsky, *Histoire*, pp. 876-877. This same formula is found in the fifteenth century *Molytovnyk-Sluzhebnyk* (edit. Kowaliv, *op. cit.*, p. 32 : " Peace in Christ, " and the response, " To your priesthood. "

[45] G. Aucher, *La versione armena della liturgia di S. Giovanni Crisostomo, fatta sul principio dell'VIII secolo*, XPYCOCTOMIKA (Rome, 1908), p. 395.

[46] *Liturgikon* of Isidore, Metropolitan of Kiev, cf. MS. *Vat. Slav.*, N. 14, fol. 144.

[47] *Cod. of Rossano*, a Gospel codex from Egypt, c. A.D. 500. Cf. A. Haseloff, *Codex purpureus Rossanensis* (Berlin, 1898), tables 6 and 7, pp. 102-106.

[48] *Liber ordinarius* of Liège (P. Volk, *Der Liber ordinarius des Lütticher St. Jakobs-Klosters* [Münster, 1923], p. 99). Circa 1256, the *Ordinarium* of the Dominicans abrogates the practice and requires only a genuflection (*Ordinarium iuxta ritum sacri Ordinis Fratrum Praedicatorum*, edit. F. Guerrini [Rome, 1921], 247).

CHAPTER LXX

THE COMMUNION OF THE CLERGY : ACCOMPANYING PRAYERS

When Justin describes the Eucharistic celebration in his day, he says nothing about any prayer accompanying the actual reception of Holy Communion. There was probably no set prayer. Later, at least during the Baptismal Eucharist, a simple prayer of administration was said. As related by Hippolytus, its text read : (1) for the Bread, " The bread of heaven in Christ Jesus "; (2) for the water, milk and wine, " In God the Father Almighty (water), and in the Lord Jesus Christ (milk), and in the Holy Spirit which is in the Holy Church (wine) "; (3) the response " Amen " was said by the recipient after each. [1]

After Nicaea in both East and West the formula of administration was merely Σῶμα Χριστοῦ, " The body of Christ, " [2] and for the chalice, Αἷμα Χριστοῦ, " The blood of Christ, " [3] or the slightly fuller Αἷμα Χριστοῦ ποτήριον ζωῆς, " The blood of Christ, the chalice of life. " [4] The formulae are probably pre-Nicene even though the evidence is all post-Nicene. Sometimes, perhaps on solemn occasions such as baptisms and ordinations, expanded versions of these were used : " This is the bread of heaven, the body of Christ Jesus " and " This is the blood of Christ Jesus our

---

[1] Hippolytus, *Apostolic Tradition*, xxiii, 5 ff.; see above, pp. 66 f.

[2] *Apostolic Constitutions*, Book VIII (see above, p. 141, or Brightman, LEW, p. 25, line 7, for the Greek); Theodore of Mopsuestia, *Sermones catech.*, VI (Rücker, *Ritus Baptismi et Missae, quem descripsit Theodorus ep. Mopsuestenus in sermonibus catecheticis* [Münster, 1933], 37); Augustine, *Serm.* 272 (PL 38, 1247); Ambrose, *De sacr.*, IV, 5, 25 (Quasten, *Monumenta eucharistica et liturgia vetustissima* [Bonn, 1935-1937], 320).

[3] Theodore of Mopsuestia, *op. cit.*; the Arabic *Testamentum Domini* (cf. A. Baumstark, " *Ein ägyptische Mess und Taufliturgie vermutlich des 6 Jh.,* " in *Oriens christ.* (1901), p. 29.

[4] *Apostolic Constitutions*, Book VIII (see above, p. 141, or Brightman, LEW, p. 25, line 11, for the Greek); the *Sahidic Ecclesiastical Canons*, chap. 64 (Brightman, LEW, Appendix A, p. 462, or P. A. de Lagarde, *Aegyptiaca* [Göttingen, 1883] pp. 276 f.).

Lord " [5]—professions of faith in the Eucharist, as the Arabic *Testamentum Domini* specifically points out : " . . . to each (recipient) when he shares the bread. . . the priest offers witness that it is the body of Christ. " [6]　　That is why the response " Amen " to each of the formulae was important—as an act of affirmation that the recipient indeed believes the same. [7]　　Later, some of the Liturgies made the professions of faith even more explicitly.　Before the end of the early Christian period, for example, we find in the *Canons of Basil* a formula which clearly states : " This is the body of Christ that he offered for our sins " [8]—both an act of faith and an expression of the purpose for which the body and blood were offered.　Purpose was also expressed in the formula given at Ancyra, *c.* A.D. 430 : " The holy body of Christ Jesus unto life everlasting. " [9]

The phrases expressing purpose are combined in the Byzantine formula : " For the forgiveness of. . . sins and for life everlasting. " The Byzantine formula was also expanded in another way : by inserting " . . .is given to N——" between its first and final clauses and by adding qualifications of the body of Christ.　Aside from these additions, the formula is ancient and simple : " The . . .body of . . .Jesus Christ is given to N——for the remission of his sins and for life everlasting. " [10]　　Thus, it closely resembles those of Ancyra and the *Canons of Basil*.　Obviously, then, the formula is centuries older than the first Byzantine source quoting it.　This is confirmed by its presence in the ancient Liturgy of the East Syrians

---

[5] This is the formula used for baptismal Liturgies in the *Sahidic Ecclesiastical Canons* (Brightman, LEW, p. 464, or P. A. deLagarde, *op. cit.*, p. 257 f.).　It is not too different from that in the baptismal Mass of the *Apostolic Tradition* of Hippolytus.

[6] Cf. A. Baumstark, *op. cit.*, p. 29; Quasten, *op. cit.*, 258.

[7] In addition to the sources quoted above, the *Amen* as a response is verified by Cyril of Jerusalem, *Catechesis*, XXIII (*Mystag.*, V) (Quasten, *op. cit.*, 108 f.); the Syrian *Testamentum Domini*, I, 23 (Quasten, *op. cit.*, 258); Pope Cornelius according to Eusebius, *Hist. eccl.*, VI, 43, 19 (NPNF, Series II, Vol. I, p. 289), and, of course, repeatedly Augustine.　Further references in Bona, *Rerum Liturgicarum libri duo*, II, 17, 3 (842 f.).

[8] Can. 97 (edit. Riedel, 275).　The present Coptic formula is similar : " This is in truth the body and blood of Emmanuel our God " (Brightman, LEW, p. 186).

[9] Cf. Mark the Hermit, *Contra Nestorianos*, 24 (Kunze, *Marcus Eremita* [Leipzig, 1895], p. 192.

[10] The formula of administration to the laity includes both body and blood, since they receive both species at once.

which has : " The body of our Lord (is given) to the discreet priest (or deacon of God, or believer) for the pardon of offenses. " [11]   Both the naming of the recipient and the wish for the remission of his sins are part of general Syrian tradition as is evident from the Liturgy of St. James, both in the Greek and in the Syriac versions. [12]   The modifiers, " precious and holy and all-pure, " however, must have been added shortly before their first appearance in the twelfth or thirteenth century documents. [13]

Besides the formula of administration, there probably were no other prayers prescribed for the ancient Communion rite, but piety demanded private prayer.   Theodore of Mopsuestia tells his followers that they should go to Communion with lowered eyes and hands extended, and " that at the same time they should speak a word of adoration, " since they are about to receive the body of the King. [14] In the Byzantine Church, this " word of adoration " was left to individual piety until about the ninth or tenth century.   Even then, there was still only one prescribed prayer. [15]   More and more Communion prayers, generally brief, are found in later sources, especially among the Slavs.   In the twelfth century concelebtrated Liturgy, for example, each concelebrant said before receiving the holy gifts : " Give me, O Lord Jesus Christ, your holy body and your precious blood, but not for judgment or for condemnation. "   On receiving the Eucharistic bread from each other, they would say substantially the same formula as today; but before partaking of the chalice, the last concelebrant would say to the first : " The Father, the Son, and the Holy Spirit, " to which the first would reply : " I will receive the chalice of salvation; I will call upon the name of the Lord. "   After partaking of the chalice, each would say :

[11] Brightman, LEW, p. 298.

[12] The formulae for both may be found in Brightman, LEW, pp. 64-65, 103.

[13] Cod. Sin., N. 1020 (Dmitrievsky, Opysanie liturgicheskikh rukopisej khranias-chikhsia v bibliotekakh pravoslavnago vostoka, Vol. II, Euchologia [Kiev, 1901], p. 145).   The twelfth century Slav form still had only one modifier : the holy Body; the precious blood (cf. Petrovsky, Histoire de la rédaction slave de la liturgie de S. Jean Chrysostome, XPYCOCTOMIKA (Rome, 1908), p. 871).

[14] Theodore of Mopsuestia, Sermones catech., VI (Rücker, op. cit., 36).

[15] Cod. of Imperial Library of St. Petersburg (Cod. Porphyrios), cf. Krasnoselt-sev, Svidinia o nikotorikh liturgicheskikh rukopis'akh Vatikanskoi biblioteki (Kazan, 1885), p. 204.

" May this be for me, O Lord, unto the remission of my sins. " [16]
Except for minor changes in the reception of the chalice, the same
order was followed when only one priest celebrated. [17]   One
difference, however, is intriguing.   After consuming the bread,
the priest would say : " This coal (of the body of Christ) is touched
to my lips [18]—an obvious import from Syria, since both East and
West Syrians have similar forms. [19]

In the thirteenth century, several significant additions were made
to the Communion rite, among them the words of the centurion
from Capernaum : " Lord, I know I am not worthy that you should
enter under my roof, " [20] added after the First Prayer before Communion, and also used in the Latin Church two centuries before. [21]
This seems to be a parallel but independent development.

Some of the additions were minor, [22] others, more important,
such as the insertion after Communion of the clergy of the words :
" Lord, I believe and confess.... " [23]   This constitutes the first
element of the present Slav prayer bearing the same name.   The
second is the *troparion*, " Receive me this day as a partaker of your
Mystical Supper..., " introduced in the fourteenth century. [24]

[16] MS. N. 342 of Moscow Synodal Library (Gorsky-Nevostrujev, *Opysanie
slavianskikh rukopisej Moskovskoj Synodal'noj biblioteky*, Vol. III [Moscow, 1859],
I, 7).
[17] Gorsky-Nevostrujev, *op. cit.*, III, 1, 7.
[18] *Ibid.*
[19] I.e., " The propitiatory coal of the body and blood of Christ our God is
given to a sinful servant for the pardon of offenses and for the remission of sins
in both worlds for ever and ever. Amen. " Cf. Brightman, LEW, pp. 103, 63-64.
[20] Petrovsky, *op. cit.*, p. 876.
[21] E.g., Sacramentary of S. Thierry (end of the tenth century); cf. Martène,
De antiquis Ecclesiae ritibus (2nd edit., Antwerp, 1736), I, 4, XXXV (I, 670 C);
Sacramentary of Moissac (eleventh century), cf. Martène, *op. cit.*, I, 4, VIII (I,
540 f.); Salzburg Missal of the twelfth or thirteenth century, cf. edit. Köck,
131; etc.
[22] Cf. Petrovsky, *op. cit.*, pp. 876-877.
[23] MS. N. 719 of Patmos Library (Dmitrievsky, *op. cit.*, II, p. 175); MS. N.
524 of Sophia Library, pp. 45-46; and MS. N. 518 of same Library, pp. 36-38
Petrovsky, *op. cit.*, p. 877).
[24] MS. N. 523 of Sophia Library, p. 44, and MS. N. 522 of same Library,
p. 36 (Petrovsky, *op. cit.*, p. 885). This *tropar* is found as a proper in the Holy
Thursday Office of solemn Vespers conjoined with the Divine Liturgy of Basil;
here it is sung in Tone VI in place of the cherubic hymn and in place of
the πλερθετο *(Da ispolniatsia)*; it also serves as the Communion hymn or
κοινονικόν *(prychasten)*.

Fifteenth century Ukrainian and Russian missals have a variety of Communion prayers, including all three elements of the present form (except the threefold exclamation of the Good Thief, found today in the Ukrainian text). [25] Neither the authors of these prayers nor the dates of their composition are known. As private prayers for Communion, they undoubtedly date back much further than the time of their incorporation into Byzantine and Slav liturgical texts. The first appears in the early eighth century Armenian version of Chrysostom : " I believe and confess that you are the Son of God who takest away the sins of the world, " [26] said three times by the priest when he took the Eucharistic Bread into his hands to adore it before consuming it. There is no Byzantine trace of this until five centuries later. Byzantine priests must also have used this act of faith at Communion, but only as an elective devotion.

The private nature of the present prayer is evident from the use of the first-person-singular. The words—addressed solely to the Son of God—are not in the ancient style. The *ecclesia* of Christian antiquity prayed as the body of Christ and addressed its prayer to the Triune God, or to the Father, in the first-person-plural. The roots, however, may be ancient, as, for instance, the third element which resembles the deacon's part in the post-Communion thanksgiving in the *Apostolic Constitutions* :

Byzantine Communion Prayer (third element)	*Apostolic Constitutions*
Lord, may the partaking of your holy sacrament be to me not for judgment or condemnation, but for the healing of my soul and body.	...to partake of his holy mysteries. Let us beseech him that it be not for our condemnation but for our salvation for the benefit of our soul and body. [27]

[25] *Liturgikon* of Isidore, Metropolitan of Kiev; cf. MS. *Vat. Slav.*, N. 14, fols. 142-144; MS. N. 1029 of Solovetzky, fols. 160-164, and MS. N. 602 of Moscow Synodal Library, fol. 46.

[26] G. Aucher, *La versione armena della liturgia di S. Giovanni Crisostomo, fatta sul principio dell'VIII secolo*, XPYCOCTOMIKA (Rome, 1908), pp. 395-396.

[27] Book VIII (cf. above, p. 142). The *Perceptio* prayer of the Latin Mass, sometimes called a " prayer of St. John Chrysostom, " is similar : " Let not the receiving of thy body, O Lord Jesus Christ, which I, all unworthy, presume to take, turn to my judgment and condemnation; but through thy goodness, may it

Other fifteenth-century prayers accepted in the Slav Liturgy disappeared a century or two later. [28]   Other changes were made in the same century. [29]

Communion prayers remained fluid during the next centuries. Present-day Orthodox missals vary in accordance with local usage. There are many other semiliturgical Communion prayers and usages, some of which are both ancient and beautiful.   Lack of uniformity may be explained in part by the absence of central authority and in part by the feeling that Communion is so intimate and private a matter that the choice of devotion should be left to the individual. Uniformity in the Catholic recensions of the Russian and Ukrainian Communion ritual took centuries because of this sense of personalism. Final achievement of unity was due to Rome.   Standardization always has its price—in this case, the charm of individualism and variety.

avail me as a safeguard and healing remedy for soul and body. ”   Encountered for the first time in Carolingian missals of the tenth century, the *Perceptio* prayer reflects a later personal and private form (cf. *Sacramentary* of Fulda, edit. G. Richter - A. Schoenfelder [Fulda, 1921], n. 24; *Sacramentary* of Tatoldus of Corbie [PL 78, 244]).   Only after the publication of Pius V's *Missale* in 1570 was its place in the Latin Mass settled definitely.

[28] E.g., compare the various manuscripts of Sophia Library : MS. N. 531, p. 49; MS. N. 536, p. 50; MS. N. 530, p. 55; MS. N. 562, p. 42; MS. N. 567, p. 44; MS. N. 529, p. 73 (Petrovsky, *op. cit.*, pp. 910-912); also MS. N. 381 of Moscow Synodal Library (Krasnoseltsev, *Materialy dlja istorii chinoposlidovania liturgii sv. Ioanna Zlatoustago* [Kazan, 1889], p. 28); MS. N. 573 of Vat. (Krasnoseltsev, *Materialy*, p. 113); etc.

[29] See all sources indicated in n. 28, above.

CHAPTER LXXI

THE COMMUNION OF THE FAITHFUL :
IN GENERAL

At the *chabûrah*, the leader or father of the house distributed the broken bread. At the Last Supper, Christ gave out the Communion. A little more than a century later, Justin Martyr leaves the impression that giving Communion was the office of the deacon. He merely mentions the fact, without elaboration, but he does mention it twice. [1] About fifty years later, Hippolytus insists more than once that, if possible, the bishop is the one who must give the bread to all the communicants " with his own hand. " The priests (presbyters) are to administer the chalice, or " if there are not enough of them, the deacons also. " [2] This arrangement is confirmed by the *Apostolic Constitutions*, which explicitly state that " the bishop should give the *prosphora* (the host), " [3] and the deacons, the chalice. [4] The thirteenth canon of the Council of Neocaesarea (*c.* A.D. 315), on the other hand, indicates that both bread and chalice are given either by a bishop or by presbyters. [5] Basil does not mention the chalice, but he does write about priests giving the bread as if that were the ordinary procedure. [6]

Clearly, then, the practice differed from place to place in Christian antiquity. The most common system seems to have been the follow-

---

[1] Justin Martyr, *First Apology*, chaps. 65 and 67 (see above, pp. 41 f.). The reference in chap. 65 is clear but chap. 67 is uncertain (" a share is taken by the deacons to those who are absent ").

[2] *Apostolic Tradition*, xxiii, 5 f. (Dix, *The Treatise on the Apostolic Tradition of St. Hippolytus of Rome* [London, 1937], 41).

[3] Book VIII (see above, p. 141).

[4] *Ibid.* The same is found also in Cyprian, *De lapsis*, 25 (CSEL, 3, 255); Augustine, *Serm.* 304, 1 (PL 38, 1395); *Testamentum Domini*, II, 10 (Quasten, *Monumenta eucharistica et liturgia vetustissima* [Bonn, 1935-1937], 273); John Moschus, *Pratum spirituale*, 219 (PG 87, 2109 C).

[5] Canon 13 of Neocaesarea reads : " Country presbyters may not make the oblation in a city church when the bishop or presbyters of the city are present; nor may they give the bread or the cup with prayer. If they are absent, however, and he [the country presbyter] alone is called to prayer, he may give them " (Mansi, *Sacrorum conciliorum nova et amplissima collectio*, Vol. II, 542 DE).

[6] Basil, *Ep.* 93 (PG 32, 485-486).

ing : In a pontifical celebration, the bishop gave the bread, the priests and/or the deacons, the chalice; in non-pontifical gatherings, the priest-celebrant gave the bread, and the deacons, the cup. This made good sense and order; also, it saved time. The distribution of Communion would have taken twice as long if the celebrant himself had given both, and the two successive line-ups would have created a further difficulty. Later, in almost all Oriental Churches, the bread was given together with the blood (by having the host permeated with the consecrated wine) and the deacon lost his part. In the Byzantine Church, however, he still administers Communion to himself as described above. He may also administer Communion to others, take the Sacrament to the sick, etc. In former times, lay people were given these privileges. Even after the persecutions, they were allowed to administer Communion to themselves if no bishop, priest or deacon were present; Canon 58 of the Trullan Synod (A.D. 692) is clear. [7] In similar circumstances, deaconesses in convents of nuns among the West Syrian Jacobites were permitted to administer Communion, not only to their fellow Sisters but also to little children. [8] Likewise, lay people brought Communion to the sick if the need arose. During the time of Dionysius of Alexandria, for example, a boy brought Communion to the aged Sarapion. [9] The Western Church had instances of Communion being given to the sick by lay people, but this was usually regarded as an abuse since various prohibitions were issued against the practice. [10]

Frequency

Until the fourth century, receiving Communion was considered so much a part of the Eucharistic Sacrifice that it would have been unthinkable to attend without partaking. The term προσενέγκειν,

---

[7] Can. 58 reads : " None of those who are in the order of laymen may distribute the Divine Mysteries to himself if a bishop, presbyter, or deacon be present " (Mansi, op. cit., XI, 969).

[8] From special containers. Cf. C. Kayser, Die Kanones Jakobs von Edessa übersetzt und erläutert, zum Theil auch zuert im Grundtext veröffentlich (Leipzig, 1886), 19.

[9] Eusebius, Hist. eccl., VI, 44 (PG 13, 251 AC [Series graeca]).

[10] E.g., Canons of Bishop Rötger of Trier (927), Canon 6 (edit. M. Blasen, Pastor bonus, 52 [1941], 67; Decretum Gratiani, III, 2, 29 (edit. Freidberg, I, 1323 f.); also cf. Browe, " Die Sterbekommunion, " ZkTh (1936), pp. 9-11.

describing the layman's part in the liturgy, means " to bring the *prosphora*," and also, " to be a communicant" (see above, p. 65). In fact, the faithful received the Sacrament more often than they attended the sacrifice, usually celebrated on Sunday only, the day of the Lord. Communion could be received at home any day. [11] The custom was founded on piety : i.e., the desire of Christians to receive their Lord more often than at the weekly Eucharist. During the persecutions, attendance at the weekday Liturgy was impossible.

In his letter of A.D. 372 to the Patrician Caesaria (or Caesarius), Basil speaks quite plainly : " All the solitaries in the desert, where there is no priest, take Communion themselves from the sacrament they keep at home. And at Alexandria and Egypt, each one of the laity regularly keeps it [the Eucharist] in his own home and partakes of it whenever he wishes. " [12] In Syria, the practice was still current in the sixth century, for John Moschus speaks of the faithful being accustomed to take home with them on Holy Thursday enough of the Eucharist to last the year. [13] In most places, however, after the persecutions had ended, the sacrament could be received only at the liturgical service.

About the time of Nicaea, the original concept was still very much in evidence. If an individual Christian's conduct or belief was incompatible with his right to receive the sacrament, he was dismissed before the Eucharistic service began; if he had a right to stay, he had the right to receive Communion. The " offerer " was also the " communicant. "

Then the approach changed suddenly : attending the Liturgy and receiving the Eucharist were no longer considered complementary. A new devotional sentiment of fear and awe prevailed. When the

[11] Cyprian tells of a woman who kept the Eucharist in an *arca* in order to be able to receive Communion in her home during the week (*De lapsis*, 27 [CSEL, 3, 256]); Tertullian indicates the practice when he asks, " Will not your husband know what it is that you secretly consume before any other food? " (*Ad uxorem*, II, 5 [CSEL, 70, 118]), and perhaps less clearly in referring to it " on the days of stations " when the Eucharist could be taken home and received in the evening (*De or.*, 19 [CSEL, 20, 192]). Cf. also Ps.-Cyprian, *De spectaculis*, 5 (CSEL, 3, 3, p. 8, 1. 11) and Hippolytus, *Apostolic Tradition* (Dix, *op. cit.*, pp. 58 f.

[12] Basil, *Ep.* 92 (PG 32, 485).

[13] John Moschus, *Pratum spirituale*, 79 (PG 87, 2936 f.). They preserved it in a locked cupboard.

" language of fear, " with terms like " dread " and " terrifying, " became commonplace in the description of the sacrament, the laity responded by feeling unworthy and afraid. During the fourth and fifth centuries, the frequency of reception decreased sharply in the East. In Syria, the introduction of the veil resulting from the same state of mind served to compound the process. Chrysostom, who combines this language of fear with his powerful rhetoric, naïvely wonders : " In vain do we stand before the altar : there is no one to partake. " [14]

The trend could not be checked. In the land of the Greeks, it found special soil in which to thrive. Many inland communities were still close to paganism, whose religious beliefs included terrifying aspects, which were all-too easily revived by the new approach to the Sacrament. The psychology of fear can explain much in the life of the Byzantine Church : its special ethos of " mystery " and " awe, " its atmosphere in which man dares to approach his God only in dread and trepidation, the all-pervading influence of the Pantocrator, the heavenly Emperor, the Supreme Lawgiver and Judge. Such psychology resulted also in a severe penitential system which granted absolution only after the penance, often severe and long, had been fulfilled. The Greek Orthodox still regard as authoritative the medieval and, to us, frightfully severe *Penitential* attributed to Patriarch John the Fuller. It is not surprising, then, that the reception of the sacrament would become a once-a-year affair.

The decline of frequent Communion, symptomatic of the same spirit, gradually seeped into the Western Church. In some places, it was swift and sudden, as it had been in the East. In Milan, for example, we find such a decline toward the end of the fourth century. This prompted the kindly Ambrose to rebuke those who received Communion only once a year, and to accuse them of acting *quemadmodum Graeci in Oriente facere consuerunt.* [15] It was typical that Gaul, so often influenced by Byzantium in liturgical matters, should have been an early victim of the same spirit. In A.D. 506,

---

[14] Chrysostom, *In Eph. homil.*, 3, 4 (edit. Montfaucon 11, 23, or PG 62, 29); also cf. *In Hebr. homil.*, 17, 4 (edit. Montfaucon 12, 169 f., or PG 63, 131 f.); *In I Tim. homil.*, 5, 3 (edit. Montfaucon 11, 577 f., or PG 62, 529 f.).

[15] Ambrose, *De sacr.*, V, 4, 25 (Quasten, *op. cit.*, 169).

the Synod of Agde found it necessary to insist on Communion three times yearly as a minimum. [16] The same legislation had to be repeated elsewhere in the West. The Lateran Council of 1215 reduced the minimum to an absolute minimum requirement : Communion once a year during Eastertime. [17]

When the Eastern Slavs accepted Christianity from Byzantium, they adopted not only its faith but also its ritualism, traditions, and Canon Law—the *Nomokanons*. All of these contributed to keeping the faithful away from the Sacrament. On the grounds of canon law alone, the myriad problems of ritual uncleanness and unworthiness were enough to make people abstain for months at a time. The ritually unclean were forbiden to kiss the cross or the Gospel Book, and even to enter a church. Much less could they receive the Sacrament. [18] The law was sometimes more lenient in case of illness. For example, sacred acts forbidden to women during menstruation were permitted to the sick—even Holy Communion provided the illness had lasted " one year or half a year. " [19] No matter how ardent their desire or the holiness of their lives, the Slavs could not receive the Sacrament frequently. The customs of centuries cannot be eradicated with a decree : the road back to frequent Communion is still long and arduous for them. It is unfortunate that the Church, so careful to preserve primitive practices, abandoned this all-important one.

Communion of Infants

One of the primitive Eucharistic practices which the Oriental Churches has not abandoned is that of imparting Communion to infants. Western authors seldom praise it, [20] yet, in the primitive Church, Communion (under the species of wine) was given to infants and children after baptism. No one seriously questions the testimony of Cyprian in this regard. [21] Augustine, in incidental

---

[16] At Christmas, Easter, and Pentecost, Canon 18 (Mansi, *op. cit.*, VIII, 327).

[17] Cf. Browe, *Die Pflichtkommunion im Mittelalter* (Münster, 1940), pp. 43 f.

[18] E.g., *Kirik*, 42; *Kirik-Sabbas*, 23; *Kirik*, 26; etc.

[19] *Kirik*, 45.

[20] Most books on the Eucharist and the Mass ignore it entirely.

[21] Cyprian, *De lapsis*, 25 (CSEL, 3, 255, or PL 4, 484).

references to child Communion, writes that it was administered either under the form of wine alone or under both species. [22] Communion under the species of wine alone to newly baptized children is also mentioned by Paulinus of Nola (*d.* A.D. 431). [23] Other sources from early times also testify to the practice. [24]

Such baptismal Communions were discontinued in the Western Church by the twelfth century. Of all the Catholic Oriental Churches, the Copts are the only ones who still administer baptismal Communion to infants. [25] To their credit, all the Orthodox still do it faithfully—generally under the form of wine, since infants may not be able to swallow the bread. The infant's hands are usually held to obviate the danger of spilling the consecrated wine.

A similar but not identical custom consisted in giving children the remainder of sacred species. In the sixth century, Evagrius Scholasticus (d. A.D. 594) reported that this was done in Constantinople from ancient times. [26] In the same century, the Synod of Macon instructed its clerics to call in the children on Wednesdays and Fridays and to administer to them the fragments of consecrated bread left over from the Sunday Communion. [27] In the Church of Constantinople, the custom must have lasted at least a thousand years. [28] As late as the early fourteenth century, Nicephorus Callistus (d. *c.* 1341) refers to his own childhood experience. [29]

[22] Augustine, *Opus imp.*, II, 30 (PL 45, 1154); *Ep.* 217, 5 (PL 33, 984 f.).

[23] Paulinus of Nola, *Ep.* 32, 5 (PL 61, 333); the phrase *cruda salutiferis imbuit ora cibis* can only be applicable to the species of wine.

[24] Cf. Martène, *De antiquis Ecclesiae ritibus*, I, xiv; Eisenhofer, *Handbuch der Katholischen Liturgik* (Freiburg, 1933), II, pp. 265 f.; J. Baumgärtler, *Die Erstkommunion* (Munich, 1929), pp. 30 ff.; Leclercq, "Communion des enfants," in DACL, III, 2249 f.

[25] Cf. L. Andrieux, *La première communion* (Paris, 1911), pp. 73-77.

[26] Evagrius Scholasticus, *Hist. eccl.*, IV, 36 (PG 86, 2796 A).

[27] Canon 6 (Mansi, *op. cit.*, IX, 952).

[28] Cf. Browe, "Wann fing man an, die in einer Messe konsekrierten Hostien in einer anderen Messe auszuteilen?" (*Theologie und Glaube*, 30 [1938], pp. 393 f.

[29] Nicephorus Callistus, *Hist. eccl.*, 17, 25 (PG 147, 280).

CHAPTER LXXII

THE COMMUNION OF THE FAITHFUL : RITE

T*he priest divides the remaining particles of the large host, then the deacon puts all the hosts in the chalice and wipes the* diskos *thoroughly with the sponge or with his thumb. Finally, he covers the chalice with the* lention *(corporal) or with the small veil.*

If the royal doors were closed, they are now opened. After making a small bow, the deacon reverently receives the chalice from the priest, proceeds to the royal doors and, raising the chalice, shows it to the people and intones :

Approach with the fear of God and with faith.

People : **Blessed is he who comes in the name of the Lord; God the Lord has revealed himself to us.** [1]

The deacon returns to the altar, puts the chalice on it and removes the veil. The priest takes the chalice, spoon, and lention, turns to face the people and recites aloud the prayer : " Lord, I believe and confess.... " After the prayer, the faithful approach, either one by one or according to any procedure dictated by local custom, to receive Holy Communion. The deacon holds the diskos *under the chin of each communicant while the priest distributes the hosts with the spoon. As he gives each a particle, he says :*

The servant of God, N——, is receiving the precious, holy, and most pure body and blood of our Lord, God, and Saviour, Jesus Christ, for the remission of his (her) sins and for life everlasting.

Weh ave already seen the historical background of the Communion rite in the preceding chapters (pp. 666 ff., 691 ff., 705 f.). The prayer, *I believe and confess,* is the same as that before the Communion of the clergy; the form of administration is also the same except

---

[1] In some places, the Russians add : " Hear, O Lord, my voice which cries to you, and have mercy on me. Alleluia, alleluia, elleluia. "

that adjustment is made to take into consideration the giving of both species together.

The only points of difference are the invitation for the faithful to approach and its response. These go back in time well beyond the early eighth century text of Chrysostom in which they first appear. The Armenian version of that period has the deacon turning to the people with the gifts and inviting them to receive as he says : " Approach with fear and with faith. " The people answered as they do today : " Blessed is he who comes in the name of the Lord : [our] God and Lord has revealed himself to us. " [2] Most probably, the Armenian Church received this item of the ritual from the Byzantines during their occupation of Armenia in the seventh century; however, it may have come earlier from Caesarea. In either case, it originated from the North Syrian Liturgy of the *Apostolic Constitutions*. According to this document, immediately after the response, " One is holy, one Lord..., " the people continued with Luke 2:14 : " Hosanna to the Son of David. Blessed is he that cometh in the name of the Lord. God is the Lord and hath appeared to us. Hosanna in the highest. " [3] The whole response, however, was completed before the people came to receive the Eucharist, since the rubric indicates that Psalm 33 was sung " during the Communion of the faithful. " The last part of this response would have been sung then in approximately the same way as it is today.

The source of the deacon's announcement, " Approach with fear of God and with faith, " may also be seen in the *Apostolic Constitutions*. After enumerating the orders of clergy who were to approach Communion in turn, the rubric states : "...and finally, all the people in order, with reverence and godly fear, without noise. " [4] This rubrical instruction later became an actual pronouncement by the deacons in their efforts to keep good order among the faithful. This is not the first time that a rubric or what had originally been a mere rubrical prescription was later incorporated into the liturgical text. By the time this direction appears again, in the eighth and ninth

---

[2] G. Aucher, *La versione armena della liturgia di S. Giovanni Crisostomo, fatta sul principio dell'VIII secolo*, XPYCOCTOMIKA (Rome, 1908), p. 396.

[3] *Apostolic Constitutions*, Book VIII; see above, p. 141.

[4] *Ibid.*; see above, p. 141.

centuries, it is definitely so. [5]   And it has not changed since then. [6]

A personal touch is given to the distribution of Communion when the Christian name of each communicant is inserted into the formula of administration.   This, of course, presupposes a true family relationship between the pastor and his parishioners.

Sanctification the Senses

When Cyril of Jerusalem described the reception of Communion in his day, he instructed his catechumens to sanctify their eyes, forehead, and other senses with the sacred species before consuming them. [7]   The practice probably originated in the Syrian Church for it is mentioned even before Cyril by another Syrian, from the East, Aphraates of Persia. [8]   " The blessing of the senses " is still found in the East Syrian Liturgy.

Other related customs arose, such as the one mentioned without disapproval by Augustine of a lady who applied on the eyes of her blind boy a compress containing the Eucharist, [9] taking the Eucharist along on a journey, [10] etc.   Such things could easily degenerate into abuse. [11]   The Byzantine Church once had a practice very similar to that described by Cyril : the priest made the sign of the

---

[5] The Armenian version (Aucher, op. cit., p. 396), and Cod. Barberini, gr. 336 (Brightman, LEW, p. 341, line 25).   The Greek St. James has : " Approach with the fear of God " (Brightman, LEW, p. 64, line 24).

[6] Except that during the thirteenth century, some of the Slav churches replaced its response with " To Christ, our God and King. . . . "   (MS. N. 518, p. 40; and MS. N. 524, p. 50, of Sophia Library contain this response; cf. Petrovsky, Histoire de la rédaction slave de la liturgie de S. Jean Chrysostome, XPYCOCTOMIKA [Rome, 1908], p. 877).

[7] Cyril of Jerusalem, Catechesis, XXIII (Mystag., V), 21-22 (Quasten, Monumenta eucharistica et liturgia vetustissima [Bonn, 1935-1937], 108-110).

[8] Aphraates of Persia (fl. 336-345), Homil. 7, 8 (BKV, Select Writings of the Syrian Church Fathers [1874], p. 99); cf. also the sixth century Canonibus ad Iacobum episcopum Insularum, Canon I (O. Braun, Das Buch der Synhados nach einer Handschrift des Museo Borgiano [Stuttgart, 1900], p. 240).

[9] Augustine, Opus imp. c. Julianum, III, 162 (PL 45, 1315).

[10] Ambrose, De excessu fratris sui Satyri, I, 43 (PL 16, 1304); Gregory the Great, Dial., III, 36 (PL 77, 304 C).

[11] Cf. Dölger, Antike u. Christentum, 5 (1936), pp. 232-247, " Die Eucharistie als Reiseschutz " and Corblet, Histoire dogmatique, liturgique et archéologique de l'eucharistie, Vol. I (Paris, 1886), 527-535.

cross on his forehead with the eucharistic bread. This is mentioned only once. [12]

In view of the Slav Church's severity in connection with physico-ritual uncleanness, it is inconceivable that any excesses regarding the sacrament had ever existed in that Church. A Church which entertained doubts as to the admissibility to Communion of " a man who has a sore from which pus is suppurating " or " if blood is oozing from his teeth, " [13] or a man " who eats garlic the day before, " [14] would surely not have countenanced anything which even remotely suggested impropriety. Old Russia and the Ukraine would have been horrified at any abuse of the sacrament, however small. The Slav Church did indeed believe that the Eucharistic Christ would heal bodies as well as souls; this is evident from some of the phrases in the pre-Communion prayers, phrases like " cure the sick, O Physician of souls and bodies, " that the sacrament be " for the healing of my soul and body. " But this was to be ac-complished by a worthy and proper reception of the sacrament and not by its application as a talisman or compress!

Communion with a Spoon

Perhaps the greatest objection to the Eastern method of imparting Communion with a spoon is that it is not hygienic. Anyone making such an objection does not know what he is talking about. One does not *eat* with this spoon. This method is actually more hygienic than distributing Communion with the fingers. If properly handled, the spoon seldom if ever touches the lips, teeth, or tongue. The recipient receives with his head held back and the mouth well open, the tongue inside. The priest *drops* the host from the spoon into the mouth. If the particle adheres to the spoon, the priest will touch the recipient's teeth with it—not the spoon. If the spoon does happen to touch any part of the recipient's mouth, it may be im-

---

[12] Esphigmenon MS. of year 1306. Cf. Krasnoseltsev, *Materialy dlja istorii chinoposlidovania liturgii sv. Ioanna Zlatoustago* (Kazan, 1889), p. 16; Dmitrievsky, *Opysanie liturgicheskikh rukopisej khraniaschikhsia v bibliotekakh pravoslavnago vostoka*, Vol. II, *Euchologia* (Kiev, 1901), p. 260.

[13] *Kirik*, 61, 62.

[14] *Precept of the Holy Fathers to Confessing Sons and Daughters*, 41.

mersed into the wine— a mild disinfectant—before Communion is given next.

Imparting Communion with the fingers has no such safeguards. If the priest happens to touch the lips or tongue of the recipient, he cannot dip his fingers. Nor can the fingers ever be as thoroughly cleansed as the spoon before the distribution of Communion. Finally, the fingers are closer to the lips of the recipient than the spoon and, hence, much more likely to touch them.

The sincere believer has no such materialistic scruple. After the example of Christ, the primitive Church had the celebrant break the common loaf and give a fragment to each one present; the precious blood was imparted from the common chalice. Then as now, it is the Divine Physician himself who is given to the faithful, the gentle, healing Christ who walked the byways of Palestine nearly two thousand years ago. The Eucharist is the divine remedy, the divine medicine that can heal all our ills of body and soul.

CHAPTER LXXIII

THE POST-COMMUNION RITUAL

After the Communion of the faithful, the priest leaves the spoon in the chalice, which he covers with the lention. Then, after returning to the sanctuary with the deacon, he places the chalice on the altar. There, the deacon covers the chalice with its veil. The priest again takes the covered chalice, goes to the royal doors and blesses the people with it, while he intones :

O God, save your people and bless your inheritance.

People : **We have seen the true light and have received the heavenly Spirit; we have found the true faith. Let us worship the undivided Trinity that has saved us.** [1]

Both priest and deacon return to the altar ; the priest sets the chalice on the altar and incenses it three times as he says :

May you be exalted above the heavens, O God, and may your glory be over all the earth.

After giving the censer to the deacon, he takes the diskos *and places it upon the head of the deacon. Holding it reverently to his forehead*

---

[1] In the Russian recension of the Liturgy, the post-Communion ritual is somewhat different. After the chalice is placed on the altar, the deacon or priest cleanses the *diskos* while he prays the following silently :

After seeing Christ's resurrection, let us adore the holy Lord, Jesus Christ, who alone is without sin. O Christ, we worship your cross; we sing and express the glory of your holy resurrection. You are our God; we know no other than you; we call upon your name. Come, all you faithful, let us worship Christ's holy resurrection. For behold, joy has come to all the world through the cross. While we continually bless the Lord, we sing of his resurrection; for he has endured the cross and has destroyed death by death.

Shine on, O new Jerusalem, shine on, for the glory of the Lord has shone upon you. Rejoice now and be glad, O Sion. Come forth in splendor, pure Mother of God, for he whom you bore is risen.

O Christ, great and most holy Passover! O Wisdom, Word, and Power of God! Grant that we may receive you more perfectly in the day of your eternal Kingdom.

The Orthodox recite the same resurrection hymns while they are putting the particles into the chalice before the Communion of the faithful. Cf. K. Nikolsky, *Posobie k izucheniu Ustava Bogosluzhenia pravoslavnoi tserkvy* (St. Petersburg, 1907), p. 446.

and looking out toward the people, the deacon says nothing but proceeds between the altar and the royal doors directly to the proskomidia table *where he sets the* diskos *down and waits for the priest.*

The priest makes a small bow, takes the chalice, and turns toward the people as he prays silently :

Blessed is our God.

Then, he intones :

At all times, now and always and for ever and ever.
People : **Amen.**

The priest goes to the proskomidia table *while the deacon incenses both the sacred species and the priest. After setting down the holy gifts, the priest makes a small bow and returns to the altar. The people in the meantime have begun the singing of the* troparion, Πληρωθήτο.

May our lips be filled with your praise, O Lord, so that we may sing your glory, because you have deigned to make us partakers of your holy, divine, immortal, and life-giving mysteries. Keep us in your holiness so that all the day long we may meditate on your righteousness. Alleluia, alleluia, alleluia.

At this point, the *Apostolic Constitutions* of the ancient North Syrian Rite reads as follows : " When all, even the women, have received (the Sacrament), the deacons should carry what remains into the sacristy. "[2] The present ceremonial developed around this simple action.

The blessing with a verse, " O God, save your people and bless your inheritance " (Psalm 27:9), appear first in the early eighth-century Armenian version of Chrysostom 's Liturgy.[3] The blessing was given with the hand and not with the chalice—as is still done in some Orthodox churches.[4] The psalm verse was said by the priest, and the people responded " Amen. "[5] This seems to have

[2] *Apostolic Constitutions*, Book VIII; see above, p. 142.

[3] G. Aucher, *La versione armena della liturgia di S. Giovanni Crisostomo, fatta sul principio dell'VIII secolo*, ΧΡΥCΟCΤΟΜΙΚΑ (Rome, 1908), p. 396.

[4] E.g., in the monasteries of Mount Athos.

[5] Aucher, *op. cit.*, p. 396.

been also the original Constantinopolitan practice.   About a century later, the Byzantine Church shortened the verse. [6]

Redemption has to be applied to each man through personal cooperation with the grace of God.   That is why the priest prays that the Lord save his people, that he endow them with efficacious grace.   The best guarantee of salvation is Communion.   We have the word of Christ for that.   " He that eateth this bread shall live forever " (John 6:59).   That is why Ignatius of Antioch insisted that the Eucharistic bread is " the drug of immortality, the remedy that will prevent our death. " [7]

We are Christ's inheritance.   " Now, inheritance is a far closer relationship than creation, " says Cabasilas, and he explains :

> The Son, in inheriting us, possesses us far more highly and excellently than he did by creating us.   Through creation, he had dominion over man's nature; through inheritance, he has become Lord of our minds and wills, and that is true dominion....
>
> But how did he, by inheritance, become Lord of our minds and wills?   In this way : we subjected them to him who came down on earth....   we submitted our minds in recognizing him as true God and sovereign lord of every creature; we submitted our wills in giving him our love, accepting his rule, and taking his yoke upon our shoulders with joy....   it was this possession that the prophet Isaiah desired so long ago, when he said : " O Lord our God, possess us. "   This is the inheritance which the Scriptures tell us that the Only-Begotten received from his Father, and which we recall in this prayer. [8]

There was a tendency to omit this beautiful proclamation during the thirteenth century—a time of liturgical indifference. [9]

---

[6] Brightman, LEW, p. 341, line 29.

[7] Ignatius of Antioch, *Ad Eph.*, chap. 20, 1-2 (edit. F. X. Funk, *Patres Apostolici* [Tübingen, 1901], Vol. I, p. 230).

[8] Cabasilas, *A Commentary on the Divine Liturgy*, chap. 40, trans. by Hussey and McNulty (London, 1960), pp. 93-94.

[9] The proclamation is not found in the Patmos MS. N. 709 (of the year 1260); nor in MS. N. 1170 of Vat. (Dmitrievsky, *Opysanie liturgicheskikh rukopisej khraniaschikhsia v bibliotekakh pravoslavnago vostoka*, Vol. II, *Euchologia* [Kiev, 1901], pp. 158, 159); nor in MS. N. 518, p. 40, MS. N. 524, p. 50, of Sophia Library (Petrovsky, *Histoire de la rédaction slave de la liturgie de S. Jean Chrysostome*,

The priest probably began to bless the people with the sacred species, before the fifteenth century. In the fifteenth century Kievan Church, the blessing with the sacred species was given only if any of the faithful received Communion, otherwise the priest blessed with the hand while the deacon held the chalice. [10] This blessing represents that which Christ imparted upon his disciples at the ascension. This is the only benediction with the Blessed Sacrament known in the Byzantine Church, Greek or Slav. The Latin Benediction was introduced chiefly to counteract a heresy, the denial of the True Presence. In the Byzantine Church and in all of the East, no such heresy arose. Those few Eastern Catholic Rites which did introduce the Benediction did so under Western influence. The Ukrainians, for example, " created " a para-liturgical ceremony similar to the Latin. Its formula was borrowed from the Divine Liturgy. In the interest of preserving the purity of the Rite, this ceremony is being discouraged.

The present response of the people, " We have seen the true light, " is in fact a *troparion* taken from the solemn Vespers of Pentecost. Proper *troparia* are used on Easter Sunday and during its octave, on Ascension Thursday and during its octave, and on the Saturday before Pentecost. [11]

Transfer of Gifts - Plerotheto

According to the *Chronicon paschale*, the *Plerotheto* was introduced into the Byzantine Liturgy in A.D. 624 by Sergius, Patriarch of Constantinople. [12] There is no reason to doubt this testimony except that Chrysostom's Liturgy in its early eighth century Armenian version has what appears to be an earlier version of it, and it is quite different from that found in later Byzantine sources :

XPYCOCTOMIKA (Rome, 1908), p. 878). It is found, however, in MS. N. 719 of Patmos and in MS. N. 381 of Moscow Synodal Library (Dmitrievsky, *op. cit.*, II, p. 175, and Krasnoseltsev, *Svidinia o nikotorikh liturgicheskikh rukopis'akh Vatikanskoi biblioteki* [Kazan, 1885], p. 29).

[10] *Liturgikon* of Metropolitan Isidore (fifteenth century), cf. MS. *Vat. Slav.*, N. 14, fol. 145.

[11] Cf. K. Nikolsky, *op. cit.*, pp. 449-450.

[12] *Chronicon paschale*, 390 (PG 92, 1001).

We have been filled with thy good things, O Lord, tasting thy body and blood. Glory be on high to thee, who hast fed us. Thou who continually feedest us, send down upon us thy spiritual blessing. Glory be on high to thee, who hast fed us. [13]

Yet, in the Constantinopolitan Liturgy of the ninth century, the *Plerotheto* is the same as it is now, except for two words. [14] Surely, the content and position of both the Armenian and Byzantine versions are too close to be the result of a mere coincidence. Both probably have their origin in a common North Syrian ancestor. Verse 8 of Psalm 70 seems to have been that common ancestor, since it is incorporated in both versions. Psalm 70 (or parts of it) was probably first sung as a Communion hymn—with the refrain, " Glory be on high to thee, who hast fed us, "—in North Syria and Cappadocia, whence it was adopted by the Armenian and Constantinopolitan Churches. While the Armenian Liturgy preserved the original in its pristine simplicity, the Constantinopolitan did not. Patriarch Sergius may have modified and embellished it.

At any rate, for centuries the Constantinopolitan version of the *Plerotheto* was used at this point in the Greco-Byzantine Liturgy. [15] It was discontinued in the Greek Church after the fifteenth century, but the Slav Church, with its spirit of literal fidelity, had kept it. The only difference between the ninth-century and the present Slav text is the addition of three descriptive modifiers : where the ancient text has " holy mysteries " the present has " holy, divine, immortal and life-giving mysteries. "

Incensing the holy gifts by the deacon was an established rite in the Armenian version of Chrysostom's Liturgy in the early eighth century, [16] but the accompanying verse (6) of Psalm 107 was intro-

---

[13] Cf. G. Aucher, *op. cit.*, p. 396.

[14] Cf. Brightman, LEW, p. 342, lines 6-9.

[15] *Cod. Sin.*, N. 1020 of twelfth or thirteenth century; *Cod. Patmos*, N. 719 of thirteenth century; MS. of Esphigmenon of 1306 (cf. Dmitrievsky, *op. cit.*, II, pp. 145, 175, 269); MS. of Panteleimon of the fourteenth century; MS. of Patriarch of Jerusalem of the fifteenth century (Krasnoseltsev, *Materialy dlja istorii chinoposlidovania liturgii sv. Ioanna Zlatoustago* [Kazan, 1889], pp. 76, 92).

[16] Aucher, *op. cit.*, p. 396.

duced only in the eleventh or twelfth century. [17] The verse which may be translated more literally, " May you be raised up, O God, above the heavens, " was added only after the action of transferring the gifts from the main altar to the *proskomidia* table was endowed with the symbolism of the ascension. [18] This is another example of an accepted symbolism introducing a liturgical text. The Slav Church did not follow suit until about three centuries later. Only after the introduction of the *Constitutions* of Philotheus did some of the missals adopt this verse. [19]

The words " Blessed is our God,... " etc., when first encountered in Chrysostom in eighth century Armenia, were said by the priest as a conclusion to the equivalent of the Byzantine *Plerotheto*. [20] When we next meet this exclamation in the eleventh or twelfth century Liturgy, translated by Leo Thuscus, it is already in the position it holds at present, serving as a signal for the people to begin the *Plerotheto*. [21]

[17] It is not contained in *Cod. Barberini, gr.* 336, of the eighth or ninth century (Brightman, LEW, p. 342), but it is in the eleventh century MS. Burdett-Coutts, III, 42 (Swainson, *The Greek Liturgies Chiefly From Original Authorities* [Cambridge, 1884], p. 141). Cf. also Dmitrievsky, *op. cit.*, II, p. 613; Krasnoseltsev, *Materialy*, p. 92.

[18] The first to explain it thus was Ps.-Germanus (PG 98, 452) in the ninth century.

[19] E.g., MS. N. 541 of Sophia Library, p. 38, gives other prayers after the incensing of the gifts, but among them it includes this verse (Petrovsky, *op. cit.*, p. 912). The fifteenth century *Liturgikon* of Isidore, Metropolitan of Kiev, was one of those which still did not have it; cf. MS. *Vat. Slav.*, N. 14, fol. 145.

[20] Aucher, *op. cit.*, p. 396.

[21] Edit. Antwerp (1562), p. 65. Compare *Cod. Sin.*, N. 1020, of the twelfth or thirteenth century (Dmitrievsky, *Opysanie*, p. 145); Cod. Patmos, N. 709, of the year 1260 (Dmitrievsky, *Opysanie*, p. 158).

CHAPTER LXXIV

THE THANKSGIVING
AFTER COMMUNION

W*hen the* Plerotheto *is being sung, the deacon unbinds his* orarion, *goes out of the sanctuary through the north door, and stands in his usual place before the royal doors. After the people have completed the hymn, he intones the following* ektenia :

Let us stand straight. After receiving the divine, holy, pure, immortal, heavenly, life-giving and awesome mysteries of Christ, let us worthily thank the Lord.

People : **Lord, have mercy.**

Deacon : **Help us, save us, have mercy on us, and protect us, O God, by your grace.**

People : **Lord, have mercy.**

Deacon : **Having prayed that this whole day be perfect, holy, peaceful, and sinless, let us commend ourselves and one another, and our whole life to Christ our God.**

People : **To you, O Lord.**

In the meantime, the priest has been reciting the prayer of thanksgiving in a low voice :

We thank you, O Lord, Lover of mankind and Benefactor of our souls, because you have deigned to make us partakers of your heavenly and immortal mysteries. Direct our way, strengthen all of us in your fear; guard our life, make our steps sure, through the prayers and intercession of the glorious Mother of God and ever-virgin Mary and of all your saints.

He folds the iliton *and returns the Gospel Book to its place in the center of the altar after first making the sign of the cross with it over the folded* iliton *and intoning the doxology :*

For you are our sanctification and we give glory to you, Father, Son, and Holy Spirit, now and always and for ever and ever.

People : **Amen.**

Then, as he goes toward the royal doors, the priest intones :

Let us depart in peace.

People : **In the name of the Lord.**

Deacon : **Let us pray to the Lord.**

People : **Lord, have mercy.**

The priest goes out of the sanctuary through the royal doors and, standing between the two choirs, he says the Prayer Behind the Ambo *in a loud voice :*

O Lord, you bless those who bless you and you sanctify those who trust in you : save your people and bless your inheritance. Preserve the fullness of your Church, sanctify those who love the beauty of your house; honor them in return by your divine power and do not forsake us who set our hope in you. Grant peace to your world and to your churches, to the clergy, to our emperor (*or* to our king, *or* to our sovereign authorities), and to all your people. For every good and every perfect gift, being from above, comes down from you, the Father of lights, and we give glory, thanksgiving, and adoration to you, Father, Son, and Holy Spirit, now and always and for ever and ever.

People : **Amen.**

As the Prayer behind the Ambo *is being sung, the deacon stands at the right side and, with head slightly bowed, holds his* orarion *towards the icon of our Lord.*

Hymns of praise were sung at the end of the first Eucharistic Liturgy, the Last Supper. In the primitive Church, the element of gratitude and thanksgiving was so forceful that the whole Eucharistic rite derived its name from it. Thanking God for the great gift of Communion was part of that rite. By the fourth century, however, some of that original fervor must have cooled. Chrysostom is very sharp with those who hurry away before the post-Communion. He accuses them of being like Judas who left the Upper Room instead of singing a hymn of praise and going out with the Lord. [1]

---

[1] Chrysostom, *De bapt. Christi*, chap. 4 (edit. Montfaucon 2, 374, or PG 49, 370).

Jerusalem was probably much better in this respect, for Cyril has no words of rebuke to the Christians of that city, but he is careful to instruct his converts " to wait for the prayer, and give thanks unto God who has accounted you worthy of such great mysteries. " [2] This refers to the common thanksgiving prayers at the end of the Liturgy.   The fervor of the Christians at Mopsuestia must have been commendable, for there is commendation in Theodore's words : " After you have received... you rightly and spontaneously offer praise and thanksgiving to God....   And you remain, so that you may also offer thanksgiving and praise with all, according to the rules of the Church, because it is fitting for all those who received this spiritual food to offer thanks to God publicly. " [3]

Other early commentators, such as Pseudo-Dionysius and Eutychius Patriarch of Constantinople, also indicate corporate prayers of thanksgiving after Communion. [4]   One of the earliest texts of such a prayer to come down to us is that in Sarapion :

> We thank thee, Master, that thou hast called those who have erred, and hast taken to thyself those who have sinned, and hast set aside the threat that was against us, giving indulgence by thy loving-kindness, and wiping it away by repentance, and casting it off by the knowledge that regards thyself.   We give thanks to thee, that thou hast given us communion of (the) body and blood.   Bless us, bless this people, make us to have a part with the body and the blood through thy only-begotten Son, through whom to thee (is) the glory and the strength in the Holy Spirit both now and ever and to all the ages of ages.   Amen. [5]

Only the celebrant's prayer is given in Sarapion, but there can be no doubt that is was preceded in the usual way by the deacon's

[2] Cyril of Jerusalem, *Catechesis*, XXIII (*Mystag.*, V), 22 (PG 33, 1125 B, or Quasten, *Monumenta eucharistica et liturgia vetustissima* [Bonn, 1935-1937], 110).

[3] Theodore of Mopsuestia, *Catecheses*, VI (edit. Rücker, *Ritus Baptismi et Missae, quem descripsit Theodorus ep. Mopsuestenus in sermonibus catecheticis* [Münster, 1933], p. 38).

[4] Ps.-Dionysius (c. A.D. 500), *De eccl. hier.*, 3, III, xiv-xv (PG 3, 469 C-472 B); Eutychius, Patriarch of Constantinople (A.D. 552-565). *De paschate et ss. eucharistia*, 3 (PG 86, 2396).

[5] *Bishop Serapion's Prayer Book*, trans. by J. Wordsworth (London, 1923), p. 66.

call, " Let us pray to the Lord. " The call evolved in the course of time. In the Ethiopian Liturgy, for example, after the usual invitation by the deacon, there is an exchange of brief prayers between the celebrant and the people : the priest recites some verses of Psalm 144 and the people answer three times : " Our Father who art in heaven, lead us not into temptation. " [6]

In the Greek Liturgies, the deacon's call developed into a short *ektenia*, to which the people respond as usual, " Lord, have mercy "; the celebrant's prayer of thanksgiving always follows. The model of such a plan can already be seen in the *Apostolic Constitutions :*

> *Deacon :* After receiving the precious body and the precious blood of Christ, let us give thanks to him who has deemed us worthy to partake of his holy mysteries.
>
> Let us beseech him that it be not for our condemnation but for our salvation, for the benefit of our soul and body, for the safeguarding of piety, the remission of sins and for life everlasting.
>
> Let us arise.
>
> By the grace of Christ let us dedicate ourselves to the only-begotten God and to his Christ. [7]

A long prayer by the celebrant follows. Thanksgiving merges with a renewed plea for the intentions of the people and for the welfare of all classes and ranks in the Church. [8] The Liturgy of Chrysostom has a similar plan, including the deacon's *ektenia*. The early eighth-century Armenian text of both ektenia and celebrant's prayer is almost identical with that of the present Byzantine-Slav. [9]

The present Greek Liturgy of Chrysostom, however, has the prayer of thanksgiving in a different position—just before the invitation, " Approach with fear of God. . . " before the Communion

---

[6] Brightman, LEW, pp. 242 f.

[7] *Apostolic Constitutions*, Book VIII; see above, p. 142.

[8] *Ibid.*

[9] The deacon's *ektenia* has one additional proclamation in this Armenian version; on the other hand, the present Byzantine-Slav has one additional adjective, " fearful, " modifying " mysteries " in the first proclamation. Cf. Aucher, *La versione armena della liturgia di S. Giovanni Crisostomo, fatta sul principio dell'VIII secolo*, XPYCOCTOMIKA (Rome, 1908), p. 397.

of the faithful. [10] This was not always so. The eighth or ninth century *Codex Barberini* still has it after the Communion of the faithful. [11] The transfer of the prayer into the new position—before the Communion of the faithful—must have come during the eleventh or twelfth century. [12] As usual, not all localities accepted this innovation immediately; the old position was kept in some places until late into the sixteenth century. [13] The deacon's *ektenia* remains in the old position, even today; so does the doxology.

When the Slavs received Christianity from Byzantium in the tenth century, they adopted the Greek Liturgy of the time, with the prayer in the original position—after the Communion of the faithful, where it remains today.

First, the deacon calls on the faithful to "stand up," which is the ancient posture for prayer to God—and to thank him worthily for the holy gifts. He calls the gifts "divine" because the Son of God himself is within them, and because they make more Godlike whoever receives them worthily. Through baptism, all are made "sons of God" as Paul told the Galatians (Gal. 4:5-6), but, through the Eucharist, that life of God in the soul is increased. The gifts are "holy" and "pure" because Christ is holy and pure, and because they will make the worthy partakers holy and pure. They are "immortal" because Christ is immortal, being God. Likewise, the Eucharist is a pledge of immortality to the communicant, for "he that eateth this bread will live forever" (John 6:59). They are "heavenly" because it is the bread "which cometh down from heaven" (John 6:50), and because those who partake of it will gain heaven itself—we have Christ's guarantee for it (John 6:33-59). They are "life-giving," since, through the redemption, Jesus brought the whole human race from death to life, and now, through the Eucharist, continues the same work by applying the fruits of

---

[10] Cf. Brightman, LEW, p. 395.

[11] Brightman, LEW, p. 342.

[12] *Cod. Sin.*, N. 973 of the year 1153 has it in the new position (Dmitrievsky, *Opysanie liturgicheskikh rukopisej khraniaschikhsia v bibliotekakh pravoslavnago vostoka*, Vol. II, *Euchologia* [Kiev, 1901], p. 85); so does the Greek Liturgy translated by Leo Thuscus, *c.* 1180 (cf. edit. Antwerp, 1562, p. 64).

[13] The Liturgy in Goar's *Euchologion* still has the prayer in its ancient position (edit. 1730, p. 67).

that redemption. Without the Eucharist, the supernatural life of the soul would soon wither and die, for "except you eat the flesh of the Son of man and drink his blood, you shall not have life in you" (John 6:54). They are "awesome" or "fearful," since Christ as Supreme Judge is indeed fearful; he will exact just retribution for all sins. Likewise, it is "fearful" for the recipient, since "whosoever shall eat this bread, or drink the chalice of the Lord unworthily, shall be guilty of the body and blood of the Lord" (I Cor. 11:27). The litany of Eucharistic attributes is applied, first, to the sacramental Christ, then to the effect produced in the recipient.

Both the *ektenia* and the celebrant's prayer are closed, as usual, with a doxology. During this particular doxology, the priest makes the sign of the cross with the Holy Gospel Book over the folded *iliton*. This has received the symbolical meaning of the sanctification of the soul by the Holy Trinity, through the holy cross, and through the teachings of Christ contained in the Gospels.

Prayer behind the Ambo

After Communion and its thanksgiving, the Divine Liturgy draws to a close. In the primitive Church, the departure rite was probably very simple : a blessing and dismissal. Even secular assemblies often had a formal announcement of their conclusion. In ancient Churches, the dismissal consisted generally in telling the people to go in peace, or in Christ.

At Antioch, Syria, and Egypt, the formula was : " Go in peace. " [14] For the early Christians "peace" was almost synonymous with Christ, as is evident in the Western *Dominus vobiscum* " the Lord be with you, " and the Eastern " *Peace be with you* " (see above, pp. 408 ff.). The same meaning is clear in the Greek Liturgies, where the " Let us depart in peace " is confirmed by the people's response, " In the name of the Lord. " [15] In the Western Church, the rite of

---

[14] Chrysostom, *In adv. Jud.*, 3, 6 (edit. Montfaucon 1, 614 C, or PG 48, 870); *Apostolic Constitutions*, Book VIII (cf. above, p. 145); the Egyptian version of Hippolytus' *Apostolic Tradition* (Brightman, LEW, p. 193).

[15] Brightman, LEW, pp. 67, 142, 343; Chrysostom's Liturgy in its early eighth century Armenian version has the same words (Aucher, *op. cit.*, p. 397).

Milan has almost the same : *Procedamus in pace*, and its response, *In nomine Christi*. [16] A similar dismissal must have been used in the Mozarabic Mass, as is evident from the *Missale mixtum*. [17] Probably the Christian farewells, " God be with you, " and " God go with you, " common to all countries of Western and Eastern Europe before they became secularized, trace their origin to the dismissal of the Christian Liturgies.

Originally, the " Go in peace " was the last item in the service. We can see this clearly in the Eucharistic Liturgy of the *Apostolic Constitutions* and the *Ethiopic Church Ordinances*, [18] as well as in the various dismissal formulae that terminate the ancient synaxis. The reason why this invitation to depart is in its present position in the Byzantine Liturgy is difficult to assess. We know that all the prayers in the present ritual following the *Prayer behind the Ambo* are post-eighth-century additions. In the eighth or ninth century *Codex Barberini*, the Liturgy ends with that prayer. [19] Most of these prayers were related originally to the distribution of the *antidoron*, which followed the Divine Liturgy. But this still does not explain why the invitation to depart is placed *before* the Ambo Prayer, i.e., Departure Blessing, instead of after it.

It seems that prior to the seventh or eighth century, there were two Ambo Prayers (Departure Blessings) : one for the Divine Liturgy followed by the invitation, " Let us depart in peace, " and the other ending the distribution of the *antidoron*. The first was dropped, probably because it was redundant, while the invitation to depart in peace was kept. The departure-blessing ending the distribution of the *antidoron* remained to become the departure-blessing for the Divine Liturgy.

In the ancient Church, such a departure-prayer-blessing was

---

[16] *Missale Ambrosianum* (edit. 1902), p. 183. It also has the *Benedicamus Domino* just before the *apolysis* just as the Byzantine does. The Roman blessing for a journey also contains an identical departure announcement and response.

[17] *Sollemnia completa sunt in nomine Domini nostri Jesu Christi;* cf. *Missale mixtum* (PL 85, 567 B).

[18] *Apostolic Constitutions*, Book VIII (cf. above, p. 145); *Ethiopic Church Ordinances* (Brightman, LEW, p. 193).

[19] Cf. Brightman, LEW, p. 352.

usually called the " Prayer of Laying on of Hands, " or the " Prayer of Inclination " (bowing of the head)—the latter deriving from the fact that all bowed their heads during its recitation; the former, from the fact that the celebrant extended his hands over the people. [20] Such a practice still existed in the East Syrian Church as late as A.D. 708, for James of Edessa writes : " ...and the prayer of the imposition of hands is said, and the deacon dismisses the people that they may depart in peace. This tradition I have received from the Fathers, which I transmit to you. " [21] In the Byzantine Church, this departure-prayer-blessing was given the name Ὀπισθάμβωνος or "Prayer behind the Ambo" because the priest went among the people behind the *ambo* (pulpit) to impart this benediction. The *ambo* at the time was placed in the center of the church, probably for the convenience of cantors and readers. Now, the priest neither extends his hands over the congregation nor imparts a blessing while reciting the prayer. Vestiges of the ancient practice, however, still exist in the Pontifical Liturgy, in which the prayer is recited by the senior priest until the words "save your people and bless your inheritance. " Then the bishop pronounces these words while imparting a blessing with the hand-cross; after the blessing, the senior priest resumes the prayer.

There was a time when the " Prayer behind the Ambo " varied for almost every major feast. The ninth or tenth century Porphyrian Missal, for example, contains twenty-eight such prayers for the Liturgy of Basil. [22] A Ukrainian Missal Prayer-Book of the fourteenth century contains fourteen different ones, besides the present

---

[20] Sarapion, *Euchologion*, no. 6; cf. edit. J. Wordsworth, *Bishop Serapion's Prayer Book* (London, 1923),p. 67.

[21] James of Edessa, *Epistula ad Thoman presbyterum*, in Dionysius bar Salibi, *Expositio liturgiae*, 3 (edit. H. Labourt, CSCO, p. 9 [39]).

[22] (1) Purification, (2) Epiphany, (3) Meat Fare Sunday, (4) First Sunday of Lent, (5) Second Sunday of Lent, (6) Third Sunday of Lent, (7) Fourth Sunday of Lent, (8) Fifth Sunday of Lent, (9) Sixth Sunday of Lent, (10) Holy Thursday, (11) Easter, (12) the Octave of Easter, (13) Patron Saint's Day of given church, (14) Christmas, (15) alternate for Christmas, (16) Assumption, (17) alternate for Assumption, (18-21) four different ones for unspecified days, (22) St. Basil, (23) another alternate for Assumption, (24) alternate for Epiphany, (25) Annunciation, (26) Ascension, (27) Pentecost, (28) Lazarus Saturday. Cf. M. Orlov, *Liturgia sviatago Vasilia Velikago. Pervoe kriticheskoe izdanie s izobrazheniem sv. Vasilia, s chetirmy spiskamy s rukopisej* (St. Petersburg, 1905), pp. 324-381.

one which appears in the text of the Liturgy. [23] Forty different formulae can be found in various manuscripts and missals. [24] The present prayer is merely that which was used on ordinary days. [25] The first time we meet it is in the early eighth-century Armenian version of Chrysostom's Liturgy. [26] The *Codex Barberini* of the next century has it too—but only for the Liturgy of Basil. [27] Ps.-Germanus calls it " the seal of all prayers. " [28]

[23] *Molytovnyk-Sluzhebnyk* of the fourteenth century; cf. Kovaliw, *Molytovnyk-Sluzhebnyk, Pamiatka XIV stolittia* (New York, 1960), pp. 90-108.

[24] Cf. M. Marusyn, " Bozhestvenna Liturhiya v Kiyevskij Mytropolii po spysku Isydorovoho Liturgikona z XV st. " in *Bohoslovia*, 25-28 (1964), p. 59.

[25] E.g., the fourteenth century *Molytovnyk-Sluzhebnyk* includes it in the text of the Liturgy itself, while the others are printed separately; cf. Kowaliv, *op. cit.*, pp. 90-108.

[26] Cf. Aucher, *op. cit.*, pp. 397-398.

[27] Brightman, LEW, pp. 343-344. An entirely different prayer appears in the Liturgy of Chrysostom.

[28] Ps.-Germanus, *Rerum eccles. contempl.* (PG 98, 452).

CHAPTER LXXV

THE ABLUTIONS, THE ANTIDORON

Immediately after the " Amen " of the " Prayer behind the Ambo, " the people continue :

Blessed be the name of the Lord, from now and unto eternity *(three times).*

Wherever customary, Psalm 33 is sung. The priest enters the sanctuary through the Royal Doors and, turning toward the holy gifts on the proskomidia *table, prays silently :*

Christ, our God, fulfillment of the Law and the Prophets, who accomplished all of the Father's plan for our salvation, fill our hearts with joy and gladness, at all times, now and always, and for ever and ever. Amen.

The deacon enters the sanctuary through the north door, consumes the sacred species, and performs the ablutions. In the meantime, the priest goes out of the sanctuary and distributes the antidoron.

Custom prescribed that the room be made tidy after the Jewish *chabûrah.* [1] The same must have applied to the primitive Eucharistic gathering. The earliest text related to any post-Communion cleansing refers, not to the vessels, but to the recipient's mouth. Chrysostom recommended drinking water and eating bread after Communion so that the last remnant of the sacred species is swallowed. The practice was unknown at the time in Constantinople, since Chrysostom was actually blamed for introducing it. [2] His advice took root, however, because such a custom is still found in many Byzantine churches. The celebrant drinks the remainder of the *zeon (teplota),* mixed with a little wine, and eats a particle of bread from the unconsecrated *prosphora.* In the Slav Church, this is called the *zapivka,* an after-drink for " washing down. " The Copts swallow some water after Communion to " cover " the sacrament;

---

[1] *Berakoth,* vii, 3.
[2] Palladius, *Dial.,* chap. 8 (PG 47, 27).

they call it " the water of covering. " [3]   The Western Church had
a similar custom in the past. [4]

Whatever rinsing of the sacred vessels was considered proper was
done after the Communion of the faithful—which also marked the
end of the Eucharistic rite in the primitive Church.

When, during the fourth century or just before it, a formal
corporate thanksgiving was added to the original rite, the ablutions
of the vessels in most churches probably took place after the end
of the service, especially if the priest celebrated alone.   If deacons
assisted, as they usually did in the Eastern Churches, then probably
one or more of them purified the sacred vessels immediately after
Communion while the corporate thanksgiving was being recited by
the other clergy.   The *Apostolic Constitutions* contains a rubric
directing deacons to " carry what remains into the sacristy " immediately after Communion. [5]   They then presumably consumed
the remains, and performed the ablutions.   Other deacons and the
celebrant continued with the service.

What if only one deacon and one priest celebrated?   In such
cases, the deacon probably took the remains of the sacrament to
the sacristy or side-table and left them there; then he went back
to perform his function in the thanksgiving rite, i.e., to chant the
ektenia.   When he finished with this, he probably went immediately
to perform the ablutions while the priest recited the departure-
prayer-blessing, distributed the *antidoron*, etc.   There is no reason
to doubt this procedure later when even more prayers were appended
to the post-Communion rite.   For the most part, this procedure is
still followed in the Byzantine Liturgy today.   When celebrating
alone, the priest performs the ablutions after the Liturgy is ended.
When a deacon or deacons assist, the only difference today is that
they wait until the Prayer for Consuming the Gifts *(Ispolneniye
zakona...)* is finished before they consume the remains, perform
the ablutions, etc.   But the ancient Church had no special prayer

---

[3] Cf. G. Graf, *Ein Reformversuch innerhalb der koptischen Kirche im zwölften
Jahrhundert* (Collectanea Hierosolymitana, II, [Paderborn, 1923], p. 85).

[4] *Regula Magistri*, chap. 24 (PL 88, 992 D); *Vita Alcuini*, chap. 15 (MGH,
Scriptores, XV, I, p. 193, 1, 9); Thegan, *Vita Chludowici*, chap. 61 (MGH, II,
638, 1, 1).

[5] *Apostolic Constitutions*, Book VIII, cf. above, p. 142.

for consuming the species; nor did it have any special prescriptions connected with the ablutions.   The rinsing was probably done with water as many times as necessary for the vessels to be perfectly clean—but without specific rubrics as to the number of rinsings. The *Sahidic Ecclesiastical Canons* urged solicitous care upon the clergy in wiping the vessels so that they should not call down upon themselves the punishment meted out to the sons of Heli for their carelessness. [6]   Later, in the Byzantine Church, either three rinsings with wine and water, [7] or only two—once with water and once with wine—were required, latter is the common practice today. [8]

An accurate estimate of the quantity of bread and wine to be consecrated always presented a problem, as it still does today.   As long as the faithful could take the Eucharist home, there seems to have been no difficulty.   But once this custom was discontinued, the remainder had to be disposed of—and it was sometimes large. Some churches, following Leviticus 8:32, burned the remainder of the consecrated bread. [9]   In the Constantinopolitan Church, the left-over species were sometimes buried. [10]   Another method of disposal which lasted more than eight centuries was to have small children consume them. [11]

Immediately after the " Amen " that followed the " Prayer behind the Ambo, " the people sing the second verse of Psalm 112, " Blessed be the name of the Lord..., " as do the Egyptians in the Liturgy of St. Mark and the Armenians. [12]   This verse of praise was already

---

[6] *Sahidic Ecclesiastical Canons*, Brightman, LEW, Appendix A, p. 463.

[7] Krasnoseltsev, *Materialy dlja istorii chinoposlidovania liturgii sv. Ioanna Zlatoustago* (Kazan, 1889), p. 76.

[8] Krasnoseltsev, *op. cit.*, p. 93; Dmitrievsky, *Opysanie liturgicheskikh rukopisej khraniaschikhsia v bibliotekakh pravoslavnago vostoka*, II, *Euchologia* (Kiev, 1901), pp. 614, 826.

[9] *Commentary on Leviticus*, II, 8 (PG 93, 886 D), a work generally ascribed to Hesychius of Jerusalem (d. *c.* A.D. 450); Humbert of Silva Candida, *Adv. Graecorum calumnias*, n. 33 (PL 143, 952 A).

[10] Cf. Browe, " *Wann fing man an, die in einer Messe konsekrierten Hostien in einer anderen Messe auszulteilen?* " (*Theologie und Glaube*, XXX [1938], 388-404), pp. 391 ff.

[11] The custom was in vogue at Constantinople during the sixth century (cf. Evagrius Scholasticus, *Hist. eccl.*, IV, 36 (PG 86, 2796 A), and Nicephorus Callistus, who died about 1341 (*Hist. eccl.*, 17, 25 (PG 147, 280), testifies to the practice in his day.   Cf. Browe, *op. cit.*, pp. 393 f.

[12] Brightman, LEW, pp. 143, 455.

incorporated in the Armenian version of Chrysostom's Liturgy in
the early eighth century; in this version it was repeated three times. [13]
The same Armenian version also had what was later to become the
" Prayer for Consuming the Gifts, " but it was used here as the
final blessing of the Liturgy.   Thus : " *The priest again goes up to the
sanctuary and adores the altar with a kiss.   He turns towards the people
and makes the sign of the cross, saying :* ' O Christ, our Redeemer, you
are the fulfillment of the Law and the Prophets, and did fulfill all
the Father's plan; fill us with thy Holy Spirit. ' " [14]   About a century
later, this is found as the " Prayer for Consuming the Gifts. " [15]   What
is now the final blessing was, in the eighth-century Armenian
version, the " Blessing after the Distribution of the Antidoron " :
" ...he makes the sign of the cross over the people, saying ' May
the blessing of the Lord [be] upon you, now and always and for
ever and ever. ' " [16]   This was made into the final blessing of the
Liturgy by the eleventh or twelfth century. [17]

The change probably came imperceptibly, and it seems to be due
to the custom of the *antidoron*.   This sacramental was given only
to those who did not receive Communion.   As the proportion of
communicants decreased, the number of those who received the
antidoron increased.   After centuries of celebrating the ordinary
Liturgy with the whole congregations staying for the *antidoron*
(since none of the faithful received Communion), the blessing after
the *antidoron* began to be regarded as the final blessing of the Liturgy.
The earlier dismissal-blessing remained—but as the " Prayer for
Consuming the Gifts. "

---

[13] Cf. G. Aucher, *La versione armena della liturgia di S. Giovanni Crisostomo,
fatta sul principio dell'VIII secolo*, XPYCOCTOMIKA (Rome, 1908), p. 398;
however, it does not appear in the eighth or ninth century *Cod. Barberini, gr.* 336.
This can be explained on grounds that many of the early MSS lack not a few of
the laity's responses.

[14] Aucher, *op. cit.*, p. 398.

[15] *Cod. Barberini, gr.* 336 (Brightman, LEW, p. 344); *Cod. Sebast.* of the tenth
or eleventh century (Krasnoseltsev, *Svidinia o kikotorikh liturgicheskikh rukopis'akh
Vatikanskoi biblioteki* [Kazan, 1885], p. 295); the Latin version of Leo Thuscus,
eleventh or twelfth century (edit. Antwerp, 1562, p. 66).

[16] Aucher, *op. cit.*, p. 398.

[17] The Latin version of Leo Thuscus (edit. Antwerp, 1562, p. 66); however,
its position was before the prayer for consuming the gifts.

We still have a vestige of the old practice when the *antidoron* is distributed, not after the Liturgy, but *before* its final blessing and *apolysis*. When it is being given out, Psalm 33 is sung. Some Slav Churches have it at this point, even if the distribution takes places after the *apolysis*; this too is a vestige of the same custom. Psalm 33, as we have seen (see above, p. 667), was used as a Communion song almost everywhere in ancient Christendom. Since formerly only noncommunicants received the *antidoron*, it was a kind of substitute for Communion; [18] hence, it is not surprising that an ancient Communion song accompany its distribution. That is probably how the sacramental received its name. *Antidoron* literally means " in place of the gift, " that is, taking the place of the infinitely greater gift of the Eucharist. [19] In actual fact, the bread used today for the *antidoron* is taken from what is left of the first *prosphora* after the main host or " Lamb " is cut out at the *proskomidia*.

A similar custom of blessed bread after Mass—the *eulogiae*—was common to all the countries of Western Europe for many centuries. There, too, it was regarded as a substitute for Communion. [20] Hincmar of Rheims, for example, says that on Sundays and holy days after Communion, the priest takes the *eulogiae*, blessed with a special formula, and distributes them to non-communicants. [21] Durandus explicitly calls it *communionis vicarius*, [22] and John Beleth regards it as a substitute at least for Sunday Communion. [23] When unleavened bread began to be used for Communion in the West, the bread for the *eulogiae* was also unleavened. After the twelfth century, however, the *eulogiae* were made to look different from the Communion bread in order to avoid confusion.

[18] Cf. Gentianus Hervetus, *Ad Lectorem*, contained in *Liturgiae sive Missae sanctorum patrum, Iacobi, Basilii Magni, Ioannis Chrysostomi, De Ritu Missae et Eucharistia* (Antwerp, 1562), p. 105.

[19] Baumstark, however, explains the *antidoron* as a " countergift " to the faithful for the usual bread offering, cf. *Die Messe im Morgenland* (Kempten-München, 1906), p. 179.

[20] Cf. Browe, *Die Pflichtkommunion im Mettelalter* (Münster, 1940), pp. 191-194.

[21] Hincmar of Rheims, *Capitula presbyteris data (*A.D. 852*), 7 (PL 125, 774); cf. also *Admonitio synodalis* (PL 96, 1378).

[22] Durandus, *Rationale*, IV, 53, 3.

[23] John Beleth, *Explicatio*, chap. 48 (PL 202, 55 D); cf. also Sicard of Cremona, *Mitrale*, III, 8 (PL 213, 144).

In the East, the custom of blessed bread is common to the Byzantine, the Armenian, and Syrian Churches. Like the Byzantine,
the Armenian distribution is accompanied by the singing of Psalm
33. [24] Among the East and West Syrians, special prayers are said
during the distribution. [25] The latter Church restricts the giving
of blessed bread to the Great Lent and the vigil Masses.

The custom of blessed bread traces its origin to the common
meals of the ancient Church, the agape. At such a " Supper of the
Lord, " the bishop used to bless (εὐλογεῖν) a loaf and the faithful
would, as Hippolytus says in his *Apostolic Tradition*, " . . .take from
the hand of the bishop one fragment of the loaf, for this is the
eulogion (blessed bread). It is, however, not the Eucharistic Body
of the Lord. " [26] If the Supper were held with only a presbyter or
deacon present, they were to " be careful to receive the blessed bread
from the presbyter's or deacon's hand.... If, however, only
laymen are present without a cleric, let them eat with understanding, for a layman cannot make the blessed bread. " [27] Such a
" Holy Supper " is still held in many Ukrainian and Russian parishes
—usually on the eves of Christmas and Epiphany. The pastor
blesses the bread with a special blessing and gives a particle to
each of the guests. A similar custom has survived in some localities
at funeral-and-anniversary Liturgies for the dead.

In most Eastern Churches, however, the common meals after the
Sunday Liturgy were held less and less frequently, probably because
of abuses. Thus, the Synod of Laodicea (A.D. 343-381) forbade
them entirely " in the Lord's Houses or Churches, " nor could the
faithful " eat and spread couches in the house of God. " [28] The
Trullan Council repeated the prohibition in A.D. 692. [29] There

---

[24] Brightman, LEW, p. 457; psalm 34=33 of Douay Rheims Version.

[25] Cf. Brightman, LEW, pp. 109-110, 304-305.

[26] *Apostolic Tradition*, chaps. xxv-xxvi (see above, p. 47). Cf. Horner, *The
Statutes of the Apostles or Canones ecclesiastici, edited with Translation and Collation
from Ethiopic and Arabic MSS; also a Translation of the Sahidic and Collation
of the Bohairic Versions; and Sahidic Fragments* (London, 1904), pp. 321-323, for
Coptic recension.

[27] *Apostolic Tradition*, chaps. xxv, xxvi.

[28] Can. 28, NPNF, Series II, Vol. XIV, p. 148.

[29] Can. 74, NPNF, Series II, Vol. XIV, p. 398.

were often no other buildings in which such meals could be held, so that they tended to disappear. This was probably the reason why both the blessing and the distribution of the *eulogiae* became separated from the meal and incorporated into the liturgical services. In the Byzantine Church, bread is also blessed and distributed at each Solemn Vesper Service with the All-Night Vigil. Since the common meals disappeared first in the West, it is significant that the first testimony of the *eulogiae* being distributed at the end of Mass comes from there. Gregory of Tours mentions this in the sixth century. [30]

In the Byzantine Church, great reverence and awe is accorded the blessed bread because, as Cabasilas explains, it " has been sanctified by being dedicated and offered to God " in the *proskomidia* and is the bread " from which the Sacred Host was taken "; [31] it is also regarded as representing the Mother of God from whose flesh the Holy Spirit fashioned the body of the Lord. [32] According to Cabasilas again, " the faithful receive this with all reverence, kissing the hand (of the priest) which has so recently touched the all-holy body of the Saviour Christ and which thus sanctified can communicate this sanctification to those who touch it.... " [33]

[30] Gregory of Tours, *Hist. Franc.*, V, 14 (PL 71, 327 B) : *Post missas autem petit (Merovech), ut ei eulogias dare deberemus.* Cf. *Hist. Franc.*, IV, 35 (PL 71, 298 B). These liturgical *eulogiae* are not to be confused with the private ones which seemed to be in vogue at the time; cf. Browe, *op. cit.*, pp. 187 f.

[31] Cabasilas, *Commentary on the Divine Liturgy*, VI, 53, trans. Hussey and McNulty (London, 1960), p. 119.

[32] Cabasilas, *op. cit.*, pp. 119-120.

CHAPTER LXXVI

THE FINAL BLESSING, APOLYSIS, AND RECESSION

Standing in the center before the royal doors and blessing the people, the priest says :

The blessing of the Lord be upon you through his grace and his love for mankind, at all times, now and always and for ever and ever.

People : **Amen.**

Facing the east, the priest says :

Glory be to you, Christ God, our hope! Glory to you.

People : **Glory be to the Father, and to the Son, and to the Holy Spirit, now and always and for ever and ever. Amen. Lord, have mercy. Lord, have mercy. Lord, have mercy. Bless (us).**

Priest (facing the people *:* **May Christ** (*on Sundays,* **who has risen from the dead) our true God, through the prayers of his pure Mother, of the holy, glorious, and most honorable Apostles, of our father among the saints, John Chrysostom, the Archbishop of Constantinople, of Saint N——** (*patron of the church*)**, and of saint N——** (*saint whose feast it is*)**, and of all the saints, have mercy on us and save us, for he is good and loves mankind.**

People : **Amen.**

If the antidoron *was not distributed before the final blessing, it is distributed at this point. Then the priest closes the royal doors, bows toward the east, and withdraws from the front of the altar.* [1] *While*

---

[1] Unlike the practice in the Western Church, the sacred vessels are not carried formally into the sacristy. Even in the Latin Church, this custom is of comparatively recent origin; in its present form, it dates back only to the time of Pius V. At concelebrated high Masses, however, the Latin Church conserves the more ancient practice of leaving the sacred vessels on the credence table until they can be put away privately without ceremony.

unvesting he recites the Canticle of Simeon, " Now thou dost dismiss thy servant... " (Luke 2:29-32). The unvesting may be done either at the diakonnyk,[2] in the sanctuary itself, or in the sacristy. When the priest finishes unvesting, he washes his hands. By this time, the deacon should have completed the ablutions of the sacred vessels and put them away. While performing this last task, he too recites the Canticle of Simeon; then he unvests, washes his hands, and joins the priest in reciting the official prayers of thanksgiving after the Liturgy :

Holy God, Holy Mighty One, Holy Immortal One,
have mercy on us. *(three times)*
Glory be to the Father...
Most Holy Trinity... (see above, p. 219)
Lord, have mercy. *(three times)*
Glory be to the Father...
Our Father...
For thine is the Kingdom. Amen.

Then they recite the dismissal hymns (troparion and kondakion) of St. John Chrysostom :

The grace of your preaching that shines forth like a torch has enlightened the universe, bestowed upon the world treasures of generosity, and has shown us the height of humility. Just as you teach us through your words, O Father, John Chrysostom, pray to Christ, God the Word, that he save our souls.

Glory be to the Father...

From heaven you have received divine grace and by your preaching you teach all men to worship the one God in the Trinity, O blessed and holy John Chrysostom. We rightly praise you, for you are indeed our teacher in revealing the things of God.

Now and always....

---

[2] The *diakonnyk* is a special cabinet-table where the vestments, church books, and sacred vessels are stored. It is usually situated on the opposite side of the sanctuary from the table of preparation.

Hymn to the Mother of God

O steadfast protectress of Christians, O unfailing mediatrix before the Creator, despise not the pleas of sinners; but since you are good, come quickly to help us who faithfully call upon you. Hasten to hear our prayer and listen to our supplication, O Mother of God, ever interceding for those who honor you.

> **Lord, have mercy** *(12 times).*
> **Glory be to the Father....**
> **Now and always.... Amen.**

We extol you since you are higher in honor than the cherubim and incomparably more glorious than the seraphim in being God's Mother by giving birth to the Word of God without violating your virginity.

> **Glory be to the Father...**
> **Now and always.... Amen.**

Finally after reciting the apolysis, *both the priest and deacon kiss the altar and depart.*

The present *apolysis,* the finale of the Divine Liturgy, was taken from the Canonical Office and as such is a relatively late addition. While many local churches adopted it during the fourteenth century, it was not used universally until the fifteenth. [3] As its name *apolysis* (dismissal) indicates, it fulfills the function of the older departure-prayer-blessings. In fact, as early as the tenth or eleventh century, we find what is now the final blessing preceded by the same preamble as that of the present *apolysis* : " Glory be to the Father.... Lord, have mercy *(three times).* Bless, Lord. " [4]

In the Canonical Office and in the Divine Liturgy, major feasts, each day of the week, the service for the dead, etc., have their proper

---

[3] Cf. A. Petrovsky, *Histoire de la rédaction slave de la liturgie de S. Jean Chrysostome,* XPYCOCTOMIKA (Rome, 1908), pp. 913-914; Krasnoseltsev, *Materialy dlja istorii chinoposlidovania liturgii sv. Ioanna Zlatoustago* (Kazan, 1889), p. 78.

[4] *Cod. Sebast.* (Krasnoseltsev, *Svidinia o nikotorikh liturgicheskikh rukopis'akh Vatikanskoi biblioteki* [Kazan, 1885], p. 295); the Latin version of Chrysostom's Liturgy, translated by Leo Thuscus (edit. Antwerp [1562], p. 66).

apolysis. This variety resembles that of the ancient " Prayer behind the Ambo, " except that many of the *apolyses* have the same basic text with an additional sentence or two relating to the occasion.

At the end of the *apolysis*, the priest does not bless the people as he did in the older departure-prayer-blessings : he makes the sign of the cross upon himself. After the *apolysis* at Easter, and during its octave, he elevates the hand-cross and proclaims joyfully : " Christ is risen! " The people reply, " Indeed he is risen! " This is done three times.

Prayers after the Liturgy

Until the thirteenth century, there were no standard prayers after the Divine Liturgy. Some missals of the fourteenth century prescribed the " O heavenly King, " and a prayer which began, " After bowing our knees and head to the ground, we sinners plead the forgiveness of our sins and pray.... " [5] A Missal Prayer Book of the same century from the Ukraine gives only one prayer, but it is different from all the texts presently used. [6] Other missals of the time prescribed other prayers or *troparia*, but none gave the *troparia* of St. John Chrysostom which are said today.

Even in the fifteenth century, matters were far from settled. Of the three general categories of prayers given in most missals, one is almost identical with today's. [7] This group of prayers, beginning with the Canticle of Simeon, is the conclusion to the Canonical Hour of Vespers, with the *troparia* proper to the feast of St. John Chrysostom. The traditional identification of Chrysostom with this Liturgy explains it.

[5] MS. N. 526, p. 31, of Sophia Library, and MS. N. 127 of Moscow Synodal Library (Petrovsky, *op. cit.*, p. 886).

[6] *Molytovnyk-Sluzhebnyk* (P. Kowaliv, *Molytovnyk-Sluzhebnyk, Pamailka XIV stolittia* [New York, 1960], p. 34).

[7] *Liturgikon* of Isidore, Metropolitan of Kiev, cf. MS. *Vat. Slav.*, N. 14, fol. 148; also the following MSS. of Sophia Library : N. 529, p. 79; N. 531, p. 55; N. 528, p. 137; N. 544, p. 87; N. 839, p. 14; N. 535, p. 48; N. 541, p. 41 (Petrovsky, *op. cit.*, p. 914, n. 2). Compare MS. N. 986 of Sinai Library (Dmitrievsky, *Opysanie liturgicheskikh rukopisej khraniaschikhsia v bibliotekakh pravoslavnago vostoka*, II, *Euchologia*, [Kiev, 1901], p. 614) and MS. N. 573 of Vat. Library (Krasnoseltsev, *Materialy*, p. 114).

The Canticle of Simeon, recited at this point, adequately expresses the sentiments of the celebrant. Finally, the Byzantine priest kisses the altar before he withdraws. It is a kiss of loving farewell, farewell for time or eternity. Perhaps its meaning is best summarized in the prayer of the Syrian Liturgy which the priest recites as he kisses the altar after the Eucharistic Sacrifice :

> Remain in peace, O holy and divine altar of the Lord. I do not know whether or not I shall ever return to you. May the Lord grant that I see you in the Church of the Firstborn in heaven. In this covenant I put my trust.
>
> Remain in peace, O holy, propitiatory altar of the Sacred Body and Expiatory Blood which I have received from you. May it be unto me for the pardon of offenses, for the remission of my sins, and for confidence before thy fearful judgment seat forever, my Lord and my God.
>
> Remain in peace, O holy altar, table of life, and entreat our Lord Jesus Christ for me. May the memory of me not leave you from now and for eternity. Amen. [8]

---

[8] From the Syrian Liturgy, as the priest kisses the altar after the Eucharistic Sacrifice. Our translation from the Latin in Hanssens, *Institutiones liturgicae de ritibus orientalibus, De Missa rituum orientalium,* Vol. III (Rome, 1932), p. 533. The original in *Missale Sarfense* (1922), pp. 97-99.

APPENDIX A

The Anaphora from the Liturgy of St. Basil

Master, Lord, adorable almighty Father, it is truly proper and right and befitting the greatness of your holiness to praise you, to sing of you, to bless you, to worship you, to thank you, to glorify you the only true God, and with a contrite heart and a humble spirit, to offer you this our sacrifice of the Word;[1] for you have bestowed on us the knowledge of your truth. And who indeed is able to describe your might adequately or make known all your praises, or proclaim all your wondrous works done at all times? Master of all, Lord of heaven and earth and all creatures visible and invisible, you sit on the throne of glory and behold the depths; you are Being without beginning, invisible, incomprehensible, ineffable, unchangeable. Father of our Lord Jesus Christ—great God and Redeemer, our hope, who is the image of your goodness, the seal of your own likeness, who shows you, O Father, in himself, the living Word, true God, eternal Wisdom, Life, Sanctification, Power, the true Light, through whom the Holy Spirit manifested himself, the Spirit of truth, the gift of the adoption of sons, the pledge of our future inheritance, the first-fruits of everlasting blessedness, the life-giving power, the font of sanctification, through whom every creature endowed with reason and understanding is given the power to serve you and send up to you an unending hymn of glory because they are all your servants. For you are praised by the angels, archangels, thrones, dominations, principalities, powers, and many-eyed cherubim; round about you stand the seraphim, each with six wings, for with two they cover their faces and with two their feet, and with two they fly, and they cry one to the other continually with unstilled hymns, as they *(aloud)* sing, cry out, proclaim and say the triumphal hymn :

(People) Holy, holy, holy Lord Sabaoth, heaven and earth are filled with your glory. Hosanna in the highest. Blessed is he who comes in the name of the Lord, hosanna in the highest.

---

[1] The slavonic expression *slovesnaya sluzhba* is rendered here as " Sacrifice of the Word. " Cf. pp. 614 f. for explanation.

With these blessed powers, Lord and Lover of mankind, we sinners too cry out and say : You are truly holy and all-holy and measureless is the majesty of your great holiness. You are blessed in all your works, for in truth and wise judgment have you brought all things to pass for us : for when you had formed man by taking dust from the earth, and graced him with your own image, O God, you have placed him in a paradise of delights and promised him, if he observed your commandments, immortality of life and the enjoyment of never-ending blessings. But man disobeyed you, the true God who created him. And so, after he was led astray by the guile of the serpent and was subjected to death by his own transgression, O God, you drove him out of paradise into this world by your just judgment and condemned him to return to the earth from which he had been taken. Yet, you did not totally turn away from your creature whom you had made, O gracious Lord; you did not forget the work of your hands but provided for him salvation through regeneration in your Christ himself.

You have visited man in various ways because of your merciful loving-kindness : you have sent the prophets, performed mighty works through your saints who in every generation have been well-pleasing to you. You have spoken to us through the mouth of your servants, the prophets, who foretold to us the salvation which was to come. You have given us the Law to help us; you have appointed angels as our guardians. Then, when the fullness of time had come, you spoke to us through your own Son himself, through whom you created the ages and who, as the reflection of your glory, as the express image of your substance, sustaining all things by the word of his power, was in his own right equal to you, God and Father, but, even as everlasting God, he appeared upon earth and lived among men. In becoming incarnate from the holy Virgin, he emptied himself by taking the form of a servant, by conforming himself to the body of our lowliness in order to conform us to the image of his glory. And, since by man sin had entered into the world, and through sin death, so your only-begotten Son, he who is in your bosom, God and Father, was pleased to be born of a woman—of the holy Mother of God and ever-virgin Mary—to live under the Law in order to condemn sin in his own flesh so that those who died through Adam might be brought to life again through him, your Christ himself.

When he lived in this world, he gave us the precepts of salvation and in turning us away from the deceits of idolatry, he brought us to know you, true God and Father; thus he acquired us for himself as a chosen people, a royal priesthood, a holy nation. After cleansing us with water and sanctifying us with the Holy Spirit, he gave himself as our ransom to the death in which we were held captive, sold under sin. Descending into hell through the cross so that through himself he might fulfill all, he loosed the pains of death. He rose again on the third day and established the way to the resurrection from the dead for all flesh, because it was not possible that the Author of life himself should be the victim of corruption; thus, he became the first risen of those who have fallen asleep, the firstborn of the dead, that he might be first over all and in all. When he ascended into heaven, he sat at the right hand of your majesty on high, whence he will come to render to everyone according to his deeds.

And he left us these memorials of his saving passion, which we have set forth according to his command. For when he was about to go forth to his voluntary and ever-memorable and life-giving death, on the night in which he gave himself for the life of the world, he took bread into his holy and all-pure hands, he showed it to you, [2] O God and Father, and gave thanks, blessed, sanctified, broke it, *(aloud)* and gave it to his holy disciples and apostles, saying :

TAKE, EAT, THIS IS MY BODY WHICH IS BROKEN FOR YOU FOR THE REMISSION OF SINS.

(People) : Amen.

In like manner, he also took the cup of the fruit of the vine, and, when he had mixed it, and had given thanks, blessed, and sanctified it *(aloud)*, he gave it to his holy disciples and apostles, saying :

DRINK OF THIS, ALL OF YOU : THIS IS MY BLOOD OF THE NEW TESTAMENT WHICH IS SHED FOR YOU AND FOR MANY FOR THE REMISSION OF SINS.

(People) : Amen.

[2] Cf. above, p. 599, for meaning of *pokazav*, ἀναδείξας, " showed, "

Do this in *anamnesis* of me : [3] for as often as you eat this bread and drink this chalice, you proclaim my death and confess my resurrection. Therefore we also, O Master, remembering his saving passion, his life-giving cross, his three days' burial, his resurrection from the dead, his ascension into heaven, his sitting at your right hand, O God and Father, and his glorious and awesome Second Coming *(aloud)*, offering you your own from what is your own, in behalf of all and for all.

(People) : We praise you, we bless you, we thank you, Lord, and we pray to you, our God.

For this reason, all-holy Master, as your sinful and unworthy servants, whom you have accounted worthy to minister at your holy altar, not because of our own righteousness, for we have done nothing good upon the earth, but because of your multifold mercy and compassion which you have so richly poured out upon us, we have the courage to approach your holy altar and, while offering you the species of the holy body and blood of your Christ, we pray and beseech you, O Holy of Holies, that through the goodness of your loving-kindness your Holy Spirit may come upon us and upon these gifts here set forth; and may he bless them, hallow and show forth this bread, [4] indeed, as the precious body itself of our Lord and God and Saviour Jesus Christ *(People :* Amen) and this chalice indeed, the precious blood itself of our Lord and God and Saviour Jesus Christ *(People :* Amen), shed for the life of the world *(People :* Amen, amen, amen). And unite with one another all of us who partake of the one bread and the one chalice in the communion of the Holy Spirit, and grant that not one of us may become liable to judgment or condemnation for partaking of the sacred body and blood of your Christ, but grant that we may find mercy and grace together with all the saints who have been well-pleasing to you through the ages : our forefathers, fathers, patriarchs, prophets, apostles, preachers, evangelists, martyrs, confessors, teachers, and every just spirit made perfect in the faith; [grant that we may find mercy and grace] especially with our all-holy, most pure, most

[3] Cf. above, p. 58, n. 8 for meaning of *anamnesis*.
[4] Cf. above, p. 599, for meaning of *pokazaty* ἀναδεῖξαι, " show forth. "

blessed and glorious Lady, the Mother of God and ever-virgin Mary *(here the people sing the hymn to the Mother of God, proper to the occasion)*; with St. John, Prophet, Precursor, and Baptist; with the holy and most honorable Apostles, with St. N——, whose memory we keep today; also with all your saints, through whose prayers may you visit us, O God.

And remember all those who have fallen asleep in the hope of a resurrection to life everlasting.

(Here the priest mentions by name all the departed for whom he wishes to pray.)

For the forgiveness and the repose of the soul of your servant, N——; give him (her) rest in a place of light from which grief and mourning have been driven away, our God.

Give them rest where the light of your countenance shines forth.

Moreover we pray to you : remember, O Lord, your holy, catholic, and apostolic Church, which extends from end to end of the universe; give peace to it [the Church] which you have redeemed with the precious blood of your Christ; also preserve this holy Church until the end of the world.

Remember, O Lord, those who offered you these holy gifts and those through whom and for whom they are offered.

Remember, O Lord, those who bring offerings (*lit.* : fruits) and those who do good work in your holy churches, and those who remember the poor; reward them with your rich and heavenly favors; in place of their earthly, temporal, and perishable gifts, give them heavenly ones, eternal and incorruptible.

Remember, O Lord, those who live in deserts, on mountains, in the dens and caves of the earth.

Remember, O Lord, those who are living in virginity, in piety, in asceticism, and those who pursue an honorable way of life.

Remember, O Lord, our (God-fearing Emperor [*or* King] N——) sovereign authorities; give them profound and enduring peace; speak into their hearts good things for your Church and for all your people, that through their serenity we may lead a quiet and tranquil life in all piety and integrity.

Remember, O Lord, all rulers and authorities and our brothers in the government and the armed forces; preserve the good in your goodness, make the wicked be good through your kindness.

Remember, O Lord, the people standing round and those who are absent for honorable reasons, and have mercy on them and on us according to the greatness of your mercy. Fill their storehouses with every good thing; preserve their marriages in peace and in harmony; foster the children; guide the young; support the aged; encourage the fainthearted; reunite the separated; lead back those who have strayed and join them to your holy, catholic, and apostolic Church; free those troubled with unclean spirits; sail with those upon the sea; travel with the travelers; defend the widows; protect the orphans; deliver those in captivity; heal the sick.

Remember, O God, all those who are in tribunals, the mines, exile, and bitter servitude; those in affliction, need, and distress.

Remember, O God, all those who need your great tenderness of heart; those who love us and those who hate us and those who have asked us, unworthy though we be, to pray for them.

Remember all your people and pour out your rich mercy upon all of them, granting to all the petitions which are for their salvation.

Remember, O God, by yourself those whom we have not remembered whether because we forgot them or did not know them or there were too many names to remember— You know the name and age of all; you know each one even from his mother's womb. Because you, Lord, are a help to the helpless, hope to the hopeless, savior to those tossed about in the tempest, a harbor for the sailor, a physician for the sick; be all things to all men— You know each one and his request, each house and its need.

Deliver, O Lord, this city (village *or* monastery) and every city and country from famine, plague, earthquake, flood, fire, sword, the attacks of foreign peoples, and civil war.

(Aloud) First of all, O Lord, remember His Holiness, the universal Pontiff N——, Pope of Rome, our Most Reverend Archbishop and Metropolitan N——, our God-loving Bishop N——; preserve them for your churches in peace, safety, honor, health, and length of days as they faithfully dispense the word of your truth.

Remember, O Lord, the servant of God, N——, for his salvation, for the pardon and forgiveness of his sins.

Remember, O Lord, every orthodox bishop who faithfully dispenses the word of your truth.

Remember, O Lord, according to the great extent of your compassion, my unworthiness; forgive my every transgression, deliberate and indeliberate, and do not withhold on account of my sins the grace of your Holy Spirit from these gifts here set forth.

Remember, O Lord, the priests, the deacons in Christ, and all the clergy, and let not one of us who surround your holy altar be put to shame.

Visit us with your kindness, O Lord; manifest yourself to us with your rich compassion.

Give us well-tempered and seasonable weather; grant gentle showers to the earth so that it may be fruitful; bless in your goodness the due cycle of seasons.

Prevent schisms in the Church; restrain the fury of the nations; quickly destroy the upsurges of heresy by the power of your Holy Spirit.

Receive us all into your Kingdom, presenting us as children of light and sons of the day; grant us your peace and your love, O Lord our God, for it is you who have given all things to us.

(Aloud) And grant that we may with one voice and one heart glorify and praise your most worthy and magnificent name, Father, Son, and Holy Spirit, now and always and for ever and ever.

(People) : Amen.

APPENDIX B

The Syro-Antiochene Anaphoras

1. *Abraham Venatoris* (date unknown, *ante* fourteenth century)
2. *St. Athanasius of Alexandria* (373)
3. *Basil VI* (?) Maphrian of Habdulgiani (1454)
4. *St. Basil of Caesarea* (379)
   a) *Basil II* is same as *Piloxenus of Mabogh I*
5. *St. Celestine of Rome* (422-432)
6. *St. Clement of Rome* (97)
7. *Cyriac*, Patriarch of Antioch (817)
8. *St. Cyril of Alexandria* (444) or *of Jerusalem* (386)
9. *Cyril* of Charka, Bishop (early 14th century)
10. *David bar Paul* (fl. 1200)
11. *Dionysius the Areopagite of Athens*, Bishop
12. *Dionysius bar Salibi* (1171) *I*
13. *Dionysius bar Salibi II*
14. *Dionysius bar Salibi III*
15. *Dioscorus of Alexandria* (454)
16. *Dioscorus of Kardu* (fl. 1285), Bishop
17. *St. Ephrem, Deacon of Edessa*
18. *Eustathius of Antioch* (330/37) *I*
19. *Eustathius of Antioch II.* Same as *Lazarus bar Sbhetha* II?
20. *Eustathius of Antioch III*
21. *Eustathius of Antioch IV* (??)
22. *Gregory Barhebraeus* (1286) *I*
    a) *Gregory Barhebraeus II.* Same as *Gregory James*
23. *Gregory James.* Same as *Gregory Barhebraeus II*
24. *Gregory John*, Bishop of Monastery of St. Matthew
25. *St. Gregory Nazianzen* (394)
26. *St. Gregory of Nyssa* (331?-396?)
27. *Holy Fathers.* Also called *Doctors* or *Theodore bar Wahbon*
28. *Ignatius of Antioch* (98-117)
29. *Ignatius V (IX) Behnam*, Patriarch of Antioch (1411-1454)
30. *Ignatius I (V) Ben Wahib*, Patriarch of Antioch (1333)
31. *Ignatius the Younger* (tenth to thirteenth centuries)

32. *St. James, Brother of the Lord I*
33. *St. James, Brother of the Lord II*
34. *James bar Kainaya* (*c.* 1358-1360)
35. *James Burde'ana* (578)
36. *James of Edessa,* Bishop (708)
37. *James of Serugh* (521) *I*
38. *James of Serugh II*
39. *James of Serugh III*
40. *St. John, Apostle and Evangelist*
41. *John bar Shushan X* (1073), Patriarch of Antioch *I*
42. *John bar Shushan X,* Patriarch of Antioch *II*
    a) *John bar Shushan X,* Patriarch of Antioch *III* = *Dionysius bar Salibi II*
43. *John XV Aaron bar Ma'dani,* Patriarch of Antiochene Jacobites (1252-1263)
44. *John of Bostra,* Bishop (650)
45. *St. John Chrysostom* (407) *I*
    a) *St. John Chrysostom II* = *John Harran*
46. *John of Dara* (fl. 830)
47. *John the Great.* Compiled from many anaphoras
48. *John of Harran,* Bishop (1165). Also known as *John Chrysostom II*
49. *John of Lechphed,* Patriarch of the Maronites (1174)
50. *John Maro,* " Patriarch of Antioch " (707)
51. *John Sabha,* First Bishop of Monastery of St. Matthew (fl. 680)
52. *John I " of the Sedros,"* Patriarch of Antiochene Jacobites (630-648)
53. *John the Scribe (XIV)* (1219)
54. *St. Julius of Rome,* Pope (352)
55. *Lazarus* (Philoxenus or Basil) *bar Sabhetha,* Bishop of Baghdad (fl. 829)
56. *St. Mark the Evangelist*
57. *Marutha of Tagrith* (628-649)
58. *Matthew the Shepherd*
59. *Michael the Elder,* Patriarch of Antiochene Jacobites (1199)
    a) *Michael the Younger,* Patriarch of Antiochene Jacobites; see *Gregory James*

60. *Moses bar Kepha* (903) *I*
61. *Moses bar Kepha II*
62. *St. Peter, Prince of the Apostles I*
    a) *St. Peter, Prince of the Apostles II.*   Same as *St. Peter I,*
    but a shorter version
63. *St. Peter, Prince of the Apostles III*
64. *Peter of Kallinikus,* Patriarch of Antioch (591).   May be the
    same as *St. Peter I* above
65. *Philoxenus of Mabogh,* Bishop *I.*   Also called *Simeon the Persian*
66. *Philoxenus of Mabogh II.*   Also called *Simeon the Persian II*
67. *Philoxenus of Mabogh III.*   Also called *Simeon the Persian III*
68. *(Holy) Roman Church*
69. *Severus of Antioch* (512-518).   Sometimes ascribed to *Timothy
    of Alexandria II*
70. *Severus of Kennenshre,* Bishop (fl. 640)
71. *Timothy of Alexandria,* Bishop (477)
    a) *Timothy of Alexandria II = Severus of Antioch*
72. *Thomas the Apostle.*   Also known as *Thomas of Harkel* (fl. 615)
73. *Twelve Apostles I.*   Also called *Luke I*
    a) *Twelve Apostles II.*   Differs somewhat from *Twelve Apostles I*
    b) *Twelve Apostles III.*   Differs greatly from preceding two
74. *St. Xystus,* Pope of Rome (125)

APPENDIX C

Printed Greek Leiturgika and Slav Sluzhebniki

XVI Century

Antwerp	1562	Greek
Paris	1560	Greek
Rome	1526	Greek (Demetrius Ducca)
Venice	1519	Slav (first Slav edit., Pachomius)
	1527	Slav
	1528	Greek
	1554	Slav
	1558	Greek
	1562	Greek
	1570	Slav
	1571	Greek
Vilna	1583	Slav (first in Slav territory)
	1597	Slav

XVII Century

Chernigov	1697	Slav
Delsky Monastery	1646	Slav
Kiev	1620	Slav
	1629	Slav
	1638	Slav
	1639	Slav
	1653	Slav
	1692	Slav
Lviv	1637	Slav
	1646	Slav
	1666	Slav
	1680	Slav
	1681	Slav
	1691	Slav

Mogilev   1616   Slav
                       1683   Slav

Moscow (all Slav edit.)

1602	1626	1639	1652	1676
1605	1627	1640	1655	1677
1615	1630	1641	1656	1684
1616	1632	1646	1658	1688
1617	1633	1647	1667	1693
1620	1635	1650	1668	1699
1623	1637	1651	1670	

Rome   1601   Greek
                       1683   Greek

Stratin   1604   Slav

Suprasl   1695   Slav

Venice   1600   Greek
                       1624   Greek
                       1626   Greek
                       1644   Greek
                       1650   Greek
                       1663   Greek
                       1687   Greek

Vilna   1607   Slav   1638   Slav
                       1617   Slav   1640   Slav
                       1624   Slav   1641   Slav
                       1634   Slav   1692   Slav

Yeve   1638   Slav

XVIII Century

Athens   1776   Greek *Hierodiakonikon*

Chernigov   1733   Slav
                       1747   Slav
                       1754   Slav
                       1763   Slav

Kiev	1708	Slav	1740	Slav
	1735	Slav	1746	Slav
	1736	Slav	1762	Slav
	1737	Slav	1785	Slav

Lviv	1702	Slav	1757	Slav
	1712	Slav	1759	Slav
	1720	Slav	1780	Slav
	1755	Slav		

Moscow	1705	Slav	1767	Slav
	1707	Slav	1770	Slav
	1708	Slav	1777	Slav
	1709	Slav	1783	Slav
	1717	Slav	1785	Slav
	1723	Slav	1789	Slav
	1732	Slav	1792	Slav
	1734	Slav	1793	Slav
	1739	Slav	1797	Slav
	1756	Slav		

Pochayiv	1735	Slav	1778	Slav
	1744	Slav	1788	Slav
	1755	Slav	1791	Slav
	1765	Slav		

Rome	1754	Greek *Euchologion*

Suprasl	1727	Slav
	1733	Slav
	1758	Slav
	1763	Slav
	1793	Slav

Uniev	1733	Slav
	1740	Slav
	1743	Slav
	1747	Slav

Venice	1714	Greek	1775	Greek
	1737	Greek	1781	Greek
	1740	Greek	1785	Greek
	1764	Greek	1795	Greek
	1765	Greek	1798	Greek
Vilna	1773	Slav		

XIX Century

Constantinople	1803	Greek *Euchologion*		
	1820	Greek *Leiturgikon*		
	1830	Greek *Leiturgikon*		
	1875	Greek *Leiturgikon*		
	1895	Greek *Hieratikon*		
Kiev	1803	Slav	1840	Slav
	1805	Slav	1846	Slav
	1806	Slav	1876	Slav
	1822	Slav		
	1838	Slav		
Kishinev	1815	Slav		
Lviv	1808	Slav		
	1842	Slav		
Moscow	1803	Slav	1850	Slav
	1804	Slav	1851	Slav
	1834	Slav	1854	Slav
	1846	Slav	1860	Slav
Przemyśl	1840	Slav		
St. Petersburg	1804	Slav		
	1850	Slav		
Pochayiv	1809	Slav		
Rome	1839	Greek *Leiturgikon*		
	1872	Greek *Euchologion*		
	1873	Greek *Euchologion*		

Tripolis	1892	Greek *Leiturgikon*
Venice	1803	Greek
	1805	Greek
	1814	Greek
	1817	Greek

XX Century

Athens	1912	Greek *Leiturgikon*
	1927	Greek *Euchologion*
Bilgorod	1928	Slav
Lviv	1905	Slav
	1929	Slav
	1930	Slav
Moscow	1901	Slav
Rome	1925	Greek *Leiturgikon*
	1937	Greek *Euchologion*
	1942	Slav (Russian recension)
	1942	Slav (Ruthenian recension)
	1952	Slav (Ruthenian recension)
Sophia	1924	Slav
Warsaw	1926	Slav
Zovkva	1917	Slav
	1927	Slav

BIBLIOGRAPHY

The following list of books is intended to provide an introduction to the study of the Byzantine-Slav Eucharistic Liturgy, its historical origin, evolution and development. It is a partial guide to an enormous wealth of documents. Some of the volumes do not agree in every respect with Catholic theology, but all of them have much to offer the judicious and perceptive student. The very length of such a list has prevented the inclusion of a bibliography of articles published in various journals during the last century; many of these are excellent and reference to them is imperative for any serious study of the Divine Liturgy.

Abramovich, D. I. *Izsl'edovanie o Kievo-Precherskom Paterikie.* St. Petersburg, 1902.

Achelis, A. *Die ältesten Quellen des orientalischen Kirchentums,* I : *Canones Hippolyti.* Leipzig, 1891.

Acta et decreta synodi provincialis Ruthenorum Galiciae, habitae Leopoli an. 1891. Rome, 1895.

Albers, Br. *Consuetudines monasticae,* 5 vols. Monte Cassino, 1905-1912.

Alkhimovich, I. *Liturgika,* St. Petersburg, 1891.

Allatius, L. *De ecclesiae occidentalis atque orientalis perpetua consensione.* Coloniae Agrippinae, 1648.
  De libris et rebus ecclesiasticis Graecorum dissertationes et observationes variae, Paris, 1646.

Alpatov, M., and Brunov, N. *Geschichte der altrussischen Kunst.* Augsburg, 1932.

Alston, A. E. and Turton, Z. H. *Origines Eucharisticae.* London, 1908.

Anaïssi, T. *Bullarium Maronitarum complectens Bullas, Brevia, Epistolas, Constitutiones aliaque documenta a Romanis Pontificibus ad Patriarchas Antiochenos Syro-Maronitarum missa.* Rome, 1911.

Andrieu, M. *Immixtio et Consecratio.* Paris, 1924.
  Les Ordines Romani du haut moyen-âge, Vol. I. Louvain, 1931.

Antoniadis, S. *Place de la liturgie dans la tradition des lettres grecques.* Leiden, 1939.

Antonov, A. *Khram Bozhij u tserkovnia sluzhby.* St. Petersburg, 1912.

Arcudius, P. *Libri VII de concordia ecclesiae occidentalis et orientalis in septem sacramentorum administratione.* Lutetiae Parisiorum, 1626.

Aristov, N. *Pervie vremena khristianstva v Rossii po tserkovnoistoricheskomu soderzhaniiu russkikh lietopisei.* St. Petersburg, 1888.

Arkhangel'sky, A. S. *Tvoreniia ottsov tserkvi v drevne-russkoi pis'mennosti,* 4 vols. Kazan, 1889-1891.

Arsen'ev, N. S. *We Beheld His Glory.* New York, 1936.

Asdvadzadourian, Archimandrite E. *The Liturgy of the Holy Apostolic Church of Armenia*, London, 1887.

Assemani, I. A. *Bibliotheca Orientalis Clementino-Vaticanae*, Vols. 3 and 4. Rome, 1719, 1728.
    Codex liturgicus ecclesiae universalis in XV Libros distributus, 13 vols. Rome, 1749-1765.

Atchley, E. G. C. *A History of the Use of Incense in Divine Worship*. London, 1909.
    Ordo romanus primus. London, 1905.

Attwater, D. *The Catholic Eastern Churches*. Milwaukee, 1935.
    The Dissident Eastern Churches, Milwaukee, 1937.

Aucher, G. *La versione armena della liturgia di S. Giovanni Crysostomo, fatta sul principio dell'VIII secolo*, XPYCOCTOMIKA, pp. 359-404. Rome, 1908.

Aunier, C. *Les versions roumaines de la liturgie de St. Jean Chrisostome*, XPYCOCTOMIKA, pp. 731-769. Rome, 1908.

Bacha, C. *Notions générales sur les versions arabes de la liturgie de St. Jean Chrysostome*, XPYCOCTOMIKA, pp. 405-471. Rome, 1908.

Badger, G. P. *The Nestorians and Their Rituals*, Vol. II. London, 1849.

Baldi, D. *La liturgia della chiesa di Gerusalemme dal IV al IX secolo*. Jérusalem, 1939.

Bannister, H. M. *Missale Gothicum*. London, 1917-1919.

Bardenhewer, O. *Geschichte der Altkirchlichen Literatur*, 4 vols. Freiburg im B., 1913-1924.

Bardy, G. *La question des langues dans l'Église ancienne*, Vol. I, Paris, 1948.

Batiffol, P. *Études d'histoire et de théologie positive, II, Eucharistie*. Paris, 1905.
    Leçons sur la Messe, 7th edit. Paris, 1920.

Baumgarten, N. *Eucharistic und Agape im Ur-Christentum*. Soleure, 1909.

Baumstark, A. *Comparative Liturgy*. Westminster, Md., 1958.
    Die Chrysostomosliturgie und die syrische Liturgie des Nestorios, XPYCOCTOMIKA, pp. 771-857. Rome, 1908.
    Die konstantinopolitanische Messliturgie vor dem IX Jh. Bonn, 1909.
    Die Messe im Morgenland. Kempten-München, 1906.
    Geschichte der syrischen Literatur mit Ausschluss der Christlich-palätinensischen Texte. Bonn, 1922.
    Missale Romanum. Seine Entwicklung, ihre wichtigsten Urkunden und Probleme. Eindhoven-Nimwegen, 1929.
    Von geschichtlichen Werden der Liturgie. Freiburg im B. 1923.

Beck, A. *Kirchliche Studien und Quellen*. Amberg, 1903.

Beckman, J. *Quellen zur Geschichte des christlichen Gottesdienstes*. Gütersloh, 1956.

Beer, G. *Pesahim (Ostern) Text, Ubersetzung und Erklärung. Nebst einem textkritischen Anhang* (Die Mišna. Text, Übersetzung und ausfuhrliche Erklärung). Giessen, 1912.

Beissel, S. *Bilder aus der Geschichte der altchristlichen Kunst und Liturgie in Italien.* Freiburg, 1899.
Entstehung der Perikopen des Römischen Messbuchs. Freiburg, 1907.

Bernardus of St. Thomas. *A Brief Sketch of the History of St. Thomas Christians.* Trinchinopoly, 1924.

Berning, W. *Die Einsetzung der heiligen Eucharistie.* Münster, 1901.

Bessarion, Bishop. *Tolkovanie na bozhestvennuiu liturgiu po chynu sv. Ioanna Zlatoustago i sv. Vasilia Velykago.* Moscow, 1884.

Bezstoronnej, I. *Objektyvnej pohljad na otnoshenia obriadove v vskhodnoj Halychyni.* Lvov, 1893.

Bickell, G. *Messe und Pascha,* Der apostolische Ursprung der Messliturgie und ihr genauer Anschluss an die Ein setzungsfeier der hl. Eucharistie durch Christus aus dem Pascharitus nachewiesen. Mainz, 1872.

Bieljustin, I. *O tserkovnom bogosluzhenii v 2 chastjakh.* St. Petersburg, 1897.

Bingham, J. *Origines Ecclesiasticae; or the Antiquities of the Christian Church,* Vols. 4 and 5. London, 1840.

Binterim, A. J. *Die vorzüglichsten Denkwürdigkeiten der christkatholischen Kirche,* 7 vols. Mainz, 1825-1841.

Bishop, E. *Liturgica historica.* Oxford, 1918.
The Liturgical Homilies of Narsai. Cambridge, 1909.

Bishop, W. C. *The Mozarabic and Ambrosian Rites.* London, 1924.

Bjerring, N. *The Offices of the Oriental Church.* New York, 1884.

Black, M. *An Aramaic Approach to the Gospels and Acts.* Oxford, 1946.

Bludau, A. *Die Pilgerreise der Aetheria.* Paderborn, 1927.

Bocian, I. *De modificationibus in textu slavico liturgiae S. Ioannis Chrysostomi apud Ruthenos subintroductus,* XPYCOCTOMIKA, pp. 929-969. Rome, 1908.

Bock, P. *Die Brotbitte des Vaterunsers.* Paderborn, 1911.

Bonsirven, J. *Judaïsme Palestinien au temps de J. C.,* 2 Vols. Paris, 1934-1935.

Borgia, N. *Il commentario liturgico di s. Germano Patriarca Constantinopolitano e la versione latina di Anastasio Bibliotecario.* Grottaferrata, 1912.
Origine della liturgia byzantina. Grottaferrata, 1933.

Botte, B. *Hippolyte de Rome.* La Tradition Apostolique. Paris, 1946.
Le Canon de la Messe Romaine. Mont César, 1935.

Bougeant, P. *Traité théologique sur la forme de la consécration de l'Eucharistie,* 2 vols. Lyon, 1729.

Bouyer, L. *Liturgical Piety.* Notre Dame, Ind., 1955.

Braun, J. *Der christliche Altar in seiner geschichtlichen Entwicklung,* 2 vols. Munich, 1924.
Das christliche Altargerät in seinem Sein und in seiner Entwicklung. Munich, 1932.

Die liturgische Gewandung im Occident und Orient nach Ursprung und Entwicklung, Verwendung und Symbolik. Freiburg, 1907.
Die liturgischen Paramente in Gegenwart und Vergangenheit. Ein Handbuch der Paramentik, 2nd edit. Freiburg, 1924.

Braun, O. *Das Buch der Synhados nach einer Handschrift des Museo Borgiano.* Stuttgart, 1900.

Bray, W. D. *The Weekly Lessons from Luke in the Greek Lectionary.* Chicago, 1959.

Brian-Chaninov, N. *The Russian Church.* London, 1931.

Brightman, F. E. *Liturgies Eastern and Western.* I : *Eastern Liturgies.* Oxford, 1896.

Brinktrine, J. *De epiclesis eucharistiae origine et explicatione.* Rome, 1923.
Die heilige Messe in ihrem Werden um Wesen. Paderborn, 1931.

Browe, P. *De frequenti communione in Ecclesia occidentali usque ad annum,* c. 1000. Rome, 1923.
Die häufige Kommunion im Mittelalter. Münster, 1938.
Die Pflichtkommunion im Mittelalter. Münster, 1940.
Die Verehrung der Eucharistie im Mittelalter. Münster, 1933.

Buchwald, A. *Die Epiklese in der römischen Messe.* Weidenau, 1906.

Buck, H. M. J. *The Johannine Lessons in the Greek Lectionary.* Chicago, 1958.

Budge, E. A. W. *A History of Ethiopia.* London, 1928.

Budilovich, A. S. *XIII slov Grigoriia Bogoslova v drevne-slavianskom perevodie.* St. Petersburg, 1875.

Buenner, D. *L'ancienne liturgie Romaine. le rite Lyonnais.* Lyons o.J., 1934.

Bukowski, A. *Die Genugtuung für die Sünde nach der Auffassung der russischen Orthodoxie.* Paderborn, 1911.

(Bulgakov), Makary. *Istoria khristianstva na Rusi do ravnoapostol'nago kniazia Vladimira,* 2nd edit. St. Petersburg, 1868.
Istoriia russkoi tserkvi, 12 vols. 2nd and 3rd edit. Moscow, 1886-1910.

Bury, J. B. *A History of the Eastern Roman Empire (A.D. 802-867).* London, 1912.

Bute, J. *The Coptic Morning Service for the Lord's Day.* London, 1882.

Butler, A. J. *The Ancient Coptic Churches of Egypt.* Oxford, 1884.

Byron, R. *The Byzantine Achievement, an Historical Perspective.* London, 1929.

Cabasilas, N. *A Commentary on the Divine Liturgy,* trans. by Hussey and McNulty. London, 1960.

Cabrol, F. *Hymnographie de l'Église grecque.* Angers, 1893.
Le livre de la prière antique. Paris, 1900.
Les origines liturgiques. Paris, 1906.

The Mass of the Western Rites, trans. by C. M. Anthony. London, 1934.

Cabrol F., and Leclercq H. *Monumenta ecclesiae liturgica*, 2 vols. Paris, 1901-1913.

Cagin, F. *L'Anaphore apostolique et ses témoins*. Paris, 1919.
L'Eucharistia, canon primitif de la Messe. Paris, 1912.

Catergian J., and Dašian, J. *Die Liturgien bei den Armeniern*. Fünfzehn Texte und Untersuchungen. Vienna, 1897.

Cavarnos, C. *Byzantine Sacred Art*. New York, 1957.

Chabot, J. B. *Synodicon orientale ou recueil de synodes Nestoriens publié, traduit et annoté* (tiré des *Notices et extraits des manuscrits de la Bibliothèque Nationale et autres bibliothèques*, v. 37). Paris, 1902.
Littérature syriaque. Paris, 1934.

Charon, C. *Le rite byzantin et la liturgie chrysostomienne dans les patriarcats melkites (Alexandrie, Antioche, Jérusalem)*, XPYCOCTOMIKA, pp. 473-718. Rome, 1908.

Chase, F. H. *The Lord's Prayer in the Early Church*. Cambridge, 1891.

Chernaiev, A. *Podrobnoe, sistematicheskoe ukazanie sostava Liturgiky, nauka o bogosluzhenii pravoslavnoi tserkvy*. Kharkov, 1859.

Chosrov, Magnus ep. Andsivensis. *Commentarius de orationibus missae*, trans. by Vetter, *Chosroae Magni, episcopi monophysitici explicatio precum missae*. Freiburg, 1880.

Cieplak, I. *De momento, quo Transsubstantiatio in augustissimo Missae sacrificio peragitur*. St. Petersburg, 1901.

Cirlot, F. *The Early Echarist*. London, 1939.

Codrington, H. W. *Studies of the Syrian Liturgies*. London, 1952.

Concilium Nationale Armenorum a. 1911—Acta et Decreta Concilii Nationalis Armenorum Romae habiti ad Sancti Nicolai Tolentinatis, Anno Domini MDCCCCXI. Rome, 1913.

Concilium Provinciale Tertium provinciae ecclesiasticae graeco-catholicae Alba-Juliensis et Fogarasiensis. Blaj, 1906.

Connolly, R. H. *Didascalia Apostolorum*. Oxford, 1929.
The Liturgical Homilies of Narsai. Cambridge, 1909.
The So-called Egyptian Church Order and Derived Documents. Cambridge, 1916.

Connolly, R. H., and Codrington, W. *Two Commentaries on the Jacobite Liturgy, by George Bishop of the Arab Tribes, and Moses bar Kepha*. London, 1913.

Cooper J., and Maclean, A. J. *The Testament of Our Lord*. Edinburgh, 1902.

Corblet, J. *Histoire dogmatique, liturgique et archéologique de l'eucharistie*, 2 vols. Paris, 1886.

Corswarem, C. *La Liturgie Byzantine et l'Union des Églises*. Avignon, 1926.

Cotroneo, R. *Il rito greco in Calabria*. Reggio di Calabria, 1902.

Couturier, A. *Cours de liturgie grecque-Melkite*, 3 vols. Jerusalem, 1912, 1914, 1930.

Croegaert, A. *The Mass, a Liturgical Commentary*, 2 vols. Westminster, Md., 1958.

Cross, S. H. *The Russian Primary Chronicle*, " Harvard Studies and Notes in Philology and Literature, " Vol. XII. Cambridge, 1930.

Cyriacus Cantzagensis (s. XIII)—Historia Armeniae, edit. Moscow, 1858.

D'Achery, J. L. *Specilegium sive collectio veterum aliquot scriptorum*, 2nd edit. in 3 vols. Paris, 1723.

Dahane, D. *Liturgie de la S. Messe selon le rite chald.* Paris, 1937.

Dalmais, H. *The Eastern Liturgies.* London, 1960.

D'Almeida, E. *Historia de Ethiopia*, edit. Beccari, C., " Rerum Aethiopicarum Scriptores Occidentales, " Vols. 5-7. Rome, 1907-1908.

Daniel, H. A. *Codex liturgicus ecclesiae universae*, 4 vols. Leipzig, 1847.

Daniel K. N. *A Critical Study of Primitive Liturgies, Especially That of S. James.* Teruvalla, 1949.

De Clercq, C. *Les Églises unies d'Orient.* Paris, 1934.

de Meester, Pl. *Les origines et les développements du texte grec de la liturgie de S. Jean Chrysostome*, XPYCOCTOMIKA, pp. 245-357, Rome, 1908.
> *Liturgies Grecques.* D.A.C.L., VI.
> *De concelebratione in Ecclesia orientali.* Rome, 1923.

de Villard, M. *Le Chiese di Mesopotamia.* Rome, 1940.

De Vries, G. *L'Oriente Cristiano ieri ed oggi.* Rome, 1950.

Denis-Boulet, N. M. *The Christian Calendar.* London, 1960.

Denzinger, H. *Ritus orientalium, coptorum, syrorum, et armenorum in administrandis sacramentis*, 2 vols. Wirceburgi, 1873, 1874.

Denzinger, H. and Umberg, J. B. *Enchiridion Symbolorum*, 15th edit. Freiburg, 1922.

Destefani, G. *La Sancta Messa nella Liturgia Romana.* Turin, 1935.

D'iakonov, M. A. *Vlast' moskovskikh gosudarei.* St. Petersburg, 1889.

Dib, P. *Étude sur la liturgie maronite.* Paris, 1919.

Dibelius, F. *Das Abendmahl.* Leipzig, 1911.

Dix, G. *The Shape of the Liturgy*, 2nd edit. London, 1945.
> *The Treatise on the Apostolic Tradition of St. Hippolytus of Rome.* London, 1937.

Dmitrievsky, A. *Bogosluzhenie strastnoj i paskhal'noj sedmytsy vo sv. Ierusalymi IX-X v.* St. Petersburg, 1894.
> *Bogosluzhenie v russkoj tserkvi v XVI v.* Kazan, 1894.
> *Drevne-judejskaya synagoga i yeya bogosluzhenia formy v otnoshenii k drevne-khristianskomu khramu i yego bogosluzhebnim formam.* Kazan, 1893.
> *Opysanie liturgicheskikh rukopisej khraniaschikhsia v bibliotekakh pravoslavnago vostoka;* Vol. I, *Tipika*, Kiev, 1895; Vol. II, *Euchologia*, Kiev, 1901; Vol. III, *Tipika*, Part II, St. Petersburg, 1917.
> *Stavlennik.* Kiev, 1904.

Dmitrievsky, I. *Istoricheskoe dogmaticheskoe i tainstvennoe izyasnenie na bozhestvennoju liturgiu.* Moscow, 1804.

Documenta Pontificum Romanorum—Historiam Ucrainae Illustrantia, edit. Welykyj, A.G., 2 vols. Rome, 1953-1954.

Dölger, F. J. *Sol salutis, Geget und Gesang im christlichen Altertum.* Münster, im W., 1920.

Dolnytsky, J. *O sviaschennykh obriadakh hrets. rusk. tserkvy.* Lvov, 1891. *Typik tserkvy rusko-katolycheskia.* Lvov, 1899.

Dowling, Archdeacon. *The Armenian Church.* London, 1910.

Drews, P. *Untersuchungen über die sogenannte clementinische Liturgie im VIII Buch der apostolischen Konstitutionem.* Tübingen, 1906. *Zur Entstehungeschichte des Kanons in der röm. Messe.* Tübingen, 1902.

Drower, E. S. *Water into Wine. A Study of Ritual Idiom in the Middle East.* London, 1956.

Drury, T. W. *Elevation in the Eucharist, Its History and Rationale.* Cambridge, 1907.

Duchesne, L. *Autonomies ecclésiastiques. Églises séparées.* Paris, 1896. *Origines du culte chrétien.* Paris, 1909.

Dugmore, C. W. *The Influence of the Synagogue upon the Divine Office.* London, 1945.

Durieux, P. *L'Eucharistie. Memento canonique et pratique.* Paris, 1925.

Dvornik, Fr. *Les Légendes de Constantin et de Méthode vues de Byzance.* Prague, 1933. *Les Slaves, Byzance et Rome au IX s.* Paris, 1926.

Dwirnyk J. *Rôle de l'Iconostase dans le culte divin.* Montreal, 1960.

Easton, B. S. *The Apostolic Tradition of Hippolytus.* Cambridge, 1934.

Ebner, A. *Quellen und Forschungen zur Geschichte und Kunstgeschichte des Missale Romanum im Mittelalter. Iter Italicum.* Freiburg, 1896.

Eisenhofer, L. *Handbuch der Katholischen Liturgik,* Vol. 2. Freiburg, 1933.

Elbogen, I. *Der jüdische Gottesdienst in seiner geschichtlichen Entwicklung,* 2nd edit. Frankfurt, 1924.

Elfers, H. *Die Kirchenordnung Hippolyts vom Rom.* Paderborn, 1938.

Engberding, P. H. *Das eucharistische Hochgebet der Basiliusliturgie.* Münster, 1931.

Engdahl, R. *Beiträge zur Kenntnis der byzantinischen Liturgie.* Berlin, 1908. *Die Proskomidie der Liturgien des Chrysostomus und Basilius während des Mittelalters.* Berlin, 1908.

Englert, C. C. *Catholics and Orthodox, Can They Unite?* New York, 1961.

Every, G. *The Byzantine Patriarchate,* 451-1204, 2nd edit. London, 1947.

Evetts, B. *The Rites of the Coptic Church, The Order of Baptism.* London, 1888.

Excavations at Dura-Europos, Preliminary Report of V. Season of Work 1931-1932. New Haven, 1934.

Fedotov, G. P. *Sviatie Drevnei Russi*. Paris, 1931.
>   *The Russian Religious Mind*, Harper, Torehbook, edit., New York, 1960.
>   *Treasury of Russian Spirituality*. New York, 1948.

Feltoe, C. L. *Sacramentarium Leonianum*. Cambridge, 1896.

Férotin, M. *Le Liber ordinum en usage dans l'église wisigothique et mozarabe d'Espagne des Ve au XIe siècle*. Paris, 1904.
>   *Le Liber mozarbicus sacramentorum et les manuscrits mozarabes*. Paris, 1912.

Festugière, M. *La liturgie catholique. Essai de synthèse*. Maredsous, 1914.

Filaret, H. *Obzor russkoi dukhovnoi literatury*. St. Petersburg, 1884.

Filograssi, J. *De Sanctissima Eucharistia*. 3rd edit. Rome, 1940.

Florovsky, G. V. *Puti russkago bogosloviya*. Paris, 1937.
>   *Vizantiiskie ottsy V-VIII v.v.* Paris, 1933.

Fortescue, A. *The Mass, a Study of the Roman Liturgy*, 3rd edit. London, 1953.
>   *The Orthodox Eastern Church*. London, 1920.
>   *The Uniate Eastern Churches : The Byzantine Rite in Italy, Sicily, Syria, and Egypt*. London, 1923.

Franco, N. *La consecrazione eucaristica nella liturgia greca*. Rome, 1913.

Frankland, W. B. *The Early Eucharist*. London, 1902.

Franz, I. T. *Die eucharistische Wandlung und die Epiklese der griechischen und orientalischen Liturgien*, I-II. Würzburg, 1880.

Frere, W. H. *Some Links in the Chain of Russian Church History*. London, 1918.
>   *Studies in Early Roman Liturgy*. London, 1930, 1934.
>   *The Anaphora or Great Eucharistic Prayer*. London, 1938.
>   *The Use of Sarum*, 2 vols. Cambridge, 1891-1901.

Fuchs, F. *Die höheren Schulen von Konstantinopel im Mittelalter*. Leipzig, 1926.

Funk, F. X. *Das Testament uns Herrn u. die verwandten Schriften*. Mainz, 1901.
>   *Der Kommunionritus : Kirchengeschicht. Abhandlungen und Untersuchunge*, I. Paderborn, 1897.
>   *Didascalia et Constitutiones Apostolorum*, 2 vols. Paderborn, 1905.
>   *Die Apostolischen Konstitutionen*. Eine literar-historische Untersuchungen. Rottenburg, 1891.
>   *Die Didache, Kirchengeschichtl. Abhandlungen und Untersuchungen*, II. Paderborn, 1904.
>   *Patres Apostolici*, 2 vols. Tübingen, 1901.

Gagin, P. *L'Anaphore apostolique et ses témoins*. Paris, 1919.

Gal'kovsky, N. *Bor'ba khristianstva s ostatkami iazychestva v drevnei Rusi*. Kharkov, 1916.

Gammurini, M. *Peregrinatio Aetheriae (Silviae) ad loca sancta*. Rome, 1887-1888.

Gass, W. *Symbolic der griechischen Kirche*. Berlin, 1872.

Gassner, J. *The Canon of the Mass. Its History, Theology and Art*. St. Louis, 1949.

Gastoué, A. *Introduction à la paléographie musicale byzantine*. Paris, 1907.

Gatti-Korolevskij. *I riti e le chiese orientali*. Genoa, 1942.

Gautier, L. *Les tropes*. Paris. 1886.

Gavanti, B., and Merati, C. M. *Thesaurus sacrorum rituum*, 5 vols. Venice, 1723.

Gaviil, Archimandrite. *Rukovodstvo po Liturgiki, ili nauka o pravoslavnom bogosluzhenii*. Tver, 1886.

Gavin, F. *Some Aspects of Contemporary Greek Orthodox Thought*. Milwaukee-London, 1923.
    The Jewish Antecedents of the Christian Sacraments. London, 1928.

Geiselmann, J. R. *Die Abendmahlslehre an der Winde der christlichen Spätantike zum Fruhmittelalter*. Munich, 1933.

Germann, W. *Die Kirche der Thomaschristen. Ein Beitrag zur Geschichte der Orientalischen Kirche*. Gütersloh, 1877.

Gewiess, J. *Die urapostoliche Heilsverkundigung nache der Apostelgeschichte*. Breslau, 1939.

Gihr, N. *The Holy Sacrifice of the Mass*. St. Louis, 1949.

Ginzel, J. *Geschichte der Slawenapostel Cyrill und Method und der slawischen Liturgie*. Vienna, 1861.

Glubokovsky, N. *Russkaya bogoslovskaya nauka*. Warsaw, 1928.

Goar, J. *Euchologion, sive Rituale Graecorum*, 2nd edit. Venice, 1730.

Goetz, L. K. *Das Kieven Höhlenkloster als Kulturzentrum des vormongolischen Russlands*. Passau, 1904.
    Kirchengeschichtliche und kulturgeschichtliche Denkmäler Altrusslands. Stuttgart, 1905.

Goguel, M. *L'Eucharistie des origines à Justin Martyr*. Paris, 1910.

Goltz, E. *Das Gebet in der altesten Christenheit*. Leipzig, 1901.

Golubinsky, E. E. *Istoriya russkoi tserkvi*, 4 vols. 2nd edit. Moscow, 1901-1917.

Goosens, W. *Les origines de l'Eucharistie Sacrament et Sacrifice*. Paris, 1931.

Gordillo, M. *Compendium Theologiae Orientalis*. Rome, 1950.
    Mariologia Orientalis. Rome, 1954.

Gorodetzky, N. *The Humiliated Christ in Modern Russian Thought*. London, 1938.

Gorski, T. *Orthodoxae Orientalis Ecclesiae Dogmata*, edit. Moscow, 1831.

Gorsky, A., and Nevostrujev, K. *Opysanie slavianskikh rukopisej Moskovskoj Synodal'noj biblioteky*, Moscow, Vol. I, 1855; Vol. II, 1857; Vol. III, 1859; Vol. IV, 1862; Vol. V, 1869.

Graf, G. *Ein Reformversuch innerhalb der koptischen Kirche im zwölften Jahrhundert*, " Collectanea Hierosolymitana, " II. Paderborn, 1923.

Greiff, A. *Das alteste Pascha-ritual der Kirche.* Paderborn, 1929.

Grekov, B. D. *Kievskaya Rus'*, 4th edit. Moscow-Leningrad, 1944.

Grondijs, L. H. *L'iconographie byzantine du Crucifié mort sur la Croix*, Bruxelles, 1941.

Grousset, R. *L'Empire du Levant.* Paris, 1946.

Gudzy, N. K. *Istoriya drevnei russkoi literatury*, 2nd edit. Moscow, 1941.

Gudzy, N. K., and Novikov, I. *Slovo o polku Igoreve.* Moscow, 1938.

Guilland, Oeconomos, and Grousset. *L'Europe orientale de 1018 à 1453.* Paris, 1945.

Gummey, H. R. *The Consecration of the Eucharist.* Philadelphia, 1908.

Halka, I. *Dukh vecherni, utreni i liturgii hr. katolytskoi tserkvy.* Lvov, 1861.

Hamm, F. *Die liturgeschen Ensetzungsberichte im Sinne vergleichender Liturgieforschung untersuch* (L.Q.F. 23). Münster, 1928.

Haneberg, B. *Canoñes S. Hippolyti.* Munich, 1870.

Hanssens, M. I. *Institutiones liturgicae de ritibus orientalibus : De Missa rituum orientalium*, 3 vols. Rome, 1930-1932.
    La Liturgie d'Hippolyte. Rome, 1959.

Hapgood, I. F. *Service Book of the Holy Orthodox-Catholic Apostolic (Greco-Russian) Church.* Boston-New York, 1906.

Harden, J. M. *An Introduction to Ethiopic Christian Literature.* London, 1926.
    The Anaphoras of the Ethiopic Liturgy. London, 1928.

Harnack, A. *Die Apostellehre und die jüdischen zwei Wege.* Leipzig, 1886.

Hauler, E. *Didascaliae Apostolorum fragmenta Veronensia.* Leipzig, 1900.

Hefele, J., and Leclercq, H. *Histoire des conciles d'après les documents originaux*, 8 vols. Paris, 1907-1921.

Heiler, F. *Urkirche und Ostkirche.* Munich, 1937.

Henke, C. *Die katholische Lehre über die Konsecrationsworte der Hl. Eucharistie.* Trier, 1850.

Hergenröther, I. *Monumenta graeca ad Photium eiusque historiam pertinentia.* Ratisbon, 1869.
    Photius, Patriarch von Constantinopel, 3 vols. Regensburg, 1867-1869.

Hermogen, Bishop. *Liturgika ili uchenie o bogosluzhenii pravoslavnoi tserkvy.* St. Petersburg, 1884.

Hoeynck, F. A. *Geschichte der kirchlichen Liturgie des Bisthums Augsburg.* Augsburg, 1889.

Hoffmann, J. *Das Abendmahl im Urchristentum.* Berlin, 1903.

Holl, K. *Enthusiasmus und Bussgewelt beim griechischen Mönchtum.* Leipzig, 1898.

Höller, I. *Die epiklese der griechisch-orientalischen Liturgien.* Vienna, 1912.

Holubev, S. *Kievskij mytr. P. Mohyla i eho spodvyzhnyky*, I. Kiev. 1883.

Hoppe, L. A. *Die Epiklesis der griech. u. oriental. Liturgieen u. der Röm. Consekrationskanon.* Schaffhausen, 1864.

Horner, G. *The Satutes of the Apostles or Canones ecclesiastici, Edited with Translation and Collation from Ethiopic and Arabic Mss.; also a Translation of the Sahidic and Collation of the Bohairic Versions; and Sahidic Fragments.* London, 1904.

Howard, G. B. *The Christians of St. Thomas and Their Liturgies.* Oxford-London, 1864.

Hrushevsky, M. *A History of Ukraine.* New Haven, 1941.

Hunkin, J. W. *The Invocation of the Holy Spirit in the Prayer of the Consecration.* Cambridge, 1927.

Hussey. J. W. *Church and Learning in the Byzantine Empire, 867-1185.* London, 1937.

Hussey, J. M. and McNulty, P. A. *Nicolas Cabasilas, A Commentary on the Divine Liturgy.* London, 1960.

Hyatt, H. M. *The Church of Abyssinia.* London, 1928.

Ikonnikov, V. S. *Opyt izsliedovania o kulturnom znachenii Vizantii v Russkoi istorii.* Kiev, 1869.

Issaverdenz, F. J. *The Armenian Ritual,* Part I, *The Armenian Liturgy.* Armenian Monastery of S. Lazzaro, 1873.

Istrin, V. M. *Ocherk istorii drevene-russkoi literatury.* St. Petersburg, 1922.

Iswolsky, H. *Christ in Russia, The History, Tradition, and Life of the Russian Church.* Milwaukee, 1960.
   Soul of Russia. New York-London, 1944.

Ivakin, I. M. *Kniaz' Vladimir Monomach i iego Pouchenie.* Moscow, 1901.

James, R. L. and Langford. *A Dictionary of the Eastern Orthodox Church.* London, 1923.

Janin, R. *Les Églises orientales et les rites orientaux.* Paris, 1929.
   Les Églises séparées d'Orient. Paris, 1930.

Joseph of Travancore, T. K. *Malabar Christians and Their Ancient Documents.* Trivandrum, 1929.

Jugie, M. *De forma Eucharistiae, De epiclesibus eucharisticis.* Rome, 1943.
   La messe dans l'église byzantine après le IXe siècle, DTC, X, 1332-1346.
   La messe en Orient du IVe au IXe siècle, DTC, X. 1317-1332.
   Theologia dogmatica christianorum orientalium ab ecclesia Catholica dissidentium, 5 vols. Paris, 1926-1935.

Jülicher, *Zur Geschichte der Abendmahlsfeier in der ältesten Kirche.* Freiburg in B., 1892.

Jungmann, J. A. *Die latinischen Bussriten in ihrer guchichtlichen Entwicklung.* Innsbruck, 1932.
   Geworden Liturgie. Innsbruck, 1941.
   Liturgical Worship. an Inquiry into Its Fundamental Principles. New York, 1941.

The Mass of the Roman Rite : Its Origins and Development (Missarum Sollemnia), 2 vols. New York, 1951.

Kahle, P. E. *Bala'izah Coptic texts from Deir El Bala'izah in Upper Egypt*, 2 vols. London, 1954.

Kalaidovich, K. F. *Ioann ekzarkh Bolgarsky*. Moscow, 1824.
Pamiatniki rossiiskoi slovesnosti XII vieka, Moscow, 1821.

Kalsbach A. *Die altkirchliche Einrichtung der Diakonissen bis zu ihrem Erlöschen*. Freiburg, 1926.

Karabinov, I. A. *Evkharisticheskaya molytva (Anaphora)*. St. Petersburg, 1908.

Karatajev, I. *Opysanie slaviano russkikh knig*. St. Petersburg, 1883.

Katansky, A. *Dogmaticheskoe uchenie o semi tserkovnikh tainstvakh v tvoreniakh drevnijshikh ottsov i uchitelej Tserkvy*. St. Petersburg, 1877.

Kattenbusch, F. *Das Apostolische Symbol*, 2 vols. Leipzig, 1894, 1900.

Kayser, C. *Die Kanones Jakob's von Edessa übersetzt und erläutert, zum Theil auch zuert im Grundtext veröffentlich*. Leipzig, 1886.

Kazansky, P. L. *Istoriia pravoslavnago russkago monashestva*. Moscow, 1855.

Khakhanov, A. S. *Ocherki po istorii gruzinskoi slovenosti*. Moscow, 1901.

Khayatt, G. *La Messa in rito siro-antiocheno*. Rome, 1942.

Khitrovo, G. *Uchenie pravoslavnoi tserkvy o bogosluzhenii ili Liturgika*. Tambov, 1869.

Khojnatsky, A. *Zapadno-russkaya Tserkovnaya Uniya v yeya bohosluzhenii i obriadakh*. Kiev, 1871.

Khorunzhov, T. *Pravoslavnaya khristianskaya Liturgika*. St. Petersburg, 1877.

Kidd, B. J. *The Churches of Eastern Christendom from A.D. 451 to the Present Time*. London, 1927.

Kimmel, E. I. *Monumenta fidei ecclesiae orientalis*, I. Jena, 1850.

King, A. *Notes on the Catholic Liturgies*. London, 1930.
The Rites of Eastern Christendom, 2 vols. Rome, 1948.

Kirch, C. *Enchiridion fontium historiae ecclesiasticae*, 4th edit. Freiburg, 1923.

Kirchhoff, K. *Die Ostkirche betet. Hymnen aus den Tagzeiten der byzantinischen Kirche*, 4 vols. Hellerau, 1934-1937.

Klauser, T. *Das römische capitulare Evangeliorum*, I. Münster, 1935.

Kliuchevsky, V. O. *A History of Russia*, 5 vols. London, 1911-1931.

Kondakov, N. P. *Ikonografiia Bogomateri*, 2 vols. St. Petersburg, 1914-1915.
Ikonografiia Iisusa Khrista. St. Petersburg, 1905.

Korolevskij, C. *Histoire des patriarcats melkites (Alexandrie, Antioche, Jérusalem) depuis le schisme monophysite du sixième siècle jusqu'à nos jours, avec une introduction sur la période antérieure*, Vols. II, III. Rome, 1911.

Kostelnik, G. *Spir pro Epiklezu mizh skhodom i zakhodom*. Lviv, 1928.

Kowaliv, P. *Molytovnyk-Sluzhebnyk, Pamiatka XIV stolittia*. New York, 1960.

Kramp, J. *Eucharistia Von ihrem Wesen und ihrem Kult*. Freiburg in B., 1926.

Krasnoseltsev, N. *K istorii pravoslavnago bogosluzhenia. (po povodu nikotorikh tserkovnikh sluzhb i obriadov nyni ne upotrebl' jayuschikhsia.* Kazan, 1889.
    Materialy dlja istorii chinoposlidovania liturgii sv. Ioanna Zlatoustago. Kazan, 1889.
    O drevnikh liturgicheskikh tolkovaniakh. Odessa, 1894.
    Svidenia o nikotorikh liturgicheskikh rukopis'akh Vatikanskoi biblioteki. Kazan, 1885.

Künstle, K. *Ikonographie der christlichen Kunst*, 2 vols. Freiburg, 1926-1928.

Kunze G. *Die gottesdienstliche Schriftlesung, I. Stand und Aufgaben der Perikopenforschung.* Gottingen, 1947.

Kyprian, Archimandrite. *Evkharistia.* Paris, 1947.

Lamy, T. I. *Dissertatio de Syrorum fide et disciplina in re Eucharistica.* Louvain, 1859.

Lavrovsky, M. A. *O drevne-russkikh uchilischakh.* Kharkov, 1854.

Lebedev, A. *O nashem symboli viri.* Sergiev-Posad, 1902.

Lebedev, P. *Nauka o bogosluzhenii pravoslavnoi tserkvy*, 2 vols. Moscow, 1904.

Lebon, J. *Le monophysisme sévérien.* Louvain, 1909.

Lebrun, P. *Explication littérale, historique, et dogmatique des prières et des cérémonies de la messe.* Paris, 1716-1726, 4 vols.

Legg J. W. *The Sarum Missal.* London, 1916.

Le Guillou, M. J. *The Spirit of Eastern Orthodoxy.* Glen Rock, N. J., 1964.

Leib, J. *Rome, Kiev, et Byzance à la fin du Xe siècle.* Paris, 1924.

Leitner, F. *Der gottesdienstliche Volksgesang im jüdischen und Christlichen altertum.* Freiburg, 1906.

Leitpold, J. *Der Gottesdienst der ältesten Kirche jüdisch? griechisch? christlich?* Leipzig, 1937.

Le Quien, M. *Oriens christianus in quatuor patriarchatus digestus, quo exhibentur Ecclesiae, Patriarchae, caeterique praesules totius Orientis,* 3 vols. Paris, 1740.

Leroquais, V. *Les Pontificaux des bibliothèques publiques de France*, 4 vols. Paris, 1937.
    Les Sacramentaires et les Missels manuscrits des bibliothèques publiques de France, 4 vols. Paris, 1924.

Levinsky, A. *Nauka o Sluzhbi Bozhii*, Lviv, 1906.

Lietzamnn, H. *Das Sacramentarium Gregorianum nach Aachener Urexemplar.* Münster, 1921.
    Klementische Liturgie. Bonn, 1910.
    Liturgische Texte zur Geschichte der orientalischen Taufe und Messe im II. und IV. Jahrhunderten. Bonn, 1923.
    Messe und Herrenmahl. Eine Studie zur Geschichte der Liturgie. Bonn, 1926.

Linton A. *The Anaphora*, London, 1922.

Lisowski, F. *Słowa ustanowienia najśw. sakramentu a ep.* Lwów, 1912.

Littledale, R. F. *The Holy Eastern Church.* London, 1870.

Loisy, A. *Les Mystères païens dans le culte juif et dans le culte chrétien.* Paris, 1919.

Loofs, F. *Nestoriana.* Halle, 1905.

Losskij, V. *Essai sur la théologie mystique de l'Église d'Orient.* Paris, 1944.

Lotockyj, I. *Der Heilige Geist in der byzantinischen Liturgie.* Vienna, 1945.

Lowe, E. A. and Wilmart, A. *The Bobbio Missal.* London, 1917-1924.

Lubeck, K. *Die christlichen Kirchen des Orients.* Munich, 1911.

Ludolfus, I. *Ad suam historiam Aethiopicam ante hac editam commentarius.* Frankfurt am Main, 1691.
   Historia Aethiopica sive Brevis et succincta descriptio Regni Habes-sinorum quod vulgo male Presbyteri Iohannis vocatur. Frankfurt am Main, 1681.

Lysytsyn, M. *Pervonachalnej slaviano-russkij tipikon.* St. Petersburg, 1911.

Maclean, A. J. *East Syrian Daily Offices.* London, 1894.
   Recent Discoveries Illustrating Early Christian Life and Worship. London, 1904.
   The Ancient Church Orders. Cambridge, 1910.

Maclean, A. J., and Browne, W. H. *The Catholicos of the East and His People.* London, 1892.

Magani, F. *L'antica liturgia romana,* 3 vols. Milan, 1897-1899.

Mai, A. *Nova Patrum Biblioteca,* 10 vols. Rome, 1852-1905.
   Scriptorum veterum nova collectio e Vaticanis codicibus edita. 10 vols. Rome, 1825-1838.
   Spicilegium romanum. 10 vols. Rome, 1839-1844.

Makarij, Metropolitan. *Istoria russkoi Tserkvy,* 12 vols. St. Petersburg 1846-1883.

Malan, S. C. *Original Documents of the Coptic Church.* London, 1875.

Malinin, V. M. *Zlatostrui. Desiat' slov Zlatostruia XII v.* St. Petersburg, 1910.

Malinovsky, M. *Izyasnenie na bozhestvennuyu Liturhiyu.* Lvov, 1845.

Maltzev, A. P. *Andachtsbuch der orthodox-katholischen Kirche des Morgenlandes.* Berlin, 1895.
   Die Nachtwache oder Abend- und Morgengottesdienst der orthodox-katholischen Kirche des Morgenlandes. Berlin, 1898.
   Die Sakramente der orthodox-katholischen Kirche des Morgenlandes. Berlin, 1898.

Mandal, M. *Nell'Oriente Greco-Byzantino.* Palermo, 1940.

Mandala, M. *La protesi della liturgia nel rito bizantino-greco.* Grottaferrata, 1935.

Mansi, I. D. *Sacrorum conciliorum nova et amplissima collectio*, 31 vols. : Vols. 1-13, Florence, 1759-1798; Vols. 14-31, Venice, 1769-1798; supplement to Vol. 31, Paris, 1901;—Collection continued— Vols. 32-53, Paris-Arnheim-Leipzig, 1923-1927.

Markovic, I. *Oevkaristiji s osobitim obzirom na Epiklesu.* Zagreb, 1894.

Martène, E. *De antiquis Ecclesiae ritibus*, 2nd edit., 4 vols. Antwerp, 1736-1738. (In our references to Martène, citations are made according to his own divisions, but volume and page numbering of 2nd Antwerp edit. are appended in parentheses.)

Masaryk, T. G. *The Spirit of Russia*, 2 vols. London-New York, 1919.

Maskell, W. *The Ancient Liturgy of the Church of England according to the Uses of Sarum, York, Hereford and Bangor*, 3rd edit. Oxford, 1882.

Mateos, J. *Le Typicon de la Grande Église*, 2 vols. Rome, 1962-1963.

Maurice-Denis, N., and Boulet, R. *Euchariste ou la Messe dans ses variétés, son histoire et ses origines.* Paris, 1953.

Maximilian of Saxony, Prince. *Praelectiones de liturgiis orientalibus*, I. Freiburg, 1908.

Maximos IV Sayegh, Patriarch. *The Eastern Churches and Catholic Unity.* Freiburg-Monreal, 1963.

Mercenier, E. *La Prière des Églises du Rite Byzantin.* 2nd edit., 3 vols. Chevetogne, 1947.

Mercier, E. *La Spiritualité byzantine.* Paris, 1933.

Mercier, S. A. S. *The Ethiopic Liturgy, Its Sources, Development and Present Form.* London, 1915.

Metallov, B. *Ocherk istorii pravoslavnago tserkovnago pieniia v Rosii*, 3rd edit. Moscow, 1900.

Michalcescu, I. *Die Bekenntnisse und die wichtigsten Glaubenszeugnisse der griechisch-orientalischen Kirche.* Leipzig, 1904.

Migne, J. P. *Patrologia Graeca.* Paris, 1857-1866. *Patrologia Latina.* Paris, 1844-1865.

Mikulas, G. *Liturgiae sancti Joannis Chrysostomi interpretatio.* Magno-Varadini, 1903.

Mindalev, P. *Molenie Daniila Zatochnika i sviazannie s nim pamiatniki.* Kazan, 1914.

Mingana, A. *The Early Spread of Christianity in Central Asia and the Far East.* Manchester, 1925. *Commentary of Theodore of Mopsuestia on the Lord's Prayer and on the Sacraments of Baptism and the Eucharist.* Cambridge, 1933. *Commentary of Theodore of Mopsuestia on the Nicene Creed.* Cambridge, 1932.

Mirkovich, G. *O vremeni presuschestvlenia Sv. Darov.* Vilna, 1886.

Mirkovich, L. *Pravoslavna Liturgika*, Sremsky Karlovtsy, 1918 (I) 1920 (II), 1926 (III).

Mirski, D. S. *A History of Russian Literature from the Earliest Times.* London, 1927.

Mishkovsky, T. *Izlozhenie Tsarehradskoi Liturgii sv. Vasyliya V. i sv. Ioanna Zlatousta po yeya drevnemu smyslu i dukhu.* Lvov, 1926.
Nash obriad i oblatynenie eho. Lvov, 1913.

Mone, F. J. *Lateinische und griechische Messen aus dem II-VI Jh.* Frankfurt, 1850.

Moreau, F. J. *Les liturgies eucharistiques. Notes sur leur origines et leur développement.* Brussels, 1924.

Muralt, E. *Briefe uber den Gottesdienst der morgelandischen Kirche.* Leipzig, 1839.

Muratori, L. A. *Liturgia Romana Vetus,* 2 vols. Venice, 1748.

Muretov, S. *Istoricheskij obzor chynoposlidovania proskomidii do Ustava patr. Filoteya.* Moscow, 1895.

Nahachevsky, I. *Rym i Vizantia.* Toronto, 1956.

Nasrallah J. *Marie dans la sainte et divine liturgie byzantine.* Paris, 1955.

Neale, J. M. *Essays on Liturgiology and Church History.* London, 1863.
Introduction to the History of the Holy Eastern Church, 2 vols. London, 1933.

Neale, J. M., and Forbes, G. H. *The Ancient Liturgies of the Gallican Church.* Burntisland, 1855.

Nesterovsky, E. *Liturgika ili nauka o Bogosluzhenii Pravoslavnoi Tserkvy,* 2 vols. Kursk, 1895 and 1900.

Netzer, H. *L'introduction de la messe romaine en France.* Paris, 1910.

Niarady, D. *Sluzhba Bozha abo Liturgia.* Diakovo, 1932.

Nicolas, M. J. *A New Look at the Eucharist.* Glen Rock, N. J., 1964.

Niechaj, M. *Oratio liturgica pro defunctis in ecclesia Russa Orthodoxa.* Lublin, 1933.

Nielen, J. M. *The Earliest Christian Liturgy,* trans. by P. Cummins. St. Louis, 1941.

Nikolsky, K. *O sluzhbakh russkoi tserkvy, byvshikh v pervikh pechatnikh bogosluzhebnikh knigakh.* St. Petersburg, 1885.
Posobie k izucheniu Ustava Bogosluzhenia pravoslavnoi tserkvy. St. Petersburg, 1907.

Nikolsky, N. K. *Materialy dlja provremennago spiska russkikh pisatelei i ikh sochinenii X-XI vv.* St. Petersburg, 1906.

Nilles, N. *Kalendarium manuale utriusque Ecclesiae.* 2nd edit. Innsbruck, 1897.

Nomocanon, 228 *canonum,* edit. Pavlov, A. S. *Nomokanon pry bol'shom Trebniku.* Iego istoria i tekst s kriticheskymy prymichaniamy. Moscow, 1897.

Nordov, V. *Besidy na bozhestvennuiu liturgiiu.* Moscow, 1842.

Novellae, edit. R. Schoell-G. Kroll, 4 th edit. 3 vols. Berlin, 1912.

O Obrzedach Grecko-Uniackich jako kwestyi czasów dzisiejszych w Galicyi wschodniej. Przez ksiedza tegoz obrzadku. Lwow, 1862.

Oakley, A. *The Orthodox Liturgy.* London, 1958.

Odintsov, N. *Porjadok obschestvennago i chastnago bogosluzhenia v drevnej Rossii do XVI v.* St. Petersburg, 1881.

Odinzov, N. *Uniatskoe bogosluzhenie v XVII i XVIII vv. po rukopisiam Vylenskoj publychnoj biblioteky.* Vilno, 1886.

Oeconomous, I. *La Vie religieuse dans l'empire Byzantin au temps des Comnènes et des Anges.* Paris, 1918.

Oesterley, W. O. E. *The Jewish Background of the Christian Liturgy.* Oxford, 1925.

Oppenheim, P. *Institutiones systematico-historicae in sacram liturgiam.* Aurini-Rome, 1941.
   Introductio historica in litteras liturgicas, 2nd edit. Turin, 1945.

Oriente Cattolico, cenni storici e statistiche. Vatican, 1962.

Orlov, A. I. *Slovo o polku Igoreve.* Moscow, 1938.

Orlov, M. *Liturgia sviatago Vasilia Velykago,* Pervoe kriticheskoe izdanie s izobrazheniem sv. Vasilia, s chetirmy spiskamy s rukopisej. St. Petersburg, 1905.

Ormanian, M. *The Church of Armenia, Her History, Doctrine, Rule, Discipline, Liturgy, Literature, and Existing Condition.* London and Oxford, 1912.

Orthodox Spirituality, by a monk of the Eastern Church. London, 1945.

Palmieri, A. *La Chiesa russa.* Florence, 1908.

Palmov, N. *O prosphorakh na prokomedii.* Kiev, 1902.

Palocaren, J. *The Syriac Mass.* Trinchinopoly, 1917.

Pamiatniki Rossijskoi Slvesnosty XII vika, izdannie s objasneniem variantam i obraztsami pocherkov K. Kalajdovichom. Moscow, 1821.

Pargoire, J. *L'Église byzantine de 527 à 847.* Paris, 1905.

Parkhomenko, V. A. *Nachalo khristianstva na Rusi.* Poltava, 1913.

Parsch, P. *Messerklärung.* Klosterneuburg b. Vien, 1937.

Pavlov, A. S. *Kriticheskie opyty po istorii drevnijshej grekorusskoj polemiki protiv Latinian.* St. Petersburg, 1878.

Pelesh, J. *Liturgyka.* Vienna, 1877.

Pelesh, J. *Pastyrskoe Bohoslovie.* Vienna, 1885.

Petrov, L. *Liturgika ili uchenie o bogosluzhenii pravoslavnoi tserkvy.* St. Petersburg, 1872.

Petrovsky, A. *Apostol'skia liturgia vostochnoi tserkvy. Liturgii ap. Iakovai Thaddeya, Mariya i sv. Marka.* St. Petersburg, 1897.
   Istoria slavianskoi redaktsii liturgii Ioanna Zlatoustago, Histoire de la rédaction slave de la liturgie de S. Jean Chrysostome, XPYCOCTOMIKA, pp. 859-928. Rome, 1908.

Pirenne, H. *Economic and Social History of Medieval Europe*, 6th edit. London, 1958. Translated from the French, *Histoire du Moyen Age*, Paris, 1931.

Pitra, J. B. *Iuris Ecclesiastici Graeci historia et monumenta*. Paris, 1868. *L'hymnographie dans l'Église grecque*. Rome, 1867.

Placidus a S. Josepho. *Ritus et libri liturgici syro-malabarici*. Thevara, 1933.

Ponomarev, A. I. *Pamiatniki drevne-russkoi uchitel'noi literatury*. Vols. I and III. St. Petersburg, 1894-1897.

Popel, M. *Liturgyka ily nauka o bohosluzhenju tserkvy hrecheskokatolucheskoi*. Lvov, 1861.

Popoviciu, N. *Epicleza eucharistica*. Sibiu, 1923.

Potebnia, A. *Slovo o polku Igorevie, Tekst i primiechaniya*. Voronezh, 1878.

Priselkov, M. D. *Istoria russkogo letopisaniya XI-XV v*. Leningrad, 1940.

Probst, F. *Die abendländische Messe vom V bis zum VIII Jahrh*. Münster i.W., 1896.
  Geschichte der katholischen Katechese. Breslau, 1886.
  Katechese und Predikt vom Anfang des IV bis zum Ende des VI Jahrhunderts. Breslau, 1884.
  Liturgie der drei ersten christlichen Jahrhunderte. Tübingen, 1851.
  Liturgie des vierten Jahrhunderts und deren Reform. Münster in W., 1893.
  Verwaltung der Euchariste als Sakrament. Tübingen, 1851.

Prokopovich, T. *Christiana Orthodoxa Theologia*, I. Leipzig, 1792.

Prylutsky, V. *Chastnoe bogosluzhenie v russkoi tserkvy v XVI v. i v pervoi polovyni XVII v*. Kiev, 1912.

Puech, A. *Histoire de la littérature grecque chrétienne depuis les origines jusqu'à la fin du IV⁰ siècle*, 3 vols. Paris, 1930.

Puniet, J. *La liturgie de la messe*. Avignon, 1928.

Quasten, J. *Monumenta eucharistica et liturgia vetustissima*. Bonn, 1935-1937.

Rabban, R. *La Messa caldea detta degli Apostoli*. Rome, 1935.

Raes, A. *Introductio in liturgiam orientalem*. Rome, 1947.
  Le Liturgicon Ruthéne depuis l'Union de Brest. Rome, 1942.

Rahlfs, K. *Die alttestamentlichen Lektionen der griechischen Kirche*. Berlin, 1915.

Rahmani, I. E. *I fadti della chiesa patriarcale Antiochena*. Conferenza d'inaugurazione tenuta in nome dell'Istituto pontificio Orientale li 18 gennaio MCMXX. Rome, 1920.
  Les liturgies Orientales et Occidentales étudiées séparément et comparées entre elles. Beirut, 1929.
  Testamentum Domini Nostri Jesu Christi. Mainz, 1899.

Rambaud, A. *L'Empire grec au X⁰ siècle*. Paris, 1870.

Ranke, E. *Das kirchliche Perikopensystem.* Berlin, 1847.

Raulin, J. F. *Historia ecclesiae malabaricae.* Rome, 1755.

Rauschen, G. *Eucharistie und Bussakrament in den ersten VI Jahrhunderten der Kirche.* Freiburg in B., 1901.
Florilegium patristicum, VII, *Monumenta eucharistica.* Bonn, 1909.

Renaudot, E. *Liturgiarum orientalium collectio,* 2 vols., 2nd edit. Frankfurt, 1847.

Rice, T. T. *A Concise History of Russian Art.* New York, 1963.

Richter, G., and Schoenfelder, A. *Sacramentarium Fuldense saec. X.* Fulda, 1912.

Riedel, W. *Die Kirchenrechtsquellen des Patriarchats Alexandrien.* Leipzig, 1900.

Riemann, H. *Sudien zur byz. Musik.* Leipzig, 1915.

Rietschel, G. *Lehrbuch der Liturgik,* 2 vols. Berlin, 1900.

Righetti, M. *Manuale di storia liturgica,* I. Milan-Genoa, 1945.

Roberts C. H.—Capelle. *An Early Euchologium, the Der Balyseh Papyrus.* Louvain, 1949.

Rocchi, A. *Codices Cryptenses, seu Abbatiae Cryptae Ferratae in Tusculano, digesti et illustrati.* Rome, 1884.

Rozkestvensky, *Izyasnenie Liturgii po chynu sv. Ioanna Zlatoustago.* St. Petersburg, 1860.

Rücker, A. *Die syrische Jakobusanaphora. Mit dem griechischen Paralleltext.* Münster, 1923.
Ritus Baptismi et Missae, quem descripsit Theodorus ep. Mopsuestenus in sermonibus catecheticis. Münster, 1933.

Runciman, S. *Byzantine Civilization.* London-New York, 1937.

Russnak, N. *Epyklyzys (Epiklesis).* Priashev, 1926.

Ryssel, V. *Ein Brief Georgs, Bischofs der Araber an den Presbyter Jesus aus dem Syrischen übersetzt und erläutert. Mit einer Eileitung über sein Leben und seine Schriften.* Gotha, 1883.

Sabas, Bishop. *Specimina palaeographica codicul graecorum et slavonicorum bibliothecae Mosquensis Synodalis saec. VI-XVIII.* Moscow, 1863.

Sakharov, V. A. *Eskhatologieeskiya sochineniya i skazaniya v dreven-russkoi pismennosti.* Tula, 1879.

Salaville, S. *An Introduction in the Study of Eastern Liturgies.* London, 1938.
Liturgies orientales : la messe, 2 vols. Paris, 1942.

Sandor, M. *Liturgika.* Ungvar, 1891.

, P. *La dottrina degli Apostoli.* Roma, 1893.

er, A. *Die Elemente der Eucharistie in der ersten drei Jahrhunderten.* Mainz, 1903.
Eucharistie in den ausserkirchlichen Kreisen. Freiburg, 1904.

Istoricheski Puti Pravoslavia. New York, 1954.

Schermann, T. *Aegyptische Abendmahlsliturgien des ersten Jahrtausends.* Paderborn, 1912.
    Der liturgische Papyrus von Der-Balizeh. Leipzig, 1910.
    Früchristliche Liturgien. Paderborn, 1915.
    Griechische Zauberpapyri und das Gemeinde- und Dankgebet im l. Klemensbrief. Leipzig, 1909.

Schmitz, H. J. *Die Bussbücher und das kanonische Bussverfahren.* Düsseldorf, 1898.

Schreiber, G. *Untersuchungen zum Sprachgebrauch des mittelterlichen Oblationswesens.* Wörishofen, 1913.

Schummer, J. *Die altchristliche Fastenpraxis.* Münster, 1933.

Schurer, E. *Geschichte des Judischen Volkes im Zeitalter Jesu Christi.* 4 vols., edit. 3-4. Leipzig, 1901-1911.

Schwartz, E. *Über die Pseudo-apostolischen Kirchenordnung.* Strassburg, 1910.

Seeberg, A. *Die Didache des Judentums und der Urchristenheit.* Leipzig, 1908.

Selam, T. M. S. *De indumentis sacris ritus aethiopici.* Rome, 1930.
    De Ss. Sacramentis secundum ritum Aethiopicum. Rome, 1931.

Semeria (Barnabite), G. *La messa nella sua storia e nei suoi simboli.* Rome, 1907.

Sfair, P. *La Messa Siro-Maronita annotata : cenno storico sui Maroniti.* Rome, 1946.

Shakhmatov, A. A. *Razyskaniya o drevnieishikh russkikh lietopisnikh svodakh.* St. Petersburg, 1908.

Sherrard, P. *The Greek East and the Latin West.* Oxford, 1959.

Shevyrev, S. P. *Istoriya russkoi slovesnosti,* 2 vols., 3rd edit. St. Petersburg, 1887.

Silva-Taruca. *Giovanni.* " *Archicantor* " *de S. Pietro a Roma e l'ordo Romanus da lui composto atti dilla Pont Accad. Rom. di archeologia,* I, 1. Rome, 1923.

Skabalanovich, M. N. *Tokovii Tipikon, (objasnytelnoe izlozhenie tipikoba s ist. vvedeniem.* Kiev, 1910.
    Vizantisskaya tserkov i gosudarstvo v XI v. St. Petersburg, 1884.

Skene, W. F. *The Lord's Supper and the Passover Ritual.* Edinburgh, 1891.

Smirnov, S. I. *Drevne-russkii dukhovnik.* Sergiev Posad, 1899.

Smolitsch, I. *Das altrussische Mönchtum (11-16 Jahrh.).* Wurzburg, 1940.

Smolodovich, D. *Liturgika ili nauka o bogosluzhenii pravoslavnoi vostochnoi katolicheskoi Tserkvy,* 2nd edit. Kiev, 1861.

Smrzik, S. *The Glagolitic or Roman-Slavonic Liturgy.* Rome-Cleveland, 1́

Sokolov, D. *Uchenie o bogosluzhenii pravoslavnoi tserkvy.* St. Pe 1892.

Solowij, M. *Bozhestvenna Liturhiya.* Istoriya, Rozvytok, ʼ Rome, 1964.

De reformatione liturgica Heraclii Lisovskyj, Archiepiscopi Polocensis (1784-1809). Rome, 1950.

Soyter, G. B. *Byzantinische Dichtung*. Ahtens, 1938.

Spacil, T. *Doctrina theologica Orientis separati de SS. Eucharistia*, 2 vols. Rome, 1928-1929.

Speransky, M. N. *Istoria drevnei russkoi literatury*, 3rd edit. Moscow, 1921.

Spinka, M. *Christianity in the Balkans*. Chicago, 1933.

Srawley, J. H. *The Early History of the Liturgy*, 2nd edit. Cambridge, 1947.

Stanley, A. P. *Lectures on the History of the Eastern Church*. London, 1884.

Stapper, R. *Katholische Liturgik*. Münster, 1931.

Stone, D. *A History of the Doctrine of the Holy Eucharist*. London, 1909.

Storf, R. *Griechische Liturgien*. München, 1912.

Strack, H. L., and Billerbeck, P. *Kommentar zum Neuen Testament aus Talmud und Midrasch*, Vol. IV. Munich, 1928.

Stromberg, A. *Studien zur Theorie und Trazis der Taufe in der christlichen Kirche der ersten 2 Jahrhunderte*. Berlin, 1913.

Strothman, R. *Die Koptische Kirche in der Neuzeit*. Tübingen, 1932.

Struckmann. *Die Eucharistielehre des hl. Cyrillen von Alexandrien*. Paderborn, 1910.

Strzygowski, J. *Orient oder Rome*. Leipzig, 1900.

Svintsytsky, I. *Kataloh knyh tserkovno-slavianskoi pechaty*. Zhovkva, 1908.

Svjetlov, P. I. *Gdi vselenskaya Tserkov?* Sergiev Posad, 1905.

Swainson, C. A. *The Greek Liturgies Chiefly from Original Authorities*. Cambridge, 1884.

Szabo, S. *Expositio ss. liturgiae s. Joannis Chrysostomi historica, dogmatica, et moralis*. Ungvar, 1902.

Tarchnisvili, M. *Die byzantinische Liturgie als Verwichlichung der Einheit und Gemeinschaft in Dogma*. Würzburg, 1939.

Tardo, L. *L'antica melurgia bizantina*. Grottaferrata, 1939.

Tarnowsky, T. *Die bedeutesten Liturgien der orientalischen Kirche*. Czernovitz, 1893.

Ter-Mikelian, A. *Die Armenische Kirche in ihren Beziehungen zur byzantinischen*. Leipzig, 1892.

Thalhofer, V., and Eisenhofer, L. *Handbuch der Liturgik*, 2 vols., 2nd edit. Freiburg in B., 1912.

Thibaut, J. B. *La liturgie romaine*. Paris, 1925.
L'ancienne liturgie gallicane. Paris, 1929.

Thiel, A. *Epistolas Romanorum Pontificum*. Braunsberg, 1868.

Tiby, O. *La musica bizantina*. Milan, 1938.

Tillyard, H. J. W. *Byzantine Music and Hymnography*. London, 1923.

Tisserant, Cardinal, E. *Eastern Christianity in India*. Westminster Md., 1957.
The Eastern Branches of the Catholic Church. New York, 1938.

Tommasi, J. M. *Opera*, edit. Vizzosi, 7 vols. Rome, 1747-1754.

Tosti, P. *La Didaiche—Traduzine italiana e commento*. Rome, 1945.

Tournebize, F. *Histoire politique et religieuse de l'Arménie depuis les origines des Arméniens jusqu'à la mort de leur dernier roi (l'an. 1393)*. Paris, 1900.

Tyciak, J. *Die Liturgie als Quelle ostlicher Frommigkeit*. Freiburg, 1937.

Tyrer, J. W. *The Eucharistic Epiclesis*. Liverpool, 1917.

Undolsky. *Ocherk slaviano-russkoi bibliografii*. Moscow, 1871.

Uspensky, F. I. *Ocherki po istorii vizantiiskoi obrazovannosti*. St. Petersburg 1891.

Vajs, J. (edit.). *Sbornik staroslovenskich literarnich pamatek o sv. Vaclavu a sv. Lidmile*. Prague, 1929.

Vandeer, E. *La Sainte Messe*. Maredsous, 1928.

Vandik, S. *De Apparatu liturgico circa verba et epiclesiam in Anaphora byzantina ; Explicatio rubricarum*. Rome, 1945.

Vansleb, I. M. *Histoire de l'Église d'Alexandrie fondée par S. Marc, que nous appelons celle des Jacobites-Coptes d'Égypte, écrite au Caire même en 1672 et 1673*. Paris, 1677.

Varaine, F. *L'Épiclèse eucharistique*. Lyon, 1910.

Varlaam. *Ob izmineniakh v chyni liturgii Ioanna Zlatoustago, Vasilia Velikago i Grigoria Dvoeslova, ukazannikh v Pomorskikh otvitakh i Mechi dukhovnom*. Kyshynev, 1860.

Vasiliev, A. A. *History of the Byzantine Empire*, 2nd edit., 2 vols. Madison, 1958.

Vernadsky, G. *A History of Russia : Ancient Russia*. New Haven, 1943.

Vladislavtsev, V. *Obijasnenie bogosluzhenia sviatoi, pravoslavnoi tserkvy*, 2 vols. Tver, 1862.

Völger, K. *Mysterium und Agape. Die gemeinsamen Mahlzeiten der alten Kirche*. Gotha, 1927.

Vykhrov, A. *Obiasnenie Bozhestvennoi liturgii sv. Ioanna Zlatoustago*. Novgorod, 1893.

Wagner, P. *Origine et développement du chant liturgique*. Tournai, 1904.

Waldenberg, V. E. *Drevne-russkiya uchenia o predielakh tsarskoi vlasti*. St. Petersburg, 1916.

Wanczura, A. *Skolnictwo v starei Rusi*. Lvov, 1923.

Ware, T. *The Orthodox Church*. Baltimore, 1963.

Warren, F. E. *The Liturgy and Ritual of the Celtic Church*. Oxford, 1881. *The Liturgy and the Ritual of the Ante-Nicene Church*. London, 1904.

Watterich, J. *Der Konsecrationsmoment im hl. Abendmahl und seine Geschichte*. Heidelberg, 1896.

Wellesz, E. *A History of Byzantine Music and Hymnography*, 2nd edit. Oxford, 1961.

Aufgaben und Probleme auf dem Gebiete der byzant. und orient. Kirchenmusik. Münster, 1923.

Wendland, P. *Die hellenistisch-römische Kultur in ihren Beziehungen zu Judentum und Christentum.* Tübingen, 1907.

Wetter, G. P. *Altchristliche Liturgien : Das christliche Mysterium. Studie zur Geschichte des Abendmahles.* Gottingen, 1921.
Altchristliche Liturgien : Das christliche Opfer. Neue Studien zur Geschichte des Abendmahles. Gottingen, 1922.

Wieland, F. *Altar und Altargrab der christlichen Kirchen im 4 Jahrhundert.* Leipzig, 1912.

Wigram, W. A. *An Introduction to the History of the Assyrian Church.* London, 1910.
The Separation of the Monophysites. London, 1913.

Wilson, H. A. *The Gelasian Sacramentary.* Oxford, 1894.
The Gregorian Sacramentary. London, 1915.

Wolley, R. M. *The Liturgy of the Primitive Church.* Cambridge, 1910.

Wordsworth, J. *Bishop Serapion's Prayerbook.* London, 1910.
The Holy Communion. Oxford, 1891.

Wright, W. *Catalogue of Syriac Manuscripts in the British Museum.* London, 1870.

Zahn, T. *Brot und Wein im Abendmahl der alten Kirche.* Leipzig, 1892.
Geschichte des Neutestamentlichen Kanons. Vol. II. Erlangen, 1890.

Zankov, S. *The Eastern Orthodox Church.* London-Milwaukee, 1929.

Zernov, N. *The Church of the Eastern Christians.* London, 1942.
The Russians and Their Church. London-New York, 1945.

MANUSCRIPTS CITED AND/OR CONSULTED

This list is intended to serve as a key to the places of origin of the principal MSS. of Greek and Slavonic liturgical (Eucharistic) interest. Russian libraries are given their pre-revolutionary names.

VIIIth TO IXth CENTURY

VATICAN : Vatican Library — *Cod. Barberini gr.* 336 (250/11, * 259/ 12/13, 271/26, 280/4, 323/20, 369/8, 384, 402/3, 405/15, 407, 409/12, 431/15, 449, 474, 478/1, 481, 515, 516, 527/24, 533/24, 536, 564, 572/4, 585/29, 603/34, 610/12, 615/3, 626/7, 641/7, 642, 643/12, 649/6, 657/40, 661, 678, 679/36, 686, 713/5, 721/17, 726, 728, 730, 734/13/15)

IXth TO Xth CENTURY

GROTTAFERRATA : Basilian Monastery of — MSS. Grottaf. Γ.β. vii (319/3, 661/11), xxix (fragments)
LONDON : British Museum — *Add.* 14518 (150/2)
MOUNT SINAI : Monastery of St. Catherine — *Cod. Sin.* No. 957
ST PETERSBURG (LENINGRAD) : (Imperial) Public Library of — MS. 226 (here designated as *Codex Porphyrios* : formerly, *Cod. Patmos* 266) (384/7, 481/6, 499/28, 610/12, 615/3, 626, 661/12, 676/18, 686, 701/15, 729)

Xth CENTURY

GROTTAFERRATA : Basilian Monastery of — MSS. *Grottaf.* Γ.β. x, xx[1]
LONDON : British Museum — *Add.* 14523 (150/2)

MESSINA : University Library — *Messina graec.* 177 (150/1)
MOUNT SINAI : Monastery of St. Catherine — Sin. 956, 958
VATICAN : Vatican Library — *Vat. gr.* 2282 (149/1, 409/10, 430/13, 482/10, 680/38)

Xth TO XIth CENTURY

JERUSALEM : Monastery of the Holy Cross — *Cod.* 40
MOSCOW : Rumiantsev Museum — *Cod.* 15 [474]; here designated as *Cod. Sebastianov* (610/12, 564/4, 481, 478/1, 686, 734/15, 740/4)
MOUNT ATHOS : Monastery of St. Panteleimon — *Pantel.* No. 162
MOUNT SINAI : Monastery of St. Catherine — *Sin.* 150
PRAGUE : Academy of Science Library — *Prague Fragments* (Glagolitic Missal) : 222.

XIth CENTURY

BURDETT-COUTTS : Private Collection — *Burdett-Coutts* iii, 42 (319/3, 409/12, 430/14, 461/16, 626/5, 721/17)
GROTTAFERRATA : Basilian Monastery of — *Grottaf.* Γ.β. II, xx, xli (fragment)
MOSCOW : Moscow Synodal Library — *Cod.* 380 [330] (266/21, 280/8)

* The figures in parentheses indicate the page and footnote numbers where a particular MS. is referred to in present book. Figures in brackets indicate alternative numbers of MSS.

THE AUTHOR

A native of Michigan, Father Casimir Kucharek changed from the Latin to the Byzantine-Slav rite in order to do specialized missionary work among the Ukrainians of Saskatchewan, Canada. He is a graduate of Maryknoll College, Lakewood, N.J., St. Joseph's Seminary, Edmonton, and the Propaganda University in Rome. In addition to regular courses in theology at the Propaganda, he studied Slavic languages and the Byzantine-Slavonic Liturgy at the Pontificio Collegio di S. Giosafat in Rome.

His facile command of modern languages (he is fluent in, or has reading knowledge of English, Ukrainian, Russian, Polish, Slovak, Italian, Spanish, French, German, besides Old Slavonic, Classical Greek, and Latin) has suited him especially for research in Byzantine-Slav liturgical studies. *The Byzantine-Slav Liturgy of St. John Chrysostom* is the result of ten years of labor in this field.

Besides his parish work since his ordination in 1956, Father Kucharek has served as a member of almost every Preparatory Commission for the First Provincial Synod of the Ukrainian Metropolitan See, held in Winnipeg in 1962, and of the various Eparchial Liturgical Commissions preparatory to Vatican II. Much of the material in this book was delivered as lectures to the students at St. Mary's Seminary, Yorkton, Saskatchewan, when Father Kucharek was professor of Byzantine Liturgy there. At present, he is the Secretary of the Ukrainian Catholic Theological Society for Canada.

19 71

TEN THOUSAND COPIES OF THIS BOOK
PRINTED BY GEDIT S. A. OF TOURNAI,
BELGIUM, IN EIGHT AND ELEVEN
POINT PLANTIN AND ELEVEN
POINT PLANTIN BOLD MAKE
UP THE ORIGINAL EDITION.

—+—

Book and jacket designed by
JOSE DE VINCK

Original Woodcut by
PHILIP HAGREEN